Information Systems and the Internet

A Problem-Solving Approach

Fourth Edition

INFORMATION SYSTEMS AND THE INTERNET

A Problem-Solving Approach

FOURTH EDITION

KENNETH C. LAUDON

New York University

JANE PRICE LAUDON

Azimuth Corporation

The Dryden Press

Harcourt Brace College Publishers

Fort Worth Philadelphia San Diego New York Orlando Austin San Antonio

Toronto Montreal London Sydney Tokyo

Publisher: *George Provol*
Executive Editor: *Wesley Lawton*
Product Manager: *Federico Arrieta*
Developmental Editor: *Larry Crowder*
Project Editor: *Michele Tomiak*
Art Director: *Scott Baker*
Production Manager: *Darryl King*

ISBN: 0-03-024797-7

Address for orders:
The Dryden Press
6277 Sea Harbor Drive
Orlando, FL 32887-6777
1-800-782-4479

Address for editorial correspondence:
The Dryden Press
301 Commerce Street, Suite 3700
Fort Worth, TX 76102

Web site address: http://www.hbcollege.com

Printed in the United States of America

7 8 9 0 1 2 3 4 5 6 021 9 8 7 6 5 4 3 2 1

The Dryden Press
Harcourt Brace College Publishers

The Dryden Press Series in Information Systems

Fenrich
Practical Guidelines for Creating Instructional Multimedia Applications

Forcht
Management Information Systems: A Casebook

Gordon and Gordon
Information Systems: A Management Approach

Gray, King, McLean, and Watson
Management of Information Systems
Second Edition

Harrington
Database Management for Microcomputers: Design and Implementation
Second Edition

Harris
Systems Analysis and Design: A Project Approach
Second Edition

Head
An Introduction to Programming with QuickBASIC

Larsen
Using Microsoft Works 4.0 for Windows 95: An Introduction to Computing

Laudon and Laudon
Information Systems and the Internet: A Problem-Solving Approach
Fourth Edition

Laudon and Laudon
Information Systems: A Problem-Solving Approach
(A CD-ROM interactive version)

Lawlor
Computer Information Systems
Third Edition

Licker
Management Information Systems: A Strategic Leadership Approach

Martin
Discovering Microsoft Office 97

Martin/Parker
PC Concepts

Mason
Using Microsoft Access 97 in Business

Mason
Using Microsoft Excel 97 in Business

McKeown
Living with Computers
Fifth Edition

McKeown
Working with Computers
Second Edition

McKeown
Working with Computers with Software Tutorials
Second Edition

McLeod
Systems Analysis and Design: An Organizational Approach

Millspaugh
Business Programming in C for DOS-Based Systems

Morgan and Lorents
Database Systems: Concepts, Management, Applications

Morley
Getting Started with Computers

Parker
Understanding Computers: Today and Tomorrow
98 Edition

Parker
Understanding Networking and the Internet

Spear
Introduction to Computer Programming in Visual Basic 4.0

Spear
Visual Basic 3.0: A Brief Introduction
Visual Basic 4.0: A Brief Introduction

Sullivan
The New Computer User
Second Edition

Thommes and Carey
Introduction to CASE Using Visible Analyst Workbench v4.3 for DOS
CASE Tools: Using Visible Analyst Workbench for Windows

Martin and Parker
Mastering Today's Software Series

Texts available in any combination of the following:

Disk Operating System 5.0 (DOS 5.0)
Disk Operating System 6.0 (DOS 6.0)
Windows 3.1
Windows 95

Microsoft Office 97
Microsoft Office for Windows 95 Professional Edition
WordPerfect 5.1
WordPerfect 5.2 for Windows
WordPerfect 6.0 for DOS
WordPerfect 6.0 for Windows
WordPerfect 6.1 for Windows
Corel WordPerfect 7.0 for Windows 95
Word 6.0 for Windows
Word 7.0 for Windows 95
Word 97
Lotus 1-2-3 (2.2/2.3)
Lotus 1-2-3 (2.4)
Lotus 1-2-3 for Windows (4.01)
Lotus 1-2-3 for Windows (5.0)
Lotus 1-2-3 97
Excel 5.0 for Windows
Excel 7.0 for Windows 95
Excel 97
Quattro Pro 4.0
Quattro Pro 6.0 for Windows
dBASE III PLUS
dBASE IV (1.5/2.0)
dBASE 5 for Windows
Paradox 4.0
Paradox 5.0 for Windows
Access 2.0 for Windows
Access 7.0 for Windows 95
Access 97
PowerPoint 7.0 for Windows 95
PowerPoint 97
A Beginner's Guide to BASIC
A Beginner's Guide to QBASIC
Netscape Communicator

THE HARCOURT BRACE COLLEGE OUTLINE SERIES

Kreitzberg
Introduction to BASIC

Kreitzberg
Introduction to Fortran

Pierson
Introduction to Business Information Systems

Veklerov and Pekelny
Computer Language C

About the Authors

KENNETH C. LAUDON is Professor of Information Systems at New York University's Stern School of Business. Ken has played an important role in defining new content, teaching materials, and techniques for business students throughout the United States. He holds a B.A. in economics and philosophy from Stanford University and a Ph.D. from Columbia University.

Ken has written 14 books and numerous articles in academic journals about the organizational and social impacts of information technology, privacy, and interactive multimedia. He has testified before Congress on many occasions and has worked as a consultant to the Office of Technology Assessment (United States Congress), the Office of the President, several executive branch agencies, and congressional committees.

JANE PRICE LAUDON is a management consultant in the information systems area and a professional writer. She has written seven books. Her special interests include systems analysis and design, software evaluation, and teaching business professionals how to design and use information systems. She has taught at the New York University Stern Graduate School of Business and at Columbia University. She received her B.A. from Barnard College, her M.A. from Harvard University, and her Ph.D. from Columbia University. For the past 15 years, Jane has been an information systems consultant for leading *Fortune* 500 companies. She and her husband, Ken, have two daughters, Erica and Elisabeth.

Information Systems and the Internet: A Problem-Solving Approach is the second book the Laudons have written together. It reflects the Laudons' personal belief that undergraduate information systems textbooks must include a multidimensional perspective involving people, technology, and organizations, and that such books must be, above all, readable, enjoyable, and informative.

Preface

Information Systems and the Internet: A Problem-Solving Approach (Fourth Edition) is based on the premise that virtually all college graduates will be expected to understand, use, and possibly design information systems in their jobs and daily life. Accordingly, we wrote this book for nontechnical undergraduate students in business, information systems, and the liberal arts who will find a knowledge of information systems vital for professional success. This book also provides a broad foundation and understanding for students who are MIS majors.

Information Systems and the Internet: A Problem-Solving Approach treats information systems as more than simply computers. Instead, we view information systems as composed of information technologies, organizations, and people. We emphasize the broader concept of information systems literacy rather than computer literacy. By information systems literacy, we mean a full understanding of organizations and individuals from a behavioral perspective combined with knowledge of information technology.

Both the business and educational worlds are finding that the major stumbling block to using computers effectively is not insufficient knowledge of how computers work but the need for greater understanding of the role of information technology in organizations and how it can be applied to business problems. Equally important is the need for students to develop critical-thinking and problem-solving skills. To remain competitive, productive, and prosperous, we need to educate people with the broader knowledge required to solve new problems they will encounter in the future. Our textbook addresses these challenges and current guidelines for foundation courses in the information systems curriculum.

OUR PROBLEM-SOLVING PERSPECTIVE

Our textbook is distinguished by its explicit problem-solving and critical-thinking perspective. It shows how businesses, nonprofit organizations, and individuals can design and use information systems to solve organizational problems, and it emphasizes the teaching of critical-thinking and problem-solving skills. Students will learn how to analyze and define a business problem and how to design an appropriate solution. In many cases, the solution requires students to visualize a new information system application. Knowing the difference between an organizational problem, a people problem, and a technology problem is central to this understanding.

Students using this text will learn:

- How to envision, design, and evaluate computer-based solutions to problems found in businesses and other organizations.
- How to use contemporary hardware and software tools, including the Internet, to develop solutions.
- Enduring concepts for understanding information systems that they can apply in their future careers or information systems courses.

•INFORMATION SYSTEMS AND THE INTERNET: A NEW ROLE FOR TECHNOLOGY IN PROBLEM SOLVING

This edition required a major revision to the text to incorporate the Internet into the introductory information systems course. Because of its ease of use and ability to link people to information from all over the world, the Internet is transforming the face of computing. It is creating a foundation for new types of products, services, and relationships among organizations. It is changing the way people access information, conduct business, communicate, and collaborate, and even how they spend their free time. We believe that the Internet has become a major problem-solving tool that is dramatically widening the role of information systems in business and daily life. Accordingly, we have changed the title of this text to *Information Systems and the Internet: A Problem-Solving Approach* to reflect this new emphasis.

•NEW TO THE FOURTH EDITION

Many changes have been made throughout the text to reflect the impact and capabilities of the Internet.

FULL CHAPTER ON THE INTERNET

A full chapter on the Internet (Chapter 8) describes the Internet's underlying technology, capabilities, and contributions to problem solving. The World Wide Web, intranets, extranets, "push" technology, and electronic commerce are among the topics given detailed coverage.

INTERNET COVERAGE IN EACH CHAPTER

The Internet and the World Wide Web are introduced in Chapter 1 and integrated throughout the text. Every chapter contains a "Focus on" box, ending case study, or in-text discussion of some aspect of the Internet relevant to the chapter topic. Here are some examples:

- Chapter 4 (Computer Hardware) contains a discussion of network computers.
- Chapter 5 (Information Systems Software) describes how Java is revolutionizing the development and distribution of software.
- Chapter 6 (Organizing Information: Files and Databases) discusses privacy issues raised by linking Web sites to internal databases.
- Chapter 10 (Designing Information System Solutions) contains a case study showing how the authors' problem-solving methodology can be used to design the user interface for a Web site.
- Chapter 13 (Basic Business Systems) describes an Internet-based sales transaction processing system.

Each chapter contains an Internet problem-solving project requiring students to use interactive Websites to develop solutions.

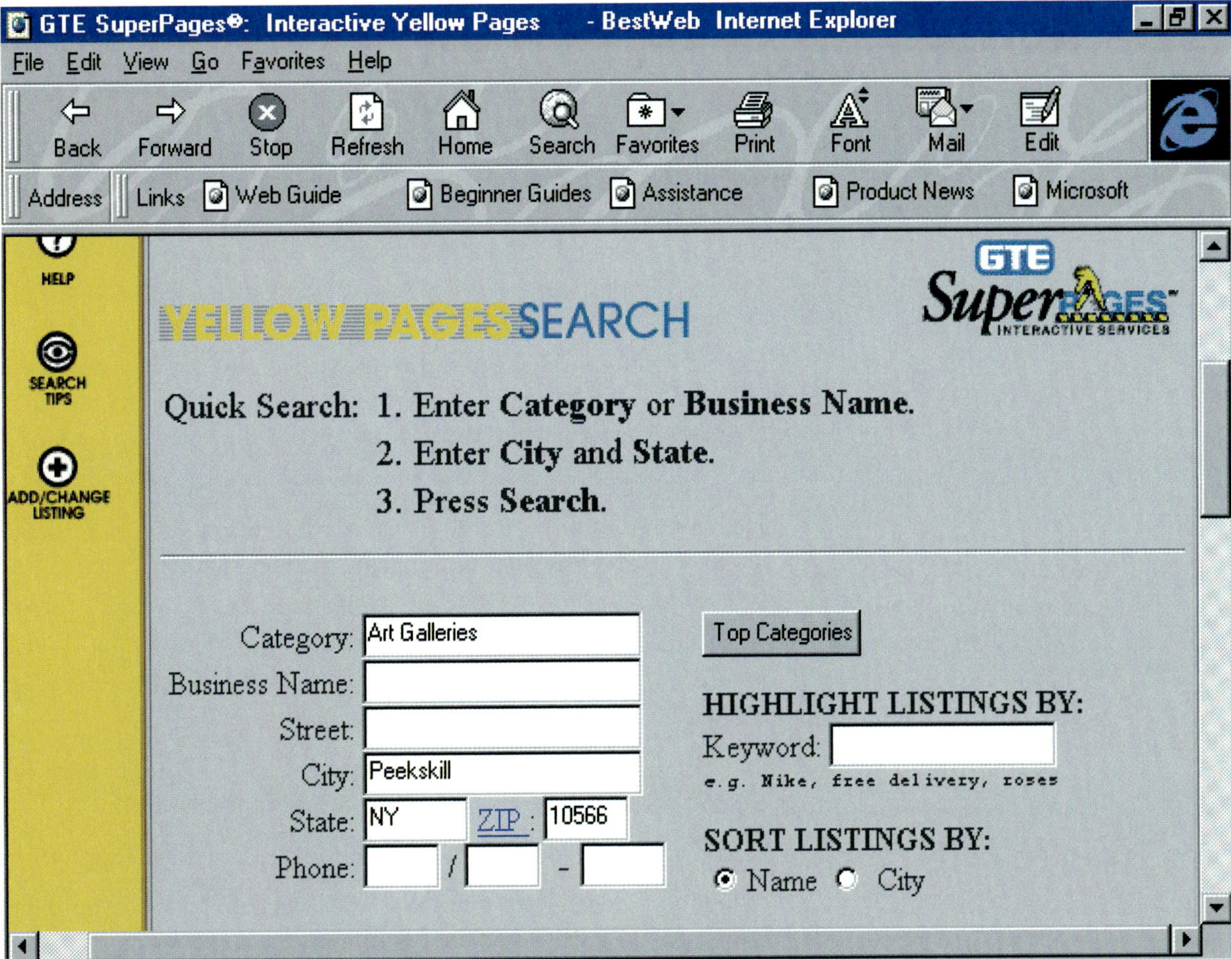

- Chapter 14 (Knowledge Work Systems) shows how the Internet can be used for group coordination and knowledge work.

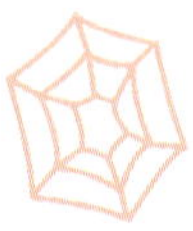

INTERACTIVE PROBLEM SOLVING WITH THE INTERNET

At the end of each chapter is an interactive Internet problem-solving project that shows students how to use the features of interactive Web sites to solve typical business problems. Students are presented with a problem requiring them to use Web sites with interactive software to develop a solution. They will be able to obtain the information required by the solution by inputting data online and using the software at that Web site to perform the required calculations or analyses. Examples of such projects are:

- Planning a business trip
- Locating a Canadian supplier
- Calculating annual shipping costs
- Conducting marketing campaigns using UseNet newsgroups
- Looking for a job by searching online databases
- Using intelligent agent software to shop for the lowest price

More extensive Internet projects can be found at the end of Chapter 10. These projects require students to develop solutions using the World Wide Web in conjunction with spreadsheet or database software.

ENHANCED WEB SITE FOR PROBLEM SOLVING

The Laudon & Laudon Web site (http://www.dryden.com/infosys/laudon/) was specifically designed to help teach students how to use the Internet for problem solving in conjunction with the text. It contains the following features:

- Interactive Internet problem-solving exercises found at the end of each chapter with hot links to the Web sites they refer to or downloadable files to be used for solving the problems. Additional instructions or files required by these projects are also provided.
- Hundreds of hotlinks to additional Web resources describing organizations or concepts covered in each chapter or in the illustrated part-ending cases.
- Hotlinks to Web sites in Canada and other non-U.S. countries for instructors and students requiring more international resources.
- Additional figures and illustrations of information systems concepts.
- Technology updates—fresh material on new developments in information systems that helps keep the learning package leading-edge.

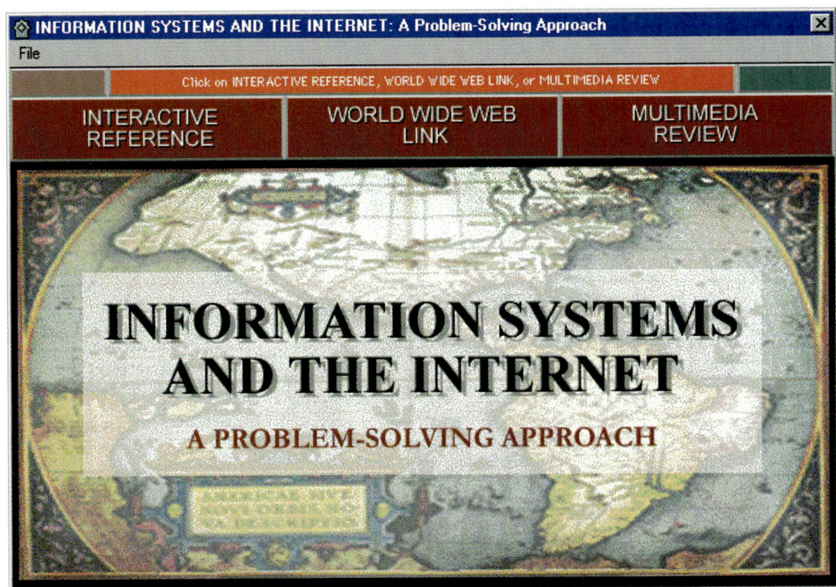

The multimedia CD-ROM accompanying this text includes links to the Web, interactive exercises, and online quizzes.

INTERACTIVE CD-ROM

An interactive multimedia CD-ROM is available as a companion to the textbook and Web site. The CD-ROM contains videos, dynamic blackboards, simulations, and online glossaries to explain key concepts as well as the complete text. Each text chapter contains a bulleted summary of key points for students to review. Interactive exercises and games require students to create and move objects to further apply text concepts. An interactive test bank provides helpful question-and-answer sessions.

The CD-ROM automatically links to the Laudon & Laudon Web site and to hundreds of other Web sites, providing additional resources and opportunities for interactive learning. Included are lessons on how to use Netscape Navigator and Internet Explorer to search for information on the Web. Additionally, full text content and features of all 16 chapters of the textbook are provided. This CD ROM can be used as an electronic interactive study guide or as a full-featured alternative to the hardcover version.

LEADING-EDGE COVERAGE OF NEW TECHNOLOGY AND BUSINESS DEVELOPMENTS

This edition features extensive treatment of leading-edge topics such as the following:

Intranets and extranets
Electronic commerce
Network computers
Java
Internet search tools

"Push" technology
Internet security and firewalls
Internet privacy
Electronic communities
Data warehousing and multidimensional data analysis
Genetic algorithms
Intelligent agents
Virtual organizations

•HOW THIS BOOK WORKS

Information Systems and the Internet: A Problem-Solving Approach, Fourth Edition, has been carefully designed to use a problem-solving framework to teach information system concepts. The following design features reflect this emphasis.

A FRAMEWORK FOR DESCRIBING AND ANALYZING INFORMATION SYSTEMS

Chapter 1 introduces the authors' framework for analyzing and solving problems by examining the people, organizational, and technological components of information systems. This framework is used repeatedly throughout the text.

Each chapter of the book opens with a vignette describing how a real-world organization used information systems to solve a problem or to respond to a new opportunity. The vignette is accompanied by a diagram analyzing the problem in terms of the authors' people, organization, and technology framework.

FOCUS BOXES

Each chapter's boxes provide real-world examples illustrating the people, organization, and technology issues relevant to each chapter. Focus box themes are:

Technology: Hardware, software, telecommunications, and data and information storage

Organizations: Histories, activities, and plans of organizations using information systems

People: Careers and experiences of individuals working with systems

Problem Solving: Examples of successful and unsuccessful solutions to problems encountered by organizations and their consequences.

Each Focus box features several questions that challenge students to think creatively and apply chapter concepts to the real-world material in the box.

PROBLEM-SOLVING EXERCISES

Each chapter concludes with a set of exercises or projects based on the material covered in the chapter. All of these exercises are designed to sharpen problem-solving skills. The problem-solving exercises encourage students to answer a question, think about a problem, use software to develop solutions, and work with a group of students to define a solution to a problem or to debate the pros and cons of an issue. The following types of problem-solving exercises can be found in each chapter:

- A group exercise to build teamwork and group skills
- A problem-solving exercise requiring students to research and write about a problem
- A hands-on exercise that can be used with any available spreadsheet or database software
- An Internet problem-solving exercise requiring students to find the information for their solution by using the interactive features of specified Web sites

CASE STUDIES

Each chapter ends with a Problem-Solving Case based on a real-world organization that helps students review the material in each chapter and apply this new knowledge to specific problems.

ILLUSTRATED CASES

Illustrated case studies conclude each major section of the text. Illustrated essays on electronic commerce, Seagram's information system strategy, CASE tools, and computers and health care provide additional opportunities to apply text concepts and sharpen problem-solving skills.

RUNNING CASE

A running case study, describing the problems faced by Macy's and efforts toward solution, further illustrates text concepts. Students can see critical thinking and problem solving in action as this retailing giant grapples with declining sales, pressure from competitors, and opportunities to use new information technology.

LEADING-EDGE TECHNOLOGY SECTION

Many chapters contain an illustration of leading-edge information technology that is related to chapter topics.

REAL-WORLD EXAMPLES

Only real-world examples are used throughout the text for cases, Focus boxes, and in-text discussions. More than 200 U.S., Canadian, and international companies and organizations are highlighted.

DIGITAL STUDENT PORTFOLIOS

Students can use the projects, problems, and exercises in the textbook to create structured portfolios of their work to demonstrate what they have accomplished in the course. The appendix "Building Your Digital Portfolio" describes how students can construct a portfolio demonstrating mastery of analytical, writing, presentation, PC software, and Internet skills that would be of great interest to future employers.

•OVERVIEW OF THE BOOK

Part 1 describes the major themes of the book and explores the role of information systems in contemporary businesses. These chapters are especially important for describing the major challenges that we all face in applying information technology more effectively. Part 1 raises several major questions: What is an information system? What is an organization? What is a business? How much do I need to know about information systems and why? How can information systems help businesses become more competitive? What broader ethical and social issues are raised by information systems in organizations?

Part 2 provides the technical foundation for understanding information system technologies and the Internet. It answers questions such as: How do information technologies work? How can organizations use their capabilities? How are these technologies likely to change in the future? Students with no prior background in computing will find Part 2 very helpful because it provides a basic foundation for computing and systems literacy. More advanced students will find that these chapters considerably extend and update their knowledge of contemporary systems.

Part 3 describes how to use the knowledge gained in Parts 1 and 2 to analyze and design solutions to problems faced by businesses and other organizations. This part focuses on the question: How can information systems be used to solve an organizational problem? Two entire chapters in Part 3 are devoted to critical thinking and problem solving. Chapter 9 describes an overall methodology for analyzing problems that considers technology, organizational, and people factors. Chapter 10 puts this methodology to work with real-world case studies of problem-solving in action, including application of this methodology to problem solving using the Internet. Chapter 11 examines various ways of building systems using basic problem-solving methods and alternative systems development methodologies, while Chapter 12 describes the issues that must be addressed to build information systems that are accurate, reliable, and secure.

Part 4 provides a more extensive introduction to real-world information systems in organizations. It answers two major questions: How do contemporary businesses and other organizations use information systems? How can systems be used to improve management decision making and distribute organizational knowledge? The emphasis here is on real-life examples and how these systems fit into the larger world of business, science, education, and government.

•CHAPTER FORMAT

We have made every effort to ensure that each chapter is lively, informative, and often provocative of further debate, discussion, and thought. Each chapter employs the following format:

A detailed outline at the beginning to provide a overview of chapter contents
A list of chapter learning objectives
A chapter-opening vignette
A diagram analyzing the people, organization, and technology issues in the opening vignette
A summary that identifies key themes, topics, and concepts introduced in the chapter
A list of key terms for students to review
A set of review questions for student use in reading
A set of discussion questions for the instructor and students to use in class discussions or individual study
Problem-solving exercises, including group, individual, hands-on software, and Internet projects
Notes with references to provide students with guidance for additional research or term papers
A problem-solving case at the end

•INSTRUCTIONAL SUPPORT MATERIALS

INSTRUCTOR'S MANUAL

The Instructor's Manual, written by Jane and Ken Laudon and Laurette Poulos Simmons of Loyola College, has been extensively revised for the fourth edition. It provides additional material to support your classroom preparation and lecture presentation. For each chapter of the text, the Instructor's Manual includes a chapter summary, learning objectives, key terms, lecture outline, answers to review questions, answers to discussion questions, answers to case questions, answers to problem-solving exercises, and answers to Focus questions.

TEST BANK

The Test Bank, extensively revised for the fourth edition by Susan Helms at Metropolitan State College, contains more than 2,000 test items, including multiple-choice, true/false, matching, vocabulary application, and short-answer questions as well as problem-solving applications. Questions are keyed to the relevant chapter objectives in the text and include an answer key noting difficulty level. The revision to the Test Bank was carefully prepared to ensure that language and vocabulary are appropriate for introductory students.

SOFTWARE APPLICATION MANUALS

A wide variety of current software application manuals is also available from The Dryden Press and can be packaged with this textbook as part of the EXACT custom-publishing program. Please contact your local Dryden/Harcourt Brace representative for the latest offering of manuals and to arrange for your custom product.

VIDEOS

Once again, The Dryden Press has created a dynamic information systems video series tailored to the educational market. This series responds to the need for real business cases instead of boring corporate training tapes or industry promotional videos. This series is custom-designed, specifically for classroom use.

The video segments range from 6 to 14 minutes in length, depending on the topic. They were all filmed on location and contain interviews with each organization's key information systems executives, managers, and system users. Most of the video segments highlight a specific use of information technology as it supports the business enterprise; others present different types of technologies in more general context. All the segments are informative, thought provoking, and enjoyable to watch.

SOFTWARE

A software problem-solving supplement called *Solve it!* is available to support the text for courses requiring additional hands-on software work. Prepared by Ken and Jane Laudon and Peter Weill and Carey Butler of the University of Melbourne, *Solve it!* consists of spreadsheet, database, and Web cases based on real-world business problems. *Solve it!* is available through The Dryden Press's EXACT custom-publishing program, or it can be obtained directly from Azimuth Corporation, 124 Penfield Avenue, Croton-on-Hudson, NY 10520. Contact your Dryden/Harcourt Brace sales representative for additional information.

ACKNOWLEDGMENTS

This book was developed over a ten-year period of teaching information systems courses at the Leonard N. Stern School of Business, New York University. We thank the more than 4,000 students who have helped us learn how to teach this material in an engaging manner. We also thank our colleagues at NYU for continually encouraging us to rethink the curriculum in information systems.

Many persons were very helpful in shaping the content and style of this book. We thank the following people for their helpful suggestions and reviews of the fourth edition: Karen A. Forcht, James Madison University; Pat Dickey-Olson, Western Illinois University; Susan Helms, Metropolitan State College; Surinder Kahai, State University of New York, Binghamton; Alwyn Richardson, Deakin University (Warrnambool Campus), Australia; Tom L. Roberts, Middle Tennessee State University; John Scott, Certified General Accountants Association, Canada; and Murali Venkatesh, Syracuse University.

We are deeply indebted to Marshall R. Kaplan and Kenneth Rosenblatt for their assistance with preparation of new Focus boxes, problem-solving cases, and updated text material. Russell Polo provided assistance with details on many technology topics.

Special thanks to Laurette Poulos Simmons for her revision of the Instructor's Manual and to Susan Helms for her work on the Test Bank.

We also thank the team of The Dryden Press, an extraordinarily professional and pleasant group to work with. Special thanks to Wesley Lawton for his encouragement as our acquisitions editor and to developmental editor Larry Crowder for his excellent recommendations and ongoing oversight of the project. Michele Tomiak, once again, has been an outstanding project editor. Our thanks also for the hard work of art director Scott Baker and production manager Darryl King.

Finally, we want to dedicate this book to our daughters—Erica and Elisabeth—and to our families for putting up with our writing on yet another project.

Kenneth C. Laudon
Jane Price Laudon
September 1997

Brief Contents

Contents

Part 1

THE WORLD OF INFORMATION SYSTEMS

Chapter

ONE

INTRODUCTION TO INFORMATION SYSTEMS

CHAPTER OUTLINE

LEARNING OBJECTIVES

After reading and studying this chapter, you will

1. Be able to define an information system and describe its basic activities.
2. Understand the basic components of information systems: organizations, people, and technology.
3. Know how knowledge, information, and data differ.
4. Know which skills are required for information systems literacy.
5. Be aware of the information system challenges ahead of you.

SELLING WITHOUT SHOE LEATHER

When Jerry Whitlock began selling seals and gaskets, he chased smokestacks, calling at every factory he could find. There was no order he wouldn't take. Twenty years later, Whitlock is still selling seals and gaskets, but he's doing most of his business from his home, often while watching daytime television on his office computer. With high-tech selling tools such as E-mail, fax, and the World Wide Web, Whitlock now does $1 million of business each year. His company, EPM Inc., is a world class supplier of industrial seals, gaskets, mechanical packings, and o-rings, specializing in oddball and hard-to-find parts.

While working as a freelance sales rep selling gaskets and seals, Whitlock accumulated piles of catalogs and bulletins. He organized and cross-referenced them in huge black binders. With the help of an investor, he launched a seal-manufacturing business that at one time had 300 employees. But he quit in 1993, weary of worrying about inventory, personnel, finance, and working with a partner.

Whitlock went back into business in 1995 as a distributor of other people's seals. This time, he vowed, he would do it without warehouses, employees, or partners. His new company, EPM Inc., consisted of a home office, the help of his wife, Rita, and his binder collection. Whitlock purchased two cell phones and a beeper so that factories could reach him if a seal failed any time of the day or night. He set up a site on the World Wide Web where people could read about his product line and order catalogs. He notified various Internet information searching services about how to locate his site on the Web so that anyone seeking "gaskets" or "seals" would find his Web site. Soon, 10 percent of EPM's sales leads were coming from the Web.

Every night Whitlock sets up his personal computer (PC) to dispatch 150 marketing faxes advertising his experience with rush jobs and hard-to-find parts. When a purchase order arrives by fax or E-mail, he looks up the product in one of his big notebooks. Then he orders it from the manufacturer for next-day delivery to his home. When the shipment arrives, Rita repackages it in EPM's packaging and ships it to the customer using Federal Express or United Parcel Service (UPS). EPM has access to over 1,000 suppliers from all over the world and can provide more than 1 million hard-to-find sealing devices as well as standard parts. Most inquiries are answered within 24 hours and shipments made within 72 hours. EPM claims it will ship to any destination in the United States or around the world, even if the order is for only one seal.

Whitlock can run his company anywhere. When he and Rita vacation along the Gulf Coast with their family, they take the business with them on a laptop computer. By using information systems to keep costs low, EPM's gross profit margins average 60 percent.

While Whitlock's high-tech systems have tremendous reach, they haven't totally replaced face-to-face selling and customer service. Whitlock might climb in his truck to deliver a shipment to a nearby customer or fly to help advise a factory having equipment problems. Technology can't totally replace shoe leather.

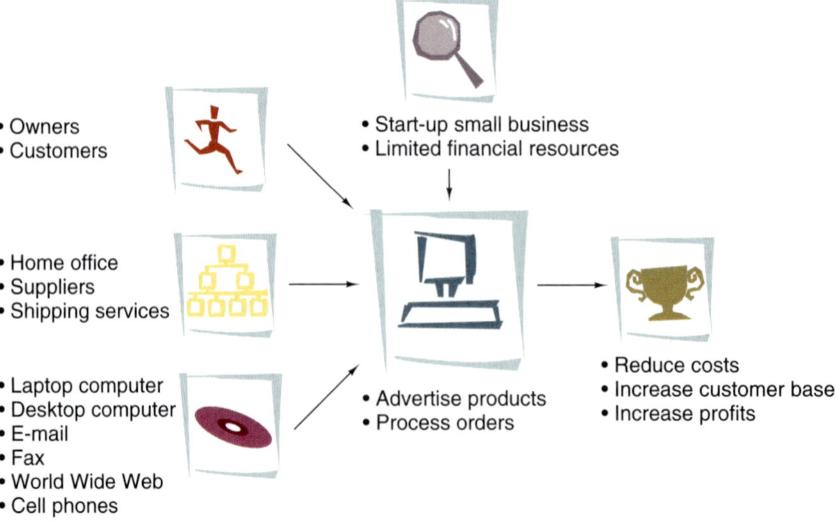

SOURCE: Thomas Petzinger, Jr., "Gasket Salesman Uses E-Mail, Fax, the Web—and Shoe Leather," *The Wall Street Journal*, April 4, 1997.

1.1 INTRODUCTION

EPM Inc. is typical of many organizations today that find information systems crucial to their day-to-day operation and long-term survival. Regardless of size, organizations increasingly need information systems to respond to the problems and opportunities of today's global business environment. Information systems are transforming the way work is conducted and the products and services that are produced. Information systems are also giving individuals new tools for improving their lives and their communities. This chapter starts our discussion of information systems by explaining how an information system works and how it uses the elements of people, organizations, and technology to solve problems.

WHY STUDY INFORMATION SYSTEMS?

Why should you be concerned about information systems? Isn't that the job of technical people? The example of EPM Inc. provides at least three reasons why you should understand how information systems work.

As a society, we are engaged in a global economic competition for resources, markets, and incomes with other nations in both Europe and Asia. For Adam Smith, the eighteenth-century Scottish economist who initiated the modern study of economics with his book *The Wealth of Nations,* the income of a nation depended on how well that society organized production in its domestic factories. Today it is clear that our society will have to organize global markets, international corporations, and multinational work forces if we are to maintain and enhance our standard of living. We will need information systems to do this effectively and successfully.

Second, we will need a thorough understanding of information systems to achieve higher levels of productivity and effectiveness within our domestic factories and offices. It simply will be impossible to operate even a small business efficiently without significant systems investments. Challenges posed by new customers, competitors, technology, political relations, economic conditions, government regulations, and labor force characteristics call for many kinds of changes, such as improved production techniques, new products and services, new administrative systems, and new employee skills. You must know how to identify problems and opportunities and how to use information systems to increase organizational responsiveness.

Finally, your effectiveness as a professional or entrepreneur—indeed, your career and income—will in part depend on how well you apply yourself to the task of understanding information systems. Whether you want to be a graphic artist, professional musician, lawyer, business manager, or small business owner, you will be working with and through information systems. The conclusion is inescapable: You will have to be information systems literate.

Before we explore the growing role of information systems in business, we must first define an information system and its basic components.

Information system
A set of interrelated components that collect, retrieve, process, store, and distribute information for the purpose of facilitating planning, control, coordination, analysis, and decision making in organizations.

INFORMATION SYSTEMS IN ORGANIZATIONS

An **information system (IS)** can be defined as a set of interrelated components working together to collect, retrieve, process, store, and distribute

FIGURE 1.1

Activities of Information Systems: Input, Processing, and Output

An information system consists of three basic activities—input, processing, and output—that transform raw data into useful information. Feedback is output that is "fed back" to appropriate people or activities; it can be used to evaluate and refine the input stage.

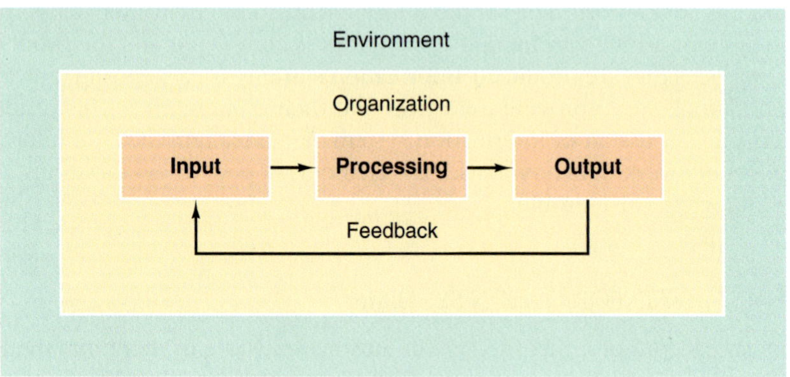

information for the purpose of facilitating planning, control, coordination, analysis, and decision making in businesses and other organizations (see Figure 1.1). Information systems contain information on significant people, places, and things in an organization's surrounding environment and within the organization itself. Information systems essentially transform information into a form usable for coordinating the flow of work in a firm, helping employees or managers make decisions, analyzing and visualizing complex subjects, and solving other kinds of problems. Information systems accomplish this through a cycle of three basic activities: input, processing, and output.

Input
The capture or collection of raw data resources from within an organization or from its external environment.

Processing
The conversion of raw input into a more appropriate and useful form.

Output
The transfer of processed information to the people or activities that will use it.

Feedback
Output that is returned to appropriate members of the organization to help them refine or correct the input phase.

Input involves capturing or collecting raw data resources from within the organization or from its external environment. **Processing** involves converting this raw input into a more appropriate and useful form. **Output** involves transferring the processed information to the people or activities that will use it. Information systems also store information, in various forms of completeness, until it is needed for processing or output. **Feedback** is output that is returned to appropriate members of the organization to help them refine or correct the input phase.

Computerized information systems capture data from either inside or outside an organization via paper forms that record them or by having them entered directly into a computer system using a keyboard or other device. Input activities, such as recording, coding, classifying, and editing, focus on ensuring that the required data are correct and complete. During processing, the data are organized, analyzed, and manipulated through calculations, comparisons, summarization, and sorting into a more meaningful and useful form. Output activities transmit the results of processing to the locations where they will be used for decision making, design, innovation, coordination, or control. The output of information systems takes various forms—printed reports, graphic displays, video displays, sound, or data to feed other information systems. The information system must also store data and information in an organized fashion so that they are easily accessible for processing or for output. Computerized information systems are essential in today's work environment because they can help people analyze problems, visualize complex subjects, create new products, communicate, make decisions, coordinate, and control.

For example, Choice Hotels International Inc. (NYSE: CHH) uses a networked information system to book and keep track of room reservations for the Quality, Comfort, Econo Lodge, Clarion, Sleep, Rodeway, and MainStay Suites hotel chains that it franchises. When travelers and travel agents call with reservations, agents at reservation centers worldwide enter the reservation data into the system using desktop computers (input). The data are transmitted to a large central computer center in Phoenix for updating Choice Hotels' reservation and client records (processing) and for storage. The system produces reservation booking forms and reports for managment (output). Figure 1.2 illustrates the input, processing, output, and feedback functions of this system.

We need to clarify our definition further by saying that we are concerned exclusively in this book with formal, organizational, computer-based information systems (CBIS). The CBIS we describe in this book are **formal systems,** which rely on mutually accepted and relatively fixed definitions of data and procedures for collecting, storing, processing, and distributing information. For instance, a manual file of customer names and addresses or an alphabetical card catalog in a library is a formal information system because it is established by an organization and conforms to organizational rules and

Formal systems
Information systems that rely on mutually accepted and relatively fixed definitions of data and procedures for collecting, storing, processing, and distributing information.

FIGURE 1.2

Input/Processing/Output Model Applied to the Choice Hotels Reservation System

In the Choice Hotels reservations system, reservation agents enter raw data into the system via desktop computer workstations. The central computer in Phoenix processes the data by updating records and storing necessary information. The output includes bookings forms and reports for management. These are sent to appropriate staff members, whose feedback can have an impact on how future input data are collected.

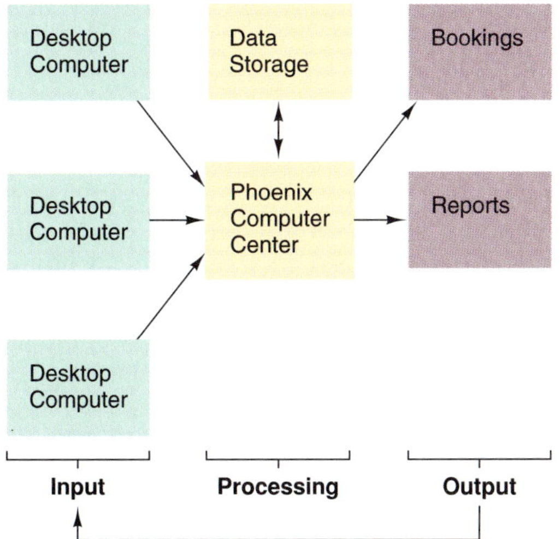

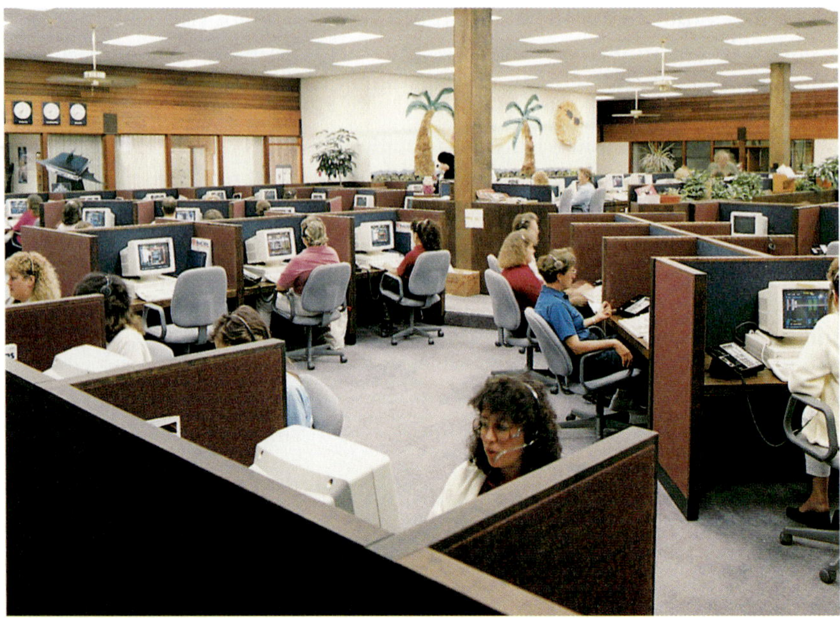

By using a networked reservation system, Choice Hotels International can instantaneously book and keep track of individual and group reservations made for the company's hotels all over the world.

SOURCE: Courtesy of Choice Hotels International.

procedures; this means that each entry in the system has the same format of information and the same type of content.

Informal systems, by contrast, do not have these features. For instance, students inevitably form small groups of friends, and these groups usually have information systems. In these informal information systems, there is no agreement on what information is, how it will be stored, and what will be stored or processed. Like office gossip networks, groups of friends freely share information on a large and constantly changing set of objects, topics, and personalities. These open, informal systems are very important—indeed, they are very powerful and flexible—but they are not the direct subject of this book.

CBIS are built for the purpose of solving significant problems as they are perceived in organizations. This insight—that systems exist to solve business and other problems—will be used often throughout this book. We can use this insight to understand not only the systems that exist now (and why) but also the way to build systems in the future and the skills you will need to have.

COMPONENTS OF INFORMATION SYSTEMS

CBIS use computer technology to perform some portions of the processing functions of an information system and some of the input and output functions as well. It would be a mistake, however, to describe an information system in terms of the computer alone. An information system is an integral part of an organization and is a product of three components: technology, organizations, and people (see Figure 1.3). One cannot understand or use information systems effectively in business without knowledge of their organizational and people dimensions as well as their technical dimensions.

Organizations Organizations shape information systems in several obvious ways. Business firms are formal organizations. They consist of specialized units with a clear-cut division of labor and experts employed and trained for different business functions such as sales, manufacturing, human resources, and finance. Organizations are hierarchical and structured. Employees in a business firm are arranged in rising levels of authority in which each person is accountable to someone above him or her. The upper levels of the hierarchy consist of management, and the lower levels consist of nonmanagerial employees. Formal procedures, or rules for accomplishing tasks, coordinate specialized groups in the firm so that they will complete their work in an acceptable manner. Some of these procedures, such as how to write up a purchase order or how to correct an erroneous bill, are incorporated into information systems. Each organization has a unique culture, or bedrock assumptions, values, and ways of doing things that have been accepted by most members of the firm.

Different levels and different specialties in an organization in turn create different interests in the organization and different points of view, which often conflict. Out of these conflicts, politics, and eventual compromises come information systems. Organizations need to build these systems to solve problems created both by these internal factors and by external environmental factors, such as changes in government regulations or market conditions.

People People use information from computer-based systems in their jobs, integrating it into the work environment. They are required to input data

FIGURE 1.3

An Information System: Not Just a Computer

A successful system has organizational and people dimensions in addition to technical components. It exists to answer organizational needs, including problems presented by the external environment created by political, demographic, economic, and social trends.

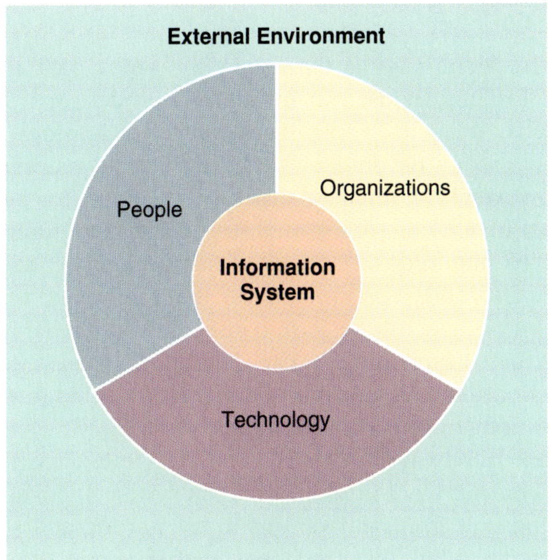

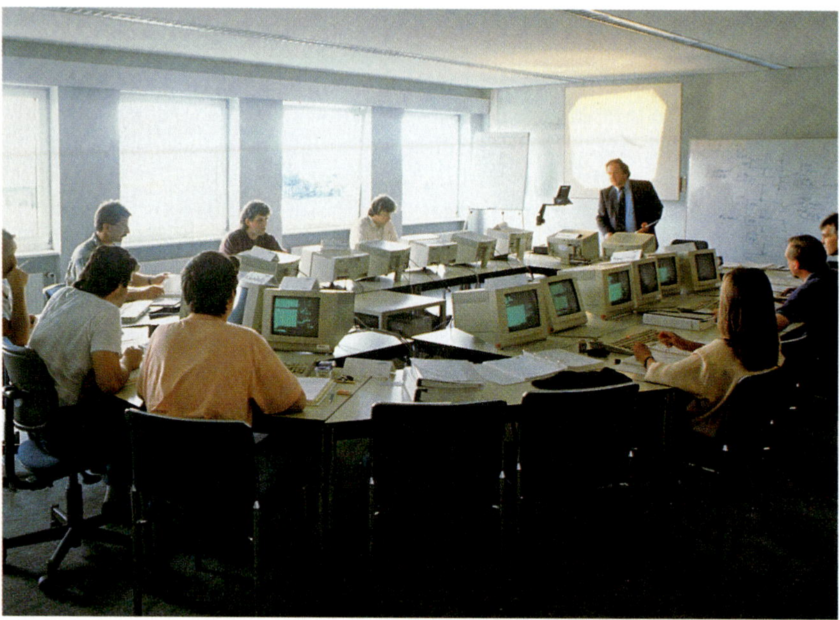

Personal computer training classes are essential to the effective use of information systems in most companies today.

SOURCE: Tony Stone Images, Inc.

into the system, either by entering data into the system themselves or by putting the data on a medium that a computer can read.

Employees require special training to perform their jobs or to use information systems effectively. Their attitudes about their jobs, employers, or computer technology can have a powerful effect on their ability to use information systems productively. Ergonomics refers to the interaction of humans and machines in the work environment; it includes the design of jobs, health issues, and the way in which people interact with information systems, and it has a strong bearing on employees' morale, productivity, and receptiveness to information systems. The user interface, or those portions of an information system with which people must interact, such as reports or video displays, also has a strong bearing on employees' efficiency and productivity.

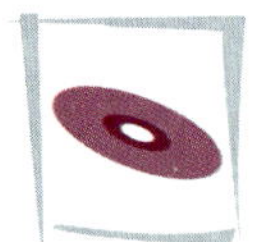

Manual system
An information system that uses only paper and pencil technology and does not rely on computers.

Technology The technology is the means by which data are transformed and organized for human use. An information system can be an entirely **manual system,** using only paper-and-pencil technology. (An example would be a professor's file folder containing course records and grades.) Computers, however, have replaced manual technology for processing large volumes of data or for complex processing work. Computers can execute millions, and even hundreds of millions, of instructions per second, performing in a matter of seconds a processing task that might take years to perform manually. Computers can also perform consistently and reliably over a longer period of time than a human being can. The information systems described in this text are computer based; that is, they rely on some form of computer technology for input, output, processing, and storage.

Computer hardware
The physical equipment used for the input, processing, and output work in an information system.

Computer hardware is the physical equipment used for the input, processing, and output work in an information system. It consists of the computer processing unit itself and various input, output, and storage devices plus physical media to link these devices together.

Input hardware collects data and converts them into a form that the computer can process. The most common computer input device is the computer keyboard, but others will be described in subsequent chapters. Processing hardware transforms input to output based on instructions supplied to the computer through software. A special processing unit in the computer itself, called the central processing unit, is primarily responsible for this task. Output hardware delivers the output of an information system to its user and commonly consists of printers or video display terminals. Chapter 4 discusses computer hardware in greater detail.

Computer software consists of preprogrammed instructions that coordinate the work of computer hardware components to perform the processes required by each information system. Without software, computer hardware would not know what to do and how and when to do it. Software consists of related programs, each of which is a group of instructions for performing specific processing tasks. Chapter 5 treats computer software in more detail.

Computer software
Preprogrammed instructions that coordinate the work of computer hardware components to perform the processes required by each information system.

The **storage technology** for organizing and storing the data used by a business is a powerful determinant of the data's usefulness and availability. Storage technology includes both the physical media for storing data, such as magnetic or optical disk or tape, and the software governing the organization of data on these physical media. Storage media are discussed in Chapter 4, and data organization and access methods are treated in Chapter 6.

Storage technology
Physical media for storing data and the software governing the organization of data on these media.

Communications technology is used to link different pieces of hardware and to transfer data from one location to another via networks. A **network** links two or more computers together to transmit voice, data, images, sound, and video or to share resources such as a printer. Communications technology consists of both physical media and software that support communication by electronic means. Chapters 7 and 8 cover communications and networks.

Communications technology
Physical media and software that support communication by electronic means, usually over some distance.

Network
Physical media and software that link two or more computers together to transmit voice, data, images, sound, and/or video or to share resources such as a printer.

Let's return to the Choice Hotels reservation system and see where each of these components fits in. The technology consists of a large central computer linked via communications technology to desktop computers and technology for storing reservation and client data. By using a computer, Choice Hotels International can process hundreds of thousands, even millions, of reservation requests each day. The people component requires training the reservations center and hotel staff to enter and receive reservation bookings and to use the computers as well as designing an appropriate user interface for these tasks. The organization component anchors the reservation system in Choice Hotels' sales and marketing function; it identifies specific procedures for booking reservations (i.e., obtaining customer identification, confirming the reservation, securing the reservation with a deposit or credit card number) and provides reports on bookings for sales staff and higher levels of management. How might hotels use information system technology in the future? The Focus on Technology explores this topic.

Review the diagram at the beginning of this chapter. It shows how people, organization, and technology elements work together to create an information system solution to a problem. The solution provides specific benefits. We begin each chapter of the text with a similar diagram to help you analyze the opening vignette and other systems you will encounter.

THE HOTEL OF THE FUTURE: IT'S HERE

When you arrive at the hotel, you introduce yourself by slipping your smart card into a doorway slot. The smart card looks like a credit card, but its tiny embedded circuitry can store and record information such as a person's name, purchase transactions, and bank account activities. Forget about the check-in desk. You can go straight to your room, which was assigned earlier by computer. The door to your room opens when you say your name. After you unpack, you punch in channel 143 on the TV and hold a videoconference with colleagues 2,000 miles away in Seattle. After the meeting, you switch to another channel to shop for a gift. Just before turning in, you use the videophone to see how the family is doing while you are on the road. This "future" scene will soon be commonplace because hotels are finding new ways to use information systems technology to please their customers.

Hotel guests habitually complain about the amount of time required for check-in. The Marriott hotel chain listened. It launched a program called 1st 10 that virtually eliminates the front desk. When a guest makes a reservation, the information system collects pertinent information such as the credit card number and time of arrival, reducing check-in time from an average of 3 minutes to 1½ minutes. With smart card technology, Marriott hopes eventually to reduce check-in time to seconds.

Other hotel chains are replacing their front desks with self-service kiosks that work like automated teller machines (ATMs). Guests slide in their credit cards to enter, punch a few buttons, and pick up their room keys. Hyatt Hotels Corp. is expanding its "Touch and Go" automated check-in system to the majority of its nonresort hotels.

The Internet provides another avenue for expanding hotel services. Travelers can bypass travel agents and reservation desks and book their own room reservations using the World Wide Web. For example, a Web site called TravelWeb, operated by a consortium of 20 major hotel companies including the Hyatt and Hilton hotel chains, enables people to search for a hotel by geographic location, room rate, or various amenities such as health club facilities, conference rooms, or babysitting services. They can pull up thousands of "electronic brochures" with pictures of rooms and information about nearby tourist attractions. Guests can then select the hotel and room they want and make their own reservations over the Web.

FOCUS Questions:
What new information system technologies are being used in this case? How could they be used to change the way the Choice Hotels reservation system works?

SOURCES: Jon Bigness, "Impersonal Touch: More Hotels Automate Front Desk," *The Wall Street Journal;* June 18, 1996; Faye Rice, "The New Rules of Superlative Service," *Fortune: The Tough New Customer,* Autumn/Winter 1993; and http://www.travelweb.com.

THE INTERNET REVOLUTION

The technical foundations of information systems today are much broader than in the past. Most computers no longer operate in isolation but as part of larger communications networks. These networks can span desktops, factory floors, or offices around the globe. They can link a company to a buyer or supplier 3,000 miles away. The most powerful advances in information processing are occurring through computers linked together in networks.

Internet
A vast interconnected network of networks linking business, governmental, scientific, and educational organizations as well as individuals around the world.

The largest and most widely used of these networks is the **Internet.** The Internet is a vast interconnected network of networks linking business, government, scientific, and educational organizations as well as individuals across the globe. At last estimate, the Internet connected more than 100,000 commercial and publicly owned networks and more than 40 million people in nearly 200 countries (see Figure 1.4).

FIGURE 1.4

The Internet

The Internet is a global network of networks that allows people to access and distribute information all over the world.

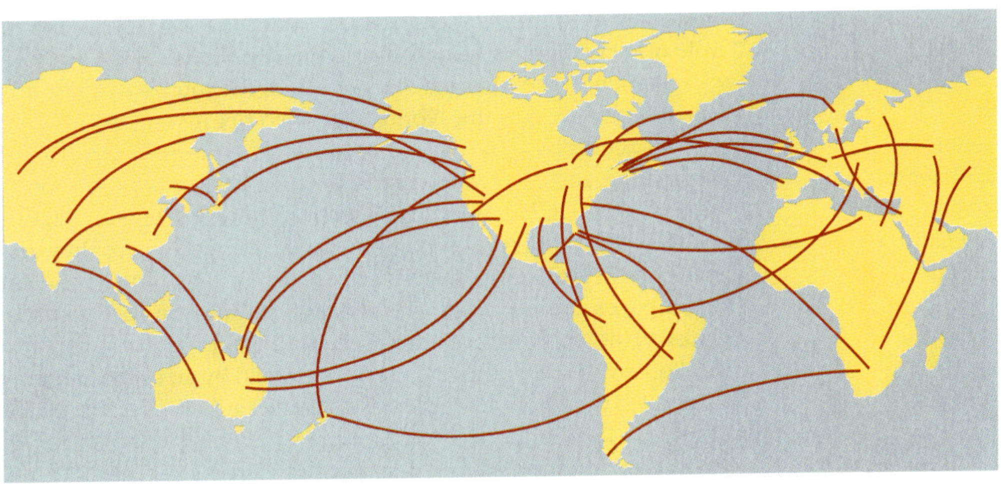

Almost every type of computer can connect to the Internet using ordinary telephone lines, even if these computers have different sizes, manufacturers, and technical standards. Once connected to the Internet, your computer becomes part of this worldwide network of computers. The Internet can transmit many types of information, including text messages, graphic images, video, and sound. Table 1.1 describes some of the many things that can be done on the Internet.

Because of its ease of use and ability to link people to information from all over the world, the Internet is transforming the face of computing. It is creating a foundation for new types of products, services, and relationships among organizations. It is changing the way people access information, conduct business, communicate, collaborate, and even how they spend their free

TABLE 1.1

The Internet: An All-Purpose Information Tool

Activity	What You Can Do on the Internet
Communication	Send electronic mail messages
	Participate in interactive discussion groups
	Transmit voice conversations
Research	Search library card catalogs
	Search for documents, articles, and books
	Transfer computer files containing text, graphics, or video to your computer
	Transfer software to your computer
Business	Display electronic brochures and advertisements
	Sell and purchase goods and services
Entertainment	Play interactive video games
	Read illustrated or animated books and magazines
	View short video clips

time. We discuss relevant features of the Internet in every chapter of this text because the Internet affects so many aspects of information systems. The Internet provides new information tools and new ways of looking at problems. The new title of this book—*Information Systems and the Internet: A Problem-Solving Approach*—reflects our belief that the Internet is recasting the role of technology in the problem-solving process.

Much of the phenomenal growth of the Internet can be attributed to a capability known as the World Wide Web because the Web makes the Internet so accessible. The **World Wide Web** is a set of standards for storing, organizing, and displaying information in a networked environment. Information is stored and displayed as electronic document-like "pages," which can be viewed by any type of computer regardless of where they are located. By clicking on highlighted words or buttons on a Web page, one can link to related pages to find additional information, software programs, or still more links to other points on the Web. Web pages can contain text, graphics, audio, or video. All of the Web pages created by an organization or individual are called a **Web site.** Figure 1.5 illustrates a Web page from EPM Inc.'s Web site described in the chapter-opening vignette. (Web pages for another company, Virtual Vineyards, are illustrated in Figure 1.11.)

World Wide Web
A set of standards for storing, organizing, and displaying information in a networked environment.

Web site
All the Web pages created by an organization or individual.

Web sites can be used to publish information, exchange messages, and even accept buy-and-sell transactions to conduct business electronically.

FIGURE 1.5

A Sample Web Page

Web pages display information as document-like pages that can include text, images, sound, video, and links to other Web pages. This Web page from EPM Inc. welcomes visitors to the company's Web site.

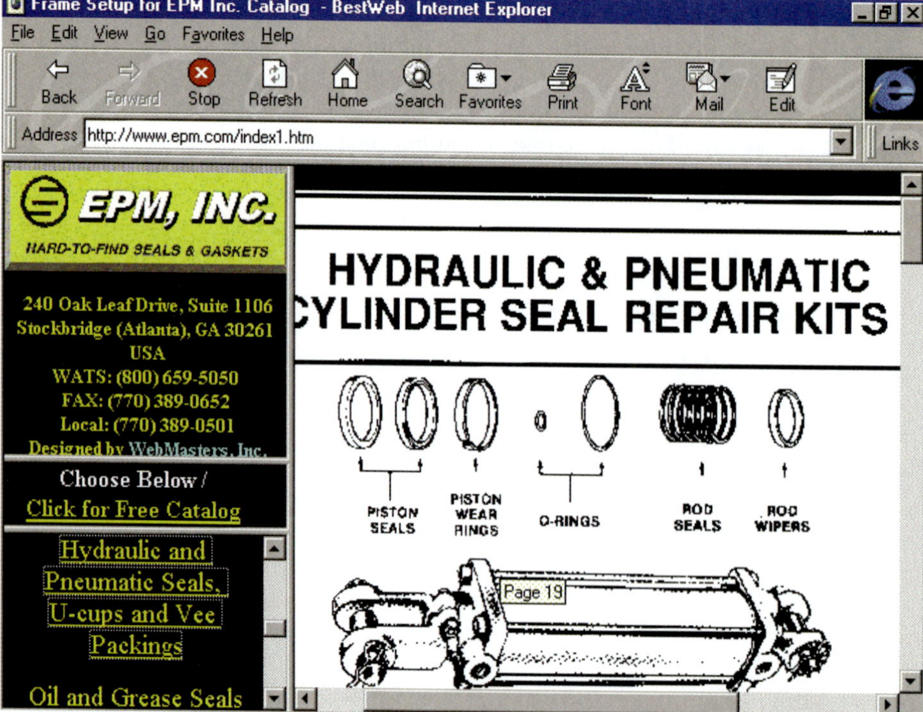

The Web's multimedia and graphic capabilities, low cost, and ease of use, make it a flexible and low-cost platform for creating new kinds of information systems. For example, EPM Inc.'s Web site creates an information system that connects buyers and sellers. Customers accessing this Web site can view an online electronic catalog of its products and contact the company via telephone or E-mail to place orders. TravelWeb, described in the Focus on Technology is an information system for providing product information and for making hotel reservations. Chapter 8 describes the Web and other Internet capabilities in greater detail.

1.2 APPROACHES TO STUDYING INFORMATION SYSTEMS

You have probably already gathered that our emphasis in this book will be on how information systems work, not just on computers. Most people think that computers and information systems are the same thing. They also think that computer literacy and information systems literacy are identical. Although this may have been true in the early days of computing and systems, it is no longer true today.

COMPUTER LITERACY AND INFORMATION SYSTEMS LITERACY

We will draw a sharp distinction in this text between a computer, a computer program, and an information system. Computers—and other information technologies—are the technical foundations or the tools of information systems. Computers and communications equipment store, process, distribute, and communicate information. Computer programs, or software, are the sets of instructions that direct computer processing.

Information systems are much broader in scope. They encompass the technologies, organizational procedures, practices, and policies that generate information as well as the people who work with that information.

Computer literacy means knowing how to use information technology. It involves a knowledge of hardware, software, telecommunications, and information storage techniques. In general, computer literacy focuses on what goes inside the box called a computer—how disk drives work, how a random access memory works, and so forth. Computer literacy is an important part of designing solutions to problems, but it is just the first step.

Computer literacy
Knowledge about the use of information technology, including hardware, software, telecommunications, and information storage techniques.

To develop information systems literacy, you need more than just computer literacy. You also need to understand the nature of problems faced by organizations: Where do they come from? How can systems be designed to solve them? Who else is involved in building system solutions? How can the work be coordinated? These issues involve design, organization, and people.

Thus **information systems literacy** consists of three elements:

- A knowledge and hands-on facility with information technologies.
- A broadly based understanding of organizations and individuals from a behavioral perspective.
- A broadly based understanding of how to analyze and solve problems.

Information systems literacy
Knowledge and hands-on facility with information technologies, a broadly based understanding of organizations and individuals from a behavioral perspective, and a similar understanding of how to analyze and solve problems.

FIGURE 1.6

Information Systems Literacy: More Than Just Using a Computer

To be information systems literate, you must develop skills in analyzing and solving problems and in dealing effectively with people at both the individual and organizational levels. Think of this course as the center of this diagram, with the three skill areas comprising the major themes of the course.

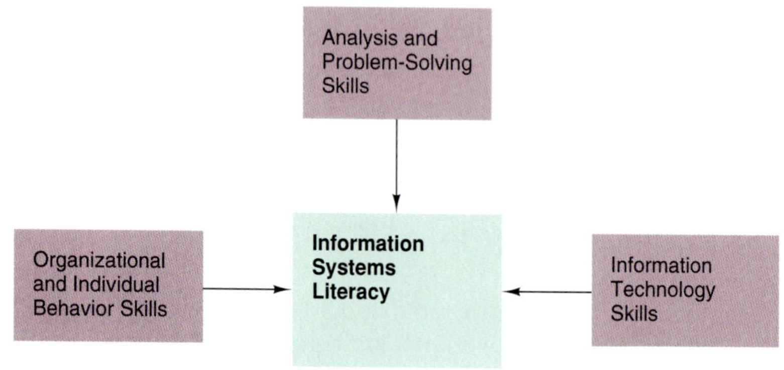

Figure 1.6 illustrates the three components of information systems literacy. Generally, students who major in information systems take courses in these three areas.

A house provides a good analogy for the difference between computer and information systems literacy. Houses are built with nails, hammers, wood, and plaster. But these alone do not make a house. Also involved in a good house are design, location, setting, landscaping, and hundreds of other features. These other considerations are crucial to the essential problem: putting a roof over one's head.

So it is with information systems: Information technologies are the tools—the hammers, nails, and materials. But to understand the systems, you need to understand the problems they were designed to solve, the proposed architectural and aesthetic solutions, and the organizational process that leads to systems.

DATA, INFORMATION, AND KNOWLEDGE

Philosophers have for centuries been struggling to define data or facts, information, and knowledge. A small library could easily be filled with their results. To arrive at some operational definitions, we can start with Plato (c. 428–348 B.C.), an ancient Greek philosopher whom you will no doubt read while in college. For Plato, pure data were a shadowy reflection on a wall of all the things going on in the world.[1] Thus **data** can be considered the raw facts, the infinite stream of things that are happening now and have happened in the past.

Data
Raw facts that can be shaped and formed to create information.

Information
Data that have been shaped by humans into a meaningful and useful form.

Knowledge
The stock of conceptual tools and categories used by humans to create, collect, store, and share information.

Information comes from the Latin word *informare,* meaning "to give form or shape." Most philosophers believe that it is the human mind that gives shape and form to data in order to create meaningful "information" and knowledge. Plato and other Greek philosophers originated this concept of a world of meaning, intention, and knowledge created by human beings. These ideas are at the heart of Western culture.

We will define **information** as data that have been given shape and form by human beings to make them meaningful and useful. **Knowledge** is the stock of conceptual tools and categories used by humans to create, collect, store, and share information. Knowledge can be stored as an artifact in a library—as a book, for instance—or in a computer program as a set of instructions that gives shape to otherwise meaningless streams of data.

Human beings have a long history of developing systems for the purpose of giving shape to data, as well as recording, storing, and sharing information and knowledge. Libraries, tabloids, writing, language, art, and mathematics are all examples of information systems. The focus of this text, and much of the course, will be on how CBIS store, collect, and share information and knowledge in organizations.

The Focus on Problem Solving shows how one of our fundamental information systems, the library, is being transformed by computers and the

FOCUS ON PROBLEM SOLVING

THE NEW LIBRARY: NO BOOKS

Every day, at libraries all over the world, workers are taking books off the shelf and throwing them away. They are creating the library of the future.

How can a library have no books? The answer lies in computer technology. A computer scans the pages of each book and stores them in digital form (often on CD-ROM disks) so that they can be retrieved by computer. The card catalog is gone, too. Instead, patrons can search for book titles, authors, and subjects using the computer. Many large public, university, and government libraries are electronically linked to each other for sharing catalogs and interlibrary loans.

Now many library card catalogs, journals, magazine articles, and government documents are available through the Internet. You need only tap into your telephone line from your desktop computer to access the catalog of the Library of Congress, Australian National University Library, or other libraries around the world using the World Wide Web. The Alex Catalog of Electronic Texts on the Internet, based at Oxford University, England (which is duplicated at North Carolina State University), links to hundreds of books and book-length manuscripts at Internet sites all over the world. You can find the full text for everything from *Alice in Wonderland* to the *Federalist Papers* or the "Hitchhiker's Guide to the Internet."

Electronic libraries and the Internet are transforming knowledge acquisition and research. When people "go to the library," they won't have to go anywhere. Communications technology, including the Internet, will bring the library to them. People will be able to sit at home browsing catalogs instead of shelves. They may even be able to obtain full documents, including text, pictures, and graphs or hear oral history collections through audio transmission. All of these features make electronic libraries more accessible, particularly for the disabled.

If computerized information could be sent cheaply from one library to another, there would be little need for libraries to maintain the same collection of books, articles, or documents. If Harvard University kept the electronic copy of the Nuremberg trials, there would be no need for Stanford or other universities to keep their own copies. Libraries would no longer have to keep dozens of copies of items on reserve for large classes, since many students could read them simultaneously on the computer.

Without the need to shelve hundreds of thousands of books, libraries will become smaller. Columbia University's law library cancelled a plan to build a $20 million addition to store new books, opting to scan and store 10,000 deteriorating old books each year on a large computer. This frees up enough shelf space for all the new copyrighted material the library acquires each year—at far less cost than new buildings or bookshelves.

FOCUS Questions: What problems are solved by using electronic libraries? How can electronic libraries benefit businesses and society in general? What are the disadvantages?

SOURCES: Kate Murphy, "Moving from the Card Catalogue to the Internet," *The New York Times*, January 6, 1997, and William M. Bulkeley, "Libraries Shift from Books to Computers," *The Wall Street Journal*, January 8, 1993.

FIGURE 1.7

A Sociotechnical View of Information Systems

In a system, technology, organizations, and people must cooperate and support one another to optimize the performance of the entire system. The three elements adjust and continue to change over time.

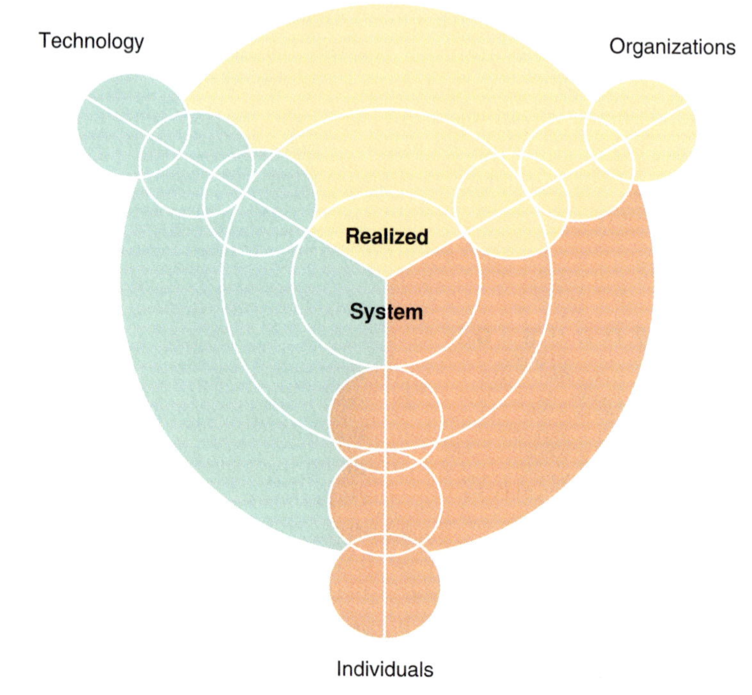

Internet and how such changes affect the acquisition of information and knowledge.

A SOCIOTECHNICAL PERSPECTIVE ON INFORMATION SYSTEMS

The view we adopt in this book is that information systems are sociotechnical systems that involve the coordination of technology, organizations, and people. The most advanced computing technology is essentially worthless unless businesses can make use of the technology and unless individuals feel comfortable using it.

Sociotechnical perspective An approach to information systems that involves the coordination of technology, organizations, and people.

In the **sociotechnical perspective,** information technology, organizations, and individuals go through a process of mutual adjustment and discovery as systems are developed. Figure 1.7 illustrates what happens over time as information systems are built. In many instances, the technology must be altered to fit the unique needs of each organization. Almost always, organizational changes must be invented and then implemented. And, of course, a considerable amount of retraining of employees must take place to develop a successful, useful system.

1.3 PURPOSE OF STUDYING INFORMATION SYSTEMS

As we pointed out earlier, the chances are very high that your employer will ask you to go out and find some sort of system solution to a business problem. The intent of this book is to prepare you for that eventuality.

But what do you really need to know about computers and information systems to succeed in today's and tomorrow's job markets? Do you have to know how a computer processes bits of data, how to program a computer in some esoteric language, how to wire together a PC workstation and a printer, how electrons behave on the surface of a chip, how a disk drive works, or how a business uses information systems for competitive advantage? Do you have to know everything about computers? These are difficult questions with which educators themselves struggle.

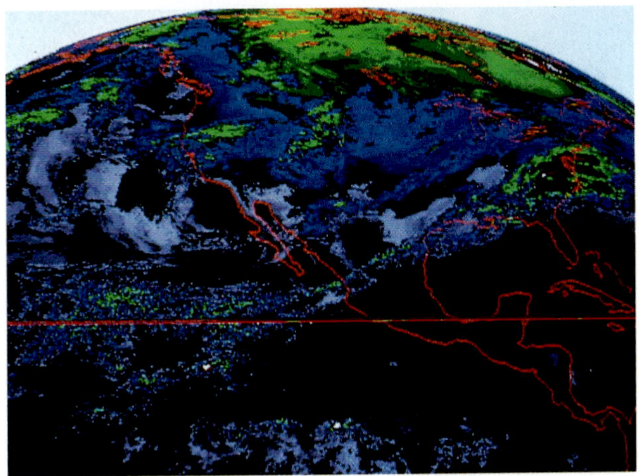

Helping business people make decisions, producing original works of art, and generating weather maps are but some of the many uses of computers today. Information systems literacy is becoming essential for careers in business, science, and the arts.

SOURCES: Courtesy of International Business Machines Corporation, Computer Associates International, Inc., and © John Bowden Uniphoto Picture Agency.

INTERSECTING SKILLS

Given the broad sociotechnical perspective on the systems just described, it is clear that no one person has all the expertise needed to put together successful information systems that can solve business problems. Even technical professionals acknowledge that no one person has a complete technical understanding of all there is to know about, say, an IBM or an Apple Macintosh PC. As it turns out, information systems are inherently a group effort involving different people with different technical, business, and analytic skills.

So, one answer to how much you need to know is that there are three skills to consider: technical, organizational, and analytic/problem-solving abilities. Some people will excel in one or two areas; most people will not excel in all three.

CAREER PATHS AND CRUCIAL SKILLS

Some of you will want to pursue a career in the information systems profession either as a technical person or as a manager of projects and systems. Others will choose a career path outside information systems, either in a technical area like engineering or biology or in a business field such as management, marketing, accounting, finance, or sales. But life and careers are un-

FIGURE 1.8

The Importance of Sociotechnical Skills in Your Career

Whether you're interested in a technical or nontechnical career, sociotechnical skills are crucial. Note that analysis and problem solving are important abilities for all four of the career paths shown.

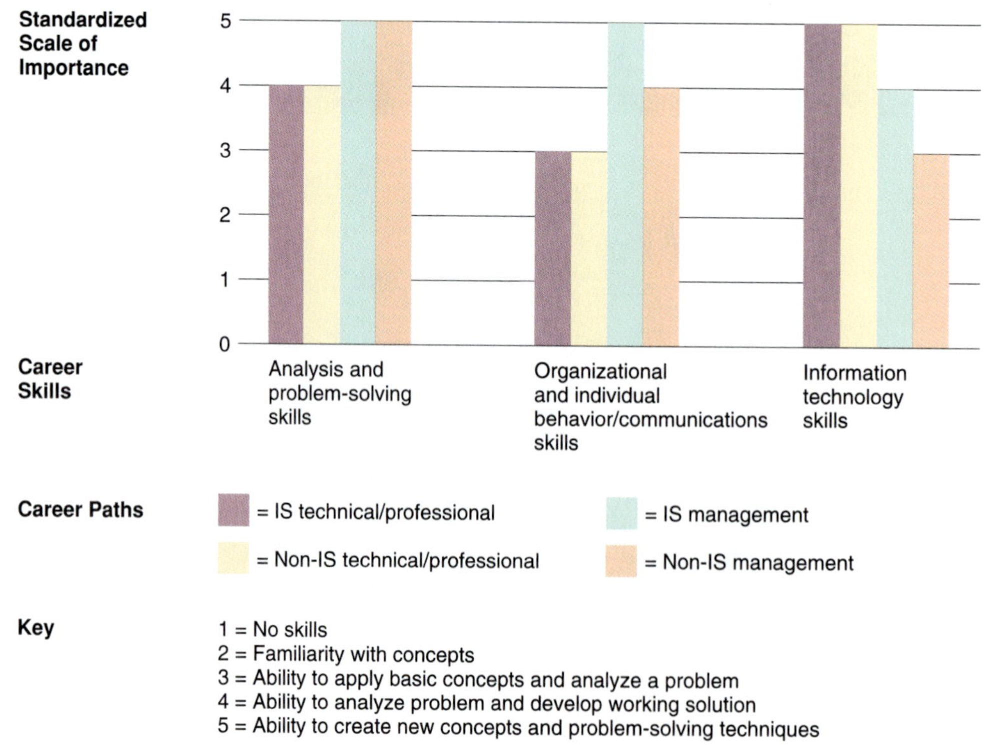

FIGURE 1.9

Courses That Will Help You Develop Important Career Skills

Each of the skill areas shown in Figure 1.8 involves an ability to perform specific organizational tasks. Here we break down each skill area into some of the particular skills that it includes. The third row lists relevant courses that will help you develop your abilities in this area.

Career Skill	Analysis/Problem Solving	Behavior and Communication Skills	Technology Skills
Specific Skills	Analytic framework Functional requirements Physical design Implementation Systems development	Organizational strategy Structure Culture Making decisions Business procedures and functions	Hardware Software Telecommunications Database
Relevant Courses	Philosophy English literature History Behavioral sciences Mathematics	Psychology Sociology Economics English literature Languages Speech	MIS Database Telecommunications Advanced software

predictable. Many current managers of information systems divisions, even entire computer companies, had little or no background in computers or systems. Hence, you will have to be prepared for several possible futures.

Depending on what kind of career path you want to pursue, you can obtain some idea of the skills you will need from Figure 1.8. There the importance of specific skills are ranked on a scale from 1 to 5, with 1 indicating that no knowledge is required and 5 indicating that extensive training is needed.

RELATED COURSES

Figure 1.9 lists specific interpersonal and on-the-job abilities that are part of these skills. It also shows courses in related disciplines that will help you develop these crucial skills. You can use this table to plan your undergraduate career and to see the relationships between diverse courses. You might wonder, for instance, what possible relevance a philosophy course has to information systems. Philosophy courses teach you about the differences among data, information, and knowledge, and they can help you understand how to conceptualize systems and how to proceed with problem solving. Psychology classes can help you understand the dynamics of individual change, interpersonal conflict, and learning. Sociology courses are useful for understanding organizational structure, change, and decision making, while economics courses provide you with the concepts needed to evaluate the return on investment in information systems and productivity.

As these figures show, information systems are no longer islands isolated from the mainstream of the corporation, staffed by technical experts. A person must have a very broad background in the liberal arts, behavioral sciences, and technology to really excel in an information systems world. Communication skills—being able to read, write, speak, and think clearly—will be more important in today's information economy than at any time in history. Therefore, you should see this course in relation to other courses in your college career and plan accordingly.

1.4 USING INFORMATION SYSTEMS WISELY: THE ROAD AHEAD

You might think from listening to advertisements or reading the newspaper that most of the significant problems with computers and information systems have been solved and that all we have to do is rely on cheaper, more powerful technology to solve our pressing productivity, quality, national wealth, and competitive problems in world markets. Nothing could be further from the truth. In fact, we are just beginning to learn how to use the currently available technology wisely, not to mention the new technology being tested in the lab.

Every technology has a development path, and it often takes almost two generations (30–40 years) before the full potential of a technology even begins to be exploited. For example, most experts would agree that although automobiles were invented in 1890, it was not until the 1920s, or even the 1930s, that the modern, mass-produced, consciously engineered automobile appeared. For a considerable period, the auto was simply a "horseless carriage" with a tiller rather than a steering wheel.

With computers and information systems we are still facing many difficult problems. Here are four issues for you to think about as you read this book: technology, productivity, strategic business issues, and people. You might want to discuss and debate these issues with your classmates or professor.

TECHNOLOGY

Briefly stated, we face two related technology problems: (1) computing hardware is advancing far more rapidly than our ability to write useful software, and (2) both are changing much faster than the ability of our organizations to understand and apply the hardware and software (see Figure 1.10). Moreover, information systems must not only perform the well-defined tasks for which they have traditionally been used, but they must also provide resources that will enable people to do their jobs more efficiently and effectively.

An appropriate analogy might be your college library. Once the library has installed and mastered the card index system and students have learned the mechanics of working with card catalogs, the college dean, president,

FIGURE 1.10

The Productivity Problem: Why Can't We Get Better Faster?

The power of software has steadily improved; it doubles approximately every eight years. The power of hardware has soared; it grows by a factor of ten every five years. Meanwhile, the average rate at which people (and organizations) learn and apply new information and knowledge in the workplace grows very slowly—an average increase in productivity of 2 percent per year.

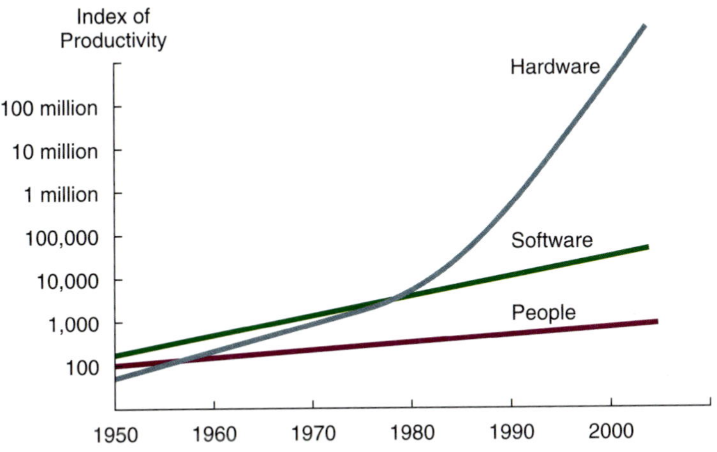

and professors must answer a more challenging question: What else is needed at the library to raise the quality of student research, thinking, and education? This is a far more complex problem than the mere mechanics of storing and accessing information. Similarly, information technology must address the broader concern of changing the way people work and think so that they will be able to take full advantage of the technology.

As we will discuss in greater detail in Chapters 4–8, while computing hardware is growing exponentially in power, and prices are falling about as fast, software—the set of instructions that controls information systems—is growing in power linearly. In contrast, the rate at which people learn is relatively constant, and the rate of change in the absorption and application of new knowledge in factories and offices is no greater than the annual rate of productivity increase (about 2 percent per year).

No one wants (or knows how) to slow down the growth of technology because it is potentially beneficial. Therefore, we must find a way to increase the rate of growth in the power of software and reduce its cost. And we must also increase the rate at which individuals absorb and understand information technology knowledge.

One possibility is to make writing software applications as simple as, say, using pen and ink to write an essay. In Chapter 5 we talk about new developments in programming and applications development that might make this possible. Another is to take advantage of the easy-to-use capabilities of the Internet and the World Wide Web (see Chapter 8).

But how can we increase the rate at which individuals in business firms increase their stock of knowledge and learn new technologies and techniques? What do we do about senior and middle managers who do not want to learn? What about other employees?

FOCUS ON **ORGANIZATIONS**

WINE FINDS ITS TIME

How does the ancient art of wine making get along with modern communications technology? Just fine, thank you. The marriage of these two contrasting industries was born out of an actual matrimony. Peter Granoff and his brother-in-law Robert Olson couldn't have had more divergent career paths. That is, until Olson quit his job as a marketing manager at Silicon Graphics, a computer company. He saw an opportunity to apply the technology behind the software he sold for Silicon to another avenue: online sales and customer administration. Olson unfortunately lacked a product to market. This was in 1994, when most people either didn't understand the Internet or didn't want to deal with it. Luckily for Olson, his brother-in-law's branch of business was in need of renovation.

Peter Granoff had spent the better part of two decades serving various functions in the wine industry, readily becoming an expert on it. He watched as it followed the lead of other retail-oriented businesses in appeasing the consumer call for lower prices by creating superstores. Such stores kept an abundance of wines in stock, but purchased fewer varieties. This enabled them to substitute regular sales clerks for wine experts who received higher wages. These savings were passed on to the customers, most of whom were willing to sacrifice knowledgeable service for convenient shopping and savings. Consequently, smaller wineries had no one to sell their product to because they could not provide the output that superstores demanded. Small wine producers were responsible for many of the industry's best wines, but they couldn't survive under the new order. Granoff knew there had to be people who were just as interested in obtaining fine, specialty wines as he was. The question was how to reach them.

The answer, it turned out, was the Internet. Olson and Granoff pooled their talents to create Virtual Vineyards, an online market that serves both the winemaker and the consumer. The key to the success of their Web site is the ability to offer the highest caliber products at the lowest possible prices. Olson and Granoff believe that the Web represents an appropriate forum for this challenge for three reasons: (1) Computers are perfectly suited for the task of searching for key words and comparing numbers, (2) online retail reduces marketing costs because it is available to potential customers 24 hours a day 365 days a year, and (3) a Web site can sell directly to customers, eliminating middlemen and distribution costs.

Olson obviously provides the technology and knowledge involved in permitting people to make purchases from Virtual Vineyards with their computers. Granoff provides credibility and expertise. Virtual Vineyards tries to do more than other wine shops on the Web by educating its visitors. The site provides Granoff's descriptions of each wine for sale and of its winery. Users can click to find out information about a particular class of wine or see a chart that visually evaluates (see Figure 1.11) each wine label. Customers of Virtual Vineyards know that the information and recommendations they receive come from one source, and they know exactly who he is. The site contains no links to other wine-related pages, leaving Granoff as the sole voice of conviction. Users learn as they shop, something they can no longer do at their local liquor superstore. A final factor adding to the air of authority around these cybergrapes is the stock, which is purchased from a wide variety of wineries. The brothers-in-law show no favorites and welcome criticism from customers.

PRODUCTIVITY

Although the United States has invested more in computers than any other country, there is an enormous—and still expanding—gap between the growth in computing power and the annual increase in productivity in the United States (see Figure 1.10 for an illustration). Why is this so? How can

FIGURE 1.11

How Virtual Vineyards Educates Visitors

Peter's Tasting Chart is another Virtual Vineyards' innovation, conveying a great deal of information at a glance. Each wine label is rated along seven dimensions of wine taste, with each line representing a range for that dimension. The placement of the red diamond indicates the status of the wine for each taste dimension.

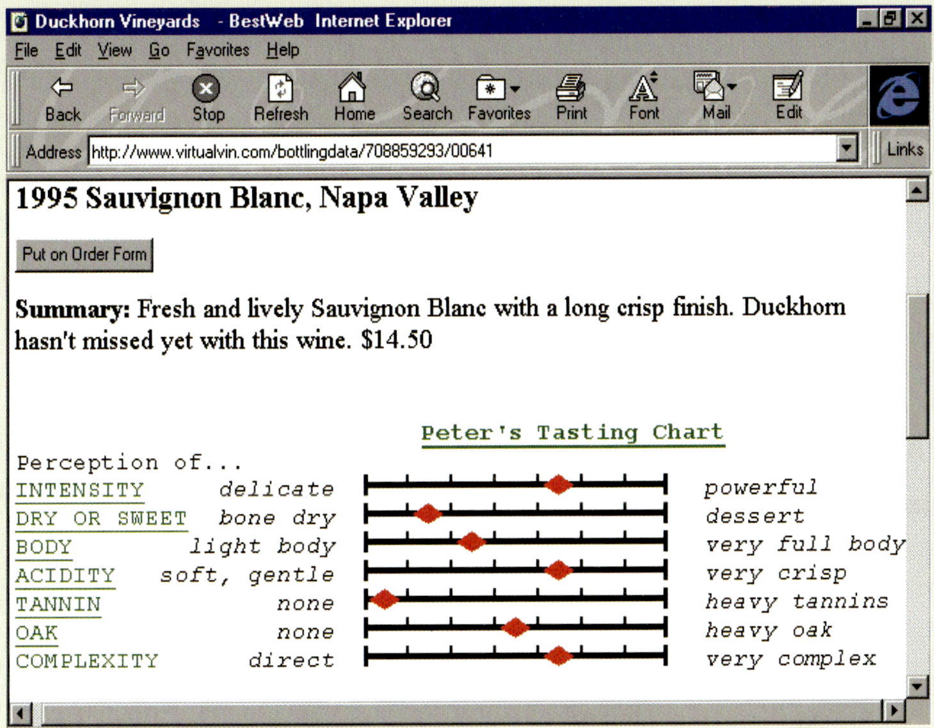

By creating Virtual Vineyards, Peter Granoff and Robert Olson have taught the business community an important lesson on how to redefine an organization in the face of a changing market. They maintain a profitable business without sacrificing the first-class service and personal touch of a small enterprise. Sales have been increasing by an average of 20 percent per month, and sales have already reached $1 million.

FOCUS Questions:
How did Virtual Vineyards rethink the wine business? What role did the Internet play? What people, organization, and technology elements had to be changed to redefine this wine business?

SOURCE: Fred Hapgood, "What Makes Virtual Vineyards Rule?," *Inc. Technology*, No. 2, 1996.

the power of hardware grow so fast, while software and ultimate productivity in offices and factories grow so slowly? One central challenge of this course is to learn how to bend the productivity curve upward so it will be more in line with the growing power of the technology.

Some people think choosing the right technology for a system is a difficult problem. Actually, the most difficult part of designing an effective information system is understanding the problem it is intended to solve. Information systems can enhance productivity only when they are applied to the right solution.

STRATEGIC BUSINESS ISSUES

As you learn more about business organizations in Chapter 2, you will discover that successful businesses become very good at doing certain things relentlessly, repetitively, and routinely, which permits them to make a great deal of money. What happens when a major change occurs in a firm's external environment, such as a change in technology or markets? How fast can a business change to take advantage of the new technology—before its competitors do? How fast can a business change its routine procedures to make new products or deliver new services?

Many expert observers believe we must redesign, rethink, and reconceptualize how we produce and deliver products and services in order to achieve breakthroughs in productivity. As the Focus on Organizations explains, this is how Virtual Vineyards is using the Internet to gain a competitive edge.

PEOPLE

Another problem we face involves the interrelationship of technology and humans. Individuals and businesses must adjust to rapid changes in technology and design systems that individuals can control, understand, and use responsibly. The estimated half-life of information systems knowledge is about five years. That means that roughly half of what you learn in this book will be outdated in five years! This is true of most other technical fields as well. Therefore, to stay current, individuals will have to invest more of their own time in retraining themselves. Obviously, business firms will have to contribute, facilitate, and even lead in this process. How much retraining a firm should undertake and how much it should invest in this process are critical questions raised throughout this book.

An important dimension of the people issue involves the need to design appropriate interfaces between human beings and machines. We must learn to design information systems—and other control systems—that permit and encourage humans to control the process and that function according to design and intentions. To understand the difficulties in designing systems that individuals can control and understand, consider the situation of American Airlines Flight 965.

In December 1995, American Airlines Flight 965 from Miami crashed into mountains near the airport at Cali, Colombia, killing 159 people. On the way to Cali, the flight had to take a nonstandard approach, descending into clouds and locking the autopilot onto navigational beacons. The air traffic controller at Cali instructed the cockpit to fly the plane toward a nearby beacon called "Rozo," identified by the letter R on navigational charts. When the letter R was entered into the flight management computer, the screen responded with a list of six navigational beacons, ranked from nearest to farthest from the plane. As was customary, the crew selected the top entry on the list, thinking it was the Rozo beacon. It was not. The R at the top of the list signified a beacon called "Romeo" in Bogotá, more than 100 miles away and in a direction more than 90 degrees off course. By the time the crew realized that the autopilot had turned the plane in the wrong direction, it was too late.

On the charts, the Rozo beacon was labelled "R." But the system was designed so that one would have to type the word "Rozo" in full to obtain the listing of the Rozo beacon from the computer. According to an American Airlines spokesman, cockpit screens only show the beacons' code letters and geographical coordinates. The coordinates appear in such tiny print on the relevant charts that a busy crew might easily overlook them. In other words, the display did not offer enough information to make sure the crew saw what it was looking for. A better display might clearly show "R-Rozo" or "R-Romeo" along with the coordinates.[2]

People in this control room monitor key system functions. Companies must take great care in designing the apparatus with which people interact to ensure that human beings can control and understand the information from computerized systems.

SOURCE: © John Zoiner, Uniphoto Picture Agency.

PEOPLE-FRIENDLY INTERFACES

Over the years, computer technology has become more and more accessible to the average person and increasingly easy to use. Computer makers are furiously working to make computers even easier to work with—as comfortable and easy as using televisions or microwave ovens.

Some theorize that the ultimate information system is one that we hardly notice. It includes housing computers in walls, desks, and even sneakers. Imagine having a system mounted on the ceiling of your office that could read and keep track of all the documents that pass through your hands. Later, you could ask it where on your desk you left a particular document. This system would also store the text of records that you read years ago.

Another way to increase the efficiency of information systems is to construct them for portable use. That forty pounds of hardware sitting on your desk accomplishes very little when you meet a potential client while waiting for a train. Beyond the already popular laptop units, researchers are developing wearable computers that contain everything from earpieces and cameras to miniature monitors and Internet connections. Portable units might be able to project images such as maps over your field of vision in case you are lost and there's no gas station around. The sneaker implanted system involves a computer activated by skin touching as in a handshake. With both people equipped, their shoe components could trade business information.

As intriguing as these possibilities are, they are long-term projects, far from perfection and availability. The more immediate focus of computer software companies for human-computer interaction is on improving the sociability of interfaces. If you work with a computer, you probably make use of a graphical interface (see Chapter 5) such as Microsoft's Windows 95 or Apple's Mac OS. These interfaces alleviated many of the more complex and intimidating aspects of computer use by having users manipulate symbols such as the desktop, folders, or other icons to represent commands. Graphical interfaces, however successful they seem to have been, appear to be just a stopping point on the way to social interfaces.

Social interfaces attempt to style interaction between computers and humans after everyday human interaction. People will be more likely to use a computer if its operation requires skills and behaviors with which they are already familiar. One of the more ambitious goals for this process is the ability of a system to understand both human speech and handwriting. Software for both methods of communication already exists and functions with varying results. Programs that only need to understand a restricted number of simple, learned voice commands have enjoyed the most success.

The spark for this revolution in computer friendliness was provided by a Microsoft program entitled, simply, Bob. Bob utilizes animal characters to assist and advise the user when questions arise. Bob was not a commercial success because few people found its design useful. Many found it either too basic or too hindering. Bob's importance lies in its intention: to be the first step toward natural human interaction with computers.

Some of Bob's friendliness can be found in the "Office Assistants" of Microsoft's Office 97

Every day we rely more and more on computerized activities, which, if they fail or are poorly used, have extremely harmful consequences. Control rooms where controls do not work, where people do not understand and are not trained to understand the system, where instruments give false signals, where time is compressed, and where mistakes are costly, perhaps deadly, are all invitations to disaster in the computer age.

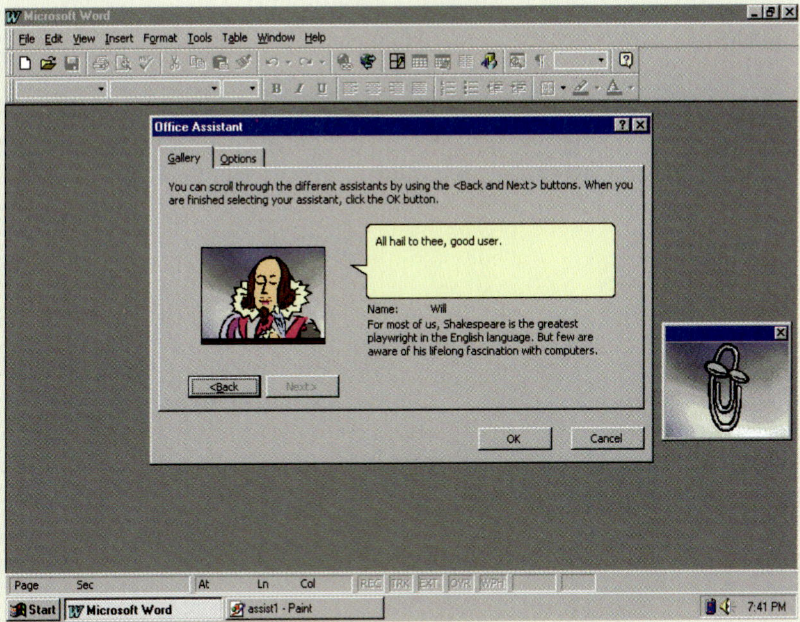

suite of software tools. The Office Assistant is a user-friendly feature that answers questions, offers tips, and provides help for a variety of tasks. The on-screen characters make the message less intimidating. They pop up with suggestions or choices when the user makes an error. The user can change the "character" of the assistant from a bug-eyed paper clip to a dog, cat, robot, red dot, Office logo, globe, Einstein, or Shakespeare character.

The next wave of social interfaces in development includes Computer Associates' Simply Village, Packard Bell's Navigator, Novell's Corsair, and Apple's Copland. Simply Village explains the functions and operations of software applications by converting the display into a graphic depiction of a village. The "mayor" of the village guides you to different buildings that contain software programs where other characters then lead you through the program contained within. Once you achieve a level of familiarity, the characters can be turned off. Simply Village also offers the option of customizing its graphic depictions and a speech recognition function.

Navigator applies a similar concept to social interface replacing the village theme with that of a house. Here, software packages are sorted into different rooms according to their user or use. Corsair hopes to extend the metaphors to online functions allowing the user to make hotel reservations by entering the hotel graphic. Copland will not operate with characters. It will accept inquiries on how to complete a task (i.e., making hotel reservations), and how to expedite the process, perhaps by obtaining the proper paperwork or providing phone numbers.

Experts believe that the move to social interfaces will be gradual, and may even face some degree of opposition much as the move to graphical interfaces from character-based systems did. Social interfaces should take root first in homes and places like ATMs where they can start helping people with limited computer experience.

FOCUS Questions:
What problems can be solved by social interfaces? Why would there be resistance to a beneficial advancement in technology?

SOURCES: Stuart J. Johnston, "Getting Sociable," *Information Week,* August 5, 1996; John W. Verity and Paul C. Judge, "Making Computer Disappear," *Business Week,* June 24, 1996; Joseph C. Panettieri, "PCs Gain Social Skills," *Information Week,* July 3, 1995.

The Focus on People shows that these disasters do not have to occur. By carefully considering the people aspects of information systems, we can design systems that can be used safely and effectively. This issue will be addressed throughout the book.

Another dimension of the people problem is the ethical issues posed by the proliferation of information systems: How do we design and use information systems in a morally as well as socially responsible and accountable manner? Should information systems be used to monitor employees? What should be done when an information system designed to increase efficiency and productivity eliminates people's jobs?

These problems of technology, productivity, business organization, and people—while daunting—also suggest that there are great opportunities for applying information technology in new and powerful ways that have not yet been discovered.

SUMMARY

- An information system is a set of interelated components designed to collect, process, store, and distribute information in order to facilitate coordination, control, analysis, visualization, and decision making.
- Input, processing, and output are the three basic activities of information systems; through these activities, raw data are transformed into useful information.
- The purpose of building information systems is to solve a variety of organizational problems.
- An information system consists of three mutually adjusting entities: people, organizations, and technology.
- The people dimension of information systems involves issues such as training, job attitudes, ergonomics, and the user interface.
- The technology dimension of information systems consists of computer hardware, software, storage, and communications technology.
- The organization dimension of information systems involves issues such as the organization's hierarchy, functional specialties, business procedures, culture, and political interest groups.
- The Internet, a global interconnected network of networks, is extending the role of information systems in organizations and daily life because it makes it easy for different types of computers in different locations to exchange information. The World Wide Web is an Internet capability that can display information as electronic pages that can contain text, graphics, audio, video, and links to other Web pages.
- Information systems literacy involves understanding the people and organizational dimensions of information systems as well as information technology.
- Knowledge, information, and data are different. Information is created from streams of data through the application of knowledge. The purpose of information systems is to create and distribute useful information and knowledge in a manner designed to solve some organizational problem.
- A sociotechnical approach to information systems combines three areas of skills: technical skills, organizational skills, and analytic problem-solving skills. Information systems courses, liberal arts courses, and math courses can be helpful in developing these skills.

• This book describes four problems in using systems wisely. Hardware technology is changing very rapidly, far faster than software or people. Productivity has not yet responded to massive investments in information technology. Organizations do not change easily, even though they must, to make optimal use of new technology. And people often must work with awkward systems, under duress, in situations that have not been anticipated or tested by designers, or that need clearer moral guidelines.

KEY TERMS

Information system (IS)
Input
Processing
Output
Feedback
Formal systems
Manual system
Computer hardware
Computer software
Storage technology
Communications technology
Network
Internet
World Wide Web
Web site
Computer literacy
Information systems literacy
Data
Information
Knowledge
Sociotechnical perspective

REVIEW QUESTIONS

1. Define an information system.
2. How do an information system, a computer program, and a computer differ?
3. What are the three basic activities of information systems?
4. What role is played by feedback in an information system?
5. What are the three components of an information system? Describe the elements of each of them.
6. What is the Internet? Why is it expanding the role played by information systems today?
7. What is the World Wide Web? Why is it an important Internet capability?
8. What is the organizational basis of information systems?
9. Distinguish between computer literacy and information systems literacy.
10. How do knowledge, information, and data differ?
11. What is a sociotechnical perspective on information systems?
12. What are the major reasons why you should study information systems?

13. What courses can you take in various disciplines to learn more about problem solving?
14. What problems and opportunities are posed by information systems?

DISCUSSION QUESTIONS

1. Some people argue that information systems should be designed and built by technical specialists, persons trained in computer science and engineering. Discuss and comment.

2. With faster and better computers, most of the problems we currently experience with information systems will disappear. Do you agree? Why or why not?

PROBLEM-SOLVING EXERCISES

1. *Group exercise:* Divide into groups. Each group should find a description of an information system in a business or computer magazine and describe the system in terms of its inputs, processes, and outputs. What are the people components of the system? The organizational components? Consider illustrating your system in a manner similar to Figure 1.2 and present your findings to the class.

2. The Yamaha Motor Corporation, one of the world's largest motorcycle manufacturers, uses a CBIS for supplying its dealers with parts. The system stores data about the quantity, price, and location of the parts in Yamaha's inventory. Each dealer has a terminal connected to Yamaha's central computer in Atlanta. When parts are needed, the dealer uses a menu on the terminal screen to select the correct parts, specifying each part with a 12-digit part number. At the end of the order, the dealer's printer prints out a shipping/packing list. The shipping/packing list states where each part will come from and indicates back-ordered parts, retail and dealer value, and preferred freight rate. Describe the inputs, processes, and outputs of this information system and its people, organizational, and technical components.

3. *Hands-on exercise:* Carole Stavis stayed two nights at West Vista Hotel. The room charge was $125 per night. Carole made a telephone call that cost $4.50 and ordered a room-service meal for $16. Hotel bills include a 5 percent state tax on hotel services. Use appropriate software to design, calculate, and produce a bill for Carole. Identify the inputs, processes, and outputs of your application.

4. *Internet problem-solving exercise:* You can start learning how to use the Internet to acquire the information you need for problem solving by taking a tour of the Internet Public Library. This "virtual library" was developed by the School of Information Studies of the University of Michigan. It allows you to access remote libraries' catalogs online and contains links to other information resources on the World Wide Web.

a. Take a tour of this "virtual library." What are its capabilities? What kind of information can you obtain using this library on the Internet? What kinds of problems can it help solve?

b. Search the collection for a list of books about Adam Smith. How much information did you find? What steps did you go through? Compare using this "virtual library" to a traditional library. What are the advantages and drawbacks?

NOTES

1. Plato, *The Republic.*
2. Stephen Manes, "A Crash Lesson: When Trust in Data Is Misplaced," *The New York Times Cybertimes,* September 12, 1996.

PROBLEM-SOLVING CASE

TECHNOLOGY THEY CAN COUNT ON

Over the past couple of years, the nation of South Africa has faced a unique set of issues raised by a dramatic change in social order. When apartheid, the legal separation of the races, ended, millions of black South Africans found themselves in possession of an assortment of rights that had previously been denied to them. Unfortunately, years of discrimination and isolation, including refusal of educational opportunities, made taking advantage of these newfound rights problematic. The people of South Africa turned to information systems to see if their problems could be solved.

The 1994 free elections in South Africa allowed millions of people who had never voted before to finally have a say in the administration of their country. The task of casting a ballot, however, was made difficult by the fact that many of the new voters could neither read nor write. In addition to having the right to vote, each citizen also needs to have the right to make an informed decision. Sandenbergh Pavon Ltd., a producer of multimedia products in Johannesburg, South Africa, acquired the responsibility of educating the nonreading community on the details of the election. The technique chosen to tackle the assignment called for the distribution of multimedia kiosks around the country. The kiosks provided standard information such as the time and place to vote and the reasons why voting was important. Motivating the public was as crucial as informing it. They also presented data on the political parties and the candidates that represented them.

Of course, the answer wasn't quite that simple. In programming the kiosks, Sandenbergh Pavon had to keep in mind that many of the people who would be using them were illiterate. Therefore, they designed them to be very understandable through heavy use of graphics, sound, video, and animation. With a simple touch of the screen, a person could listen as candidates and parties explained their views and official platforms. With 19 different parties running in this particular election, the value of the kiosks and their flexibility could not be overstated. The software used enabled alterations to be made as parties declared their eligibility or changed position. Thirty units traveled to seventy different locations. By the time election day arrived, in excess of a million people had taken advantage of the kiosks. The United Nations Economic, Scientific, and Cultural Organization, one of three groups that funded the effort, found this use of information technology so worthwhile that it hopes to duplicate it throughout Africa and Europe.

South African banks now have approximately 20 million new clients, a figure that represents an astoundingly high segment of the total population. Most of these people have never had the freedom to use a bank, let alone make an investment or take out a loan. At the time of the first general election, 1 percent of the 20 million black adults in South Africa had a credit card, and only one-quarter accessed automatic-teller machines. Mike Jarvis, the general manager of information systems for First National Bank, asserts that only 20 percent of all money transactions are made in something other than hard currency. The burden of bringing banking options to a wider segment of the population and decreasing the use of straight cash rests with a bank's ability to implement new technology. To that end, First National has embarked on an ambitious campaign to network its branches with new computer and communications hardware at cost of nearly $60 million.

In addition to making more services available at their branches, banks are also literally bringing innovations to the customers. A significant portion of South Africans reside in rural areas where setting up permanent modern facilities is not currently feasible. First National has initiated a program in one such area to distribute pensions to retirees more efficiently. In the region of KwaZulu Natal, half a million men and women of retirement age receive the equivalent of $67 from the government every two months. In the past, they waited in long lines to have their retirement status confirmed by officials. The new system, called Cash Paymaster Services (CPS), has equipped the pension trucks with automated machines that scan thumbprints for identification and then distribute the pensions. The CPS benefits both the customer and the bank. The ordeal of receiving one's payment is not nearly as taxing as it once was, and the new identification system dramatically reduces incidences of fraud.

The introduction of advanced computer technology into the banking industry of South Africa has produced positive results while solving numerous problems. It has also fostered a sense of community among financial organizations rather than just competition. This development is best exemplified by South Africa's network of ATMs, known as Saswitch. Saswitch allows customers access to every machine in the country, no matter which bank they establish as their own. Such collaboration may be imperative for moving South Africa's diverse segments into the next century as one.

SOURCES: Simon Cashmore, "Networking a Nation," *Computerworld,* September 9, 1996; Mitch Betts, "Multimedia Kiosks Provide Voter Education in South Africa Election," *Computerworld,* May 9, 1994.

CASE STUDY QUESTIONS

1. What problems can be solved by the systems described in these examples? What problems can't be addressed by these systems?

2. What are the people components of these systems? The organizational components? The technology components?

3. Analyze one of these systems in terms of inputs, processing, and outputs.

Chapter

→ TWO ←

HOW BUSINESS FIRMS USE INFORMATION SYSTEMS

CHAPTER OUTLINE

LEARNING OBJECTIVES

After reading and studying this chapter, you will

1. Be able to define a business organization.
2. Understand the major functions and processes performed by businesses.
3. Know why business organizations need information systems.
4. Understand how the core business information systems support the manufacturing and production, finance and accounting, sales and marketing, and human resources functions.

MARKETING ON THE INTERNET—KNOW YOUR BUSINESS

Many companies are furiously at work spending hundreds of thousands—even millions—of dollars to create sites on the World Wide Web. They hope that their electronic presence on the Internet will add to their riches, bringing them more customers and sales. But very few have profited this way.

Many Web sites are "hip, cool" designs with all the bells and whistles—audio, video, hot buttons, dazzling graphics displays, interactive simulations. But they do very little for the business itself. Successful Web sites require strategy, planning, and clear thinking. According to Larry Smith and Richard Masterson of US Interactive, "It's not how to put your business on the Internet, but how to put the Net into your business." If a Web site can't increase sales or reduce expenses, it's a waste of resources. US Interactive provides Web-site design and consulting services for companies such as American Express, ZD Net, and United Parcel Service (UPS).

When planning a Web program, US Interactive first develops marketing and media plans for a client's Internet presence. It learns as much as it can about the business it represents—how the company does business and its key business processes. Armed with that information, US Interactive can then determine what should be presented on a site and how the Internet will support that business model.

This approach—understanding the client's business first before applying Internet technology—helped US Interactive create a successful Web site for UPS. The consulting firm found that a Web site could help UPS enhance customer service and sign on new customers. Customers can use UPS's Web site to track their packages by submitting their package tracking numbers where prompted on the site. They can also download UPS's proprietary online package tracking software from the site into their own computers.

US Interactive counseled UPS against using its Web site to supply a brochure that includes software free of charge. The Web site requires potential customers to submit a request and supply a credit card number to receive a package for $9.95, but they receive $9.95 worth of shipping credit. By asking for credit card information, the site filters out casual visitors who might order a free brochure but who aren't prepared to pay for anything, and it generates a little revenue for the marketing department as well.

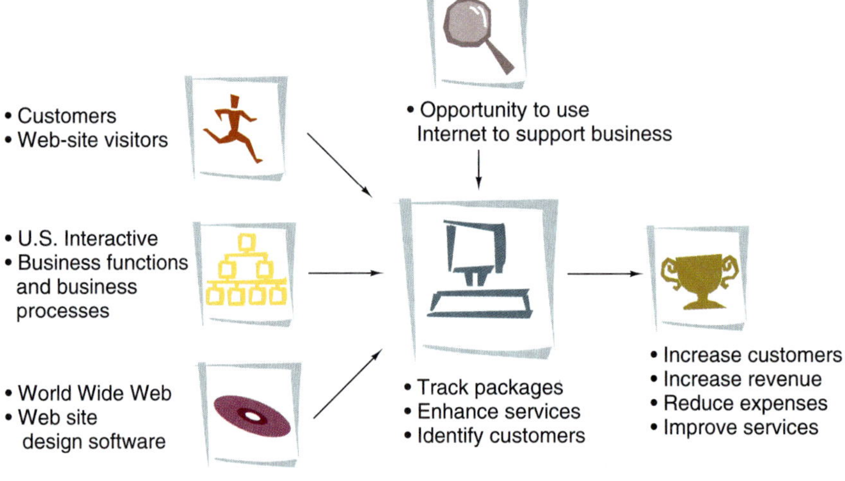

SOURCE: Erica Smith, "Marketing, US Interactive Style," *Interactivity,* February 1997.

The experience of US Interactive in designing UPS's Web site shows that information systems can be effective only if they are deliberately designed to fit the needs of the business. To do this, business and technical specialists must have a clear understanding of the nature of the business and how information systems can be used to make that organization more productive and competitive. Business people need to become more aware of the contributions that can be made by information systems, and information technology experts need to become more aware of how the business works. This chapter explains what business organizations are and how they use information systems.

2.1 COMPONENTS OF BUSINESS

A **business organization** is a complex, formal organization whose aim is to produce products or services for a profit—that is, to sell products at a price greater than the cost of producing the product. Customers are willing to pay a price greater than the cost of production because they believe they receive a value equal to or greater than the sale price. Of course, there are nonprofit firms (the Society for the Blind produces goods but does not aim to make a profit), nonprofit organizations (like churches and public interest groups), and government agencies, all of which are complex formal organizations that do not operate to produce a profit. In general, the information systems found in nonprofit organizations are remarkably similar to those found in private industry.[1]

Business organization
A complex, formal organization whose goal is to produce a product or service for a profit.

ORGANIZING A BUSINESS

Imagine that you wanted to set up your own business. Just deciding to go into business, of course, would be the most important decision, but next would come the question of what product or service you would produce. The decision of what product or service to produce is called a strategic choice because it will determine the kinds of employees you need, the production methods, the marketing themes, and a host of other factors.

Once you answer these questions, what kind of an organization would you need? First, you would have to design some sort of production division—an arrangement of people, machines, and procedures to be followed to produce the product (which could be a service). Second, you would need a sales and marketing group or division whose principal job would be to sell

The human resources group at The Travelers Corporation conducts training sessions for employees, encouraging them to share ideas and expertise. In organizing a business, vital functions like human resources cannot be neglected.

SOURCE: © R. J. Muna.

FIGURE 2.1

The Four Major Functions of a Business

Every business, regardless of its size, must perform these four functions to succeed. It must *produce* something, whether a physical product or a service, and it must *market and sell* the product. The firm must perform *finance and accounting* tasks to manage its financial assets and fund flows, and it must also focus on *human resources* issues.

the product or service at a profitable price. Third, you would need a finance and accounting group. These people would seek out sources of credit or funds and would keep track of current financial transactions such as orders, purchases, disbursements, and payroll. Finally, you would want a group of people to focus on recruiting, hiring, training, and retaining people to work for you. In other words, you would want a human resources group (see Figure 2.1).

Of course, if your business was very small with only a few employees, you would not need, nor would you have the resources, to create specialized groups or divisions to perform these tasks. You would be doing all the work yourself with the assistance of one or two others. But your business would still entail the **business functions** of production, marketing, finance and accounting, and human resources activities.

Business functions
The specialized tasks performed in a business organization—for example, manufacturing and production, sales and marketing, finance and accounting, and human resources activities.

Specialization
The division of work in an organization so that each employee focuses on a specific task.

Hierarchy
The arrangement of people in an organization according to rank and authority; people at one level of the hierarchy report to those on the next level who have more authority.

Informal structure
A network of personal relationships within an organization.

How would you go about actually organizing a business? Most organizations go through several stages. First, work is divided among a large number of employees, which permits **specialization:** each employee focuses on a specific task and becomes adept at it. Next, a **hierarchy** of reporting and authority relationships is developed to assure that the work is completed. Over time, an **informal structure** emerges in a formal organization as people get to know one another. Birthday parties, births, new hires, and retirements are all occasions for informal relationships to grow and for a culture to emerge. An organization needs both informal relationships and culture to help coordinate work and to provide meaning to work. In general, organizing is never completed but is instead an ongoing process driven by constant environmental changes and changing perceptions within the organization.

BUSINESS FUNCTIONS, PROCESSES, AND LEVELS

Like your hypothetical business, most organizations typically perform the four specific business functions: manufacturing and production, sales and marketing, finance and accounting, and human resources (see Figure 2.1). In fact, many large companies are organized along functional lines, with a specialized department or division created for each function. Under the head of the company would be a manufacturing division, a sales and marketing division, a finance and accounting division, and a human resources division. The organizational hierarchy shown in Figure 2.6 is based on these functional divisions.

Of course, these organizational functions do not operate independently from one another. In order to sell a product to a customer, the sales and marketing function would have to locate potential customers, sell the product to the customer, and pass an order for the product to manufacturing. Manufacturing would produce the product to fulfill the order and arrange for it to be delivered to the sales outlet or directly to the customer. The customer would pay for the product, and this payment information would flow to accounting. One could look upon this series of interrelated activities through which work is organized and focused as a **business process.** Business processes reflect the unique ways in which organizations coordinate work, information, and knowledge. Business processes that are well designed and executed can make the entire organization more efficient and competitive. Figure 2.2 illustrates the business process of generating and fulfilling an order. Designing and developing a new product or hiring an employee are other examples of business processes. These processes often require people from different functional specialties to work together.

Business process
A series of interrelated activities through which work is organized and focused to produce a product or service.

Another way of looking at organizations is by describing them as a series of these interrelated processes. This *business process view of organizations* has recently gained popularity because it focuses attention on how the organization actually accomplishes its tasks and coordinates work. It is believed to encourage organizations to be more customer oriented and more action oriented than the traditional functional approach. Organizations can focus on designing processes that cut across functional lines and that deliver greater service and value to the customer. For example, instead of evaluating manufacturing in terms of how well it lowers the cost to produce each unit

FIGURE 2.2

The Order Generation and Fulfillment Process

Generating and fulfilling an order is a multistep process involving the coordination of the sales and marketing, manufacturing and production, and finance and accounting functions.

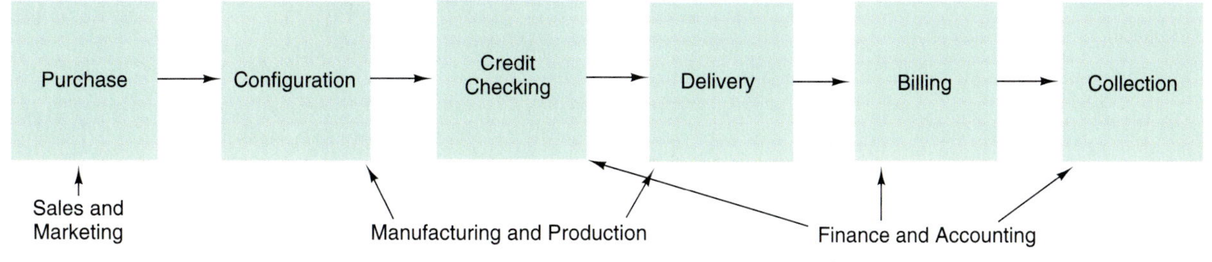

of a product and shipping in terms of how rapidly it ships out each unit, the organization might evaluate the entire production process from receipt of raw material to final delivery to the customer.

Senior management
The people at the top of the hierarchy in an organization; they have the most authority and make long-range decisions for the organization.

Middle management
The people in the middle of the hierarchy in an organization; they carry out the programs and plans of senior management by supervising employees.

Knowledge and data workers
The employees in an organization who create and/or use knowledge (e.g., engineers) or data (e.g., clerical workers) to solve problems.

Production workers
The employees in a business organization who actually produce the firm's products or services.

Levels in a Business Organization Like all organizations, business firms coordinate the work of employees through a hierarchy in which authority is largely concentrated at the top. The hierarchy is typically composed of a **senior management** group, which makes long-range decisions about what products and services to produce; a general or **middle management** group organized into specialized divisions, which carries out the programs and plans of senior management by supervising employees; a group we call **knowledge and data workers,** who design the product or service (such as engineers) and administer the paper work associated with a business (such as clerical workers); and, finally, **production** or service **workers,** who actually produce the products or services of the firm (see Figure 2.3).

Organizations differ in terms of how much authority is concentrated in each layer. Some organizations are "flat" with a small group of senior managers and a single layer of middle management, followed immediately by production workers. Other organizations are much more bureaucratic and may have as many as 7 to 15 layers of management between the senior group and the production worker. Never, however, is all authority concentrated solely at the top. Indeed, production workers can often stop production entirely; hence what they do and feel is quite important to the firm. Perhaps the most important strategic business decision employees make every day is the decision to come to work.

As you can see, a business firm is a complicated entity that requires many different kinds of skills and people, who must be organized rather

FIGURE 2.3

The Organizational Pyramid: Levels in a Firm

Business organizations are hierarchies consisting of four principal levels: senior management, general or middle management, knowledge and data workers, and production and service workers. Each level of employees specializes in performing an important organizational role.

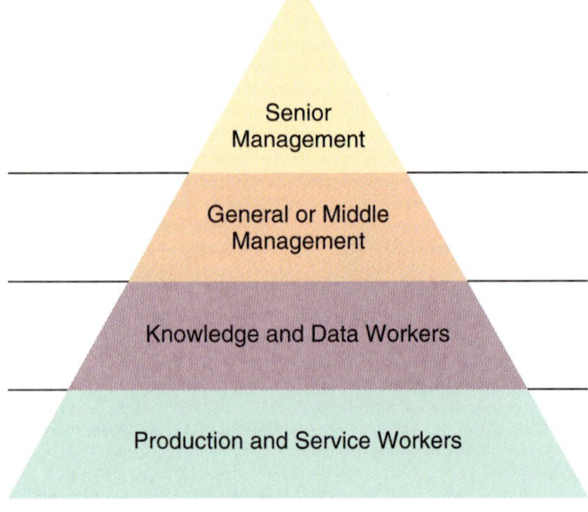

tightly to enable the firm to operate efficiently and make a profit. Imagine, then, how difficult it is to start a new business and make it successful.

THE BUSINESS ENVIRONMENT

So far we have considered business firms as if they existed in a vacuum. Actually, organizations depend heavily on their surrounding **business environment** to supply resources like capital and labor, to supply symbolic support or legitimacy (which helps in getting capital and labor), to provide protection, and, usually, to provide new technology, techniques, and education. Most importantly, the environment provides customers to the business, for without customers the business would fail.

Business environment
The external conditions in which a business organization operates; the general environment includes government regulations, economic and political conditions, and technological developments, while the task environment includes customers, suppliers, and competitors.

The business environment can be divided into two components: a general environment and a specific task environment (see Figure 2.4). The general environment encompasses the political, economic, and technological conditions within which the business must operate. To stay in business, organizations must monitor changes in their general environment. A business, for

FIGURE 2.4

The Complex Environment of a Business

To be successful, an organization must constantly monitor and respond to—or even anticipate—developments in both its general environment and its task environment. The task environment involves specific groups with which the business must deal directly, such as customers, suppliers, and competitors. The broader general environment involves socioeconomic trends, political conditions, technological innovations, and global events.

instance, must comply with government directives and laws, respond to changing economic and political conditions, and continually watch for new technologies. In addition to having this broad view, businesses must also keep track of important groups with which they are directly involved. This is the task environment, which includes customers, suppliers, competitors, regulators, and stockholders.

Environments are always changing and fluid: new technology, economic trends, political developments, or regulations that affect businesses emerge constantly. When capital and labor can move freely, competitors are always present to take away customers. In general, when businesses fail, it is because they have neglected to respond adequately to their changing environments.

NEW ORGANIZATIONAL TRENDS

Some of these environmental changes are leading to smaller, more flexible organizations that can respond more quickly to external events. In the United States, the average number of employees per company has been decreasing since 1970. Many large companies will still be large, but they will have fewer employees than in the past. For instance, Caterpillar Inc., a world-leading heavy equipment manufacturer, can produce the same total product output today that it did in 1979 with 40,000 fewer employees (see the problem-solving case at the end of this chapter). In the future, the average company will be smaller and will employ fewer people. More people will be in business for themselves.

Computerized information systems contribute to these changes by automating more types of work, from guiding machines to transmitting information within the organization. "Coordinating" activities, such as processing orders or keeping track of inventory can be performed with far fewer clerks and managers. Organizations can become "flatter," accomplishing the same work with fewer levels of management.

Many firms will find it cheaper to acquire a product or service from an external vendor than to produce it in-house. They will be able to use networked information systems to work closely with other companies in new organizational arrangements. One emerging arrangement is the virtual organization. In a **virtual organization,** a company can create a partnership with other companies to create and deliver goods and services outside the traditional organizational framework. One company can take advantage of the capabilities of another company without actually being physically tied to that company. For example, one company might be responsible for product design, another for manufacturing, another for transporting the product, and another for administration and sales. Information systems are used to facilitate communication and coordination among the participating organizations.

Virtual organization
An organizational arrangement whereby companies create partnerships with other companies to deliver goods and services outside the traditional organizational framework and without having physical ties among the companies.

Calyx & Corolla, which pioneered in using networked information systems to sell flowers directly to customers, is an example of a virtual organization (see Figure 2.5). The company uses a toll-free telephone number to take orders, entering them into a central computer, where they are transmitted directly to flower growers. Farmers pick the flowers and ship them directly to the customer in refrigerated vans supplied by Federal Express. The flowers are delivered a day or two after being picked, weeks fresher than flowers provided by traditional florists. In this virtual organization, Calyx & Corolla uses the capabilities of Federal Express instead of having its own logistics systems.

FIGURE 2.5

Calyx & Corolla's Virtual Company

Calyx & Corolla sells flowers directly to customers by using networked information systems and the services of other organizations such as Federal Express.

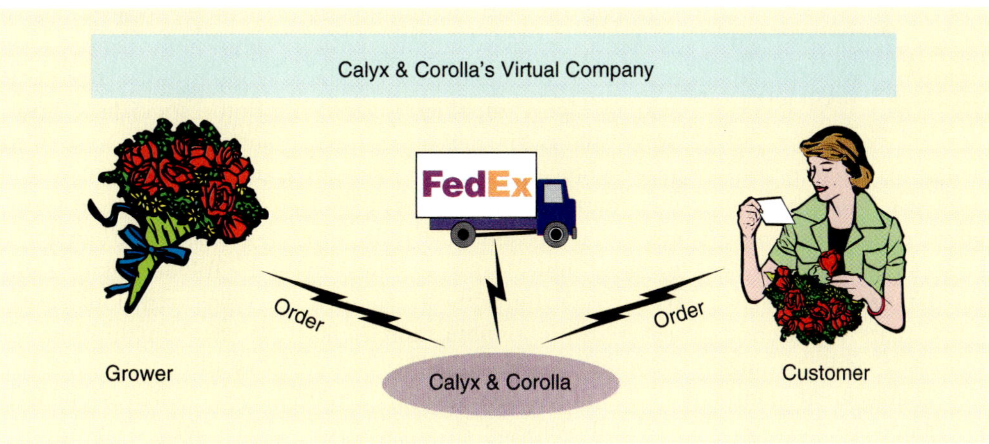

Information systems have also made it possible to run an organization without tying employees to a central work location. Many people now work at home or use information systems to bring work home with them. Armed with laptop computers, cellular telephones, and modems, insurance agents, sales representatives, or advertising account executives can do much, if not all, of their work away from the office. Today many types of work can be done any time or any place, regardless of physical location. We will be looking more closely at virtual work environments in Chapter 14.

Today, more than ever, the pace of global change is calling for much higher levels of organizational responsiveness—monitoring and responding

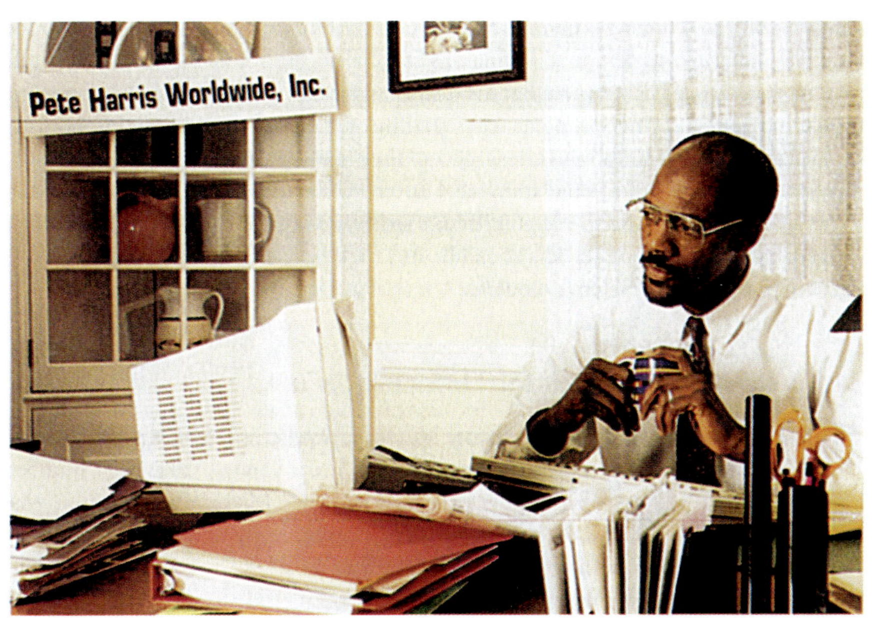

Desktop computers and communications devices such as cellular phones, modems, and fax machines make it possible for people to run small businesses such as Pete Harris Worldwide, Inc. entirely from their homes. In the twenty-first century, more and more people will use information systems to work at home or in nontraditional settings.

SOURCE: © Chuck Savage, Uniphoto Picture Agency.

FOCUS ON **PEOPLE**

WANTED: THE EVERYTHING EXPERT

The job market is tighter than ever. If you listen to corporate recruiters and read the want ads, you might conclude that employers want the impossible person: "under 25, five years experience in programming, with strong demonstrated management skills. Internet experience a plus." Organizations not only want technical prowess in new employees but business and management savvy as well. Businesses are looking beyond the typical computer science and information systems major. They want more students with liberal arts, finance, marketing, and human resources skills. And they want technical skills as well—all in the same person.

People with strong communication and people skills are especially valued. A series of employer surveys has found an overwhelming need for "soft" skills, such as listening, sensitivity, writing, speaking, and team building. In many leading-edge companies, information systems specialists are held accountable not only to information systems management but also to management within the business units, such as sales, finance, or manufacturing. In such instances, communication skills are indispensable.

Employment experts agree that soft skills are even more important to an information systems career than technical ability. Because the direction of both business and technology changes so rapidly, the individual must be able to master new technologies while using soft skills to stay in touch with the needs of the business and the direction of the marketplace.

Many believe that business effectiveness is enhanced when an information systems specialist can take a tour of duty into business operations to see how the technology is applied, or when a business specialist has experience with information systems. Combining both perspectives helps both specialists spot ways of using information technology to improve the business. John Zarb, Chief Information Officer (CIO) of Libbey, Inc., a tableware maker in Toledo, Ohio, reads business philosophy books as well as technology publications. He recommends that his information systems staff attend industry seminars, take trips to user sites, and receive formal training in speech, writing, or interpersonal communication skills.

FOCUS Questions:
What skills should the "everything person" have? Why? Why are soft skills important?

SOURCES: Marianne Kolbasuk McGee, "Soft Skills Can Boost Careers," *Information Week,* August 19, 1996, and John P. McPartlin, "Generation Exasperated," *Information Week,* October 25, 1993.

to changes in the surrounding environment—than ever before. Throughout this text, we will be looking at ways that information systems can contribute to organizational responsiveness. Most organizations will need to make significant changes, and some may have to rebuild themselves completely, just to stay in business. Businesses will increasingly seek people who are flexible and creative and who understand both business and information systems. The Focus on People explains what this means for you and your career.

2.2 PLACEMENT OF INFORMATION SYSTEMS IN A BUSINESS

Until now we have not mentioned information systems or described their place in the organizational structure because we wanted to introduce the

FOCUS ON ORGANIZATIONS

A NEW MEANING FOR "TOURIST SITE"

"You wanna what?"

That frequently uttered reply combined with a wealth of knowledge, a demand for information, and proper timing has created a new outlet for the tourism industry. Mark Ruthenberg, whose extensive travels and equally extensive travel logs fashioned him into a human information booth, is the founder of UWanna What Intermedia Inc., a business based on the World Wide Web. It is a searchable directory of what to see and do in Calgary, Alberta, with its own site on the Web (www.UWannaWhat.com). Ruthenberg's company can now tell visitors to the city of Calgary exactly what they wanna do. And where they wanna do it.

UWanna What's Web site, which has expanded to cities such as Vancouver and Edmonton (with other Canadian and U.S. cities showing interest), lists thousands of sporting, entertainment, and recreational events taking place in Calgary. In addition, UWanna What provides thousands more listings for restaurants, hotels, and other tourist-friendly businesses. Visitors to the site can search for specific wants and needs at no charge. What is the best hotel for a business traveler in downtown Calgary for under $100 a night? Now you don't have to be Mark Ruthenberg's friend to find it.

UWanna What relies on a carefully planned sales strategy to ensure its prosperity. A basic listing on the site costs nothing. Ruthenberg, however, trusts that businesses will pay to have their listing appear more appealing than a standard directory line. A $50 per month fee attaches a logo to the listing, while $100 links their listings to additional information such as a map, menu, or the advertiser's own Web site. Sponsorship banners from breweries and credit card companies, a major source of funding for many Web sites, now adorn UWanna What as well.

Ruthenberg launched his enterprise with $400,000 of his own money, money that he made from previous business ventures and careers. His personal investment now stands at nearly double that figure. An additional $1 million came from private investors, and this is the method by which he would prefer to continue funding the project. Running the Web site in a particular city costs approximately 50 cents per capita, so taking on the task of expanding to cities with populations in the millions appears unlikely for now. In addition to the necessary capital, UWanna What also requires a 25-person staff just to run the Calgary site. Forty percent of the personnel comprise the editorial department, with the rest involved in technical support or marketing and sales. Growth of the staff will coincide with the creation of Web pages in other markets.

Ruthenberg feels that Calgary provides the perfect climate for his organization to flourish. Computers are widely used there due to the presence of the oil industry, and the population is very enterprise minded. Now they also have someone to help guide their way into the future.

FOCUS Questions: Could this business have been created without the Internet? Why or why not? Why has this business been successful?

SOURCE: Paula Jacobs, "The Ruthenberg Bible," *Webmaster*, September 1996.

traditional business organization, structure, and environment. Now let's bring systems into the picture.

PURPOSES OF INFORMATION SYSTEMS

All businesses face two generic problems: how to manage the internal forces and groups that produce their products and services and how to deal with customers, government agencies, competitors, and general socioeconomic trends in their surrounding environment. The most powerful explanation of why businesses build systems, then, is to solve organizational problems and to respond to a changing environment.

Businesses build systems to respond to competitors, customers, suppliers, and social or technological changes in a dynamic and fluid environment. As external forces and organizational problems change, new systems are required and old systems must be modified. The Focus on Organizations shows how systems can be created to respond to new opportunities in the external environment, including the emergence of new technologies.

Businesses also build systems to track materials, people, and activities inside the firm and to manage their internal problems, such as the production of goods and services or the tracking of parts, inventories, and employees. Some information systems deal with purely internal problems, some with purely external issues, and some with both internal and external phenomena. Typically, systems are categorized by the functional specialty they serve and by the type of problem they address.

BUSINESS SYSTEMS: FUNCTIONS AND PROCESSES

No single system governs all the activities of an entire business. Businesses have different kinds of information systems to address different levels of problems and different business functions. Figure 2.6 provides a single

FIGURE 2.6

An Integrated View of the Role of Information Systems within a Firm

Specialized information systems serve different functions and organizational levels. Strategic-level systems help senior managers plan the firm's long-term course of action. Tactical systems help middle managers supervise and coordinate day-to-day business activities. Knowledge and data workers use knowledge systems to design products, streamline services, and cope with paperwork, while operational systems deal with day-to-day production and service activities.

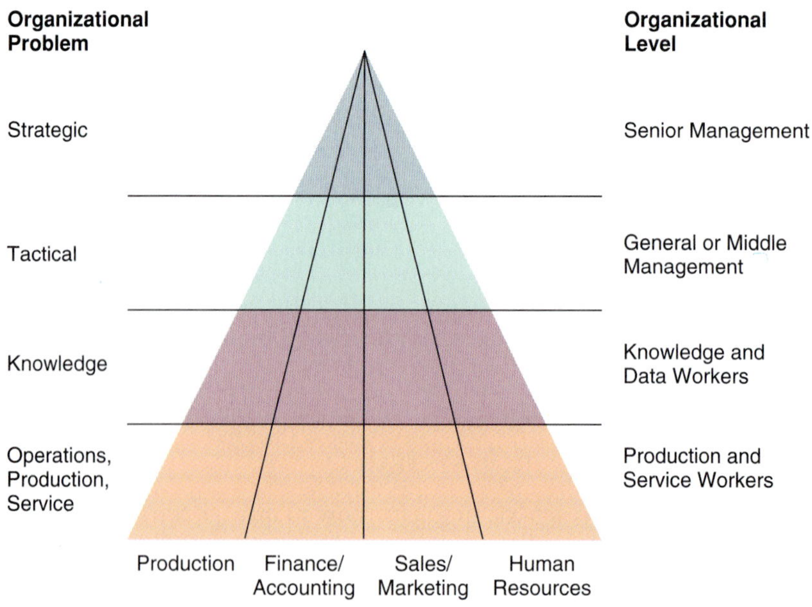

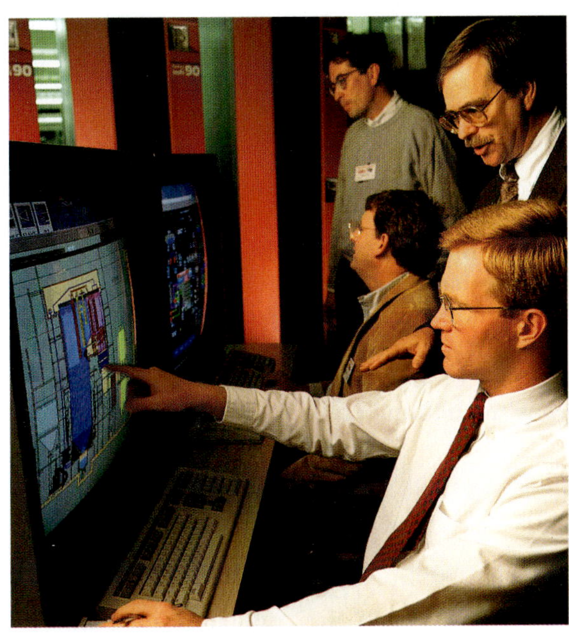

Businesses large and small use information systems to solve organizational problems and to respond to changing environments. Information systems help Boise Cascade engineers take part in a quality audit to ensure that Baily Control's Ohio plant meets specified quality standards.

SOURCE: © John Madere.

integrated view of the role of information systems in business firms. Here you can see that business firms do not have one huge system but, instead, many different specialized systems. Each functional area of a firm develops systems: There are manufacturing and production systems, finance and accounting systems, sales and marketing systems, and human resources systems. Organizations also have systems supporting processes that span more than one function. The systems also serve different levels: Strategic-level systems help senior managers plan; middle-management systems help control an organization's day-to-day activities; knowledge systems assist engineers and office workers; and operational systems are used in manufacturing and service delivery.

Systems can be classified according to the type of organizational problem they solve. This usually corresponds to the level in the corporation that the system serves. For instance, some problems are clearly strategic because they involve questions of organizational goals, products, services, and long-term survival. Such problems in organizations are typically handled by senior management, and often **strategic-level systems** and applications are developed. Strategic-level systems might be used in deciding whether to introduce new products, invest in new technology, or move to a new location. Other problems in an organization are clearly tactical because they involve questions of how to achieve goals and how to control and evaluate the process of achieving goals. These problems are the province of middle management and typically involve the development of **tactical,** or management support, **systems.** Tactical systems might be used in such applications as monitoring sales to see if annual or quarterly targets were met or reviewing departmental budgets to make sure the firm is not wasting its resources.

Strategic-level systems
Information systems used in solving a business organization's long-range, or strategic, problems.

Tactical systems
Information systems used in solving a business organization's short-term, or tactical, problems, such as how to achieve goals and how to evaluate the process of achieving goals.

A very different set of newly recognized problems faced by organizations involves questions of knowledge and technical expertise. Knowledge problems encompass a very wide range of questions: What is the optimal production mix? Where should factories be located? How should a bolt assembly be designed? How should training be performed? and What kind of

Knowledge systems
Information systems used by knowledge workers in business organizations to solve questions requiring knowledge and technical expertise.

Operational systems
Information systems used in monitoring the day-to-day activities of a business organization.

information technologies should be employed? Knowledge problems are the province of knowledge and data workers, who create, distribute, and use knowledge and information on behalf of the firm. **Knowledge systems** are used in applications that serve these groups and solve this class of problem, In general, knowledge workers hold university degrees and often are professionals such as engineers, doctors, lawyers, or scientists. Data workers have primarily clerical skills and backgrounds.

Finally, **operational systems** are used to solve problems related to operations, services, and production: How fast should machines be operated? How should today's letters be produced? How many orders were shipped out today? How can an angry queue of customers best be handled? These problems are the province of technical, production, service, and operations workers and involve monitoring the day-to-day activities of the firm.

2.3 EXAMPLES OF BUSINESS INFORMATION SYSTEMS

Next, we discuss how organizations use information systems to solve problems in specific functional areas, although many support processes spanning multiple functions. The examples of systems in this chapter provide an overview. More detail on how various types of information systems in the firm deal specifically with operational, tactical, knowledge, and strategic problems can be found in Chapters 13–16.

FIGURE 2.7

Stages of the Production Process

The manufacturing or production process typically has three stages: inbound logistics, production, and outbound logistics.

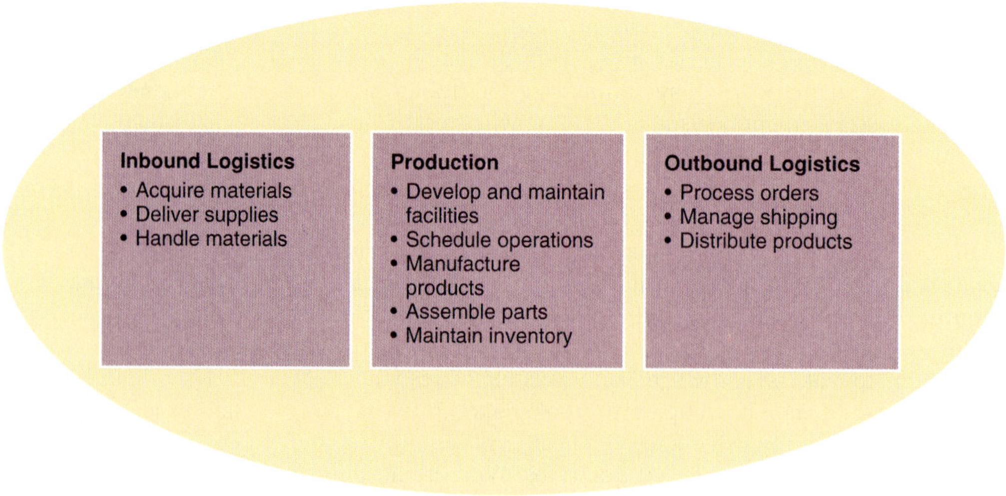

MANUFACTURING AND PRODUCTION SYSTEMS

Goods-producing organizations typically develop a **manufacturing and production function,** with a division or department of manufacturing that specializes in the production of the goods or services that the firm produces for the environment (customers). In service industries these departments are called "operations" or "production" functions rather than "manufacturing."

Manufacturing and production function
The division of a business organization that produces the firm's goods or services.

The typical production process can be divided into three stages: inbound logistics, production, and outbound logistics (see Figure 2.7).

To support this production process, a number of key strategic, management, knowledge, and operational systems are required. Manufacturing and production systems deal with the planning, development, and maintenance of production facilities; the establishment of production goals; the acquisition, storage, and availability of production materials; and the scheduling of equipment, facilities, materials, and labor required to fashion finished products.

Manufacturing and production systems help provide answers to the following questions: What production technology will be used? What production plan will produce the required quantity of products and services

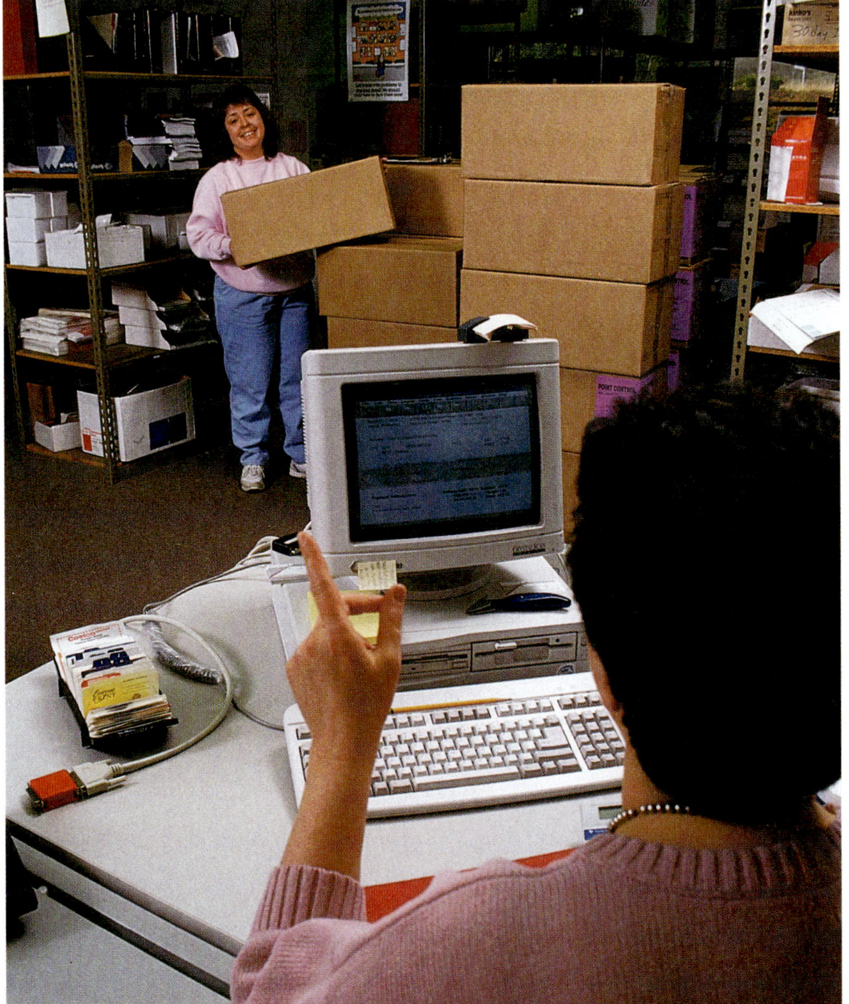

One of the most popular uses of computers in manufacturing is to keep track of the location and number of component parts and finished products held in inventory by firms. By tracking exactly what items are in stock and where they are located, inventory control systems enable businesses to keep just the right number of parts and products on hand to fill orders.

SOURCE: © Oscar Palmquist, Lightwave.

within the required time frame and budget? How will parts and operations be designed and tested? How will the flow of production be controlled?

Table 2.1 shows some typical manufacturing and production information systems arranged by the organizational level of the problem. Strategic-level manufacturing systems deal with the firm's long-term manufacturing goals, such as where to locate new plants or whether to invest in new manufacturing technology. Tactical manufacturing and production systems deal with the management and control of manufacturing and production costs and resources. Knowledge manufacturing and production systems create and distribute design knowledge or expertise to drive the production process, and operational manufacturing and production systems deal with the status of production tasks.

An example of a manufacturing and production system would be a bill-of-materials system, which is typically found in most factories today (see Figure 2.8). A bill-of-materials system provides managers and factory supervisors with a list of all the manufactured items that require a specific part—in this case, a six-foot power cord used in home and industrial air fan assemblies. The list can be "hard copy" (on paper) or on a computer screen.

As the figure indicates, the system itself is quite simple. Key data elements (pieces of information) in the system include the component description, cost, unit, and component part number. The system must also keep track of the item code of the end product that uses the part, a description of the end product, the quantity needed for each product produced, and the extended cost (unit times cost).

The component in the report shown is the "Triple S power cord," which is a three-conductor, six-foot-long, grounded cable with a plug at one end and soldered lugs at the other and which attaches to the fan motor. This component costs $0.47 a foot and is used in three different fans, each of which requires a single unit (quantity = 1.0), with an extended cost of $2.82.

A bill-of-materials system has several uses. In the event of a part shortage or failure, factory supervisors can look on the screen to see immediately which ultimate end products may be affected and change delivery schedules accordingly. Perhaps most important, the bill-of-materials system can feed directly into the firm's tactical systems that coordinate orders, available parts, cost, and delivery dates.

TABLE 2.1

Manufacturing and Production Information Systems

Strategic-Level Systems	*Knowledge Systems*
Production technology scanning applications	Computer-aided design systems (CAD)
Facilities location applications	Computer-aided manufacturing systems (CAM)
Competitor scanning and intelligence	Engineering workstations
Tactical Systems	Numerically controlled machine tools
Manufacturing resource planning	Robotics
Computer-integrated manufacturing	*Operational Systems*
Inventory control systems	Purchase/receiving systems
Cost accounting systems	Shipping systems
Capacity planning	Labor-costing systems
Labor-costing systems	Materials systems
Production scheduling	Equipment maintenance systems
	Quality control systems

FIGURE 2.8

A Bill-of-Materials System

A common example of a manufacturing/production system is the bill-of-materials system, which helps firms keep track of all products that require a particular part such as the Triple S power cord. A bill-of-materials system is useful for determining costs, coordinating orders, and managing inventory.

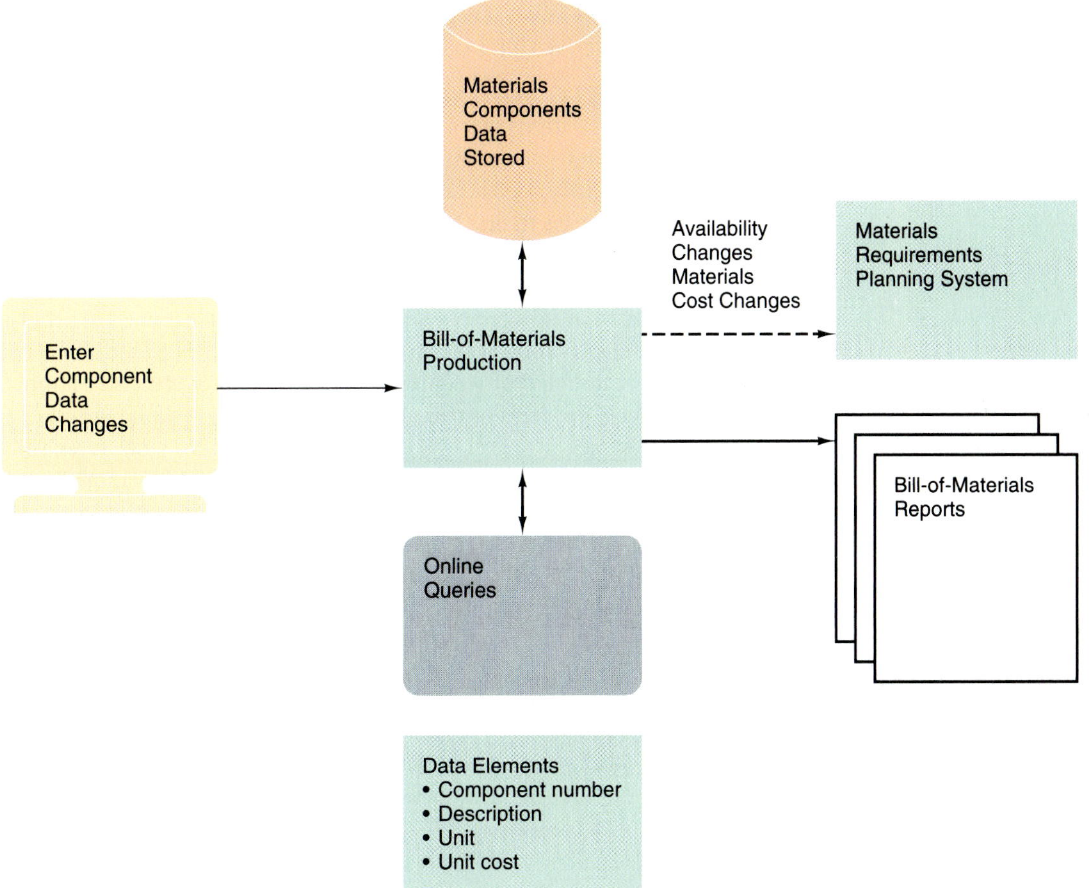

Hard-Copy Report

Week No.: 11 Where Used Bill of Material Report Date: 7/9/98

COMPONENT: Triple S Power Cord COST: $0.47 PART NO.: 2085
UNIT: 6ft

ITEM CODE	DESCRIPTION	QUANTITY	EXTENDED COST
662	Double window fan	1.0	$2.82
175	12" utility fan	1.0	$2.82
227	15" utility fan	1.0	$2.82

FOCUS ON
PROBLEM SOLVING

FASTER THAN A SPEEDING DELIVERY TRUCK

Since businesses exist primarily to make a profit, they focus constantly on how to increase their profit margin. Increasing the efficiency of a company's operation is one of the leading ways to raise a profit margin. Manufacturing companies rely on carefully orchestrated procedures to turn out their products in the most efficient manner possible. Through the years, problems with supply chains have been a significant hindrance to members of the manufacturing industry in their quest to reach optimal levels of production. Inefficiencies result when companies have either too many or too few raw materials and parts in inventory to fulfill incoming orders. Now, technological advances in software applications are providing new ways to address these problems.

Supply-chain management software applications have given manufacturing firms an alternative to buying larger factories and more equipment. Companies like Timken Steel, Selectron, and furniture maker Herman Miller Inc. have increased productivity without spending tens of millions of dollars on expansion. All they had to do was overhaul the supply chains in their present facilities. The idea of improving supply chains has achieved such impressive results that new software companies have been emerging just to fill the demand for the new systems.

The advantage that this new generation of manufacturing software has over previous generations is that it can run through and simulate the entire production process. Thus, applications like i2 Technologies' Rhythm can sense scheduling glitches before they occur. Should the program detect a problem in the supply chain, it can suggest ways to overcome the problem. The technology reduces the anxiety that accompanies not knowing if a deadline can be met. A manufacturer can know as soon as an order comes in whether it is feasible. Supply-chain management software also eliminates the need to stockpile supplies in case of emergency by forecasting precisely which parts will be needed and exactly when they must be available.

A computer's ability to handle procedural issues so adeptly makes a manufacturer more marketable. Selectron's master scheduling manager, Jeffrey Lawrence, now produces reliable production plans in a matter of minutes where it used to require an entire working day to create a less accurate one. Customers who order circuit boards from Selectron appreciate having firm confirmation of their orders so quickly. Industry leaders have realized that this kind of responsiveness has become the critical step in keeping up with competitors.

FOCUS Questions:
What are the advantages to using supply-chain management software? What problems does it solve? Are there any disadvantages? Describe two other problems that could benefit from the use of supply and schedule management software.

SOURCE: Amal Kumar Naj, "Manufacturing Gets a New Craze From Software: Speed," *The Wall Street Journal,* August 13, 1996.

Many firms are trying to create a seamless manufacturing process by integrating the various types of automated manufacturing systems using computers and communication technology. The data produced in one system are immediately available to be used by other systems.

With these integrated manufacturing systems, companies can respond much more rapidly to customers. For example, businesses can use information systems to carefully track orders and the materials or products needed to fulfill those orders, so that only enough supplies are kept in inventory to meet the day's production requirements. These systems would send requests for more materials directly to suppliers' information systems. The suppliers could then use this information to prepare and deliver the needed materials to the production line the day that they were needed, keeping inventory to a minimum. Such systems are called **just-in-time production systems (JIT).**

Just-in-time production systems (JIT)
Systems that minimize inventory by ensuring that materials required for production are made available exactly at the time they are needed.

Systems that further automate the process of supply chain management represent a further step toward seamless manufacturing. The Focus on Problem-Solving describes how these supply chain management systems work by simulating the entire production and supply process in great detail. These systems help companies predict whether their production schedules will encounter bottlenecks in the supply chain and suggest ways the manufacturer could circumvent these supply problems to fulfill their orders.

Leading-edge applications are even using the data from computer-generated designs to drive the actual fabrication and assembly of products. Traditionally, design engineers drafted plans and then handed them over to experts in manufacturing. The Focus on Technology illustrates how techniques can be used to test the consequences of design decisions before products are built, sharply reducing the amount of time required to develop a new product.

Although we describe some of these systems in greater detail in later chapters, you should also be aware that production systems and problems are discussed in courses on Operations Management, or Production Management, in most business schools. If you are interested in a more detailed view of production systems, you should be sure to take one of these courses.[2]

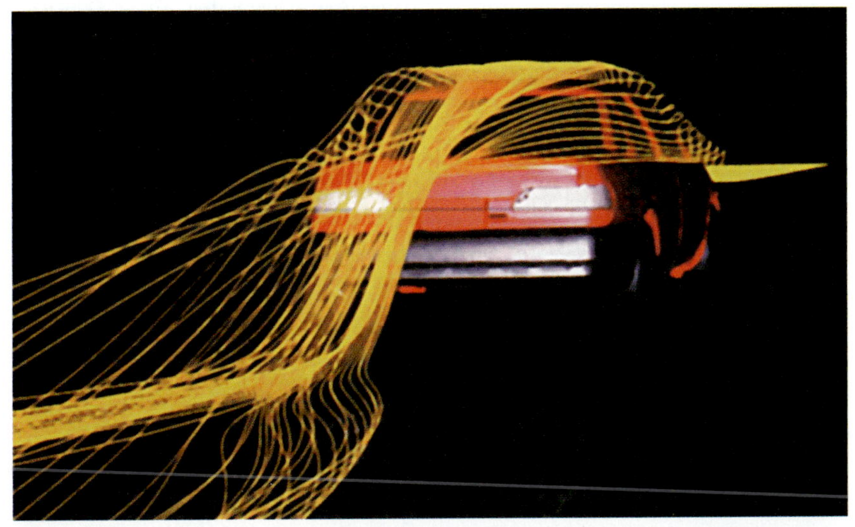

Ford Motor Company's computer-aided design (CAD) system can provide three-dimensional simulations of its automobile designs. Because sophisticated CAD systems allow many aspects of a design to be tested on computer screens before physical prototypes are built, companies like Ford can save considerable time and money developing new products.

SOURCE: Courtesy of Ford Motor Co.

3-D COMPUTING BRINGS INFORMATION TO LIFE

You've designed a beautifully styled new telephone casing that is sure to be popular. But will it break when dropped? Now you can find out by sitting in front of your computer. A $5,000 desktop computer equipped with an Autodesk "cyberspace development kit" allows designers to assign physical properties such as mass, density, springiness, and roughness to images they create. Before any physical prototype is built the designer can test the new casing by "dropping" it on a concrete floor.

Such computerized simulations are so accurate and economical that many automobile makers now perform most of their crash tests without real cars. A Cray supercomputer and software from Mecalog of Paris were used to model a broadside collision between two Opel sedans. The crash unfolds in slow motion, the cars appearing like ghostly x-ray images on the screen. The engineers can freeze the action at any point to study the effect of the impact on the key internal parts, the body work, and the passengers. This "accident" produces detailed results at a cost of $5,000 per crash; using real cars, the price would be $1 million.

The development of powerful desktop computers and workstations has made it possible to apply visualization to manufacturing. Using computer-aided design (CAD) systems, engineers can create product designs on their screens and test them before building a physical prototype. They can also send the design specifications to computerized manufacturing systems to electronically direct the machines that build the products.

Smith-Meter, a measurement and control device manufacturer in Erie, Pennsylvania, used CATIA computer-aided design/computer-aided manufacturing (CAD/CAM) software to design a new meter to measure the delivery of petroleum products to tank trucks at liquid terminals. CATIA, which stands for "computer-aided three-dimensional interactive application," was initially developed by Dassault Systems of France for the aerospace industry to automate the process of developing numerical control machining from three-dimensional models. The software is also used for designing appliances, automobiles, electronics, and sensing/control devices in other industries. Smith technicians used CATIA for developing the initial design and for numerical control programming as they came closer to the manufacturing stage. CATIA could simulate all aspects of the meter at each step. By creating real-life simulations of the meter during the early stages of development, Smith engineers could make appropriate adjustments before the meter was physically produced.

Other uses for three-dimensional computing abound in science, architecture, medicine, oil exploration, and air-traffic control. Three-dimensional computer visualization is a powerful means of bringing designs to life. Design consequences and total effect can be seen and modified as needed. Almost half of the human brain is devoted to processing what the eyes see: People can grasp data presented as a three-dimensional object much more quickly than they can interpret columns of numbers or flat two-dimensional charts.

FOCUS Questions:
What are the advantages of using this kind of software? Describe two other problems that could benefit from the use of three-dimensional visualization software.

SOURCE: Matt Clarkson, "Reengineering CAE," *Desktop Engineering,* January/February 1996, and Gene Bylinsky, "The Payoff from 3-D Computing," *Fortune: Making High Tech Work for You,* Autumn 1993 special issue.

SALES AND MARKETING SYSTEMS

Sales and marketing function
The division of a business organization that sells the firm's product or service.

The basic purpose of the **sales and marketing function** is to sell the product or service to customers willing to pay the asking price. While this sounds simple enough, to accomplish these goals you will have to identify the customers, their needs, how to create awareness and need for your product,

FIGURE 2.9

The Sales and Marketing Process

There are three basic steps involved in sales and marketing: identifying and creating a market, developing it, and maintaining it. Identifying market needs, locating potential customers, and satisfying those customers require a great deal of information that must be effectively analyzed and applied.

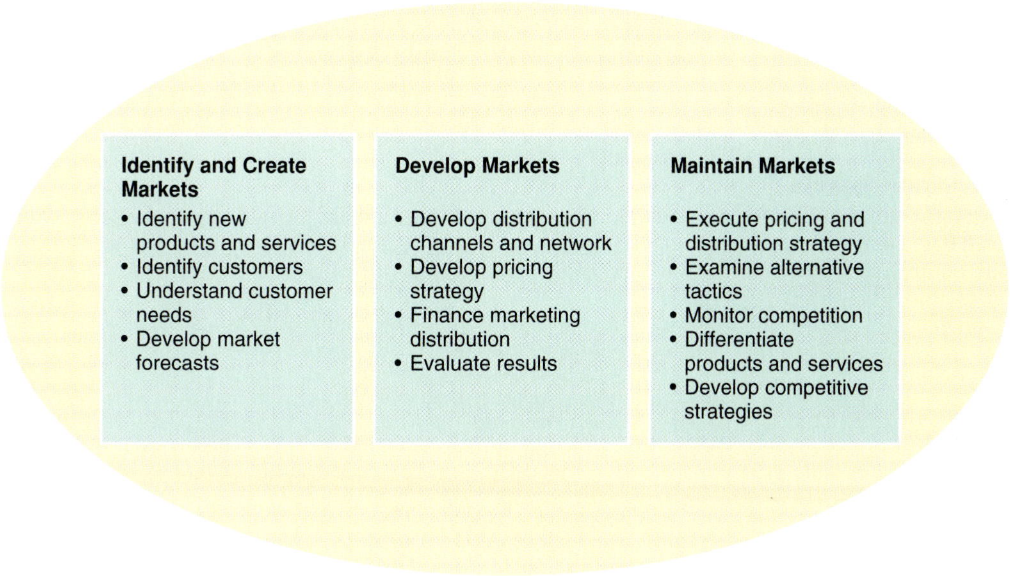

how to contact the customers, what channels of distribution to use, how to record and track sales, how to physically distribute the product, how to finance marketing, and how to evaluate the results (see Figure 2.9).

Information systems are used in marketing in a number of ways. Strategic-level sales and marketing systems monitor trends affecting new products and sales opportunities, support planning for new products and services, and monitor the performance of competitors. Tactical-level sales and marketing systems support market research, advertising and promotional campaigns, and pricing decisions, and analyze sales performance and the performance of the sales staff. Knowledge-level sales and marketing systems support marketing analysis workstations. Operational level systems assist in locating and contacting prospective customers, tracking sales, processing orders, and providing customer service support (see Table 2.2).

TABLE 2.2

Sales and Marketing Information Systems

Strategic-Level Systems	*Knowledge Systems*
Demographic market forecasting systems	Marketing workstations
Economic forecasts	*Operational Systems*
Competitor scanning applications	Salesperson support systems
Tactical Systems	Order entry systems
Sales management systems	Point-of-sale systems (POS)
Pricing strategy decision support systems	Telemarketing systems
Sales personnel management systems	Credit information systems
Marketing data analysis	

One straightforward example of a sales information system (see Figure 2.10) is used by business firms like The Limited, The Gap, and many other retailers. In this Sales Analysis and Reporting System, data are captured from point-of-sale devices (typically hand-held scanners), which record each sale by item and item identification code. This sales information is recorded immediately in some systems, permitting precise and timely analysis of inventory levels, market trends, advertising effectiveness ("Did the television campaign really work?"), and sales targets.

FIGURE 2.10

A Sales Information System

A sales information system can capture sales data for the computer at the moment the sale takes place for further analysis. The report displayed here compares sales figures for various items with the figures for the same items one week or one year ago as a means of pinpointing sales trends and identifying popular and unpopular items.

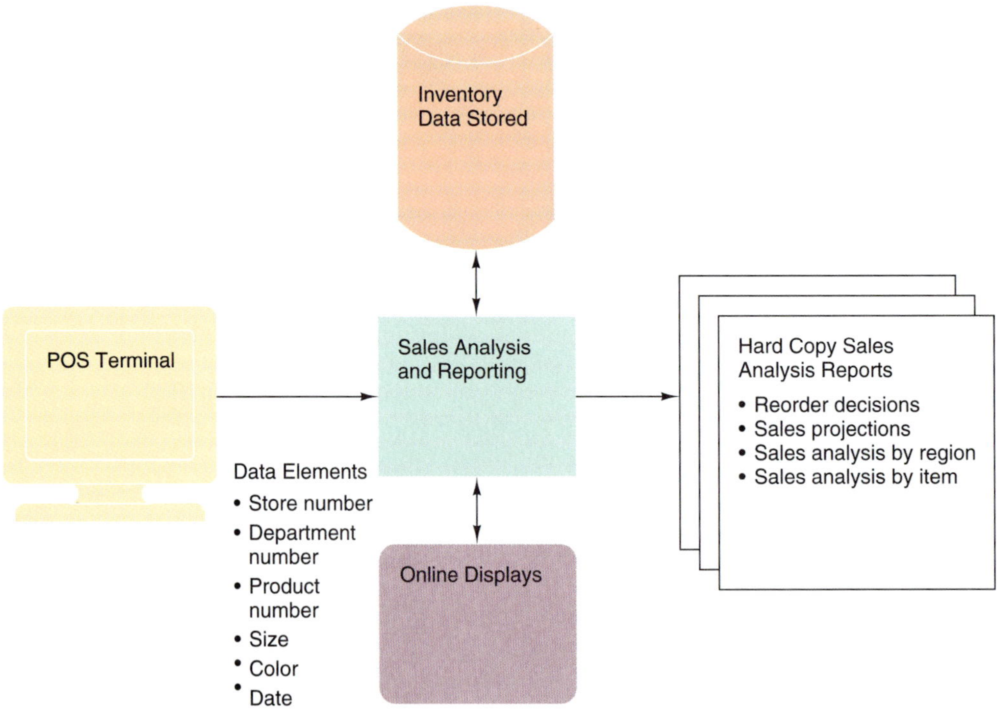

Week No.: 4   Sales Analysis by Item and Week   Report Date: 5/7/98

ITEM CODE	DESCRIPTION	VOLUME 1998	VOLUME 1997	PERCENT INCREASE
447	Red slouch sox	71,020	65,662	8.15
762	Tennis sox, multi-stripe	44,875	49,722	-9.02
331	Sports bag	22,611	20,553	10.01

This scanning gun captures data about each item of clothing sold, such as style, size, and color, as the purchase passes the checkout counter. Sales information systems use these data to determine which items are in inventory, which items need to be restocked, and which items are selling well.

SOURCE: Courtesy of International Business Machines Corporation.

FINANCE AND ACCOUNTING SYSTEMS

In many firms, finance and accounting are handled as a single division even though they are relatively distinct functions (see Figure 2.11). Finance involves the proper management of a firm's financial assets: cash on hand, securities, stocks, bonds, and the like. The purpose of finance is to maximize the return on the firm' s financial assets and to manage the capitalization of the firm (i.e., find new financial assets in stocks, bonds, or other forms of

FIGURE 2.11

The Finance and Accounting Process

Finance is the function of managing a firm's financial assets; the accounting process manages financial records. While these can often be supported by separate systems, a great deal of information flows between the two functions.

Finance
- Manage financial assets
- Maximize return
- Manage capitalization of firm

Accounting
- Manage financial records
- Track flow of funds
- Develop financial statements

RUNNING CASE PART 1

MACY'S THRIVES ON SALES

Founded in 1858, the R.H. Macy Co. was the first department store in the United States. It was a large open-floor building with a wide variety of goods for sale. From its home store at Herald Square, Macy's expanded to over 114 locations, making it one of America's biggest department store chains. The flagship store at Herald Square was considered the largest department store in the world.

Macy's thrives on sales—if there's no sale, there's no business. Macy's still stocks a wide array of goods—clothing for men, women, and children, jewelry, dishes, appliances, linens, television sets. Some items feature nationally known brand names such as Polo by Ralph Lauren. Others are private-label items that are produced and marketed as a Macy's brand name. The merchandise mix for each store varies depending on geographic location and the tastes of the clientele. Some stores do better selling brand-name housewares or expensive designer-label fashions; others have customers who look for value and lower prices. Stores in Texas and Minnesota need to stock larger sizes than stores in New York. A key problem for Macy's is determining which items to stock in which stores. Continuing success depends on stocking merchandise the customers want—the right items and styles in the right colors and sizes.

Merchandise buyers play a powerful role in determining what items each Macy's store will carry. At one time, Macy's had 425 buyers. The buyers select the items that will be sold—which brand of dresses, shoes, lipstick, or dinnerware. The buyers plan advertising and promotions, call on suppliers, order, and allocate merchandise to the stores. Until recently, stores called the buyers directly to ask for merchandise. The buyer for women's purses, for example, could get calls from more than 50 stores in his or her division. Buyers had to juggle all of these responsibilities and worry about whether they were making their sales targets. Often they could not return calls for several days.

Macy's management training program taught young buyers and executives the "more is always better than less" theory of inventory management. The idea was to make sure that the stores were well-stocked, because stocking desirable merchandise would increase Macy's chance of selling more and make sales more profitable. To make sure no customer went away empty-handed, Macy's buyers filled the stores with many more goods than were actually sold, carrying both best-selling items and goods that were difficult to move off the shelves. Macy's, the world's largest department store, became one of the world's most fully stocked department stores as well.

SOURCE: Stephanie Strom, "A Key for a Macy Comeback," *The New York Times*, November 1, 1992.

RUNNING CASE Questions

1. How important is the sales function at a store such as Macy's? Why?
2. What role do merchandise buyers play in the sales and marketing process at Macy's?

3. What pieces of information do merchandise buyers need to do their job effectively?
4. How could a point-of-sale system such as the one illustrated in this chapter help a Macy's merchandise buyer?
5. How do decisions made by merchandise buyers affect the other business functions at Macy's?

debt). In many large companies, these financial assets are so large that the financial function is a significant contributor to the firm's profits. Hence finance has grown in importance from a mere support activity to a "primary" activity in many firms.

The accounting function involves the management of financial records—receipts, disbursements, depreciation, payroll, and so forth. The purpose of accounting is to "account" for the flow of funds in a firm. Both the **finance and accounting functions** share related problems: how to keep track of a firm's financial assets and fund flows. What is the current inventory of financial assets? What records do we have for disbursements, receipts, payroll, and other fund flows?

Finance and accounting functions
The division of a business organization that manages the firm's financial assets (finance) and maintains the firm's financial records (accounting).

The finance function must obtain a considerable amount of information from sources external to the business. Finance ultimately must answer the question, "Are we getting the best return on our investments?" This can only be answered by obtaining a steady flow of daily financial information from outside the firm.

Table 2.3 shows some of the leading finance and accounting systems found in a typical large organization. Strategic-level systems for the finance and accounting function establish long-term investment goals for the firm and provide long-range forecasts of the firm's financial performance. Tactical financial information systems help managers oversee and control the firm's financial resources. Knowledge systems support finance and accounting by providing analytical tools and workstations for evaluating the firm's financial performance. Operational systems in finance and accounting track the flow of funds in the firm through transactions such as paychecks, payments to vendors, stock reports, and receipts.

A simple but powerful example of a finance and accounting system that is found in all businesses is an accounts receivable system (see Figure 2.12). An accounts receivable system keeps track of every customer invoice: Each invoice generates an "account receivable"—that is, the customer owes

TABLE 2.3

Finance and Accounting Information Systems

Strategic-Level Systems	*Knowledge Systems*
Financial and securities market data analysis	Financial management workstations
Economic and demographic forecasting systems	Portfolio analysis systems
	Security analysis systems
Budget forecasting systems	Trader workstations
Tactical Systems	*Operational Systems*
Fixed assets accounting	Accounts payable/receivable
Cost accounting systems	General ledger
Budgeting systems	Payroll

FIGURE 2.12

An Accounts Receivable System

An accounts receivable system tracks and stores important customer data such as payment history, credit rating, and billing history. Input to the system includes payment and invoice data; answers and information can arrive both on paper and on a screen.

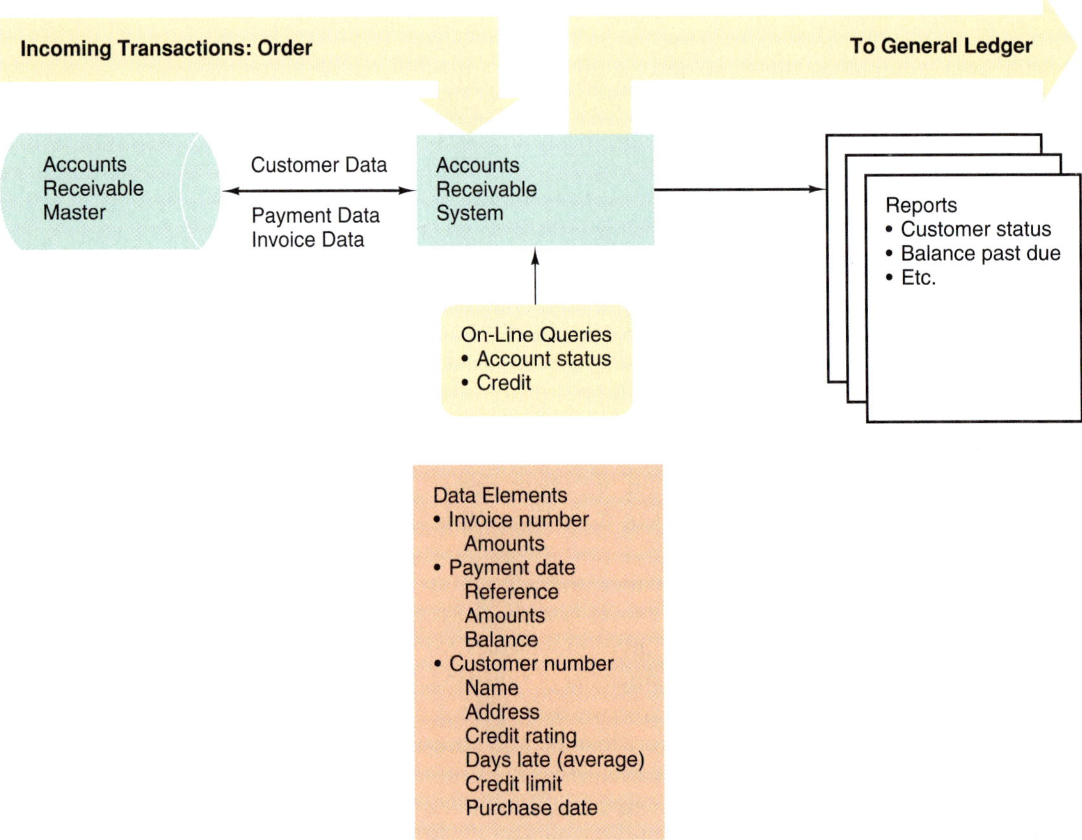

REPORTS

Customer Status

CUSTOMER NUMBER	CUSTOMER NAME	CREDIT RATING	CREDIT LIMIT	CURRENT BALANCE	AMOUNT RECEIVED	TOTAL BALANCE
61298	Nelligan Co.	2	4,500.00	2,000.00	0	2,000.00

Aged Accounts Receivable

CUSTOMER NUMBER	CUSTOMER NAME	CURRENT BALANCE	1-30 DAYS PAST DUE	31-60 DAYS PAST DUE	60+ DAYS PAST DUE	TOTAL BALANCE
61298	Nelligan Co.	0		2,000.00		2,000.00

the firm money. Some customers pay immediately in cash, and others are granted credit. As the business owner, you must decide if you wish to grant credit (some people really don't pay their bills).

The accounts receivable system records each invoice in a master file that also contains information on each customer, including credit rating. As the business goes on day after day, the system also keeps track of all the bills outstanding and can produce a variety of output reports, both on paper and on computer screens, to help the business collect bills. The system also answers queries regarding a customer's payment history and credit rating.

Note, however, that although this system is important on its own, it is connected directly to the general ledger system, which tracks all cash flows of the firm. We describe more extensive financial systems in later chapters.

HUMAN RESOURCES SYSTEMS

The purpose of the **human resources function** is to attract, develop, and maintain a stable, effective, and appropriately trained labor force (see Figure 2.13). Crucial to this mission are the identification of potential employees, the maintenance of complete records on existing employees, and the creation of training programs.

Human resources function The division of a business organization that concentrates on attracting and maintaining a stable work force for the firm; it identifies potential employees, maintains records on existing employees, and creates training programs.

Human resources managers use many types of human resources systems to solve problems. In some cases these "systems" are specific applications that can run on a small desktop computer (for instance, a small desktop-based system can help managers plan for the succession of key managers). In other instances, such as employee compensation and benefits, a

FIGURE 2.13

The Human Resources Process

The role of the firm's human resources function is to attract, develop, and maintain an effective labor force. This includes locating and hiring new employees, measuring and improving the performance of current employees, and maintaining an appropriate and competitive staff over time.

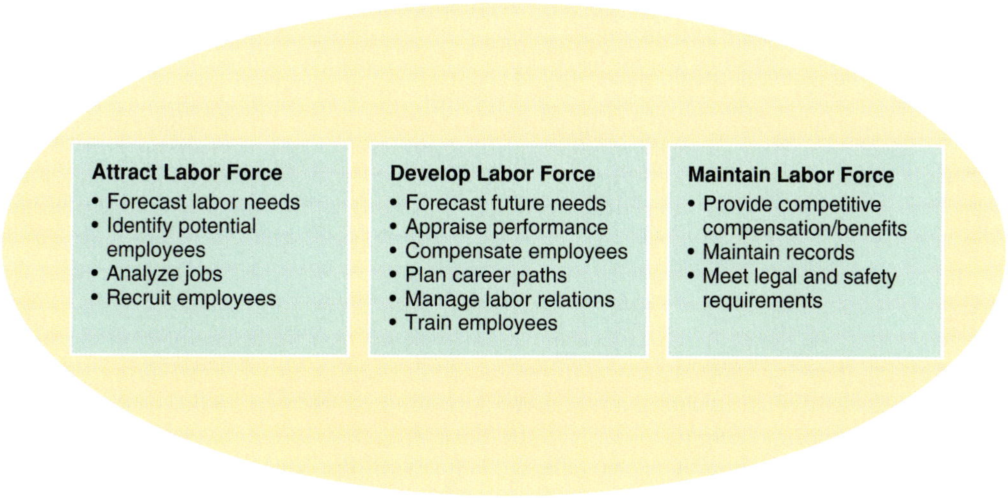

Attract Labor Force
- Forecast labor needs
- Identify potential employees
- Analyze jobs
- Recruit employees

Develop Labor Force
- Forecast future needs
- Appraise performance
- Compensate employees
- Plan career paths
- Manage labor relations
- Train employees

Maintain Labor Force
- Provide competitive compensation/benefits
- Maintain records
- Meet legal and safety requirements

FIGURE 2.14

A Typical Personnel Record-Keeping System

All businesses need to keep records of their employees to satisfy government regulations as well as their own internal requirements. A typical personnel record-keeping system maintains data on the firm's employees, identifying those who have been newly hired or terminated.

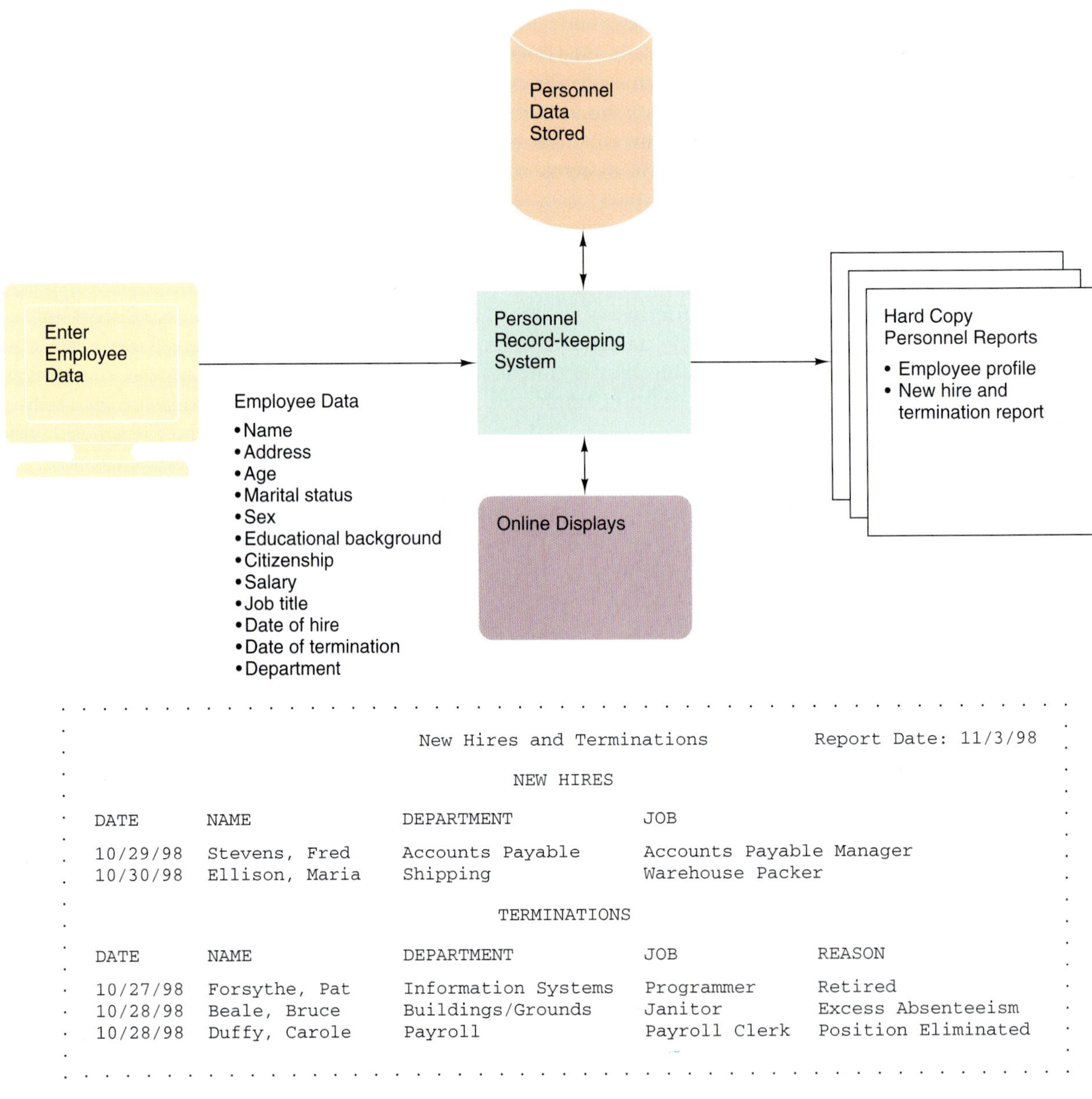

major commitment of organizational resources is required to build very large systems.

As we have done for the other organizational functions, let's examine some human resources information systems by type and level. Strategic-level human resources systems identify the manpower requirements (skills, educa-

TABLE 2.4

Human Resources Information Systems

Strategic-Level Systems	*Knowledge Systems*
Human resources planning	Career path systems
Labor force forecasting systems	Training systems
Demographic analyses	Human resources workstations
Succession planning systems	*Operational Systems*
Tactical Systems	Personnel record keeping
Labor force budgeting systems	Applicant tracking
Positions control systems	Benefits systems
Compensation and job analysis systems	Training and skills inventory systems
Contract cost and labor relations systems	Positions tracking
Equal employment opportunity (EEO) compliance systems	

tional level, types of positions, number of positions, and cost) for meeting the firm's long-term business plans. At the tactical level, human resources systems help managers monitor and analyze the recruitment, allocation, and compensation of employees. Knowledge systems for human resources support analysis activities related to job design, training, and the modeling of employee career paths and reporting relationships. Human resources operational systems track the recruitment and placement of the firm's employees (see Table 2.4).

A typical human resources system for personnel record keeping maintains basic employee data, such as the employee's name, age, sex, marital status, address, educational background, citizenship, salary, job title, date of hire, and date of termination (see Figure 2.14). The screen in the figure shows a report on newly hired and recently terminated employees. Another output of the system might be a "profile" of data on each individual employee showing all of the details of his or her employment record.

SUMMARY

- To understand business systems, you need to know what a business is and how business firms operate.
- A business firm is a formal, complex organization that seeks to maximize profits.
- The major business functions are manufacturing and production, sales and marketing, finance and accounting, and human resources.
- Organizations can also be viewed as collections of interrelated business processes that span multiple functional areas. Business processes organize, coordinate, and focus work to produce a valuable product or service.
- Business organizations are arranged hierarchically in levels composed of senior management, middle management, knowledge and data workers, and production workers.
- Organizations are becoming smaller and more flexible, using information systems to accomplish the same amount of work using fewer production

workers and management or by having some of their functions performed by other organizations. Mobile offices and virtual organizations are examples of new ways of working outside the traditional organizational framework.

• Businesses develop information systems to deal with internal organizational problems and to ensure their survival in a changing external environment.

• Information systems can usefully be seen in two perspectives. First, information systems serve specific functional areas of the firm. Second, different kinds of systems are designed to solve different kinds of problems at different levels of the business.

• Manufacturing and production systems solve problems related to production technology, planning for production, design of products and operations, and controlling the flow of production.

• Sales and marketing systems help businesses promote products, contact customers, physically distribute products, and track sales.

• Finance and accounting systems keep track of the firm's financial assets and fund flows.

• Human resources systems develop staffing requirements; identify potential employees; maintain records of the firm's employees; track employee training, skills, and job performance; and help managers devise appropriate plans for compensating employees and developing career paths.

KEY TERMS

Business organization
Business functions
Specialization
Hierarchy
Informal structure
Business process
Senior management
Middle management
Knowledge and data workers
Production workers
Business environment
Virtual organization
Strategic-level systems
Tactical systems
Knowledge systems
Operational systems
Manufacturing and production function
Just-in-time production systems
Sales and marketing function
Finance and accounting function
Human resources function

REVIEW QUESTIONS

1. How would you define a business organization?
2. What are the major steps you would go through in organizing a business?
3. What are the major business functions typically found in all business firms?

4. What are business processes? What role do they play in organizations?
5. What are the levels of a business firm?
6. Why are external environments important for understanding a business?
7. How will organizations and jobs change as we move into the twenty-first century?
8. Why do business organizations develop information systems?
9. What are the major functional information systems of business? Give some examples of each.
10. What are the different levels of information systems in a firm? Give some examples of each.

DISCUSSION QUESTIONS

1. Some people argue that computers will reduce the need for managers in an organization. They believe fewer managers will be required because employees using computers will supervise themselves. The results of their work will be monitored by computer and passed directly to senior management without the need for middle managers. Discuss and comment.

2. How would the framework for describing business information systems introduced in this chapter have to be adjusted for a small business such as a drugstore consisting of an owner and several sales clerks?

PROBLEM-SOLVING EXERCISES

1. *Group exercise:* Divide into groups and have each group obtain an annual report of a business or find an article describing a business in *Business Week, Fortune,* or another publication. The group should use the information provided to describe the kinds of information systems one might find in that business. Each group should present its findings to the class.

2. Describe an operational process that you think can be radically improved by the introduction of information systems. You could focus on your college or university bookstore, cafeteria, or registrar's office or a local delicatessen.

3. *Hands-on exercise:* Select appropriate software that could produce the new hires and terminations report illustrated in Figure 2.14. Design an input transaction that would capture this information, enter the information, and produce the report.

4. *Internet problem-solving exercise:* Your company specializes in manufacturing kits for prefabricated outdoor wood storage sheds. You would like to locate Canadian suppliers of lumber and other building materials to use in your product. Use the Internet Directory of Canadian Web sites to locate companies that you could contact in British Columbia supplying lumber and building materials. Make a list of these companies.

NOTES

1. Kenneth C. Laudon, "Information Technology and Non-Profit Organizations: A Concepts Paper" (Teaneck, N.J.: Reference Point Incorporated, an online public information utility for the nonprofit sector, 1989).
2. An excellent text, likely to be found in most university libraries, is Roger G. Schroeder, *Operations Management: Decision Making in the Operations Function* (New York: McGraw-Hill, 1993). In this text, as well as in others, you will find useful descriptions of the manufacturing and operations process as well as many examples of where information systems are and could be used.

PROBLEM-SOLVING CASE

CATERPILLAR MOVES MOUNTAINS WITH NEW INFORMATION SYSTEMS

Caterpillar Inc., based in Peoria, Illinois, is the largest construction equipment maker in the world and for years was a world market leader. But in 1982, sales tumbled by almost 30 percent. Losses continued to mount as Caterpillar grappled with Japanese competition, a downturn in the construction trade, and rising manufacturing costs.

Caterpillar management initially responded to the downturn in the usual way, by closing plants, laying off workers, and cutting expenses. But the usual ways were not enough to overcome Caterpillar's inefficient factories and excessively bureaucratic management. Management decided to pursue new production and business solutions using information systems.

In 1985 Caterpillar began a remarkable turnaround by launching a $1.85 billion program to modernize its factories and improve customer satisfaction. The goal was to increase product quality and plant flexibility while slashing inventories and production time. Caterpillar's "Plant with a Future" program was designed to eliminate wasted motion, excess inventory, and superfluous labor by simplifying, consolidating, and automating various tasks.

Here's an example of how the new program works. Caterpillar's Aurora, Illinois, plant makes earthmoving vehicles. It used to build several different models on only two assembly lines, which required frequent and lengthy set-up changes. Caterpillar redesigned its manufacturing process, spending $250 million on new information systems and equipment. Now, as vehicles move down its assembly line, automatically guided cranes and a monorail system deliver parts as needed from one of 500 or more storage locations next to the factory floor. The redesigned factory can run eight shorter, more specialized assembly lines.

At Caterpillar's plant in East Peoria, Illinois, partially assembled tractors move along the assembly line on air-driven dollies. Instead of continually moving units along an assembly line, the system holds a unit steady while parts and subassemblies are mounted. This means that workers can alter the pace of assembly to resolve any quality problems that might arise. Overhead monorails deliver major subassemblies such as radiator housings or the cab unit.

Networked computer terminals on the factory floor require workers to alert the system at key stages of the assembly process. Components are automatically replenished by having workers respond to computer queries, often with a single keystroke. The system monitors parts consumption, automatically transmitting reorders to suppliers and information on inventory levels and finished products to the financial tracking system at Caterpillar headquarters in Peoria. The integrated materials handling system has cut inventories of tens of thousands of components by nearly 40 percent. The company has reduced the time it takes to produce equipment such as wheel-loaders, which scoop, carry, and dump materials such as sand or gravel, from 16 days to only five days. On-time deliveries to customers have risen by 70 percent. Customers benefit from faster delivery, lower prices, and a defect rate that is 50 percent lower than before.

Caterpillar sells nearly all its tractors, loaders, and bulldozers through dealers. Seventy dealers run more than 300 outlets in the United States alone. Since the dealers are the firm's only direct link with the customers, Caterpillar wants to make it easy for dealers to do business with them. New information systems help by linking dealers' local computers to Caterpillar's central computers. A Dealer Business System enables dealers to access product and repair data from the central computers. Another system, Antares, allows dealers to order parts and process invoices and warranties from their local computers; parts can be obtained by 6:30 A.M. the day after an order is placed. A Service Information System electronically delivers catalogs of Caterpillar's engine parts to the dealers. The system provides a graphical diagnostic tool that dealers can use to identify and repair problems with Caterpillar machines or parts. Caterpillar's equipment commonly stays in use for 15 years or more, so dealers and field technicians have an ongoing need for parts data.

These systems eliminate time and paperwork because dealers don't have to call different people to obtain copies of invoices or information on customers and parts; they can now obtain this information directly from the computer. The systems expedite order fulfillment by allowing the immediate transmission of parts orders to Caterpillar's manufacturing and production systems. Thus, managers have an easier time scheduling production.

For instance, when a customer places an order with a Caterpillar dealer for six new bulldozers, the dealer first tries to fill the order from stock. If the equipment has to be built, the dealer places the order directly to Peoria through his or her computer. The order is transmitted immediately to Caterpillar's planning system, where it is matched against a master production forecast plan and given a slot on a master production schedule. Caterpillar then transmits the order to the plants that will produce the parts and assemble the machines through a global telecommunications network that connects 23 warehouses in 11 countries as well as the main supply hub in Morton, Illinois.

This process contrasts with traditional manufacturing, in which companies manufactured large volumes of parts and items for stock based on sales forecasts. The new "pull" approach lets a customer's order trigger a series of actions throughout the plant, ultimately generating an order to suppliers. Production is more closely tied to actual sales.

An executive information system built by Caterpillar's corporate information systems group lets business units project the profitability of various activities by performing "what if" scenarios. For example, a manager in the engine division can extract warranty information to identify the dealers who spend an unusual amount on customer warranty claims. An activity-based cost information system helps managers calculate each plant's contribution to the production cost of a particular product.

Caterpillar has cut the amount of time required to develop a new product and bring it to market by using a computer-aided design system with vehicle simulation software. By using the system to simulate products, engineers can eliminate up to 90 percent of the unworkable design ideas before even building a physical prototype. Time to market for new designs, which used to be six to eight years, is now two to four years. Caterpillar broadcasts a monthly "CAT TV" program to dealers, informing them of new offerings, product changes, and service-related announcements. This "business television" consists of a one-way video service with two-way audio. Communication with dealers and integration of Caterpillar headquarters, warehouses, and plants depends on the firm's global telecommunications network. The network provides more than 180 Caterpillar dealers in more than 1,000 locations with voice, data, and video, including electronic mail and electronic exchange of transactions between dealers and suppliers.

Caterpillar's new information system technology has also helped it add 220 new or upgraded products. For example, Caterpillar designed farm tractors that run on rubber tracks instead of wheels. The tracks, which were originally developed for its heavy construction gear, cut soil compaction, improve yields, and enable farmers to work in the fields in bad weather.

Since Caterpillar implemented its flexible manufacturing program, sales and profits have been steadily rising. Because the company can make different products without reconfiguring its assembly lines, Caterpillar has cut manufacturing time by 75 percent and inventories by 60 percent.

Caterpillar's business redesign had another goal: to help employees keep their jobs. Although slightly more than half of Caterpillar's products are sold abroad, three-fourths of these products are made in the United States. Nearly three out of four Caterpillar employees work on U.S. soil. Instead of cutting costs by farming out production to foreign plants, Caterpillar chose an information system plan that would preserve jobs at home. By concentrating on service, quality, mass customization, and lead time rather than cheap labor, Caterpillar is the world market leader once again.

Yet Caterpillar has been plagued by poor labor relations. While management made a sustained effort to keep jobs in the United States, it still had to find ways to rein in costs, including the cost of labor. The company has been locked in a five-year struggle over wages and benefits with the United Auto Workers (UAW), which represents about 24 percent of its employees. Although the union returned to work in December 1996 after a bitter 18-month strike, members have refused to ratify the no-frills contract offered by the company. Caterpillar will eventually have to find common ground with the UAW. It needs worker participation in order to benefit from introducing new products.

SOURCES: Peter Elstrom, "This Cat Keeps on Purring," *Business Week,* January 20, 1997; Doug Bartholomew, "Caterpillar Digs In," *Information Week,* June 7, 1993; Bob Violino, "Unearthing a New Approach," *Information Week,* April 13, 1992.

CASE STUDY QUESTIONS

1. What were Caterpillar's problems? What people, organization, and technology factors helped to create those problems?

2. What role did Caterpillar's systems play in solving these problems? How successful were they? What problems could they solve? What problems couldn't they solve?

3. What business functions and processes are supported by Caterpillar's information systems?

4. What levels of the business do Caterpillar's systems support?

Chapter

→ THREE ←

INFORMATION SYSTEMS: CHALLENGES AND OPPORTUNITIES

CHAPTER OUTLINE

Opening Vignette: Tracking the Virtual Customer

3.1 Achieving Competitive Advantage with Information Systems

Countering Competitive Forces

The Value Chain

3.2 Competing on a Global Scale

Global Opportunities

The Challenge of Building International Information Systems

3.3 Promoting Quality with Information Systems

What Is Quality?

How Information Systems Can Enhance Quality

3.4 Transforming Organizations: Reengineering

Reengineering Business Processes

Examples of Reengineering

3.5 Promoting Ethical and Social Responsibility

The Relationship between Information Technology and Organizations

Basic Ethical Concepts: Responsibility, Accountability, and Liability

Leading Social and Ethical Impact Areas

Ethical Guidelines

LEARNING OBJECTIVES

After reading and studying this chapter, you will

1. Know how businesses can use information systems for competitive advantage.
2. Be aware of the challenges to the development of information systems that support businesses on a global scale.
3. Understand how information systems can be used to promote quality in organizations.
4. Understand how organizations can be redesigned through reengineering to maximize the benefits of information technology.
5. Be aware of information system ethics and the major social and organizational effects that computer-based systems have had on advanced societies.

TRACKING THE VIRTUAL CUSTOMER

Europe has a counterpart to America's G.I. Joe and he is called Action Man. Action Man has his own Web site, created by Hasbro Europe, the United Kingdom-based division of toymaker Hasbro International. The company hopes to benefit from its investment in designing and maintaining this Web site by finding out new marketing information. Julian Jones, Hasbro Europe's Graphics Services manager, installed a software tool called Market Focus to analyze how people were using the Web site. Market Focus's Web site analysis reports told him that fully 40 percent of the visitors to Action Man's Web site never actually made it to the site because the site's elaborate graphics were too data intensive for their computers to process quickly. They didn't want to wait.

Hasbro's Web design team reduced the size of the opening image to the Action Man Web site so that it did not take so long for visitors to access. The design group also reorganized the Web site so that visitors would be taken deeper into the site on their first click. These efforts increased the duration of the average visit to Action Man's Web site by almost 50 percent, to 11 minutes, and reduced the number of visitors who bailed out before entering the site to 25 percent.

Many companies, like Hasbro, carefully scrutinize the data about visitors to their Web sites because it can provide valuable marketing information about the people they are spending thousands of dollars to reach. They want to glean anything they can about the age, sex, geographic location, and income of their Web-site visitors, as well as information about their hobbies, buying patterns, values, and attitudes. They can then use this information to contact potential customers and to develop messages and creative strategies for selling.

The software for maintaining a company's Web site automatically creates an access log of usage data, showing the number of visitors to a site, the dates and times of access, the Internet location of the visitor's computer, which files were viewed, and the type of Web browsing software the visitors used. A number of special Web-site auditing tools such as Market Focus are available to help companies tally, slice, and present usage log data so that it yields valuable information. Other software can track what other Web sites the visitors accessed and visitors' E-mail addresses, information rich in clues about visitors' interests and potential spending habits. Some Web sites are even able to capture visitors' names and addresses by asking them to fill out registration forms or to sign "guest books."

The Action Man site includes a guest book. Although it is optional and can be easily bypassed, most people choose to fill it in. The guest book consists of a blank message space on which people can write whatever they please, plus space for entering their name and country of residence. Visitors taking part in the Action Man competition are asked to provide more information. From analyzing the entry forms, Hasbro knows that participants are generally between the ages of 25 and 35 and had the Action Man toy when they were children. "We know quite a bit about them, actually," observed Jones.

That's exactly what some observers are worried about, because tracking these virtual visitors raises some thorny privacy questions. When companies examine what Web sites you have visited, it's like standing behind someone at the newsstand and writing down every magazine they pick up. Is this a form of voyeurism? And what happens when companies start pooling their Web visitor data with that of other companies and organizations? Providing valuable demographic data that marketers can use to finely target consumers for personalized advertising may be one of the principal ways that most World Wide Web sites will pay for themselves. They could create centralized databases of information detailing exactly who we are and what we do every day.

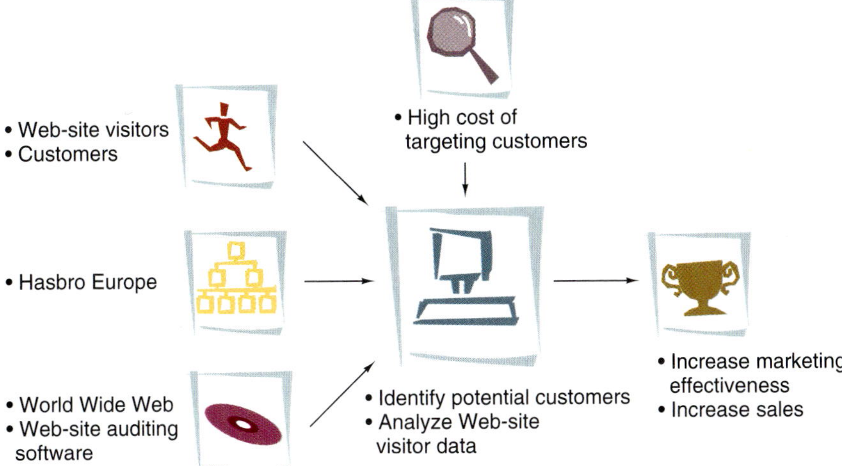

SOURCE: Miryam Williamson, "Getting to Know You," *Webmaster,* September 1996.

The Internet and the World Wide Web are creating new opportunities for businesses to increase sales and market their products more effectively. But at the same time, the use of this technology raises serious ethical questions, including the threat to individual privacy. The financial benefits of information systems need to be balanced against their ethical and social impact.

Information systems cannot be used effectively without addressing these and other challenges. These challenges include the drive toward competitive advantage; the need to understand the information system requirements for competing on a global scale; the need to ensure quality of products and services; the need to redesign organizations to make them more efficient; and the need to ensure that information systems are used in an ethically and socially responsible manner. This chapter describes each of these challenges and the opportunities they have created for information systems.

3.1 ACHIEVING COMPETITIVE ADVANTAGE WITH INFORMATION SYSTEMS

A new role for information systems has been their application to problems concerning the firm's competitive advantage. Such systems are considered **strategic information systems** because they focus on solving problems related to the firm's long-term prosperity and survival. Such problems may entail creating new products and services, forging new relationships with customers and suppliers, or finding more efficient and effective ways of managing the firm's internal activities. The objective of such systems is to provide solutions that will enable firms to defeat and frustrate their competition. You

Strategic information systems Information systems used in solving a business organization's long-range, or strategic, problems.

will find many examples of information systems used strategically throughout this book.

Although any information system application is "important" in the sense that it solves some important business problem, a strategic information system is one that places the firm at a competitive advantage. Strategic impact systems are far-reaching and deeply rooted; they fundamentally change the firm's goals, products, services, or internal and external relationships.

COUNTERING COMPETITIVE FORCES

To stay in business, almost all firms must worry about their competitive advantage—that is, their ability to compete with other firms. This competitive advantage is shaped by a series of competitive forces, such as substitute products and services, the bargaining power of customers and suppliers, and the threat of new competitors entering the market. These forces, in turn, affect the balance of power between the firm and its traditional competitors in the industry. Figure 3.1 illustrates how these competitive forces would affect the position of a cable television company.

Firms can pursue four basic strategies to counter these competitive forces; these are summarized in Table 3.1.[1]

Low-cost leadership: produce products and services at a lower price than competitors.

FIGURE 3.1

Competitive Forces in the Cable Television Industry

Various forces affect a firm's ability to compete in the television industry and its balance of power with competitors.

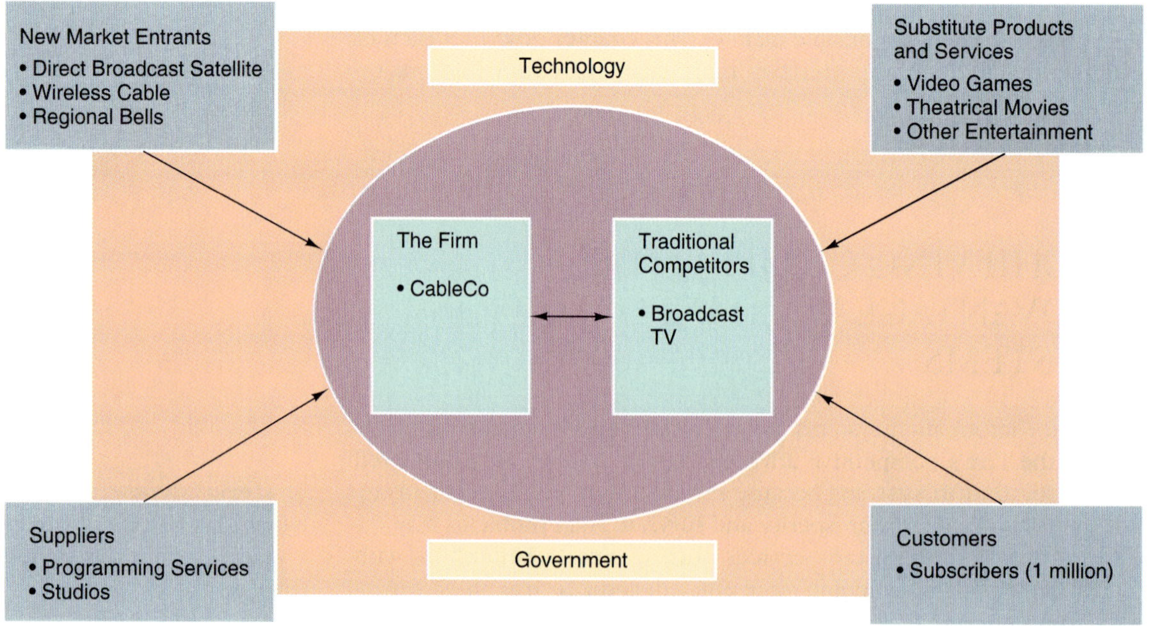

TABLE 3.1

Four Basic Competitive Strategies

Strategy	Problem to Be Solved	Solution
1. Low-cost leadership	Competition from firms with comparable products and services at the same cost is taking away customers.	Produce products and services at a lower price than competitors without sacrificing quality and level of service.
2. Focus on market niche	Multiple firms are competing for the same market.	Identify a specific focal point for a product or service. The firm can serve this narrow target area better than competitors and attract a specific buyer group more easily.
3. Product differentiation	Customers have no brand loyalty, and competitors can lure them away with lower prices.	Create brand loyalty by developing unique new products that are distinct from competitors' products.
4. Linkage	Customers can easily switch to another firm. Suppliers deliver late or at unfavorable prices.	"Lock in" customers and suppliers, making it difficult for customers to switch and tying suppliers into a price structure and delivery timetable shaped by the firm.

Focus on market niche: create new market niches by pinpointing a target market for a product or service that the firm can provide better than its competitors.

Product differentiation: develop unique new products or services.

Linkage: develop tight linkages to customers and suppliers that "lock" customers into the firm's products and suppliers into the price structure and delivery timetable determined by the purchasing firm.

Firms can use information systems to support each of the four competitive strategies. Information systems can create unique products or services that cannot easily be duplicated so that competitors cannot respond. Information systems can also target marketing campaigns more precisely or "lock in" customers and suppliers, making switching to competitors too costly and inconvenient to be worthwhile. Finally, information systems can have a strategic effect if they enable firms to do what they have been doing in a more efficient, cost-effective manner and to offer their goods and services at higher quality or lower prices than competitors. The following examples illustrate how leading U.S. and foreign firms have used strategic impact systems for competitive advantage.

New Marketing Strategies Powerful new sales and marketing information systems enable firms to "mine" existing information as a resource to increase

FOCUS ON ORGANIZATIONS

FINDING THEIR NICHE

Getting your foot in the door of the athletic equipment sales industry is one thing. Not getting it stuck is another. Such was the problem confronting Mike and Brendan Moylan during the summer months of 1994. The brothers co-own Sports Endeavors Inc., an organization that sells soccer and lacrosse equipment by catalog out of Hillsborough, North Carolina. Mike Moylan founded the business in 1984 when he was just 18 years of age. He focused on establishing a strong connection with the tastes of his customers. This task became more difficult as the business increased both its revenues and its number of clients. Enter Brendan, the more detail- and technology-oriented of the two. His goal was to enhance the systems by which Sports Endeavors managed itself, converting Mike's visions into strategies.

Despite all their planning, the Moylans found themselves in a potentially disastrous situation. One of their purchasing agents had bought 30,000 pairs of soccer cleats believing that the catalog would need two months to move all of them. After two months, approximately half of the inventory remained unsold. Mike and Brendan realized that the time had come to make a change in the operation of their organization.

Sports Endeavors hired a consultant to help guide the implementation of a database-marketing system. Over the years, the Moylans had updated their information systems processing technology often but had never reached the level of efficiency that their industry demanded. For example, one system they used required several days of sorting through data in order to determine the rate of sales for shorts. More specific information, such as the sales rate for shorts of a certain color, entailed repeating the procedure. The system could store information on everything from customer purchases to inventory status and vendors' names, but it couldn't do anything with the data. Sports Endeavors couldn't even find out what products customers were buying the most.

In other words, Sports Endeavors needed a system that could analyze data instead of just producing numbers. Their consultant recommended a system capable of addressing issues such as which catalog items were most popular, which vendors made the best profit, and what effect seasonal factors have on certain items.

This newfound capacity to analyze data and sales trends so intricately permitted Mike and Brendan to develop more ambitious and effective marketing strategies. They began to study trends in the flow of their products, and these trends could be employed to predict future tendencies in the market. Equipped with that advantage, Sports Endeavors could avoid clogging up its shelf space with superfluous items. Indeed, reading the market and the desires of the customers became a focus of the organization. As a result, Mike and Brendan cut down their inventory drastically and witnessed an impressive increase in their sales.

Many small companies are starting to follow the Moylans' example by incorporating massive amounts of customer-related information into their businesses. What was once only possible for large corporations due to the expense and complexity of the technology is now a viable option for smaller organizations.

FOCUS Questions: What problems did analyzing sales data solve for Sports Endeavors? How important was it to the success of the company? How did it alter the way the Moylans ran their business?

SOURCE: Anne Field, "State-of-the-Art Precision Marketing," *Inc. Technology*, No. 2, 1996.

profitability and market penetration. Firms can use this information to identify and target products for a particular market or product niche, or they may use it to determine ways to serve specific market segments more effectively.

Many companies mine their sales and customer data for marketing information. The Avon Corp. issues 15 million product brochures every two

Customer service representatives can collect valuable information for the firm when they respond to customer complaints or questions. Information systems can analyze the data they gather about customer purchases and problems with products to identify problem products, expedite repairs, and target customers that might be interested in purchasing warranty services or additional items.

SOURCE: Courtesy of Whirpool Corporation.

weeks for use in direct marketing. Avon's sales campaign management group uses information captured from invoices to plan the brochures. Invoice information is also employed to link the special offers in the brochures, such as a necklace offered for $6.99 when accompanied by a perfume purchase. Avon thus can link its promotions more effectively to a range of objectives—profitability, movement of inventory, or giveaways to boost customer service. The Focus on Organizations shows how data mining can benefit small businesses as well as large ones.

Companies can also examine customer service data to target sales campaigns and improve the quality of their products. The Whirlpool Corp. searches its customer-call data early in the life of its washing machine, dryer, and refrigerator models to identify faulty parts. Analysis of the data lets Whirlpool identify the customers who have purchased the machines so that mechanics can be dispatched to replace any defective parts before more complaints surface and customers become unhappy. Whirlpool also uses customer service data to target customers who might want to purchase warranty services or new appliances.

New Products and Services Information systems have been used to create appealing new products and services that cannot easily be replicated by competitors. Many of these new products and services have been created for the financial industry. Classic examples are the bank debit card and automatic teller machine (ATM) systems, which were first developed by Citicorp in 1977. Citicorp's ATMs were so successful that other banks formed their own ATM networks, such as NYCE (New York Case Exchange) in the northeast, Yankee 24 in New England, and the Star System in California. NYCE and Yankee 24 merged in late 1993 to offer new services such as bill payments by telephone or personal computer and the use of bank cards to make purchases in stores. Banks such as Citibank and Wells Fargo Bank now offer online banking services. Security First Network Bank in Atlanta, actually

Security First Network Bank in Atlanta created a unique new banking service that allows customers to do all of their banking over the Internet.

created a "virtual bank" with no physical branches, only an outpost on the Internet. All banking is done electronically, although customers need to mail in their deposits. Wells Fargo Bank now offers online account access through its World Wide Web site as well.

Solidifying Relationships with Customers and Suppliers Information systems have also been used to "lock in" customers, making it costly or inconvenient for customers to switch to a competitor. The Federal Express Corp. has compiled a list of more than 20,000 steady customers. To prevent them from defecting to rivals like the United Parcel Service, FedEx installed free personal computers linked to its Memphis headquarters. Shippers using FedEx can use the machines to check the status of the packages they send each day. Even customers that are not large enough to qualify for free computers can receive free FedEx package tracking software to use with their own PCs for this purpose, or they can track their packages using FedEx's World Wide Web site.

Information systems can also create new relationships with suppliers that maximize the firm's purchasing power. For example, the Chrysler Corp. and all the major U.S. auto companies have established electronic links with major suppliers. The Budd Co. of Rochester, Michigan, a leading supplier of sheet metal parts, wheel products, and frames, receives manufacturing releases directly from Chrysler terminals installed in all its work areas. Chrysler achieves savings from strict delivery requirements that specify parts to be supplied on the day they are needed.

Improved Operations and Internal Management Companies can also gain competitive advantage by performing their business tasks more efficiently and by improving productivity, reducing costs, or enhancing the quality of products or services. Basic business systems (such as those described in

Chapter 13) that cut administrative costs, reduce costs from excess inventory, or speed production can be strategic if they help a firm become the low-cost leader in its field.

For example, Wal-Mart Stores Inc. rose to the top of the U.S. retail business by keeping its prices low and its stores well stocked and by minimizing inventories. It uses a legendary inventory replenishment system triggered by point-of-sales purchases that is considered the best in the industry. The "continuous replenishment system" sends orders for new merchandise directly to suppliers as soon as consumers pay for their purchases at the cash register. Point-of-sale terminals record the bar code of each item passing the checkout counter and send a purchase transaction directly to a central computer at Wal-Mart headquarters. The computer collects all the orders and transmits them to suppliers. Because the system can replenish inventory so rapidly, Wal-Mart does not need to spend much money on maintaining large inventories of goods in its own warehouses. The system also allows Wal-Mart to adjust purchases of store items to meet customer demands. Competitors such as Sears spend nearly 30 percent of each dollar in sales to pay for overhead (i.e., expenses for salaries, advertising, warehousing, and building upkeep). Kmart spends 21 percent of its sales dollars on overhead. But by using information systems to keep operating costs low, Wal-Mart pays only 15 percent of sales revenue for overhead. By focusing on ways to maximize sales while minimizing inventory costs, Wal-Mart has become larger than Kmart and Sears combined and nearly as big as the entire U.S. department store industry.

THE VALUE CHAIN

The concept of the value chain can be used to identify the specific activities in each organization for which information systems can be used most effectively

Point-of-sale systems capture data about purchases at the moment a sale takes place, often using bar-code scanners and computerized cash and computerized cash registers. Firms can use this data to determine what items in inventory need restocking, buying patterns, and sales trends.

SOURCE: Courtesy of International Business Machines Corporation.

Value chain
The viewing of a business firm as a series of basic activities that add value to the firm's products or services.

to enhance the firm's competitive position. The **value chain** views the firm as a series or "chain" of basic activities that add value to a firm's products or services. These activities can be categorized as either primary activities or support activities.

Primary activities include inbound logistics, operations, outbound logistics, sales and marketing, and service. The first four of these primary activities are described in the discussions of the manufacturing and production and sales and marketing processes in Chapter 2. The service activity involves maintenance and repair of the firm's goods and services. Support activities make the delivery of the primary activities possible and consist of administration and management, human resources, technology, and procurement.

An information system could provide strategic impact if it helped the firm perform its value activities at a lower cost than competitors or if it provided the firm's customers with added value or service. Figure 3.2 illustrates the value chain and provides examples of strategic information systems that could be developed for each of the value activities. For instance, an automated warehouse system that identified and assigned warehouse locations for incoming goods could support inbound logistics. Operations could be supported by computer-controlled machine tools that cut materials into various shapes, and outbound logistics could be supported by a system that automatically generated packing lists and scheduled shipments. A system to

FIGURE 3.2

Examples of Strategic Information Systems in the Value Chain

Systems can be built to support each of the activities in the value chain. For activities that add the most value to the firm's products and services, such systems can provide a competitive advantage.

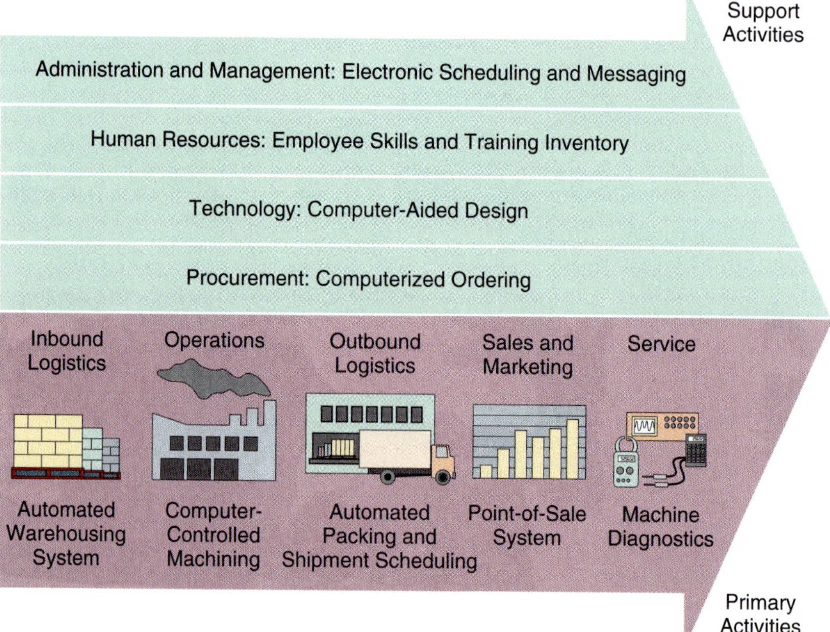

diagnose problems with machine tools would support the service activity. A system that scheduled meetings electronically and sent messages from one employee's desktop to another would support administration and management. A system that inventoried the training and skills of employees would support the human resources activity. A computer-aided design system similar to the applications described in Chapter 2 would support the technology activity. Wal-Mart's continuous replenishment system supports both the sales and marketing activity and the procurement activity. The precise activities that add the most value to products and services depend on the specific features of each firm. Businesses should develop strategic information systems for the value activities that add the most value to their particular firm.

3.2 COMPETING ON A GLOBAL SCALE

Look closely at your jeans or sneakers. Even if they have a U.S. label, they were probably designed in California and stitched together in Hong Kong or Guatemala using materials from China or India. Many of the items we use every day come from other countries or have foreign components; the firm where you work probably engages in business abroad as well. Foreign trade now accounts for over 25 percent of the goods and services produced in the United States and even more in Germany and Japan. Today, and even more in the future, the success of many firms will depend on their ability to compete internationally.

Globalization has created new opportunities for using information systems to coordinate the work of different parts of the company and to communicate with customers and suppliers. But building and using information systems on an international scale creates new challenges. In this section, we describe both the challenges and opportunities created by global information systems.

GLOBAL OPPORTUNITIES

While hundreds of thousands of small companies conduct business abroad from a single domestic location, larger corporations often have factories, design centers, sales headquarters, and retail outlets in foreign countries. Very large corporations, like General Motors or PepsiCo, have entire subsidiaries for each major country in which they do business, each with its own products, production facilities, and information systems based on national boundaries.

Quaker Oats, the food products company with headquarters in Chicago, Illinois, used to market its products on a country-by-country basis. The products used the Quaker Oats logo but had country-specific brand names. Quaker Oats organized its information systems around each country and the unique products in that country. Quaker used a **multinational** approach to organizing its business: Financial management and control were maintained out of a central home office while production, sales, and marketing were distributed to units in other countries. After the creation of the

Multinational
Approach to organizing a business in which financial management and control are maintained out of a central home office while production, sales, and marketing operations are located in other countries.

European Community, which seeks to eliminate trade barriers and tariffs between countries and to create a single unified market, Quaker Oats began to develop more products like Gatorade, which is marketed under the same brand name in Italy, Canada, and Germany. Quaker Oats hopes to take advantage of the changes in Europe to restructure its operations and systems to span many countries and serve large economic blocks. The company will have to rebuild its systems to support common products sold to large geographic regions. The firm is moving from a multinational toward a **transnational** business organization in which sales and production activities are managed from a global perspective without reference to national borders.

Transnational
Approach to organizing a business in which sales and production activities are managed from a global perspective without reference to national borders.

Ford Motor Co. reorganized along transnational lines. In order to compete more effectively in emerging car and truck markets in Asia and in established European and North American markets, the company created a single worldwide automotive organization called Ford Automotive Operations. Ford has plants in 30 countries and over 300,000 employees worldwide. (Figure 3.3 shows the location of Ford plants and design centers.) Consolidating into a single global operating unit will eliminate redundant engineering and production activities and reduce the cost of materials so that the firm can cheaply and rapidly produce a wider variety of cars and trucks for diverse markets from Michigan to Malaysia. Instead of organizing its operations country by country, Ford created global vehicle development centers. Ford's objective is to create basic car models that can be sold in large numbers around the globe, with modifications for local tastes in styling and local pollution regulations.

THE CHALLENGE OF BUILDING INTERNATIONAL INFORMATION SYSTEMS

What would it take to create information systems that could support Ford's new global organization or that could provide the management of Quaker Oats in Chicago with reliable information on the profitability of Gatorade in Germany and Italy? Systems spanning international boundaries pose special people, organization, and technology challenges.

People Challenges Cultural and linguistic differences are a powerful impediment to building common international systems that can be used by business units in different countries.[2] If the user interface of a system is written in English, how can it be understood and used by other employees in Greece, Turkey, Spain, Italy, or France? Not all workers in international companies are fluent in English. To make the system work across national boundaries special data entry screens, output forms, reports, and handbooks explaining how the system works will need to be created in the language of each country where the system will be used. The educational levels in some nations are lower than others, making it more difficult to assemble an educated workforce that can easily acquire computer and information system skills.

Organization Challenges Cultural and political differences have a profound effect on the way people work and on organizational procedures. For example, it is standard practice among Hong Kong garment manufacturers for the

FIGURE 3.3

Ford Revamps with Eye on the Globe

Ford Motor Company created a single automotive operation worldwide with global vehicle development centers. The idea is to develop specific types of cars that Ford will sell worldwide.

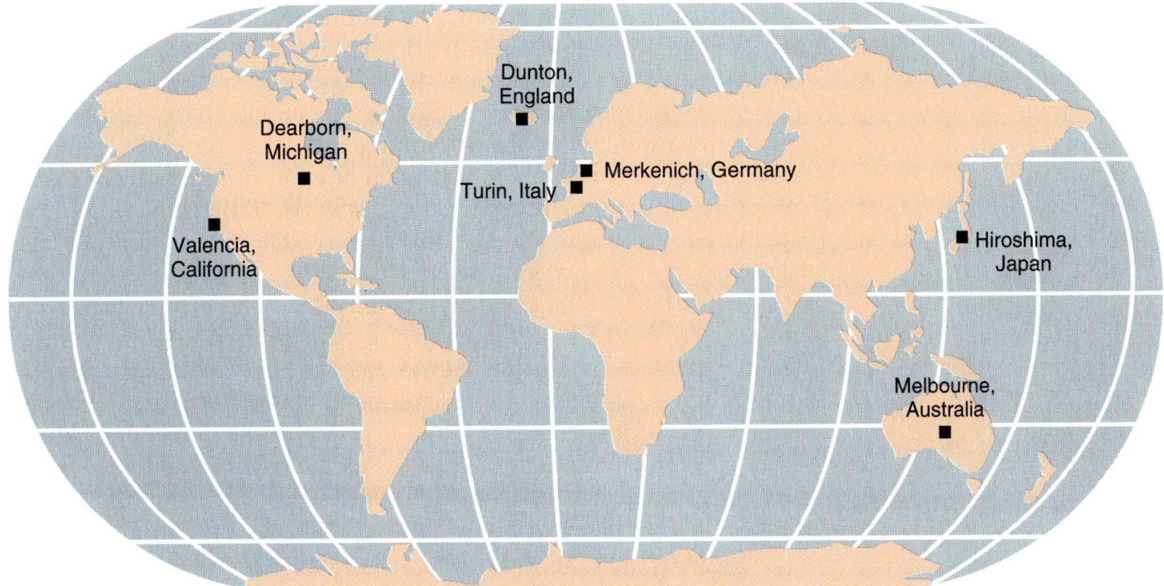

Ford's Existing Design Centers

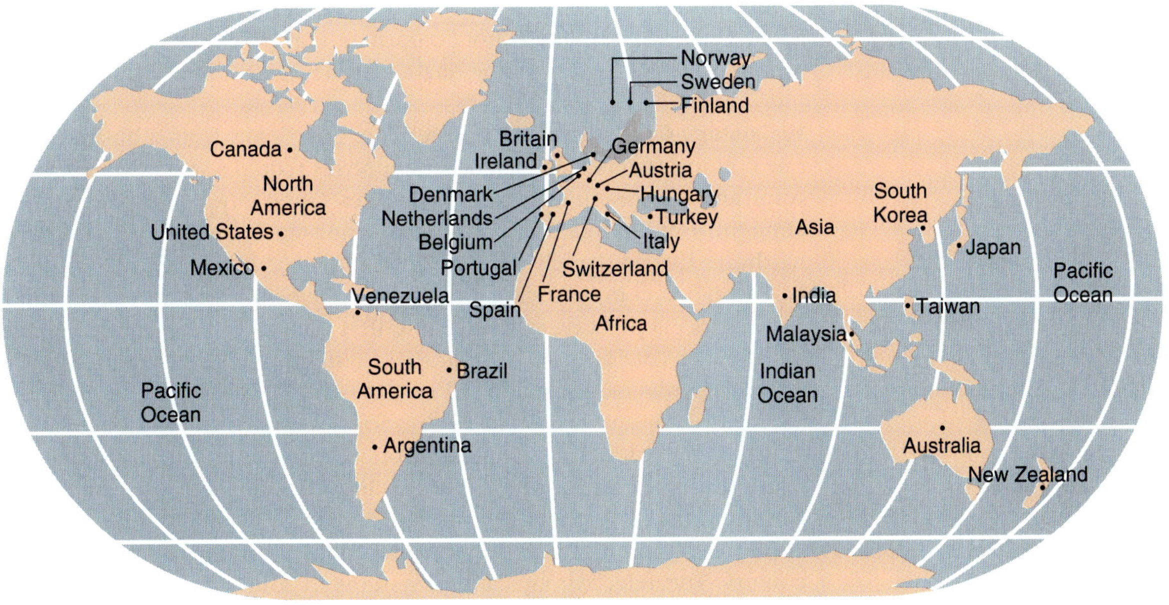

Where Ford Has Plants

shop sewing the garment to handle the final steps of finishing and washing. In the United States, in contrast, the individual steps are contracted out to different parties.

National laws and traditions have created disparate accounting practices in various countries that affect the way profits and losses are analyzed. German companies generally do not recognize the profit from a venture until the project is completely finished and they have been paid. British firms, on the other hand, begin posting profits before a project is completed when they are reasonably certain they will get the money.

How can an organization have an accounting system that serves two countries with different practices and goals? And how can a large international company with units in ten different countries obtain consistent data to monitor its performance? If a company wants to use the same information system in several countries, it may have to create special software that can take each country's tax laws into account.

The use of diverse national currencies and currency fluctuations offer further complications. A product that appears profitable in France may suddenly produce a loss because of changes in foreign exchange rates.

It is also difficult to understand how units of the business operate in different countries when they use disparate conventions for naming and identifying essential pieces of business data. A sale may be called an "order produced" in France, an "order scheduled" in Germany, and an "order booked" in the United Kingdom.

Transborder data flow
The movement of information in any form from one country to another.

Countries have different laws governing **transborder data flow,** the movement of information in any form from one country to another. Some European nations, for instance, prohibit the transmission of information about employees to foreign countries. The European Commission, which is the highest planning body for the integration of Europe, has been considering measures to restrict the flow of personal information to countries such as the United States that do not conform to Europe's strict requirements governing the transmission of personal information.

Technology Challenges To transfer data effortlessly from a business unit in one country to other units in other countries requires special hardware, software, and telecommunications capabilities. Often different divisions or operating units of an organization use different brands and models of computer hardware that are largely incompatible with each other. Information systems based on one computer cannot automatically be used on another computer. For instance, operating units that use IBM computers would not be able to transfer the data and software in their systems to Digital Equipment Corp. (DEC) computers, nor would all models of IBM computers be able to run the same information system applications automatically. Although different kinds of computers can be linked through the Internet, many systems do not use Internet technology, nor can the Internet be used for many types of applications.

Telecommunications services are handled differently from country to country. The telecommunications systems in some countries cannot fulfill even the most basic business needs, such as providing reliable circuits (telecommunications lines in southern and eastern Europe and underdeveloped countries in Africa, Asia, and South America are notoriously unreliable), issuing bills in a common currency, or coordinating among different

FORD DESIGNS FOR GLOBAL MARKETS

The striking 1994 Ford Mustang represented a revolution in the way Ford designs cars. Thanks to powerful computer-aided design (CAD) tools and global networking, Ford transformed a collection of design studios scattered all over the world into a single global design organization.

In the past, automobile design was a slow, step-by-step effort in which artists carved clay models from design drawings (each costing $100,000 and a great deal of time); design changes were then made, new designs were drawn, and new models were created. This process was repeated many times until management was satisfied. Production engineers then took over; inevitably the production process forced additional design changes. Design and development consumed 60 months or more.

CAD created an automobile design revolution. Starting in Japan, more and more design work has been done on powerful workstations. Work progresses more quickly and efficiently because sophisticated CAD software can identify many design flaws while simultaneously allowing designers to "see" the actual product without carving expensive models at each step. Ford designed its 1994 Mustang in 35 months; Jack Telnack, Ford's design chief, believes design time can be reduced to 24 months.

Hardware technology developments have been partially responsible for these improvements. For example, three-dimensional graphics designs with photograph-like reality that can be rotated and viewed from all sides require enormous quantities of data and processing power. CAD workstations able to handle this processing are now readily available. Today a workstation can "crunch" more numbers per second than a person working nonstop could deal with in 2,400 years.

The newest wrinkle in technology support of automobile design is termed "virtual co-location"—designers scattered throughout the world working together as if they were in one location. A typical, transmittable CAD automobile design file now takes about 7.5 minutes to transmit on a network. Prior to satellite transmission and fiber optics, the transmission of such gigantic files was so slow as to be impractical.

Why the need for virtual co-location? Ford designers work in offices in the United States, Europe, Japan, and Australia. Each location has unique knowledge workers and equipment with specialties not available elsewhere. The original designs are usually created in Dunton, England. They are then transmitted to Dearborn, Michigan, where they are modified. Dearborn and Dunton designers work together on networked computers to make modifications, even rotating the three-dimensional images to view them from all sides. When the model is acceptable to all, designers and engineers in Turin, Italy, take over, using the data files transmitted from Dearborn to drive a computerized milling machine to turn out full-size, styrofoam clay models. Production engineers at scattered production sites also participate during the design process.

In December 1995 Ford signed a $200 million contract with Structural Dynamics Research, Inc. of Milford, Ohio, to replace its home-grown software with a system that combines computer-aided design, manufacturing, engineering, and product information management. The new software provides a single system for electronically designing, simulating, testing, and optimizing vehicle manufacturing.

FOCUS Question: What people, organizational, and technical issues should be addressed by companies attempting to use virtual co-location design?

SOURCES: Doug Bartholomew, "Ford Retools," *Information Week,* April 1, 1996, and Julie Edelson Halpert, "One Car, Worldwide, with Strings Pulled from Michigan," *The New York Times,* November 6, 1993.

telecommunications carriers and the regional telecommunications authority. Europe's efforts to create a unified economic community have been thwarted by a hodgepodge of disparate national technical standards for telecommunications technology and levels of service.

Special software is required to translate between different brands of computer hardware and different telecommunications standards. Although standards for connecting networks, computers, and diverse pieces of software are starting to be developed, there are no universal standards that all businesses or countries have agreed upon. Organizations address this problem by developing special software to translate between one system and another, but this process is very costly, especially if an organization needs to develop such software for all its information systems. We describe some of the software challenges in Chapters 5 and 7.

The Focus on Technology illustrates how the Ford Motor Co. overcame these challenges when it built its global design organization.

The rest of this text will provide you with the understanding of information system technology and problem solving to help you meet these and other people, organization, and technology challenges.

3.3 PROMOTING QUALITY WITH INFORMATION SYSTEMS

During the last decade of the twentieth century, quality has developed from a business buzzword into a growing and very serious goal for many businesses. The imperative of becoming and remaining globally competitive is the primary cause for this trend. Information systems have a major contribution to make in this drive for quality. After briefly defining quality, we will examine some of the way information systems can help.

WHAT IS QUALITY?

A number of definitions exist for quality. A very common one is conformance to specifications (or the absence of variations). This definition is a producer view of quality rather than a consumer view. Using this definition, one can easily measure quality by first establishing specifications and then checking the product (or service) to make certain it meets those specifications. In an information system, for example, one specification for an online corporate payroll might be a 3-second response time 90 percent of the time when no more than 20 clerks are using the system. A simple statistical tracking of the system will allow those involved to determine whether the system is conforming to the specification. Similarly, the specifications for a telephone might include one that states the strength of the phone should be such that it will not be dented or otherwise damaged by a drop from a 4-foot height onto a wooden floor. Again, a simple test will allow this specification to be measured. For this producer perspective on quality to pay off, the organization must be willing to take the action needed to bring its products up to specifications when they fall short.

Today, as the quality movement in business progresses, the definition of quality is increasingly from the perspective of the customer. Customers are concerned with getting value for their dollar and product fitness, performance, durability, and product support.

Consumers define quality from three aspects. The first is the physical materials: the ease of installation and use of the product; product safety, reliability, serviceability, and durability; and the style and appearance of the product. Quality of service is a second aspect: truth in advertising; billing statement accuracy; responsiveness to expressed or implied warranties; support of product. Finally, psychological impressions are a significant aspect of consumer-defined quality: staff appearance, courtesy and sympathy; staff knowledge of their products and their job; and brand name reputation.[3]

The consumer definition of quality has become important for two reasons. Studies and experience have shown that lower quality is actually costly. For example, if a furniture manufacturer produces a folding chair with a defect rate of 8 percent, that means eight of every 100 chairs shipped are defective. It has long been obvious that returning a product can cost a great deal in extra shipping costs, spare parts, and staff time for repair as well as in customer loyalty. A list of some of the costs arising from producing those eight defective chairs includes

- Cost of materials for eight chairs
- Labor to build eight defective chairs
- Production machinery wear and tear resulting in maintenance and replacement 8 percent more often
- Higher work-in-process inventory costs
- Higher storage costs due to the need to warehouse 8 percent more raw materials, work in process, and finished goods
- An 8 percent larger inspection staff to inspect the extra chairs
- Increased insurance liability costs and even legal defense costs due to harm caused by the defective chairs

A second reason firms now focus more on customer definitions of quality is the need to survive in an increasingly competitive market. Consumer preferences have changed. Customers have shown in recent years that they are willing to pay more to receive quality. The low-price, lower-quality producer or retailer often cannot remain in business.

Total quality management (TQM), a concept made popular in Japan, has become the central approach to quality. TQM makes quality the responsibility of everyone within an organization. Everyone must improve quality, from the typist who reduces typing errors to the line worker who spots product defects, the engineer who eliminates design errors, and the sales person who sells only what the firm can deliver. With TQM quality is not achieved by eliminating defective products. Rather, whenever possible, quality is built in at the source; that is, the defect never happens. Some TQM companies adopt a goal of zero defects.

Total quality management (TQM)
Concept that makes quality improvement the responsibility of all members of an organization.

HOW INFORMATION SYSTEMS CAN ENHANCE QUALITY

How can information systems contribute to the enhancement of a company's products or services? Many ways exist, but the answer will depend on the individual company, its business, its competitive environment, and its current needs. Let us examine some of the ways companies face the challenge of improving quality to see how information systems can be part of the process.

Simplify the Product and/or the Production Process One way to achieve quality is to reduce the number of steps in any process and the number of parts in any product, thus reducing "opportunities" for problems. Pitney Bowes, the $3.3 billion manufacturer of postage meters and mailing machines, decided to redesign its entire production process in response to a drop in market share. They held 88 percent of the market, but considering that historically they had almost no competition, this was a clear indication of trouble. They decided

- To reduce manufacturing costs, allowing them to either lower the price or increase quality for the same price (either way becoming more competitive and giving the customer more quality for the dollar); and
- To simplify their products, thus reducing opportunities for production errors and allowing the firm to establish higher quality standards.

Pitney Bowes used several computer software packages, including the Advanced Planning System (APS), a simulation software package from Carp Systems of Lexington, Massachusetts, and computer-aided design (CAD) engineering software. First, Pitney Bowes redesigned its products, switching from metal castings and mechanical parts to plastics and electronics, thus reducing not only the weight but also the number of moving parts. Their engineers were able to cut the total number of parts per product in half, thus simplifying the production process. Next, using simulation, they redesigned their production facilities, enabling them to consolidate previously scattered factories into one facility. They also moved production steps closer to each other. This combination of changes simplified the production process, resulting in an improved ability to control product quality. The process redesign also increased their output per square foot by 50 percent while making them much more efficient.

Pitney Bowes used simulation and computer-aided design (CAD) software to redesign its production process. It increased quality by reducing the number of moving parts and the number of steps required to create its business equipment products.

SOURCE: Courtesy of Pitney Bowes. Photo by Bill Freeman.

Benchmarking One way to improve quality is to benchmark—to statistically measure your products and activities and compare the results against your own high standards or external industry standards. As described in the Focus on Problem Solving, when Florida Power and Light decided to benchmark outages, customer complaints, customer time without power, and causes for power interruptions, they required a great deal of information. With the aid of their information systems groups, they collected and distributed the needed information. As a result, they improved customer service while reducing other serious problems such as downtime due to lightning strikes.

Direct the Product or Service toward Customer Demands For example, improving customer service will improve quality, as demonstrated by both the Pitney Bowes and the Florida Power and Light projects. In both cases, information systems played a central role.

Reduce Cycle Time Studies have shown that probably the best single way to reduce quality problems is to reduce cycle time (the amount of time from the beginning of a process to its end). Shorter cycle times mean that problems are caught earlier in the process, often before the production of the defective product is completed, saving some of the hidden costs of producing it. Moreover, because a shorter cycle time is easier to grasp and understand than a longer cycle time, employees are less likely to make mistakes. Finally, finding ways to reduce cycle time often means finding ways to simplify production steps, as in the case of Pitney Bowes. Information systems can contribute by eliminating critical time delays, as Rockwell International discovered. The Downey, California, defense contractor found that slow communication between their manufacturing plant in Palmdale, California, other Rockwell design facilities, and the Kennedy Space Center in Florida was causing errors to be made or to go undetected as the Space Center staff was preparing for a space shuttle launching. To correct the problem, the Rockwell IS department installed an automated imaging system and networked it to all relevant sites. Now engineers can transmit design changes instantaneously to wherever they are needed or review problems at the space center immediately. The case study concluding Chapter 14 decribes Rockwell's efforts in greater detail.

Improve Design Quality and Precision Computer-aided design software has made a major contribution to quality improvements in many companies, from producers of automobiles to producers of razor blades. One typical but interesting example of CAD's contributions to quality is Alan R. Burns's use of it to design a newly invented product, a modular tire. Burns, a Perth, Australia, mining engineer, developed the idea of a tire made of a series of removable, replaceable tread segments. The modules are not pneumatic and so cannot go flat, but they can be damaged. If that occurs, the damaged segment can simply and easily be replaced. Burns started a company, Airboss, and quickly found a major outlet for his product in the heavy equipment vehicle market, which manufactures equipment such as tractors and earth movers. He first established tire and tire usage quality criteria for the modules, such as speed, load, temperature, surface characteristics, wear life, and traction. Then, after entering this data into the CAD software, he iteratively designed, modified, and tested the product on the computer until he was satisfied with the results.

MEASURING FOR QUALITY

Florida Power and Light (FPL), with about $5 billion in revenues, provides electrical power to over three million Floridians, including residents of Miami, Sarasota, and Jacksonville. When FPL instituted its quality program, the Florida Public Power Commission was receiving about 2,100 complaints annually about FPL's service and billing, and FPL's average customer time without service after an outage report was 100 minutes. During the first five years of their Quality Improvement Program (QIP), complaints fell at an average rate of 15 percent per year and were down to just 900 per year, an even more impressive gain in the light of a customer-based growth of 3.5 percent per year. Customer electrical outage time dropped during the same period to 48 minutes, a reduction of 52 percent. The central methodology of FPL's quality program was to measure as much as possible and use benchmarks to set target goals. Extensive measuring also allowed FPL to identify and control problems at an early stage. As Al Horner, manager of information planning, system, and programming, put it, "There are ways to measure everything."

Information systems (IS) played a central role in FPL's achievements by extracting data from existing systems whenever possible and by building new systems to measure activities when necessary. IS then collected all the data and made them available for everyone who needed them. A key to the IS contribution was its decision to make the data available in an easy-to-read graphics format so users could effortlessly spot deviations early enough to prevent serious problems from developing. IS built three systems to support FPL's QIP.

The Divisions Management Information System (DMIS) collects and analyzes customer survey and check-sheet data in 101 categories from all divisions. With this data users can measure their performance against benchmarks and also analyze the source of problems in more detail in search of a solution. For example, data from this system helped FPL to realize that many of its outages were caused when improperly grounded transformers were hit by lightning (Florida has the highest lightning rate in the United States). DMIS data from all five FPL divisions are available to all the divisions. Thus, if the Eastern Division has a particular problem and sees from the DMIS report that the Southern Division does not experience the same problem, staff members of the Eastern Divisions can analyze Southern's data or consult with its staff.

The Trouble Call Management System (TCMS) aids customer service personnel in locating electrical trouble and outages from customer service complaints and automatically notifies repair crews of the nature and location of the problem, thus significantly reducing response time. The same data are also used by technicians to analyze past problems in order to predict where future problems are likely to occur. TCMS is partly responsible for the 52 percent drop in outage response time and the resulting reduction in customer complaints.

The Distribution Construction Management System (DCMS) combines data from FPL's more than 400 locations to enable FPL users to estimate labor and material costs for the 150,000 work orders the utility processes every year. The system also supports and improves work-crew scheduling.

These information systems themselves were vulnerable because of Florida's frequent hurricanes and severe storms. Florida Power and Light made them more reliable, and therefore more capable of supporting its customer service improvements by instituting measures for backing up the data they contained so that the data would not be lost in the event of power outages. With the help of IBM, the utility company created an elaborate disaster recovery system where the data contained in most of its systems are backed up nightly.

FOCUS Questions: What aspects of quality was Florida Power and Light concerned about? How did information systems help the firm improve quality?

SOURCES: "Backup and Recovery at Florida Power and Light," *IBM Storage Software,* December 4, 1996; Daniel Greising, "Selling a Bright Idea," *Business Week,* August 8, 1994; and Alan J. Ryan, "Where Quality Takes Command," *Computerworld,* December 11, 1989.

Only late in the process did he have to develop an actual working model. By using CAD software, Burns was able to test with such precision that he produced a much higher quality product than would have been possible had he been able to test only by making repeated, manually tested models.

Improve Production Precision and Tighten Production Tolerances Computer-aided design software has been a major boon in designing improved production processes. Many CAD software systems include the capability of using the product design specifications to design production tooling and the actual production process. The user of this software is able to design a more precise production system, a system with tighter tolerances, than could ever be done manually. Burns used his CAD software to do just this. In testing the production process through the CAD software, he identified in advance such problems as uneven cooling. In addition, his design cycle time was short, thus saving money and allowing him to meet changing customer demands more quickly.

Reduce Opportunities for Human Error Usually this requires either reducing the number of steps or automating steps. With Airboss, for example, Burns did not need to enter data for design of the production process into the computer. Instead, he used the data developed within the CAD system for the process design step. Florida Power and Light used its TCMS system data to automatically notify repair crews of problems called in by customers. The data did not need to be reentered into a separate system.

Many of these efforts to promote quality were also successful because they were based on teamwork. The McKesson case study concluding this chapter is an excellent example of the value of such teamwork.

3.4 TRANSFORMING ORGANIZATIONS: REENGINEERING

Technology alone is often not enough to make organizations more competitive, efficient, or quality oriented. The organization itself may need to be changed to take advantage of the power of information systems. Our sociotechnical perspective on information systems suggests that organizations and people need to change in order to make information technology work properly. Sometimes these changes can be accomplished by adjusting and streamlining procedures; often the organization itself must be redesigned. The organization may need to rethink its goals, its relationships to customers and suppliers, and its fundamental operating procedures.

REENGINEERING BUSINESS PROCESSES

One way that organizations can maximize the benefits of information system technology is by redesigning their business processes. **Reengineering** is the rethinking and radical redesign of business processes to achieve dramatic improvements in cost, quality, service, and speed. Chapter 2 introduced the

Reengineering
The rethinking and radical redesign of business processes to significantly improve cost, quality, service, and speed and to maximize the benefits of information technology.

concept of business processes. A business process is a set of related activities involving the coordination of work and information, such as the development of a new product or the processing of a sales order. In reengineering, the steps required to accomplish a particular task are combined to cut waste, reduce paperwork, and eliminate repetitive or redundant work. Often this means breaking down the traditional divisions among functional areas, such as sales, marketing, manufacturing, and finance, and redeploying workers in multifunctional teams. Thus, instead of processing an order by passing the order from sales to manufacturing to warehousing to inventory to billing, a streamlined, reengineered ordering process might combine representatives from all these departments to work on order fulfillment simultaneously.

EXAMPLES OF REENGINEERING

To reengineer successfully, the organization must ask basic questions: Why do we do what we do? Why do we do it in the way we do? If we could start from scratch, what would we do now, and how would we do it? The organization needs to examine the tacit rules and assumptions underlying its standard operating procedures and the way it conducts business. Then it needs to reinvent these processes anew, without regard to traditional responsibilities of work groups, departments, or divisions.

Here's how reengineering worked at IBM Credit Corp., a large subsidiary of IBM that provides financing for the computers, software, and services that IBM sells. In the past, when an IBM field sales representative called with a request for financing, the call was logged by 1 of 14 people sitting at a conference room table in Greenwich, Connecticut. The person taking the call wrote the financing request on a piece of paper (step 1).

The paper was then taken upstairs to the credit department, where a specialist entered the application into a computer system to check the potential borrower's credit worthiness (step 2).

The credit specialist wrote the results of the credit check on the piece of paper and sent it to the business practices department, which used its own computer system to modify IBM's standard loan terms in response to the customer request (step 3). A business practices department member would attach the special terms to the request form.

Next the request went to a pricer, who entered the data into a PC spreadsheet to determine the appropriate interest rate to charge the customer. The pricer wrote the interest rate on another piece of paper (step 4) that was delivered with the other paperwork to a clerical group.

An administrator in the clerical group combined all the information into a quote letter for delivery to the field sales representative using Federal Express (step 5). An average of six days—sometimes up to two weeks—elapsed before the entire process was complete. The sales reps were dissatisfied because within those six days, customers could find another source of financing or turn to another computer vendor.

Two senior managers at IBM Credit learned that the actual work required to process a financing request took only 90 minutes. The work was primarily clerical—finding a credit rating, plugging numbers into a standard model, pulling standard "boilerplate" clauses from a file. Most of the six days was taken up by moving the form from one department to another. So IBM Credit restructured the process itself, replacing its credit checkers, pricers, and other specialists with generalists. Instead of sending a financing application from office to office, one person (called a deal structurer) processes the entire application from beginning to end. IBM Credit developed a new information system to support the deal structurers that provides access to all the required data and tools. Only in complicated credit situations does the deal structurer need to turn elsewhere. IBM Credit still maintains a small pool of real specialists in credit checking, pricing, and so forth to work with the structurers as a team.[4] Even under these special circumstances, the process has been reduced to a single step. Figure 3.4 compares the finance application process before and after reengineering.

FIGURE 3.4

Reengineering the Finance Application Process at IBM Credit Corporation

By reengineering, IBM Credit Corporation drastically reduced the number of steps required to obtain financing.

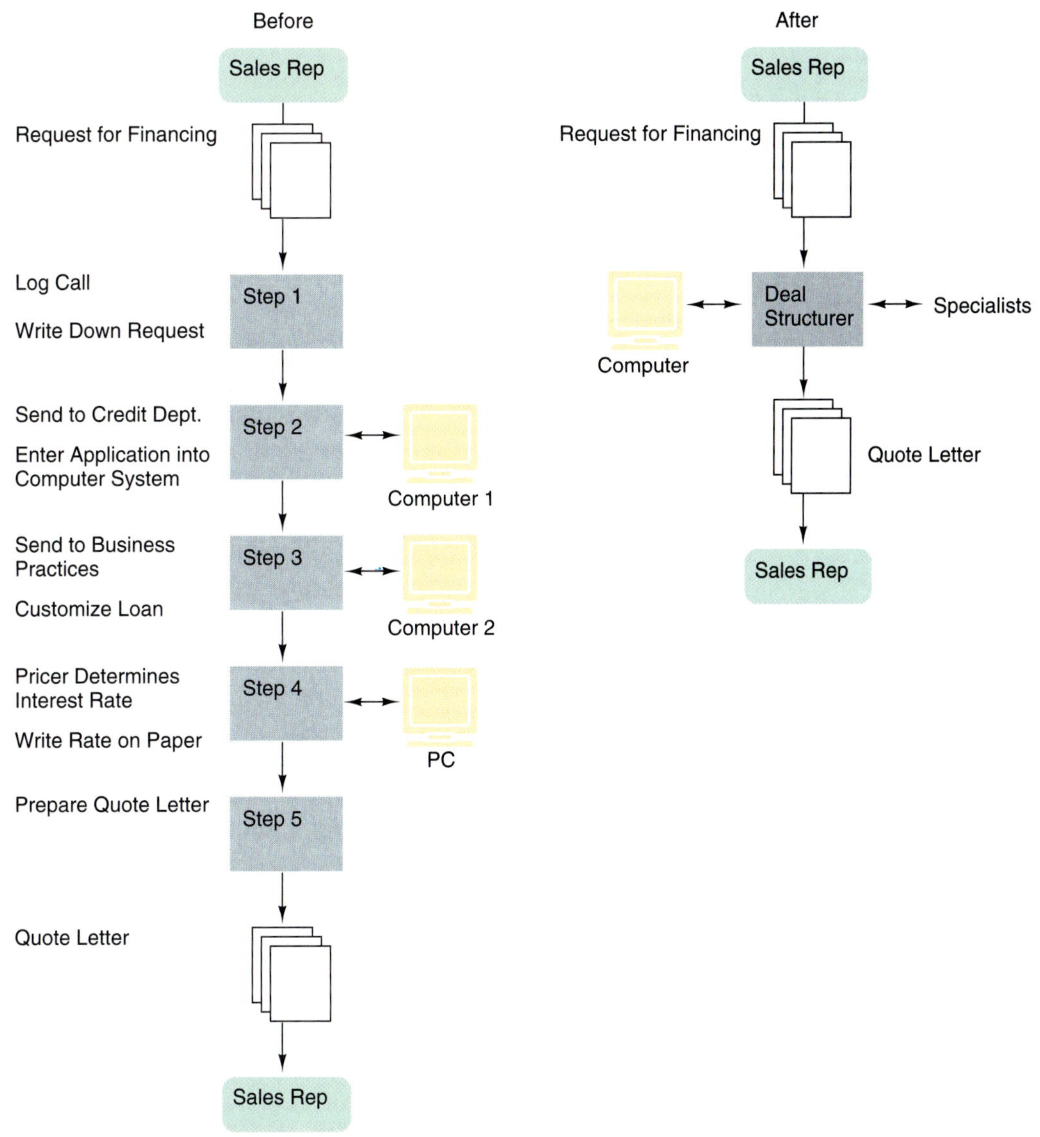

3.5 PROMOTING ETHICAL AND SOCIAL RESPONSIBILITY

Building global, competitive organizations is a significant information systems challenge. But information systems and technologies have ethical, social, and political dimensions as well. A central challenge facing us all—and discussed throughout this book—is how to build powerful and effective systems and organizations that are socially and ethically responsible. What ethical objectives can we expect organizations to pursue? When faced with a choice between building a system that affords a strategic competitive advantage to your organization, but costs the jobs of hundreds of loyal employees, versus the alternative of building a system that is less effective but preserves existing jobs, what is the correct course of action? What new alternatives should you seek?

Ethics
Principles of right and wrong that can be used to guide the behavior of free moral agents who make choices.

Ethics refers to the principles of right and wrong that can be used to guide the behavior of free moral agents who make choices. What should I do in this situation? What principles of right and wrong apply? Information systems present an array of ethical issues because they involve so many ways in which an individual's actions can affect other people. For example:

- Firms such as airlines or telephone companies may routinely monitor the telephone conversations of reservation agents or operators in the interest of improving productivity or customer service. This monitoring may violate the agents' expectations of privacy and create resentment even as it improves the quality of agent responses.
- A software project to develop a new customer billing system will take longer to complete than originally planned. To deliver the system on time and within the original budget specified by management, the project leaders eliminate some safeguards, such as error correction and detection, and reduce the testing of the system. Safeguards and the finer details of testing will take place after the system is in production.
- A firm under intense competitive pressure to reduce costs in order to stay in business installs a new streamlined, state-of-the-art, online order-entry system that is expected to eliminate the jobs of 50 order-entry clerks.

None of these situations involves violating a law, but in each situation different principles and sets of interests may be at odds. For instance, a firm might have to balance its need to reduce costs in order to stay in business against its responsibility toward the welfare of its employees. Monitoring employees' telephone conversations or electronic mail to make sure they are using the firm's telephone or electronic-mail facilities only for work-related purposes could run counter to the need to respect employee privacy.

THE RELATIONSHIP BETWEEN INFORMATION TECHNOLOGY AND ORGANIZATIONS

Computers themselves can't change society. Whatever good or evil comes from computers can be traced to some key design decisions about how they will be used by organizations and people. Behind all computing equipment (hardware and software) are engineers and designers who made conscious decisions about how the technology will perform in a technical sense. Once the equipment leaves the factory, systems analysts, programmers, managers, and end-users—people like you—determine how the computing equipment will actually perform its tasks. Through their decisions, these same people, sometimes unconsciously or unintentionally, determine how computer-based systems will change jobs, organizations, and people's lives. There is a long chain of decisions and decision makers in the journey from a simple "computer" to the "social impacts of computers."

BASIC ETHICAL CONCEPTS: RESPONSIBILITY, ACCOUNTABILITY, AND LIABILITY

In this chapter we want to emphasize the concepts of ethical moral responsibility, organizational accountability, and legal liability. There can be no ethics without these concepts. The concept of moral **responsibility** is based on the idea that individuals, organizations, and societies are free moral agents who act willfully and with good intentions, goals, and ideas. Because individuals, organizations, and societies are free moral agents, they are morally responsible for their actions. Organizational **accountability** means that actions can be traced throughout an organization to identify responsible individuals who can be held accountable by their fellow citizens and other governments and societies. These "higher authorities" can morally exact a payment for any harm done.

Responsibility
The idea that individuals, organizations, and societies are free moral agents who act willfully and with intentions, goals, and ideas; consequently, they can be held accountable for their actions.

Accountability
The ability to trace actions to identify individuals responsible for making the decisions to take those actions.

Liability
The idea that people may be obligated by law to compensate those they have injured in some way; liability is established by laws that set out legal remedies for proscribed behavior.

Liability extends the ideas of responsibility and accountability to the law. Liability is the legal obligation of someone who has engaged in proscribed behavior to make a payment to those they have harmed; liability is established by laws that set out legal remedies for proscribed behavior. In societies governed by laws, individuals, organizations, and even governments are legally liable for their actions. No social actors are above the law.

These considerations of responsibility and liability are important for understanding the ethical implications of using computers. Changes "caused" by computers cannot occur without human intervention. People and organizations who use computers in such a way that harm comes to others are morally responsible and can be held accountable just as the operators of motor vehicles can be held accountable for their actions. In some instances, specific laws govern the use of computers. Because computers are relatively new, however, the legal framework governing their use is still evolving.

LEADING SOCIAL AND ETHICAL IMPACT AREAS

The concerns raised about the effects of computers are actually not about computers but about traditional, long-standing issues of an industrial society. For instance, people are concerned about how computers affect freedom, creativity, and education because these are important, enduring human concerns. Computers are important because they potentially affect long-standing social issues like autonomy, creativity, liberty, vulnerability, and morality. We can classify the impact of computers into five major areas: information rights, property, accountability, system quality, and quality of life (see Figure 3.5).

FIGURE 3.5

Computer Impact Areas

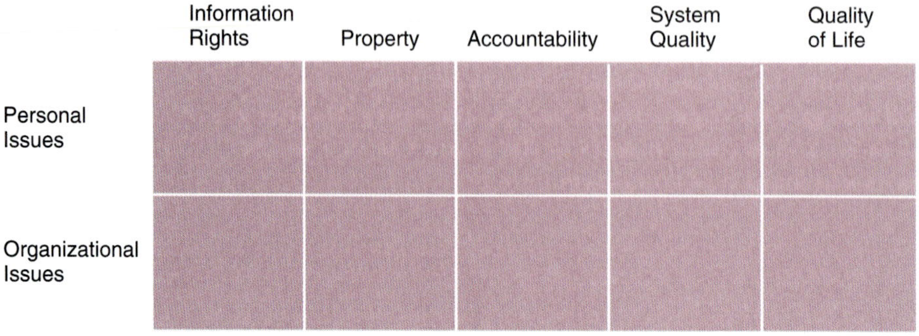

	Information Rights	Property	Accountability	System Quality	Quality of Life
Personal Issues					
Organizational Issues					

The personal issues involve your deciding on the proper course of action: What should you do in situations in which the law is unclear? The organizational issues involve developing business policies to govern the behavior of employees: What should the policy of our firm be? Next we discuss each of these social impact areas and point out some of the personal and organizational choices in each area.

Information Rights In George Orwell's 1947 novel entitled *1984,* a centralized machine-based surveillance system referred to as "Big Brother" keeps track of the minute details of what people say, what they purchase, whom they speak with, and what materials they read. Perhaps no single image of the modern computer-based information system has had such a lasting effect. Orwell's best-selling novel raises many questions central to the modern computer-based age: How much should government snoop on its citizens? What rights do citizens have to be free from government surveillance? Do citizens have a right to keep personal information from private industries such as banks, credit bureaus, and retailers? Should schools, other citizens, and even foreign governments be given access to any or all of a person's personal files and records, purchase patterns, medical records, and telephone records? If France has stronger privacy laws than the United States, should any data on French citizens be processed in the United States? These problems existed before computers. Indeed, some of the world's most notorious dictatorships existed long before computers. But with computer-based information systems, huge private and government databases that contain detailed personal information on citizens can be created inexpensively and efficiently. What information is available on you, and where does it come from? Table 3.2 lists the kinds of information about you that is available to just about any business (or individuals in business) and government in the United States.

Most of this information originates with you through the process of borrowing money, participating in a government program, or purchasing goods. Consumers and borrowers—that's all of us—routinely give information voluntarily to retailers and creditors so we can purchase goods on credit. At least once a month, millions of banks, retailers, credit card companies, and mail-order houses send computer tapes or other electronic files detailing their customers' purchases and payment activities to credit bureaus. These files contain detailed personal information on bank balances, credit history, income, family makeup, employment, driving record, and the like for nearly every consumer in the United States and many foreign countries as well. The three largest national credit bureaus (TRW, Inc., Trans Union, and Equifax, which together have 500 million records on Americans) resell this information either as ordinary credit reports or as lists of names to marketing companies who want to know about you. In addition to these national bureaus, there are more than 200 "superbureaus" that serve small businesses in local and state regions. Credit reports cost about $10 to $50, depending on the detail requested. The chapter-opening vignette describes some of the ways that the Internet can be used to collect personal information by tracking visitors to Web sites.

Federal, state, and local governments are a second major source of personal information about you. Citizens routinely and voluntarily provide a large amount of personal information to obtain college loans, small business loans, or other government benefits.

Why does the existence of huge, computerized, national information systems threaten freedom, privacy, and due process? **Privacy** is the right of individuals and organizations to be left alone and to be secure in their personal papers. Consider that both government and private industry have used information from computer-based data files to intimidate their opponents. As a result, these institutions have had what the courts call a "chilling effect" on political debate and have interfered with the exercise of political freedoms. For instance, if you take a public position against a corporation or a state agency, damaging information may be found about you in national data files and released to the press in order to destroy your credibility. Have you ever visited a mental health professional? Have you ever had a medical condition that you would not like to be made public? Have you ever committed an infraction of a law, statute, or regulation? Does your record include frank and critical comments by teachers or others? If you fall into any of these categories—and most of us have something negative on our many records—then you can be

Privacy
The right of individuals and organizations to be left alone and to be secure in their personal papers.

TABLE 3.2

Information on Individuals Available to Businesses

- Credit records
- Income
- Debts and payment history
- Personal data (e.g., Social Security number, age, birth date, family history, ethnicity)
- Reading materials, including magazines and book clubs
- Listening materials, including record clubs
- Motor vehicle information
- Driver license information, including infractions
- Federal and state loans
- Telephone calls
- Medical records
- Insurance records
- School records
- Employment history
- Legal judgments, hearings, and related data
- Marital history

potentially embarrassed or even neutralized politically. You may not have done anything wrong or illegal, but chances are you have done something embarrassing that is filed on a national record system somewhere. The contents of these data files also could be used to deny you insurance or a job.

Second, consider whether the information is accurate. Have you inspected the information held about you in national files? What if it is used to make decisions about you but is not really accurate or true, or is no longer true? This raises the issue of due process. The right to **due process** is the right to be treated fairly in accordance with a set of published legal procedures, including such things as the right to appeal and the right to an attorney.

Due process
The right to be treated fairly in accordance with established legal procedures, including such things as the right to appeal and the right to an attorney.

What can you, your business firm, and society do about these issues of privacy, freedom, access to information, and due process? The U.S. Congress and all state legislatures have passed many significant laws that attempt to govern record keeping in American society. European countries and Canada have even stronger legislation. These U.S. laws are described in Table 3.3.

Despite a number of laws seeking to protect privacy, the pressure of commercial interests to obtain access to personal information, coupled with powerful new technologies, has served to weaken existing laws. Nevertheless, the principles laid out by Congress in its preamble to the **Privacy Act of 1974** can be useful in extending legislation to cope with the age of electronic networks, personal computers, and huge, easily accessed private databases. (Note: Material in brackets is the authors'.)

Privacy Act of 1974
A federal statute that defines citizens' rights in regard to federal government records and management's responsibilities for them; sets out some of the principles for regulating computer technology in order to protect people's privacy.

The Privacy Act of 1974
Public Law 93-579

Be it enacted by the Senate and House of Representatives of the United States of America in Congress assembled, That this Act may be cited as the "Privacy Act of 1974."

Sec. 2.

(a) The Congress finds that—

(1) the privacy of an individual is directly affected by the collection, maintenance, use, and dissemination of personal information by Federal agencies;

(2) the increasing use of computers and sophisticated information technology, while essential to the efficient operations of the Government, has greatly magnified the harm to individual privacy that can occur from any collection, maintenance, use, or dissemination of personal information;

(3) the opportunities for an individual to secure employment, insurance, and credit and his right to due process, and other legal protections are endangered by the misuse of certain information systems;

(4) the right to privacy is a personal and fundamental right protected by the Constitution of the United States; and

(5) in order to protect the privacy of individuals identified in information systems maintained by Federal agencies, it is necessary and proper for the Congress to regulate the collection, maintenance, use, and dissemination of information by such agencies.

(b) The purpose of this Act is to provide certain safeguards for an individual against an invasion of personal privacy by requiring Federal agencies, except as otherwise provided by law, to—

TABLE 3.3

Major U.S Privacy Legislation

Freedom of Information Act (1966): This statute gives citizens and all organizations the right to inspect information about themselves held in government files and gives individuals and organizations the right to request disclosure of government records. This legislation has been the single most powerful information legislation in American history, giving individuals, writers, reporters, and even private corporations unprecedented access to unclassified government records.

Fair Credit Reporting Act (1970): Under this statute, credit agencies cannot share credit information with anyone but authorized customers; the act also gives citizens the right to inspect their records and be notified of their use for employment or credit. The law is easily circumvented because access is given to anyone with "a reasonable business need."

Privacy Act (1974): This law defines citizens' rights and management's responsibilities for federal government records. The law has had little effect because its language is vague and the Office of Management and Budget (the president's budget agency) does not enforce the law vigorously.

Family Educational Rights and Privacy Act (1974): This law requires schools and colleges to give students and parents access to student records and the right to challenge and correct those records.

Right to Financial Privacy Act (1978): This statute limits federal government searches of your bank records. State and local governments are not covered.

Cable Communications Policy Act (1984): This law regulates the cable industry's collection and disclosure of information on subscriber viewing habits.

Electronic Communications Privacy Act (1986); Computer Fraud and Abuse Act (as amended in 1986); Computer Security Act (1987): These laws protect the confidentiality of personal electronic communications and computer-based digital files against government and/or private abuse and intrusion. The Communications Privacy Act protects the privacy of electronic messages sent on public networks only against government surveillance (not against private surveillance) and does not cover internal corporate E-mail networks.

Video Privacy Protection Act (1988): Under this act, video rental records cannot be sold or released without a court order or consent of the person renting the videos.

Computer Matching and Privacy Act (1988): This statute regulates computer matching of computer files in different agencies to verify eligibility for federal programs and to identify delinquent debtors. The law does nothing about law enforcement and tax-matching programs, and it has many other loopholes.

(1) permit an individual to determine what records pertaining to him are collected, maintained, used, or disseminated by such agencies [No secret records or record systems];

(2) permit an individual to prevent records pertaining to him obtained by such agencies for a particular purpose from being used or made available for another purpose without his consent [Informed consent];

(3) permit an individual to gain access to information pertaining to him in Federal agency records, to have a copy made of all or any portion thereof, and to correct or amend such records [Right of inspection];

(4) collect, maintain, use, or disseminate any record of identifiable personal information in a manner that assures that such action is for a necessary and lawful purpose, that the information is current and accurate for its intended use, and that adequate safeguards are provided to prevent misuse of such information [No record systems without statutory authority and the principle of management responsibility];

FOCUS ON PEOPLE

THEFT BY INTERNET

If you could copy a spreadsheet program like Microsoft's Excel from your campus network, would you do it? How about WordPerfect, Lotus 1-2-3, and popular entertainment programs like Sim City? Several thousand people did in fact copy a wide range of programs from an Internet bulletin board in one of the largest software piracy cases in U.S. history. Just about any user can create an electronic bulletin board on the Internet where other users—if they know the password—can leave messages or digital copies of software.

David LaMacchia, a 20-year-old electrical engineering and computer science student at the Massachusetts Institute of Technology, was charged by the U.S. Attorney in Boston with distributing more than $1 million worth of copyrighted software. LaMacchia was not charged with personally copying software, or placing software on the Internet, or selling software. Instead LaMacchia was charged with operating a bulletin board, distributing the bulletin board address and password, and letting others "avail themselves of the opportunity to copy . . . software and computer files." The U.S. Attorney charged LaMacchia under the federal Computer Software Copyright Act of 1980 (amended in 1992).

LaMacchia created the bulletin board and then sent coded messages to potential users using a codename like "John Gaunt,sysop" seeking specific software products like WordPerfect. A few Internet users who received these messages would then send copies of the requested software via the Internet to an anonymous remailer service in Finland. The remailer service is used to strip the sender's name from the message, adding the remailer name, thus protecting the privacy of the sender. If you are going to steal, why advertise your name? People who wanted to copy the software would send their requests through the remailer service in Finland. The use of a remailer service makes it difficult (but not impossible) for authorities to discover who is placing stolen software on the Internet and who is making copies.

LaMacchia was indicted on April 7, 1994. If convicted, he

(5) permit exemptions from the requirements with respect to records provided in this Act only in those cases where there is an important public policy need for such exemption as has been determined by specific statutory authority [Exemptions only by law]; and

(6) be subject to civil suit **for any damages which occur as a result of willful or intentional action which violates any individual's rights under this Act** [Civil liability for damages]. (Emphasis added.)

Sections 3 and 4 of the Act define the key terms of the above preamble and the mechanisms for enforcing and administering the Act.

Note that Congress did not claim computers were the cause of privacy problems. Rather it is the use of computers by the federal government and private organizations that constitutes the threat. The Internet makes it even easier to invade others' privacy because it is so inexpensive to contact other people via E-mail.

Spamming, the practice of sending unsolicited E-mail and electronic messages, is growing because it costs only a few cents to send thousands of messages advertising one's products or services to subscribers of online services or users of Internet bulletin boards.

The personal ethical issue is: Under what conditions will you as an individual invade the privacy of others, with or without the use of computers?

could have received a prison term plus a $250,000 fine. Defenders of LaMacchia, many of them Internet users, claimed that the First Amendment protection of freedom of speech should apply. They argued that AT&T is not liable for criminal conspiracies being discussed over its phone lines, and newspapers are not liable for gambling activities that rely on accurate sports page reporting. So why should a bulletin board operator be held liable for activities that take place over his or her bulletin board? These defenders also claim that a successful federal suit could stifle the free flow of information on the information superhighway.

Judge Richard D. Stearns of the U.S. District Court for the District of Massachusetts dismissed the indictment on December 29, 1994. He, too, expressed concern that conviction of information intermediaries on the Internet for activities of persons using their services would raise serious First Amendment questions. The U.S. government decided not to appeal the dismissal.

Software piracy on the Internet continues. The Software Publishers Association (SPA) filed lawsuits charging copyright infringement against Internet service providers Community ConneXion, Inc. in Oakland, California, and GeoCities, Inc. in Beverly Hills, California. Tripod, Inc., a Web-hosting service in Williamstown, Massachusetts, was also served with legal papers. SPA filed the suits on behalf of three software manufacturers: Adobe Systems, Inc., Claris Corp., and Traveling Software Inc. The suits allege that these service providers allowed their users to infringe on software copyrights by posting unauthorized copies of copyrighted software, publishing illegal software authorization serial numbers, publishing utility software programs that could be used to illegally penetrate other computer systems, or allowing users to maintain links to Internet sites where they could download pirated software.

FOCUS Questions: Should operators of bulletin boards like David LaMacchia or Internet service providers be prosecuted if their facilities are used for software piracy? Why or why not? Are there any circumstances in which software copying is justified?

SOURCES: Stewart Deck, "Internet Providers Sued for Software Piracy," *Computerworld,* October 14, 1996, and Peter H. Lewis, "Student Accused of Running Network for Pirated Software," *The New York Times,* April 9, 1994.

For example, EPM Inc., described in the Chapter 1 vignette, sent out 150 unsolicited faxes per day to advertise. Was this an invasion of privacy? How can you use computer-based systems to protect your privacy and that of others? The organizational ethical issue is: Does your firm have a privacy policy in place that informs employees about the kinds of surveillance and privacy invasion practiced by the firm? Many organizations handle information rights questions by developing formal policies and informing their employees about these policies. These are called "informed consent" policies.

Property Who owns the information that is so readily available in computerized information systems or on networks? How can that ownership be established when computerized information is so easily copied, distributed on networks, or accessed from a computer system? Information technology has made it difficult to protect intellectual property and other types of intangible property created by individuals and organizations.

Copyright laws are the most frequently used protection for computer software. A copyright protects the creator of intellectual property against copying by others for a commercial purpose for up to 28 years to reward the creators of books, music, artwork, and motion pictures. Unfortunately, copyright law does not protect the ideas behind a work, but only the work itself.

The literal copying of software is illegal, but developing a software program that produces similar or exactly similar results is not illegal. Congress passed the Computer Software Copyright Act of 1980 to strengthen the protection of software.

The growth of networks and the Internet has made protecting intellectual property more difficult. Software, books, and articles can be easily copied and transmitted to others through online bulletin boards, the World Wide Web, and other online services (see the Focus on People).

The personal ethical issue is: How will you protect the property rights of others? What will you do when handed a piece of software that has obviously been copied? If your colleagues at work copy software, and the management tolerates this copying, what action should you take? The organizational ethical issue is to devise a business policy to ensure that employees observe the law and protect the property rights of vendors who provide the firm with software and other services. This involves writing a corporate policy that clearly establishes who owns what software, prohibits loading illegally copied software on corporate machines, and specifies penalties for infraction of copying rules.

Accountability and Liability Who is responsible for the personal damages caused by a computer-controlled x-ray machine that occasionally administers lethal doses of radiation to patients undergoing radiation therapy for cancer? The software vendor, the hardware manufacturer, or the hospital that administers the test? Should Prodigy be held liable for pornographic messages posted to electronic bulletin boards and sent to customers' E-mail addresses? If a student puts copyrighted software programs on the Internet, who is liable for the damages done to the software company? The university (or other Internet provider) that provided the student access to the Internet, or the student, or all those who read the bulletin board and downloaded the software to their computers?

These are just a few of the accountability problems raised by information technology and systems. Accountability is a basic prerequisite for an ethically responsible system: It is a system in which the actions and consequences of individual behavior can be traced, a system in which actors can be held responsible. Liability extends this idea to include the legal recovery of damages: If someone harms you, you can recover damages done to you.

Generally, existing legal protections for liability apply only to products, and not to services or intellectual products like books, magazines, and software. Courts have refused to hold publishers of books, magazines, or newspapers liable for their contents except under unusual circumstances in order to protect First Amendment rights to freedom of speech. Hence, software and its creator are rarely held liable.

But software is different from books: We are more critically dependent on software; it is difficult to perceive errors in software until they happen; and people come to believe that software is infallible. We can expect that in the future courts will extend liability protections to software in order to hold software manufacturers, sellers, and users liable for the damages they produce through the use of software.

The personal ethical issue is to decide the extent to which you are responsible for the consequences of the software that you create or use. For example, if you prepare a spreadsheet projecting business cash flow for the next year, are you personally liable for the accuracy and integrity of the spreadsheet? The organizational ethical issue is to understand the liabilities your business firm incurs to customers and employees through the use of software. Firms should carefully examine their responsibilities to customers, including implied warranties of fitness for consumption and reliability.

System Quality Dan Beckner was using accounting software from Peach Tree Software to run his Elbridge, New York, security devices business. One day he recorded the sale of a video camera costing $325, only to find that the software had miscalculated the camera's cost as $4,567,896. He then started double-checking his data and found other cost miscalculations. If he hadn't detected the errors, Beckner would have miscalculated the value of his May inventory and his tax payments to the Internal Revenue Service. Beckner is not alone. Many software makers knowingly ship products with minor defects in order to bring their products quickly to market. For other companies as well, software errors and poor data quality practices result in decisions that otherwise might not have been taken.[5]

What level of quality is adequate for systems to achieve? Is a systems error rate on the order of 1 in 100,000 transactions acceptable? How about software program errors—is an error of 1 in 1,000,000 acceptable or morally unacceptable? If you fail to edit data input into a computer system and accept poor data quality, are you responsible for the errors produced? What if lives depended on these decisions? The main sources of poor system quality are software bugs and errors, hardware and equipment failures (often due to natural disasters—so-called acts of God), and poor input data quality. We discuss these sources of poor system quality in Chapter 12 in greater detail.

The challenge facing managers today is to build systems that achieve the highest levels of system quality within the firm's technological and economic

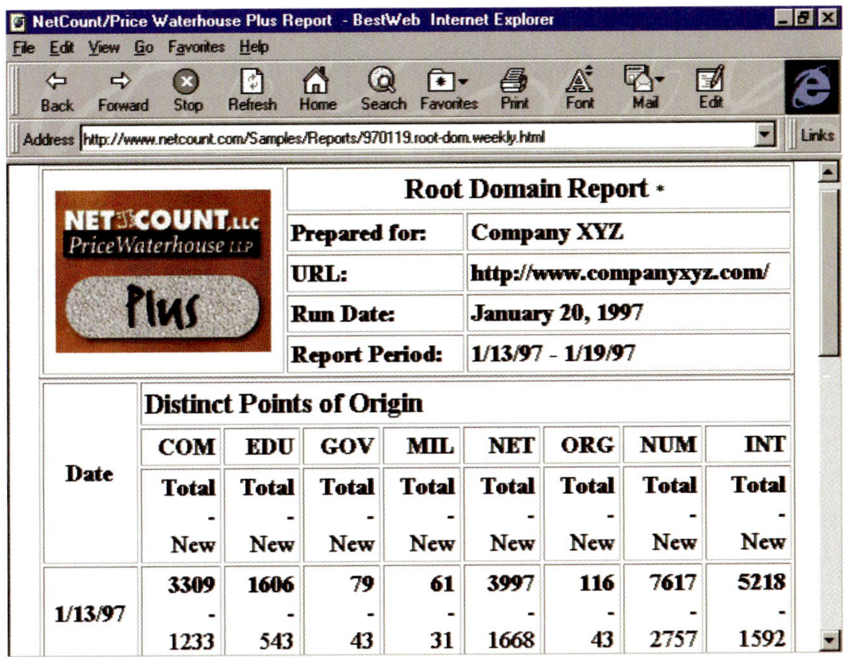

Root Domain Report

Prepared for:	Company XYZ
URL:	http://www.companyxyz.com/
Run Date:	January 20, 1997
Report Period:	1/13/97 - 1/19/97

Date	Distinct Points of Origin							
	COM	EDU	GOV	MIL	NET	ORG	NUM	INT
	Total - New	Total - New	Total - New	Total - New	Total - New	Total - New	Total - New	Total - New
1/13/97	3309 - 1233	1606 - 543	79 - 43	61 - 31	3997 - 1668	116 - 43	7617 - 2757	5218 - 1592

Many commercial software products are available to help companies collect and analyze data about visitors to their Web sites. Collecting data about Web site visitors can provide valuable marketing information but raises worries about protecting individual privacy.

resources. For instance, it is impossible to achieve zero defects in software code in large programs because all the paths through the program cannot be tested. Moreover, at some point testing must stop because of the cost of testing and the growing infrequency of error detection. But at what point should testing be stopped? No definitive standards have been established.

The personal ethical issue is to decide at what point you have exhausted the technological and economic resources available to you to deliver systems of high quality. What levels of error, and what consequences of errors, are you willing to live with? The organizational ethical issue is to investigate and gather data on the quality and performance of your systems, and then to develop policies and benchmarks for improving system quality. These policies are discussed in Chapter 12.

Quality of Life Aside from concerns of privacy and freedom of information, computers are associated with a number of other broad social and organizational impacts (see Table 3.4). Social impacts include the changes in the location of work brought about by computers (telecommuting), dependence on computers, the speed of social change, the erosion of boundaries between work and family life, and the growth of computer crime (described in Chapter 12). Organizational impacts include computer-generated changes in the quality of work life and organizational structure and the role of middle managers in downsizing organizations.

Telecommuting

Telecommuting
Working at home on a computer tied into corporate networks.

One area of social concern is how computers affect the distribution of workers, jobs, and businesses. The traditional distribution is changing as **telecommuting,** the ability to work for a company from one's home by using a telephone and networked computer, increases in the United States. Approximately 9 to 14 million workers in the United States and 1.25 million in Europe telecommute, and some predict these numbers will rise quickly.

Telecommuting was predicted to have several benefits: Fuel consumption would decline dramatically as commuters abandoned the highways for home offices; working parents would be able to spend more time with their families; and efficiency would increase as workers no longer struggled just to get to work each day. Several negative effects were also predicted: Urban areas would be abandoned for suburbs and exurbs (communities even far-

TABLE 3.4

Quality of Life Issues and Computers

Few would deny that computers have had a large impact on social and organizational life. One way to classify these impacts is to distinguish between broad social impacts and more narrow organizational impacts.

Social Impacts	Organizational Impacts
Telecommuting	Quality of work life
Dependence	Change in structure
Speed of change	Reduced employment
Erosions of boundaries	
Computer crime	

Computers and communications networks make it possible for people to work at home, without traveling to an office. However, the "do anything, anywhere" computing environment can blur the traditional boundaries between work and family time.

SOURCE: Tony Stone Image, Inc. © Walter Hodge.

ther from central cities than suburbs); poor people who needed jobs would live in cities with declining employment; and the isolated workers at home would tend to be women and minorities who would miss out on promotion opportunities at central headquarters. It is too early to tell whether computers are creating faster growth of suburbs or exurbs or the extent to which telecommuting is producing benefits or drawbacks.

Dependence on Computers

A second broad area of social concern involves computer dependence—the fact that we as a society increasingly depend on computers to provide vital services. If computer hardware or software malfunctions, people are not merely inconvenienced, as they would have been a few years ago; instead, their lives may be in jeopardy. If the telephone system's computerized switches break down for only a few minutes, entire industries (from mail-order retailing to data communications) can lose revenues amounting to hundreds of millions of dollars. As our dependence on computer hardware and software grows, so does our vulnerability. In general, information technology is advancing much faster than our ability to develop related moral principles and legal doctrines. The choices are not easy to make.

Speed of Social Change

Have you met people in the past year who said they were having a hard time keeping up with all the work they have to do? While we tend to dismiss these complaints as commonplace, many experts believe that fax machines, electronic mail, portable phones, cellular phones, and portable computing have all resulted in an acceleration of social change that many people find hard to cope with. The workloads and pressures on middle managers have expanded as their colleagues are laid off and they are expected to pick up the slack.

Erosion of Boundaries

Families are social units that provide a powerful bulwark against the demands of society, employers, and the state. Historically, the family has played a central role in training children, developing social values, encouraging original and radical thought, and nurturing emotions that cannot be expressed anywhere else. The digital revolution means, among other things, that more and more people will be working (at home, on vacation, on the weekend) when they should be communicating with their families and loved ones. This will erode traditional boundaries that separate work from play and family.

Computer Crime

Almost every new technology—electricity, telephones, automobiles—has created opportunities for criminal behavior. For instance, automobiles greatly enhanced the mobility of bank robbers, making it more difficult for authorities to apprehend them. Likewise with computers: Criminals will use computers to commit traditional and perhaps new kinds of crime. We discuss this topic in greater depth in Chapter 12.

Quality of Work Life

Although the use of computers raises significant issues at the social level, it is in the workplace, where computers are primarily used, that their effects first become apparent. The organizational impact of computers has affected the quality of work life, organizational structure, and employment.

Next to "Big Brother," the most common and long-standing fear of computer-based information systems is that they will degrade the quality of work by removing skill and craftsmanship, increase the authority of superiors by tightening surveillance, and reduce the training of workers as machines take on more and more sophisticated tasks. Other concerns center on the impact of computers on the **quality of work life**—the degree to which jobs are interesting, satisfying, and physically safe and comfortable. Table 3.5 summarizes the major aspects of work potentially affected by computerization.

Quality of work life
The degree to which jobs are interesting, satisfying, and physically safe and comfortable.

Some have predicted that the mental and physical health of workers will decline as they are exposed to high-pressure jobs paced by a computer that requires them to use small muscle groups in the hands, arms, and eyes, leading to strain and fatigue. Research has found that in some instances, computer-based systems do indeed result in significantly negative changes in

TABLE 3.5

Aspects of Work Potentially Affected by Computerization

Nature of Work	Quality of Employment
• Productivity	• Job satisfaction
• Frequency of tasks	• Job quality
• Ease of tasks	Variety
• Quality of training	Satisfaction with work group
• Quality of service and product	Autonomy
	Challenge
	Ability to see results of work
	• Pressure
	• Mental health
	• Quality of management

FIGURE 3.6

How Computerization Affected Clerical Employees at One Company

The chart illustrates that automation does not always affect people's jobs in a totally negative way. It became easier for workers to perform common tasks, for instance, and employees' mental health improved. Computerization exerted some negative effects as well: The variety and challenge of tasks declined.

SOURCE: Robert Kraut, Susan Dumais, and Susan Koch, "Computerization, Productivity and Quality of Work-Life," *Communications of the ACM* 32, no. 2 (February 1989): 226.

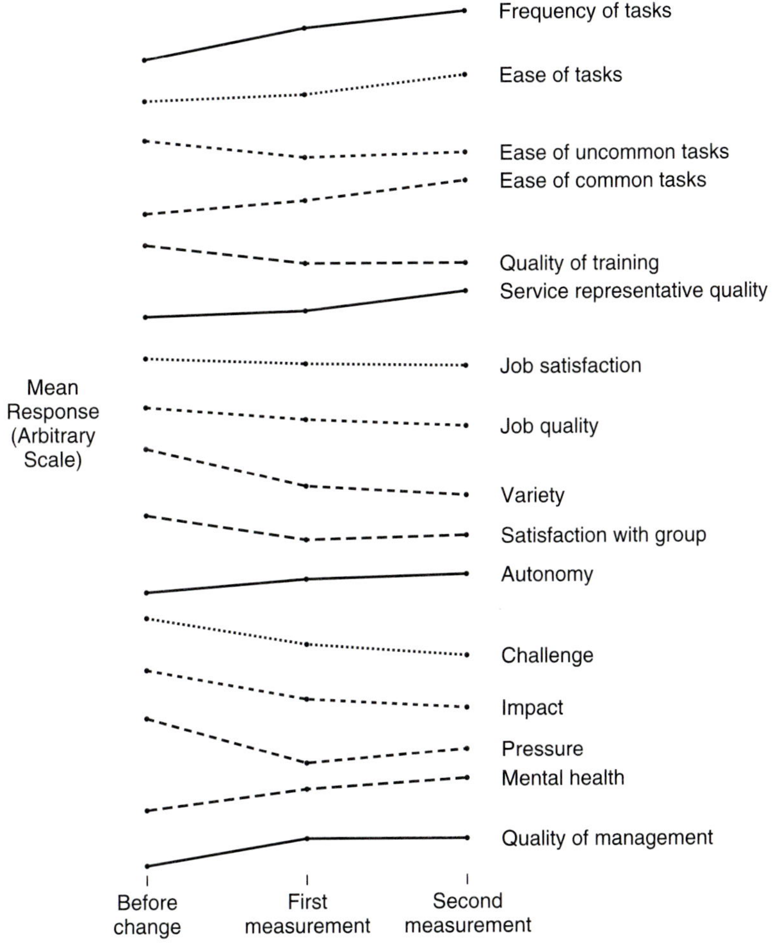

the quality of working life. At the same time, many other instances have been documented in which systems had positive effects on work: In these cases, work was upgraded and made more interesting and self-paced. Systems can boost workers' productivity as well. Much depends on the kinds of jobs examined, the kinds of management involved, and the history and culture of the company. Researchers now believe that the effects "produced" by computers result from management decision making and the designs of systems developers.

One study of the impact of computers on clerical work found that computerizing a customer record system made doing simple things easier, but also made it harder to perform complicated tasks (see Figure 3.6).[6] Job pressure declined, happiness increased, and mental health improved. On the down side, skills were lost because customer service representatives' jobs were less complex, interesting, and challenging; previous training was made irrelevant; and there was decreased involvement with other workers. The researchers also found the effects of the technology depended on the quality of management. In offices with better management, the negative consequences were decreased.

Computers have tended to have far more positive effects on professional and knowledge workers: Their skills are amplified by computing equipment, and they tend to have more control over their work. Computers have also tended to enhance most qualities of work in factories. In general, most researchers have found that information technologies have enhanced the cognitive skills of the labor force.[7]

Changes in Organizational Structure

Organizational structure
The number of different levels, the type of work, and the distribution of power in an organization.

While work and supervision are affected almost immediately when new computer systems are installed, over longer periods of time the structure of organizations can change as well. By **organizational structure** we mean the number of different levels in an organization, the type of work and workers involved, and the distribution of incomes and power. Computers have helped some organizations become "flatter" by reducing the number of middle managers, making organizations more efficient and productive. Computers also automate tasks that formerly were performed by people, so that organizations can increase the output of their products and services with a smaller labor force to manage. Computers may empower lower-level workers to take over supervisory tasks previously done by managers. But there is no data to show that computers will necessarily produce these changes in all organizations.

Reduced Employment

Since commercial computers first began to be widely used, there has been a persistent fear that computers would reduce the need for all kinds of workers and lead to much higher levels of unemployment. The number of secretaries would decline radically, so it was thought, because computers would reduce paperwork. The number of blue-collar factory workers would decline because robots would take over their jobs. Today, the argument is that because of business "reengineering" and enormous investments in information technology to create extensive telecommunications and computing facilities, organizations no longer need a large labor force of managers and specialists. Instead, business firms can rely on external contractors in an electronic marketplace to do the work, supervising them electronically and accepting or rejecting their work on a contract basis.

On the whole, only anecdotal evidence exists to support these arguments, and there are many counter trends. While some industries have reduced their workforce (airlines, aircraft production, railroads, highway construction, home construction, manufacturing), others have expanded (retailing, health care, restaurants, finance, security, information technology).

Although computers have proved useful for producing letters, quickly calculating spreadsheets, and printing lists of customers, this use has not led to any wholesale decrease in white-collar jobs. Employers have taken advantage of the higher efficiencies created by computers in selected tasks to assign additional kinds of work to secretaries, accountants, and managers. Instead of firing accountants who used to manually calculate a few spreadsheets a week, employers have retrained accountants to use computers to produce hundreds of spreadsheets a week, analyze many different scenarios by using the new software, supervise expenditures more closely, and achieve higher quality work. Instead of firing large numbers of secretaries, employers have tended to retain or even hire more secretaries to put out more letters to achieve more sales and greater market penetration. In fact, computers have tended to increase—not decrease—the amount of paperwork in advanced economies.

The personal ethical issue in these quality of life issues is to decide how you as an individual will use information technology. To what end will you put the new technology? What price are you personally willing to pay to make full use of the new possibilities? Likewise at the organizational level: You and your colleagues will have to decide what ends your organization serves and how it will use the technology to pursue those ends. Often there will be no clearly defined right or wrong answers. But whatever you decide, you will be held accountable for the results.

ETHICAL GUIDELINES

In searching for ethical principles to guide you and your colleagues through difficult decisions, there are many sources. First, know the law, because it is a synthesis of what your society believes is the minimal level of ethical behavior. Second, look for corporate ethics codes, published by nearly all Fortune 500 firms, or ethical guidelines published by various professional associations (see Table 3.6). These corporate codes guide employees in diverse situations for which laws may not exist, from personal harassment behavior to sharing computer disks and corporate information. Third, look to various religious and philosophical treatises to discover general principles

TABLE 3.6

The Ten Commandments of Computer Ethics

1. Thou shalt not use a computer to harm other people.
2. Thou shalt not interfere with other people's computer work.
3. Thou shalt not snoop around in other people's computer files.
4. Thou shalt not use a computer to steal.
5. Thou shalt not use a computer to bear false witness.
6. Thou shalt not copy or use proprietary software for which you have not paid.
7. Thou shalt not use other people's computer resources without authorization or proper compensation.
8. Thou shalt not use other people's intellectual output.
9. Thou shalt think about the social consequences of the program you are writing or the system you are designing.
10. Thou shalt always use a computer in ways that demonstrate consideration and respect for your fellow humans.

SOURCE: Computer Ethics Institute, Washington, D.C.

of ethical conduct. Some principles are well known, like the Golden Rule (do unto others as you would have them do unto you) and the Utilitarian principle (select the action that produces the greatest good for the greatest number). There are many others that you should discuss with your friends and professors.

SUMMARY

• Information systems can be used to gain a strategic competitive advantage over rival firms. Information systems can be used to develop new market niches, lock in customers and suppliers, differentiate products and services, and lower operational costs.

• The value chain can be used to identify business activities that offer opportunities to use systems with strategic impact.

• Information systems can help companies operate internationally by supporting coordination of geographically dispersed units of the company and by supporting communication with distant customers and suppliers.

• Disparate linguistic and cultural traditions, organizational procedures, and computer hardware, software, and telecommunications standards are obstacles to building international information systems.

• Quality can be defined from both a producer viewpoint (conformance to specifications) and from a consumer viewpoint (physical materials, quality of service, and psychological impressions). Total quality management (TQM) makes quality the responsibility of everyone in the organization.

• Information systems can enhance quality by simplifying a product or service; supporting benchmarking; reducing product development cycle time; improving quality and precision in design and production; and reducing opportunities for human error.

• Organizations may maximize the benefits of information system technology by redesigning their business processes. The rethinking and radical redesign of business processes to achieve dramatic improvements in cost, quality, service, and speed is called reengineering.

• The five major areas in which computers have social and ethical impacts are information rights, property, accountability, system quality, and quality of life.

• The Internet poses new ethical challenges because it makes it even easier to assemble, copy, and distribute information all over the world. Protection of intellectual property and individual privacy are especially threatened.

• Privacy has been threatened by the ease with which computerized information systems can collect, process, transmit, and store vast quantities of detailed data about individuals. The U.S. Congress has passed many pieces of legislation to promote privacy, including the Privacy Act of 1974.

• The major effects of computers on the quality of life in society have been the growth of telecommuting, computer dependence, accelerated change, erosion of boundaries between work and family, and computer crime.

- Computers have both positively and negatively affected the quality of work life, organizational structure, and employment. Computer effects depend on the nature of management and the organization.

KEY TERMS

Strategic information systems
Value chain
Multinational
Transnational
Transborder data flow
Total quality management (TQM)
Reengineering
Ethics
Responsibility
Accountability
Liability
Privacy
Due process
Privacy Act of 1974
Telecommuting
Quality of work life
Organizational structure

REVIEW QUESTIONS

1. Give examples of how information systems can support each of the four competitive strategies.
2. What is the value chain? How can it be used to identify opportunities for strategic information systems?
3. List and describe some of the obstacles to creating global information systems.
4. What is quality from a producer perspective? From a consumer perspective? What is total quality management?
5. How can information systems help organizations enhance quality?
6. What is reengineering? How can information systems aid this process? How can reengineering make information systems more powerful?
7. Define accountability, responsibility, and liability. How are they related to ethics?
8. Define and describe the five major areas in which information systems have social and ethical impacts.
9. What is privacy? Why is it endangered by information systems?
10. Name and describe three laws enacted by Congress to protect privacy.
11. What new problems does the Internet pose for protection of privacy and intellectual property? Why?
12. Why is it difficult to hold providers of software and software services liable for failure or injury?
13. Why is system quality important? What are the common sources of system quality problems?

14. List and describe those aspects of society in which computers have affected the quality of life.
15. List and describe those aspects of organizations in which computers have affected the quality of work life.

DISCUSSION QUESTIONS

1. Reengineering not only eliminates redundant work and excess paperwork but may also eliminate excess jobs. Should employers care about the unemployment caused by reengineering?

2. Is it acceptable to copy software used on your job so you can continue your work at home?

PROBLEM-SOLVING EXERCISES

1. *Group exercise:* Divide into groups. Each group should develop an information system code of ethics for your university. The group should prepare a report describing the issues that should be addressed by the code and the recommended standard of conduct. The groups should present their reports to the class.

2. Obtain an annual report of a business or find an article describing a business in *Business Week, Fortune,* or another publication. Analyze the business in terms of the value chain to suggest strategic information systems for that business.

3. *Hands-on exercise:* Pacific Value Co. is a growing San Diego firm that sells low-cost computer and office equipment and supplies. It has six sales representatives, who are paid on a straight commission basis. Steven Ricciardi, the firm's owner, would like to pay his staff well to reward them for their efforts and to motivate them to sell more. On the other hand, the firm's competitive advantage lies in keeping operating costs, including employee expenses, low. Ricciardi has guaranteed his sales representatives a minimum of 15 percent commission on the sales they make. He is thinking of raising commissions to 16 percent or 17 percent. Use appropriate software and the data in the following report to analyze the impact of paying 15 percent, 16 percent, and 17 percent commissions to Pacific Value's sales reps.

Pacific Value Co.

1997 Salesperson Annual Sales Report

Salesperson Name	Sales
Carl Arneson	$203,000
Delia Baker	$265,000
Albert Giordano	$259,000
Michael Hubbard	$271,000
Alice Lerner	$276,000
Paula Townsend	$234,000

4. *Internet problem-solving exercise:* You have developed your own brand of swimming goggles that are more watertight and comfortable than any you have seen in the marketplace. You would like to start marketing and selling the goggles on your own by targeting potential customers among the participants in Internet discussion groups interested in swimming. You can quickly locate Internet discussion groups interested in swimming by accessing Deja News's Web site, which archives postings from more than 13,000 newsgroups and allows you to search messages by keyword, author's name, newsgroup, date, or subject. Find and make a list of all the discussion groups interested in swimming by accessing the Deja News Web site. Select one of the messages listed, and carefully examine all the information that is available about the posting and its author. How could you use this information to market your product? Does this raise any ethical issues or problems?

NOTES

1. Michael Porter, *Competitive Strategy* (New York: Free Press, 1980). See also Kenneth Laudon and Jon Turner, eds., *Information Technology and Management Strategy* (Englewood Cliffs, NJ: Prentice-Hall, 1989).
2. Paul John Steinbart and Ravidner Nath, "Problems and Issues in the Management of International Data Networks," *MIS Quarterly* 16, No. 1 (March 1992).
3. For an excellent discussion of quality control and management, see Lee J. Krajewski and Larry P. Ritzman, *Operations Management: Strategy and Analysis,* 4th ed. (Reading, MA: Addison-Wesley, 1996).
4. Michael Hammer and James Champy, *Reengineering the Corporation* (New York: HarperCollins, 1996).
5. Joan E. Rigdon, "Frequent Glitches in New Software Bug Users," *The Wall Street Journal,* January 18, 1995.
6. Robert Kraut, Susan Dumais, and Susan Koch, "Computerization, Productivity, and Quality of Work-Life," *Communications of the ACM* 32, No. 2 (February 1989).
7. D. R. Howell and E. N. Wolff, "Changes in the Information Intensity of the U.S. Workplace Since 1950: Has Information Technology Made a Difference?" Starr Center for Applied Economics, New York University, No. 93-08.1993.

PROBLEM-SOLVING CASE

McKESSON DRUG COMPANY REDESIGNS FOR QUALITY

McKesson Drug Co. of San Francisco, California, is a $10 billion wholesaler and distributor of pharmaceuticals and other goods used in drugstores. McKesson's 45 warehouses nationwide stock 20,000 items, including aspirin, antacids, hair conditioners, and dozens of other personal-use products. McKesson has managed to obtain an impressive 28 percent market share amid extreme competition that has reduced everyone's profit margins.

McKesson has been a pioneer in the use of computerized ordering and bar coding. It installed a system called Economost in its customers' stores that enables druggists to order products with essentially no typing. An Economost customer places orders by using a laser scanner to read product bar codes, noting which items on its shelves need reordering. The item numbers are transmitted to the system, which enters the order, automatically entering the usual quantity. Only if the quantity is not "normal" does the druggist need to type, and then only the new quantity. Thus, order quality is improved because typing errors are all but eliminated. The order is instantaneously transmitted to McKesson's central computer in Rancho Cordova, California. The computer captures the orders and relays them to a minicomputer in one of the company's regional distribution centers. The minicomputer assigns the orders to several pickers, who walk through the warehouse pushing totes on rollers to fill the orders. The warehouses are designed so that their shelves correspond to pharmacy departments. A minicomputer in the distribution center issues invoices, bar-code order identification labels, price tags, and pick lists.

Approximately 99 percent of McKesson's pharmaceutical items and 93 percent of its over-the-counter items are delivered the next day. The orders are delivered in cartons that match the aisle arrangements and departments in the drugstore. With this reliable next-day service, many pharmacies have eliminated inventory other than shelf stock. According to P. Tracy Currie, one of McKesson's directors of computers, the pharmacists "count on the McKesson truck showing up at 10 A.M. So the order-processing cycle drives the rest of the business. We can't let order processing run late, otherwise the truck is late."

However, the order-processing system initially did not address the issue of picking errors. Picking orders in warehouses accurately and quickly had been a problem. As McKesson spokesperson Jim Cohune put it, "It's a business of 'oneseys' and 'twoseys' and things can get confused." Cohune estimates that every mispick costs McKesson about $80 in lost time and shipping costs, not to mention customer dissatisfaction when the wrong product arrives. McKesson has used information technology to attack the problem with signs of genuine success.

Because picking a few of this and a few of that easily leads to wrong items or quantities being picked, McKesson developed a bar-code reader for the pickers to carry. Before picking each product, the pickers would use the reader to read the product bar code to verify that they were choosing the correct item. However, the system did not work well. The pistol-shaped scanner had to be unholstered for each product, requiring the use of both hands. The pickers, who use both hands to pick, found the scanner gun very inconvenient and slow. Most simply did not use it. McKesson's senior vice-president of distribution services summarized the problem this way. "The warehouse employee must be able to electronically read bar codes to verify the incoming order against the purchasing order, while keeping both hands free to lift and move shipping containers"—a tall order indeed.

The solution was a genuine innovation called AcuMax. It was developed jointly by McKesson and Electronic Data Systems, a leading information systems consulting firm. McKesson had learned a critical lesson

Strapped onto one arm, McKesson's AcuMax computer lets warehouse pickers scan in bar-code data about items selected to fulfill orders while freeing both hands to lift and move shipping containers. By using a team approach that includes line workers to design and implement a system, companies like McKesson have been able to raise quality and productivity.

SOURCE: Courtesy of McKesson Corp.

in the previous failure—involve the line workers, the pickers, in designing and implementing a solution. McKesson established a team that included technicians, managers, and line workers.

AcuMax is a computer with an attached laser bar-code reader. It straps onto one arm, weighs only about three-quarters of a pound, and is in constant radio communication with the warehouse's minicomputer. The computer first plans the most efficient route for the picker to follow through the giant warehouse, thus reducing picking time. The AcuMax screen lists the first item and displays the route to that item. When the picker arrives, he or she points an index finger at the item's bar-coded shelf label. As the pointing finger is lifted, it throws a switch that activates the laser bar code reader. The bar code is fed into AcuMax, which compares the bar code to the stored purchase order product number to determine whether the picker is pointing at the desired product. Assuming the item is correct, the arm-borne computer then displays the next product and the path to it, and the process is repeated until the order is filled. AcuMax has proven very effective. McKesson estimates that order-picking errors have been reduced by 70 percent, while the productivity of the pickers has risen dramatically.

How does the new system rate in McKesson's drive for quality? From the perspective of the producer, it has achieved a 70 percent reduction in errors. From the consumer perspective, the system gives the buyer greater value for the dollar, less work in ordering, minimal bother with returns and problems with the order, and overall improved service. The productivity of the pickers has increased sharply. Given what has been learned over the past several decades about ways to improve quality, it is no surprise that the improvement was partly the result of teamwork that involved both line workers and managers.

The AcuMax project raised a major ethical issue for McKesson's management. One of their goals was productivity. If successful, McKesson's management realized, order processing data entry jobs and warehouse picking jobs would be eliminated (including a reduction in billing work as fewer errors would need manual correction). Thus, new technology would improve the profit position of the company by eliminating jobs. However, McKesson management also saw another side to the issue. McKesson needed the cooperation and input of the very workers whose jobs were threatened in order for the project to be successful. Management thought they had addressed the picking problem when they installed the pistol laser reader system, but the project failed precisely because the line workers were not involved.

This time several managers spent a few days working as clerks. When a preliminary version of the new picking system was developed, workers in the distribution center were asked to try it out. Management told the workers that the new hand-held computers were a tool to do their jobs better and asked them what they thought. Using worker feedback, EDS made more than 50 modifications to the device. For instance, moving the thumb to trigger the laser scanners gave some people sore hands. The device was redesigned so that workers activate the laser by pointing at the item and tapping a button with their index finger. Management learned its lesson—line workers were essential to the design process. Management took the obvious and ethical step, promising that no one would lose their job as a result of this project. The result was a successful project for McKesson and for its staff.

Sources: Eugene M. Grygo, "McKesson Finds the Right Prescription," *Client/Server Computing,* July 1995; James Daly, "What Happens When 'Close Enough' Isn't Close Enough Anymore," *Computerworld,* December 12, 1993; "McKesson Drug Curing Inaccuracy of Warehouse Labor with Wearable PCs," *Computerworld,* May 11, 1992, and "Making It All Worker-Friendly," *Fortune Special Issue: Making High Tech Work for You,* Autumn 1993.

CASE STUDY QUESTIONS

1. Use the three perspectives of people, organization, and technology to categorize and analyze the problems faced by McKesson.

2. How strategic was the Economost system? Why? Use the perspective of competitive strategies and the value chain to analyze its strategic benefits. What do you think McKesson needs to do to maintain its advantage over competitors?

3. Analyze the McKesson quality program in terms of the seven ways to improve quality listed in this chapter. Did they use any other methods, and if so, what? How did information systems help McKesson improve quality?

4. How ethical was the solution McKesson developed? Should McKesson have promised no job losses if management believed that line worker involvement was not critical in designing the solution? How would you justify your position to corporate management?

Part 1

✧ILLUSTRATED CASE✧

INFORMATION SYSTEMS HELP SEAGRAM STAY ON TOP

Joseph E. Seagram & Sons, Inc. was founded in 1933 and currently has major offices in 36 countries on six continents. The Seagram empire includes high-end cognacs, champagnes, vodkas, and whiskeys, as well as music, movies, book publishing, and theme parks. The list of leading brands Seagram markets includes Chivas Regal scotch, Perrier-Jouet champagne, Crown Royal Canadian whiskey, Martell cognacs, and Tropicana orange juice. In late 1993, Seagram added Absolut vodka to the list. With such an excellent product portfolio and such high profits, what industry problems could possibly concern Seagram management?

The liquor industry is focusing its main efforts on premium brands, betting that consumers will maintain product loyalty. The strategy is to create value for premium brands and increase marketing efforts focused on brand name. While this strategy has been successful, it has also created an opening for cheap brands and private labels that have recently gained a larger share of the market.

Seagram has followed the premium brand strategy by selling off such lower-priced labels as Lord Calvert Canadian whiskey and Wolfschmidt vodka and acquiring rights to market Absolut. In addition,

Seagram's distillery in Keith, Scotland, is one of the firm's facilities for producing high-quality, top-of-the-line spirits. Seagram's global business strategy has focused on promoting premium brands and on increasing sales abroad in emerging markets such as China and Eastern Europe.

SOURCE: Courtesy of Joseph E. Seagram & Sons, Inc.

the company is pursuing a global strategy, seeking growth in the emerging markets of Eastern Europe and China; analysts cite this strategy as the primary reason for Seagram's obtaining the marketing rights to Absolut. Edgar Bronfman, Jr., CEO of Seagram, predicted that the proportion of Absolut's sales outside the United States will double by 1999.

Part of Seagram's response to these challenges is its worldwide multimedia document management system. According to Seagram's Chief Information Officer, Jack Cooper, the Open Document Management System (ODMS) is meant to achieve "boundary-less document access anywhere in the world." Using this system, a document created in Hong Kong can be reviewed in the United States and stored in London. The documents are multimedia—they can contain video, voice, and graphics as well as text. For example, Seagram may use ODMS to store its companywide operational procedure manuals, use a video clip to illustrate a new procedure, or allow users to send and receive faxes from their desktop computers.

ODMS uses a worldwide network to connect Seagram's various sites, not only its larger offices but its staff members who work outside of established offices but who nonetheless need to be linked with the rest of the company.

The first Seagram department to make use of the system was Accounts Payable, located in White Plains, New York. Prior to ODMS, invoices were hand-sorted by type of bill and then delivered to the appropriate specialist (such as a phone specialist). The invoices were then passed from processor to processor in a time-consuming serial, paper-based work flow. Once the original processing was completed, the document was sent to be microfilmed for permanent storage, a process that took as long as two weeks. With an average of 450 invoices per day, the procedure was time consuming and expensive. It was also a headache for suppliers. Supplier inquiries were directed to one of the 18 specialists handling the supplier's area. To answer the supplier's question, the specialist hunted through a stack of bills until the appropriate one was found. Suppliers' phone hold time could be long, while their patience could become short. In addition to these billing and supplier problems, when staff in California needed access to documents, the documents had to be located in the White Plains office and then faxed to California.

The new system changes all that. Incoming bills are now scanned directly into ODMS upon receipt, making them immediately available to the accounts payable processors. Managers can add voice annotation to documents; for example, a specific processor can be instructed to give a designated invoice special handling. Now, no matter which specialist answers the phone, he or she will be able to answer a supplier's questions quickly by online accessing of document information. Seagram staff time is saved, and suppliers are not kept waiting. Accounts Payable is also redesigning its work flow by eliminating the traditional slow, serial, manual processing. It will institute a more efficient approach that will give various

The Seagram headquarters in New York City oversees operations in 36 countries on six continents. Global information systems such as Seagram's Open Document Management System (ODMS) help companies coordinate the work of offices and staff members and communicate with customers and suppliers in many different parts of the world.

SOURCE: © Arlene Collins, Monkmeyer Press Photos.

processors simultaneous access to the same document. Microfilming is obsolete. Finally, because the system is networked, California staff will have direct access to needed data.

Accounts Payable productivity has benefited in still other ways from ODMS. Managers can now track the productivity of both the accounts payable process and of individual employees. Perhaps even more significant, Accounts Payable Supervisor Candice Puleo says that ODMS is a "real time-saver" for auditing, a critical aspect of the accounts payable function. No longer will auditors need to spend long hours digging through old microfilm or paper to find needed documentation (Puleo remembers once waiting four months to obtain 400 boxes of paper needed for an Internal Revenue Service audit).

With Accounts Payable now on board, Cooper plans to sell the system to other departments. His hope is that three new groups will implement the system each month.

How does ODMS contribute to Seagram's strategy for survival in a declining market? In several ways. First, if sales fall and competition from lower-priced products increases, one classic response is to lower costs through improved productivity. ODMS contributed significantly to reducing costs in Accounts Payable. It can probably do the same throughout the company by allowing departments to redesign their work flow, reduce manual labor costs, and improve relations with suppliers and customers. In that way, the system will likely make a major contribution to survival.

Seagram's experience in developing this information system application also leaves the firm poised to take competitive advantage of the ongoing developments in computer and telecommunications technology. Seagram will be able to upgrade its technology both at minimal cost and with minimal disturbance if it finds a competitive value in doing so.

Ultimately, to make the most significant contribution to the future of a company, an information system must be aligned with the company's business strategy. ODMS, a global system, is definitely strategic for Seagram. With the ODMS worldwide telecommunications system in place, Seagram can support its planned global expansion. More efficient departments and instant communications around the world should also allow the company to respond more rapidly to customer orders and to solve customer problems as needed. Finally, the network technology not only gives corporate management access to critical, worldwide data, but it also puts the local data where needed in a global market, on the desktop of the local clerk, manager, or executive.

SOURCES: Bill McDowell, "Spirit Sales Grow Merrier in '96 after 15-year Slide," *Advertising Age* (January 6, 1997); T.L. Stanley and Gerry Khermouch, "Edgar Bronfman, Jr." *Mediaweek* (October 9, 1995); Johanna Ambrosio, "High Spirits at SEAGRAM," *Computerworld Client/Server Journal* (August 11, 1993); and Julia Flynn and Laura Zinn, "Absolut Pandemonium," *Business Week* (November 8, 1993).

CASE QUESTIONS

1. What problems did Seagram face?

2. How did Seagram use information systems to deal with its problems? What people, organization, and technology factors did they address?

3. How did Seagram deal with the major information system challenges described in this section?

4. Assuming Seagram is able to gain maximum benefit from ODMS and other systems meant to lower costs and globalize the company, do you think these information systems are an adequate base for a successful strategy of survival in a declining market?

Part 2

FOUNDATIONS OF INFORMATION TECHNOLOGY

Chapter

FOUR

COMPUTER HARDWARE

CHAPTER OUTLINE

Opening Vignette: Technology Helps UPS Keep Its Promise

4.1 Computer Concepts and Components
- The Computer System
- The Central Processing Unit and Primary Storage
- Measuring Time, Size, and Processing Power
- How Computers Represent Data
- Generations of Computer Hardware

4.2 Mainframes, Minicomputers, Personal Computers, Workstations, and Supercomputers
- Mainframes, Minis, and PCs: What's the Difference?
- Workstations, Supercomputers, and Parallel Processing
- Microprocessor Technology: The Chips behind the Machines
- Reduced Instruction Set Computing

4.3 Storage Technology
- Magnetic Tape
- Magnetic Disk
- Optical Disk Technology

4.4 Input and Output Technology
- Input Technology
- Batch versus Online Input and Processing
- Output Technology

4.5 Information Technology Trends
- Multimedia
- Superchips and Fifth-Generation Computers
- Leading-Edge Technology: Network Computers

LEARNING OBJECTIVES

After reading and studying this chapter, you will

1. Know the components of a computer and how they work.
2. Be able to distinguish among different types of computers.
3. Know how to measure computer speed, storage capacity, and processing power.
4. Know the major secondary storage technologies and be able to describe how they work.
5. Be familiar with how the major input and output technologies work.
6. Be familiar with multimedia, network computers, and future information technology trends.

TECHNOLOGY HELPS UPS KEEP ITS PROMISE

United Parcel Service (UPS), the world's largest air and ground package distribution company, began in 1907 with a promise of "best service and lowest rates." UPS still strives to fulfill that promise, providing both traditional and overnight delivery of close to 3 billion parcels and documents each year to any address in the United States and to more than 180 countries and territories. How can UPS manage this immense volume of packages with such efficiency and speed? The answer lies in advanced information systems technology.

UPS links its 1,750 offices with a network of PCs connected to five mainframe computers located in its Paramus and Mahwah, New Jersey, data centers. The PCs are located in UPS customer service telephone centers, which take calls from customers requesting that a package be picked up or traced.

UPS replaced its familiar driver's clipboard with a handheld, battery-powered Delivery Information Acquisition Device (DIAD). The DIAD captures customers' signatures, scans barcode tags to identify packages and their destinations, and displays the day's delivery route. It stores the input until the end of the day and then transfers the information to UPS's computer network. The information entered into the DIAD can then be retrieved to trace a shipment or to provide proof of delivery to the customer. Previously, UPS had to track ground deliveries manually. With these technologies, UPS hopes to entirely remove paper documents—delivery records, COD slips, even time cards—from the domestic delivery process.

Several systems allow packages to be monitored at various points in the delivery process. A package tracking system uses shipping information contained on the package label that is scanned with a bar-code device at various points in the delivery process and fed into a central mainframe computer. Customer service representatives can then use their PCs to access information on the status of packages and respond immediately to customer inquiries. An Advanced Label Imaging System (ALIS) scans data from UPS Next Day Air and 2nd Day Air labels. When a customer calls, a UPS customer service representative can bring up the image of the airbill on a screen in seconds. The on-line image is exactly as it appeared when the driver recorded it on the air label. An international shipments processing system supports UPS package delivery services abroad by transmitting package information directly to customs prior to the arrival of shipments, thereby expediting customs clearance.

UPS customers can even schedule shipments and track their packages themselves using special software supplied by UPS on the World Wide Web. Anyone with a package to ship can use the UPS Web site to check delivery routes, calculate shipping rates, and schedule a pickup. Eventually they will be able use the Web to pay for their shipments using a credit card. (Regular customers with large accounts will continue to be billed monthly.) The data collected at the UPS Web site are transmitted to the UPS central computer and then back to the customer after processing.

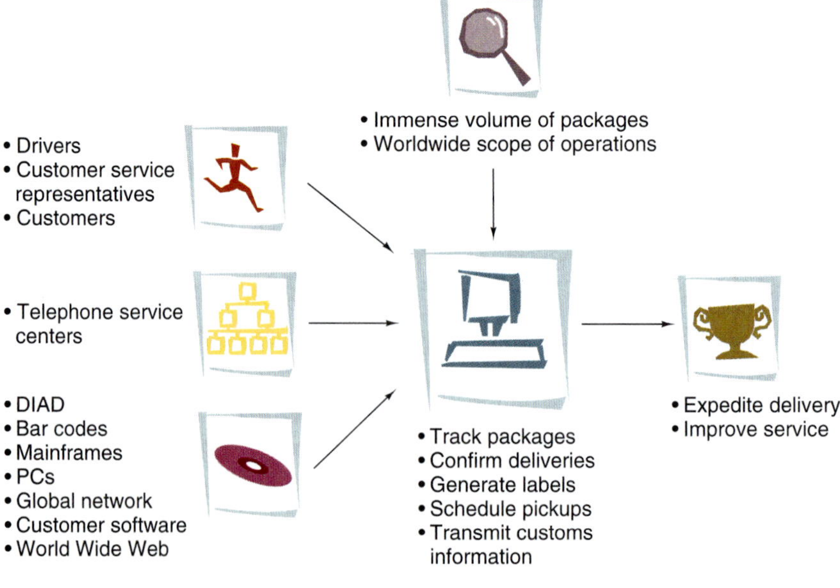

SOURCES: "UPS Launches New Delivery and Information Options," *UPS Public Relations,* January 2, 1997; Kim Nash, "Overnight Services Duke It Out On-Line," *Computerworld*, April 22, 1996; and Lynda Radosevich, "When Overnight Isn't Good Enough," *Computerworld,* May 31, 1993.

UPS's use of bar coding, scanning, pen-based input, PCs, and mainframes illustrates how organizations can become more efficient and competitive by using the proper computer hardware technology. In this chapter we examine computer processing, input, storage, and output technologies.

4.1 COMPUTER CONCEPTS AND COMPONENTS

Contemporary information technologies range far beyond the computer alone and include communications networks, fax machines, "smart" printers and copiers, workstations, image processing, graphics, multimedia, and video communications. Increasingly, problems will be solved not by an isolated mainframe or desktop computer but by an array of digital devices networked together. In this chapter, we show how hardware components work together to create a computer system. Other chapters in this section treat related information technologies—software, telecommunications, and files and databases.

THE COMPUTER SYSTEM

A **computer** is a physical device that takes data as an input, transforms these data by executing a stored program, and outputs information to a number of devices. As Figure 4.1 illustrates, a contemporary computer system consists

Computer
A physical device that takes data as an input, transforms them by executing a stored program, and outputs information to a number of devices.

FIGURE 4.1

Components of a Computer System

A contemporary computer system consists of a central processing unit, primary storage, secondary storage, and input/output and communications devices. Buses are the pathways or connections that data and signals travel along between the central processing unit, primary storage, and the other components of the computer system.

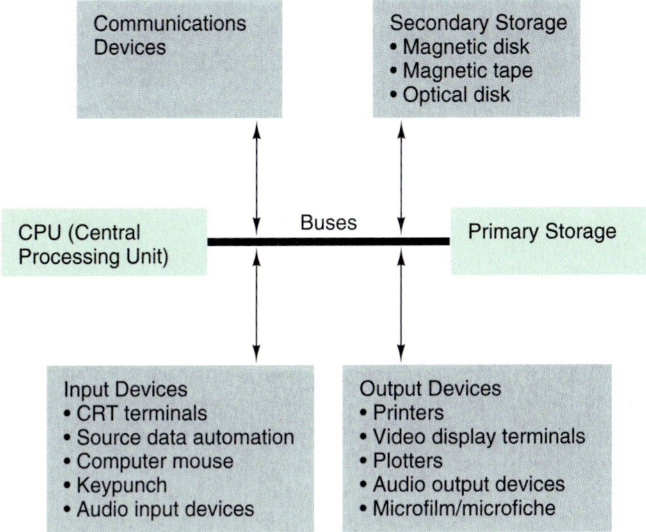

Central processing unit (CPU)
A hardware component of a computer system that processes raw data and controls other parts of the computer system.

of a **central processing unit (CPU),** primary storage, input devices, output devices, secondary storage, and communications devices. The characteristics of the central processing unit and primary storage largely determine a computer's speed and capacity to solve problems. The CPU manipulates raw data into a more useful form and controls the other parts of the computer system, while primary storage temporarily stores data and program instructions during processing. Input devices, such as keyboards, optical scanners, and computer mice, convert data into electronic form for input into the computer. Output devices, such as printers and video display terminals, convert electronic data produced by the computer into forms intelligible to humans. Secondary storage devices store data and program instructions when they are not being used in processing. Communications devices allow the computer to be connected to communications networks. Buses are paths for transmitting data and signals among the various parts of the computer system.

THE CENTRAL PROCESSING UNIT AND PRIMARY STORAGE

The CPU is responsible for the manipulation of symbols, numbers, and letters and also controls the other parts of the computer system. As Figure 4.2 shows, the central processing unit consists of a control unit and an arithmetic-logic unit. The central processing unit is often contained on an individual semiconductor chip (a silicon chip on which hundreds of thousands, or even millions, of circuit elements can be etched) with semiconductor chips for primary storage located nearby.

FIGURE 4.2

Closeup of the Central Processing Unit and Primary Storage

Primary storage temporarily stores data and program instructions. Each byte in primary storage has a unique address. The central processing unit contains a control unit and an arithmetic-logic unit. The control unit coordinates the transfer of data among the central processing unit, primary storage, and input/output devices. The arithmetic-logic unit performs calculations and logical operations on data. The data bus, the address bus, and the control bus transfer signals among the central processing unit, primary storage, and other devices in the computer system. The system clock helps pace the sequence of events occurring in the system.

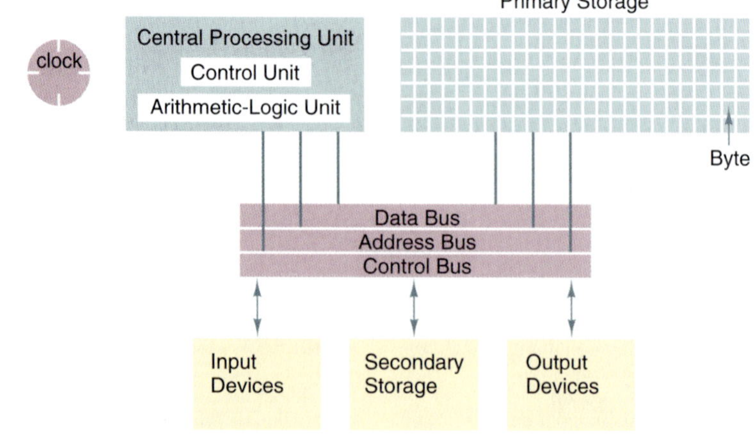

Primary Storage **Primary storage** (also called main memory or primary memory) stores program instructions and the data being used by those instructions. Data and programs are placed in primary storage before processing, between processing steps, and after processing has terminated before being released as output. Once the computer is finished with specific pieces of data and program instructions, they are overwritten by new incoming data or program instructions, released as output, or returned to secondary storage.

Primary storage
The component of a computer system that temporarily stores program instructions and the data being used by these instructions.

Whenever data or program instructions are placed in primary storage, they are assigned to storage locations called **bytes.** Each byte stores only a single character of data and has a unique address so that it can be located when needed. A byte may be compared to a mailbox, with its number being the address. As Figure 4.2 shows, primary storage contains many bytes.

Byte
A single character of data made up of a combination of bits that the computer processes or stores as a unit; the unit in which computer storage capacity is measured.

Figure 4.2 also shows that three kinds of buses connect the CPU, primary storage, and other devices in the computer system. The address bus carries signals used to locate a given address in primary storage. The data bus carries data to and from primary storage. The control bus carries signals indicating whether to "read" or "write" data to, or from, the address specified in primary storage and to, or from, input or output devices. The system clock helps regulate the pace of operations in the computer.

The Arithmetic-Logic Unit The **arithmetic-logic unit (ALU)** performs arithmetic and logical operations on data. It adds, subtracts, multiplies, divides, and determines whether a number is positive, negative, or zero. The ALU can make logical comparisons of two numbers to determine whether one is greater than, less than, or equal to the other. The ALU can also perform logical operations on letters or words.

Arithmetic-logic unit (ALU)
The component of the CPU that performs arithmetic and logical operations on data.

The Control Unit The **control unit** controls and coordinates the other components of the computer. It reads stored program instructions one at a time and, based on what the program tells it to do, directs other components of the computer to perform the required tasks. For example, it might specify which data should be placed in primary storage, which operation the ALU should perform on the data, and where the results should be stored. It might also direct the result to an appropriate output device, such as a printer. After each instruction is executed, the control unit proceeds to the next instruction.

Control unit
The component of the CPU that controls and coordinates the other components of the computer.

The Machine Cycle The control unit plays a key role in the most basic and fundamental CPU operation, called a **machine cycle.** As you will see, a machine cycle has two parts. One part is called the **instruction cycle (I-cycle),** in which an instruction is retrieved from primary storage and decoded. A second part is called the **execution cycle (E-cycle),** in which the required data are located, the instruction executed, and the results stored.

Machine cycle
The series of operations involved in executing a single instruction.

Instruction cycle (I-cycle)
The portion of a machine cycle in which an instruction is retrieved from primary storage and decoded.

Execution cycle (E-cycle)
The portion of a machine cycle in which the required data are located, the instruction is executed, and the results are stored.

Figure 4.3 shows in greater detail how the machine cycle works. The control unit fetches an instruction from the program stored in primary storage, decodes the instruction, and places it in a special instruction register. **Registers** are special storage locations in the ALU and the control unit that act like high-speed staging areas. There are several different kinds of registers. The control unit breaks each instruction into two parts. The part of the instruction telling the ALU what to do next is placed in an instruction register. The part of the instruction specifying the address of the data to be used

Register
A storage location in the ALU or control unit; it may be an instruction register, address register, or storage register, depending on what is stored in it.

FIGURE 4.3

A Machine Cycle

Each machine cycle consists of two smaller cycles: the instruction cycle (I-cycle) and the execution cycle (E-cycle). These involve a series of steps in which instructions are retrieved from a software program, decoded, and performed. Running even a simple software program involves thousands of machine cycles.

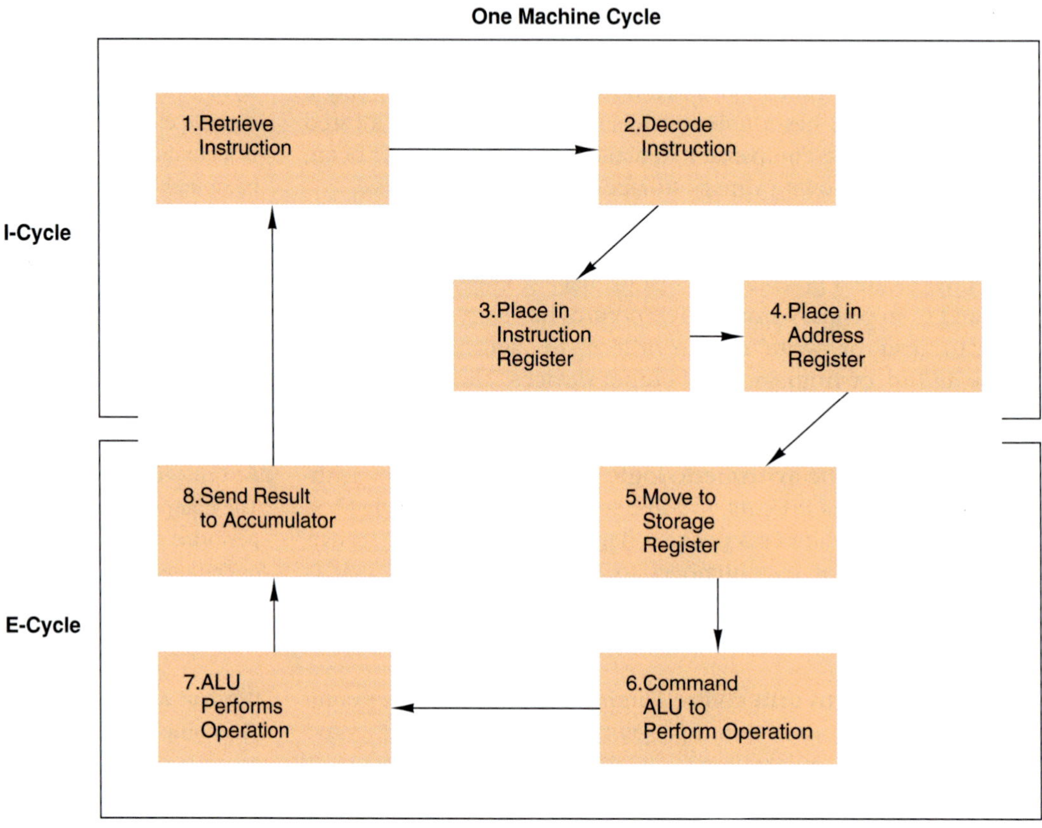

in the operation is moved to an address register. A storage register is used to store any data that have been retrieved from primary storage. Last, an accumulator is used to store the results of an operation.

In this manner, the modern digital computer methodically reads through a computer program and executes the program, one instruction at a time, in sequential order. There may be millions, or hundreds of millions, of such machine cycles to perform in a program. However, because the machine works very fast—processing millions of instructions per second—extremely large programs can be executed in a few moments.

RAM
A memory device used for short-term storage of data or program instructions; stands for random-access memory.

Memory Devices Several kinds of semiconductor memory chips are used in primary storage. Each serves a different purpose. **RAM,** or random-access memory, is used for short-term storage of data or program instructions. RAM is located in RAM chips physically close to the CPU. The contents of RAM can be read and changed when required. RAM is volatile: This means that if the computer's electricity supply is disrupted or the computer is turned off, its contents will be lost.

Another kind of memory found in a computer is **ROM,** or read-only memory, which stores important program instructions permanently. For example, in the IBM PC, ROM permanently stores instructions concerning the display screen, keyboard, and printer. ROM is nonvolatile, meaning that its contents will not be lost if electric power is disrupted or the computer is turned off. Nor can it be destroyed if someone tries to write over the instructions.

There are several other categories of nonvolatile memory chips. **PROM,** or programmable read-only memory, is similar to ROM in that it can only be read from and cannot be changed once the chips have been programmed. Initially, however, PROM chips contain no program instructions. These are entered by the purchaser, usually a manufacturer, who programs the chips and implants them in manufactured products where they serve as control devices. For example, instead of fabricating a specialized chip to control small motors, a manufacturer can program a PROM chip with the control instructions. **EPROM** (erasable programmable read-only memory) chips are also nonvolatile. Unlike PROM chips, however, EPROM chips can be erased and reprogrammed. Consequently, they are used in robots and other devices in which the program may have to be changed periodically.

ROM
A memory device used for permanent storage of program instructions; stands for read-only memory.

PROM
A memory device in which the memory chips can be programmed only once and are used to store instructions entered by the purchaser; stands for programmable read-only memory.

EPROM
A memory device in which the memory chips can be erased and reprogrammed with new instructions; stands for erasable programmable read-only memory.

MEASURING TIME, SIZE, AND PROCESSING POWER

How can we determine whether a given computer will help us with problem solving? How can we determine which model or size of computer to use? We need to know how fast a computer can work, how much data it can store, and whether it can store the data required to solve our problem. Therefore, knowing the measures of computer speed and processing capacity is essential.

Very slow, older computers or hardware devices measure machine cycle times in **milliseconds** (thousandths of a second). More powerful machines use measures of **microseconds** (millionths of a second) or **nanoseconds** (billionths of a second). A few very powerful computers measure machine cycles in **picoseconds** (trillionths of a second). Large business computers have a machine cycle time of less than 10 nanoseconds. Thus, such computers can execute more than 200 million instructions per second. MIPS, or millions of instructions per second, is a common benchmark for measuring the speed of larger computers.

Computer storage capacity is measured in terms of bytes. A thousand bytes (actually 1,024, or 2^{10} storage positions) are a kilobyte. The **kilobyte** used to be the typical measure of personal computer (PC) storage capacity. Thus, when someone speaks of a PC with a 640 K memory, this means that the machine has an internal RAM capacity of 640 kilobytes. PCs today have storage capacities in the **megabyte** (over 1 million bytes) range, and larger machines have storage capacities in the **gigabyte** (over 1 billion bytes) range. External computer storage devices can store trillions of bytes **(terabytes)** of data. Table 4.1 summarizes the key measures of computer time and storage capacity.

Millisecond
A measure of machine cycle time; equals one one-thousandth of a second.

Microsecond
A measure of machine cycle time; equals one one-millionth of a second.

Nanosecond
A measure of machine cycle time; equals one one-billionth of a second.

Picosecond
A measure of machine cycle time; equals one one-trillionth of a second.

Kilobyte
The usual measure of PC storage capacity; approximately 1,000 bytes.

Megabyte
A measure of computer storage capacity; approximately 1 million bytes.

Gigabyte
A measure of computer storage capacity; approximately 1 billion bytes.

Terabyte
A measure of computer storage capacity; approximately 1 trillion bytes.

HOW COMPUTERS REPRESENT DATA

A computer represents data by reducing all symbols, pictures, or words into a string of binary digits. Binary means having two states, and each binary digit can have only one of two states or conditions, based on the presence or

TABLE 4.1

Key Measures of Computer Time and Storage Capacity

Time		Storage Capacity	
Millisecond	1/1000 second	Kilobyte	1,000 (2^{10}) storage positions
Microsecond	1/1,000,000 second	Megabyte	1,000,000 (2^{20}) storage positions
Nanosecond	1/1,000,000,000 second	Gigabyte	1,000,000,000 (2^{30}) storage positions
Picosecond	1/1,000,000,000,000 second	Terabyte	1,000,000,000,000 (2^{40}) storage positions

absence of electronic or magnetic signals. A conducting state in a semiconductor circuit represents a one; a nonconducting state represents a zero. In magnetic media, a magnetized spot represents a one when a magnetic field is in one direction and represents a zero when the magnetism is in the other direction.

Bit
A binary digit that can have only one of two states, representing 0 or 1.

A binary digit is called a **bit** and represents either a zero or a one. The binary number system, or base 2 system, can express all numbers as groups of zeroes and ones. As in the decimal (base 10) system, which we ordinarily use, the value of each number depends on the place of each digit in a string of digits. Figure 4.4 illustrates how the decimal system works. Each digit has been broken down according to its place value to show how numbers are created. In Figure 4.5 we apply the same approach to show how to convert a binary number to its decimal equivalent. Any number in the decimal system can be expressed as a binary number and vice versa. For example, the decimal number 25 would be represented as 11001 in the binary system; the decimal number 27 would be the binary number 11011.

FIGURE 4.4

Converting a Decimal Number to Its Decimal Components

The value of a number depends on the place of each digit within a series of digits. In the decimal (or base 10) number system, each number can be expressed as a power of the number 10.

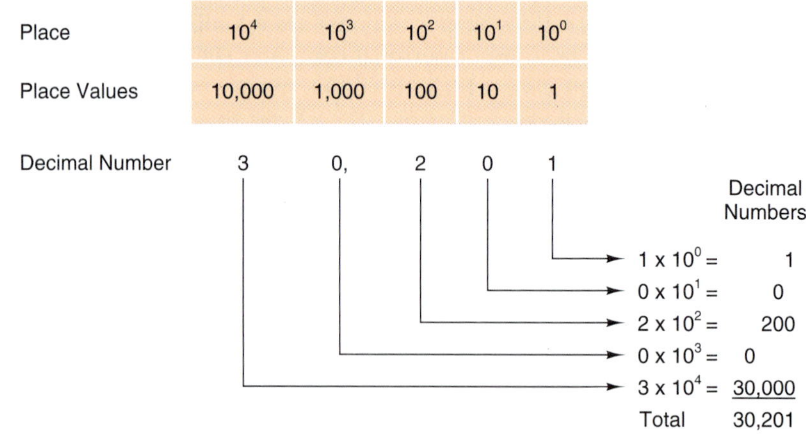

FIGURE 4.5

Converting a Binary Number to Its Decimal Equivalent

In the binary, or base 2, number system, each number can be expressed as a power of the number 2.

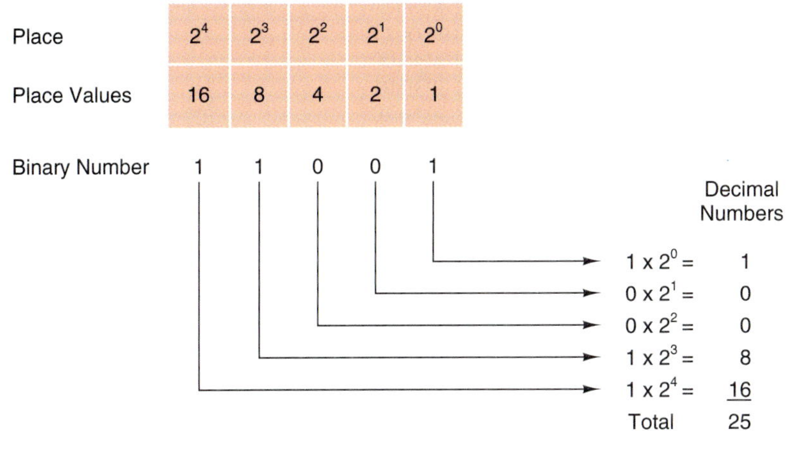

What about letters and symbols such as $ and &? These can also be represented in binary form using special coding schemes. The two most popular binary coding schemes are EBCDIC (Extended Binary Coded Decimal Interchange Code) and ASCII (American Standard Code for Information Interchange). **EBCDIC** (pronounced ib-si-dick), developed by IBM, is used in IBM and other mainframe computers. **ASCII** was developed by the American National Standards Institute (ANSI) as a standard code that could be used by many different computer manufacturers to make their machines compatible. ASCII is used in data transmission, in PCs, and in some larger computers.

EBCDIC
An eight-bit binary coding scheme used in IBM and other mainframe computers; stands for Extended Binary Coded Decimal Interchange Code.

ASCII
A seven- or eight-bit coding scheme used in data transmission, PCs, and some larger computers. Stands for American Standard Code for Information Interchange.

EBCDIC is an eight-bit coding scheme; that is, eight bits are grouped together to form a byte. Each byte represents a single letter, symbol, or number and consists of a unique combination of bits. For example, the decimal digit *8* is represented by the EBCDIC code as 11111000. An *A* is represented in EBCDIC as 11000001. ASCII was originally designed as a seven-bit code, but most computers use eight-bit versions of ASCII. Table 4.2 compares the EBCDIC and ASCII-8 bit coding schemes.

EBCDIC and ASCII also contain an extra bit position called a parity bit. This bit is automatically set to zero or one to make all the bits in a byte add up to an even or odd number. Computers are constructed to have either even or odd parity. An even-parity machine expects the number of "on" bits in a byte to add up to an even number. An odd-parity machine expects the number of "on" bits in a byte to be odd. If the number of "on" bits in a byte is even in an odd-parity machine, the parity bit will be turned on to make the total number of "on" bits odd. Figure 4.6 shows both valid and invalid representations of a character in an odd-parity computer. Parity bits are used to detect errors caused by environmental disturbances or garbled data transmission.

TABLE 4.2

EBCDIC and ASCII Coding Systems

Character	EBCDIC Binary	ASCII-8 Binary
A	1100 0001	1010 0001
B	1100 0010	1010 0010
C	1100 0011	1010 0011
D	1100 0100	1010 0100
E	1100 0101	1010 0101
F	1100 0110	1010 0110
G	1100 0111	1010 0111
H	1100 1000	1010 1000
I	1100 1001	1010 1001
J	1101 0001	1010 1010
K	1101 0010	1010 1011
L	1101 0011	1010 1100
M	1101 0100	1010 1101
N	1101 0101	1010 1110
O	1101 0110	1010 1111
P	1101 0111	1011 0000
Q	1101 1000	1011 0001
R	1101 1001	1011 0010
S	1110 0010	1011 0011
T	1110 0011	1011 0100
U	1110 0100	1011 0101
V	1110 0101	1011 0110
W	1110 0110	1011 0111
X	1110 0111	1011 1000
Y	1110 1000	1011 1001
Z	1110 1001	1011 1010
0	1111 0000	0101 0000
1	1111 0001	0101 0001
2	1111 0010	0101 0010
3	1111 0011	010 10011
4	1111 0100	0101 0100
5	1111 0101	0101 0101
6	1111 0110	0101 0110
7	1111 0111	0101 0111
8	1111 1000	0101 1000
9	1111 1001	0101 1001

GENERATIONS OF COMPUTER HARDWARE

Computer hardware has undergone a series of transitions, each of which has made computers increasingly easy to use, widening the range of problems computers can solve. Each stage, or generation, in the history of computing has used a different technology for the electronic components used in the computer's processing work. Generational changes in computer hardware have been accompanied by generational changes in computer software (see Chapter 5).

The First Generation (1951–1958): Vacuum-Tube Technology The first generation of computers used vacuum tubes to store and process information. These tubes consumed large quantities of electric power, generated a great deal of heat, and had short lives. First-generation computers were colossal in size, yet they had very limited memories and processing capacity. The maxi-

FIGURE 4.6

Detecting Errors with a Parity Check, Using Odd Parity

With odd parity, the correct representation will involve an odd number of "on" bits. Having an even number of "on" bits alerts the computer that an error has occurred.

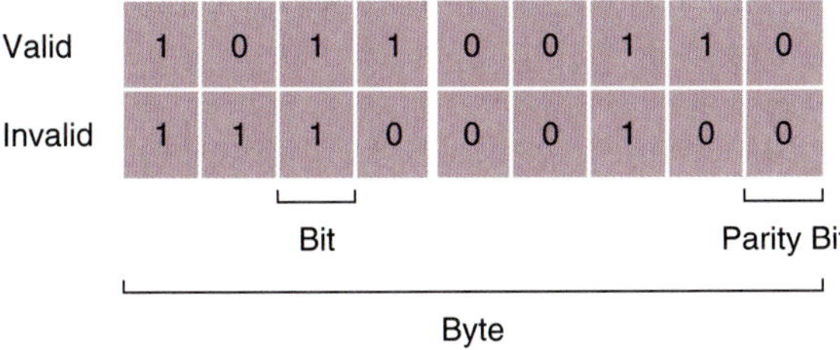

mum memory size was only about 2 kilobytes, with a speed of 10 kilo instructions per second. Rotating magnetic drums were used for internal storage, and punched cards were used for external storage. Jobs such as running programs or printing output had to be coordinated manually. First-generation computers were used primarily for very limited scientific and engineering problems.

The Second Generation (1959–1963): Transistor Technology Second-generation computers were based on transistor technology, with individual transistors wired into printed circuit boards. Not only were transistors smaller, cheaper, and more reliable than vacuum tubes, but they also generated far less heat and consumed less power. Memory size expanded to 32 kilobytes of RAM, and speeds reached 200,000–300,000 instructions per second. Internal storage used magnetic cores (small doughnut-shaped devices strung together on racks within the computer, which have much faster access speeds than magnetic drums). Magnetic tape and disks started to be used for external storage. Second-generation computers saw more widespread use for scientific and business problems.

The Third Generation (1964–1979): Integrated Circuit Technology Third-generation computers relied on integrated circuits, which printed thousands of tiny transistors onto small silicon chips. Computers thus could expand to 2 megabytes of RAM and accelerate processing speed to as much as 5 MIPS. Third-generation machines also supported software that was even closer to the English language and easier to use. This meant that persons without a technical background could use these machines and associated software without having to rely heavily on specialists. Third-generation computers played a larger role in business.

The Fourth Generation (1980–Present): Very-Large-Scale Integrated Circuit Technology Fourth-generation computers use very-large-scale integrated circuits (VLSIC), which contain hundreds of thousands to millions of circuits per chip; a single chip may be the size of a fingernail. Fourth-generation technology has enabled conventional mainframes to achieve memory sizes over 2 gigabytes and speeds over 300 MIPS. Supercomputers exceed these capacities and speeds.

Microprocessor
A silicon chip containing an entire CPU; used in PCs.

Another feature of fourth-generation hardware is the **microprocessor.** A microprocessor actually consists of an entire CPU on a single silicon chip. Personal computers and "intelligent" features in automobiles, watches, toys, and other items are based on microprocessor technology. Microminiaturization has produced computers that are so small, fast, and cheap that they have become ubiquitous in daily life. Software for such computers is becoming increasingly easy to use, so nontechnical specialists can use personal computers to solve problems on their own.

4.2 MAINFRAMES, MINICOMPUTERS, PERSONAL COMPUTERS, WORKSTATIONS, AND SUPERCOMPUTERS

Computers are typically classified as mainframes, minicomputers, personal computers, workstations, or supercomputers based on their size and processing speed. Because of continuing advances in computing technology, these definitions change constantly. Here we describe each category of computer and the microprocessor technology they use.

MAINFRAMES, MINIS, AND PCS: WHAT'S THE DIFFERENCE?

Mainframe
A large computer, generally used for business or military problems.

Minicomputer
A medium-sized computer, generally used in universities or research labs.

Personal computer (PC)
A small desktop or portable computer.

Generally speaking, a **mainframe** is the largest computer, a powerhouse of a machine with huge memory and extremely rapid processing power. Mainframes are typically used for solving very large commercial, scientific, or military problems where a computer must handle massive amounts of data or many complicated processes. A **minicomputer** is a mid-range computer, about the size of an office desk; minicomputers are often used in universities, factories, or research laboratories. A **personal computer (PC),** which is sometimes referred to as a microcomputer, is small enough that it can be placed on a desktop or carried from room to room. (Small laptop and notebook PCs are fully portable, weighing less than 6 pounds.)

Today's PCs have the same computing power as the mainframes of the 1980s plus new graphic and interactive capabilities. (However, mainframes and minicomputers can still perform many more tasks simultaneously than PCs and can be used more easily by large numbers of people at the same time.) PCs can be used either as individual stand-alone machines with their own processing power, stored data, and software or as part of a departmental or company-wide network. Lightweight, portable laptop PCs make it possible to use computers in many locations—at home, on the train, or on an airplane.

Distributed processing
The distribution of processing among multiple computers linked by a communications network.

Distributed Processing PCs can be linked to minicomputers and mainframes, forming company-wide information networks that share hardware, software, and data resources. The use of multiple computers connected by a communication network for processing is called **distributed processing.** Instead of relying exclusively on a large central mainframe computer or

FIGURE 4.7

Distributed Processing Linking a Computer Network

The network can include various combinations of mainframes, minicomputers, and PCs.

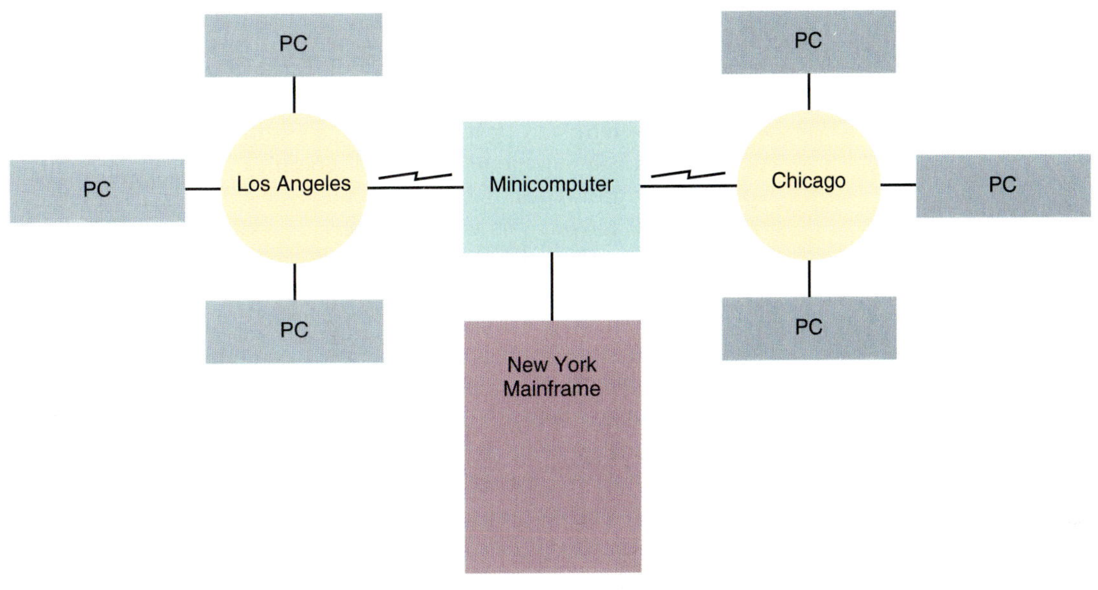

several independent computers, processing work is distributed among the various PCs, minicomputers, and mainframes linked together. The network can be simple, as shown in Figure 4.7, or it can involve hundreds or thousands of separate computers.

Downsizing and Cooperative Processing Because PCs can now perform many problem-solving tasks that were formerly reserved for much larger machines, many organizations are **downsizing,** or shifting problem-solving applications from large computers to smaller ones. As firms replace mainframes and minicomputers with PCs, the PCs are often networked to share data and communication with one another (see Chapter 7).

Downsizing
The process of moving software applications from large computers, such as mainframes or minicomputers, to smaller computers, such as PCs.

Every MIPS on a mainframe costs about 100 times more than on a personal computer. A megabyte of primary memory on a mainframe runs about ten times the cost of equivalent memory on a PC, and mainframe disk storage runs about twice as much. However, these cost savings must be balanced against the need to write new software and provide training to use the new technology.

Another computing pattern divides processing work for a particular application between mainframes and PCs. They communicate with one another on a network, and each type is assigned the functions it performs best. For example, the PC might be used for data entry, while the mainframe would be responsible for processing the input data and handling data stored by the system. This division of labor is called **cooperative processing.**

Cooperative processing
The division of processing work for applications among mainframes and PCs.

WORKSTATIONS, SUPERCOMPUTERS, AND PARALLEL PROCESSING

Workstation
A desktop computer with powerful graphics and mathematical processing capabilities and the ability to perform several tasks at once.

Workstations are desktop machines with powerful graphics and mathematical processing capabilities plus the ability to perform several tasks at once. They are typically used by scientists, engineers, designers, and other knowledge workers. Their graphics and CPU capacity allow them to present fully rendered, multiple views of a physical object, such as an airplane wing; rotate the object three dimensionally; give its physical parameters, such as dimensions and weight; and provide its design history and cost factors. Workstations can easily integrate text and graphics, displaying multiple tools, applications, and types of data simultaneously. They are used increasingly in the financial industry, in which powerhouse desktop machines simultaneously provide financial data and news services, analyze portfolios, and process securities and commodities trades.

Low-cost workstations and PCs are becoming harder to distinguish. Some of the more sophisticated personal computers have workstation-like features, and as PCs become more powerful and graphics oriented, the distinction is likely to blur further. Distinctions based on price (the purchase price of an inexpensive workstation starts at $4,000; a high-end PC can cost $5,000) are also evaporating, although the most sophisticated workstations can cost hundreds of thousands of dollars.

Supercomputer
A very sophisticated and powerful computer that can perform complex computations very rapidly.

A **supercomputer** is a sophisticated and powerful computer used for problems requiring extremely rapid and complex computations with hundreds or thousands of variable factors. Because supercomputers are very expensive, they have been used mainly for military and scientific applications, although business firms are starting to use them. For example, Dow Jones & Co. uses two supercomputers to handle its customer information requests and extra database services. Traditionally, supercomputers have been used for weapons research, weather forecasting, and petroleum and engineering applications, which involve complex mathematical models and simulations.

Parallel processing
A type of processing in which more than one instruction is processed at a time using multiple processors; used in supercomputers.

Supercomputers perform complex and massive computations much faster than conventional computers because they process up to 64 bits in less than 1 nanosecond—many times faster than the largest mainframes. Supercomputers do not process one instruction at a time but instead rely on **parallel processing.** In parallel processing, the computer processes more than one instruction at a time by dividing a problem into smaller parts and parceling out the parts to multiple processors. (In contrast, conventional computers use sequential or serial processing, in which the CPU executes only one instruction at a time in sequential order.) Figure 4.8 illustrates parallel processing for a hypothetical problem involving four parts (A–D). The problem is divided into smaller parts and assigned to multiple processing units, which work on it simultaneously. Some supercomputers have hundreds and thousands of microprocessors all working simultaneously.

Powerful parallel processing capabilities can be found in high-end workstations (see the Focus on Technology). However, only supercomputers can perform the billions of mathematical calculations per second required for the most complex problems.

Server computer
A computer designed or optimized to support a computer network.

Any category of computer could be used to support a computer network. **Server computers** are computers specifically designed for network use so that users can share files, software, printers, and other network resources. They typically have powerful processing, storage, and communications capabilities.

FIGURE 4.8

Parallel Processing: An Important Ingredient in Supercomputers

Supercomputers can perform complex calculations much faster than even a mainframe can. This is possible in part due to parallel processing, in which multiple CPUs break down a problem into smaller portions and work on them simultaneously.

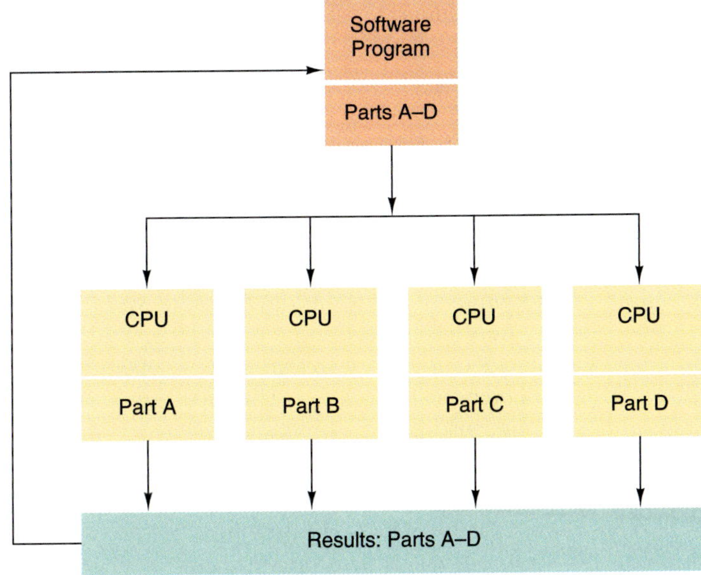

MICROPROCESSOR TECHNOLOGY: THE CHIPS BEHIND THE MACHINES

The processing capabilities of computers depend heavily on the speed and performance of the microprocessor on which they are based. They can be affected by word length, bus width, and clock speed.

PCs have been labeled as 16-bit or 32-bit machines according to their **word length.** A word is the number of bits that may be processed together as a unit. A 16-bit chip can retrieve or process 16 bits in a single machine cycle; a 32-bit machine, 32 bits. Thus, the bigger the word size, the more data and instructions the computer can handle at one time, and the greater its speed.

Word length
The number of bits that a computer can process or store together as a unit.

Another factor affecting performance is **bus width.** The width of the data bus affects how much data can be moved at one time among the central processing unit, primary storage, and other devices in the computer system. The 8088 chip used in the original IBM Personal Computer, for example, had a 16-bit word length but only an 8-bit data bus width. This meant that data were processed within the CPU chip itself in 16-bit chunks but could be moved only 8 bits at a time among the CPU, primary storage, and external devices.

Bus width
The number of bits that can be moved at one time among the CPU and the other devices of a computer.

The width of the address bus determines the maximum size of memory. The 20-bit address bus width on the 8088 meant that the computer could address only 1 megabyte of memory at a time. On the other hand, the 80486 chip has a 32-bit word length and 32-bit data bus and address bus widths.

PETRO-CANADA TURNS TO PARALLEL PROCESSING

Petro-Canada, an oil refiner in Calgary, Alberta, with $3.5 billion in annual revenue, had run its information systems on a variety of departmental and mainframe computers. Many of these information systems were homegrown and did not work together to provide the company with a unified picture of its operations or data. So Petro-Canada decided to implement SAP's R/3 software, which integrates a wide range of business functions, including manufacturing, inventory, accounting, and human resources, so that they could automatically share data. An order entered by the sales department, for example, could be viewed by the factory and the warehouse to help them with scheduling. Headquarters could tap into up-to-the-minute data on sales, inventory, and production. The company could access single views of its business data with this new application, but it also meant that Petro-Canada's computers would have to process an enormous volume of data to do so. The company believed that computers with conventional processing could not do the job.

Petro-Canada turned to parallel processing. It decided to use IBM's RS/6000 SP Server to store this information because the server could handle parallel operations on data while providing users with a single view of data. The RS/6000 SP has up to six processing units, each with 512 megabytes of memory and a total of 300 gigabytes of disk storage. Petro-Canada opted for IBM's 7133 Serial Storage Architecture (SSA) disk drives, which are faster than the parallel SCSI drives conventionally used in parallel processing systems. The RS/6000 is networked to 2000 PCs, which will handle E-mail, fax, and printing services.

The company started the system transition by using the new RS/6000 and the SAP software in two refineries in eastern Alberta. Two western refineries and Petro-Canada's natural gas exploration and production activities started using the new system later. The system was completely rolled out by the end of 1996.

The cost savings from the new system have not yet been calculated, but the company believes that the system will improve its bottom line.

FOCUS Question: How did parallel processing technology help Petro-Canada achieve its business goals?

SOURCE: Barbara DePompa, "Petro-Canada Goes Parallel," *Information Week,* April 8, 1996.

Megahertz (MHz)
A measure of clock speed, or the pacing of events in a computer; represents 1 million cycles per second.

Cycle speed also affects speed and performance. An internal system clock sets the pace for sequencing events in the computer by emitting millions of electronic pulses per second. This clock speed is measured in **megahertz (MHz),** or millions of cycles per second. Each type of chip is equipped to handle clock speeds within a certain range. For example, the Intel Pentium microprocessor operates at 75–166 MHz.

Even more powerful are Intel's Pentium Pro and Pentium II chips, Digital Equipment's Alpha chip, and the PowerPC chip developed jointly by IBM and Apple Computer Corp. The following section describes the capabilities of these and other "superchips." Table 4.3 compares the capabilities of the leading microprocessor chips.

Reduced instruction set computing (RISC)
Technology for increasing microprocessor speed by embedding only the most frequently used instructions on a chip.

REDUCED INSTRUCTION SET COMPUTING

Microprocessor speed and performance can also be enhanced by using **reduced instruction set computing (RISC),** which drastically simplifies computer design. Conventional chips, which are based on complex instruction set computing, have many internal instructions built into their circuitry and take

TABLE 4.3

Popular Microprocessors

Name	Manufacturer	Word Size	Bus Width	Clock Speed (MHz)	MIPS	Used In
80486DX	Intel	32	32	25-100	25-66	IBM and other PCs
68040	Motorola	32	32	25-40	15-35	Mac Quadras
Pentium	Intel	32	64	75-166	100-180	IBM and other PCs
PowerPC	Motorola, IBM, Apple	32-64	64	60-300+	100-300+	Power PC, Power Mac, work-stations
Alpha	DEC	64	64	150-400+	275-1332	Digital PC, AXP 150
Pentium Pro	Intel	64	64	150-200	300	High-end PCs and work-stations
Pentium II	Intel	64	64	233-300		High-end PCs and work-stations

several clock cycles to execute an instruction. However, only 20 percent of these instructions are needed for 80 percent of the computer's tasks. The most frequently used instructions are the simple operations that can be performed at peak efficiency.

RISC chips, on the other hand, have only the most frequently used instructions embedded in them. With pared-down circuit design, a RISC CPU can execute most of its instructions in one cycle and may be able to execute many instructions at the same time. The Alpha chip is a 64-bit RISC micro-

The Intel Pentium II microprocessor contains more than 7 million transistors and has supercomputing processing capabilities. Powerful chips will continue to advance information technology.

SOURCE: Courtesy of Intel Corporation.

processor that can reach speeds of over 300 MHz, which gives it the performance of a small supercomputer.

RISC is most appropriate for scientific and workstation computing, which requires repetitive arithmetical and logical operations on data and sometimes three-dimensional image rendering. RISC technology is unlikely to be used for all microprocessors. Because software written for conventional processors cannot automatically run on RISC computers, new software is required. Conventional microprocessors are being enhanced and streamlined to keep them competitive with RISC.

4.3 STORAGE TECHNOLOGY

Storage technology is important because it affects how quickly and flexibly data can be accessed and used by the CPU. Even in the biggest computers, the amount of data that can be kept in primary storage is very limited, and the cost of storing information there is high. Moreover, data stored in primary storage can easily be lost or destroyed if the electric power is disrupted. Most data is stored outside primary storage in secondary storage.

Secondary storage
The relatively long-term storage of data outside the CPU.

Secondary storage refers to the relatively long-term storage of data outside the CPU and primary storage. Secondary storage is nonvolatile; that is, it will retain data even if the electric power is turned off. Secondary storage is slower than primary storage because it uses a number of electromechanical components, whereas primary storage is electronic and occurs nearly at the speed of light. Nevertheless, secondary storage media must still be able to transfer large bodies of data rapidly to primary storage. The principal secondary storage technologies are magnetic tape, magnetic disk, and optical disk.

MAGNETIC TAPE

Magnetic tape
A secondary storage medium in which data are stored by means of magnetized and unmagnetized spots on tape; can store information only sequentially.

Magnetic tape is considered a fading storage technology, but it is still used in older computer systems and for storing large amounts of data at low cost. A **magnetic tape** is much like a tape cassette for storing music, in that records are stored in sequential order, from beginning to end. Magnetic tape comes in reels of up to 14 inches in diameter with tape approximately .5-inch wide and up to 3,600 feet long (or in cartridges with .25-inch-wide tape). Magnetic tapes have a range of densities for storing data, measured in bytes per inch (bpi). A low-density tape has 1,600 bpi, and a high-density tape has 6,250 bpi. A 10.5-inch high-density tape reel can store over 200 megabytes of data. A quarter-inch tape cartridge can store over 10 gigabytes.

The principal advantages of magnetic tape are that it is very low in cost and is a relatively stable storage medium (although the tape can age and crack over time and the environment in which it is stored must be carefully controlled). Magnetic tape is also reusable; its contents can be erased so that it can be used for storing new information. It is often used as a "backup" storage medium for data.

The disadvantages of magnetic tape are that it can store information only sequentially and that it is relatively slow. To find an individual record on magnetic tape, such as your Social Security earnings history, the tape must be read from beginning to end, one record at a time, until the desired record has been located.

MAGNETIC DISK

The most popular and important secondary storage medium today is the **magnetic disk.** Disk technology permits direct and immediate access to data. The computer can proceed immediately to a specific record or piece of data on the disk instead of reading through records one by one. For this reason, disk technology is often referred to as **direct-access storage devices (DASD).** There are two kinds of magnetic disks: hard disks and floppy disks.

Magnetic disk
The most popular secondary storage medium; data are stored by means of magnetized spots on hard or floppy disks.

Direct-access storage device (DASD)
Magnetic disks, including hard and floppy disks; called *direct access* because in this technology the computer proceeds immediately to a specific record without having to read all the preceding records.

Hard disk
A type of magnetic disk resembling a thin platter, where relatively large quantities of data can be stored and data can be rapidly accessed.

Hard Disks Magnetic **hard disks** are thin metallic platters—large ones are about the size of phonograph records—with an iron oxide coating. Several disks may be mounted together on a vertical shaft, where they rotate at speeds of approximately 3,500 to 7,200 revolutions per minute. Electromagnetic read/write heads are mounted on access arms. The heads fly over the spinning disks and read or write data on concentric circles called tracks. Data are recorded on tracks as tiny magnetized spots forming binary digits. Each track can store thousands of bytes. The read/write head never actually touches the disk but hovers a few thousandths or millionths of an inch above it.

Disk storage capacity depends on the type, quantity, and arrangement of disks in a unit. Individual disk packs or fixed disk drives may have storage capacities ranging from several megabytes to several gigabytes. PC hard disks can store several gigabytes.

Removable-pack disk systems consist of hard disks stacked into a pack or indivisible unit that can be mounted and removed as a unit. They are primarily found on mainframe and minicomputer systems. Figure 4.9 illustrates

FIGURE 4.9

Side and Top Views of a Removable-Pack Disk System

Each disk contains concentric tracks; the 20 tracks located on the same vertical line form a cylinder. Data are stored in records, each of which has a unique location, or address, which refers to the specific cylinder, recording surface, and data record number.

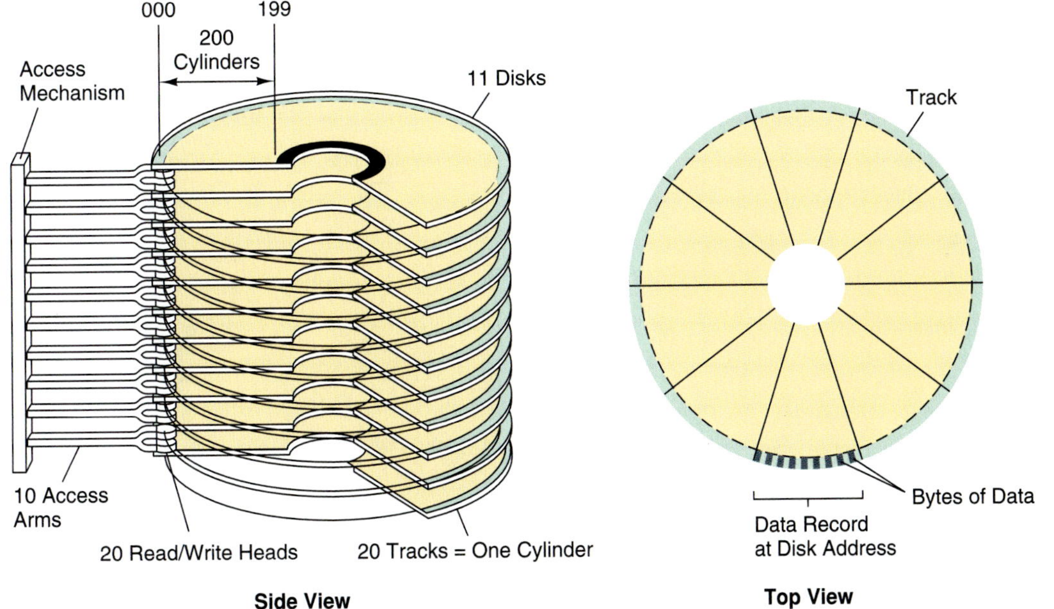

a commercial removable disk pack with 11 disks, each with two surfaces. Only 20 surfaces on the disk pack can be used for recording data, however, because the top and bottom surfaces are not used for this purpose. Each surface area, in turn, is divided into tracks where data are recorded. A cylinder consists of 20 circular tracks located at one position of the read/write access arms; they are on the same vertical line, one above the other. Read/write heads are directed to a specific record using a disk address consisting of the cylinder number, the recording surface number, and the data record number.

RAID (redundant array of inexpensive disks)
High-performance disk storage technology that can deliver data over multiple paths simultaneously by packaging more than 100 smaller disk drives with a controller chip and specialized software in a single large box.

A disk technology called **RAID (redundant array of inexpensive disks)** is becoming a popular high-performance disk storage system. RAID devices package more than 100 small 5.25-inch disk drives, a controller chip, and specialized software in one large unit. In contrast to traditional disk drives, which deliver data from the disk drive along a single path, RAID technology delivers data over multiple paths simultaneously to produce a faster disk access time. If one RAID drive fails, other drives are available to deliver data, making the technology potentially more reliable than traditional disk drives.

Magnetic disks offer several advantages. Individual records can be accessed directly within milliseconds, permitting solutions to problems requiring immediate access to data, such as airline reservation systems or customer information systems. Moreover, as we discuss in Chapter 6, disk storage permits records and pieces of related data to be organized and combined easily.

The principal drawbacks of disk technology are the need for backup, susceptibility to environmental disturbances, and cost. In disk technology there is only one copy of the information because the old record on the disk is written over if the record is changed. Disk technology also requires a pure and stable environment, since smoke or other particles can cause a disk pack to "crash." Technical advances have boosted disk storage capacity while reducing cost, but it is still more expensive than magnetic tape.

FIGURE 4.10

The Sector Method: How a Floppy Disk Stores Data

Floppy disks contain concentric tracks where data are stored as magnetized bits. In addition, the disk surface is divided into triangular sectors, each of which has a unique number. Data can be accessed directly by using an address that includes the sector and data record number.

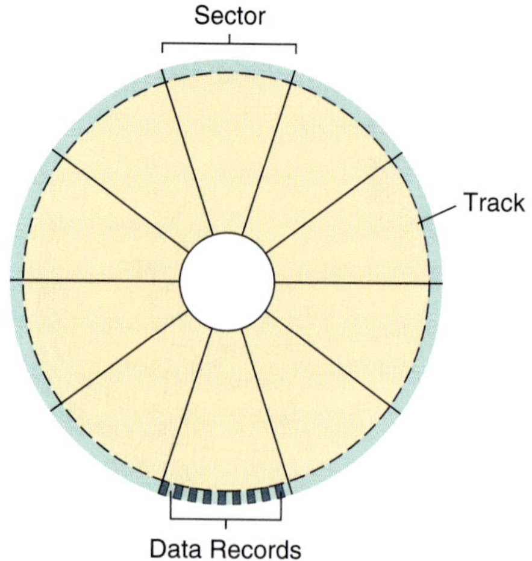

FIGURE 4.11

How a WORM Drive Works

To write data on a write once, read many (WORM) optical disk drive, a high-power laser beam (panel a) heats the disk substrate, leaving a permanent pit on its surface for a binary 0 and leaving the disk surface smooth and reflective for a binary 1. A low-power laser (panel b) is used to read the data. The laser reflects from areas with no pits to read a binary 1. The pits diffuse the laser, creating no reflection, to read a binary 0.

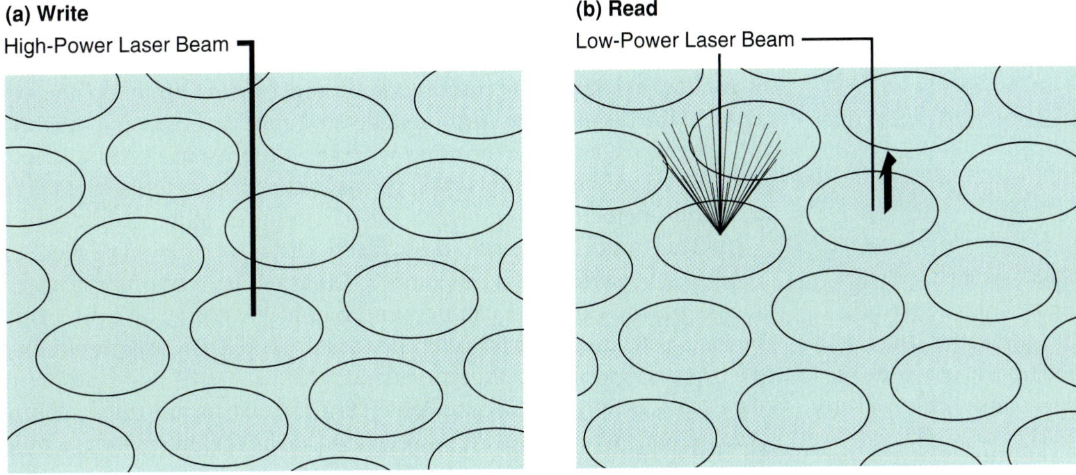

Floppy Disks **Floppy disks** are used primarily with PCs. These disks, which are very inexpensive, are an ideal medium for storing data and programs that are not in constant use or for transporting data and programs. Floppy disks are available in 3.5-inch and 5.25-inch sizes, but the 5.25-inch disk is largely obsolete. High-density 3.5-inch disks can store from 1.44 MB to nearly 3 MB of data.

Floppy disk
A flexible, inexpensive magnetic disk used as a secondary storage medium; primarily used with PCs.

Floppy disks use a sector method for storing data. The disk surface is divided into eight or nine wedges like a pie; the actual number depends on the disk system used (see Figure 4.10). In most disks, each **sector** has the same storage capacity, since data are recorded more densely on the inner disk tracks. Each sector is assigned a unique number. Data can be located by using an address consisting of the sector number and an individual data record number.

Sector
A method of storing data that divides a disk into pie-shaped pieces, each with a unique number that becomes part of the address.

OPTICAL DISK TECHNOLOGY

Using a laser device that records data by burning microscopic pits in a spiral track, **optical disks** (also called compact disks or laser optical disks) store data at densities much greater than those of magnetic disks. There are two basic ways in which information is placed on an optical disk. The most common way is by using a small laser to burn permanent pits into the surface of the plastic optical disk (called an ablative technique). The resulting pattern of pits and clear surface is used to define a single bit of information. A pit can be defined as a "0" and a clear area as a "1." A small reading laser is used to read the pattern of bits (see Figure 4.11).

Optical disk
A disk on which data are recorded and read by laser beams rather than by magnetic means; such disks can store data at densities much greater than magnetic disks.

Massive quantities of data can be stored in a highly compact form on optical disks. For example, a 4.75-inch optical disk can store up to 660 megabytes, equivalent to the storage capacity of 300 high-density floppy disks. Consequently, optical disks are most appropriate for problems requiring enormous quantities of data to be stored compactly for easy retrieval.

The second technique, used for rewritable optical disks, employs a laser and a magnetic field to melt and magnetize tiny areas on the surface of an optical disk. The magneto-optical disk consists of layers of magnetic film deposited on a rotating disk substrate. A strong laser beam strikes the disk as it rotates, heating a microscopic spot and causing atoms in the recording layer of the disk to form into a magnetized zone representing one bit of data. The size of each spot determines whether it represents a 0 or a 1. To read the disk, a weaker laser beam scans the magnetized spots. This beam is reflected to a photodetector that converts the variations in spot size into binary data.

CD-ROM
An optical disk system used with microcomputers; it is a form of read-only storage in that data can only be read from it, not written to it; stands for compact disk/read-only memory.

The optical disk system most often used with PCs is called **CD-ROM** (compact disk/read-only memory). CD-ROM is read-only storage, which means that no new data can be written to it; it can only be read. CD-ROM has been most widely used for reference materials with massive amounts of data, such as encyclopedias, directories, and large databases. For example, financial data from Dow Jones are available on CD-ROM, as are titles such as *Street Atlas U.S.A.,* which provides street-level maps for every square mile of the United States. CD-ROM is also becoming popular for storing images (described in later chapters), for delivering software, and for interactive entertainment and multimedia[1] (see Section 4.5, "Information Technology Trends").

WORM
An optical disk system in which data can be recorded only once on the disk by users and cannot be erased; stands for write once, read many.

WORM (write once, read many) optical disk systems allow users to record data only once on an optical disk. Once written, the data cannot be erased, but they can be read indefinitely. WORM has been used as an alternative to microfilm for archiving digitized document images. For instance, California's

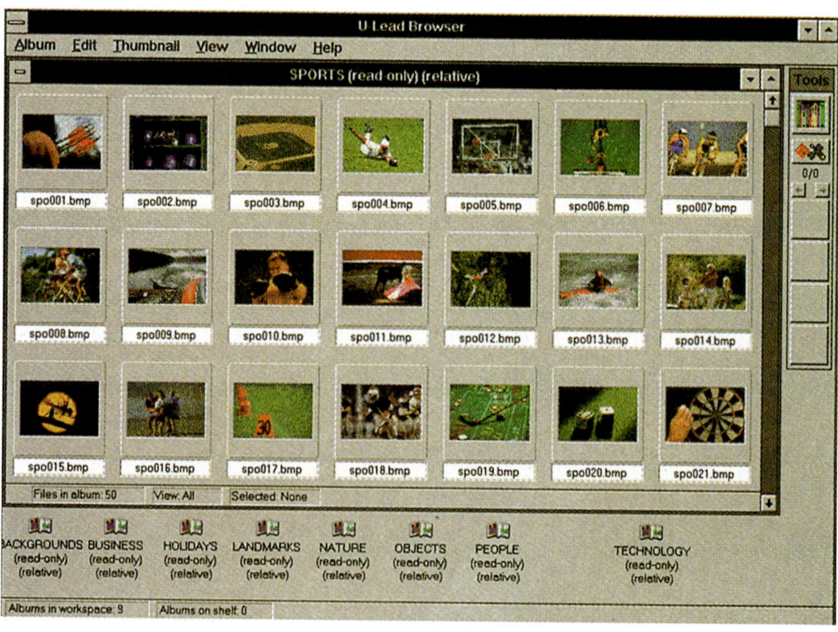

Because a single CD-ROM can store vast quantities of data, the technology is often used for storing images, color illustrations, books, and multimedia applications.

Mass storage systems provide automated retrieval from a library of tape cartridges. They can provide very rapid access to vast amounts of data.

SOURCE: Storage Technology.

Department of Motor Vehicles used WORM media to store pictures, signatures, and fingerprints so that no one could tamper with permanent information.

Digital video disks (DVDs) (also called digital versatile disks) are optical disks of even higher capacity, with the ability to hold up to 5 gigabytes of data—enough to store a full-length motion picture. Initially they will be used to store movies and multimedia applications using large amounts of video and graphics, but they may replace CD-ROMs because they can store digitized text, graphics, audio, and video data.

Digital video disk (DVD) A very-high-capacity optical storage device that can store full-length videos and massive amounts of data.

Erasable, rewritable optical disks are becoming faster and cheaper than tape storage. Optical disk drives operate at around 200 to 500 milliseconds, much faster than the 60 seconds required for a person to mount a tape and up to 30 minutes to read an entire tape. Erasable optical disks can also be more reliable than magnetic disks. Because they use laser beams instead of mechanical read/write heads to read and record data, they are immune to "head crashes." They also are not as easily affected as magnetic disks by stray magnetic fields, which can alter data. Magneto-optical disks are the most popular erasable optical disk technology.

4.4 INPUT AND OUTPUT TECHNOLOGY

Input and output devices make it possible for human beings to interact with computers. The speed, capacity, and ease of use of input and output devices have a direct bearing on the performance of an entire information system.

INPUT TECHNOLOGY

Traditionally, data have been input through a keyboard. In the past, data entry clerks used a keypunch machine to code their data onto 80-column punched cards; each character was identified by a unique punch in a specific location on the card. Another alternative was a key-to-tape or key-to-disk machine that allowed data to be keyed directly onto a magnetic tape or magnetic disk for computer processing. Such methods have been largely discarded in favor of more direct methods of entering data. Data can now be entered directly into a computer system by using a keyboard and computer terminal or by using new tools such as touch screens, digital scanners, the computer mouse, pen-based input, optical character recognition, sensing devices, and voice input.

Computer mouse
A hand-held device that can be moved on a desktop to control the position of the cursor on a video display screen.

Touch screen
A sensitized video display screen that allows data to be input by touching the screen surface with a finger or pointer.

Source data automation
Advanced forms of data input technology that generate machine-readable data at their point of origin; includes optical character recognition, magnetic ink character recognition, digitizers, and voice input.

Magnetic ink character recognition (MICR)
A form of source data automation in which an MICR reader identifies characters written in magnetic ink; used primarily for check processing.

Optical character recognition (OCR)
A form of source data automation in which optical scanning devices read specially designed data off source documents and translate the data into digital form for the computer.

Bar code
Specially designed bar characters tht can be read by OCR scanning devices; used primarily on price tags and supermarket items.

The Computer Mouse The **computer mouse** is a hand-held device connected to the computer by a cable; the mouse can be moved around on a desk top to control the position of the cursor on a video display screen. Once the cursor is in the desired location, the operator can push a button on the mouse to make a selection. The mouse can also be used to "draw" images on the graphics display screen. The "point and click" capability of the electric mouse is an alternative to keyboard and text-based commands.

Touch Screens **Touch screens** allow limited amounts of data to be entered by touching the surface of a sensitized video display monitor with a finger or a pointer. The operator makes selections by touching specified parts of the screen. Although the applications of touch screens are limited at present, they are easy to use and appeal to persons who are not familiar with a keyboard. Stores, banks, restaurants, and some offices use them.

Source Data Automation **Source data automation** collects machine-readable data at the time they are created. Source data automation technologies, including magnetic ink character recognition, optical character recognition, pen-based input, digital scanners, voice input, and sensors, eliminate the need for special data entry staff and are more accurate than keying in data. The error rate for bar-code scanners, for example, is less than 1 in 10,000 transactions (keypunchers make up to 1 error per 1,000 keystrokes).

Magnetic ink character recognition (MICR) technology is used primarily by the banking industry for processing large numbers of checks. The characters in the lower left portion of a check are preprinted in special magnetic ink to indicate the bank identification number, the checking account number, and the check number. After the check has been cashed and sent to the bank for processing, an MICR reader senses the MICR characters on the check and feeds them into the computer. The amount of the check, which is written in ordinary ink, must be keyed in by hand.

Optical character recognition (OCR) devices read marks, characters, and codes and translate them into digital form for the computer. Optical character reading devices reflect light off characters with special fonts or shapes on source documents and convert them into digital patterns that the computer can recognize. The most widely used optical code is the **bar code,** which is used by supermarkets, clothing stores, hospitals, libraries, military operations, transportation facilities, and every kind of manufacturing operation. Scanning devices built into countertops or hand-held wands are employed to read the bar codes. Bar codes frequently utilize a Universal Product Code that records data based on the width of the bars and the space between them. The codes include manufacturer and product identification numbers (see Figure 4.12). Some point-of-sale systems, such as those found at Shoprite supermarket checkout counters, capture bar-coded data and use them to obtain the item's price from the firm's computer system. These data can also immediately update the firm's sales and inventory records.

Because bar codes can contain other useful pieces of information, such as time, date, and location data in addition to identification data, they can be used to track an item, analyze its movement, and calculate what has happened to it during production or other processes.

With **pen-based input,** users print directly on a tablet-sized screen using a penlike stylus. The screen is fitted with an additional transparent layer composed of a grid of fine wires. The screen detects the presence of the special stylus, which emits a faint signal from its tip. The screen can also interpret gestures made with the stylus such as tapping and flicking. Letters and numbers written by users on the tablet can be recognized and changed into digital form, where they can be stored or processed and analyzed. The opening vignette about United Parcel Service described some of the benefits of this technology, although it is still difficult for pen-based devices to read handwriting .

Pen-based input
Input devices that accept handwritten input by allowing users to print directly on a sensitized screen using a penlike stylus.

Digital scanners translate images such as drawings, photographs, charts, documents, and other printed information into digital form so that they can be stored or manipulated by the computer.

Digital scanner
An input device for translating images and printed information into digital form.

Voice input devices convert spoken words into digital form. Special voice recognition software (see Chapter 5) compares the electrical patterns produced by the speaker's voice to a set of prerecorded patterns. If the patterns match, the input is accepted. Sophisticated voice systems with "vocabularies" of more than 30,000 words have been developed, but many voice input applications currently are used for simple commands. For instance, the

Voice input devices
Input devices that convert the spoken word into digital form.

FIGURE 4.12

Bar Codes: The Most Commonly Used Optical Codes

Here we see a common type of bar code, the Universal Product Code, which identifies each product with a unique code based on the width of the bars and the spaces between them. The codes include manufacturer and product identification numbers.

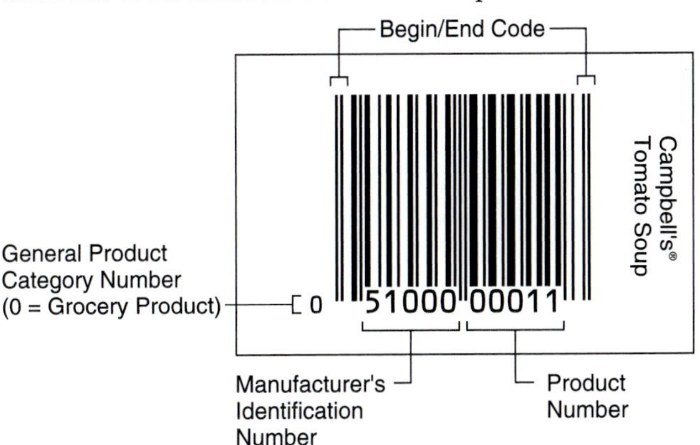

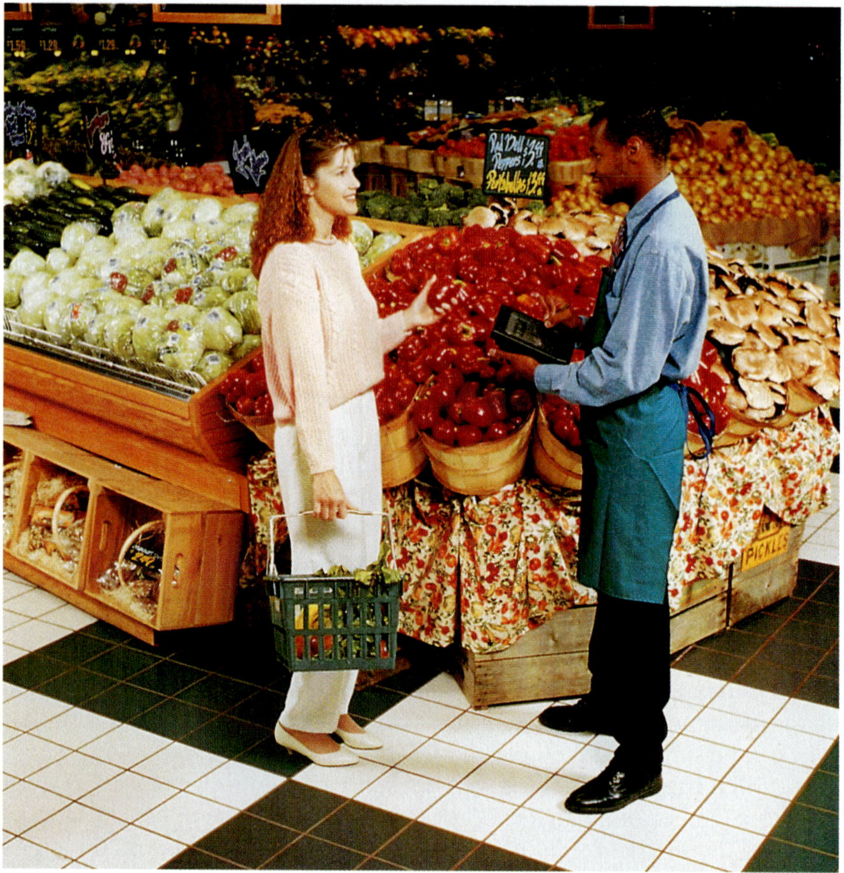

Pen-based input allows users to enter data by writing with a penlike device on a special screen. It is useful for entering small amounts of data.

SOURCE: Courtesy of International Business Machines Corporation.

U.S. Postal Service uses a voice recognition system to expedite mail sorting. Users can speak ZIP codes instead of keying them in, leaving their hands free to sort packages. The Focus on People describes how voice input and some other advanced input technologies have helped disabled people to contribute and communicate.

Sensors
Devices that collect data directly from the environment for input into the computer.

Sensors collect data directly from the environment for input into a computer system. For instance, sensors are used in General Motors cars with on-board computers and screens that display a map of the surrounding area and the driver's route. Sensors in each wheel and a magnetic compass supply information to the computer for determining the car's location. The South Coast Air Quality Management District's system uses sensors in smokestacks to supply data for monitoring pollution emissions. The sensors continuously measure emissions; they are linked to PCs at the site of each smokestack that send the data collected by the sensors to the district's central computer for analysis.

Batch input and processing
An approach to input and processing in which data are grouped together as source documents before being input; once input, they are stored as a transaction file before processing, which occurs later.

BATCH VERSUS ONLINE INPUT AND PROCESSING

The manner in which data are collected for input is closely tied to processing. In **batch input and processing,** data are collected in the form of source documents such as orders or payroll time cards; these are accumulated and stored for a period of time in groups called batches. Then the batches of documents are keyed into the computer and stored in computer-usable form as a transaction file until they are needed for processing; that may be a few hours, a few weeks, or even months later. Finally, the batch is processed as a group in

FOCUS ON PEOPLE

ENABLING THE DISABLED

How can someone who is completely paralyzed hold a job in a major corporation—and be productive? Mike Ward is an editor at Intel Corp., the giant maker of computer chips. He edits articles written by engineers about failure analyses of components used in various high-technology projects for *Failure Analysis Summit,* an Intel newsletter. Ward was diagnosed with Lou Gehrig's disease, or amyotrophic lateral sclerosis, which progressively destroys the motor neurons that control all a person's muscles. He has been confined to a wheelchair and can move only his eyeballs. He requires a ventilator to breathe and must be fed artificially. But his mind is fully productive. The key technologies that allow him to work are input and output devices that enable him to communicate with the computer, which, in turn, communicates with others for him.

Ward uses the Eyegaze computer system, which reads eye movement with great precision. The system uses a low-power infrared system mounted below the computer monitor. The system illuminates the eye lens and takes a picture 30 times per second. It can detect where the person is looking to within 1/4 inch, allowing the user to activate keys as small as 5/8 inch wide. A key is "pressed" by the user looking at the key for 1/4 second or longer. The screen Ward uses contains a keyboard and other symbols as well to allow him to accomplish other tasks—typing, turning on lights or television, even "speaking" on the telephone. Ward claims the system works so well and so fast that he can now write using full sentences and punctuation without a loss of time. To do his writing and editing, he uses an ordinary PC running standard software.

To "talk," Ward uses a special text-to-speech output system called MultiVoice from the Institute of Applied Technology of the Children's Hospital in Boston. This system runs on a laptop PC that is mounted to his wheelchair. Ward's MultiVoice speaks with a deep voice, although the quality and intonation of the voice can be adjusted.

Computer technology is helping other physically challenged people as well. Daniel Lawrence's vocal cords had been removed because they were cancerous, but he found work as a voiceless disk jockey at KHUM-FM, a free-form rock-n-roll station in Ferndale, California. Using a speech synthesizer called DECtalk from the Digital Equipment Corporation, he types comments which are then "spoken" by the computer. The computerized speech is fed directly into the station's control board, bypassing the microphone to improve fidelity. "Digital Dan" has increased KHUM's popularity in a crowded market, and the job has given Dan Lawrence a new purpose in life.

Don Dalton, who is paralyzed from the chest down and confined to a wheelchair, started Micro Overflow Corp. in his garage. He relied heavily on a PC, initially operating the keyboard with a stick held in his mouth. Now he uses a microphone in a headset connected to the PC and can activate all the computer's functions by voice, type 100 words per minute, and manage the company's finances and scheduling. Micro Overflow is a distributorship that adapts computer technology for the disabled. Dalton is helping other disabled entrepreneurs to profit from computer technology, just as he did.

FOCUS Question: Suggest other computer systems that have been or could be developed to aid people with various disabilities, such as blindness, deafness, or the inability to walk.

SOURCES: Bruce Felton, "Technologies That Enable the Disabled," *The New York Times*, September 14, 1997; Andrea Adelson, "Cancer Survivor Finds a 'Lifeboat,'" *The New York Times,* April 9, 1996; and Thomas Hoffman, "Knocking Down Barriers," *Computerworld,* August 30, 1993.

a computer job (see Figure 4.13). The output is created only when new batches are processed. This was the earliest approach to input and processing and is still used today for processing payrolls and utility bills.

In contrast, with online input, data are immediately captured for computer processing instead of being collected and stored on source documents. In **online realtime processing,** the data are processed immediately upon input into the system. There is no waiting, and output and information stored by the system are always up to date. Airline reservation systems, which must respond immediately to new data, require an online realtime approach.

Online realtime processing
An input approach in which data are input into the computer and processed as they become available.

In online input with delayed processing, data are directly translated into computer-usable form, but they are not processed immediately. Instead, the data are held in temporary storage until scheduled processing occurs. For instance, some merchandise catalog sales firms input orders directly into terminals as the orders are taken over the telephone. The computer holds the orders in a transaction file until the end of the day, when they are all processed together.

OUTPUT TECHNOLOGY

When computers were in their infancy, printers were the primary output medium. Today, there are many more options for displaying computer output, such as video display terminals, color graphic output devices, and audio output.

Printer
An output device for producing permanent hard-copy output.

Printers and Plotters **Printers** are still the medium of choice when permanent paper output is required. A wide range of printer options is available, based on their speed and the way they print. The speed, cost, and quality of printer output are important considerations in selecting the right printer. The two main types of printers are impact printers and nonimpact printers.

Nonimpact printers form characters without physical contact between the printing mechanism and the paper. The most common type of nonimpact printers are laser printers and inkjet printers. *Impact printers,* such as the dot-matrix printer, form characters by pressing a typeface device such as a print hammer or wheel against paper and inked ribbon.

Plotter
A device used for outputting high-quality graphics; pen plotters move in various directions to produce straight lines.

Plotters are special devices for outputting high-quality graphics, such as maps, charts, drawings, and graphs. They are commonly used by engineers and architects. A pen plotter is programmed to move in various directions to produce a series of straight lines; it draws curves as a series of very short lines.

Video display terminal (VDT)
A screen on which output can be displayed; varieties include monochrome, color, text, and text/graphics.

CRT
An electronic tube that shoots a beam of electrons that illuminates pixels, or tiny dots, on a video display screen; stands for cathode ray tube.

Video Display Terminals Displaying output on a **video display terminal (VDT)** is appropriate when there is no need for a permanent paper record or when an immediate response is required. VDTs can be classified in terms of whether they are monochrome or color and whether they can display text only or text and graphics. The traditional technology for displaying output on a terminal screen is the cathode ray tube, or **CRT.** CRTs work much like television picture tubes, in that an electronic "gun" shoots a beam of electrons that illuminate tiny dots, called pixels, on the screen. The more pixels (a contraction of the phrase *picture element*) per screen, the higher the resolution, or sharpness, of the screen image.

FIGURE 4.13

Three Approaches to Input and Processing

In batch processing, source documents are collected and entered into the computer as a batch, or group. There they are stored in a transaction file, and eventually the entire batch is processed together. Thus, the system is updated only when each batch is completed. With online realtime processing, data are processed immediately as they are entered, so the system is constantly updated. A third approach combines the first two: data are entered immediately but are stored temporarily in a transaction file. At scheduled intervals the computer processes the new input.

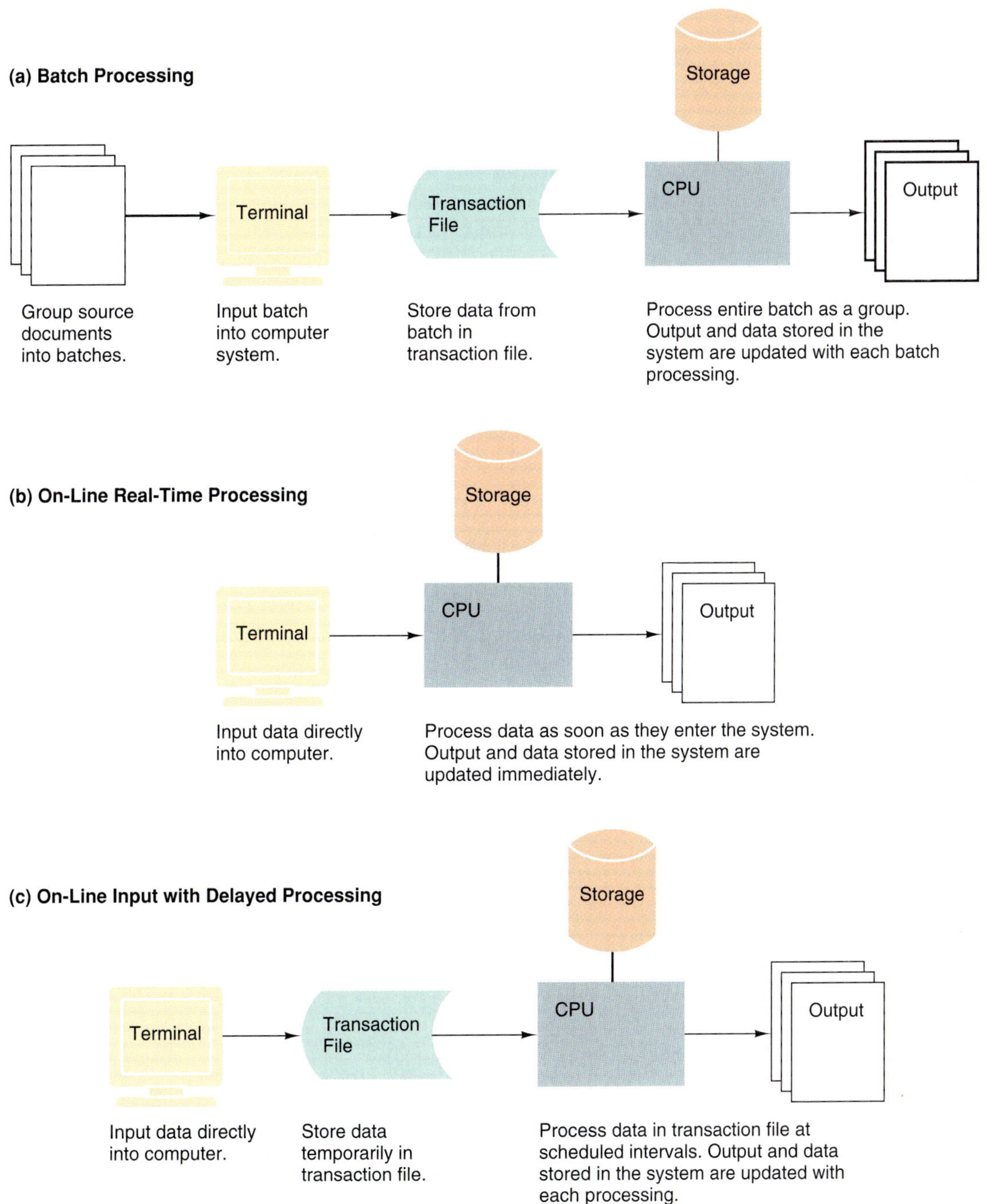
(a) Batch Processing
Storage
Terminal
Transaction File
CPU
Output
Group source documents into batches.
Input batch into computer system.
Store data from batch in transaction file.
Process entire batch as a group. Output and data stored in the system are updated with each batch processing.
(b) On-Line Real-Time Processing
Storage
Terminal
CPU
Output
Input data directly into computer.
Process data as soon as they enter the system. Output and data stored in the system are updated immediately.
(c) On-Line Input with Delayed Processing
Storage
Terminal
Transaction File
CPU
Output
Input data directly into computer.
Store data temporarily in transaction file.
Process data in transaction file at scheduled intervals. Output and data stored in the system are updated with each processing.

Bit mapping
A technology often used for displaying graphics on a video display terminal; it allows each pixel on the screen to be addressed and manipulated by the computer.

Display devices for graphics often use **bit mapping,** which allows each pixel on the screen to be addressed and manipulated by the computer (as opposed to blocks of pixels in character-addressable displays). This requires more computer memory, but it permits finer detail and the ability to produce any kind of image on the display screen. A high-resolution color monitor using the Extended VGA standard to support graphics work displays much clearer, sharper images because it has a 1,024 × 768 resolution (786,432 pixels).

Other Output Devices Microfilm and microfiche have been used to record output as microscopic filmed images that can be stored compactly for future use. These media are cumbersome to search through, however, and are gradually being replaced by optical disk technology.

Audio output
Output that emerges as sound rather than as a visual display.

Audio output includes voice, music, and other sounds. Voice output devices convert digital data into speechlike form. When you call for information on the telephone, for example, a computer "voice" may respond with the telephone number you requested. Sounds needed to process inquiries are prerecorded, coded, and stored on disk to be translated back as spoken words. Voice output is gaining popularity in toys, automobiles, and games as well as in situations in which visual output is not appropriate.

4.5 INFORMATION TECHNOLOGY TRENDS

For the past 30 years, each decade has seen computing power increase by a factor of 100 while costs have dropped by a factor of 10. Advances in science, technology, and manufacturing will enable this momentum to continue. The future will see even more "intelligence" built into everyday devices, with mainframe-like computing power packed into a device the size of a shirt pocket or notebook. The most powerful microprocessors, such as Intel's Pentium Pro or DEC's Alpha, have mainframe and even supercomputer-like computing power.

Smart cards are being used to collect subway and bus fares electronically and have become popular alternatives to coins in public telephone booths.

SOURCE: Courtesy of MetroCard.

FOCUS ON **ORGANIZATIONS**

HERE COME THE SMART CARDS

If you think you are carrying too many cards in your wallet now, just wait. The smart cards are coming, and they have the potential of either filling up your wallet even more or replacing most of your other cards. A smart card is a plastic card the size of a credit card that contains a tiny microprocessor. Bank and credit cards already carry some digital information on their electronic strips, but the amount of information they can carry is very limited—owner identification data, a password, and standard account data. Replace the strip with a tiny microprocessor, and the card can carry a great deal more information and even do some processing.

What are some of its uses? The card can carry vital health-care records so that you can take those records with you very easily. The U.S. military is considering using a smart card to replace the traditional military dog tags (they can carry much more data). Smart cards are already being used in digital cellular telephones, in satellite pay-TV, and in pay-telephone cards. The New York City Transit Authority offers smart cards as alternatives to subway and bus tokens and for toll collection on its highways and bridges. Smart cards could be used to replace existing credit cards, carry a photograph for identification purposes, hold a list of phone numbers, or contain other data people carry with them. They can even replace cash.

The organization that has pioneered in producing and marketing smart cards is Gemplus SCA, a German company headed by Marc Lassus. While his dream of widely used smart cards was once not taken seriously, smart card sales have grown from about 250 million in 1992 to about 750 million in 1996. Projections are that sales will approach 2 billion cards in 1998.

A trial use of cash cards is already underway in Swindon, which is in southern England. Swindon residents can pay for purchases with their cash cards, enabling them to carry no coins or bank notes at all. French, Austrian, and German banks have adopted smart cards, as has the Spanish social security system.

Many places in the United States already accept debit cards, enabling the holder to pay for purchases by a card. But debit cards are not smart cards. They merely result in the purchase amount being deducted from the holder's bank account and transferred to the vendor's bank account. Debit cards carry no electronic cash. The cash card differs in that it actually contains electronic cash, cash that has already been withdrawn from the bank and electronically transferred to the card. The value to the merchant is that the process of collecting for his or her goods and services is quicker, cleaner, and safer. The banks must play a role in cash cards because the cards must be "filled" with cash by the bank. Therefore, banks must have a way to make a profit. Their plan is to charge a fee for the card once the trial periods are over. In addition, banks plan to earn interest on the float of the cash—the actual cash will remain with the bank from the time the customer's cash card is loaded until the merchant collects.

Many questions exist about the value and viability of smart cards. Some fear the loss of privacy if medical records are carried around in electronic format. In Germany, more than 60 million medical smart cards have been issued, but they carry little actual medical information because of privacy protection laws. Other critics fear the cards can be used for fraud or can be stolen and used by others. Computer hackers in Ireland used the card system to steal television signals, forcing British Sky Broadcasting PLC to change its code. Still others claim that these will not replace all the other cards people carry and so will end up only stuffing wallets even further.

FOCUS Questions:
What people, organization, and technology factors should a business consider if it is considering accepting cash cards? Suggest other applications for smart cards.

Sources: Douglas Lavin, "French Smart Card Proves a Bright Idea," *The Wall Street Journal,* April 22, 1996, and Nicholas Bray, "Future Shop: 'No Cash Accepted; Microchip-Card Purchases Only,' " *The Wall Street Journal,* July 13, 1995.

Computers on a chip will increasingly guide automobiles, military weaponry, robots, and everyday household items as well as large and small computers. Computers and related information technologies will have the ability to blend data, images, and sound and send them coursing through vast networks with equal ease.[2] The Focus on Organizations examines one effect of microminiaturization—the growing use of smart cards and the move toward a cashless society.

Other important information system technology trends include the widening use of multimedia, fifth-generation computers, and network computers.

MULTIMEDIA

Multimedia
The integration of two or more types of media such as text, graphics, sound, full-motion video, or animation into a computer-based application.

Multimedia can be defined as the technologies that facilitate the integration of two or more types of media, such as text, graphics, sound, voice, full-motion video, still video, and/or animation into a computer-based application. By pressing a button a user can access a screen of text; another button might bring up video images. Still another might access related talk or music. Products and services that already use multimedia include imaging, graphics design tools, electronic books and newspapers, electronic presentations, interactive entertainment, multimedia video conferencing, and interactive kiosks. Many sites on the World Wide Web use multimedia.

Digitizing graphics, full-motion video, and sound produce enormous quantities of data, requiring high-capacity microprocessor, storage, and communications technology to meld text, graphics, sound, and video data into a single application. A simple multimedia system that can run multimedia applications can be constructed from a PC with a 32-bit microprocessor and a CD-ROM drive. A 5-inch optical disk holding more than 600 megabytes of information can store an hour of music, several thousand full-color pictures, several minutes of video or animation, and millions of words.

Figure 4.14 shows the input, output, and storage devices for a multimedia system that can be used to create and run multimedia applications:

- A PC with a 32-bit (or larger) microprocessor and 8 megabytes or more of RAM
- Special adapter cards (sound, video, and video compression cards) to digitize sound and video, integrate them into the computer, and digitally compress full-motion video
- A keyboard, mouse, or digitizer to input text and still images
- Microphones, CD players, music keyboards, and cassette players for audio input
- Camcorders, VCRs, and laser video disk players for video input
- CD-ROM drive
- A high-capacity hard disk (800 megabytes or more of storage)
- A very-high-resolution color monitor with a large screen
- Stereo speakers

FIGURE 4.14
Components of Multimedia Systems

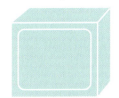

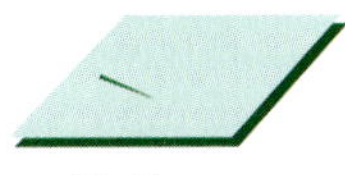

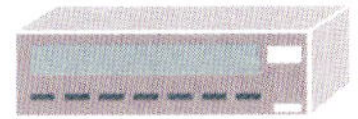

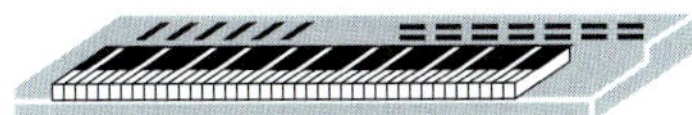

The most difficult element to incorporate into multimedia information systems has been full-motion video because so much data must be brought under the digital control of the computer. The process of actually integrating video with other kinds of data requires special software or compression boards with dedicated video processing chips. The massive amounts of data in each video image must be digitally encoded, stored, and manipulated electronically using techniques that "compress" the digital data.

Performance can be enhanced by using special microprocessors optimized for multimedia. Intel's MMX (MultiMedia eXtension) microprocessor is a Pentium chip that has been modified to increase performance in many applications featuring graphics and sound. Games, video, and other visually intensive software will be able to run more smoothly, with more colors, and be able to do more things at once. For example, multiple channels of audio, high-quality video or animation, and Internet communication could all be running in the same application.

SUPERCHIPS AND FIFTH-GENERATION COMPUTERS

Conventional computers are based on what is called the Von Neumann architecture, which processes information serially, one instruction at a time. In the 1940s, John Von Neumann, an influential mathematician at Princeton Univer-

Corporations are taking advantage of new multimedia software and hardware to train employees and to upgrade their work skills. Multimedia training permits people to respond to questions posed by the computer and to learn at their own pace.

SOURCE: Courtesy of International Business Machines Corporation Multimedia Training.

sity, sketched out the design elements of digital computers in which a computer works through a list of instructions one at a time. In contrast, "fifth-generation computers" are supercomputers designed to function like the human brain in the sense that they carry out multiple streams of activity at once.

In the future, more computers will use parallel and massively parallel processing to work on many parts of a problem at the same time, producing solutions 10 to 100 times faster than the most powerful sequential processors. **Massively parallel processing** harnesses very large numbers of processor chips interwoven in complex ways to solve a problem simultaneously. In contrast to parallel processing, which uses a small number of expensive, specialized microprocessor chips working together, massively parallel processing chains hundreds and even thousands of inexpensive, commonly used chips to work on a single computing problem. Massively parallel systems can achieve supercomputer speeds at as little as one-tenth to one-twentieth the cost of conventional parallel computers.

Massively parallel processing
Computer processing in which a very large number of inexpensive processor chips are chained together to work on a single computing problem simultaneously.

While contemporary supercomputers can perform hundreds of billions of calculations per second, massively parallel technology has made it possible to create super-supercomputers that can perform more than a trillion mathematical calculations each second—a teraflop. (The term *teraflop* comes from the Greek *teras,* which for mathematicians means 1 trillion, and *flop,* an acronym for floating point operations per second.) Teraflop machines will help scientific researchers in the twenty-first century to map the surface of planets and simulate the mechanisms of biological brains.[3]

LEADING-EDGE TECHNOLOGY: NETWORK COMPUTERS

If you purchase a personal computer, the figure on the price tag probably does not represent your total investment. You may need to purchase software or to upgrade that software as more powerful capabilities are added. You may need to repair your disk drive or add to RAM as time goes on. Now, imagine that you own a business that requires the use of PCs by most of your employees. How would you keep expenses bearable with tens or even hundreds of machines to maintain? Network computers are a front-running solution to this problem.

Network computers are smaller, simpler, and cheaper versions of the traditional personal computer. A network computer does not store any data permanently. Instead, users download any software and data they need from a central computer over the Internet or from an organization's own internal network. The central computer also saves information for the user and makes it available for later retrieval, effectively eliminating the need for hard disks, floppy disks, CD-ROMs, and their drives. A network computer need consist of little more than a gutted PC, a monitor, a keyboard, and a network connection.

Network computer
A pared-down desktop computer that does not store software programs or data permanently, obtaining them when they are needed over a network.

Network computers have their champions and critics. Network computers cost between $500 and $1,000 to purchase. They are considered less expensive to operate and maintain than a conventional PC. Most estimates place a corporation's yearly cost of owning a PC between $5,000 and $12,000. This includes maintenance, software upgrades, training, and troubleshooting help. Designers of network systems claim to be able to reduce that number by as much as 80 percent. They point to the following as factors in their favor:

Network computers have fewer components than PCs because they download the software and data users need from a network.

SOURCE: Courtesy of International Business Machines Corporation.

- A network computer unit itself costs significantly less than a PC.
- The network computer has fewer parts and is therefore less likely to experience problems.
- With only one central distribution point, software packages and applications do not have to be purchased and then updated for each user.
- All work can be saved on one backup system.
- Company secrets cannot be leaked, and software cannot be stolen because users have no way of copying from their machines to a secondary storage tool such as a disk drive.
- The system is protected from viruses because users cannot install their own applications.
- Worker efficiency increases because the management controls which software to make available and can eliminate distractions.

For business owners, perhaps the greatest advantage to computer networking lies in the control they can exert over daily operations. Every time a worker decides to take ten minutes to play a game or check a favorite Web site, money disappears. By supplying only essential programs from the mainframe, time wasting would diminish significantly. Also, if the network computers use a programming language such as Java, organizations will no longer have to purchase software for different brands of computers or specific operating systems (see Chapter 5).

Opposition to the very idea of a stripped-down, inexpensive computer has come from both PC makers and users. They acknowledge the convenience of network computers but question the necessity of removing all

TO NETWORK OR NOT TO NETWORK

Kevin Smith, director of corporate technology services at Pro Staff Inc., a temporary-services company in Minneapolis, is smiling. His company decided to install 700 network computers at 140 offices across the country. The NCs will let Pro Staff employees access the firm's customer-management system and other applications, all running on a computer at one of the company's computer centers.

With this arrangement, Pro Staff's information systems team of 13 can easily service hundreds of widely dispersed users. All applications, and changes to these applications, are controlled centrally in Minneapolis. If a user in the field experiences a problem, the information systems staff can provide immediate help by copiloting the application from his or her own desk. Employees traveling to another office can always log onto their own personal screen because their desktop isn't actually on a desktop. The system is also available to employees who don't use NCs. Salespeople with notebook computers and staff at headquarters using desktop PCs can still communicate with the system.

Other companies point to low purchase and maintenance costs as their rationale for switching to NCs. Don Resh, senior VP and CIO of Retired Persons Services Inc. in Alexandria, Virginia, the pharmaceutical group of the American Association of Retired Persons (AARP), runs one of the first large NC systems to be installed in the United States. It consists of 1,000 NCs at three locations, with 200 more to be installed later. According to Resh, "There's nothing a user can do to screw them up." The NC system requires much less technical support than 1,000 PCs. Resh calculates that five years of support and maintenance for 1,000 PCs would cost $35 million, compared with $2.5 million for the network computer system.

Holsten Medical Group, a physician practice in Kingsport, Tennessee, installed 250 NCs at its 13 clinics. Each examining room, doctor's office, and nurse's station has an NC to provide constant access to the group's medical records. Chip Childress, Holsten's information systems director, opted for NCs because the hardware is less expensive than PCs. Holsten wanted to have five terminals per doctor. At the time Holsten was making its decision, it could afford only 50 PCs for 50 doctors. Even with software costs, the affordability of the NCs let Holsten do what it wanted.

FOCUS Question: What people, organization, and technology factors should be addressed when considering whether to use network computers?

SOURCE: Edward Cone, "NCs Impress," *Information Week,* March 31, 1997.

independence from the computer. Some researchers believe that removing this technology would allow management to overregulate the network, stifling worker initiative and creativity. Several studies of the cost of owning PCs question whether the savings promised by network computers will actually be realized. The cost of licensing software for network use has not been firmly established. Some commercial software packages will require hourly usage rates on a network that could result in rather high fees. Once a company has switched to network computers, software and communications service providers could easily raise their fees, knowing that network computer users were "locked in." If a network failure occurred, no one could use his or her computer, whereas people could keep on working if they had full-function PCs. A poorly supervised network computer system could prove to be just as inefficient as PCs sometimes are.

Simplified network computers are being promoted by Sun Microsystems Inc., the creator of the Java programming language. Sun offered its Javastation network computer in the fall of 1996. IBM and Oracle have also aligned themselves on the side of the simplified network unit. Microsoft and Intel, each a driving force behind the PC explosion, originally dismissed the network computing concept as a step back to an earlier time in computer history. After some consideration, Microsoft and Intel now recognize the need for a more economical PC and have announced plans for their own version of the network computer. The NetPC features the same sharing capabilities as Sun Microsystems' Javastation but will also include a Windows operating system and an Intel chip allowing businesses to continue using the software they already have. Users would have some local processing and storage capability. PC manufacturers such as Compaq, Hewlett-Packard, Digital, and NEC indicated they would support the NetPC.[4]

The exact role network computers will play in the years to come remains somewhat unclear. The Focus on Problem Solving decribes how some organizations are deciding whether to use this technology.

SUMMARY

- The principal hardware components of a contemporary computer system are a central processing unit, primary storage, secondary storage devices, input devices, output devices, and communications devices.
- The central processing unit (CPU) is where the computer manipulates symbols, letters, and numbers. The CPU consists of an arithmetic-logic unit and a control unit.
- Primary storage stores program instructions and data being used by those instructions. Primary storage locations are called bytes. RAM and ROM are the principal semiconductor memory chips used with primary storage.
- The generations of computer hardware evolution are vacuum tube technology, transistor technology, integrated circuit technology, and very-large-scale integrated circuit technology.
- Computers can be classified as mainframes, minicomputers, personal computers (PCs), supercomputers, and workstations. Server computers are optimized for networks.
- The capabilities of microprocessors depend on their word length, bus width, and clock speed.
- Distributed processing distributes computer processing work among multiple computers linked by a communications network.
- The principal secondary storage devices are magnetic tape, magnetic disk, and optical disk.
- Optical disks use laser technology to store vast amounts of data in a compact space. CD-ROM disk systems can only be read from. WORM optical disk systems can write data supplied by the user only once but can be read many times. Rewritable optical disks are starting to be used.
- There are several approaches to input and processing: a batch approach, an online real-time approach, and an online input with delayed processing approach.
- The principal input devices are keyboards, touch screens, computer mice, digital scanners, pen-based input, magnetic and optical character recognition, voice input, and sensors.

- The principal output devices are printers, plotters, video display terminals, microfilm and microfiche, and audio output devices.
- Multimedia technology can integrate text, graphics, sound, and video into a single computer-based application.
- Network computers are stripped-down computers with no secondary storage and minimum processing power. They use a network to obtain software and store data on a large central computer.

KEY TERMS

Computer
Central processing unit (CPU)
Primary storage
Byte
Arithmetic-logic unit
Control unit
Machine cycle
Instruction cycle (I-cycle)
Execution cycle (E-cycle)
Register
RAM (random-access memory)
ROM (read-only memory)
PROM (programmable read-only memory)
EPROM (erasable programmable read-only memory)
Millisecond
Microsecond
Nanosecond
Picosecond
Kilobyte
Megabyte
Gigabyte
Terabyte
Bit
EBCDIC
ASCII
Microprocessor
Mainframe
Minicomputer
Personal computer (PC)
Distributed processing
Downsizing
Cooperative processing
Workstation
Supercomputer
Parallel processing
Server computer
Word length
Bus width
Megahertz (MHz)
RISC (reduced instruction set computing)
Secondary storage
Magnetic tape
Magnetic disk
Direct-access storage device (DASD)
Hard disk
RAID (redundant array of inexpensive disks)
Floppy disk
Sector
Optical disk
CD-ROM (compact disk/read-only memory)
WORM (write once, read many)
Digital video disk (DVD)
Computer mouse
Touch screen
Source data automation
Magnetic ink character recognition (MICR)
Optical character recognition (OCR)
Bar code

Pen-based input
Digital scanner
Voice input devices
Sensors
Batch input and processing
Online realtime processing
Printer
Plotter
Video display terminal (VDT)
CRT
Bit mapping
Audio output
Multimedia
Massively parallel processing
Network computer

REVIEW QUESTIONS

1. Name the components of a contemporary computer system and describe the functions of each.
2. Name the components of the CPU and describe the function of each.
3. What is the difference between RAM, ROM, and EPROM?
4. Name and define the principal measures of computer time and storage capacity.
5. How are data represented in a computer? Distinguish between a bit and a byte.
6. List the major generations of computers and the characteristics of each.
7. Define and describe the various categories of computers.
8. Define downsizing, distributed processing, and cooperative processing.
9. Name and describe the factors affecting the speed and performance of a microprocessor.
10. List and describe the major secondary storage media. What are the advantages and disadvantages of each?
11. List and describe the major input devices.
12. Distinguish among the following: batch input and processing; online input and real-time processing; online input with delayed processing.
13. List and describe the major output devices.
14. What is multimedia? What technologies does it involve?
15. What is the difference between serial, parallel, and massively parallel processing?
16. What is the difference between a network computer and a PC?

DISCUSSION QUESTIONS

1. How will various jobs and occupations change with the growing availability and power of microprocessor technology?

2. How do input, output, and storage technologies affect the design and performance of an information system?

PROBLEM-SOLVING EXERCISES

1. *Group exercise:* Divide into groups. Each group should use magazine articles and research materials available in your library to prepare a report and oral presentation on VDT safety. Each group's report and presentation should include conclusions about VDT hazards. If possible, each group should take a position for or against VDT legislation, and opposing groups should debate whether government should regulate how VDTs are used in the marketplace.

2. The Bancroft Chemical Corporation is required by law to store employee medical histories for 25 years. Currently, employee medical claim forms are stored in document retention centers, where they are very difficult to access. Write an analysis of how you could use information technologies to help Bancroft fulfill its legal requirements.

3. *Hands-on exercise:* Many organizations need to compile and analyze the information collected on handwritten paper forms. Use appropriate software to design and create an application that analyzes medical emergency report forms. The forms contain the following information:

Date	Patient Name	Age	Type of Accident	Trauma?	Medical Insurance?	Procedure Administered?
01/28/98	John Kelly	17	Auto	Y	N	Y
01/29/98	Audrey Stern	6	House	N	Y	N
02/03/98	Scott Schram	67	House	Y	Y	Y
02/05/98	Kara Wauters	33	Auto	N	Y	N
02/07/98	Pat Bohlen	18	Auto	Y	N	Y
02/12/98	Ben Thomas	51	House	Y	N	Y

Use your software to create a report or series of reports with the following information:

The total number of emergency report forms.

The number of reports in January 1998.

The total number of trauma cases.

The total number of emergency cases in which patients had no medical insurance coverage.

A list of all emergency patients under the age of 18 who had auto accidents.

4. *Internet problem-solving exercise:*
You work in the human resources department of your company and do analysis of employee records, insurance costs, adherence to government regulations, payroll data, and a great deal of other data. You need a new, more powerful desktop computer to carry out your responsibilities. You have set the following minimum requirements:

Speed	166 MHz
Memory (RAM)	16 MB
Monitor	17″ SVGA
Storage	2-gigabyte hard drive
CD-ROM drive	

Check the Web sites for buying a computer listed on the Laudon & Laudon Web site and find the lowest-priced computer that meets or surpasses your specifications.

NOTES

1. Mark Mehler, "Desktop Multimedia: Up to the Task?" *Beyond Computing,* June 1996; Clinton Wilder, "Data on a Silver Platter," *Information Week,* March 21, 1994.
2. Alan E. Bell, "Next-Generation Compact Discs," *Scientific American,* July 1996; Eric Brown, "Will Multimedia Make College Obsolete?" *Newmedia,* July 1993; and Terry Schwartz, "Corporate Paperwork Gets Sound and Action," *The New York Times,* July 7, 1993.
3. Otis Port, "Speed Gets a Whole New Meaning," *Business Week*, April 29, 1996.
4. Bob Francis, "How Much Will It Cost?" *Information Week*, March 3, 1997; Steve Lohr, "The Network Computer as the PC's Evil Twin," *The New York Times,* November 4, 1996; David Simpson, "Who Needs a Network Computer?" *Datamation,* October 1996.

PROBLEM-SOLVING CASE

STORING THE WORLD'S DOCUMENTS

Few organizations have documents as important to the entire world as the treaties signed by the nations of the world that are in the custody of the United Nations (UN). These treaties are the basis of world trade. They are essential to solving world health, hunger, and environmental problems. And they are fundamental to maintaining peace among nations. Therefore, these documents must be guarded carefully. They must be neither destroyed nor altered. In addition, governments and people from all over the world want and need access to them. The UN's problem has been how to achieve both the protection and access.

The 600,000 pages of international treaties that have been signed over the past 50 years have been stored in bound volumes that are not cross-indexed. Diplomats, reporters, researchers, and anyone else wanting to gain access to them had to go to UN headquarters in New York City and rifle through the volumes until they found the desired document—a process that could take several weeks. Meanwhile, these original documents were being handled and were subject to damage. To allow people rapid access to these documents from anywhere in the world (without having to go to New York and without having to handle the originals), the UN turned to document imaging and optical storage.

Using imaging technology, the United Nations is able to translate the documents into digital format and then read them into the computer. The documents are digitized using scanning hardware and software. As a result, copies of the text can be read and manipulated in word processors. Maps, pictures, and other graphic material are stored in graphic format so that copies can also be viewed and manipulated. Ron Van Note, the information systems consultant in charge of the project, turned to write once, read many (WORM) optical storage technology to store the document images. A WORM disk system enables the user to record only once, so that once stored the documents can never be altered. However, the optical disks can then be read as many times as needed using laser disk readers. The disks are stored in an optical jukebox (a device for storing many optical disks), where they are kept online for almost instant access. Each optical disk can store 1.3 gigabytes of data while the jukebox holds 32 disks, more than enough to contain all 600,000 pages of documents. Once the documents are scanned and then stored on these disks, the originals almost never need to be touched again and are thus protected from damage.

The project did go down one false-technology path. Because the treaties had been microfiched, Van Note tried to scan these copies into the computer, an approach that would have avoided handling the original documents. However, he quickly found that the documents scanned this way were less than 100 percent accurate and therefore of inadequate quality. The project swiftly abandoned this approach and went back to the originals as the source for scanning. They had learned that the quality of the stored document can be no better than the quality of the document that is scanned.

While the documents were being scanned, each page of each document needed to be indexed so that it could be easily found when needed. This presented a problem that corporations are also facing more and more—dealing with multiple languages. According to United Nations rules, all treaties must be written in both English and French as well as in all the languages of the signatories. Moreover, the various languages often are interspersed within one page. Thus, the indices themselves are a major complication.

Next, Van Note and the UN had to find ways to make the documents available to people throughout the United Nations and around the world. The first step was relatively simple. The United Nations already had in place an in-house local area network (LAN). All that needed to be done was to connect the jukebox and the document system to that LAN, and anyone within the UN could gain access. Van Note decided to connect the system to the Internet so that anyone could view the documents using a Web browser from anywhere on the globe without the UN's having to build a new network and without the viewer's having to obtain and support a viewing system. When completed, the project will also enable the UN to maintain a secure audit trail of the documents and the access to those documents.

SOURCE: Ron Levine, "Archiving and Distributing the United Nations' Documents," *Digital Publishing World,* February/March 1997.

CASE STUDY QUESTIONS

1. What people, organization, and technology issues did the UN have to address in selecting a document storage system?

2. What problems were solved for the UN with this project? What problems do you think were not solved?

3. Suggest other applications for which the combination of imaging and optical storage technologies is particularly appropriate. Also suggest whole industries where this technology would be especially applicable.

Chapter

→ FIVE ←

INFORMATION SYSTEMS SOFTWARE

CHAPTER OUTLINE

LEARNING OBJECTIVES

After reading and studying this chapter, you will

1. Understand the roles systems software and applications software play in information systems.
2. Be familiar with the generations of computer software.
3. Know how the operating system functions.
4. Understand the strengths and limitations of the major programming languages.
5. Be able to select appropriate software for business applications.

COLLEGE APPLICATIONS IN A FLASH

Remember when you were a high-school senior? The hardest part about getting into college was probably filling out all those applications. Completing one by hand or typewriter is tough enough, but filling out seven or eight might constitute cruel and unusual punishment.

Today, much of that ordeal can be eliminated thanks to software called Apply '97. The software is supplied on a CD-ROM with digitized applications to over 500 popular colleges, including top-ranked schools such as Harvard, Princeton, and Duke, small private colleges such as Bard and Kenyon, and even some state universities in Massachusetts and Illinois. All the college applicant need do is select a school, fill in the blanks on the screen, and hit the "print" button. Out comes a completed application with all the proper fonts and graphics, ready for mailing. Unlike filling out paper applications, if you make a mistake, you can simply delete it and correct it on the computer—no need for correction fluid. While Apply '97 won't write your application essays, it will allow you to paste a word-processing document directly onto the form.

The software was produced by Apply Technology of Burlington, Massachusetts. It is available free of charge because companies such as Apple Computer, Chase Manhattan, Citibank, Amtrak, J. Crew, Discover Card, Saturn, and Sprint paid for the software development in exchange for some subtle on-screen advertising.

Apply '97 actually consists of two software programs. One provides an on-screen interview to help students match their academic records and personal preferences to a database of 1,200 colleges and universities. The other software program contains the computerized school applications. These computerized versions actually look like the real application forms. Apply Technology guarantees that the admissions offices of the participating colleges and universities have agreed to accept applications created with Apply '97.

Another valuable feature of the software is that it remembers what was typed into the first application. When you fill out a new one, the program fills in the corresponding blanks. You need type your name, address, telephone number, and Social Security numbers only once. But while the software works well at replicating basic items such as names and addresses, it isn't consistent with other items—you'll still want to proofread your applications. Although the publisher claims that Apply '97 can run on a 486 PC with 8 megabytes of memory, it really needs a minimum of 16 megabytes of memory and a Pentium processor to run effectively. More memory is advisable if you want to run a Web browser simultaneously; the software comes with links to many college sites on the World Wide Web. Even with these drawbacks, Apply '97 beats wading through a stack of paper applications.

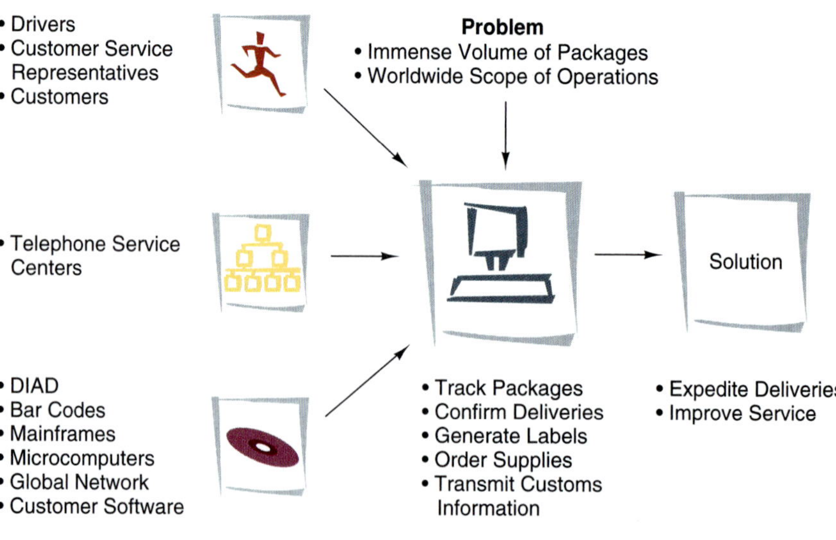

SOURCE: Michael J. Himowitz, "College Applications 1-2-3," *Fortune,* November 25, 1996.

The capabilities of Apply '97 illustrate some of the ways that software can enhance the problem-solving process. Without such software, students could not use their computer hardware to prepare college applications. Special software had to be written to tell the computer how to collect, store, process, and display the information required in a college application and how to link the computer to World Wide Web sites on the Internet.

This chapter shows how computer software and computer hardware combine into useful information systems. We describe the features and capabilities of the two major types of software, systems and application software, and show how to select appropriate software for problem solving.

5.1 INTRODUCTION

Software refers to the detailed instructions that control the operation of computer hardware. Without the instructions provided by software, computer hardware is unable to perform any of the tasks we associate with computers. Software has three principal functions: (1) it develops the tools for applying computer hardware to problem solving; (2) it enables an organization to manage its computer resources; and (3) it serves as an intermediary between an organization and its stored information.

SOFTWARE PROGRAMS

A software **program** is a series of statements or instructions to the computer. The process of writing or coding the program is called programming, and the individual who performs this task is called a programmer.

Program
A series of statements or instructions to the computer.

In order to execute, or have its instructions performed by the computer, a program must be stored in the computer's primary storage along with the required data. This is called the **stored-program concept.** Once a program finishes executing, the computer hardware can be used for another task by loading a new program into primary storage.

Stored-program concept
The concept that a program cannot be executed unless it is stored in the computer's primary storage along with the required data.

MAJOR TYPES OF SOFTWARE

The two major types of software are systems software and applications software. Each handles a different set of problems.

Systems software consists of generalized programs that manage computer resources such as the central processing unit (CPU), printers, terminals, communications links, and other peripheral equipment. In other words, systems software serves as the intermediary between the software used by end users and the computer itself.

Systems software
Generalized software that manages computer resources such as the CPU, printers, terminals, communications links, and peripheral equipment.

Applications software consists of programs designed for applying the computer to solve a specific problem. Payroll-processing programs or sales order entry programs are examples of applications software. Systems software provides the platform on which applications software runs. The relationships among people, the two different kinds of software, and computer hardware are illustrated in Figure 5.1. As the figure shows, people send

Applications software
Programs designed to handle the processing for a particular computer application.

FIGURE 5.1

The Relationships between Hardware, Systems Software, Applications Software, and the User

Software serves as the intermediary between people and computer hardware. Most of the software that business professionals use directly is applications software. Systems software coordinates the various parts of the computer system and transforms instructions from applications software into instructions that will operate the hardware. Information flows both ways; the results of the hardware's operations travel through the systems software, and the applications programs transform them into results that people can use.

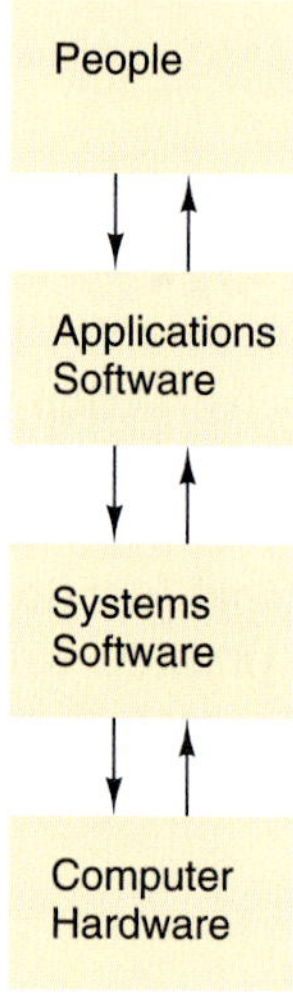

instructions to the applications software, which "translates" the instructions for the systems software, which in turn forwards them to the hardware. Information flows in two directions: from the person using the computer to the hardware and back again.

GENERATIONS OF SOFTWARE

The sophistication and range of problems that can be addressed by programming languages can be attributed to the increased capacity of computer hardware. Just as computer hardware evolved over time, software has developed over several generations.

Machine language
The programming language used in the first generation of computer software; consists of strings of binary digits (0 and 1).

The first generation of computer software was **machine language.** Machine language, consisting of strings of the binary digits 0 and 1, was the only way to communicate with the primitive computers of the 1940s. It took highly trained, specialized programmers to understand, think, and work directly with the machine language of a particular computer. Machine language instructions must specify the storage location for every instruction and data item used. Consequently, writing software in this language was excruciatingly slow and labor intensive; very few problems could be addressed this way.

Machine language is no longer used to develop software, having been replaced by symbolic and high-level languages. Symbolic languages, or assembly languages, use symbols and alphabetic abbreviations in place of the 0s and 1s of machine language for representing operation codes, storage locations, and data elements. **High-level languages** consist of statements that, to varying degrees, resemble natural languages (e.g., English).

High-level language
A programming language that consists of statements that, to some degree, resemble a natural language such as English.

Assembly language
A programming language used for second-generation software; consists of natural language-like acronyms and words such as add, sub(tract), and load and is considered a symbolic language.

The second generation of software, which began in the early 1950s, consisted of **assembly language.** Assembly language is considered a symbolic language because it consists of language-like acronyms and words such as add, sub (for "subtract"), and load. Today, assembly language has limited use for problems that require maximum execution efficiency or highly intricate manipulations.

Third-generation computer software, which prevailed from the late 1950s to the 1970s, featured high-level languages that were more sophisticated, easier to use, and directed toward specialized classes of problems. High-level languages also are less machine dependent and often can be used on more than one type of computer. Popular third-generation languages include FORTRAN (FORmula TRANslator) for scientific and mathematical problems, COBOL (COmmon Business-Oriented Language) for business problems requiring extensive file manipulation and large lists, and BASIC (Beginner's All-Purpose Symbolic Instruction Code), a generalized programming language popular for microcomputers. Third-generation software is still in wide use today.

Fourth-generation software was developed in the late 1970s and is widely used today for application development. Fourth-generation tools include query software, report generators, graphics software, application generators, and other tools that dramatically reduce programming time and make some development tasks easy enough to be performed by nontechnical specialists.

The first three generations of software languages were procedural. Program instructions had to detail a sequence of steps, or procedures, telling the computer what to do and how to do it. In contrast, fourth-generation software has nonprocedural features. Program instructions need specify only *what* has to be accomplished rather than provide details about *how* to carry out the task. Consequently, the same process can be accomplished with

Speech scientist Vladimir Sejnoha carefully analyzes Kurzweil applied intelligence voice recognition software for mistakes. The screen displays the pattern made when the word *baby* is spoken. Voice input technology is useful for applications where the input consists primarily of simple spoken commands.

SOURCE: © Hank Morgan, Rainbow.

fewer program steps and lines of program code than with third-generation languages.

Some fourth-generation software has natural-language features, meaning that commands are expressed in English-language form. Offices and factories are starting to take advantage of voice recognition software, in which users communicate with computers through spoken commands. For example, the Boeing Company uses voice recognition software in its receiving and warehousing operations. Instead of handwriting information about incoming parts and having clerks enter the information into a computer, workers describe each incoming part by speaking. The software converts what is said into computer input. High-end voice recognition software can recognize natural speech patterns and consider the context of an entire phrase.[1] Software will increasingly feature more prominent use of such natural-language tools, as well as graphical interfaces, touch screens, and other features that will make it easier for nontechnical specialists to use.

5.2 SYSTEMS SOFTWARE

Operating system
The systems software that manages and controls the activities of the computer.

Systems software consists of programs that coordinate the various parts of a computer system and mediate between applications software and computer hardware. The **operating system** is the systems software that manages and controls the activities of the computer. It supervises the operation of the CPU; controls input, output, and storage activities; and provides various support services. Other vital services, such as computer language translation facilities and utility programs for common processing tasks, are provided by language translators and utility programs (discussed later in this chapter).

THE OPERATING SYSTEM

The operating system can be visualized as the chief manager of the computer system. Like a human manager in a firm, the operating system determines which computer resources will be used for solving which problems and the order in which they will be used. As shown in Figure 5.2, the operating system has three principal functions:

- Allocating and assigning system resources
- Scheduling the use of resources and computer jobs
- Monitoring computer system activities

Allocation and Assignment A master control program called a supervisor, executive, or monitor oversees computer operations and coordinates all of the computer's work. The supervisor, which remains in primary storage, brings other programs from secondary storage to primary storage when they are needed. As each program is activated, the supervisor transfers control to that program. Once that program ends, control returns to the supervisor.

A command language translator controls the assignment of system resources. The command language translator reads special instructions to the

FIGURE 5.2

The Tasks of the Operating System

The operating system is the systems software that manages the computer's operations. It has three major roles: It allocates hardware resources as needed; it schedules the various functions, such as input and output; and it monitors the functioning of the system.

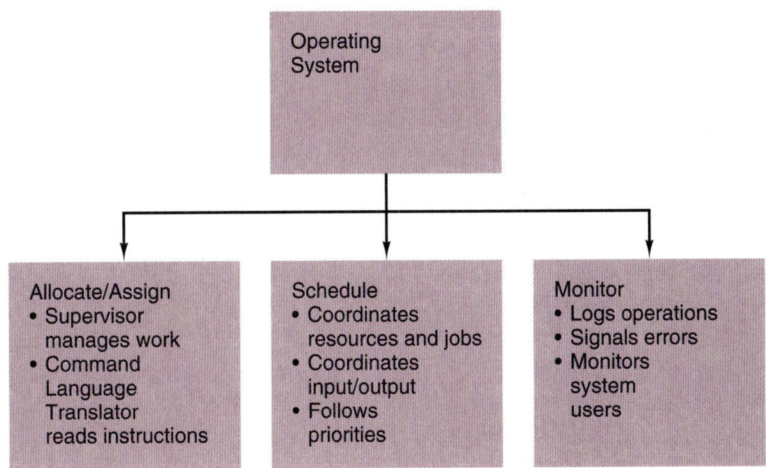

operating system that contain specifications for retrieving, saving, deleting, copying, or moving files; selecting input/output devices; selecting programming languages and applications programs; and performing other processing requirements for a particular application. These instructions are called command language.

Scheduling Thousands of pieces of work can be going on in a computer at the same time. The operating system decides when to schedule them—computer jobs are not necessarily performed in the order in which they are submitted. For example, payroll or online order processing may have a higher priority than other kinds of work. Other processing jobs, such as software program testing, would have to wait until these jobs were finished or left enough computer resources free to accommodate them.

The operating system coordinates scheduling in various areas of the computer so that different parts of different jobs can be worked on simultaneously. For example, while some programs are executing, the operating system is also scheduling the use of input and output devices.

Monitoring The operating system is also responsible for keeping track of the activities in the computer system. It maintains logs of job operations, notifying end users or computer operators of any abnormal terminations or error conditions. It also terminates programs that run longer than the maximum time allowed.

Operating system software may also contain security monitoring features, such as recording who has logged on and off the system, what programs they have run, and any unauthorized attempts to access the system. Security issues are explored in greater detail in Chapter 12.

If a computer can execute only one instruction from one program at a time, how can thousands of American Airlines reservation clerks use the computer simultaneously to book flights? How can American Airlines run its online reservation software 24 hours a day and still use its computers for accounting and other activities? Operating system software has special capabilities for these purposes.

Multiprogramming
The concurrent use of a computer by several programs; one program uses the CPU while the others use other components such as input and output devices.

Multiprogramming **Multiprogramming** allows multiple programs to use the computer's resources at the same time through concurrent use of the CPU. Only one program actually uses the CPU at any given moment, but at this same instant the other programs can use the computer for other needs, such as input and output. Thus, a number of programs can be active in the computer at the same time, but they do not use the same computer resources simultaneously.

Figure 5.3 shows three programs (1, 2, and 3) stored in primary storage. The first program (1) uses the CPU to execute until it comes to an input/output event (in this case, output). The CPU then moves to the second incoming program and directs a communications channel (a small processor limited to input/output processing functions) to read the input and move the output to a printer or other output device. The CPU executes the second program until an input/output statement occurs. It then switches to program 3, moving back and forth among all three programs until they have all finished executing.

The advantage of multiprogramming is that it enables computers to be used much more efficiently. Before multiprogramming, computers were a single-program environment; only one program at a time could be executed. The CPU had to stop and wait whenever a program had to read input or write output. With multiprogramming, more problems can be solved at the same time using a single computer.

Multitasking
The multiprogramming capability of single-user operating systems such as those for PCs; it enables the user to run two or more programs at once on a single computer.

Multitasking **Multitasking** refers to multiprogramming capability on single-user operating systems such as those for PCs. It enables one person to

FIGURE 5.3

Multiprogramming Uses the CPU More Efficiently

Early computers could execute only one software program at a time. This meant that the CPU had to stop all processing until the program it had just processed finished outputting. Multiprogramming means that the systems software allows the CPU to work on several programs simultaneously (see panel b). Even though the computer can still *process* only one program at a time, it can simultaneously perform input and output functions on other programs.

(a) Single Program Environment

Operating System
Program 1
Unused Memory

(b) Multiprogramming

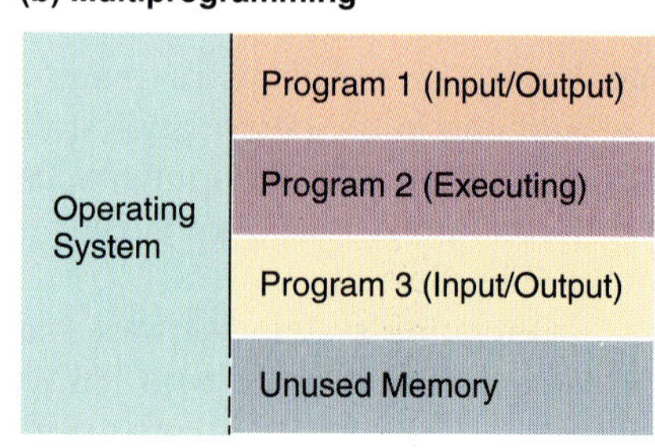

run two or more programs concurrently on a single computer. For example, a stockbroker could write a letter to clients with a word-processing program while simultaneously using another program to record and update client account information. Multitasking enables the broker to display both programs on the computer screen and work with them at the same time instead of having to terminate the session with the word-processing program, return to the operating system, and then initiate a session with the program that handles client account information.

Multiprocessing The use of two or more CPUs linked together to work in parallel is **multiprocessing.** Two CPUs may be assigned to execute different instructions from the same program simultaneously so that they can be accomplished more rapidly than on a single machine, or instructions from more than one program can be processed simultaneously. The operating system is responsible for scheduling and coordinating the tasks of the various processors. The two CPUs can "communicate," or exchange information, in order to execute programs more efficiently.

Multiprocessing
The simultaneous use of two or more CPUs under common control to execute different instructions for the same program or multiple programs.

Time Sharing A technique that enables many users to share computer resources simultaneously is **time sharing.** It differs from multiprogramming in that the computer spends a fixed amount of time on one program before proceeding to another. Each user is allocated a tiny slice of time (say, two milliseconds). The computer performs whatever operations it can for that user in the allocated time and then releases two milliseconds to the next user. (In multiprogramming, the computer works on one program until it reaches a logical stopping point, such as an input/output event. Then the computer starts processing another program.)

In a typical time-sharing environment, a CPU is connected to thousands of users at terminals. Many people can be connected to the same CPU simultaneously, with each receiving a tiny amount of CPU time. Because computers now operate at the nanosecond level, the CPU can actually do a great deal of processing in two milliseconds.

Time sharing
A technique in which many users share computer resources simultaneously (e.g., one CPU with many terminals); the computer spends a fixed amount of time on each user's program before proceeding to the next.

Virtual Storage **Virtual storage** is a way of splitting up programs so that the operating system can manage them more efficiently. Before virtual storage was developed in the early 1970s, only a few programs could be loaded into primary storage. A certain portion of primary storage usually remained underutilized because the programs did not take up the total amount of space available. In addition, very large programs could not be loaded as whole programs in primary storage. Programmers had to split up such programs to find portions that would fit into limited memory space.

Virtual storage is based on the realization that only a few program statements can actually be used by the computer at any one time. Virtual storage divides programs into fixed-length portions called pages (each page is approximately 2–4 kilobytes) or into variable-length portions called segments.

A page is read into the CPU when needed. All other program pages are stored in secondary storage, or disk, until they are required. When it is no longer needed, a page is sent back to secondary storage. The CPU executes the instructions from each page and then moves on, either to the next page

Virtual storage
A way of dividing programs into small fixed- or variable-length portions with only a small portion stored in primary memory at one time so that programs can be used more efficiently by the computer.

FIGURE 5.4

Virtual Storage Expands the Computer's Memory

Virtual storage is a feature of operating systems that expands the potential memory of the computer. Software programs are split into portions called pages (fixed length, as shown here) or segments (variable length). The pages are stored in secondary storage and shuttled into and out of main memory as needed for processing. Thus the CPU can process pieces of many programs almost simultaneously.

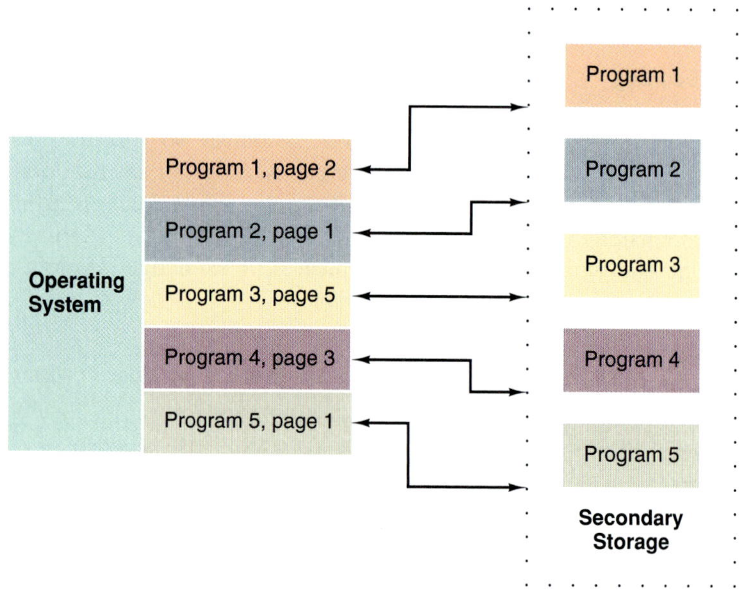

of the program or to a page from a different program (see Figure 5.4). Many portions of programs, broken down into pages, can reside in primary storage at once. All other program pages are stored in a secondary storage peripheral disk unit until they are required for execution.

Virtual storage has several advantages. Not only does it promote fuller utilization of the CPU, but programmers no longer have to worry about program size because any program can be broken down into pages or segments. In addition, large programs do not need large machines to run; they can be executed on smaller computers.

LANGUAGE TRANSLATORS AND UTILITY PROGRAMS

Source code
Program statements in a high-level language that are translated by systems software into machine language so that the high-level programs can be executed by the computer.

Object code
The machine-language version of source code after it has been translated into a form usable by the computer.

Compiler
A language translator program that translates an entire high-level language program into machine language.

Another important function of systems software is to translate high-level language programs into machine language so that they can be executed by the computer. The program statements in the high-level language are called **source code,** and the machine-language version is called **object code.** Before actually being executed by the computer, object code modules normally are joined together with other object code modules in a process called linkage editing. The result, called the load module, is what the computer executes.

There are three kinds of language translator programs: compilers, interpreters, and assemblers. A **compiler** translates an entire high-level language program into machine language. An **interpreter** translates each source code statement, one at a time, into machine code and executes it. Consequently, interpreted programs run more slowly than compiled programs. Many versions of BASIC use interpreters. An **assembler** is similar to a compiler but is used only for assembly languages (see Section 5.3). Figure 5.5 illustrates the language translation process for a compiler, the most common type.

Interpreter
A language translator program that translates a high-level language program into machine code by translating one statement at a time and executing it.

Assembler
A program that translates assembly language into machine code so that it can be used by the computer.

Utility Programs Systems software typically includes utility programs for important but common, routine, repetitive tasks, such as sorting records or copying programs from tape to disk. Utility programs are stored in libraries where they can be shared by all users of a computer system.

FIGURE 5.5

Language Translation

A compiler translates software that people use into instructions that the computer can use. The compiler transforms high-level language instructions (called source code) into their machine language equivalent (object code). A linkage editor combines modules of object code with those from other incoming programs into a load module, the group of instructions that the computer follows.

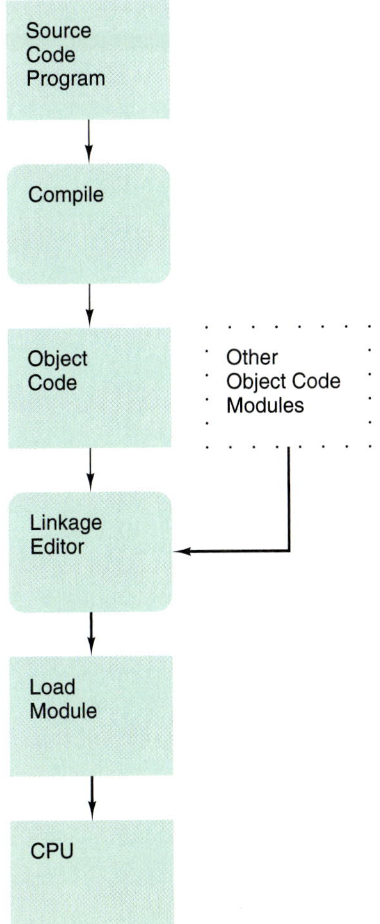

GRAPHICAL USER INTERFACES

Graphical user interface (GUI)
The feature of an operating system that uses graphical symbols, or icons; rather than typing in commands, the user moves the cursor to the appropriate icon by rolling a mouse on a desktop.

When people work with a computer, the interaction is controlled by an operating system. Users interact with the operating system through the user interface of that operating system. Users communicated with earlier operating systems by using text-based commands. For instance, to delete a file named FILED using the older DOS operating system for PCs, the user would have to type the command DELETE FILED. In contrast, a **graphical user interface** (often called a **GUI**) uses icons, buttons, bars, and boxes instead of text-based commands to represent common operations. Icons are symbolic pictures that are used in GUIs to represent programs and files. Commands are activated by rolling a mouse to move the cursor to the appropriate icon and clicking a button on the mouse to make a selection. Many GUIs use a system of pull-down menus to help users select commands and pop-up boxes to help users select among various command options. Windowing features allow users to create, stack, size, and move various boxes of information.

How do GUIs affect problem solving? Proponents claim that they are easier to master for computing novices without prior training. For example,

Windows 95 has a streamlined graphical user interface that arranges icons to provide instant access to common tasks.

FOCUS ON **PEOPLE**

ARE GUIs THE ULTIMATE USER INTERFACES?

The graphical user interface (GUI) was one of the great computer developments of the past decade because it made it easy for ordinary people (those who are not computer experts) to use computers. No technical terminology had to be learned to issue commands—just point the mouse at an easy-to-understand icon and click. So far, the GUI has depended on the use of graphics and icons, and such technology has its limits.

In the early days of personal computers, people communicated with the computer via the keyboard. Commands were frequently confusing and all but required the user to be a programmer. The use of icons became popular after Apple introduced its personal computers in 1984. It was a gigantic leap—the icon culture became enmeshed with pride in not having to use any words at all.

At first, icons were easy to understand. A picture of an opening manila file folder represented the command to open a file. A blank sheet of paper represented the setup for a new document. A "trash" icon represented the delete command. But problems arose as computer users developed wider applications—spreadsheets, graphics, telecommunications. As each application became more sophisticated, more functions were added, each requiring a new icon. GUI developers discovered that many actions are difficult to depict as icons. How, for example, is it made clear that one small picture deletes a document, another deletes a paragraph, a third deletes a line, and yet a fourth deletes a word?

Attempts at solutions can aid individual users but cause confusion among groups. For example, some applications, such as Microsoft Windows, include software to allow users to make their own icons or modify existing icons. These solutions may work well for an isolated computer user but can cause serious problems when people share computers.

Other issues complicate the problem. Many blind people are stymied by graphical user interfaces. They can use text-to-speech "screen readers" and keyboards that work with the character-based DOS operating system but not with graphical user interfaces, including Internet Web browsers. Text-based Internet sites opened up a new world of information to blind users. But the World Wide Web is becoming increasingly graphic intensive and mouse-driven—another problem for blind users, who need keyboards. As companies put applications on graphic-intensive Web sites, they may be closing the door on both employees and customers who are sight impaired. According to Dan Oliver, director of information systems at the Massachusetts Commission on the Blind (who is himself blind), the GUI nature of the Web raises major concerns because "people may start to lose their jobs over this. Some already have."

Some technology solutions are being developed. Microsoft's Internet Explorer Web browser software has a text-only option for screen readers. A version of the Netscape Navigator Web browser runs on IBM's OS/2 Warp 4, which has speech recognition capabilities that can aid visually impaired users. PWWebSpeak from Productivity Works in Trenton, New Jersey, is a speaking Web browser designed to understand the software used to create Website pages.

FOCUS Questions:
What are the strengths and problems of graphical user interfaces? What other approaches to user interfaces might be successful?

SOURCES: Mindy Blodgett, "Blind Users Stymied by New Internet Graphics," *Computerworld,* September 30, 1996, and Dave Kansas, "The Icon Crisis: Tiny Pictures Cause Confusion," *The Wall Street Journal,* November 17, 1993.

using the Macintosh PC operating system GUI, a file can be deleted simply by dragging the file icon to the "trash" icon. A complex series of commands can be issued by linking icons. Commands are standardized from one program to the next, so new programs can often be used without additional training or studying reference manuals. For example, the steps involved in printing a letter created by a word-processing program or a financial statement generated by a spreadsheet program should be the same. GUIs also encourage solutions communicated through graphics.

However, GUIs have not fully achieved these possibilities. The Focus on People shows that graphical symbols are not always easy to use or to understand.

PC OPERATING SYSTEMS

Personal computer software is based on specific operating systems and machines. Operating systems software defines the "personality" of the computer by specifying the way in which programs are controlled, files are stored and retrieved, and how the system's hardware components are held together. Software written to run on a specific PC operating system can't run on another. To use PCs effectively, one must understand the capabilities of their operating systems software.

DOS
An operating system for 16-bit microcomputers based on the IBM microcomputer standard.

Table 5.1 compares the leading PC operating systems—DOS, Windows 95 (and Windows 98), Windows NT, OS/2, UNIX, and the Macintosh operating system. **DOS** (which stands for Disk Operating System) was the most popular operating system for IBM and IBM-compatible 16-bit personal computers. There are two versions of DOS: PC-DOS, used exclusively with IBM PCs, and MS-DOS, used with other personal computers with 16-bit processors that function like the IBM PC. DOS is no longer widely used because it

TABLE 5.1

PC Operating Systems: A Comparison

Operating System	Features
Windows 95 and Windows 98	32-bit operating system with a streamlined GUI and the capability to run programs requiring more than 640 K of memory. Supports multitasking and has built-in networking and Internet capabilities.
Windows NT	32-bit operating system for powerful PCs and workstations in networked environments that is not limited to Intel microprocessors. Supports multitasking, networking, and multiprocessing and can run programs requiring more than 640 K of memory.
DOS	Operating system for IBM (PC-DOS) and IBM-compatible (MS-DOS) PCs. Uses text-based commands and limits use of memory to programs requiring less than 640 K.
OS/2	Operating system for IBM and IBM-compatible PCs. Can take advantage of the 32-bit microprocessor. Supports multitasking and networking and can run large programs requiring more than 640 K of memory.
UNIX	Operating system for powerful PCs, workstations, and minicomputers that is portable to different models of hardware. Supports multitasking, multiuser processing, and networking.
Mac OS	Operating system for the Macintosh computer. Supports multitasking and has powerful graphics, and multimedia, and Internet capabilities.

has a number of limitations: It requires text-based commands and it cannot take advantage of the power of today's 32-bit microprocessors because it can address data in only 16-bit chunks. DOS can run only one application at a time, and it limits the size of a program in memory to 640 K.

Microsoft **Windows,** a GUI shell that runs in conjunction with the underlying operating system, provides DOS with a graphical user interface. Windows supports limited forms of multitasking and networking but can run programs using only 640 K of memory or less. Early versions of Windows had problems with application crashes when multiple programs contended for the same memory space.

Windows
A GUI shell that runs in conjunction with the DOS operating system.

Microsoft's **Windows 95** is a complete operating system designed to replace DOS or DOS running Windows. It is a 32-bit operating system, achieving much more power and speed than DOS because it can address data in 32-bit chunks. It can run software written for DOS and Windows, but it can also run programs taking up more memory than 640 K. Windows 95 features a simplified graphical user interface that arranges icons to provide instant access to common tasks, multitasking, and multithreading (the ability to manage multiple independent tasks simultaneously). This operating system has powerful networking capabilities, including built-in fax, E-mail, and Internet access.

Windows 95 (Windows 98)
A powerful 32-bit operating system with a streamlined graphical user interface and built-in multitasking, networking, and Internet capabilities.

Windows 98, the newest version of the Windows operating system, provides further integration with the Internet. It provides an alternative interface so that users can look at their desktop information or the Internet and Web through a single interface and includes a built-in Web browser and Web publishing tools. It also supports technologies such as the MMX multimedia processor and the digital video disk (DVD) standard.

Windows NT, also developed by Microsoft Corporation, is a powerful yet flexible operating system designed for large applications in networked environments with massive memory and data requirements. There are two versions of NT: a server version for the network's server computer and a workstation version for the computers connected to the network. NT features the same GUI as Windows 95 but has even more powerful multitasking and memory management capabilities. Windows NT can run software written for DOS and Windows but was designed to take advantage of 32-bit microprocessors. It can support multiprocessing with multiple CPUs. Windows NT can be used with Intel microprocessors as well as workstations and PCs based on other microprocessors such as DEC's Alpha chip. The server version of NT has capabilities for developing Web pages and operating a server for Web pages.

Windows NT
A powerful operating system for use with 32-bit microprocessors in networked environments; supports multitasking and multiprocessing and can be used with Intel and some other types of microprocessors.

OS/2 (Operating System/2) is a robust operating system that can support multitasking and is used with powerful 32-bit IBM or IBM-compatible PCs. OS/2 runs faster than DOS because it can address data in 32-bit chunks and is useful for applications that require massive amounts of memory (e.g., networking or multitasking). It can run large, complex programs that require more than 640 K of memory. It provides a powerful desktop computer with many of the capabilities of mainframe operating systems, such as the ability to run multiple applications simultaneously and support for multiple users in networks. OS/2 is a more protected operating system than Windows running under DOS; an application that crashes is less likely to disrupt other applications or the entire operating system. OS/2 can run DOS and Windows applications at the same time in its own resizable

OS/2
A powerful operating system used with 32-bit IBM PCs that supports multitasking and multiple users in networks.

UNIX
A machine-independent operating system for microcomputers, minicomputers, and mainframes; it is interactive and supports multiuser processing, multitasking, and networking.

windows, and it has its own graphical user interface. Later versions of OS/2, called OS/2 Warp, have multimedia, voice recognition, and Internet access capabilities.

UNIX, which was developed at Bell Laboratories in 1969 to link different types of computers together, is an interactive, multiuser, multitasking operating system that is highly supportive of communications and networking. Many people can use UNIX simultaneously, or one user can run many tasks

FOCUS ON TECHNOLOGY

LONDON BEGINS TRADING IN UNIX FOR WINDOWS NT

Why would London's financial market companies be changing operating systems, moving from UNIX into Windows NT? Before we can answer such a question, we must first understand the computing needs of the industry. The financial markets deal with massive amounts of data that are constantly changing, so it is critical that financial systems be stable and reliable. Also, traders need computers on their desks that not only operate very fast but can calculate prices and projected values on several financial instruments simultaneously. Most traders are not willing to work with a system unless its interface is easy to use. Finally, systems must be quick and easy to program because of the continual appearance of new types of investments.

UNIX has been the obvious operating system in the past because of its lead in the two most critical areas—its known stability and its great speed. Yet UNIX has not been satisfactory because its interface is difficult to use. Moreover, program development under UNIX is slow and expensive and requires highly trained professionals. On the other hand, Windows NT interfaces are known to be user friendly and are familiar to users throughout the world. In addition, small programs can be quickly and easily developed using programming tools that operate under Windows. Until recently, Windows NT would not have been suitable for London financial companies. It has long been considered both slow and unstable. Two developments have changed all that and given Windows NT a growing edge.

Microsoft has been steadily improving Windows NT over the years, and since the release of version 3.5, the operating system has gained the reputation of genuine stability. People in the financial industry have now begun to trust it. In the case of its lack of speed, however, the source of the problem was not the software but the computer chip. Windows NT runs primarily on Intel's family of PC processing chips, which have been slow compared with the chips used to run the UNIX workstations. The problem was addressed several years ago with the release of the faster, 32-bit Pentium chips, but even these were too slow because they were engineered to run existing 16-bit software. Intel subsequently released the Pentium Pro chip, a true, dedicated 32-bit operations chip. Using the Pentium Pro, financial trading systems not only run very fast but can now recalculate four different financial instruments simultaneously. Windows NT finally can compete with UNIX in speed and reliability while it outclasses UNIX in ease of use and development speed.

Two other factors have influenced the competition in London between UNIX and Windows NT. UNIX financial systems usually run on costly Sun workstations. Windows NT systems run on desktop computers that sell for less than one-third their price. The cost per MIPS (million instructions per second) is much lower using Windows NT systems. Moreover, Windows NT-based financial industry commercial software is now becoming available. For example, a leading risk management system, Monarch by SunGard, has been released in a Windows NT version but is only partially available in a UNIX version.

FOCUS Questions:
What people, organization, and technology factors would you consider in deciding whether to move from UNIX to Windows NT? Why do you think the move to Windows NT in the United Kingdom has appeared first in the financial trading market?

SOURCE: Andy Webb, "London's Falling for NT," *Wall Street & Technology*, April 1996.

on UNIX concurrently. UNIX was initially designed for minicomputers, but now there are versions for PCs and mainframes. At present, UNIX is primarily used for workstations, minicomputers, and server computers in multiuser environments. Applications software that runs under UNIX can be transported from one computer to another with little modification.

UNIX does have limitations. It uses a complicated set of commands. (Some versions offer a graphical user environment to address this problem.) It cannot respond well to problems caused by overuse of computer resources. It has weak security features because it allows multiple users and multiple computer jobs to access the same file simultaneously. It requires huge amounts of RAM and disk storage capacity. There are several versions of UNIX, and each is slightly different.

Mac OS, the latest version of Macintosh system software, supports multitasking and networking and has a highly praised graphical user interface. It can take advantage of the power of 32-bit microprocessors. Multimedia capabilities of this operating system allow Macintosh users to integrate video clips, stereo sound, and animated sequences with conventional text and graphics software. (See Chapter 4 for a discussion of multimedia.) New features of this operating system allow users to connect to, explore, and publish on the Internet and World Wide Web.

Mac OS
Operating system for the Macintosh microcomputer, with multitasking, graphics, Internet, and multimedia capabilities.

As this brief survey suggests, the various PC operating systems offer a variety of features as well as advantages and disadvantages. Therefore, when selecting a PC operating system, one should ask several key questions:

What kind of computer hardware is required? How much processing power and storage capacity are required to run the operating system?

What kinds of applications software does it support?

How easy is it to learn and use?

How quickly does it run?

Are many problems anticipated that would best be solved in a multitasking environment?

Is the operating system primarily designed for single users or for networking?

How much technical and support assistance is available?

The Focus on Technology shows how London financial market companies used these criteria when selecting a new operating system.

5.3 PROGRAMMING LANGUAGES AND TOOLS

Each major kind of software consists of programs written in specific programming languages. Each programming language was designed to solve a particular class of problems. It is important to understand the strengths and limitations of each of these languages and other programming tools in order to select appropriate software.

MAJOR PROGRAMMING LANGUAGES

Assembly Language As explained in Section 5.1, assembly language was developed to overcome some of the difficulties of machine language. Mnemonic (easy-to-remember) codes and symbols are used to represent operations (such as adding or moving) and storage locations. For example, A stands for "Add," and L stands for "Load." Assembly language is very machine oriented because assembly-language instructions correspond closely to the machine-language instructions for a specific computer and specific microprocessor. Each assembly-language instruction corresponds to a single machine-language instruction (see Figure 5.6).

Assembly language emphasizes efficient use of computer resources. Minimal memory and CPU activity are required for processing with assembly language. Therefore, execution of assembly-language programs is extremely rapid and efficient.

Although assembly language is easier to use than pure machine language, it is still extremely difficult to learn and requires highly skilled programmers. Assembly language is used primarily for writing operating systems software, when highly detailed programs that are sensitive to a specific computer's machine language must be designed.

FORTRAN
A programming language developed in 1954 for scientific, mathematical, and engineering applications; stands for FORmula TRANslator.

FORTRAN **FORTRAN** (which stands for FORmula TRANslator) was developed in 1954 to facilitate the writing of scientific, mathematical, and engineering software. Although business applications can be written in FORTRAN, the language is most appropriate for scientific, engineering, and mathematical problems that use complicated formulas.

FORTRAN's great strength lies in its facilities for mathematical computations. It does not have strong facilities for input/output activities or for working with lists. Thus, it would not be appropriate for business problems that involve reading massive numbers of records and producing reports. On the other hand, for business problems requiring sophisticated computations, such as forecasting and modeling, FORTRAN has been used successfully.

FIGURE 5.6

Examples of Machine Language Code and Assembly Language Code to Add the Value of B to A

Assembly language is primarily used today for writing software for operating systems. As you can see, it is very different from English and much closer to machine language in its commands. Although this can make it inefficient for humans to learn, it is very efficient for computers to execute.

Machine Code

```
111110100101001010010000000000001001000000001100
```

Assembly Code

```
AP TOTALA,     VALUEB
```

SOURCE: Figure 4-15, "Examples of Machine Language Code and Assembly Language Code to Add the Value of B to A (A = A + B)," from *Computer Information Systems* by Jerome S. Burstein and Edward G. Martin, p. 113, copyright © 1989 by The Dryden Press. Reprinted by permission of the authors.

COBOL **COBOL** (which stands for COmmon Business-Oriented Language) was introduced in the early 1960s and remains the predominant language for business problems. It was designed to process large data files with alphanumeric characters (mixed alphabetic and numeric data), which are characteristic of business problems. COBOL can read, write, and manipulate records very effectively. Business specialists also find it easier to learn than most other programming languages. It uses relatively English-like statements, is easily readable, and supports well-structured programs. COBOL does not handle complex mathematical calculations well, however, and its programs tend to be wordy and lengthy.

COBOL
A programming language with English-like statements designed for processing large data files with alphanumeric characters; the predominant programming language for business applications; stands for COmmon Business-Oriented Language.

PL/1 IBM created **PL/1** (which stands for Programming Language 1) in 1964 as a general-purpose programming language to support both business and scientific problem solving. PL/1 is very powerful but not widely used. Companies that had already invested heavily in COBOL and FORTRAN software and programmers did not want to convert to another language. They were reluctant to spend millions of dollars rewriting software when software written in COBOL and FORTRAN was already solving problems well. It has also been difficult to teach PL/1 to programmers versed in COBOL.

PL/1
A programming language developed in 1964 by IBM for business and scientific applications; not as widely used as COBOL or FORTRAN.

BASIC **BASIC** (which stands for Beginner's All-Purpose Symbolic Instruction Code) was developed in 1964 to teach Dartmouth College students how to use computers. It has become an extremely popular programming language for PCs and for teaching programming in colleges and high schools. BASIC is easy to learn and has minimal memory requirements for conversion into machine code. Beginners with only a few hours of instruction can use the software to solve small problems.

BASIC can handle many kinds of problems, although experts point out that it performs few tasks very well. BASIC also lacks strong structures for enforcing a clear flow of logic and well-organized programs, so it is not conducive to teaching structured programming practices.

BASIC
A programming language frequently used for teaching programming and for PCs; although it is easy to learn, it does not easily support sound programming practices.

Pascal Named after Blaise Pascal, the seventeenth-century mathematician and philosopher, **Pascal** was developed by the Swiss computer science professor Niklaus Wirth of Zurich in the late 1960s. Wirth wanted to create a language that would teach students structured programming techniques. Pascal programs consist of smaller subprograms, each of which is a structured program itself.

Pascal programs can be used on PCs, but Pascal itself is used primarily in computer science courses to teach sound programming practices. Pascal has limited features for input and output, so it is not well suited for most business problems.

Pascal
A programming language that consists of smaller subprograms, each of which is a structured program in itself; used on PCs and for teaching programming.

Ada **Ada** was developed in 1980 to provide the U.S. Defense Department with a standard structured programming language for all its applications. In addition to military command and control systems, Ada is used in some nonmilitary government applications. The language is also useful for business problems: it can operate on PCs, is portable across different brands of computer hardware, and promotes structured program design.

Ada was named for Ada, Countess of Lovelace, the daughter of the English poet Lord Byron. The Countess was an able nineteenth-century

Ada
Programming language developed for the Department of Defense to be portable across diverse brands of hardware; also has nonmilitary applications.

mathematician who developed the mathematical tables for an early calculating machine. For this reason she is sometimes called the first programmer.

Ada has many attractive features. It was explicitly designed so that it could be uniformly executed in diverse hardware environments. The language also promotes structured software design and reusable software components.

Nevertheless, the question remains as to whether Ada will ever be widely applied to business problem solving. Many firms are not convinced that it is worth the investment and risk to abandon COBOL as the business standard.

C
A programming language with tight control and efficiency of execution like assembly language; portable across different microprocessors and easier to learn than assembly language.

C Developed under the auspices of AT&T's Bell Laboratories in the early 1970s, **C** is the language in which most of the UNIX operating system is written. C has much of the tight control and efficiency of execution of assembly language, yet it is easier to learn and portable across different microprocessors.

Much commercial PC software has been written in C, and C is starting to be used for business, scientific, and technical applications on larger computers.

FOURTH-GENERATION LANGUAGES

Fourth-generation languages
Programming languages that are less procedural than conventional languages and contain more English language-like commands; they are easier for nonspecialists to learn and use than conventional languages.

Fourth-generation languages offer two major advantages: they allow end users to develop software on their own with little or no technical assistance, and they offer dramatic productivity gains in software development.

Fourth-generation languages tend to be less procedural than conventional languages, making them more suitable for end users. Thus, these languages have created the technical platform for nonspecialists to play a larger role in problem solving with information systems. In addition, fourth-generation languages can be employed by less-skilled programmers, a quality that helps improve productivity. Studies have shown that fourth-generation languages can produce productivity gains of 300 to 500 percent over conventional languages.[2]

Several major types of fourth-generation software tools are available:

1. Query languages
2. Graphics languages
3. Report generators
4. Application generators
5. Very-high-level programming languages

Query language
A high-level, easy-to-use, fourth-generation language for accessing stored data.

Query languages are high-level, easy-to-use languages for accessing data stored in information systems. They are valuable for supporting ad hoc requests for information that are not predefined (as opposed to routine, predefined requests), which are one-time requests for information that cannot be produced by existing applications or reporting software.

Query languages tend to be very end-user oriented, although some may have sophisticated capabilities for updating data as well. Some query languages have strong natural-language features, such as statements that use English-like words and syntax. An example of an ad hoc query might be, "List all products with a unit price over $12.00."

FIGURE 5.7

Nomad2: A Query Language

Query languages are fourth-generation languages that make it easier than ever before to access stored data. They allow nonprogrammers to "ask" computers questions pertaining to stored information. This Nomad2 query lists total salary for each department in a firm.

```
>LIST BY DEPT SUM (SALARY)
PAGE 1
DEPARTMENT    SUM CURRENT SALARY
MARKETING     66,700
PERSONNEL     54,900
SALES         77,300
```

Figure 5.7 illustrates the query language capabilities of Nomad2. Most query languages are highly interactive, allowing users to satisfy requests for information immediately online. Chapter 6 describes SQL (Structured Query Language), which is the most widely used query language today.

Graphics languages are specialized software for displaying computerized data in graphical form. Most numeric data can be understood more easily when presented as graphs. This is particularly true when making comparisons or spotting trends. Graphics software can retrieve stored data and display them in the graphic format requested by users. Some graphics languages can also manipulate data and perform calculations. Microsoft's PowerPoint, Lotus Freelance Graphics, and Aldus Persuasion are leading presentation graphics packages for PCs. SAS Institute's SAS System and SYSTAT Inc.'s SYSTAT are examples of powerful analytical graphics software.

Graphics language
A fourth-generation language for displaying computerized data in graphical form.

Report generators are software tools that extract stored data to create customized reports that are not routinely produced by existing applications. In contrast to query languages, report generators give users more control over the way data are formatted, organized, and displayed. For example, report generators such as RPG have facilities for specifying report headings, subheadings, page headings, column positioning, page numbering, and totaling of numbers. Report generators may have online capabilities, but they typically run in a batch-processing environment.

Report generator
A software tool that extracts stored data to create customized reports that are not routinely produced by existing applications.

Application generators are related pieces of software that can generate entire information system applications without customized programming. The end user need only specify *what* needs to be done, and the application generator will create the appropriate program code. The most versatile and powerful application generators integrate tools such as a query language, screen painter, graphics and report generators, modeling software, and a special programming language. Application generators typically are too complex for end users to work with alone, but they require less technical assistance than does conventional programming and can create entire applications more rapidly. Some features of application generators, such as the query language or graphics languages, can be employed directly by end users. Application generators have been developed to speed the creation of Web sites. Microsoft FrontPage is an example of a Web site development tool.

Application generator
Software that can generate entire information system applications without customized programming.

Very-high-level programming languages are primarily tools for professional programmers, but they have some capabilities that can be employed

Very-high-level programming language
A programming language that produces program code with far fewer instructions than conventional languages; used primarily by professional programmers.

by end users. These languages are distinguished by their productivity-promoting features, which produce program code with far fewer instructions than conventional languages such as COBOL or PL/1. APL and Nomad2 are examples of such very-high-level programming languages.

OBJECT-ORIENTED PROGRAMMING

What if all cars had nonstandard engines that were built by hand? Automobiles could not play a large role in everyday life because they would be prohibitively expensive to run and hard to repair. Yet this is the situation that has prevailed for software. Most software is still constructed piece by piece by highly trained craftsmen, somewhat like medieval blacksmiths or woodcarvers.

Object-oriented technology promises to create an "industrial revolution" for software by allowing the use of interchangeable parts similar to those in modern manufacturing. These interchangeable software parts are called *objects* and consist of chunks of computer code that describe entities ranging from the concrete, such as an automobile part, to the more abstract, such as an airline reservation. Each object is an encapsulated collection of data and operations performed on that data.

Traditional software development methods treat data and procedures as independent components, similar to the ingredients and instructions in a cookbook recipe. A separate programming operation must be performed every time someone wants to take an action on a particular piece of data. For instance, a credit card company would have to store data on its customers' purchases and have the instructions for using that data to calculate a customer's balance in a separate billing program.

Object-oriented programming
Approach to software development that combines data and the instructions acting on that data into one "object."

Object-oriented programming, on the other hand, combines data and the specific instructions acting on that data into one "object." In the credit card application, a customer object would contain both the data on

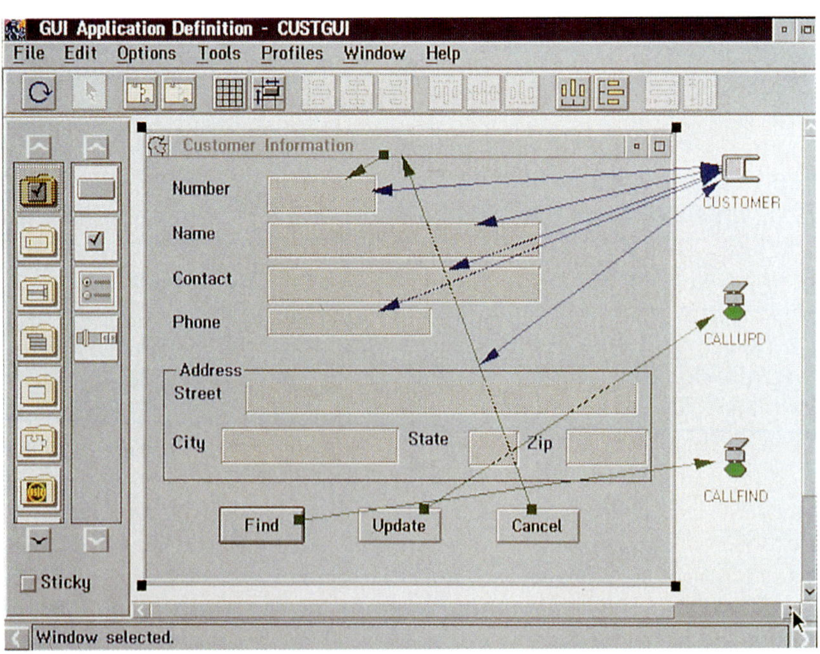

An object-oriented development environment makes creating a customized application relatively quick and simple.

FIGURE 5.8

A Banking Application of Object-Oriented Programming

Object-oriented programming divides the program into objects that contain both data and instructions and can be reused in different combinations. One object can be defined as a subcategory of another so that the savings and checking account objects are subcategories of the customer account object. The bank can create a new interest-bearing checking account object by merely specifying the difference between the interest-bearing checking account and the checking and savings accounts. The new object can easily be linked to the objects in the existing program.

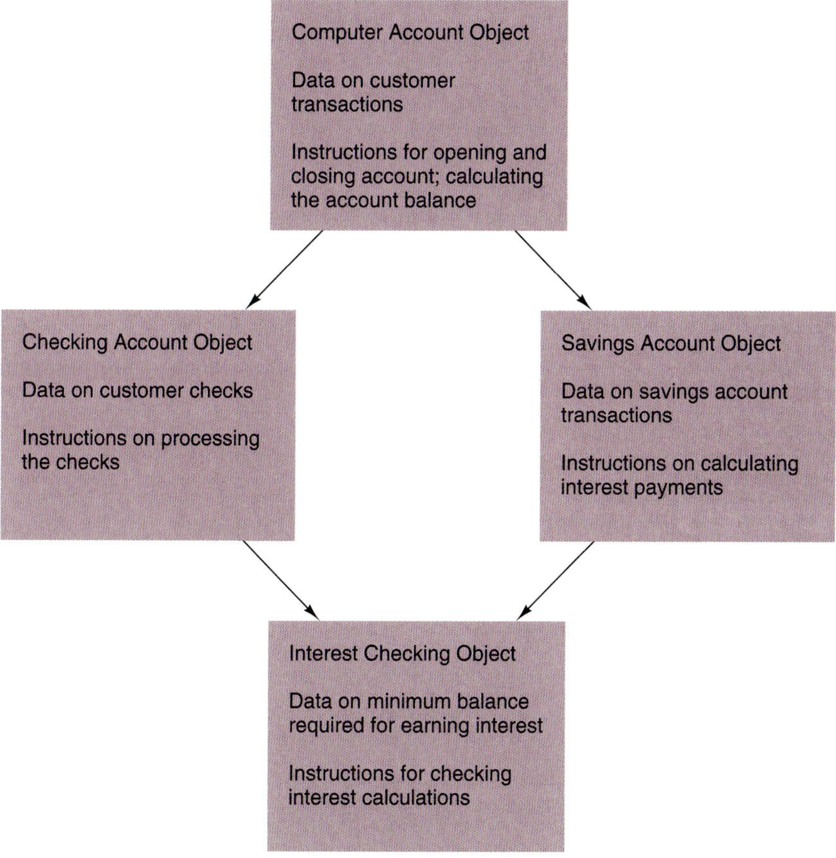

the customer's purchases and the techniques for calculating the customer's balance. Because data and operations are combined, each object is an independent software building block that can be used in many different systems without changing the program code. Objects can be assembled by combining various objects; the objects themselves don't need to be altered. If modifications are required, the programmer can design new objects that "inherit" attributes from existing objects.

The main benefit of object-oriented programming is the reusability of the code. The various objects can be reused in different combinations. After programmers build processing routines and data sources into objects, they can retrieve and insert them into other software applications without having to reinvent the wheel each time. Figure 5.8 illustrates how these features of object-oriented programming could be used in a bank program.

Future software work can draw upon a library of reusable objects. For example, Bank of America has been designing and building business objects that can be reused within the bank and sold to other financial institutions.[3]

One of the challenges of object-oriented programming is analyzing business functions so that they can be portrayed as objects. Programmers trained in traditional software development techniques require extensive retraining because object-oriented software represents a fundamental shift in thinking.

Visual programming
A programming method in which programs are created by working with objects onscreen.

Object-oriented programming has been the foundation for a new technology known as **visual programming,** which can enhance the productivity of both programmers and end users. Visual programming allows the programmer to create a program by working with a group of objects, clicking on a specific object and moving or copying it to another location, or drawing a line to connect one object to another (see Figure 5.9). Visual BASIC is a widely used visual programming tool that is being used to build many software applications today. The Focus on Problem Solving explores this topic.

SELECTING A PROGRAMMING TOOL

To select the right software tool for problem solving, you must know the capabilities and limitations of the major programming languages and tools

FIGURE 5.9

Visual Programming

Visual Basic simplifies the creation of programs that run under Microsoft Windows.

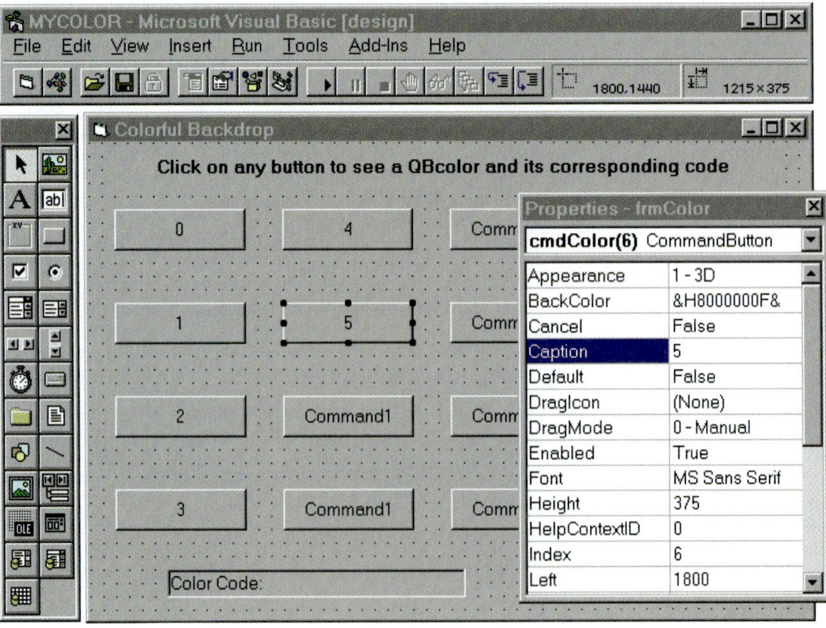

FOCUS ON PROBLEM SOLVING

VISUAL PROGRAMMING

If you use a Windows-based word-processing or spreadsheet program, you may unknowingly be doing visual programming. To customize the button bars, you would point at the button you wanted to place on your button bar and then drag it to the desired location on the bar—that's visual programming.

Programmers find visual programming especially useful in building user interfaces. The Dreyfus Corporation, the giant mutual fund company, needed to bring together financial and client information found in six separate storage locations on two separate mainframes. It wanted the data to be stored on the mainframes but the processing to be controlled by users at their desktops. The company's goal was to create a "transparent" interface in which users would be unaware of how the data were accessed or where they were stored. Using visual programming software called SQL Windows, the programmers were able to create the interface much more easily and rapidly than had they used more traditional tools.

The key to the productivity improvements is the SQL Windows "drag-and-drop" capability. The programmer selects a needed object (such as a button bar) from a list of objects, clicks on it, drags it to the position in the interface program where it is needed, and drops it there. The object brings with it all its data and processing code.

Visual programming helped Purolator Courier build systems to keep pace with its rapidly changing information requirements. Located in Mississauga, Ontario, Purolator is Canada's largest courier service, with 10,000 employees moving 1 million packages each day. Purolator risked losing business to competitors if it could not respond quickly to customers' changing needs. For example, some companies wanted Purolator to provide additional information, such as the exact warehouse location where products Purolator shipped and delivered were stored. Purolator used tools such as Microsoft's Visual C++ and Component Object Model (COM) paired with component modeling tools from Rational Software in Santa Clara, California, to model the company's business processes as software component building blocks. If the company adds a new service, programmers merely need to "snap" the new service component into the system. If a date calculation has to be changed, the date component can be replaced, leaving other programs that use the date component unaffected by the change.

FOCUS Questions: What problems does visual programming solve? What other useful applications can you suggest for visual programming?

SOURCES: Rich Levin, "Programming Goes Prefab," *Information Week,* January 13, 1997, and Barnaby J. Feder, "Sophisticated Software Set for Exotic Financial Trades," *The New York Times,* March 30, 1994.

TABLE 5.2

Comparison of Programming Languages and Tools

Programming Language	Key Features	Appropriate Tasks
Assembly language	Machine dependent; highly efficient; symbolic; difficult to learn.	Systems software.
FORTRAN	Strong facilities for mathematical computations and formulas; poor input/output facilities.	Scientific and mathematical problems requiring complex formulas; modeling.
COBOL	Strong input/output and file manipulation facilities; weak facilities for mathematical computations.	Business problems requiring extensive reading and printing of records and file manipulation.
PL/1	Powerful, multipurpose language developed by IBM; complex and somewhat difficult to learn.	Both scientific and business problems.
BASIC	General-purpose language; easy to learn; runs on PCs; does not promote good program structure.	Problems that can be solved primarily with PCs; teaching programming.
Pascal	Used to teach structured programming; limited input/output capabilities.	Education; scientific problems that can be solved with PCs.
Ada	Developed by Defense Department for weapons systems and business applications; powerful; portable across different machine environments.	Weapons systems; business problems.
C	Highly efficient and portable across different computer machine environments; somewhat difficult to learn.	General-purpose problems, especially those that can be solved with PCs;development of systems software
Fourth-generation languages	Query languages, report generators, application generators, graphics languages, very-high-level programming languages; largely nonprocedural with many "user-friendly" features.	Simple problems that can be solved primarily by nontechnical specialists.
Object-oriented programming tools	Combine data and procedures into objects that can be reused.	Problems where solutions can be modeled as objects or where objects can be reused.

(see Table 5.2 for a comparison of the various languages and tools). The following are the most important considerations for selecting a programming language or tool:

1. **The nature of the problem to be solved:** Is it a scientific problem, a business problem that requires mathematical modeling, or a problem that entails extensive file manipulation and input/output work?

2. **Computer hardware requirements:** Is the language or tool compatible with your computer hardware resources? Is it essential that it be able to run on more than one kind of machine? Will it work on the operating system for your computer hardware (see Section 5.2)? Are there any limitations on memory size or computer resources?

3. **Ease of use:** Is the language or tool one that you can use, one that your technical staff is already familiar with, or one that can easily be learned?

4. **Maintainability:** Is it important that the language be highly structured? Can the language or tool support programs that can be modified and maintained by others over a long period of time?

5.4 APPLICATIONS SOFTWARE PACKAGES

A computer application is the use of a computer to solve a specific problem or to perform a specific task for an end user. Applications software is a major category of software that handles the processing for a particular computer application. Applications software has been written for numerous computer applications: business functions, such as accounts receivable or sales forecasting; scientific and engineering functions, such as molecular modeling or microprocessor design; law enforcement functions, such as computerized criminal-history recordkeeping; educational functions, such as computer-based mathematics instruction; artistic functions, such as the production of computer-generated music and art; and the transmission of data via telecommunications.

SOFTWARE PACKAGES

Software packages are prewritten, precoded, commercially available programs that eliminate the need for writing software programs. Software packages are available for systems software, but the vast majority of software packages are **applications software packages.** The spreadsheet, database, and word-processing software for your personal computer are all software packages. A mainframe-based payroll system that issues checks each week for 30,000 employees and the checking and savings account processing system of a bank also typically use software packages.

The Focus on Organizations describes examples of state-of-the-art applications software packages that can represent data geographically.

Applications software package
A prewritten, precoded, commercially available program that handles the processing for a particular computer application (e.g., spreadsheet or data management software for a personal computer).

PC APPLICATIONS PACKAGES

Some of the most popular examples of applications software are the general-purpose applications packages that have been developed for personal computers. Word-processing, spreadsheet, data management, graphics, desktop-publishing, and Web browser software have been widely adopted for business and other kinds of problem solving. Some of this software also has been widely copied and distributed, raising questions about violations of software copyrights and improper use (see Chapter 3).

Word-Processing Software **Word-processing software** has dramatically enhanced the productivity of clerical workers, managers, and knowledge workers by automating the creation, editing, and printing of documents. Text data are stored electronically rather than typed on paper. The word-processing software allows changes to be made in the document electronically in memory so that it does not have to be typed again. Changes in line spacing, margins, character size, and column widths can be made with formatting options in the software. Microsoft Word and WordPerfect are popular word-processing packages.

Word-processing software
Software that handles such applications as electronic editing, formatting, and printing of documents.

Most word-processing software has advanced features that automate other aspects of the writing process. Spelling checkers use built-in dictionaries to locate and correct spelling errors. Style checkers analyze grammar and punctuation errors and may even suggest ways to improve writing style.

FOCUS ON ORGANIZATIONS

SOFTWARE THAT READS MAPS

The giant Exxon Valdez oil spill in Prince William Sound, Alaska, in the late 1980s caused many environmental organizations to examine their ability to react to such spills in their own geographic areas. The California Department of Fish and Game was one such organization. The department did take steps and so was prepared when an estimated 2,000 gallons of oil spilled from a broken pipeline into McGrath Lake in California. One key tool at Fish and Game's disposal was a geographic information system (GIS) that it had developed in the years following the Vadez spill. Using this software, environmental specialist Randy Imai's Office of Oil Spill Prevention and Response knew exactly where to go and what to do. The system pinpointed the lake locations where gulls, grebes, and brown pelicans gathered. Veterinarians were quickly dispatched to rescue the birds. Later, other specialists followed. Their task was to follow the plan previously stored in the GIS—to replant native plants and to help the environment recover from the disaster in other ways.

GIS software, often called mapping software, presents its data in the form of maps rather than as lists of numbers. Data presented in this format are usually much easier for people to absorb than are data presented in the form of written reports. To establish its GIS, the Department of Fish and Game first had to collect, catalog, and store in a database data on California's sensitive marine and wildlife areas and on the populations that inhabit those areas. The department's system uses Arc/Info GIS software from Environmental Systems Research Institute. The system includes the graphical mapping interface. Imai explained the value of the software by saying, "You can visualize, you can see, here are the red dots which represent a sensitive area."

Such mapping software has many uses. Quaker Oats Co. uses it to target stores and regions in geographic areas with specific products. The software displays and analyzes customer data, store locations, and sales volume geographically on electronic charts, maps, and graphs. Quaker uses this information to develop cost-effective advertising programs targeted at specific stores and areas.

Banks are using GISs to ensure that their lending practices are equitable. The Community Reinvestment Act requires that banks lend money back to the same neighborhoods from which they receive deposits. The legislation is designed to prevent redlining, a practice in which banks circled low-income areas on a map in red. Even if applicants had respectable incomes and credit ratings, they were either denied mortgage loans or subject to more stringent credit-granting standards than residents of more affluent areas. Banks can use GIS to perform the analysis needed to create the required loan/deposit reports and to present the data in map form. When banks identify neighborhoods where the loan/deposit ratio is out of balance, they can use the GIS to target neighborhoods for special programs.

FOCUS Questions: What people, organization, and technology factors should a business examine when considering whether to use mapping software? Can you suggest other applications for mapping software?

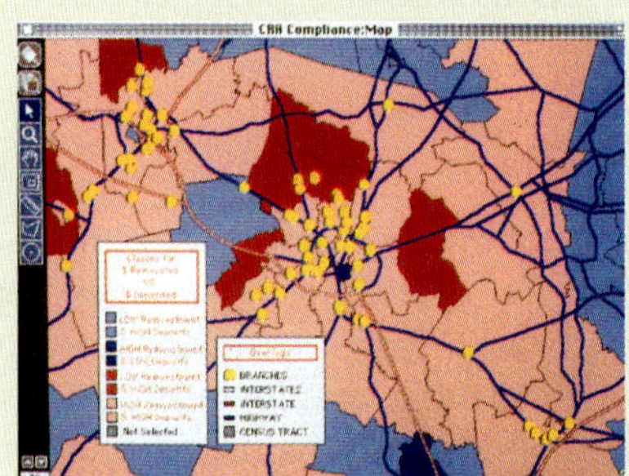

Banking and demographic census data are combined to analyze Community Reinvestment Act compliance. Census tracts are color coded by level of reinvestment in comparison to level of deposits.

SOURCE: Courtesy of Tactics International Ltd.

SOURCES: Michael Goldberg, "GIS helps curb oil spill damage," *Computerworld,* January 22, 1996; Nora Sherwood Bryan, "A Look at GIS," *Computerworld,* July 26, 1993; and David Forrest, "Seeing Data in New Ways," *Computerworld,* June 29, 1992.

Thesaurus programs provide online lists of synonyms and antonyms. Mail merge programs link letters or other text documents with names and addresses in a mailing list.

Spreadsheets Electronic **spreadsheet software** provides computerized versions of traditional financial modeling tools—the accountant's columnar pad, pencil, and calculator. A spreadsheet is organized into a grid of columns and rows. The intersection of a column and row, which is called a cell, can store a number, formula, word, or phrase.

Spreadsheet software
Software that provides the user with financial modeling tools; data are displayed on a grid and numerical data can easily be recalculated to permit the evaluation of several alternatives.

Spreadsheets are valuable for solving problems in which numerous calculations with pieces of data must be related to one another. After a set of mathematical relationships has been constructed, the spreadsheet can be recalculated immediately using a different set of assumptions.

Spreadsheet software readily lends itself to modeling and "what if" analysis. A number of alternatives can easily be evaluated by changing one or two pieces of data without having to rekey the rest of the worksheet. Figure 5.10 illustrates how spreadsheet software could be used to answer the question, "What if sales revenue increased 10 percent each year over a five-year period?" Many spreadsheet packages include graphics functions that can present data in the form of line graphs, bar graphs, or pie charts. The most popular spreadsheet packages are Excel and Lotus 1-2-3.

Data Management Software Although spreadsheet programs are good at manipulating quantitative data, they are poor at storing and manipulating lists or at extracting parts of files from larger sets of data. **Data management software,** on the other hand, is weak at manipulating quantitative data but is very good at creating and manipulating lists and at combining information from different files for problem solving. It has programming features and easy-to-learn menus that enable nonspecialists to build small information systems.

Data management software
Software that is used for such applications as creating and manipulating lists, creating files and databases to store data, and combining information for reports.

Data management software typically has facilities for creating files and databases, storing data, modifying data, and manipulating data for reports and queries. Data management software and database management systems are treated in detail in Chapter 6. Access is the most popular data management software for PCs.

FIGURE 5.10

Spreadsheet Software—An Important Business Tool

Spreadsheets have become very popular in business because they can perform "what if?" analysis. The top worksheet displays the results of asking the software to determine sales revenues over a five-year period if sales increased 10 percent each year. The bottom worksheet shows the formulas and data relationships that were entered to ask this question.

		Breakdown of Sales by Region			
SALES REGION	1997	1998	1999	2000	2001
Northeast	$2,304,000	$2,534,400	$2,787,840	$3,066,624	$3,373,286
South	$1,509,300	$1,660,230	$1,826,253	$2,008,878	$2,209,766
Midwest	$3,309,800	$3,604,780	$4,004,858	$4,405,344	$4,845,878
WEST	$2,667,000	$2,933,700	$3,227,070	$3,549,777	$3,904,755

% Annual Growth 10%

		Breakdown of Sales by Region			
SALES REGION	1997	1998	1999	2000	2001
Northeast	$2,304,000	+C23*(1+$C$11)	+D23*(1+$C$11)	+E23*(1+$C$11)	+F23*(1+$C$11)
South	$1,509,300	+C24*(1+$C$11)	+D24*(1+$C$11)	+E24*(1+$C$11)	+F24*(1+$C$11)
Midwest	$3,309,800	+C25*(1+$C$11)	+D25*(1+$C$11)	+E25*(1+$C$11)	+F25*(1+$C$11)
WEST	$2,667,000	+C26*(1+$C$11)	+D26*(1+$C$11)	+E26*(1+$C$11)	+F26*(1+$C$11)

% Annual Growth 10%

Integrated software package
A software package that provides two or more applications, such as spreadsheets and word processing, allowing for easy transfer of data between them.

Integrated Packages Problem solving often requires a combination of software skills—some writing, some quantitative analysis, and some record management. To produce a polished sales forecast report using unintegrated word processing and spreadsheet programs, one would have to develop a sales forecasting spreadsheet and then reformat that spreadsheet as a report by separately keying the data into both programs. **Integrated software packages** eliminate the redundant work by performing such tasks without having to switch from one program to the other. Using an integrated software package, the spreadsheet data could be reworked in word-processing mode by merely pressing a few keys on the keyboard.

Integrated packages such as Microsoft Works typically combine the most common kinds of personal computer applications software—spreadsheet, database, and word processing. Some have recently added data communications, graphics, and project management functions.

Integrated software packages should be distinguished from applications software suites, which are collections of applications such as a spreadsheet, database, and presentation graphics that are sold as a unit. An example would be Microsoft Office, which consists of Excel spreadsheet software, Microsoft Word word-processing software, Access database software, PowerPoint presentation graphics software, and Outlook, a program for E-mail, contact management, and scheduling. (The software tools in the Office 97

FIGURE 5.11

The Internet Explorer Web Browser

Web browser software enables the user to access World Wide Web pages with text, graphics, video, and audio and to link to other Web pages and Web sites. The Web browser illustrated here displays the welcoming page of the user's Internet service provider.

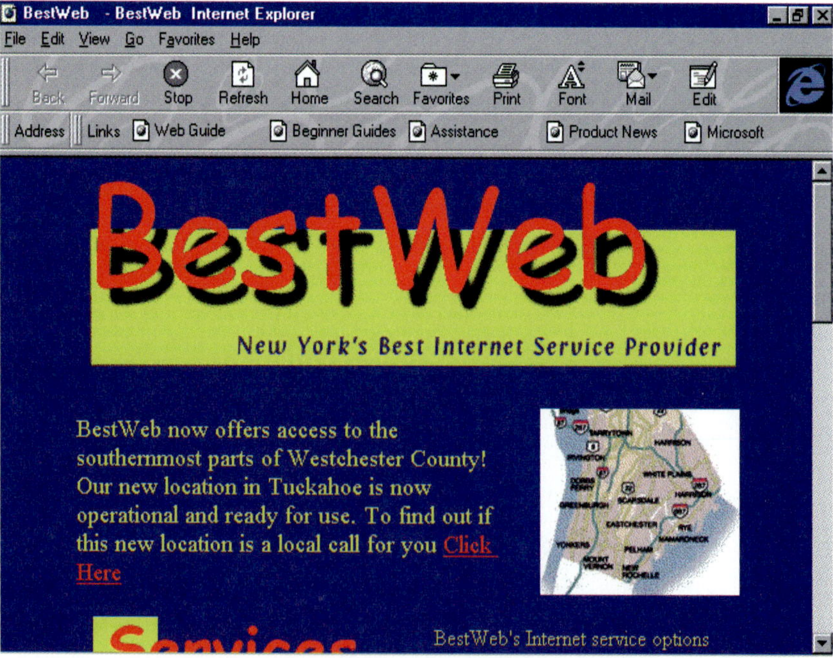

suite allow users to create and import files for the World Wide Web and create links to specific Web sites.) Software suites have some features of integrated packages, such as the ability to exchange data among different applications in the suite, but they consist of the full-featured versions of each type of software. Integrated packages generally offer fewer features and less versatility than the stand-alone versions.

Web Browsers **Web browsers** are becoming increasingly important as software tools for accessing the World Wide Web. Web browser software features a point-and-click graphical user interface that can be employed throughout the World Wide Web so that it can access and display information stored on other computers connected to the Internet. Browsers can display or present graphics, audio, and video information as well as traditional text, and they allow you to click on-screen buttons or highlighted words to link to related Web sites. Netscape Navigator, Netscape Communicator, and Microsoft's Internet Explorer are the most popular Web browsers, with additional features for using E-mail, online bulletin boards and discussion groups, and other Internet services (see Figure 5.11).

Web browsers
Software with a graphical user interface that can access and display Web pages.

5.5 LEADING EDGE TECHNOLOGY: JAVA

Java, a programming language that Sun Microsystems designed for network-based computing, represents a revolutionary concept in software development. First, it is an object-oriented language that allows developers to create applications that can be distributed over the Internet. Second, it is platform independent. The software can run on any computer or computing device, regardless of which microprocessor or operating system the computer uses. In other words, Java can run on a smart cellular phone, a personal digital assistant (PDA), a laptop running Windows 95, a UNIX workstation or server, or even an IBM minicomputer or mainframe. All kinds of systems using Java can talk to one another and share applications.

Java
Platform-independent, object-oriented programming language that can deliver miniature applications as software "applets" downloaded from networks.

Traditional software applications typically address many functions in the same software package. For example, a word-processing program includes not only commonly used functions such as deleting text, setting margins, and changing line spacing, but many other features for more specialized purposes—merging documents, inserting footnotes, automatic numbering, inserting graphics, and so forth. Most people use only a small number of these functions at one time. Such software usually requires a computer with large amounts of memory, secondary storage, and processing power. The software must be run on the specific computing platform for which it was designed. For example, different versions of the Microsoft Word word-processing package are required for PCs with Intel processors running Windows 95 and Macintosh PCs running the Mac OS operating system.

Java, in contrast, allows users to create miniature applications called "applets" that reside on a network in centralized servers (see Figure 5.12). The network delivers only the applets for the specific functions you need. With Java applets residing on your network, you could analyze the sales results from the northeast region of your company by merely asking for the

FIGURE 5.12

Java—the Universal Interface

A browser using Java acts as a universal interface that lets users access applications written in the Java language regardless of the type of computer or operating system the users have.

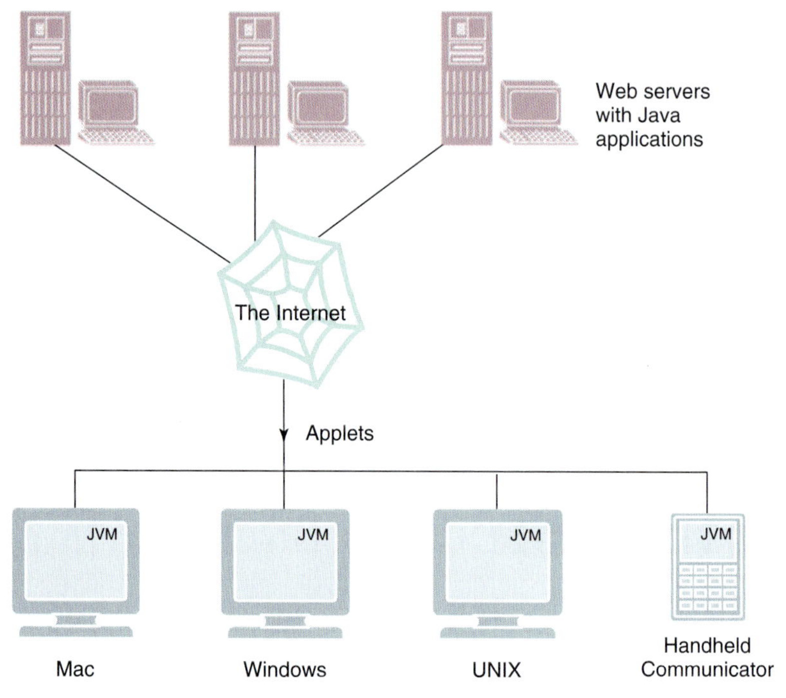

data and a sales analysis applet; the network would then deliver them to your computer. You would not need to store either the data or the program on your hard disk, so you could use a much less powerful machine for your work. Java and similar software are spurring the development of network computers, described in the previous chapter. You can see Java applets at work in many Web sites that feature animated cartoons or rolling stock tickers. Java can handle text, graphics, sound, and video, all within one program if needed.

To run Java applets, a computer needs an operating system containing a Java Virtual Machine. (A Java Virtual Machine is incorporated into Web browser software.) The Java Virtual Machine is a compact program embedded in a computer operating system that enables the computer to run Java applications. The Virtual Machine lets the computer simulate an ideal standardized Java computer, complete with disk drives, memory, display, and everything else that would be needed on a computer to run the program. The Virtual Machine executes Java programs by interpreting their commands one by one and commanding the underlying computer to perform all the tasks specified by the command. Because no Java program actually penetrates your computer, the design helps safeguard against computer viruses.

Widespread use of Java could potentially transform the way software is developed, used, and marketed. Because the same Java software will work on millions of otherwise incompatible computers, software companies would no longer have to create unique versions of their products for computers running Windows or UNIX. Moreover, the Virtual Machine program is tiny, so it could easily be used in devices such as cellular phones or television sets. A cheap hand-held device, for instance, could browse airline flight data on a wireless network, book a seat, and pay for it. The phone would need only the computing capacity to run the required Java applets. All types of computing hardware devices would be able to take advantage of a broad array of software solutions. Sun Microsystems terms this phenomenon "write once, run anywhere."

The way you use and pay for software will also change. Instead of paying a one-time fee to purchase the program, you might pay a small fee each time you use a software applet. Or your company might pay for one network copy of Java applets that would be available to all employees. There would be no need for companies to purchase hundreds or thousands of copies of commercial software to run on individual computers.

There may be less need to purchase powerful PCs if there is no need to store software and data on individual computers. Inexpensive network computers could do the job by downloading applets when needed. Data and computing functions that used to be stored on desktop computers could be stored in network servers at one location, making it easier for organizations to administer their hardware and software resources from one central point. Users would merely need to plug in and do what they needed to do without worrying about underlying hardware and software technology, much like making a telephone call.[4]

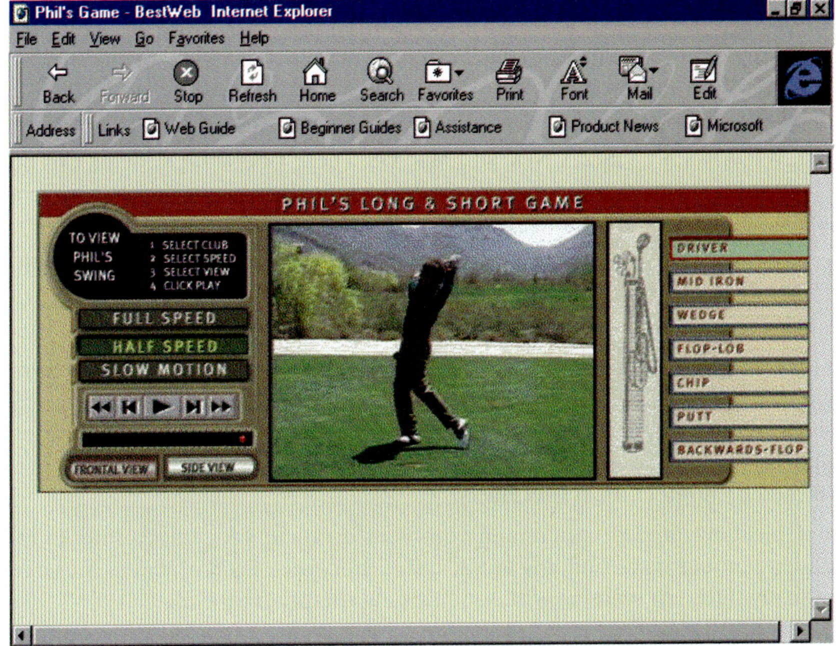

This Web site is driven by a Java applet developed for professional golfer Phil Mikelson and IBM. Visitors to this Web site can select videos to view in full, half, or slow motion that show Phil's swing using different types of clubs.

SUMMARY

- There are two major types of software: systems software and applications software. Systems software consists of generalized programs to manage computer resources and mediate between applications software and computer hardware. Applications software consists of programs designed for applying the computer to solve a specific problem, such as a business problem.

- There have been four generations of software development: (1) machine language; (2) symbolic languages such as assembly language; (3) high-level languages such as FORTRAN and COBOL; and (4) fourth-generation languages, which are less procedural and closer to natural language than earlier generations of software.

- The operating system acts as the chief manager of the computer system, allocating, scheduling, and assigning system resources and monitoring the use of the computer.

- Multiprogramming, multitasking, multiprocessing, virtual storage, and time-sharing enable computer system resources to be used more efficiently so that the computer can attack many problems at the same time.

- Multiprogramming (multitasking in microcomputer environments) allows multiple programs to use the computer's resources concurrently.

- Multiprocessing is the use of two or more CPUs linked together, working in tandem to perform a task.

- Time sharing enables many users to share computer resources simultaneously by allocating each user a tiny slice of computing time.

- Virtual storage splits up programs into pages or segments so that primary storage can be used more efficiently.

- To be executed by the computer, a software program must be translated into machine language via special language translation software—a compiler, an assembler, or an interpreter.

- A graphical user interface (GUI) allows users to interact with the operating system by using a mouse to select icons representing commands.

- The leading PC operating systems are DOS, Windows 95 (and Windows 98), Windows NT, OS/2, UNIX, and Mac OS. These operating systems can be classified according to whether they support multitasking and multiple users and whether they are command driven or use a graphical user interface.

- The most popular programming languages are assembly language, FORTRAN, COBOL, BASIC, PL/1, Pascal, C, and Ada. Each has been designed to solve a special class of problems.

- Fourth-generation languages are more nonprocedural than earlier programming languages and include query software, report generators, graphics software, application generators, and other tools that dramatically reduce programming time and make some software tasks easy enough to be performed by nontechnical specialists.

- Object-oriented programming combines data and procedures into an independent software building block called an object. Each object is reusable in many different systems without changing the program code.

- Software packages are prewritten, precoded, commercially available programs that eliminate the need for writing software programs. The most popular software packages for PCs are productivity aids such as word-processing software, spreadsheet software, data management software, integrated software packages, and Web browsers.

- Java is an object-oriented programming language designed to run on any computer and operating system. It can deliver only the software needed for a particular task as an applet transmitted through a network.

KEY TERMS

Program
Stored-program concept
Systems software
Applications software
Machine language
High-level language
Assembly language
Operating system
Multiprogramming
Multitasking
Multiprocessing
Time sharing
Virtual storage
Source code
Object code
Compiler
Interpreter
Assembler
Graphical user interface (GUI)
DOS
Windows
Windows 95 (Windows 98)
Windows NT
OS/2
UNIX
Mac OS
FORTRAN
COBOL
PL/1
BASIC
Pascal
Ada
C
Fourth-generation languages
Graphics language
Report generator
Query language
Application generator
Very-high-level programming language
Object-oriented programming
Visual programming
Applications software package
Word-processing software
Spreadsheet software
Data management software
Integrated software package
Web browsers
Java

REVIEW QUESTIONS

1. Why do we need software to use computers?
2. What are the major types of software? How can they be distinguished?
3. What are the major software generations? When were they developed? Describe the characteristics of each generation.

4. Define an operating system. What functions does it perform?
5. How do a compiler, an assembler, and an interpreter differ?
6. Define multiprogramming, multitasking, time sharing, multiprocessing, and virtual storage.
7. What is a graphical user interface? Describe some of the features that make graphical user interfaces easy to use.
8. Name the leading PC operating systems. How can they be distinguished?
9. Name and describe four popular high-level programming languages.
10. What is a fourth-generation language? Give examples of fourth-generation software tools.
11. What is object-oriented programming? How does it differ from the traditional method of developing software?
12. What is an applications software package? Name and describe the major kinds of software packages used with PCs.
13. What is Java? Why is it so revolutionary?

DISCUSSION QUESTIONS

1. Why is the operating system considered the chief manager of a computer system?

2. Software will continue to become more user friendly. Discuss.

PROBLEM-SOLVING EXERCISES

1. *Group exercise:* Divide into groups to research the features of a major Web browser tool using computing magazine articles, vendor literature, and personal observation. For instance, one group could describe the features and advantages of Netscape Navigator or Netscape Communicator; another could discuss Microsoft's Internet Explorer. Each group should present its findings to the class.

2. David Ashton is the superintendent of schools for the Herron Lake School District. His staff consists of a business manager, who performs all the accounting for the district and manages the budget; a manager of pupil and personnel services, who maintains enrollment and test score data; and two secretaries. The secretaries are in charge of the superintendent's appointments and correspondence with district staff and parents. The district office has one terminal connected to a countywide computer system that maintains student enrollment data and prints mailing labels. Otherwise, all work is performed with calculators, electric typewriters, or pen and pencil. Write a memo describing how the leading microcomputer software packages could help the superintendent and his staff. Identify applications that should be computerized and the type of software most suitable for each. What software selection criteria should be considered?

3. *Hands-on exercise:* The following list displays some of the information that needs to be maintained by waste management companies such as John

Sexton Contractors Co., which handles trash and waste disposal for other parties. The "Amount" column represents tons of waste.

Landfill	Truck Owner	Type of Waste	Amount	Party Charged
Buford	Sherman	Garbage	10	Conti
Ulster	Higgins	Construction	14	O'Callahan
Buford	DeWitt	Garbage	14	Johnson
Buford	Sherman	Yard	22	Conti
Stony Ridge	DiNardo	Floor cleaner	15	McPherson
Ulster	Oliva	Garbage	17	Conti

Use appropriate software to develop an application that can store this data and create reports that would be of interest to companies such as Sexton Contractors. Some of these reports would be:

A list of all types of waste dumped at the Ulster site.

The total amount of garbage dumped at the Buford site.

All waste paid for by Conti classified by type of waste and landfill size.

4. *Internet problem-solving exercise:* You are head of dispatching for the logistics department of BBZ Industries, a manufacturer of cabinets for kitchens and other household areas. BBZ's factory is located in Aurora, Illinois, and finished cabinets are shipped from there to distributors. It is your responsibility to help BBZ's drivers plan their routes to be sure that goods are transported as efficiently as possible. Use the Tripquest feature of the Mapquest geographic information software on the Web to help plan the route from Aurora to Rochester, Minnesota. Use the software to determine the most direct route and the fastest route.

NOTES

1. John Swenson, "Dictating to Your PC Gets Easier," *Information Week,* June 24, 1996, and Walter S. Mossberg, "Dragon Systems Takes a Giant Step in Speech Recognition," The *Wall Street Journal,* June 12, 1994.
2. Jesse Green, "Productivity in the Fourth Generation," *Journal of Management Information Systems* 1 (Winter 1984—85).
3. Rich Levin, "Programming Goes Prefab," *Information Week,* January 13, 1997.
4. Bill Semich and David Fisco, "Java: Internet Toy or Enterprise Tool?" *Datamation,* March 1, 1996, and Sun Microsystems, Inc., "Strategic Overview: Java Computing Changes Everything," 1996.

PROBLEM-SOLVING CASE

THE YEAR 2000 PROBLEM: THE FUTURE IS NOW

As the year 2000 approaches, we can make one safe prediction: the year 2000 will bring a lot of headaches to computer users.

The next time you use a computer, check to see whether any of the applications or the operating system itself uses the date as a method of storage or organization. Now look to see how the year is expressed. Does it have two digits or four? The difference between 1997 and 97 carries with it a lot more consequences than you might think. And the so-called Year 2000 problem has the business world in a frenzy.

Unfortunately, most computer programs use a decades-old convention to represent the date that contains six digits: two for the month, two for the day, and two for the year (MM-DD-YY). This was done as a way of saving space, time, and resources. It also makes the task of entering data more convenient: Imagine having a job that requires you to punch in numbers all day. Not having to type "19" every time you had to enter a date would make a big difference. This programming standard also saved computer storage space. But as the turn of the century grew nearer, someone finally asked, "What happens after 99?" Much to people's dismay, the answer is that in a two-digit representation of the year, 00 comes after 99. To a human mind, that does not pose a problem. We know it stands for 2000. To a computer, however, it stands for 00. That is to say zero, or 99 less than 99, not 99 plus 1.

Consider the consequences if nothing is done about changing date formats. Suppose you own a life insurance policy that lasts through the year 2005. According to you, the policy will cover you into the next century. According to the insurance company's computer, your policy expires in 05, which it knows how to interpret only as 1905. So, in effect, your policy expired before you were even born.

If you took out a long-term loan in 1995 that was scheduled to be paid off in full in 25 years, you would complete payments in the year 2020. But not if you knocked off the first two digits, the way the computer does. Doing so results in wonderful news for you: Your loan payments ended in 1920—congratulations! It is doubtful that the bank would be as excited.

Billions of lines of computer programming code must be examined and rewritten simply to change year representations from two to four digits. Companies may need to test every system they own to locate the problems, assess risk factors, and schedule conversions. Prudential Insurance estimates that its systems alone hold 125 million lines of code. The vast majority of programs that require reworking are COBOL programs. And even if your company solved its Year 2000 problem, its systems could be polluted by bad date data from customers and suppliers.

Time is running out. Peter de Jager, a Year 2000 consultant from Brampton, Ontario, calculates that a company that started the conversion process in January 1996 would be 99 percent finished by the year 2000. The figure drops to 80 percent for a January 1997 start date and plummets to 30 percent if an organization holds off until 1999. As disquieting as that sounds, most companies figure that they must conclude the overhaul by January 1999, not 2000, so that they can test the results for at least a year—before they become critical. Despite this urgency, by late 1996, 40 percent of executives in charge of information systems still had not developed a strategy for dealing with the matter.

A survey conducted in April 1996 by the U.S. House of Representatives found that only six U.S. government agencies had estimated the amount of money and resources they needed to solve their Year 2000 problem. The Department of Defense hadn't yet finished inventorying its roughly 358 million lines of program code. The Department of Energy started to address the issue a week after receiving the House survey questionnaire, and the Department of Transportation didn't respond to the survey at all.

The question of exactly who should deal with the matter once a strategy is in place remains somewhat unsettled. GTE expects to have 1,000 people working on the problem. Some organizations are hiring outside firms to tackle the project, especially where non-COBOL programs are involved. The cost of these efforts reveals another pothole in the road to 2000. The Stamford, Connecticut, consulting firm, Gartner Group, puts the cost of conversion anywhere from $.90 to $1.50 per line of program code. Figures like that explain why Prudential will pay IBM's Integrated Systems Solutions Corp. $340 million to work with one of its division's mainframe applications. Some companies will not even disclose the fees they are paying to combat the problem because either the numbers are so outrageously high or their board of directors has not yet been told the figure. Frighteningly, costs will skyrocket even more as time and available help diminish.

Prudential tackled the problem by assembling accounting executives from each of its major business groups as well as from its legal, auditing, human resources, and information systems departments. By December 1995 the teams had completed an inventory of their systems and started identifying applications that needed modification to correct Year 2000 problems. Prudential found 900 applications that run on mainframes. The remainder are newer, network-based applications, where processing is distributed, and don't have as many Year 2000 problems. Prudential also classified its applications according to their importance to the business, identifying which applications needed to be converted first, which needed the date field expanded, and which could be handled by "work-around" solutions that trick applications into year 2000 compliance. By conducting this analysis, Prudential found that 30 percent of its applications could be retired or replaced and that 75 percent could be managed with work-around solutions.

Sharing knowledge about how to fix the Year 2000 problem has led to a period of unprecedented cooperation in the business world. A Web site containing the latest strategies even exists. Of course, not all developments related to the year 2000 have a positive ring. The other trend gathering momentum involves lawyers gearing up to pursue cases against companies whose systems do fail and cause damages.

SOURCES: Richard Adhikari, "Conversion Urge: Others to Get Started Now," *Information Week,* October 7, 1996; Kris Brown, "Beat the Clock," *Information Week,* September 30, 1996; Roger Lowenstein, "The Year 2000 and the CEO's Big Secret," *The Wall Street Journal,* July 25, 1996; and Thomas Petzinger, Jr., "Businesses Make a Date to Battle Year 2000 Problem," *The Wall Street Journal,* July 26, 1996.

CASE STUDY QUESTIONS

1. Why is preparing for the year 2000 a critical business decision?

2. What people and organizational issues should be considered when making preparations to handle the year 2000?

3. What problems do you see with businesses trying to convert their systems to ensure smooth sailing into the next century?

4. It has been said that if information systems were all thoroughly object oriented, the Year 2000 problem would probably be a minor annoyance. Do you agree or disagree?

Chapter

→ SIX ←

ORGANIZING INFORMATION: FILES AND DATABASES

CHAPTER OUTLINE

LEARNING OBJECTIVES

After reading and studying this chapter, you will

1. Understand how the usefulness of information is affected by file organization.
2. Be familiar with traditional file organization methods.
3. Be able to describe how a database management system overcomes the limitations of a traditional file environment.
4. Be familiar with the three database models.
5. Know how to design a simple database.
6. Be able to describe new database trends.

SQUIBB INTEGRATES DATA FOR MANAGED CARE

In the pharmaceutical industry, weak information systems are a formula for failure. Fierce competition among the major pharmaceutical companies has led to intense price wars and the consolidation of smaller companies into industry giants. Under these conditions, not having a solid grasp on essential business data could prove disastrous. Bristol-Myers Squibb, located in Plainsboro, New Jersey, and a major player in the pharmaceutical industry, found its competitive position weakened because of its fragmented and inconsistent data. The company needed a consolidated view of its data on doctors, their prescription-writing habits, and managed care facilities.

Squibb's data analysis suffered because the data itself lacked organization. Reports were generated by an external body based on information that arrived infrequently. Squibb analysts would receive updated prescription information about once a month. It would take two to three weeks for the external body to process requests for batch reports, which were processed by an outside source. The data kept on Squibb's own systems contained many inaccuracies and inefficiencies. For instance, a single company name might appear in more than 20 different forms. Kathy Serfin, the associate director of Squibb's data warehouse management group, attributes those difficulties to the focus of the company. Squibb had always been a product-oriented operation. Its information systems maintained data based on products. But to keep in step with the industry, it needed to become more customer oriented, and it needed to be able to analyze data based on customers as well as products. Data consolidation would help accomplish that goal.

To begin the process, Squibb consolidated its data into a single database, selecting an Oracle database management system running on powerful Hewlett-Packard workstations. That solved the problem of organizing the data. Then began the task of cleaning up the problem data already in its systems, including correcting errors and eliminating repetitive entries. The software that Squibb chose for the task was the Integrity Data Reengineering Tool produced by Vality Technology in Boston. By consolidating and cleaning up its data, Squibb had found a way to analyze the way doctors prescribe medication, spot emerging trends, and create more targeted marketing efforts.

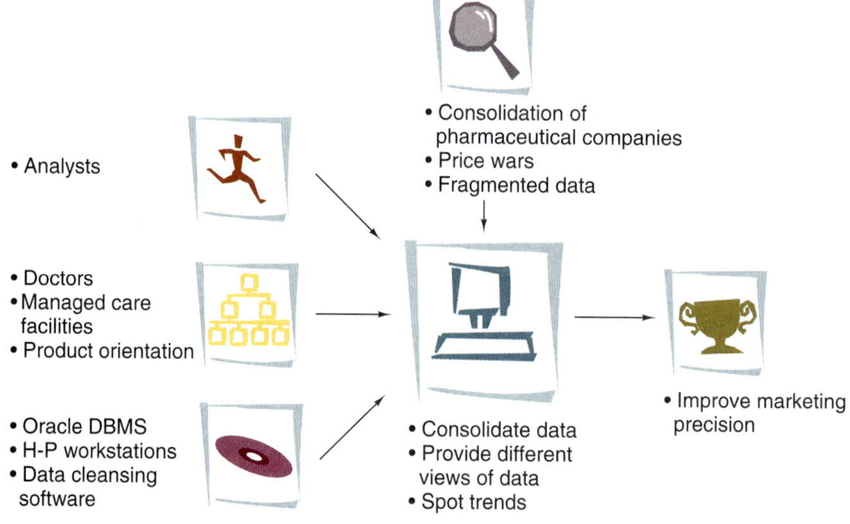

SOURCE: Sentry Market Research, "Squibb Needed a Single View of Managed Care: Data Warehousing Directions," *Software Magazine,* October 1996.

The usefulness of information depends a great deal on how it is stored, organized, and accessed. Solving problems is difficult—sometimes impossible—unless the requisite information is easily available in the right form. Consequently, an understanding of files and databases is crucial for using information systems effectively. This chapter describes traditional file management technologies and database management systems, showing how a database approach can overcome problems in accessing data such as those faced by Squibb.

6.1 INTRODUCTION

Information systems cannot provide solutions unless their data are accurate, timely, and easily accessible. Various file organization and management techniques have been developed to achieve these objectives. Each of these techniques works best with a different class of problems.

WHY ARE FILE ORGANIZATION AND MANAGEMENT IMPORTANT TO PROBLEM SOLVING?

In all information systems, data must be organized and structured so that they can be used effectively. But unless information can be easily processed and accessed, the system cannot achieve its purpose. Due to disorganized methods of storing and retrieving information, many firms with excellent hardware and software cannot deliver timely and precise information. Poor file organization prevents some firms from accessing much of the information they maintain.

Imagine how difficult it would be to write a term paper with your notes on index cards if the cards were in random order. No matter how neatly they were stacked and stored, you would have no way of organizing the term paper. Of course, with enough time, you might be able to arrange the cards in some order. But often, imposing an organization scheme after the fact or modifying it to accommodate a change of viewpoint in your paper will cause you to miss your deadline. Thus, the role of file organization and management cannot be underestimated.

DATA ORGANIZATION TERMS AND CONCEPTS

Data are structured in information systems in a manner that keeps track of discrete data elements and related groupings of information. The data are organized in a hierarchy that starts with bits and bytes and progresses to fields, records, files, and databases (see Figure 6.1).

A bit, as you have seen, represents the smallest piece of data the computer can handle. A byte is a group of bits that represents a single character, which can be a letter, number, or other symbol. A grouping of characters into a word, group of words, or complete number, such as a person's name or age, is called a **field.** A collection of related data fields, such as a person's name, age, and address, is called a **record.** A group of related records is called a **file.** For example, we could collect all the records described in Figure 6.1 into a personnel file. Related files, in turn, can be grouped into a **database.** For example, our personnel file could be grouped with a payroll information file into a human resources database.

Entities and Attributes An **entity** is a person, place, or thing on which information is maintained. For example, *employee* is a typical entity in a personnel file that maintains information on people employed by the firm. Each characteristic or quality describing a particular entity is called an **attribute.** For example, name, address, or number of dependents would each be an

Field
A grouping of characters into a word, a group of words, or a complete number.

Record
A grouping of related data fields, such as a person's name, age, and address.

File
A group of related records.

Database
A group of related files; more specifically, a collection of data organized to appear to be in one location so that they can be accessed and used in many different applications.

Entity
A person, place, or thing on which information is maintained.

Attribute
A characteristic or quality of a particular entity.

FIGURE 6.1

The Data Hierarchy

In an information system, pieces of data are organized into a hierarchy. The smallest piece of data is the bit. Next is the byte, a group of bits that forms a character. A field is a group of characters that forms a word, a group of words, or a number. A record is a collection of related fields; a file is a collection of related records. The largest element in the hierarchy, a database, consists of related files.

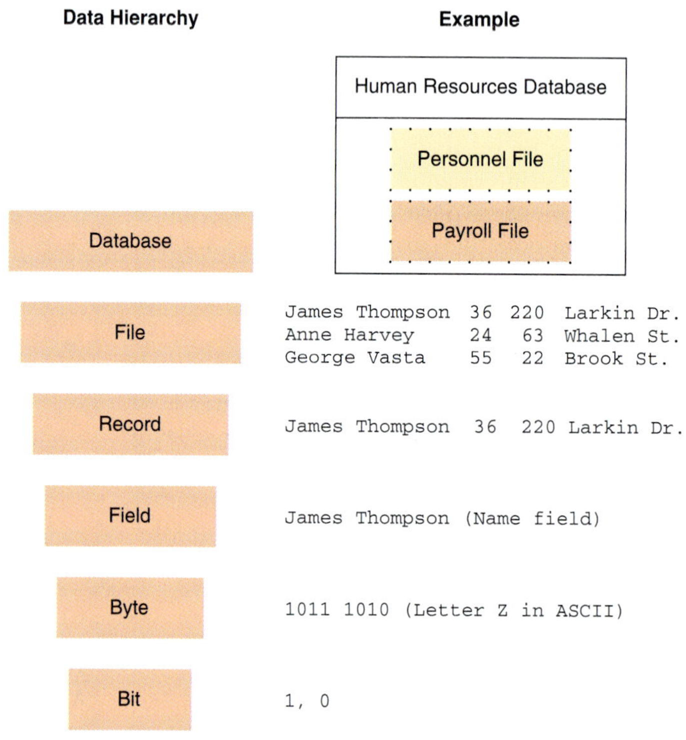

FIGURE 6.2

A Sample Record Containing Data about the Entity "Employee"

A personnel record with information about employees contains separate fields for attributes such as last name, first name, and so on. Social Security number is the key field because each employee has a unique Social Security number that can be used to identify that employee.

Entity = "Employee"

SSN Field	Last Name Field	First Name Field	Birth Date Field	Address Field
444367890	Johnson	Maureen	01/02/60	12 Valley Road, Croton, NY 10520
113467098	Kanter	Steven	11/04/44	33 Hillsdale Dr., Peekskill, NY 10566
224569801	Minton	Helen	08/04/57	46 Wood Road, Bedford, NY 10593
576018935	Thomas	George	04/04/59	11 Avery Drive, Croton, NY 10520

Key Field

Attributes

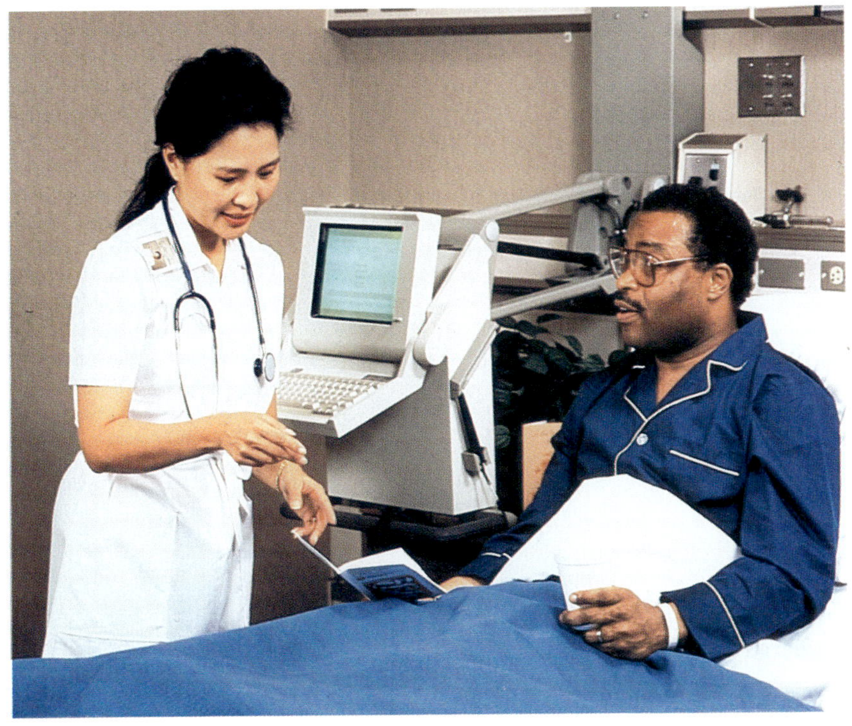

Computers are used in hospitals to help diagnose patients, design treatments, prescribe drugs, and teach medicine. Records for patients typically include the patient's name and address, medical problems, allergies, and prescribed medications.

SOURCE: Courtesy of International Business Machines Corporation.

attribute of the entity employee. The specific values that these attributes have can be found in the fields in a record describing a particular entity.

Key Fields Every record in a file or database must contain at least one field that uniquely identifies that record so that it can be retrieved (accessed), updated, or sorted. This identifier field is called a **key field.** An example of a key field would be an employee number or Social Security number for a personnel file or a product number for an inventory file. In the sample personnel record in Figure 6.2, which contains information about the entity employee, the Social Security number is the key field for the record because each employee has a unique Social Security number.

Key field
A field in a record that uniquely identifies that record so that it can be retrieved, updated, or sorted.

6.2 THE TRADITIONAL FILE ENVIRONMENT

The way data are organized on storage media determines how easily they can be accessed and used. In Chapter 4 we discussed the difference between sequential-access storage devices, such as magnetic tape, and direct-access storage devices (DASDs), such as magnetic disk. In a **traditional file environment,** data records are physically organized on storage devices using either sequential file organization or random (or direct) file organization.

Traditional file environment
The storage of data so that each application has its own separate data file or files and software programs.

FIGURE 6.3

Two Methods of Organizing Data

The sequential file access method (panel a) retrieves records in the same sequence as that in which they are physically stored. In the indexed sequential-access method (ISAM) (panel b), records are also stored sequentially but can be accessed directly by using an index. The index lists every record by its unique key field and gives its storage location.

(a) Sequential File Access Method

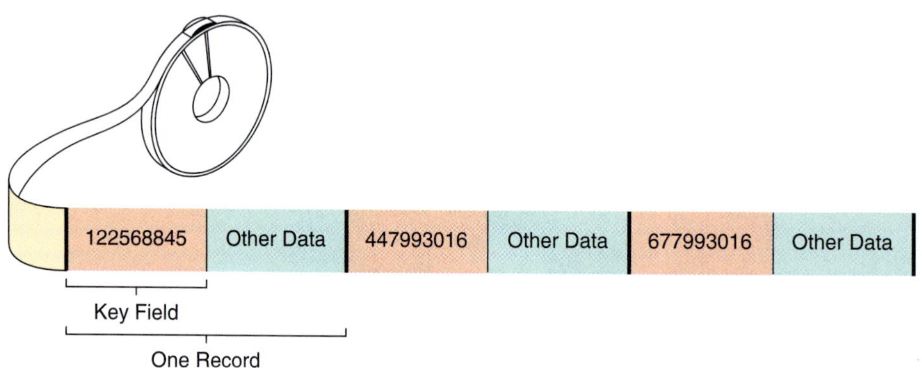

(b) Indexed Sequential Access Method (ISAM)

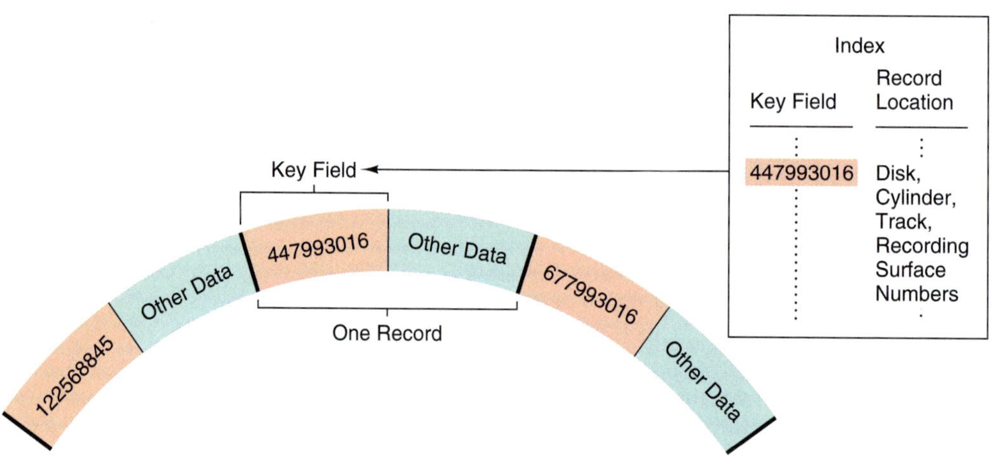

Sequential file organization A way of storing data records so that they must be retrieved in the physical order in which they are stored; the only file organization method that can be used with magnetic tape.

Random file organization A way of storing data records so that they can be accessed in any sequence, regardless of their physical order; used with magnetic disk technology.

SEQUENTIAL FILE ORGANIZATION

In **sequential file organization,** data records must be retrieved in the same physical sequence as the one in which they are stored. In **random** (or direct) **file organization,** data records can be accessed in any sequence, independent of their physical order. Sequential file organization is the only file organization method that can be used with magnetic tape. Random file organization is used with magnetic disk technology.

Sequential files are becoming outmoded, but they are still used for older batch-processing applications, which access and process each record in sequential order. The classic example is a payroll system; the system must process all a firm's employees one by one and issue each a check. Most applications today, however, including those based on PCs, rely on some form of random file organization method.

Figure 6.3 compares sequential file access with the **indexed sequential-access method (ISAM),** which stores records sequentially on a DASD but also allows individual records to be accessed in any desired order by using an **index** of key fields. Like the index for a book, the index for a file consists of a list of record keys and their associated storage location. The index shows the actual physical location on disk of each record that can be found via its key field. Any specific record can be located directly by checking the index for its storage address. ISAM is most useful for applications requiring sequential processing of large numbers of records in batch mode but with occasional direct access of individual records.

Indexed sequential-access method (ISAM)
A way of storing records sequentially on a direct-access storage device that allows individual records to be accessed in any desired order using an index of key fields.
Index
A list, for a file or database, of the key field of each record and its associated storage location.

RANDOM FILE ORGANIZATION

Random, or direct, file organization also uses a key field to locate the physical address of a record but accomplishes this without an index. This access method uses a mathematical formula called a randomizing algorithm (also called a transform or hashing algorithm) to translate the contents of a key field directly into the record's physical storage location on disk. The algorithm performs some mathematical computation on the record's key field, and the result of that calculation is the record's physical address. For example, in Figure 6.4, the randomizing algorithm divides the record's key field number (4467) by the prime number closest to the total number of records in the file (997). The remainder designates the address on disk for that particular record.

This access method is most appropriate for applications requiring location of individual records directly and rapidly for immediate online processing. Only a few records in the file need to be retrieved, and the records are selected randomly, in no particular sequence. An example might be an online order processing application.

FILE ORGANIZATION AND TRANSACTION PROCESSING

File organization not only determines how quickly data can be accessed from an information system, it determines how quickly data can be entered

FIGURE 6.4

Direct File Access Methods

Direct file access involves a mathematical operation called a randomizing algorithm. In this example, the algorithm divides the record's key field contents (4467) by the prime number closest to the total number of records in the file (997). The remainder (479) is the record's storage address on disk. Thus, one can go directly to this record rather than sift through all the records that may be stored ahead of it.

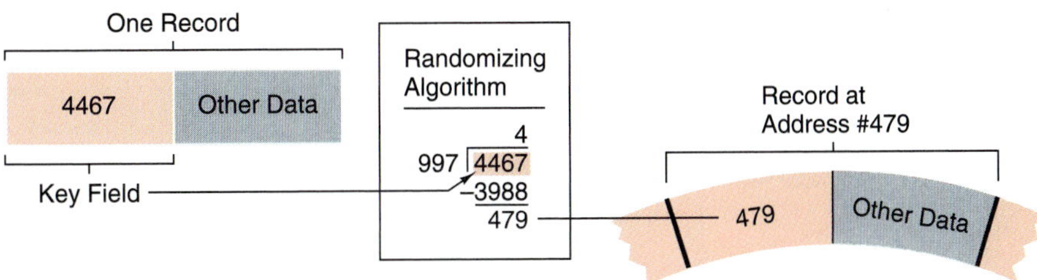

and processed as well. At their most elementary level, information systems keep track of the day-to-day transactions of a business, such as processing orders, airline reservations, or payroll checks. A transaction is an event to which a business must respond by collecting data relevant to the transaction and storing that data in either a manual or computerized information system. Transactions are used to update the firm's records and to produce documents required for business operations. The personnel record illustrated in Figure 6.2, for instance, could be created by entering a transaction to add an employee to the firm's personnel file. Other types of personnel transactions might involve changing an employee's address or deleting an employee record from the firm's personnel file if employment is terminated.

Chapter 4 introduced the concepts of batch and online input and processing. Transactions can be processed in either batch or online mode. Online transaction processing requires a direct-access storage device and some form of direct file organization. Making an airline reservation, illustrated in Figure 6.5, is a classic online transaction processing application. Airline reservation or travel agents key in airline reservations at desktop terminals. The key fields in the airline reservation transaction (date, destination, and flight number) are used to locate the address of the appropriate reservation record

FIGURE 6.5

Online Transaction Processing

Online transaction processing is used for airline reservations and other applications in which information must be processed immediately. Direct file organization is required so that the reservation transaction can directly locate the appropriate reservation record and update it.

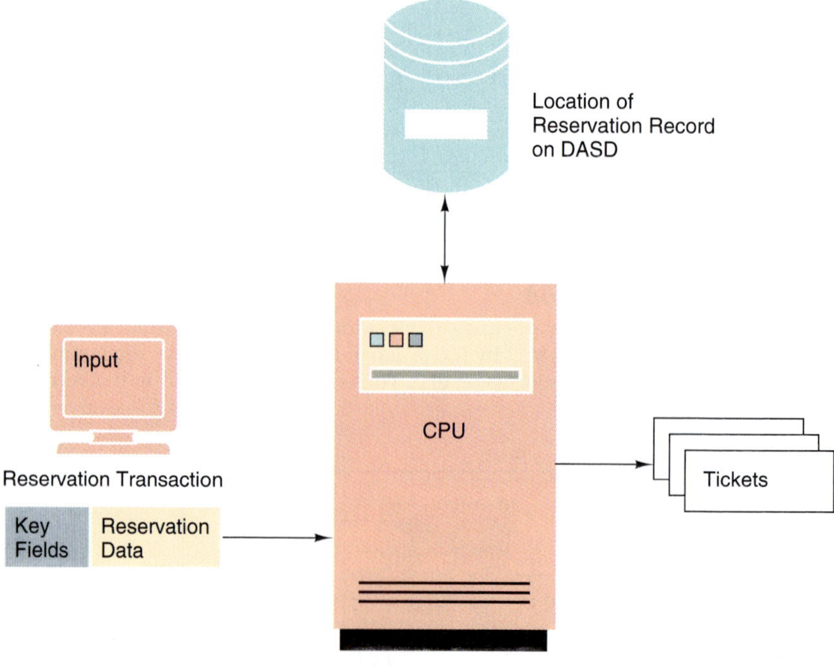

and update that record. Passengers are immediately booked on the flight of their choice. If requested to do so by passengers, agents with desktop printers can print out their tickets at the same time as they are making the reservations.

The processing of transactions necessary to conduct the day-to-day activities of the business is the distinctive feature of a special category of information systems called transaction processing systems. Chapter 13 provides a detailed description of the role of transaction processing systems in business.

PROBLEMS WITH THE TRADITIONAL FILE ENVIRONMENT

All these methods of file organization are associated with individual files and individual software programs. But what if the information required in order to solve a particular problem is located in more than one file? Often, extra programming and data manipulation will be required to obtain that information.

For example, suppose you want to know all the orders outstanding for a particular customer. Some of the information is maintained in an order file for an order entry application. The rest of the information is contained in a customer master file. Thus, the required information is stored in disparate files, each of which is organized in a different way. To extract the required information, you will need to sort both files repeatedly until the records are arranged in the same order. Records from the two files will have to be matched, and the data items from the merging of both files will have to be extracted and output. Obtaining this information entails additional programming and the creation of more files. Sometimes the effort to extract this information is so enormous that the problem remains unsolved.

Even with the most up-to-date computer hardware and software, the traditional file environment presents many obstacles to efficient and effective problem solving—high costs, poor performance, inflexible response to information requests, and information processing chaos. Most organizations have developed information systems one at a time, as the need arose, each with its own set of software programs, files, and users (the people in the organization who use that system). Over time, these independent applications and files can proliferate to the point that the firm's information resources may be out of control. Some symptoms of this crisis are data redundancy, program/data dependence, data inconsistency, and excessive software costs. This predicament is illustrated in Figure 6.6 for a bank in which customers maintain several accounts.

Data redundancy refers to the presence of duplicate data in multiple data files. The same piece of data, such as employee name and address, is maintained and stored in several different files by several different systems. Separate software programs must be developed to update this information and keep it current in each file in which it appears.

Data redundancy
The presence of duplicate data in multiple data files.

Program/data dependence refers to the close relationship between data stored in files and the specific software programs required to update and maintain those files. Every computer program must describe the location of the data it uses. In a traditional file environment, any change to the format or structure of data in a file necessitates a change in each software program that uses these data. The program maintenance effort required, for example, to change from a five-digit to a nine-digit ZIP code may be exorbitant.

Program/data dependence
The close relationship between data stored in files and the specific software programs required to update and maintain those files, whereby any change in data format or structure requires a change in all the programs that access the data.

FIGURE 6.6

The Traditional Approach to Organizing Data

Most organizations have developed information systems one at a time, as they needed them, each with its own set of software programs and files. Often, this involves storing duplicate information in each system.

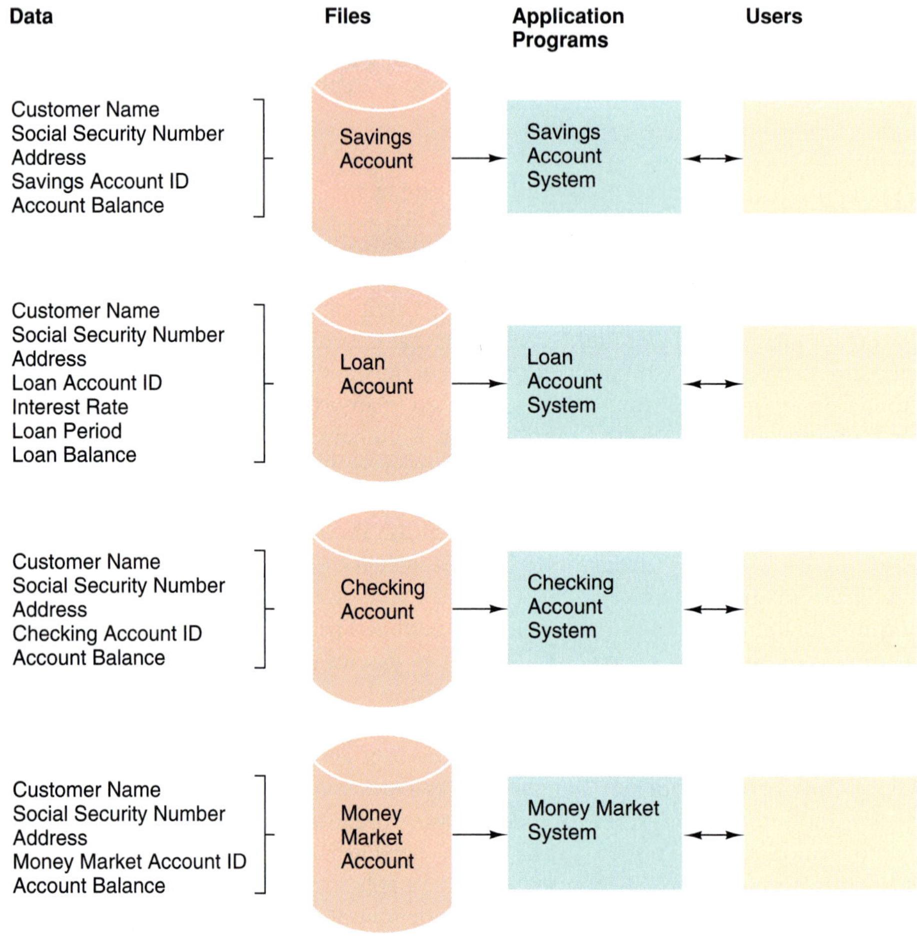

Data inconsistency refers to inconsistencies among various representations of the same piece of data in different information systems and files. Over time, as different groups in a firm update their applications according to their own business rules, data in one system become inconsistent with the same data in another system. For example, the student names and addresses maintained in a school student enrollment system and in a separate system to generate mailing labels may not correspond exactly if each system is updated with different software programs, procedures, and time frames.

Excessive software costs result from creating, documenting, and keeping track of so many files and different applications, many of which contain redundant data. Organizations must devote a large part of their information systems resources merely to maintaining data in hundreds and thousands of files. New requests for information can be satisfied only if professional programmers write new software to strip data from existing files and recombine them into new files.

6.3 THE DATABASE VISION

Many of the problems of the traditional file environment can be solved by taking a database approach to data management and storage. Here is a stricter definition of a database: a collection of data organized so that they can be accessed and used by many different applications. Instead of storing data in separate files for each application, data are stored physically so that they appear to users as being stored in one location. A single common database services multiple applications. For example, instead of a bank storing customer data in separate information systems and separate files for savings accounts, money market funds, loans, and checking accounts, the bank could create a single common client database, as in Figure 6.7.

FIGURE 6.7

How a Database Management System Helps a Business Organize Data

Here we see how a database management system could help the bank solve the data problems shown in Figure 6.6. The bank can combine all its data into a single customer database, and the database management system can make the data available to multiple applications and users. Combining all data into one database avoids duplicating data. It also means that a particular data element needs to be updated only once; all systems will use the same updated piece of information.

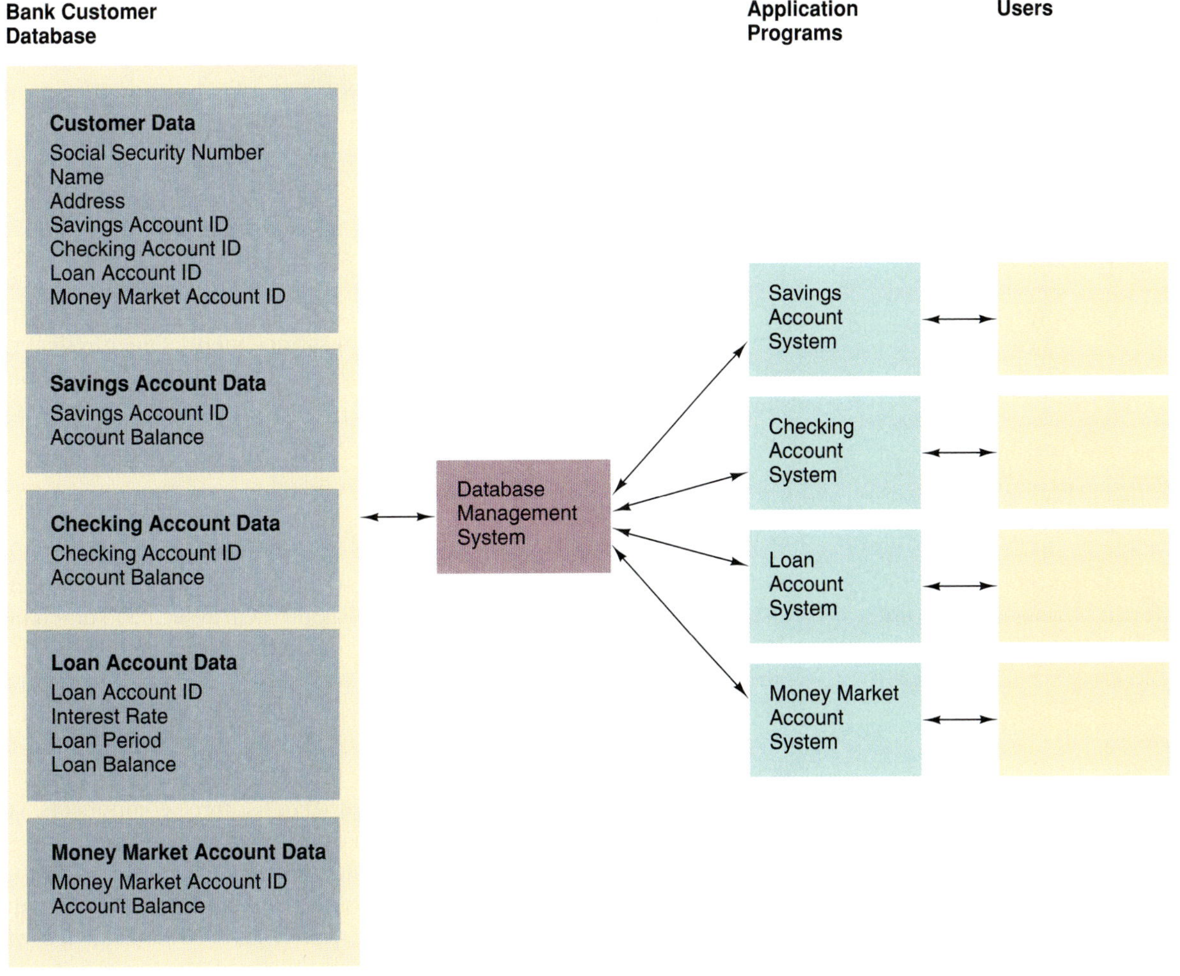

To improve the detection of severe weather, data on storms, such as wind speed and direction, are collected and analyzed by the NEXRAD system created by Unisys Corporation. The information is stored in a database and sent to U.S. government weather bureaus and air traffic controllers.

SOURCE: Courtesy of Unisys Corporation.

LOGICAL VERSUS PHYSICAL VIEWS OF DATA

Logical view
The presentation of data as they would be perceived by end users or business specialists.

Physical view
The presentation of data as they are actually organized and structured on physical storage media.

Database management system (DBMS)
Software that serves as an interface between a common database and various application programs; it permits data to be stored in one place yet be made available to different applications.

Data definition language
The part of a database management system that defines each data element as it appears in the database before it is translated into the form required by various application programs.

The database concept distinguishes between logical and physical views of data. In the **logical view,** data are presented as they would be perceived by end users or business specialists. The **physical view** shows how data are actually organized and structured on physical storage media. One physical view can support many logical views. A database management system uses special database management software to make the physical database available for different logical views presented by various application programs.

COMPONENTS OF A DATABASE MANAGEMENT SYSTEM

Special software called a **database management system (DBMS)** permits these data to be stored in one place while making them available to different applications. Database management software serves as an interface between the common database and various application programs. When an application program calls for a data element like hourly pay rate, the database management software locates it in the database and presents it to the application program. There is no need for the application programmer to specify in detail how and where the data are found. A database management system has three components: a data definition language, a data manipulation language, and a data dictionary.

The **data definition language** defines each data element as it appears in the database before it is translated into the form required by various application programs. Database programming specialists use this language when they are developing the database.

The **data manipulation language** is a special tool for manipulating data in the database. It is used along with some conventional third- or fourth-generation programming languages. It has features that both end users and technical specialists can use to extract data from the database, satisfy information requests, and develop applications. The most prominent data manipulation language today is **SQL, or Structured Query Language,** which is the data manipulation language for mainframe database management systems such as IBM's DB2, with versions for PC database management software.

A **data dictionary** is an automated file that stores definitions of data elements and other characteristics such as usage patterns, ownership (who in the organization is responsible for maintaining the data), relationships among data elements, and security. If properly documented, the data dictionary is an important problem-solving tool. It identifies for end users and business specialists which data reside in the database, their structure and format, and their business usage.

Figure 6.8 shows a sample data dictionary entry for a human resources database. This entry describes the size, format, meaning, alternate name

Data manipulation language
A special tool in a database management system that manipulates the data in the database.

SQL (Structured Query Language)
A data manipulation language for relational database management systems that is a business standard.

Data dictionary
The component of a database management system that stores definitions and other characteristics of data elements; it identifies which data reside in the database, their structure and format, and their business usage.

FIGURE 6.8

An Example of a Data Dictionary Entry

Here is a sample entry from a data dictionary for a human resources database. The data element is AMT-YTD-EARNINGS; its "alias" or alternative name is YTD-EARNINGS. The entry gives such helpful information as the size of the data element, which programs and reports use it, and which department is responsible for updating it.

NAME : AMT-YTD-EARNINGS
ALIAS : YTD-EARNINGS

DESCRIPTION : EMPLOYEE'S YEAR-TO-DATE EARNINGS

SIZE : 9 BYTES

TYPE : NUMERIC

OWNERSHIP : PAYROLL

UPDATE SECURITY : PAYROLL DATA ENTRY CLERK

ACCESS SECURITY : PAYROLL DATA ENTRY CLERK
PAYROLL MANAGER,
ACCOUNTS PAYABLE MANAGER
PERSONNEL COMPENSATION ANALYST
BENEFITS ADMINISTRATOR

BUSINESS FUNCTIONS USED IN : PAYROLL
PERSONNEL
BENEFITS

PROGRAMS USED IN : PLP1000
PLP2020
PLP4000
PLP6000

REPORTS USED IN : PAYROLL REGISTER
PAYROLL CHECK STUB
W-2 FORMS
941A REPORT
PENSION BENEFITS REPORT

(alias), and usage of the data element AMT-YTD-EARNINGS, which is an employee's accumulated year-to-date earnings. The dictionary also shows which individuals, programs, reports, and business functions use this data element and which business function "owns" or has the responsibility for maintaining this piece of data. The "security" entries identify the people who have the right to access this information.

ADVANTAGES OF DATABASE MANAGEMENT SYSTEMS

Database management systems and a database approach to organizing information overcome many of the limitations of the traditional file environment:

- Data are independent of application programs. The DBMS distinguishes between logical and physical views of data so that many different application programs can use data from a common, shared database.
- Data redundancy and inconsistency are reduced. Because data are independent of application programs, there is no need to build isolated files in which the same data elements are repeated each time a new application is called for. Data are maintained in only one place.
- Complexity is reduced by consolidated management of data, access, and use via the DBMS.
- Information is easier to access and use. The database establishes relationships among different pieces of information. Data from different records and applications can be more easily accessed and combined.

THE THREE DATABASE MODELS

The way data are organized in a database depends on the nature of the problems they are required to solve. There are three principal logical database models: the hierarchical model, the network model, and the relational model. Each model is best suited to solving a particular class of problems.

Hierarchical database model
The organization of data in a database in a top-down, treelike manner; each record is broken down into multilevel segments, with one root segment linked to several subordinate segments in a one-to-many, parent-child relationship.

The Hierarchical Model The **hierarchical database model** organizes data in a top-down, treelike manner. Each record is broken down into pieces of records called segments. The database looks like an organizational chart with one root segment and any number of subordinate segments. The segments, in turn, are arranged into multilevel structures, with an upper segment linked to a subordinate segment in a parent-child relationship. A "parent" segment can have more than one "child," but a subordinate "child" segment can have only one "parent."

The hierarchical model thus works best for one-to-many relationships among pieces of data. Figure 6.9 shows a hierarchical database for personnel in a work department. The root segment, *Department,* is the point of entry into the hierarchy. Data are accessed by starting at the root and moving progressively downward in the hierarchy. Thus, to find information about employees, jobs, and performance ratings, one must start at Department and then access related data about the employees and jobs in a particular department. IBM's IMS (Information Management System) is the most widely used hierarchical DBMS.

FIGURE 6.9

A Hierarchical Database: A Child Has Only One Parent

The design of a hierarchical database resembles a tree: it has a single "root" segment (in this case, "department") connected to several lower-level segments ("employee"). Each employee segment, in turn, connects to other subordinate segments ("performance ratings" and "job assignments"), each subordinate segment being the "child" of the "parent" segment immediately above it in the design. In a hierarchical database, each child segment can have only one parent; in order to access that child, one must "go through" the parent.

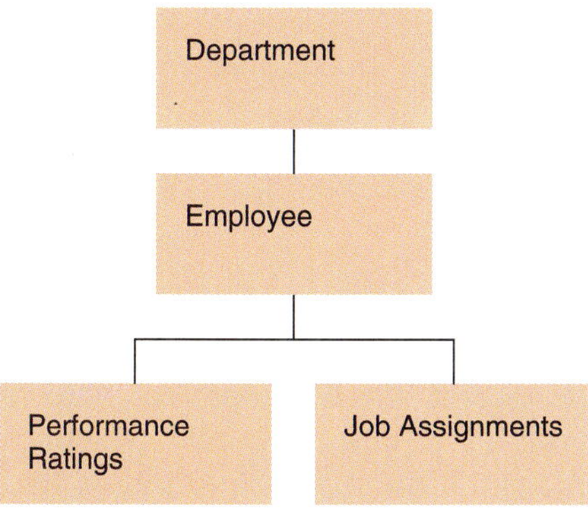

Hierarchical DBMSs thus have well-defined, prespecified access paths. Any piece of data in the database must be accessed from the top downward, starting with the root segment and proceeding through successive layers of subordinate segments. Hierarchical DBMSs are best suited for problems that require a limited number of structured answers that can be specified in advance. Once data relationships have been specified, they cannot easily be changed without a major programming effort. Thus, the hierarchical model cannot respond flexibly to changing requests for information.

Hierarchical DBMSs are also noted for their processing efficiency, making them ideal for systems in which massive numbers of records and changes to the database must be processed. Hierarchical DBMSs would be ideal for solving problems such as the daily processing of millions of airline reservations or automated teller banking transactions.

The Network Model The **network database model** is best at representing many-to-many relationships among data. In other words, a "child" can have more than one "parent." For example, in the network structure for personnel in work departments in Figure 6.10, an employee can be associated with more than one department. Computer Associates' IDMS is a network DBMS for computer mainframes.

Network database model
The organization of data in a database to depict a many-to-many relationship.

Network DBMSs are more flexible than hierarchical DBMSs, but access paths must still be specified in advance. There are practical limitations to the number of links, or relationships, that can be established among records. If they are too numerous, the software will not work efficiently. Neither network nor hierarchical database management models can easily create new relationships among data elements or new patterns of access without major programming efforts.

FIGURE 6.10

A Network Database: A Child Can Have More Than One Parent

A network database permits many-to-many relationships. If we wanted to retrieve information on Employee 3, for example, we could access that information by going through either Department A or Department B. This means that network databases are somewhat more flexible than their hierarchical counterparts, although there are practical limits to the number of links that can be designed into them.

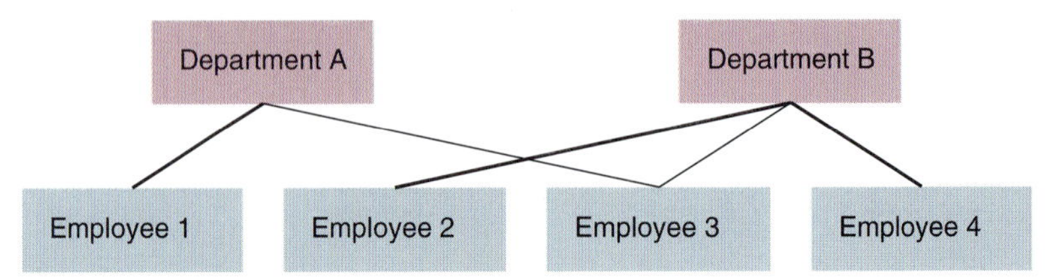

Relational database model
The organization of data in a database in two-dimensional tables called relations; a data element in any one table can be related to any piece of data in another table as long as both tables share a common data element.

The Relational Model The most recently developed database structure, the **relational database model,** was developed to overcome the limitations of the other two models in representing data relationships. The relational model represents all data in the database in simple two-dimensional tables called relations. The tables appear similar to flat files, but the information in more than one file can be easily extracted and combined.

The strength of the relational model is that a data element in any one file or table can be related to any piece of data in another file or table as long as both tables share a common data element. IBM's DB2 and Oracle from the Oracle Corporation are examples of mainframe relational database management systems. Microsoft Access is a PC relational database management system. (Oracle also has a PC version.)

Figure 6.11 illustrates how personnel in work departments would be treated by a relational database. The relational database consists of four tables or files: a department file (Department), an employee file (Employee), a performance rating file (Performance), and a job assignment file (Job). Each file or table consists of columns and rows. Each column represents a different field, and each row represents a different record in the file. The database was arranged this way because most of the time these files or tables are updated and accessed independently. When information is needed from more than one table, however, it can be combined by using DBMS commands. Therefore, a request to show which department is associated with a particular job assignment and the department's name and location could easily be satisfied by a relational database model.

The standard data manipulation language for relational database management systems is SQL (Structured Query Language). SQL was developed by IBM in the mid-1970s for mainframe and minicomputer environments and was commercially introduced in 1979. It has been incorporated into some PC environments. In SQL, we can combine information from several tables or files using the operations SELECT, FROM, and WHERE.

The basic structure of an SQL query for retrieving data is as follows:

```
SELECT <columns>
FROM <tables>
[WHERE <condition>]
```

FIGURE 6.11

A Relational Database: The Most Flexible Approach to Data Retrieval

A relational database arranges data into tables, or relations. A data element in one table can be related to any data element in any other table as long as the two tables share a common data element. Thus, in the example here, the employee table can be combined with the job assignment table because each table has a field containing a job code. Similarly, the employee table can be combined with the performance rating table because each holds an employee ID field.

Table (Relation)

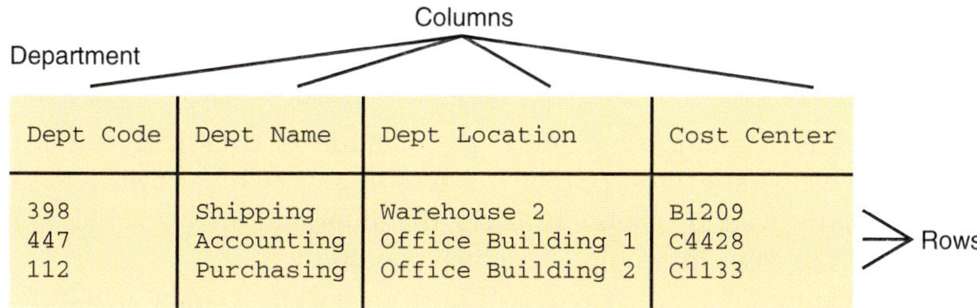

Dept Code	Dept Name	Dept Location	Cost Center
398	Shipping	Warehouse 2	B1209
447	Accounting	Office Building 1	C4428
112	Purchasing	Office Building 2	C1133

Employee

Employee ID	Employee Name	Address	Age	Hire Date	Term Date	Salary	Job Code
113223394	David Sniffen	11 Scenic Dr, Rye, NY 11233	33	02/04/90		22,000	S88
432669764	Paula Hayes	22 Brook St, Croton, NY 10520	67	05/03/49	04/30/90	27,000	C42
135770964	Mark Hastings	6 Nordica, Elmsford, NY 11677	44	11/01/85		66,000	M55
445890264	Robert Flynn	3 Oak Pl, Harrison, NY 10767	55	11/01/77		46,000	M77

Job Assignment

Job Code	Job Description	Date Created	Salary Range	Dept Code
C42	Clerk	01/01/45	13,000-29,000	447
S88	Shipping Clerk	05/01/49	15,000-25,000	398
M55	Manager	01/01/45	40,000-150,000	112

Performance Rating

Employee ID	Performance Rating	Evaluation Date
113223394	2	12/14/98
432669764	3	11/23/98
135770964	1	12/07/98
445890264	2	12/14/98

FIGURE 6.12

A Sample Query Using SQL

SQL (Structured Query Language) is a popular data manipulation language for retrieving information from relational databases. Here we see an SQL query to obtain information by joining two different tables.

```
SELECT Job.Job__Code,Job__Description,Job.Dept__Code,Dept__Name,
Dept__Location
FROM Job,Department
WHERE Job.Dept__Code = Department.Dept__Code
```

The SELECT command identifies the columns or data fields to retrieve. The FROM clause specifies the tables or files from which to retrieve this information. The WHERE clause restricts the information output to only those records or rows matching a specified condition.

Figure 6.12 illustrates a typical SQL query to extract data from the Department and Job tables illustrated in Figure 6.11. The two tables share a common field, Dept_Code, which identifies each department. In the SQL query, the department code field in the Job table, called Job.Dept_Code, is given a prefix of Job to distinguish it from the department code field (Department.Dept_Code) in the Department table. The query described in Figure 6.12 joins the Department and Job tables to form a new table with the required information.

6.4 APPLYING DATABASE CONCEPTS TO PROBLEM SOLVING

In applying database concepts to problem solving, several points must be kept in mind: (1) how the database should be designed; (2) whether a traditional file access method or a database approach should be chosen; and (3) if a database approach is appropriate, which database model should be selected. The solution should also specify whether data should be stored in one central location or distributed in multiple locations in the organization.

DESIGNING DATABASE SOLUTIONS

Because file or database organization has a profound effect on how information can be delivered, the design of a database must be very carefully considered. An information system solution must include the logical design and physical design of the database.

The logical design of the database shows how data are arranged and organized from a business, as opposed to a technical, perspective. There are three steps in logical database design:

1. Identifying the functions the solution must perform.
2. Identifying the pieces of data required by each function.

3. Grouping the data elements in a manner that most easily and efficiently delivers the solution.

We will illustrate the data modeling for a simple purchasing system. (Real-world systems of this sort are more complex; we have simplified here for instructional purposes.) The problem consists of finding a way to track the orders for all the parts a ventilator manufacturer purchases from outside vendors. There may be more than one order for each part. The solution consists of a purchasing system with three basic functions:

- Issuing and tracking purchase orders.
- Keeping track of parts on order.
- Tracking parts suppliers.

The system will need to maintain the following data for each function:

1. Issue purchase orders:

   Order number

   Part number

   Part description

   Unit cost

   Number of units

   Total cost of order

   Vendor identification code

   Vendor name

   Vendor address

   Order date

   Delivery date

2. Track parts:

   Part number

   Part description

   Unit cost

   Vendor identification code

   Vendor name

   Vendor address

3. Track suppliers:

   Vendor identification code

   Vendor name

   Vendor address

   Vendor payment terms

This laundry list of data must then be analyzed to identify redundant items and to find the most useful way to group data elements. From our list and description of functions, we can identify three basic data groupings or entities: orders, parts, and suppliers. Each grouping represents a single subject, or entity, and defines an individual file or record. The data elements are the details that are appropriate for describing each entity. We also need to add key fields so that we can identify unique records. Thus, part number is the key field for the parts file, vendor identification code is the key field for the suppliers file, and order number is the key field for the orders file.

The final logical design describes all the data elements to be stored in the database, the records and files into which they will be grouped, the relationships among these data elements, and the structure of the database (hierarchical, network, or relational). Figure 6.13 shows that the logical design for solving this problem uses a relational model with three separate tables, or files: a suppliers file, a parts file, and an order file. The key field in each table is marked with an asterisk.

Note that vendor name, vendor address, part description, and unit cost appear in only one file, although they are required for more than one function. Ideally, redundant data elements should be represented only once—in the group in which they are most appropriate. The data elements in each file pertain to the subject of that file, but they can be combined with one another if required. This is accomplished by using certain fields to establish links or relationships between files, a task facilitated by the relational database model. The vendor identification code in the parts file, for example, allows us to access further details about the vendor of a particular part from the suppliers file.

Once the logical database design has been finalized, it is translated into a physical database, the form in which the data are actually arranged and stored on computer storage media. The goal of physical database design is to arrange data in a manner that makes updating and retrieval as rapid and efficient as possible. Business specialists' data access patterns and frequency of data usage are important considerations for the physical design. The physical database design for our purchasing system using Microsoft Access software appears in Figure 6.14.

FIGURE 6.13

The Logical Design for Building a Purchasing System's Relational Database

The logical design for a database organizes the data according to an end-user perspective rather than a technical perspective. The final design groups the data elements into records and files that will best serve the information needs of the organization. It must also identify the key field of each file. In this illustration, we have marked the key field with an asterisk.

Order File	*Parts File*	*Suppliers File*
Order number*	Part number*	Vendor identification code*
Part number	Part description	Vendor name
Number of units	Unit cost	Vendor address
Total cost of order	Vendor identification code	Vendor payment terms
Order date		
Delivery date		

FIGURE 6.14

Building a Physical Design from a Logical Design

Here we see the physical database design developed from the logical plan in Figure 6.13. Microsoft Access software was used to create the physical version.

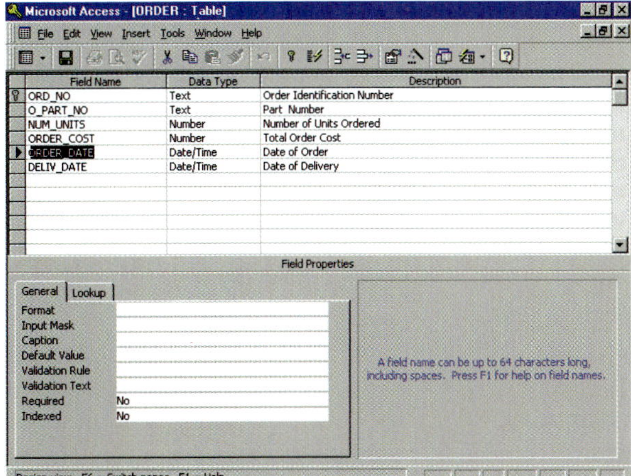

A Order Table

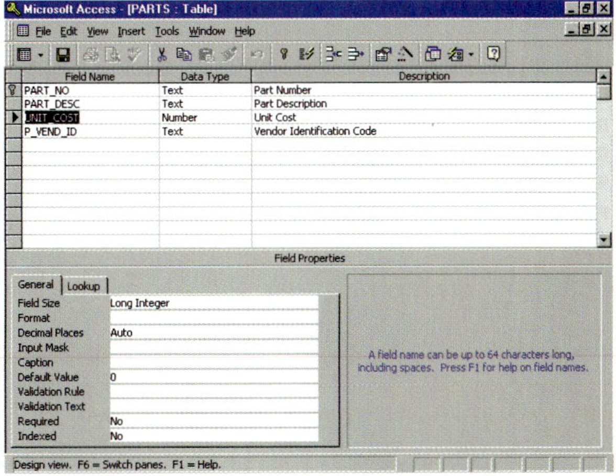

B Parts Table

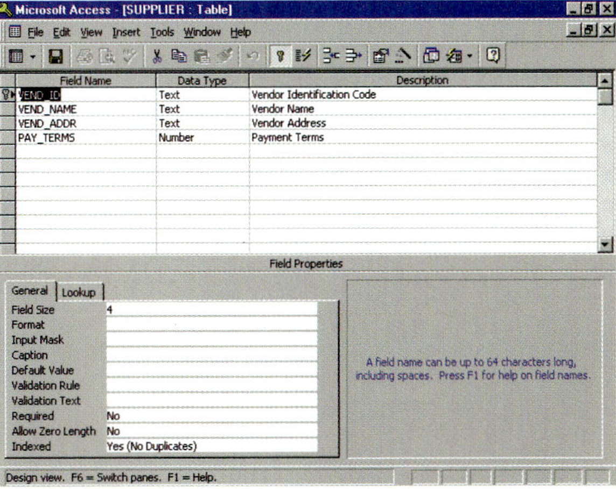

C Supplier Table

CHOOSING A TRADITIONAL FILE ACCESS METHOD OR A DATABASE APPROACH

Problem solving must consider alternative file organization and access methods. The nature of the problem at hand largely determines whether one of the traditional approaches to file management or a database approach should be built into the solution design.

Very few application solutions today will be based on magnetic tape sequential files. But files using indexed sequential or random-access methods may be appropriate if the solution best stands alone as an independent application or if the firm does not have the economic or organizational resources to commit to a database approach.

Stand-alone PC databases for personal or small business applications are easy to implement compared with large companywide databases residing on mainframes or minicomputers. The data requirements of personal or small business databases tend to be quite simple; PC database management software is much less complex and easier to master than mainframe DBMSs. However, a true database approach for a large corporation is a large-scale, long-term effort requiring deep-rooted organizational and conceptual changes. In order to fashion an application-independent database, organizational discipline must be applied to enforce common standards for defining and using data among diverse groups and functional areas. Defining and building files and programs that take into account the entire organization's interest in data is a long-term effort.

If a database approach is selected, the nature of the problem likewise dictates the most appropriate database model. Table 6.1 shows the kinds of problems each database model is best able to solve.

DISTRIBUTED DATABASES AND ONLINE INFORMATION SERVICES

Distributed database
A complete database or portions of a database that are maintained in more than one location.

Replicated database
A central database that is duplicated at all other locations.

Databases can be centralized in one location or distributed among multiple locations. The movement away from centralization toward distribution of computing resources and the growth of computer networks has also spawned a trend toward **distributed databases.** With a distributed database, a complete database or portions of it are maintained in more than one location. As Figure 6.15 shows, there are essentially two kinds of distributed databases: replicated and partitioned.

With a **replicated database,** a central database is duplicated at all other locations. This is most appropriate for problems in which every loca-

TABLE 6.1

A Problem-Solving Matrix for Database Models

Problem Dimension	Hierarchical DBMS	Network DBMS	Relational DBMS
Data relationships	One-to-many	Many-to-many	Flexible
Transaction volume	High	Medium	Medium but improving
Flexibility of information retrieval	Low	Low	High
Ease of use for end users	Low	Low	High

FIGURE 6.15

The Two Types of Distributed Databases: Replicated and Partitioned

A distributed database distributes data among several locations. There are two ways of doing this. A replicated database (panel a) places copies of the central database in each location. Every database is a duplicate of the central one. A partitioned database (panel b) "partitions" its data according to the needs of each location. Thus, each local database contains a different portion of the organization's data, and none of the local databases contains all the data.

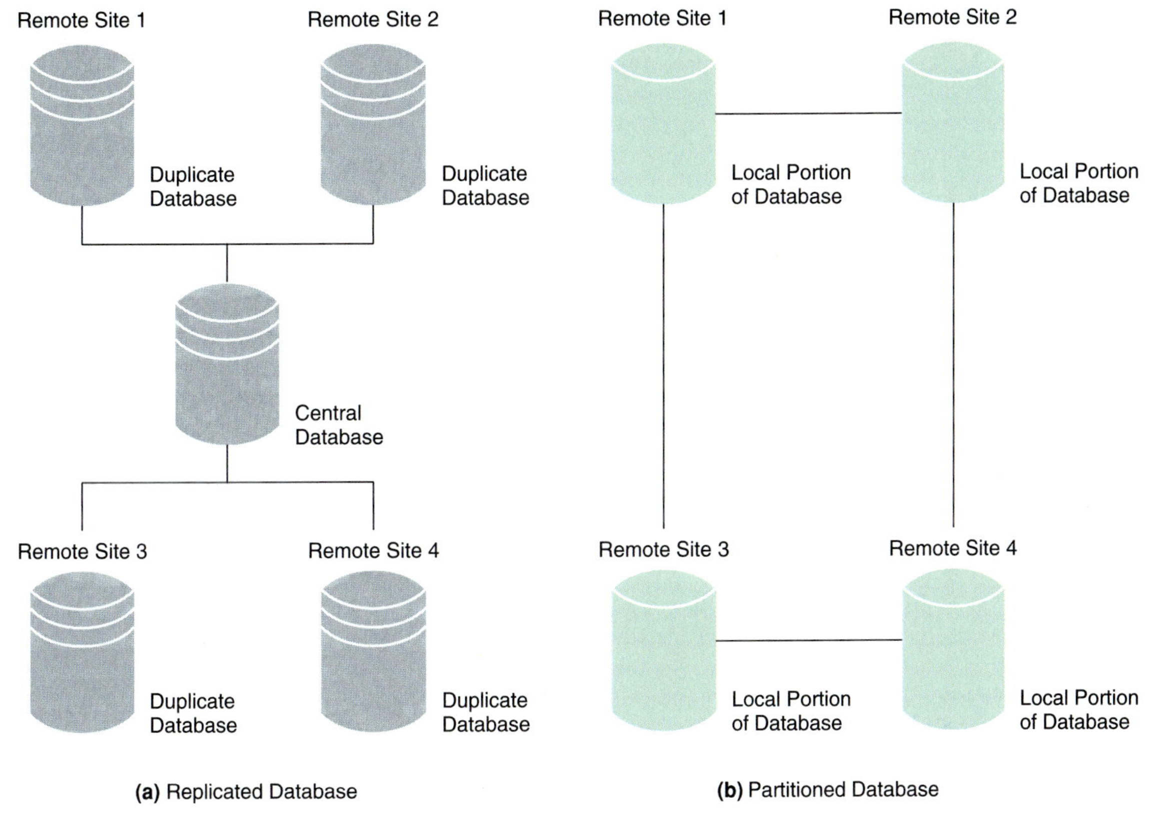

tion needs to access the same data. A **partitioned database** is subdivided so that each location has only the portion of the database that serves its local needs.

Partitioned database
A database that is subdivided so that each location has only the portion of the database that serves its local needs.

Distributed databases provide faster response time and service at each business location. Firms can fill orders or service customer requests faster if their data are locally available. Distributed databases also reduce the vulnerability of consolidating all the firm's essential data at only one site. They can also increase security problems, however, because of their dependence on telecommunications links and widened access to sensitive data.

Distributing databases increases data redundancy, especially if a replicated database is chosen. Inconsistencies can easily arise among the data in central and local systems, especially if changes to the data in one system are not immediately captured by the other. These problems can be compounded if data from a central database are informally "distributed" by downloading portions of them to PCs.

FOCUS ON **PEOPLE**

MEDICAL DATABASES GIVE A SECOND OPINION

The assertion that everyone has an opinion generally does not carry much weight where medical issues are concerned. When discussing an area as important as one's health, an informed opinion—in other words, that of a doctor—is the one that matters. Now, however, thanks to database technology and the World Wide Web, individuals can formulate their own informed medical opinions without the help of a physician. Some people find this to be a very valuable asset, while others warn that it might produce harmful results.

Anyone who has access to the Internet or commercial online data services can do medical research, and it seems that more and more people have turned to medical databases to investigate the findings of their doctors. In its first four months of operation, Health Responsibility Systems of Herndon, Virginia, logged more than 1 million consumer searches of its medical article database through the America Online information network. The National Library of Medicine in Bethesda, Maryland, reported that the amount of text downloaded from its massive Medline database of medical journal abstracts has more than doubled in the past five years.

Performing amateur medical research can be a complicated and time-consuming process, and organizations that will do the research for you have begun to thrive. Groups like MedCetera of Houston, and Health Resource of Conway, Arkansas, will search medical databases and send you the resultant articles for fees starting at around $100. Other companies such as HealthGate Data Corp. of Malden, Massachusetts, have Web sites that allow for searches geared toward educating patients. Tens of thousands of people bring up HealthGate's site each day, and several thousand have opened credit card accounts that permit them to view medical paper summaries. They can pay by the article or fork over a monthly fee for unlimited access.

So, what exactly has caused people to respond to their medical evaluations by returning to the doctor with their own diagnoses? Many people hint that it is because the doctor-patient relationship has eroded so much over the years. The days of family doctor house calls have long passed. Nowadays, health care plans bring people together with physicians they do not know and who sometimes do not have the time to investigate a case fully. Furthermore, some health maintenance organizations provide financial incentives to doctors for not mentioning treatments that the HMO's plan does not include. Such circumstances contribute to a lack of trust among patients. These patients want assurance that all possibilities have been explored; using medical databases can answer questions and satisfy patients' minds.

Some people have found success in seeking different courses of treatment on their own. By using the MedCetera medical database search service, Meg Eaton found that the surgeon scheduled to perform delicate surgery on her son's perforated eardrum had previously performed only 12 such operations. She consulted another specialist, who recommended a less invasive procedure that proved successful.

Not surprisingly, doctors have expressed concern over this trend. They fear that too much exposure to medical data will beset people with a problem that some medical students experience: the more symptoms and maladies you read about, the more likely you are to falsely attribute some to yourself. Doctors also point out that a lot of the available material uses scientific language that the average person cannot readily understand. And in the worst scenarios, people with terminal conditions might find information somewhere that fosters false hopes in them. Even doctors who support the idea of patients participating actively in their treatment prescribe proceeding with a sense of caution.

FOCUS Questions:

How do people benefit from computerized medical databases? How can they be harmed? What steps could be taken to prevent this data from being harmful?

SOURCE: Laura Johannes, "Patients Delve Into Databases to Second-Guess Doctors," *The Wall Street Journal,* February 21, 1996.

TABLE 6.2

Leading Online Database Services

Company	Service Provided
America Online	General interest and business information
CompuServe	Business and general interest information
Prodigy	Business and general interest information
Dow Jones News Retrieval	Business and financial information
Dialog	Scientific, technical, medical, and business information
Lexis	Legal research

In addition to maintaining information internally, many firms are using information from **online databases and information services.** Such services supply information such as stock market quotations, general news and information, or specific legal and business information. Some of these services are commercial, requiring subscribers to pay a fee for their use (see Table 6.2). Other online databases are available at no cost through the Internet. Users can search these online databases for specific information using as keywords and phrases, and extract reports. If you were doing research about CAD workstations, for example, you could request references using the key words *workstation, CAD,* and *computer-aided design* and receive a list of articles containing those key words.

Online database and information service
A service that supplies information external to the firm, such as stock market quotations, general news and information, or specific legal and business information.

The Focus on People illustrates some of the benefits—and some of the challenges—that prevail when people use the Internet or commercial information services to obtain medical information from online databases.

6.5 LEADING-EDGE TECHNOLOGY: NEW FORMS OF DATABASES AND DATA WAREHOUSES

As information needs change, methods of data storage and retrieval must also change. Object-oriented and hypermedia databases, along with data warehouses, are transforming the way we manage data.

OBJECT-ORIENTED DATABASES

Database management systems (DBMS) were initially designed to store only homogeneous, predefined, structured numeric and character data into fields and records. Many applications today need to store such traditional data together with drawings, images, photographs, voice, and even full-motion video within one database. CAD (computer-aided design) is a typical application. An engineer's design usually includes design specifications (numeric data), written descriptions (characters), and images (graphics) that are often complex three-dimensional representations that can be viewed from all angles. A

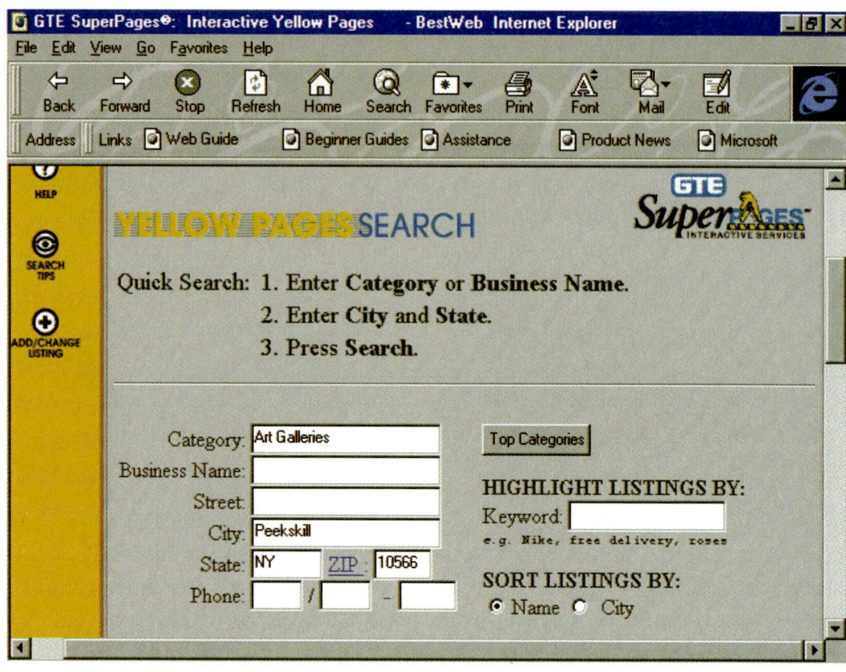

Visitors to the GTE SuperPages Web site can access information from a massive object-oriented database.

medical database might need to include doctor notes, laboratory reports, test results, chronological charts, X rays, and magnetic-resonance image videos. A traditional DBMS could not automatically manipulate and link these different types of data in a single application.

Object-oriented database
A database that stores data and processing instructions as objects that can be automatically retrieved and stored.

Object-oriented databases store data as objects that can be automatically retrieved and shared. Included in the object are processing instructions to complete each database transaction (see Chapter 5 for a discussion of object-oriented programming). These objects can contain various types of data, including sound, graphics, and video as well as traditional data and processing procedures. The objects can be shared and reused. These features of object-oriented databases promise to facilitate software development through reuse and the ability to build new multimedia applications that combine multiple types of data. For example, Cold Spring Harbor Laboratory, a biology research center in Cold Spring Harbor, New York, has used the GemStone object-oriented database management system (OODBMS) to store images of DNA molecules. The OODBMS lets the laboratory model the DNA molecule in three dimensions, as it actually appears in the real world.

Another benefit of OODBMSs is their ability to support applications for the World Wide Web, as described in the Focus on Technology.

Object-oriented databases are still a relatively new technology and can be much slower than relational systems for handling large quantities of data where there is a high volume of transaction processing. Hybrid object-relational databases have been developed that combine the capability of handling large numbers of transactions found in relational DBMSs with the capability of handling complex relationships and new types of data found in OODBMSs.

FOCUS ON TECHNOLOGY

REACH OUT AND TOUCH EVERYONE

Most homes keep their copy of the local yellow pages wherever it happens to fit: in a closet, on a shelf, next to the phone. When people do need to find a listing—for a restaurant for a cozy candlelit dinner—they have to lug out the fat, heavy tome and page through until they find something they like. Then they have to call, make a reservation, and get directions. But what if they could do the same thing with only a few keystrokes at their computer? That is the motivation behind SuperPages, a Web site created by GTE.

SuperPages is a database that stores listings of 11 million businesses across the United States. The advantage of placing such a database on the World Wide Web stems from both the Internet's ability to deliver large amounts of information and the Web's graphical and multimedia faculties. This was important to GTE because it did not want to limit its Web page to simple text listings. To counter growing competition from other phone companies and directory services, GTE aspired to set up an environment in which advertisers could incorporate multimedia elements such as sound, graphics, and video into their listings as well as large quantities of text data.

For instance, to find a restaurant, one accesses the GTE SuperPages site on the World Wide Web and fills in an online form with search criteria such as "all Chinese restaurants in Medford, Massachusetts." The query passes over the Internet to one of GTE's two Sun SparcServer 1000 workstations in Dallas. A search capability identifies and gathers the appropriate multimedia objects (in this case, restaurant listings) from a database. This information is sent back over the Internet to the user. By selecting one of the restaurants on the list and clicking on a hypertext link, the user can zoom in on a map showing the restaurant's location.

To accomplish their goal, members of GTE Directories' new media services department needed to select an appropriate database management system. The company decided that an object-oriented database would provide the technology necessary to make SuperPages most effective. Unlike relational databases, object-oriented databases combine and manage graphics, text, audio, and other information as a single unit, which can make for faster access. Relational database vendors claim that object-oriented database technology is still new and unproven.

GTE opted for ObjectStore, a database program from Object Design in Burlington, Massachusetts. GTE had been using Oracle as its relational database management system for other applications. Oracle had added object-management capabilities, but only in a relational file system. GTE found the response time for retrieving objects from Oracle too slow because relevant information had to be extracted from several locations in the database. ObjectStore, on the other hand, was a pure object-oriented database that could consolidate text, images, and sound into one easily activated component. GTE found that the pure object-oriented database required much less preparation than a relational database by eliminating as much as 40 percent of the application coding that would have been required by a relational database approach.

The technology driving SuperPages solves the problem of how to keep the site current. Making changes to an object database can take just minutes. Furthermore, GTE never has to shut down the site to add new listings, product information, or additional graphics or audio. Advertisers enjoy relative flexibility as well. They can now update their listings in one business day, and the process will eventually be an immediate one through the use of online forms. A plain text listing carries a fee of $25 per month, while an advertisement with a basic graphical display costs $10 more per month plus an initial construction fee. SuperPages also offers the option of linking an independent Web site for $45 plus the setup cost. GTE declares that sales have been quite successful and that its original investment should be recovered by 1999.

FOCUS Questions:
Was an object-oriented database an appropriate solution for GTE? Why or why not?

SOURCE: Bronwyn Fryer, "Let Your Browser Do the Walking," *Information Week,* October 14, 1996.

HYPERMEDIA DATABASES

Hypermedia database
A database organized to store text, graphics, audio, or video data as nodes that can be linked in any pattern established by the user.

Hypermedia databases manage data differently from object-oriented DBMSs, but they can also contain diverse types of data. They store data as "chunks" of information, with each chunk in a separate node. Each node can contain traditional numeric or character data or whole documents, software programs, graphics, and even full-motion video. Each node is totally independent—the nodes are not related by a predetermined organization scheme as they are in traditional databases. Instead, users establish their own links between nodes (see Figure 6.16). The relationships among nodes are less structured than in a traditional DBMS. Searching for information does not have to follow a predetermined organization scheme. Users can branch directly from one node to another in any relationship they establish. For instance, a hypermedia database on automobiles might link basic product information (auto model name, model number, color, body type, suggested dealer price) with descriptive sales brochures, a video showing the automobile in action, and the location of authorized dealers.

DATA WAREHOUSES

Data warehouse
A database that consolidates data from various operational systems for use in reporting and analysis.

Many companies have allowed their data to be stored in many separate systems that are unable to provide a consolidated view of information usable companywide. One way to address this problem is to build a data warehouse. A **data warehouse** is a database that consolidates data extracted from various production and operational systems into one large database that can be used for management reporting and analysis. The data from the organization's core transaction processing systems are reorganized and combined with

FIGURE 6.16

Hypermedia

In a hypermedia database, the user can choose his or her own path to move from node to node. Each node may contain text, graphics, sound, full-motion video, or executable programs.

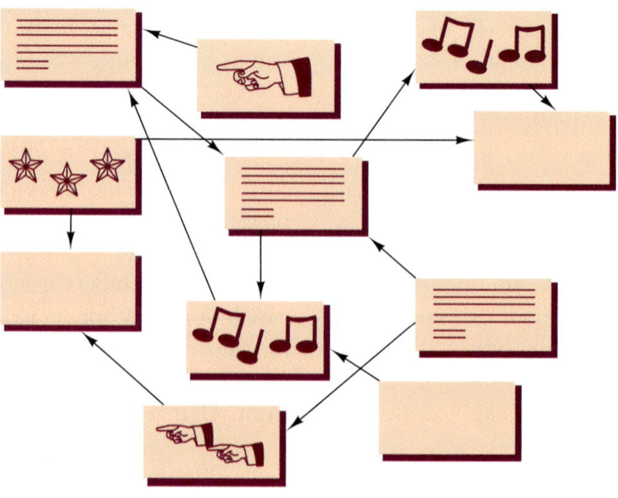

FOCUS ON PROBLEM SOLVING

PUTTING THE WORLD IN A BOX

DHL Worldwide Express, the number-one delivery company in the world, serves businesses and individuals daily in over 200 countries. Transporting and keeping track of hundreds of thousands of packages requires close attention to data control. For DHL, handling such great quantities of data becomes even more of a challenge when you consider that the company functions without a central headquarters. Fourteen worldwide regional centers oversee smaller facilities in each country in their region. Considering these circumstances, analyzing data on a full-scale level was once a daunting task. Generating a report is difficult when the data contributors follow their own conventions for collecting and organizing the information.

This was a problem that DHL could not ignore. The company had to address its customers' desire for detailed reports on the services they were receiving. Before choosing a plan of attack, DHL had to accept two facts: Different people had different data needs, and the information technology group could not impose its conventions on the regional centers. Once those factors were clear, so was the choice of a method for managing data. DHL opted to construct a data warehouse.

DHL Systems initially intended to incorporate a number of applications into its data warehouse. The company decided to proceed cautiously, however, and the project team narrowed the scope to just a marketing application and a costing application. DHL Systems' Dee Copelan stressed that combining those two data sources alone made a significant difference for the company, and the versatile nature of the warehouse will allow them to add other components systematically in the future. In the meantime, DHL's data warehouse has vastly improved analytical capabilities by converting inconsistent data into uniform terms. Automating this process means that workers can concentrate on performing detailed analysis rather than only compiling and translating different forms of data. DHL can now produce polished reports on its operations anywhere in the world in a matter of hours, which customers find appealing.

The business benefits of data warehousing are driving other organizations to develop gigantic databases for this purpose. In fact, some companies, including MCI, MasterCard, and Wal-Mart, have compiled databases that can be measured in terabytes, or *trillions* of bytes. MCI is using its three-terabyte data warehouse to reduce the cost of finding new customers. MCI matches the internal billing and call-detail information on its customers with demographic data provided by external sources. The data are analyzed using 21 models with 10,000 variables that define customer behavior. The warehouse is growing at a rate of 100 gigabytes per month. Creating and maintaining a data warehouse so enormous carries a multimillion-dollar price tag, but their users insist that the systems pay for themselves quite easily by increasing efficiency and cutting extraneous costs. Databases have reached this level of growth because organizations are gathering more data and keeping it longer for the purpose of long-term analysis. Some experts fear that the growth will run beyond anyone's control. In the period of only a few years, two-terabyte databases are expected to expand to at least 30 terabytes. Anne Grim, vice-president of global information services for MasterCard, admits that large databases may eventually have to be divided up for the sake of efficiency—when databases reach terabyte size, it takes conventional computers a long time to access information. Managing giant databases is complicated, and many fail to provide the desired results.

FOCUS Questions: What kinds of problems are data warehouses designed to solve? What kinds of problems do they create?

SOURCES: John Foley, "Towering Terabytes," *Information Week,* September 30, 1996, and "DHL Worldwide Makes Warehousing Work," *Computerworld,* February 13, 1995.

other information, including historical data so that they can be used for management decision making and analysis. In most cases, the data in the data warehouse can be used only for reporting—they cannot be updated—so that

FOCUS ON ORGANIZATIONS

THE WORLD WIDE WEB: THE NEW DATA MARKETPLACE

Does your mailbox overflow with catalogs and offers for free trips to Acapulco? Does your phone ring off the hook at around 6 P.M. with offers to sell you a product for which you have been specially chosen? If so, welcome to the controversial age of data selling.

A wide variety of organizations maintain databases chock-full of personal data on their customers. Often, they use this data to analyze customer preferences and sales trends. Equally important, such data are an additional source of revenue. Businesses that do not maintain such data will pay for access to databases that can help them target potential customers. For instance, catalog companies might sell their customer databases to other catalog companies looking for new customers.

The World Wide Web provides new avenues for sharing and selling personal data. Organizations can link their internal databases to the World Wide Web, where they can be accessed by their business partners. Outsiders can also query and analyze the data stored in the databases. For example, ShopKo Stores of Green Bay, Wisconsin, plans to let its suppliers access its 400-gigabyte database via the Web so that they can analyze sales trends. ShopKo has accumulated several years' worth of "market basket" data, representing the daily sales of 200,000 items in 130 stores, in an Oracle7 Parallel Edition database running on IBM parallel SP servers. ShopKo's suppliers will be able to know what is in every shopping basket so that they can determine what is selling and the effectiveness of their advertisements.

Why is this blossoming business controversial? Because it raises thorny privacy questions. Some of these data consist of personal information that people may not want other organizations to know about. Consumers do not always respond positively to the idea of having their incomes or buying habits sold around. Equally as seriously, companies that sell such data increase the risk of having the government step in to impose strict standards for the practice. One company has already experienced the downside of marketing personal data firsthand. Word that the information service provider LEXIS-NEXIS was making critical information such as Social Security numbers and maiden names available for sale spread quickly by E-mail. The company's Dayton, Ohio, headquarters received a deluge of communications from individuals

With its new data warehouse, DHL Worldwide Express can quickly generate reports on its operations anywhere in the world.

SOURCE: Courtesy of DHL Airways, Inc.

who requested that their names be deleted from the LEXIS-NEXIS P-Trak service. When the furor died down, it was revealed that the service provided Social Security numbers for only a very short period. The remainder of the data provided through P-Trak (name, address, two prior addresses, maiden name, birthdate, and telephone numbers) is header information from credit reports and is not protected by the Fair Credit Reporting Act. (The Fair Credit Reporting Act restricts the use of consumer credit data. Review Chapter 3.)

As a result of the LEXIS-NEXIS incident, the Federal Trade Commission has recommended broadening the Fair Credit Reporting Act to extend confidentiality guidelines to cover items such as Social Security numbers, birthdates, former addresses, and mothers' maiden names. The Senate even designated a subcommittee to explore the dangers of circulating personal data publicly. The subcommittee recognizes that a great deal of data has already reached the public arena, but it wants to investigate whether the data's presence on the Internet makes the problem much more severe because the data is easy to find and to access.

Despite the drawbacks, perfecting the union of data warehouses and the Internet remains a priority for some organizations. They are encouraged by findings such as those by the META Group in Stamford, Connecticut. Meta foresees "a new breed of data providers" that will shortly create a multibillion-dollar industry by distributing information over the Web to businesses and consumers. For instance, MicroStrategy, which sells online analytical processing (OLAP) software for relational databases, announced a joint venture with Acxiom Corporation, which accumulates data on 95 percent of U.S. households. These data include names, addresses, phone numbers, approximate incomes, hobbies, and personal interests. The combined product from these two companies can help other companies make money by allowing other companies to combine their internal data with demographic data and access that information through the Web. Even LEXIS-NEXIS intends to proceed with projects that involve using the Web to sell data. Will the federal government allow these efforts to proceed? Or will it issue new restrictions to protect individual privacy?

FOCUS Question:

What people, organization, and technology factors need to be addressed in using the Web for accessing data warehouses?

SOURCE: John Foley and Bruce Caldwell, "Dangerous Data," *Information Week,* September 30, 1996.

the performance of the company's underlying operational systems is not affected. The Focus on Problem Solving describes some of the benefits companies have obtained by using data warehouses.

Data warehouses often contain capabilities to remodel the data. A relational database allows views in two dimensions, such as sales by region. A multidimensional view of data lets users look at data in more than two dimensions—for example, sales by region by quarter. To provide this type of information, organizations can either use a specialized multidimensional database or a tool that takes multidimensional views of data in relational databases. Multidimensional analysis enables users to view the same data in different ways using multiple dimensions. Each aspect of information—product, pricing, cost, region, or time period—represents a different dimension. So a product manager could use a multidimensional tool to learn how many items were sold in the Southwest sales region in June, how that compares with the previous month and the previous June, and how it compares with the sales forecast. Another term for multidimensional data analysis is **online analytical processing (OLAP).**

Online analytical processing (OLAP)
Viewing data in different ways using multiple dimensions.

Database technology has provided many benefits, but it also allows organizations to maintain data that could threaten individual privacy. The threat to privacy is further magnified when organizations allow internal databases and data warehouses containing personal information to be accessed by outsiders using the World Wide Web. This issue is explored in the Focus on Organizations.

SUMMARY

- Data are organized in computerized information systems in a hierarchy that starts with bits and bytes and proceeds to fields, records, files, and databases.
- In the traditional file environment, data records are organized by using either a sequential file organization or a random file organization.
- Transactions can be processed in either batch or online mode. Online transaction processing requires a direct-access storage device and some form of direct file organization.
- Problems associated with the traditional file environment include data redundancy, program/data dependence, data confusion, and excessive software costs.
- A true database approach to organizing information stores data physically in only one location and uses special database management software so that this common pool of data can be shared by many different applications.
- The three components of a database management system are a data definition language, a data manipulation language, and a data dictionary.
- Advantages of using a database approach to organizing information include independence of data from application programs, reduction of data redundancy and inconsistency, elimination of data confusion, consolidation of data management, and ease of information access and use.
- The three principal database models are the hierarchical model, the network model, and the relational model. The suitability of each model depends on the nature of the problem to be solved—specifically, the nature of the data relationships (one-to-many or many-to-many), the need for flexibility, and the volume of requests or changes to the database to be processed.
- The standard data manipulation language for relational database management systems is Structured Query Language (SQL).
- With a distributed database, a complete database or portions of it are maintained in more than one location. The two major types of distributed databases are replicated databases and partitioned databases.
- Commercial online databases can provide essential information to firms easily and inexpensively.
- Object-oriented and hypermedia databases can store graphics and other types of data as well as numeric data and text, making them suitable for multimedia applications. Data in hypermedia databases can be linked together in any pattern established by the user.

• A data warehouse is a database consisting of current and historical data extracted from operational systems and consolidated for analysis and decision making. Data warehouses often have capabilities for multidimensional data analysis.

KEY TERMS

Field
Record
File
Database
Entity
Attribute
Key field
Traditional file environment
Sequential file organization
Random file organization
Indexed sequential-access method (ISAM)
Index
Data redundancy
Program/data dependence
Logical view
Physical view
Database management system (DBMS)
Data definition language
Data manipulation language
SQL (Structured Query Language)
Data dictionary
Hierarchical database model
Network database model
Relational database model
Distributed database
Replicated database
Partitioned database
Online database and information service
Object-oriented database
Hypermedia database
Data warehouse
Online analytical processing (OLAP)

REVIEW QUESTIONS

1. Why should businesses be concerned about file organization and management?
2. List and define each of the components of the data hierarchy.
3. Why are indexes and key fields important tools for file management?
4. What is the difference between the indexed sequential-access method and the sequential-access method? Distinguish between the indexed sequential-access method and the random-access method.
5. What is the relationship between file organization and batch and online transaction processing?
6. Define a database and a database management system.
7. What problems associated with a traditional file environment can be overcome by a DBMS?

8. What is the difference between a logical view and a physical view of data?
9. List and describe the components of a DBMS.
10. Why are data dictionaries important tools for businesses?
11. Describe the three principal database models and indicate the strengths and limitations of each.
12. What are the three steps in logical database design?
13. What is a distributed database? List and define the two major types of distributed databases.
14. How do hypermedia and object-oriented databases differ from a traditional database? What kinds of problems are they most useful in solving?
15. What is a data warehouse? What kinds of problems can it help solve?
16. What is online analytical processing (OLAP)?

DISCUSSION QUESTIONS

1. Compare the database approach with the traditional approach to file management. What are the advantages and disadvantages of each?

2. It has been said that you do not need database management software to have a database environment. Discuss.

3. Which of the components of a DBMS (data definition language, data manipulation language, data dictionary) would you use for each of the following?

   a. The field for annual salary must be expanded from six to seven digits.

   b. A report listing all employees who work in the purchasing depart ment must be produced.

   c. A new data element, taxable life insurance, must be added to the database. Personnel and payroll programs must be modified to keep track of the amount of company-funded life insurance that is taxable.

PROBLEM-SOLVING EXERCISES

1. *Group exercise:* A university typically maintains information about students and courses. Some of the pieces of data that must be maintained are student names and addresses, student identification numbers, course names, course descriptions, course numbers, grades, majors, course enrollments, number of credits per course, faculty member teaching each course, term offered, and department offering the course. Using the guidelines presented in Section 6.4, divide the class into groups, and have each group design a database for this application.

2. Develop a data dictionary for the purchasing system described in this chapter. List all of the data elements in the system and show their format, size, definition, and business usage.

3. *Hands-on exercise:* Use appropriate application software to create the relational database illustrated in Figure 6.11. Then develop an application to create the following reports:

   a. All employees with salaries over 30,000, listing the employee's name, identification number, job code, and salary.

   b. All employees with performance ratings of 2 or 3, listing the employee's name, identification number, and performance rating code.

   c. Jobs in the Shipping Department, listing the department name, department code, job description, and job code.

4. *Internet problem-solving exercise:* You have just graduated from college and want to find a marketing job somewhere in New Mexico, where you grew up. You decide to search online, using the Online Career Center (http://www.occ.com/). Explore the site, first of all, to determine whether a large number of corporations and organizations list with the site, making it an appropriate place to search. Then search for actual listed jobs, selecting New Mexico as the location and marketing as the job category. Describe the various kinds and breadth of skills required of candidates for the jobs that are listed. Include in that description the computer skills and knowledge that are generally required. Indicate how having taken this course would help with those skills.

PROBLEM-SOLVING CASE

A GUESSING GAME

When the popular clothing manufacturer Guess? evaluated its production process recently, CIO Joseph Fink discovered that Guess? lost millions of dollars in preparing each upcoming season's new product line. Fink set about the task of determining what was wrong and how the business could make up for the money it had been losing.

The evaporating money resulted mostly from inefficiencies in the process of creating samples for a new line of apparel. Too many of the samples simply never made it to market. At times, that number could reach an astounding 80 to 90 percent. How did this happen? A severe lack of communication among the different departments at Guess? was responsible. Designers, production workers, salespeople, and managers concentrated on their divisions without accurate knowledge of what was happening throughout the rest of the company. One division would make a decision, and the others would continue on, unaware that anything had changed. As a result, only 10 or 20 pieces of sample clothing out of 100 became part of a season's lineup.

Fink, recognizing that Guess?'s operations needed alteration, turned to Kurt Salmon Association, a systems integrator from Atlanta. In addition to the aforementioned problems at Guess?, Kurt Salmon also addressed the issue of overproduction. The number of samples being made was simply too high.

Overall, Guess? hoped to increase its ability to control product development data and to improve communication among all key groups in the production process. Kurt Salmon programmed a product-line development system to achieve these goals as well as solve the specific production problems of the company. The system uses a Microsoft SQL Server database that houses vital records on fabrics, vendors, styles, bodies, and costs, all of which are an integral part of the preproduction process.

In the past, the data were stored on either a host computer or in separate paper spreadsheets and reports in the various departments. The new system makes all the information available to everyone at all times. More significantly, the database reflects any changes automatically so that no department is ever left in the dark as to what actions the others have taken. When one user changes information in the database, others can see these changes in realtime. The system has also evolved from a one-dimensional system that dealt only with sample design into a comprehensive system that ties into Guess?'s Hewlett-Packard 3000 manufacturing system. Previous incarnations required that data for style and fabric be entered into both systems individually, an obvious hindrance to efficiency.

By implementing the product-line development system, Guess? has engineered a revolutionary idea in retail-oriented manufacturing. Sales and production departments have access to sketches generated on designers' computer-aided design (CAD) systems, where they can view clothing designs before the garments have been fabricated. If the designs in progress do not match the wants of the consumers, the salespeople can relate the discrepancies to the designers.

Production workers can place orders for materials as soon as the materials are incorporated into a design. More importantly, they learn of changes in a scheme immediately, so precious weeks do not pass with the production team thinking it has the correct materials, only to find that a reorder must be made that will take several more weeks. The structure of the system prevents one department from holding up the rest of the company. In the past, designers could hold up an entire line by changing a zipper to a button if the button had a ten-week lead time for orders and the zipper had only a two-week lead. To ensure that designers do not throw an unexpected wrinkle into the operation, the data for the plans are locked in once they are transferred from the server to the HP manufacturing system. At this stage, they can be viewed but not modified.

Future enhancements expected from Kurt Salmon include an online calendar that will display all the major deadlines at Guess? from the earliest phase of design through the last detail of going to market. Users will be able to track their own department's progress as well as the headway being made by the other parties.

The overall effectiveness of Guess?'s new database relies less on the technology than it does on the users. Humans represent the biggest obstacle to making the new method of data sharing function smoothly and, thereby, profitably. As Joseph Fink puts it, "We were fine as far as the technical aspects of the system go. Our biggest problem has been changing our procedures." That means that every employee must be conscientious about entering every decision made into the database. Fink realizes that the various departments at Guess? have never had to share data in this fashion before. The new system presents a challenge that may take some time to grow accustomed to but that in the end will bring highly favorable results. Fink expresses optimism regarding the system's implementation. Early indications were that communication throughout the company had taken a turn for the better and that employees were adapting to the new technology quite well.

SOURCE: Candee Wilde, "No More Guess? Work," *Information Week,* September 23, 1996.

CASE STUDY QUESTIONS

1. Why did Guess? need to convert to a database system? What people, organization, and technology problems had to be addressed?

2. What did Joseph Fink hope to accomplish by bringing in Kurt Salmon Association?

3. Which of the problems that caused Guess? to initiate this project seem to be well addressed by the solution? Are any of the problems experienced by Guess? not addressed by the solution?

Chapter

SEVEN

TELECOMMUNICATIONS AND NETWORKS

CHAPTER OUTLINE

LEARNING OBJECTIVES

After reading and studying this chapter, you will

1. Understand the basic components of a telecommunications network.
2. Know how to measure telecommunications transmission rates.
3. Be familiar with the three basic network topologies.
4. Know the major types of telecommunications networks.
5. Be able to address telecommunications issues when designing a solution.
6. Be aware of important business applications using telecommunications.

BRITISH COLUMBIA'S PHARMANET CUTS COSTS, IMPROVES SERVICE

Governments in the United States and other countries don't have to look very far to find workable ways to bring down health care related costs and to provide better service at the same time.

British Columbia's PharmaNet, a $15 million integrated pharmaceutical network, promises to slash claim processing costs and speed claim reimbursements while at the same time providing pharmacists crucial information on the interaction of prescribed drugs.

A three-tier TCP/IP network links 16 different in-store pharmacy systems with the Ministry of Health wide area network; prescriptions are processed through an IBM RS/6000 UNIX workstation. There are no visible changes in the front-end applications because pharmacists link to the system using a Ministry of Health application-programming interface.

Prescription claims that were paper-based and processed manually are now automatically processed online, saving the Ministry of Health the equivalent of 30 full-time jobs. The Ministry of Health has projected a six-month return on the system in reduced labor and claims processing costs alone.

In addition, British Columbia residents are realizing better service. Low-income and other residents who aren't covered by PharmaCare (a prescription drug program similar to the one in the U.S. Medicare system) now save hundreds of dollars in up-front pharmaceutical copayments under PharmaNet's payment delivery system. They now pay only 30 percent of their prescription costs up front after meeting their annual $600 deductible. Under the old system, those same residents had to pay 70 percent of the prescription costs even after paying their $600 deductible and were not reimbursed for six to ten weeks.

The automatic processing of prescriptions also benefits pharmacists because PharmaNet lets them know exactly when they will get paid by the government for a prescription.

Probably the most important feature of PharmaNet is the speed with which pharmacists can access information on drug interactions. Within minutes, PharmaNet allows pharmacists to access the last 14 months of prescription histories on 2.8 million people. The information is used by pharmacists to ensure that newly prescribed drugs won't create adverse side-effects when they interact with a patient's existing prescriptions.

IBM, which installed PharmaNet, put 675 pharmacies online in the Canadian province last June. The company originally promised 5-second response times for pharmacists. Instead, pharmacists are seeing a 15- to 20-second response time. But because the previous process for claims processing, prescription reimbursement, and drug interaction checks took 45 to 60 days, PharmaNet users see a real improvement.

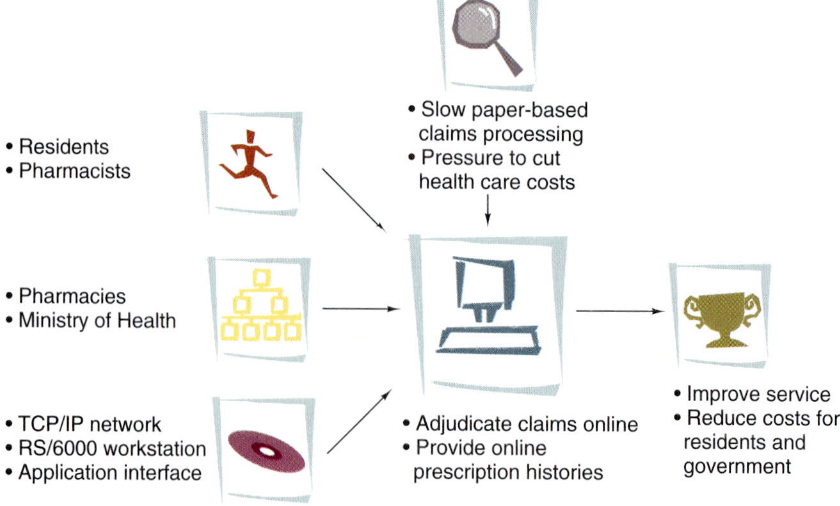

SOURCE: Thomas Hoffman, "Prescription for Savings," *Computerworld,* July 1, 1996.

The use of PharmaNet illustrates one of the many ways in which communications technology can be used to overcome barriers of distance for the benefit of communities and businesses alike. Today telecommunications networks are a critical ingredient for linking people, factories, stores, and offices in different locations, for improving organizational efficiency, and for creating new products and services. Many of the advanced features of information systems, such as online processing and access to information, are the products of telecommunications technology.

This chapter describes the elements of telecommunications technology and shows how they can be arranged to form various types of networks. We show the major kinds of network-based applications that can help organizations solve problems and the factors that must be considered when designing a network-based solution.

7.1 INTRODUCTION

Telecommunications can be defined as communication by electronic means, usually over some distance. A telecommunications system transmits information, establishes an interface or path between sender and receiver, directs messages along the most efficient paths and ensures they reach the right receiver, edits data by performing error checking and reformatting, converts messages so that they flow from one device to another, and controls the overall flow of information. Telecommunications systems can transmit text, graphic images, voice, or video information.

Without communications technology, it would be impossible to solve problems requiring immediate, online access to information, sharing of information among different geographic locations, or transmission of information from one location or one information system to another. Table 7.1 lists some typical applications based on telecommunications and the problems they solve.

Recent changes in communications technology and in the ownership and control of telecommunications services have blurred the distinction between telecommunications and computing. Before 1984, telecommunications in the United States was virtually a monopoly of American Telephone and Telegraph Company (AT&T). But, in that year, legal action by the Department of Justice forced AT&T to give up its monopoly and allowed competing firms to sell telecommunications services, presenting firms with a bewildering array of alternative vendors and technologies from which to choose.

Telephone companies are starting to provide information services as well, as the Focus on Organizations points out.

Consequently, since many more communications choices are available than in the past, you will need some background knowledge on telecommunications systems in order to choose wisely among them. To understand how telecommunications systems work, you must become familiar with certain characteristics of data transmission, the capabilities of various transmission media, the manner in which the components of a telecommunications network work, and alternative ways of arranging these components into networks.

TABLE 7.1

Common Uses of Telecommunications

Application	Purpose
Finance	Reducing the time and cost of funds transfer
Automated teller machines	
Electronic funds transfer	
Electronic clearinghouses	
Securities trading	
Online account inquiry	
Sales and Marketing	Making it easy for customers to purchase
Point-of-sale terminals	
Telemarketing	
Airline and hotel reservation systems	
Online order processing	
Credit cards and credit authorization	
Manufacturing and Production	Reducing production costs
Process control	
Online inventory control	
Computer-integrated manufacturing	
Human Resources	Managing human resources
Online personnel inquiry	
Online applicant tracking	
Communication and Knowledge Work	Reducing the cost of knowledge and information transfer
Electronic mail	
Groupware	
Online information services	
Shared design databases and specifications	
Videoconferencing	

Analog signal
A continuous sine waveform over a certain frequency range, with a positive voltage representing a 1 and a negative charge representing a 0; used for voice transmissions.

Digital signal
A discrete flow in which data are coded as 0-bits and 1-bits and as a series of on-and-off electrical pulses.

Modulation
The process of converting digital signals into analog form.

Demodulation
The process of converting analog signals into digital form.

Modem
A device used to translate digital signals into analog signals and vice versa, a necessity when computers communicate through analog lines; stands for MOdulation and DEModulation.

TYPES OF SIGNALS

Two types of signals are used in telecommunications systems: analog and digital (see Figure 7.1). An **analog signal** takes the form of a continuous sine wave over a certain frequency range. A positive voltage charge represents a +1 and a negative charge represents a 0. Analog signals are used to handle voice traffic and to reflect variations in pitch.

A **digital signal** is a discrete burst rather than a continuous wave; it represents data coded into two discrete states: 0-bits and 1-bits, which are transmitted as a series of on-and-off electrical pulses. Most computers communicate with digital signals, as do many local telephone companies and some larger networks. (Although telephone lines used to be analog only, digital lines, which can transmit data faster and more accurately than analog lines, are beginning to be used.) If computers communicate through analog lines, all digital signals must be converted into analog form and then reconverted into digital form for the receiving computer.

The process of converting digital signals into analog form is called **modulation,** and the process of converting analog signals back into digital form is called **demodulation.** A device called a **modem** (MOdulation and

FOCUS ON ORGANIZATIONS

THE RACE FOR THE INFORMATION SUPERHIGHWAY

The race for the information superhighway could be the greatest business race of the century. Communications giants are locked in a struggle to build and control a vast web of electronic networks delivering information, education, and entertainment services to offices and homes. These networks will be information highways that could affect life as profoundly in the twenty-first century as railroads and interstate highways did in the past.

The Telecommunications Act of 1996 freed telephone companies, broadcasters, and cable companies to enter one another's markets. Local telephone companies could enter the long-distance phone business, while long-distance and cable companies such as AT&T, MCI, and Time Warner could enter the local telephone business. Telephone companies can sell cable TV services over their phone lines. Earlier federal court rulings allowed the telephone companies to provide information and entertainment services, such as news reports, electronic white and yellow pages, electronic retrieval of books and periodicals, movies, and television.

Telephone lines can now be linked to television sets or computer monitors in the home. Movies, home shopping, two-way interactive educational services, the ability to see real estate before traveling, exchanging purchase orders and product designs—all could take place on the network.

To provide a full range of information services, including video, the telephone companies need more transmission capacity than can be provided by traditional twisted-pair telephone wire. To meet this need, they are laying millions of miles of high-capacity fiber-optic cable and are purchasing cable companies or forming joint ventures with them. The coaxial cable used by cable companies already has the capacity to transmit the graphics and video that most of these new information services require.

The telephone companies are expected to help with the construction of another electronic superhighway that the federal government is proposing. This information superhighway will be a national network connecting universities, hospitals, research centers, and other institutions that need to exchange vast amounts of data. The Clinton administration wants to extend this national data highway into homes and schools to give students and families immediate online access to libraries and other rich sources of information. Although this national data highway will be public oriented, the government expects it to be constructed by private enterprise.

The information superhighway race is heating up in Europe as well. Telecommunications in continental Europe have been more tightly regulated than the United States. But in July 1996, cable companies, railways, and utilities were freed to lease their phone lines to anyone. By early 1998, 20 European countries will be open to telecommunications competition. Companies are also allying to build networks that challenge existing monopolies. For instance, Bell Atlantic, France Telecom, and Deutsche Telekom have joined to combat Telecom Italia's monopoly.

FOCUS Questions:
What problems are solved by having telephone companies deliver information services? How could businesses and individuals benefit? Are there any drawbacks to using the information superhighway?

SOURCES: Mark Landler, "Pacific Telesis and Two Other Bells Feud Over Future of TV Venture," *The New York Times*, January 16, 1997; Mary E. Thyfault, "Big Bang II," *Information Week*, February 5, 1996; and Gail Edmondson and Karen Lowry Miller, "Europe's Markets Are Getting Rewired, Too," *Business Week*, April 8, 1996.

DEModulation) is used for this translation process. As Figure 7.2 shows, when computers communicate through analog telephone lines, two modems are needed—one to convert the first computer's digital signals to analog, the other to convert the analog signals back to digital for the second computer.

A Panhandle Eastern Corporation technician makes a routine check of a gas pipeline measurement station near Indianapolis. A telecommunications system at this station electronically sends volume data to the Houston operating headquarters.

SOURCE: Courtesy of Panhandle Eastern Corporation.

FIGURE 7.1

Analog and Digital Signals

An analog signal is a continuous wave over a particular range of frequencies. A positive voltage charge represents a "1," and a negative voltage charge represents a "0." A digital signal contains discrete bursts representing "on" and "off" electrical pulses.

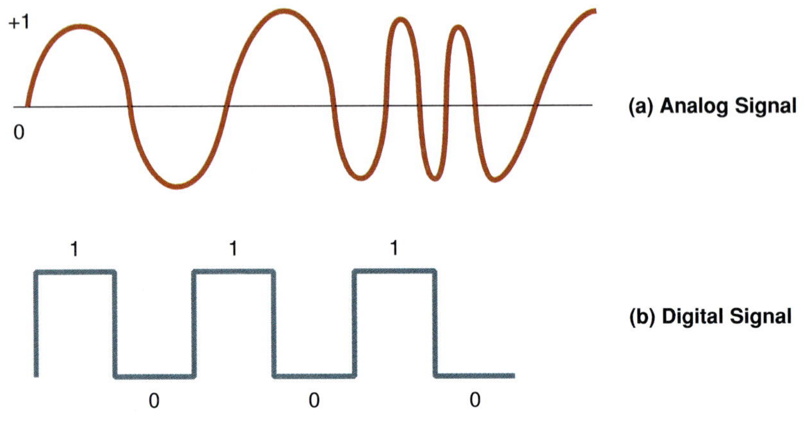

DIGITAL TRANSMISSION MODES

Once the signal type has been determined, the user must be aware of the alternative ways of arranging bits of data for transmission and must also consider the direction of data flow supported by the telecommunications medium.

Asynchronous transmission A method of transmitting one character or byte at a time when data are communicated between computers, with each string of bits comprising a character framed by control bits.

Synchronous transmission The transmission of characters in a block framed by header and trailer bytes called flags; allows large volumes of data to be transmitted at high speeds between computers.

Simplex transmission A form of transmission over communications lines in which data can travel in only one direction at all times.

Asynchronous and Synchronous Transmission Data are transmitted from one computer to another as a stream of bits. How, then, does a receiving computer know where one character ends and another begins? Several conventions have been devised for communicating when a character begins or ends. In **asynchronous transmission,** characters or bytes are transmitted one at a time. Each string of bits composing a character is "framed" by control bits—a start bit, a parity bit, and one or two stop bits. The parity bit is set on or off, depending on whether the parity scheme is odd or even (see Chapter 4).

In **synchronous transmission,** several characters at a time are transmitted in blocks, framed by header and trailer bytes called flags. Synchronous transmission is faster than asynchronous transmission because the characters are transmitted as blocks with no start and stop bits between them. Consequently, it is used for transmitting large volumes of data at high speeds. Figure 7.3 compares synchronous and asynchronous transmission.

Simplex, Half-Duplex, and Full-Duplex Transmission Transmission must also consider the direction of data flow over a communications line. In **simplex transmission,** data can travel in only one direction at all times; thus, data can flow from a computer processing unit to a printer but cannot flow

FIGURE 7.2

The Function of Modems in Telecommunications

A modem (short for MOdulation/DEModulation) is a device that translates digital signals into analog, and vice versa. It is a vital piece of equipment in telecommunications systems that employ both types of signals.

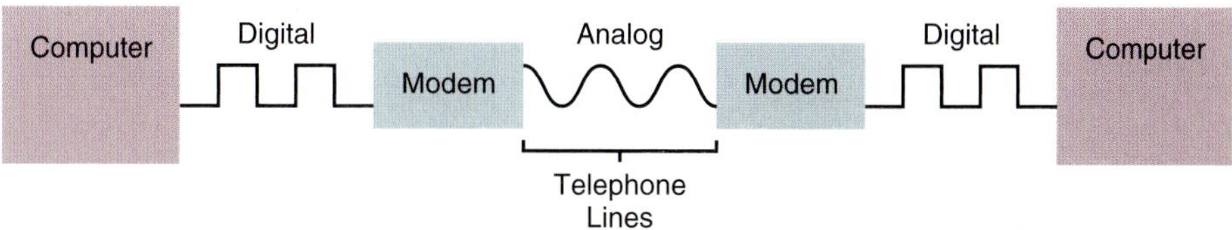

from the printer to the computer. **Half-duplex transmission** supports two-way flow of data, but the data can travel in only one direction at a time. In **full-duplex transmission,** data can move in both directions simultaneously. Figure 7.4 compares the simplex, half-duplex, and full-duplex transmission modes.

Half-duplex transmission A form of transmission over communications lines in which data can move in both directions, but not simultaneously.

Full-duplex transmission A form of transmission over communications lines in which data can be sent in both directions simultaneously.

FIGURE 7.3

Asynchronous and Synchronous Transmission

Asynchronous and synchronous transmission represent two ways of sending bits of data along telecommunications lines. Asynchronous transmission usually sends one byte (one character) at a time; each byte is preceded by a start bit and followed by a parity bit (for error checking) and a stop bit (to signal the end of that particular byte). Synchronous transmission sends several bytes at one time, preceded and followed by bytes called flags. Not surprisingly, synchronous transmission is much faster than asynchronous transmission.

(a) Asynchronous Transmission

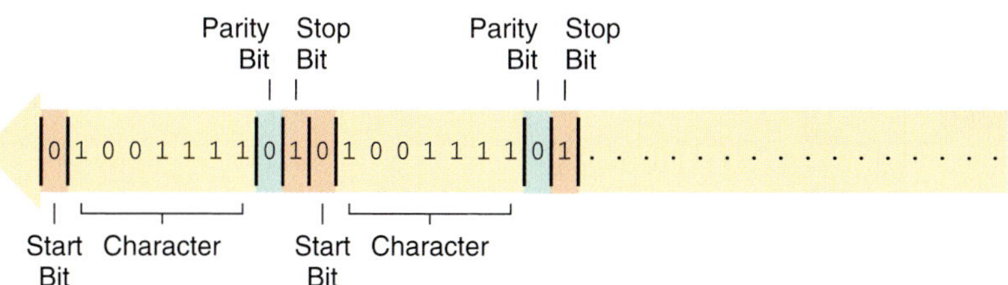

(b) Synchronous Transmission

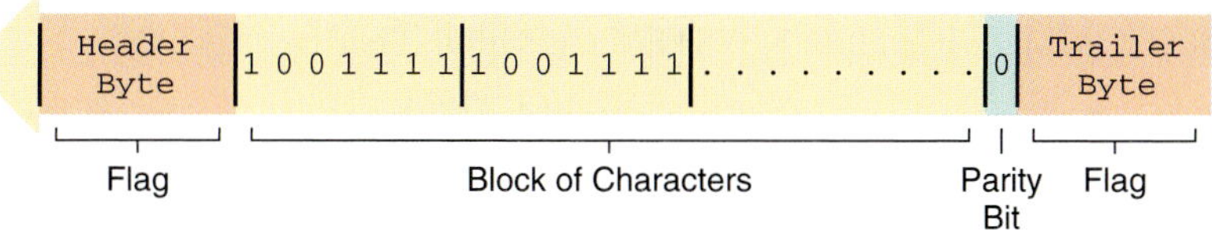

FIGURE 7.4

How Data Flows: Simplex, Half-Duplex, and Full-Duplex Transmission

Simplex transmission (panel a) allows data to flow in only one direction—in this case, from a computer to a receiving device. Half-duplex transmission (panel b) allows two-way flow, but data can travel in only one direction at a time. Full-duplex transmission (panel c) can transmit data in both directions at the same time.

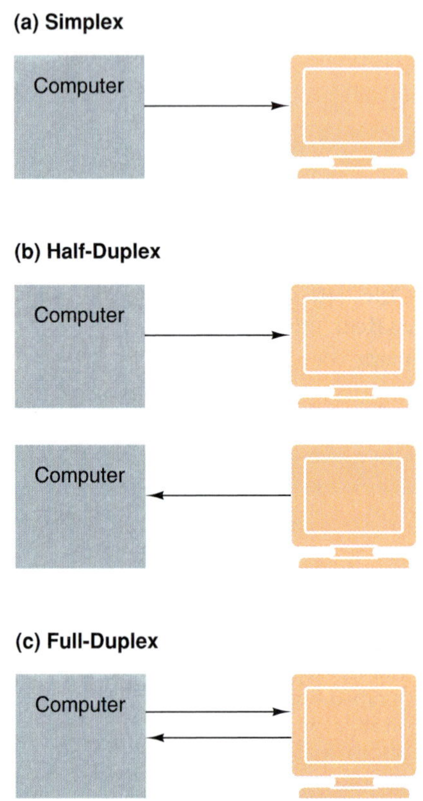

7.2 TELECOMMUNICATIONS TECHNOLOGY

A telecommunications system is a collection of both hardware devices and the software needed to control these devices. We examine the major components of telecommunications systems in this section and then describe how these components are used to build networks in the following section.

TELECOMMUNICATIONS SYSTEM COMPONENTS

A telecommunications system is a network of interconnected hardware and software components that perform the telecommunications functions described above. Its essential components are as follows:

1. Computers to process information.

2. Terminals or any input/output devices that send or receive data.
3. Communications **channels,** the links by which data or voice communications are transmitted between sending and receiving devices in a network. Communications channels use various transmission media, such as twisted wire, fiber-optic cables, coaxial cables, microwave, satellite, and other forms of wireless transmission.
4. Communications processors, such as modems, front-end processors, multiplexers, controllers, and concentrators, which provide support functions for data transmission.
5. Telecommunications software, which controls input and output activities and other functions of the communications network.

Channel
A link by which voices or data are transmitted in a communications network.

Communications Processors A telecommunications system in a large-computer environment contains a number of computer-like "intelligent" devices, each of which plays a special role in a network.

The **front-end processor** is a computer (often a programmable minicomputer) that is dedicated to communications management and attached to the **host computer** (main computer). It takes some of the load off the host computer by performing error control, formatting, editing, controlling, routing, and speed and signal conversion. The front-end processor is largely responsible for collecting and processing input and output data to and from terminals, and it also groups characters into complete messages for submission to the central processing unit (CPU).

Front-end processor
A computer that manages communications for a host computer to which it is attached.

Host computer
The main computer in a network.

A **multiplexer** is a device that enables a single communications channel to carry data transmissions from multiple sources simultaneously. The multiplexer divides the communications channel so that it can be shared by several transmission devices. The multiplexer may divide a high-speed channel into multiple channels of slower speed or may assign each transmission device a very small slice of time in which it can use the high-speed channel. Figure 7.5

Multiplexer
A device that enables a single communications channel to carry data transmission from multiple sources simultaneously.

FIGURE 7.5

The Components of a Telecommunications System

The five major components of a telecommunications system are a computer, communications processors, communications channels, terminals (or other input/output devices), and telecommunications software. Here we see a telecommunications system that uses two multiplexers as communications processors. The multiplexers divide the communications channel to allow several devices to share it. The separate streams of data entering from terminals are routed through the channel into the computer.

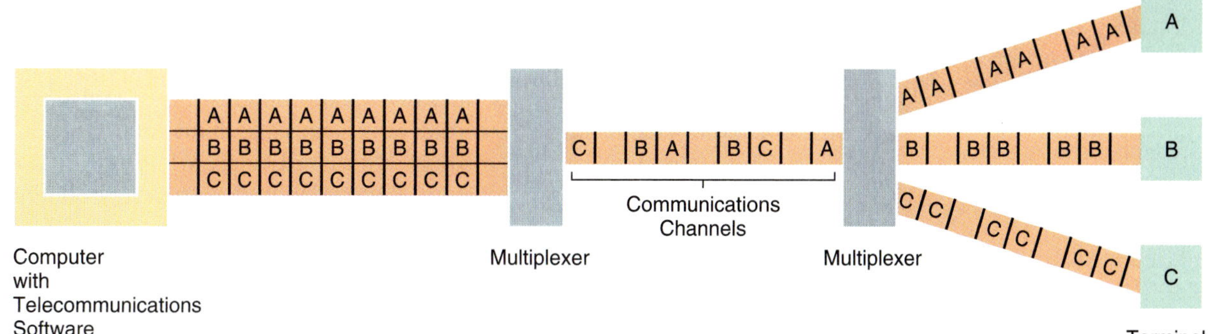

Concentrator
A device that collects and temporarily stores messages from terminals in a buffer or temporary storage area and sends bursts of signals to the host computer.

Controller
A device that supervises communications traffic between the CPU and peripheral devices such as terminals and printers.

Protocol
The set of rules governing transmission between two components in a telecommunications network.

Twisted wire
The oldest transmission medium, consisting of strands of wire twisted in pairs; it forms the basis for the analog phone system.

illustrates components of a telecommunications system that includes two multiplexers.

A **concentrator** is a type of "store and forward" device (often called a specialized minicomputer) that collects and temporarily stores messages from terminals in a buffer, or temporary storage area. When the messages are ready to be sent economically, the concentrator "bursts" signals to the host computer.

A specialized minicomputer called a **controller** supervises communications traffic between the CPU and peripheral devices such as terminals and printers. The controller manages the flow of messages from these devices and communicates them to the CPU, and it also routes output from the CPU to the appropriate peripheral device.

Telecommunications Software Special software is required to control and support the activities of a network. This software resides in the host computer, front-end processor, and other processors in the network. The main functions of telecommunications software are network control, access control, transmission control, error detection/correction, and security.

Network control software routes messages, polls network terminals, determines transmission priorities, maintains a log of network activity, and checks for errors. Access control software establishes connections between terminals and computers in the network and controls transmission speed, mode, and direction. Transmission control software enables computers and terminals to send and receive data, programs, commands, and messages. Error control software detects and corrects errors and then retransmits the corrected data. Security control software uses log ons, passwords, and various authorization procedures (see Chapter 12) to prevent unauthorized access to a network.

Telecommunications networks typically consist of a wide variety of hardware and software technologies. In order for different components in a network to communicate, they must adhere to a common set of rules, called a **protocol,** that enables them to "talk to" each other. Each device in a network must be able to interpret the other devices' protocols. There are both hardware and software protocols.

Although the need for standard protocols is widely recognized, different vendors have developed their own systems. Section 7.3 describes some of these systems of protocols and efforts to create universal standards that can be accepted and used by all manufacturers.

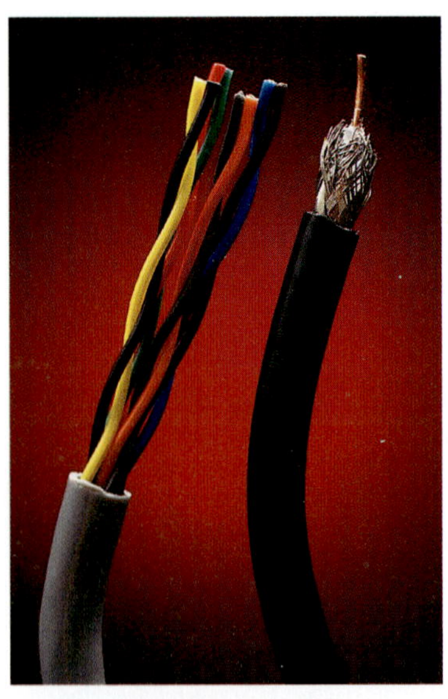

Twisted wire used in analog telephone lines can be used for low-speed data transmission of up to 10 megabits per second, while coaxial cable supports high-speed data transmission reaching 200 megabits per second.

SOURCE: © Dan Bryant.

TYPES OF TRANSMISSION MEDIA

There are five principal telecommunications transmission media: twisted wire, coaxial cable, fiber optics, microwave (and other forms of radio transmission), and satellite. Each has certain advantages and limitations.

The oldest transmission medium is **twisted wire,** which consists of strands of wire twisted in pairs. Most of the telephone system in a building relies on twisted wires installed to operate the analog phone system. Most buildings have extra cables installed for future expansion, so every office usually has a number of unused twisted wire cables that can be used for digital communications. Although it is low in cost and is already in place, twisted wire is relatively slow for transmitting data, and high-speed transmission causes interference called crosstalk. On the other hand, new software and hardware have raised the transmission capacity of existing twisted wire cables up to 10 megabits per second, which is often adequate for connecting microcomputers and other office devices.

Coaxial cable, like that used for cable television, consists of thickly insulated copper wire that can transmit a larger volume of data than twisted wire. It is often used in place of twisted wire for important links in a telecommunications network because it is a faster, more interference-free transmission medium. Speeds of up to 200 megabits per second are possible. However, coaxial cable is thick and hard to install in many buildings; it usually has to be moved when the computer and other devices are moved.

Coaxial cable
A transmission medium consisting of thickly insulated copper wire; it can transmit a larger volume of data than twisted wire and is faster and more interference-free.

Fiber optics technology consists of thousands of strands of clear glass fiber, the thickness of a human hair, that are bound into cables. Data are transformed into pulses of light that are sent through the fiber-optic cable by a laser device at a rate of 500 kilobits to 1.7 gigabits per second. Fiber-optic cable is considerably faster, lighter, and more durable than wire media and is well suited to solutions requiring transfers of large volumes of data. (See the Focus on Problem Solving.) On the other hand, fiber-optic cable is more difficult to work with, more expensive, and harder to install. It is best used as the "backbone" of a network rather than for connecting isolated devices to a backbone. In most networks, fiber-optic cable is used as the high-speed trunk line, while twisted wire and coaxial cable are used to connect the trunk line to individual devices.

Fiber optics
A transmission medium consisting of strands of clear glass fiber bound into cable through which data are transformed into pulses of light and transmitted by a laser device.

Fiber-optic cable can transmit data that have been transformed into pulses of light at speeds of up to 1.7 gigabits per second.

SOURCE: Matthew Borkoski, Stock, Boston.

THE CHRYSLER TECHNOLOGY CENTER

In the late 1980s, the Chrysler Corporation was sliding into another financial crisis. Its market share was slipping away to the Japanese. How could it sell more cars? Chrysler slashed its operating costs and decided to emphasize designs that would make its cars as striking as possible.

To support its new approach to product design and development, Chrysler built a 3.5 million-square-foot Chrysler Technology Center (CTC) 30 miles north of Detroit at a cost of $1.3 billion. Seven thousand people are employed in "platform development teams" that can have as many as 700 members. In the past, Chrysler and the other U.S. automobile makers used a rigid "stovepipe" method of creating new cars in which functionally separate departments such as the engine department or the design department each performed one aspect of development in sequence. In contrast, the platform teams combine experts from diverse areas such as design, manufacturing, marketing, and purchasing to share ideas and expertise.

The CTC represents the heart of Chrysler's effort to re-engineer the automobile design process by coordinating the talents of its staff and information systems to speed high-quality products to market. At the new design center, engineers, manufacturing specialists, and even accountants review designs from their conception forward. As a result, they have more time to anticipate and work out problems. Designers are more

The Chrysler Technology Center's massive fiber-optic network has enhanced productivity by allowing platform development teams to share and simultaneously work on automobile designs.

SOURCE: Courtesy of Chrysler Corporation.

Microwave
A transmission medium in which high-frequency radio signals are sent through the atmosphere; used for high-volume, long-distance, point-to-point communication.

Communications satellite
A satellite orbiting the earth that acts as a relay station for transmitting microwave signals.

Microwave systems transmit high-frequency radio signals through the atmosphere and are widely used for high-volume, long-distance, point-to-point communication. No cabling is required. Because microwave signals follow a straight line and do not bend with the curvature of the earth, terrestrial transmission stations must be positioned 25 to 30 miles apart, which adds to the expense of microwave. This problem can be solved by using microwave systems with other communications methods, such as satellites.

Communications satellites are preferred for transmitting large quantities of data over long distances because they do not have the distance limitations of terrestrial microwave transmission stations. Communications satellites orbiting more than 22,000 miles above the earth can receive, amplify, and retransmit microwave signals; thus, the satellites act as relay stations for earth stations (microwave stations on the ground).

sensitive to the manufacturability of their creations. Will a door permit enough side-impact protection? Will too much steel be wasted if the manufacturer tries to stamp this shape? Manufacturing and engineering, in turn, try to make the innovative designs work. For instance, when the Dodge Stratus and Chrysler Cirrus cars were on the drawing boards, designer Michael Santoro wanted to emphasize curves in the car sides. The curves would make the sedan feel roomier and artfully reflect light. But from an engineering standpoint, the curve was a nightmare. No hinge ex-isted that would make car doors swing properly when a car's sides curved so sharply. A few years ago, the curve would have been straightened. But the curve survived because the team concept allowed designers and engineers to work out their mutual problems.

The CTC houses ten mainframe computers, two supercomputers, and control systems for all the center's computer networks. Every room in the CTC has 8-inch raised floors covering 10,000 fiber-optic cables. These cables can transmit massive volumes of data, such as design specifications and graphics, at very high speed. The cables also link CTC's buildings to its main computer center.

The CTC provides the technology—state-of-the art workstations and CAD/CAM software—to enable the platform teams to test designs by computer.

Software programs are available to perform computer simulations for external aerodynamics and internal fluid dynamics. The software can perform analyses of engine cooling systems, catalytic converters, defroster ducts, and many other components.

Designs can be easily passed among team members and modified in the computer. Instead of building a series of expensive physical models of a car for crash tests (hand-built prototypes cost $250,000 to $400,000), designers can use their computers to compare crash data from a test with theoretical predictions, moving closer to a solution with succeeding prediction cycles. Only when they need to test a final solution would they actually have to crash a real model. Using this approach, engineers refined the design of the LH car so that it passed its first crash test.

The first new product from the CTC was the LH, a "cab-forward" line of midsized cars that directly competes with Japanese automobiles on price and quality. The design of these cars expands passenger space and increases the driver's feeling of control by pushing the cabin out over the front wheels and moving the wheels out to the corners of the car to give the sense that it clings to the road.

Using the team concept and the CTC's advanced technology, Chrysler has greatly increased its productivity. New products such as the LH can be developed with half the design and production staff in 30 percent less time than before.

FOCUS Questions: Why was fiber-optic cabling so important in the CTC? What kinds of problems are solved by using telecommunications technology in the CTC?

SOURCES: Chrysler Technology Center (http://www.chryslercorp.com/); James Bennet, "The Designers Who Saved Chrysler," *The New York Times,* January 30, 1994; and Edward Cone, "Chrysler," *Information Week,* September 7, 1992.

Satellite is not optimal for problems requiring extremely rapid exchanges of data because delays occur when data are sent thousands of miles into space and back down again. However, satellite is very appropriate for transmission of large quantities of information in one direction at a time. Figure 7.6 shows a typical VSAT (very small aperture terminal) private satellite communications system. Satellite networks are typically used for communications in large, far-flung organizations with many locations that would be difficult to tie together through cabling media. For example, the Chrysler Corporation uses a private VSAT network to connect its corporate headquarters in Detroit, Michigan, with nearly 5,000 dealerships and offices throughout the United States. Section 7.5 describes other forms of wireless communication.

Satellite dishes facilitate telecommunications transmission to geographically remote areas.

SOURCE: © Stacy Pick, Stock, Boston.

FIGURE 7.6

A VSAT Satellite Communications System

A VSAT (very small aperture terminal) satellite system uses a satellite that orbits the earth. At the central site, a hub earth station and a host computer with a front-end processor manage the earth. At the remote sites—there can be hundred of these—an outdoor VSAT or antenna links the remote site with the central location by picking up transmissions from the satellite. A control center at the remote site handles data from telephones, facsimile machines, and broadcasts.

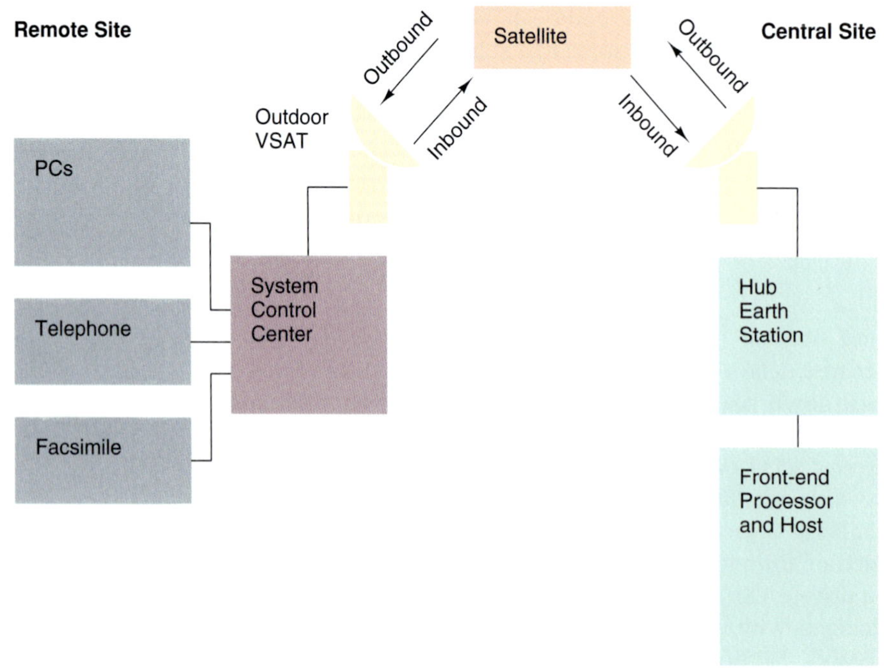

MEASURING TRANSMISSION RATES

The total amount of information that can be transmitted via any telecommunications channel is measured in bits per second (BPS) for digital transmission. (The analog measure is the range of frequencies supported.) Sometimes this is referred to as the **baud** rate; a baud represents a voltage switch (signal change) from positive to negative or vice versa. The baud rate is not always identical to the bit rate, however. At higher speeds, more than one bit at a time can be transmitted in a single signal change, so the bit rate will generally surpass the baud rate. Because one signal change, or cycle, is required to transmit one or several bits per second, the transmission capacity of each type of telecommunications medium is a function of its frequency—that is, the number of cycles per second that can be sent through that medium measured in hertz (see Chapter 4). The range of frequencies that can be accommodated on a particular telecommunications medium is called its **bandwidth.** The bandwidth is the difference between the highest and lowest frequencies that can be accommodated on a single channel. The larger the range of frequencies, the greater the bandwidth and the greater the medium's telecommunications transmission capacity.

Baud
A change in voltage from positive to negative and vice versa. The baud rate at lower speeds corresponds to a telecommunications transmission rate of bits per second. At higher speeds, the baud rate is less than the bit rate because more than one bit at a time can be transmitted by a single signal change.

Bandwidth
The range of frequencies that can be accommodated on a particular telecommunications medium.

Deciding which telecommunications medium to employ depends not only on cost but also on how often the channel is used. For example, the monthly charges for satellite links are much higher than for twisted wire, but if a firm uses the link 100 percent of the time, the cost per bit of data could be much lower than leasing a line from the telephone company. Table 7.2 compares the speed and cost of the various transmission media.

7.3 TELECOMMUNICATIONS NETWORKS

There are several ways of organizing telecommunications components to form a network and, hence, several ways of classifying networks. They can be classified by their shape, or **network topology;** they can also be classified by their geographic scope and the type of services they provide. Wide area networks, for example, encompass a relatively wide geographic area, from

Network topology
The shape or configuration of a network; the most common topologies are the star, bus, and ring.

TABLE 7.2

Transmission Capacity of Telecommunications Media

In general, the high-speed transmission media are more expensive, but they can handle higher volumes (which reduces the cost per bit). A wide range of speeds is possible for any given medium, depending on the software and hardware configuration. Most microwave and satellite commercial systems support a standard of 6.2 MBPS for high-speed communication but theoretically have much higher transmission rates.

Medium	Speed
Twisted wire	500 BPS to 10 MBPS
Microwave	256 KBPS to 100 MBPS
Satellite	256 KBPS to 100 MBPS
Coaxial cable	56 KBPS to 200 MBPS
Fiber-optic cable	500 KBPS to 10 GBPS

NOTE: BPS = bits per second; KBPS = kilobits per second; MBPS = megabits per second; GBPS = gigabits per second.

several miles to thousands of miles, whereas local area networks link local resources such as computers and terminals in the same department or office of a firm. This section examines both the topological and geographical classifications of networks.

NETWORK TOPOLOGIES

The three most common network topologies are the star, the bus, and the ring, which are compared in Figure 7.7. Each configuration is appropriate for a particular class of problems.

Star network
A network in which a central host computer is connected to several smaller computers and/or terminals; all communications between the smaller computers or terminals must pass through the host computer.

In the **star network** (panel a), a central host computer is connected to a number of smaller computers, terminals, and other devices such as printers. This topology is popular for organizations in which some aspects of information processing must be centralized while others can be performed locally. For instance, company-wide files such as a master customer list are best stored on a central host. A star network allows data from the master list to be downloaded, or transferred to local computers for processing, and then uploaded back to the central file when the work is complete. The star topology is primarily used in mainframe environments.

One problem with the star network is its vulnerability. All communication between points in the network must pass through the host computer. Another computer cannot send output to a printer, for example, without first channeling it through the host. Because the host computer is the traffic controller for the other computers and terminals in the system, communication in the network will come to a standstill if the host computer stops functioning.

Bus network
A network in which a number of computers are linked by a single loop circuit made of twisted wire, coaxial cable, or optical fiber; all messages are transmitted to the entire network and can flow in either direction, with special software identifying which component receives each message.

The **bus network** (panel b in Figure 7.7) links a number of computers and other equipment by a single circuit made of twisted wire, coaxial cable, or optical fiber. All the messages are broadcast to the entire network; messages can flow in both directions along the cable. When data are sent, a destination address is included in the transmission to identify the appropriate receiving device. No central host computer controls the network, although a host computer can be one of the devices on the network. If one of the computers in the network fails, none of the other components in the network is affected; hence, the network is far less vulnerable than a star network to a machine failure. The bus and ring topologies are commonly used for local area networks (LANs); these are discussed in the following section.

One difficulty of bus networks is that for many users, the system slows down because messages start colliding with one another and have to be sent again. Bus networks perform best for applications such as electronic mail, sharing of resources such as printers, and file transfers from one machine to another.

Ring network
A network in which a number of computers are linked by a closed loop of wire, coaxial cable, or optical fiber in a manner that allows data to be passed along the loop in a single direction from computer to computer.

Like the bus network, the **ring network** (panel c in Figure 7.7) does not rely on a central host computer and does not break down if one of the component computers malfunctions. The connecting wire, coaxial cable, or optical fiber forms a closed loop that allows each computer in the network to communicate directly with any other computer. Data are passed along the ring from one computer to another, always flowing in one direction, but each computer processes its own applications independently. The most common ring network for microcomputers is IBM's Token Ring Network. Ring networks offer similar advantages and disadvantages as bus networks.

FIGURE 7.7

Three Common Types of Networks: Star, Bus, and Ring

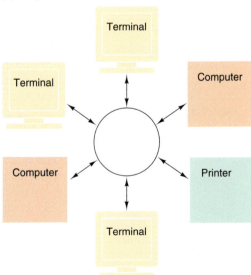

The star network (panel a) is managed by a central or host computer that is connected to all the other devices in the network. All communications must pass through the host computer. The bus network (panel b) connects equipment via a single circuit. There is no host computer to control the network, and all data are transmitted to the entire network in both directions. A third topology is the ring network (panel c), in which the connecting channel (wire, cable, or optical fiber) forms a closed loop. This allows each member of the network to communicate directly with any of the others, with data always flowing in one direction.

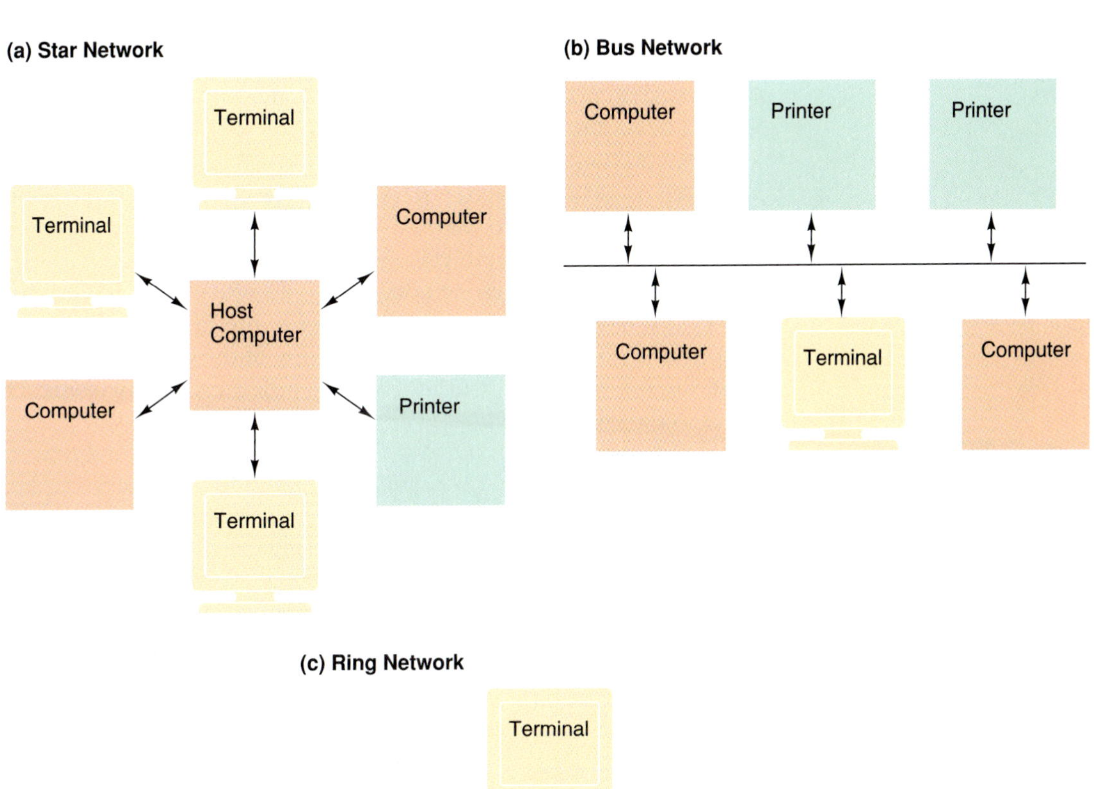

PRIVATE BRANCH EXCHANGES AND LOCAL AREA NETWORKS

The most common kinds of local networks are local area networks and private branch exchanges.

Private branch exchange (PBX)
A central private switchboard that handles a firm's voice and digital communications needs.

Private Branch Exchanges A **private branch exchange (PBX)** is a private telephone exchange that handles a firm's internal voice and digital communications needs. A branch exchange is simply the equipment—found in many buildings—that switches incoming and outgoing telephone calls from the telephone company trunk line to individual offices. In the past, most private exchanges were owned by the telephone company and manually operated by human operators. Today, many are fully automated and owned by the building or business firm.

Like the switching equipment in central offices, today's PBX is a special computer originally designed for handling and switching voice telephone calls. PBXs not only store, forward, transfer, hold, and redial telephone calls, but they also can carry both voice and data to create local networks, switching digital information among computers and office devices. For example, a person can write a letter on a PC, connect to the PBX using his or her own modem and telephone, and distribute a copy of the document to other people in the office or have it printed on the office copying machine. The PBX serves as the connection among all these various devices.

PBXs create networks without the expense of installing new cable or wire because they rely on the existing phone wires. Devices can be linked wherever there is a phone jack. Therefore, PCs can be networked together or linked to mainframes or minicomputers using existing telephone lines.

The primary disadvantage of PBXs is that they are limited to telephone lines and, therefore, cannot easily handle large volumes of data. Although they are good at connecting low-volume digital devices, they are less well developed than local area networks for accessing massive central databases such as customer files.

Local area network (LAN)
A transmission network encompassing a limited area, such as a single building or several buildings in close proximity; widely used to link PCs so that they can share information and peripheral devices.

Local Area Networks A **local area network (LAN)** encompasses a limited area, usually one building or several buildings in close proximity. Most LANs connect devices located within a 2,000-foot radius and are widely used to link PCs. In contrast to PBXs, which use existing telephone lines, LANs require their own communications channels.

LANs have higher transmission capacities than PBXs. LANs generally have bus or ring topologies and a high bandwidth. A very fast PBX may have a transmission capacity of over 2 megabits per second, whereas LANs typically transmit at a rate ranging from 256 kilobits per second to over 100 megabits per second, depending on the model and transmission medium. They are recommended for solutions requiring high volumes of data and high transmission speeds. For example, a problem requiring a solution expressed with graphics would need a LAN because graphic output is data intensive.

LANs have become popular for network-based solutions for several reasons: Networks can be built independently of central computer systems. Instead of relying on a central main computer for processing (which can fail), LANs can be installed wherever the business need is the greatest. A LAN solution can be economical since hardware and software can be shared by many locations. For instance, several offices or departments in a firm may share an expensive laser or color printer. Finally, LANs may be the only viable alternative for electronic mail, video conferencing, graphics, and online applications requiring a high-capacity network solution.

LANs are most commonly used to link PCs within a building or office so that they can share information and expensive peripheral devices such as laser printers. Another popular application of LANs is in factories, where they link computers and computer-controlled machines. Figure 7.8 shows a typical LAN for an office environment. It consists of several PC workstations, a file server, a network gateway, and a laser printer. We have shown a LAN that uses the ring topology.

A **server** is a computer—often a high-capacity PC or workstation—with a large hard disk. Its function is to allow other devices to share files and programs. The server typically contains the LAN's network management software, which manages the server and routes and manages communications on the network. The **network gateway** connects the LAN to public networks, such as the telephone network, or to other corporate networks so that the LAN can exchange information with dissimilar networks external to it.

Server
A computer with a large hard disk whose function is to allow other devices to share files and programs.

Network gateway
The communications processor that links a local area network to another dissimilar network, such as the public telephone system or another corporate network.

LAN technology components consist of metallic or fiber-optic cable or wireless transmission media linking individual computer devices, special adapters that serve as interfaces to the cable, and software that controls LAN activities. LANs employ either a baseband or a broadband technology. Baseband products provide a single path or channel for transmitting text, graphics, voice, or video data. Broadband networks provide several paths or

FIGURE 7.8

A Local Area Network (LAN)

LANs are networks that link a limited area, such as one office building or several buildings located close to one another. Here we show a LAN with the ring topology. LANs with the bus topology are also common.

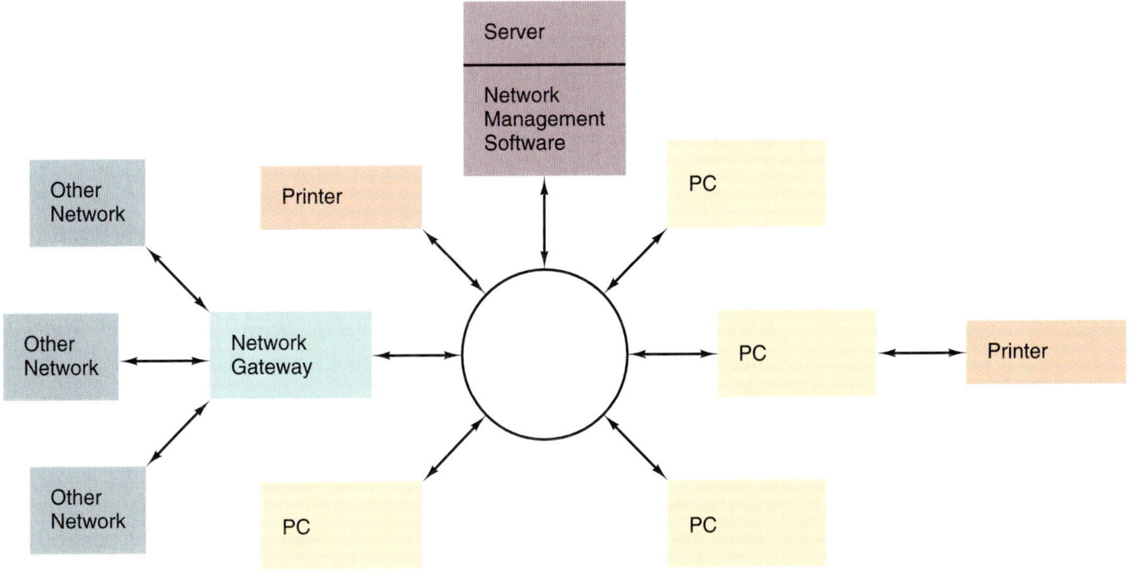

channels so that different types of data, or different messages, can be transmitted simultaneously.

LAN capabilities are also defined by the network operating system employed. The network operating system works with applications software, such as word processing or electronic mail, to keep data traffic flowing smoothly. The network operating system can reside on every PC in the network, or it can reside on a single designated computer, which acts as the server for all the applications on the network.

The primary disadvantages of LANs are that they can be more expensive to install than PBXs and are more inflexible, requiring new wiring each time the LAN is moved (unless the LAN uses wireless transmission). LANs also require specially trained staff to manage and run them.

WIDE AREA NETWORKS

Wide area network (WAN)
A telecommunications network covering a large geographical distance; provided by common carriers but managed by the customer.

Wide area networks (WANs) span a broad geographical distance, ranging from several miles to entire continents. WANs are provided by common carriers, which are companies (such as AT&T or MCI) that are licensed by the government to provide communications services to the public. The common carrier typically determines transmission rates or interconnections between lines, but the customer is responsible for the content and management of telecommunications. In other words, individual firms are responsible for establishing the most efficient routing of messages, error checking, editing, protocols, and telecommunications management.

WANs may consist of a combination of switched and dedicated lines and microwave and satellite communications. Switched lines are telephone lines that a person can access from his or her terminal to transmit data to another computer; the call is routed, or switched, through paths to the designated destination. Dedicated lines, or unswitched lines, can be leased or purchased from common carriers or private communications media vendors and are continuously available for transmission. The lessee typically pays a flat rate for total access to the line. Dedicated lines are often conditioned to transmit data at higher speeds than switched lines and are more appropriate for transmitting high volumes of data. Switched lines, on the other hand, are less expensive and more appropriate for low-volume applications requiring only occasional transmission.

The largest wide area network in use today is the Internet, which connects hundreds of thousands of smaller networks and many millions of users around the world. The Internet was originally set up for research scientists and academics, but it is now accessible to anyone with a computer and a modem. The Internet allows millions of people to access vast stores of information in computer systems throughout the world and to exchange information anywhere in the world at any time. Chapter 8 describes the wonders of this vast network of networks.

Value-added network (VAN)
A multipath data-only network managed by a private firm that sets up the network and charges other firms a fee to use it.

Value-Added Networks **Value-added networks (VANs)** are an alternative to firms designing and managing their own networks. VANs are private, multipath networks for data only. They are managed by third parties that can provide economies of service and management to participating businesses. A private firm establishes and manages the VAN and sells subscriptions to other firms willing to use it. The network may use ordinary telephone or voice-grade lines, satellite links, and other communications channels leased by the value-added carrier. Subscribers pay only for the amount of data they transmit plus a subscription fee. Note that VANs are not common carriers in the sense that they are not regulated monopolies; instead, they are private firms offering a service for a fee. They cannot provide long-distance voice service, however, which is reserved for common carriers.

The term *value-added* refers to the extra "value" added to communications by the telecommunications and computing services these networks provide to clients. Customers do not have to invest in network equipment and software or perform their own error checking, editing, routing, and protocol conversion. They may also save online charges and transmission costs because the costs of using the network are shared among many users. Thus, the resulting rates may be lower than if the clients had leased their own lines or satellite services. VANs are also attractive because they provide special services, such as electronic mail and access to public databases and bulletin boards. Tymnet and GE Information Services Company (GEIS) are popular VAN suppliers.

Another way VANs achieve economies is through **packet switching.** This entails breaking up a lengthy block of text into packets, or small bundles of data approximately 128 bytes long. The VAN gathers information from many users, divides it into small packets, and continuously searches for available communications channels that it leases from common carriers and others on which to send the packets. In contrast, an individual firm might use a single leased line for an hour and then not use it for two or three hours. Packets of data originating at one source can be routed through different paths in the network and reassembled into the original message when they reach their destination. Packet switching enables communications facilities to be used more fully and shared by more users.

Packet switching
The breaking up of a block of text into packets of data approximately 128 bytes long; a value-added network gathers data from its subscribers, divides the data into packets, and sends the packets on any available communications channel.

Frame relay is a faster and less expensive type of packet switching. Since so many of today's digital lines are cleaner than in the past and networks have features for correcting transmission problems, frame relay transmits data in packets without performing error correction. Frame relay works successfully over reliable lines that do not require frequent retransmission because of error.

Frame relay
Network technology that organizes data into packets without error correction routines to transmit data over networks faster and cheaper than packet switching.

CLIENT/SERVER COMPUTING

Networks with powerful servers have created a new model of computing called **client/server computing,** in which diverse pieces of hardware work on the same processing problem. In addition to managing the activities of the network, the server can store applications programs and data files and can distribute programs or data files to other computers on the network as they request them. Servers can be mainframes or minicomputers, but often they are large workstations or powerful PCs. In the client/server model, some processing tasks are handled by the server and others by the subordinate machines, called "clients," with each function being assigned to the machine best suited to perform it (see Figure 7.9). In large, complex applications, more than one server can supply services to clients. The client portion of the application usually handles user interfaces, data input, querying a database,

Client/server computing
Model of computing that divides processing tasks between "clients" and "servers" on a network, with each machine assigned the functions it performs best.

FIGURE 7.9

The Client/Server Model of Computing

In client/server computing, processing is divided among client and server machines linked by a network.

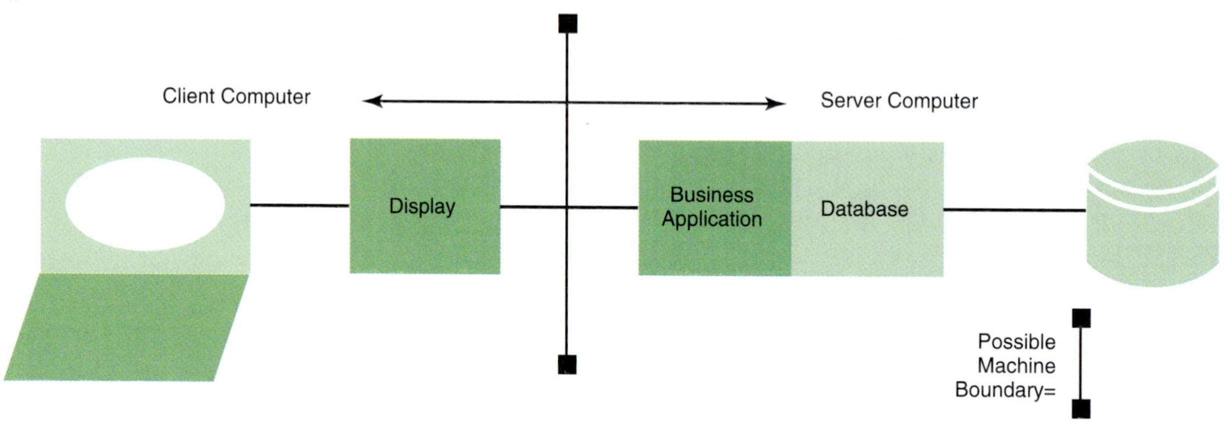

and obtaining reports, whereas the server part usually retrieves or processes data. The exact division of tasks varies with each application. The client/server model requires that applications programs be written as two separate software components that run on different machines but that appear to operate as a single application.

Because of the immense power and range of capabilities of desktop computers, client/server computing has emerged as a serious alternative to traditional computing based on centralized mainframes. Many companies are trying to downsize by replacing the work performed by mainframes with some type of client/server network. For example, the Burlington Coat Factory in Burlington, New Jersey, replaced a system that collected transactions from its retail stores and that was based on a Honeywell mainframe computer with one based on six smaller Sequent 2000/750 computers and Sun workstations. Cash registers in each Burlington store are connected by LANs to the Sun workstation, which serves as the main store processor. The Sun machines act as servers for the registers and as communications gateways to the company's host computers. They send each store's transactions via satellite to several Sequent computers at company headquarters. Users no longer have to request reports in advance, as they did with the mainframe system. They can access company databases from their desktops and use the data in their own spreadsheets and word-processing applications. The network can run even if individual parts are not working properly.[1]

Client/server computing has become attractive because it appears to be less expensive yet more flexible than using a centralized mainframe. The hardware for a client/server network costs much less than a mainframe, significantly reducing computer processing expenses. However, client/server computing has some hidden costs. Companies need to write new software that can divide the processing among clients and servers. Client/server networks are still not as reliable as centralized mainframes, with the potential for crippling the organization if they malfunction. Information systems specialists and end users require extensive training to use client/server technology properly.

THE DRIVE TOWARD STANDARDS

Telecommunications networks are most effective when digital information can move seamlessly from one type of computer system to another, without regard for the hardware or software technology being used. This goal has been difficult to achieve because of the many disparate types of communications equipment and software. Government, industry, and professional groups are working to create telecommunications standards that can be accepted by all computer manufacturers. Some of the most important standards used today are Transmission Control Protocol/Internet Protocol (TCP/IP) and Integrated Services Digital Network (ISDN).

Transmission Control Protocol/Internet Protocol (TCP/IP) An important networking standard is called **Transmission Control Protocol/Internet Protocol (TCP/IP),** which was developed in 1972 by the U.S. Department of Defense to help scientists link disparate computers. The Internet, described in Chapter 8, is based on TCP/IP. TCP/IP divides the telecommunications process into five layers. Data from the sending computer are broken down into bits and grouped into packets that can travel through communications channels to the receiving computer. The receiving computer then reassembles the data into a form it can use. If the receiving computer found a damaged packet, it would ask the sending computer to retransmit it. Two different computers using TCP/IP would be able to communicate, even if they were based on different hardware and software platforms. TCP/IP is used in both WAN and LAN environments.

Transmission Control Protocol/Internet Protocol (TCP/IP)
Networking standard for linking different types of computers; used in the Internet.

Integrated Services Digital Network (ISDN) **Integrated Services Digital Network (ISDN)** is an emerging international standard for extending common-carrier digital service to homes and offices from central telephone company facilities. Imagine sitting in your office or dormitory room looking at your computer screen; in one window is a spreadsheet, and in the other is the moving picture of a friend or colleague located across the country with whom you are working. You can both share voice messages, digital information, and video pictures. All this information comes over a single twisted-wire telephone line that is completely managed by the local phone company. That means you have integrated voice, digital, and video service and great flexibility with no expensive rewiring with coaxial cable; you simply plug your computer/telephone into the wall socket. Briefly, ISDN is the "everything network." The goal and promise of ISDN is to provide a more functional network to transport all kinds of digital information, regardless of its source or destination. It is a vision of the public switched-phone network turning into a vast digital superexpressway.

Integrated Services Digital Network (ISDN)
Standard for transmitting voice, data, and video over public switched telephone lines.

Two levels of ISDN service are available. Basic rate ISDN delivers two 64-kilobit-per-second channels for voice, data, and video and one 16-kilobit-per-second channel for control information (such as the phone number of the calling party) to the desktop or room through ordinary phone wire. Primary rate ISDN offers 1.5 MBPS of bandwidth divided into 23 channels for voice, video, and data and one channel for control information. This service can connect PBXs, central office switches, or computer systems with a need for high-speed data transmission. Plans are under way to increase the transmission capacity of both basic rate and primary rate ISDN. National ISDN service is emerging as local telephone companies upgrade their equipment. Currently, implementation of ISDN is restricted by its cost, regional limitations, and the difficulties organizations have experienced in learning how to use the technology. Once the technology is fully developed, however, and prices fall, ISDN will become a leading network alternative.

Asynchronous transfer mode (ATM)
Protocol for transmitting voice, data, and images over LANs and wide area networks using computers from different vendors by parceling information into uniform cells of 53 groups of 8 bytes.

Asynchronous Transfer Mode (ATM) Most corporations today use separate networks for voice, private-line services, and data, each of which is based on a different technology. **Asynchronous transfer mode (ATM)** may overcome some of these problems because it can seamlessly and dynamically switch voice, data, images, and video between users. ATM also promises to tie local and wide area networks together more easily (LANs are generally based on lower-speed protocols, whereas WANs operate at higher speeds.) ATM is a protocol that parcels information into uniform "cells," each with 53 groups of eight bytes, thus eliminating the need for protocol conversion. It can pass data between computers from different vendors and permits data to be transmitted at any speed the network handles. ATM currently requires fiber-optic cable, but it can attain transmission speeds of hundreds of megabits per second.[2]

7.4 TELECOMMUNICATIONS APPLICATIONS

Many of the information system applications discussed throughout this text employ telecommunications technology to help people make decisions faster and to accelerate the production of goods and services. Telecommunications has become essential to organizations with multiple geographic locations that must be closely coordinated. Here we discuss some of the leading telecommunications applications for communicating, coordinating, and speeding the flow of information: electronic mail, voice mail, fax, teleconferencing and videoconferencing, and electronic data interchange.

ELECTRONIC MAIL, VOICE MAIL, AND FAX

Electronic mail
The computer-to-computer exchange of messages.

Electronic mail, or E-mail, is the computer-to-computer exchange of messages that has become a way of eliminating "telephone tag" and costly long-distance telephone charges. It is possible for a person with a PC attached to a modem or a terminal to send notes and even lengthier documents simply by typing the name of the message's recipient. Many organizations have created their own internal E-mail systems, but people can also send and receive E-mail by subscribing to a commercial (public) E-mail service such as MCI Mail and AT&T Mail. Value-added networks and online information services such

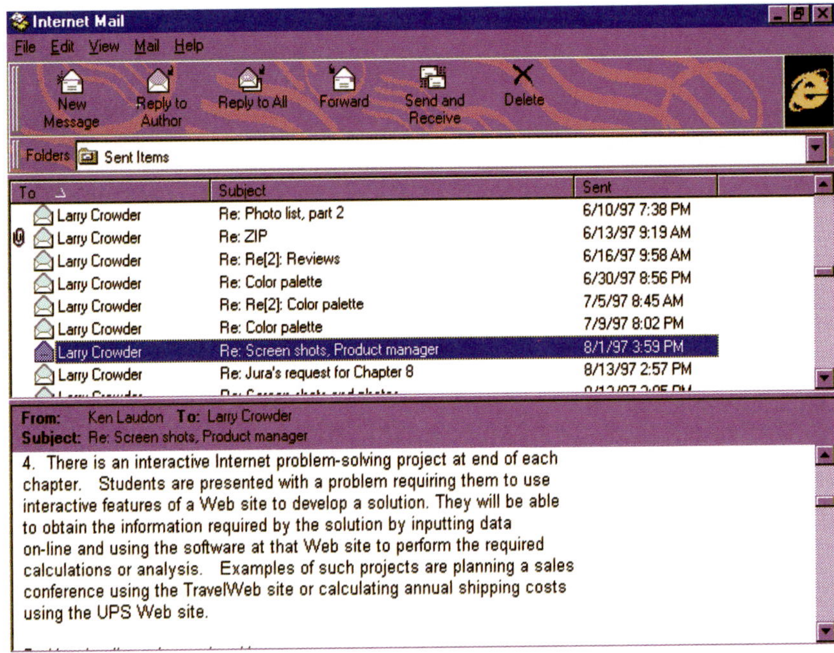

This E-mail program displays an outgoing message that was selected from a list of "Sent Items." With E-mail, people can easily send notes, messages, or letters directly from their computer to another computer.

as CompuServe and Prodigy also offer E-mail facilities. E-mail capabilities are also available on the Internet.

Because E-mail is generally more efficient than sending letters or using the telephone, it has become the preferred method of communication for many organizations, changing the way people interact. The Focus on People explores this phenomenon, showing the impact of E-mail and networking on campus life.

Voice Mail In a **voice mail** system, the spoken message of the sender is digitized, transmitted over a telecommunications network, and stored on disk for later retrieval. When the recipient is ready to listen, the messages are reconverted to audio form. Various "store and forward" capabilities notify recipients that messages are waiting. Recipients can save these messages for future use, delete them, or route them to other parties. Sophisticated mainframe- or minicomputer-based voice mail systems can store hundreds of hours of messages and handle over 100 incoming phone lines; PC-based systems are much smaller in scope.

Voice mail
A telecommunications system in which the spoken message of the sender is digitized, transmitted over a telecommunications network, and stored on disk until the recipient is ready to listen, when the message is reconverted to audio form.

Facsimile **Facsimile (fax)** machines can transmit documents containing both text and graphics over ordinary telephone lines. The image is scanned, digitized, and transmitted by a sending fax machine and reproduced in hard-copy form by a receiving fax machine. The process results in a duplicate, or facsimile, of the original.

Facsimile (fax)
A machine that can transmit documents containing both text and graphics over telephone lines; the sending machine digitizes and transmits the image, which is reproduced as a facsimile (fax) by the receiving machine.

TELECONFERENCING AND VIDEOCONFERENCING

Telecommunications technology provides **teleconferencing** capabilities that allow people to meet electronically. In electronic meetings, several people "confer" via telephone or E-mail group communications software (see

Teleconferencing
The use of telecommunications technology to enable people to meet electronically; can be accomplished via telephone or electronic mail.

FOCUS ON PEOPLE

COMPUTER NETWORKS TRANSFORM THE CAMPUS

Where did everybody go? That is what some visitors to college campuses are asking these days. Meeting on the quad or at the local hangout for a chat seems to have gone the way of the record player, a development that has some scholars concerned about whether technological advances adversely affect social interaction. The blame would lie directly with networks, which have dramatically altered the way in which college students function, both academically and socially.

At colleges such as Dartmouth in Hanover, New Hampshire, students can accomplish just about every task they need to during the day without leaving their rooms, with the possible exceptions of eating and physically attending classes. And even those aren't always necessary. With dorm rooms wired for connection to the college's computer network, a student can perform research using library materials, ask questions of professors, submit papers and assignments, have food delivered, and chat with friends across campus and around the country—all while sitting in front of a computer at a desk amidst piles of laundry.

From a purely academic standpoint, Dartmouth's network enhances the students' learning experience by giving them greater and more convenient access to resources in a multimedia format. Professors can use Web sites to display works of art or anatomy charts. "Smart" classrooms provide each student with a computer so that information and examples can be shared during a discussion. Dartmouth's E-mail system, dubbed Blitzmail, has evolved into somewhat of a lifeline for the campus. The college has placed public computer terminals at strategic points on the campus so that students can check their messages without having to return to their rooms. If they have a question for a professor, they can send it immediately instead of waiting until the instructor's office hours. It is not uncommon to witness long lines of students waiting for their turn at one of these terminals.

Not everyone is enthusiastic about the dynamic presence of computers on college campuses, however. Some academics believe that human interaction represents a significant part of the educational experience. They also contend that networks have changed normal socialization for the worse. Instead of getting to know each other on a personal, face-to-face basis, students just sit in their rooms, typing back and forth to each other. They miss out on opportunities to develop important conversational and social skills with other students and with professors because they do not interact in person. Some students critical of the trend liken electronic interaction to the relationships often established at parties: casual, brief, and not all that meaningful.

Still, experts dispute the idea that E-mail and computer networks convert thriving institutions into social ghost towns. While it may be true that some students could benefit from more face-to-face conversation with a professor, others, especially those who have difficulty overcoming shyness or whose first language is not English, might actually make more of an impact electronically. David G. Brown, provost and professor of economics at Wake Forest University, insists that he communicates much more with students as a result of the network and that the level of communication spills over to their personal encounters. Apparently, the university agrees with him. Each member of Wake Forest's class of 2000 received a laptop computer at the beginning of their first semester, paid for by an increase in tuition. Paperless courses have made the transition from concept to reality.

Networking college campuses will remain a cause for debate for some time. College surveys have started to rate schools on their network capabilities. Some institutions of learning simply do not have the financial resources to compete with others technologically. When roommates type messages to each other on their computers while they are both in the same room, obviously much has changed. Whether the development of wired campuses will help or hinder the university experience over the long run remains to be seen.

FOCUS Questions: What problems do computer networks solve for college campuses? What problems do they create? What new opportunities do they create?

SOURCE: Trip Gabriel, "Computers Help Unite Campuses but Also Drive Some Students Apart," *The New York Times,* November 11, 1996.

Chapter 14). With video teleconferencing, or **videoconferencing,** participants can see one another on video screens.

Videoconferencing
Teleconferencing in which participants can see each other on video screens.

Teleconferencing helps bring ideas and people together from remote locations, reducing the need for costly business travel and saving travel time. For example, the British firm ICL adopted videoconferencing as a means of reducing executive travel and facilitating global sharing of information.

In the past, videoconferencing was very expensive, requiring complex video conference facilities, technology to integrate images with data and voice transmission, and appropriate transmission media to relay the massive volume of data for images. Advances in transmission technology have reduced these costs. In addition, PC desktop videoconferencing systems, where users can see one another and simultaneously work on the same document, have made videoconferencing even more affordable and easier to implement. The Focus on Technology explores these videoconferencing options, including desktop videoconferencing through the Internet.

ELECTRONIC DATA INTERCHANGE

Electronic data interchange, or **EDI,** is the direct computer-to-computer exchange of standard business transaction documents, such as invoices, bills of lading, and purchase orders, between two separate organizations. EDI saves money and time because transactions can be electronically transmitted, eliminating the printing and handling of paper at one end and the inputting of data at the other. Figure 7.10 illustrates how EDI streamlines information processing.

Electronic data interchange (EDI)
The direct computer-to-computer exchange of standard business documents between two separate organizations.

EDI differs from electronic mail in that it transmits an actual transaction, as opposed to a primarily text message, and features standardized transaction formats, content-related error checking, and actual processing of the information.

FIGURE 7.10

Electronic Data Interchange (EDI)

EDI is the computer-to-computer exchange of standard business documents between two separate organizations. This diagram illustrates an EDI system that transmits a purchase order (P.O.) from the buyer to the seller.

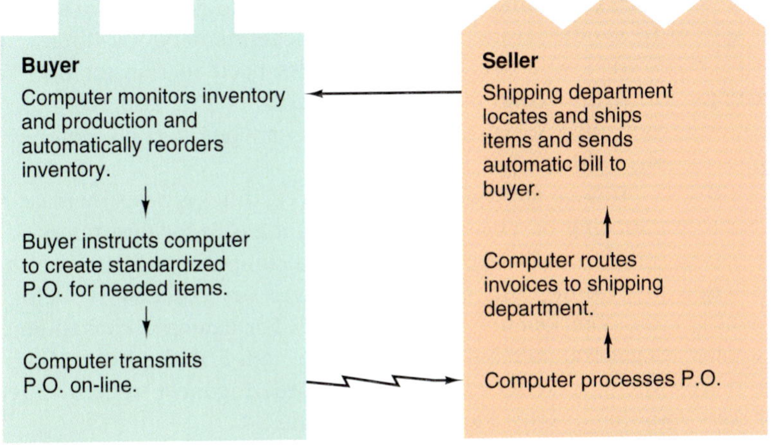
Buyer
Computer monitors inventory and production and automatically reorders inventory.
Buyer instructs computer to create standardized P.O. for needed items.
Computer transmits P.O. on-line.
Seller
Shipping department locates and ships items and sends automatic bill to buyer.
Computer routes invoices to shipping department.
Computer processes P.O.

FOCUS ON TECHNOLOGY

NOW YOU SEE ME

Of all the organizations on the planet, one with the greatest need to stay connected is the World Bank. With headquarters in Washington, D.C., and bureaus or affiliates in almost 200 countries, keeping the lines of communication flowing presents serious challenges. Conference calls do not always suffice to take the place of meetings, but budget and time restrictions can put a damper on conducting business in person. In videoconferencing, organizations such as the World Bank finally have a solution to such logistical problems.

PictureTel Corporation provides one of the platforms on which the World Bank engages in videoconferencing. Systems in various branches around the globe host large meetings and training classes networked under the watch of the organization's Information and Technology Services department. This setup can incur rather high costs, but it is a necessary expenditure. For smaller-scale gatherings, however, the World Bank has discovered a less expensive method of communicating. Cornell University's CU-SeeMe desktop system allows for videoconferencing on the Internet. After two years of using CU-SeeMe, the World Bank adopted an upgraded commercial version of the system from White Pine Software. The biggest advantage to these Internet-based systems is indeed the price. They require very little extra equipment, virtually none for parties who only need to sit in on a conference. Those who need to be an active part of a meeting would spend a few hundred dollars for a camera, microphone, and other hardware.

Naturally, with the savings come some sacrifices. The video image that CU-SeeMe produces does not measure more than 4-inches square, and the feed does not always appear very smooth. Peter Knight, chief of World Bank's electronic media center, is not really bothered by this, saying that the system fits his organization's small-scale conferencing needs just fine. He does think that it will require some time before employees get used to videoconferencing, but he sees that as an obstacle easily overcome.

Researchers forecast that the number of videoconferencing systems sold to both businesses and homes will jump enormously by the end of the century. Improvements in cost, quality, and user friendliness will contribute to the trend. Before too long, PCs will arrive fully equipped for videoconferencing, with video and audio software and camera included. Already, numerous organizations have adopted the technology successfully.

Kimmel Cancer Center at

Various transaction documents, such as purchase orders and invoices, can be generated electronically and passed from one organization's information system to another using a telecommunications network. Routine processing costs are lower because there is less need to transfer data from hard-copy forms into computer-ready transactions. EDI also reduces transcription errors and associated costs that occur when data are entered and printed out many times.

EDI can produce strategic benefits as well; it helps firms increase market share by "locking in" customers—making it easier for customers or distributors to order from them rather than from competitors. EDI also reduces transaction processing costs and can cut inventory costs by reducing the amount of time components are in inventory. For example, by handling 80 percent of its general merchandise orders through EDI, the Kmart Corporation in Troy, Michigan, reduced lead time for ordering most stock by three or four days, resulting in substantial interest savings.

Thomas Jefferson University has used desktop videoconferencing to enable doctors at other hospitals to consult each other when making diagnoses or setting a course of treatment for cancer patients. Doctors can actually share images of patients and discuss their opinions of the scans without leaving their offices. Virtual Mortgage Network of Newport Beach, California, has worked in conjunction with Flagstar Bank in Bloomfield, Michigan, to reduce the complicated process of obtaining a mortgage down to a matter of hours. Customers can speak to a mortgage counselor via a PC connection from a real estate office, often coming to terms on a loan in one videoconferencing session.

Like any new step in technology, videoconferencing will experience growing pains before being widely accepted in the business world. Like any step in business, an organization must analyze its problems and potential solutions first.

By using videoconferencing technology, people can meet and work together from many locations.

FOCUS Questions: What problems can videoconferencing solve for individuals and organizations? What people, organization, and technology factors would you use to decide whether to use videoconferencing?

SOURCE: Matt Hamblen, "Desktop Video Surge Forecast," *Computerworld,* October 14, 1996, and Lynda Radosevich, "Sizzle and Steak," *WebMaster,* November 1996.

PROBLEM SOLVING WITH NETWORKS: CAUTIONS AND CONCERNS

Several factors must be considered when a solution involves the use of a network, including the Internet:

1. *Response time:* This refers to the amount of time an online system takes to send a transaction or query over a network and receive a response. An example might be an inquiry about the balance in a client's checking account in an online banking system. Many factors other than the network can affect response time, including the processing speed of applications software and the ease of extracting information or records from databases. Many of these factors are network related, however, such as the transmission capacity of a telecommunications channel and related equipment, the distance data must be communicated, and the amount of traffic on the network. High error rates, which are primarily caused by

line noise or power surges, also degrade response time because messages must be retransmitted.

2. *Reliability:* A network may be unable to deliver the required solution if it is crippled by excessive "downtime" (the period of time a network is nonoperational). Businesses such as MasterCard would come to a standstill if their network operations were interrupted for more than a few minutes. Network reliability is a function of the quality of telecommunications channels and equipment, error rates, and the quality of the personnel managing the network.

3. *Cost:* There are extra costs for using a network solution, such as the cost of installing or renting the channels, purchasing telecommunications equipment, and employing and training personnel to manage the network. Alternative network solutions may have different cost structures that should be considered—for example, a PBX is less costly to install than a LAN but has a lower transmission capacity. Savings may also be realized by increasing response time or by reducing transmission errors. The cost and performance trade-offs of alternative network structures must be figured into the solution design.

4. *Security:* Networks are vulnerable to disruption and penetration by outsiders at many points. A network solution must consider the critical nature of the data flowing through the network and the extent to which they need to be safeguarded by special security measures. This issue is discussed in detail in Chapter 12.

5. *Standards:* The vast array of existing hardware, software, and network standards makes it difficult for different devices and different networks to communicate with each other and exchange information. Designing a network-based solution requires consideration of compatibility and standards.

6. *Ethics:* Widespread use of networks raises new ethical issues for businesses when they need to determine whether to monitor the way their employees use their networks and set standards of professional conduct for managers and employees. We explore this topic in the case study at the end of the chapter.

RUNNING CASE PART 2

AUTOMATING THE SALES FLOOR

Which specific information system technologies would be most useful to large retail stores such as Macy's? Discounters such as Kmart and department stores such as JCPenney, Sears, and Saks Fifth Avenue have benefited from technology that helped them automate their sales floors. They are using point-of-sale terminals, store-based local area networks, hand-held radio frequency scanners, and sophisticated customer databases to expedite purchases and to supply information to improve marketing and inventory management.

Point-of-sale devices: Point-of-sale devices such as hand-held scanning wands or guns or scanners built into countertops near the cash register record sales data at the point where the sales transaction is taking place. The captured data, which usually include the item sold, the number of units of the item sold, and perhaps the flavor, color, or size of the item, are transmitted to a computer. These data are used in information systems that track items in inventory, reorder items that are running out of stock, and analyze customer buying patterns.

Store-based local area networks (LANs): Stores can link their point-of-sale terminals via local area networks to in-store PCs to maintain their own sales data. Data specific to each store can also be transmitted to a central database for company-wide analysis. For example, branches of Neiman Marcus, the Dallas-based luxury department store, maintain their own data on purchases made locally using an in-store IBM RS/6000 workstation. The data are captured as purchases and are entered in point-of-sale devices. Neiman Marcus sales associates use this data to call or write their customers. The in-store data are also transmitted to corporate headquarters, where Neiman Marcus maintains a large companywide database of all customer purchases made in all stores and all customer purchases made by mail order.

Hand-held radio frequency scanners: Hand-held wireless radio-frequency–based scanners can be easily used by store employees as they roam the aisles to capture data about items on store shelves for automatic transmission to sales and inventory management systems. For example, New York-based Saks Fifth Avenue uses hand-held radio frequency scanners supplied by Telxon Corporation to transmit data on style, size, and color directly to a PC running under OS/2. The scanners are in constant radio communication with the PC, which acts as the store server. The PC then transmits the data to Saks's corporate mainframe. By automating the tedium of counting inventory, the scanner gives sales staff more time to spend with customers.

Customer databases: The information maintained by department stores on customers and their credit card purchases is a veritable goldmine for direct marketing and sales promotions. By analyzing customer purchases and sales data captured by point-of-sale devices, department stores can target ads or direct marketing campaigns at customers most likely to respond to a specific type of promotion. Individual stores can tailor their particular product assortments to the brands, styles, sizes, and colors of merchandise that their customers are most likely to buy. In combination with sales data, customer databases can help stores fine-tune their inventory to ensure that the merchandise their customers want to buy is on the shelves when they want to buy it.

SOURCE: Linda Wilson, "The Big Stores Fight Back," *Information Week*, April 26, 1993.

RUNNING CASE Questions:

1. How could sales floor automation technology help Macy's merchandise buyers?
2. How could sales data be used to give a firm a competitive advantage?
3. What kinds of problems can sales floor automation solve? What kinds of problems can't be solved by using this technology?

7.5 LEADING-EDGE TECHNOLOGY: WIRELESS COMMUNICATION

Until the past few years, telephones, computers, faxes, and other communications devices have been tethered to wires. But advances in microprocessors and software are changing that, and powerful wireless networks are emerging. Wireless networks allow people to communicate cheaply and easily without being tied to their desktop telephones or computers. These networks could change the way many people do their jobs; more employees could work at home or in the field, with central offices run by fewer people. As the work force becomes more mobile, the ability to move information without wires is essential.

The range of wireless technologies includes some we have already described: microwave and satellite transmission media. Other wireless technologies include the use of radio-based mobile data networks, paging systems, enhanced cellular telephones, personal communication services, and new satellite networks. Wireless LANs can also be created using infrared or radio-frequency–based transmission.

Mobile data networks
Radio-based wireless networks for two-way transmission of digital data.

Mobile data networks are radio-based wireless networks for two-way transmission of digital data. These systems employ a network of radio towers to send text data to and from hand-held computers. They can send long data files efficiently and cheaply by transmitting them in packets (see the discussion of packet switching in Section 7.3).

Ram Mobile Data and ARDIS are two data-only national digital networks. These networks are used primarily by workers such as field technicians or sales representatives. For instance, from a single office in Connecticut, Otis Elevators uses the ARDIS network to dispatch repair technicians all over the United States and to receive their reports. These radio-based data networks could be expanded to provide electronic mail and other network services.

Paging systems
Wireless system for notifying users of telephone calls that can also be used to transmit short alphanumeric messages.

The most common use of portable **paging systems** has been to beep when the user receives a telephone call. Since the mid 1980s, paging devices have also been used to transmit short alphanumeric messages that can be read on the pagers' screens. These paging systems can now send data to mobile computers. Paging services operate at very low speeds, making them useful primarily for sending very short messages. Some organizations find one-way paging more economical and efficient than faxing. For example, Ethos Corporation, a software maker in Boulder, Colorado, developed commercial mortgage-processing software that uses a paging system to electronically deliver mortgage rates from financial firms to nearly 2,000 brokers daily. These firms used to spend $30,000 per month to fax the same information from a service bureau, whereas paging costs $10,000 or less per month. Even more important, data transmitted through the paging network can be downloaded and manipulated, saving brokers perhaps 1½ hours of work each day.

Cellular telephones
Telephones working in a system that uses radio waves to transmit voice and data to radio antennas placed in adjacent geographic areas.

Cellular telephones work by using radio waves to communicate with radio antennas placed within adjacent geographic areas called cells. When you place a call from a cellular phone, the call moves through a radio highway of these transmission towers, directed by advanced digital switches and computers. As a cellular call moves from one cell to another, a computer that monitors signals from the cells switches the signal to a radio channel assigned to the next cell. Although cellular phones are primarily used for voice transmission, cellular companies have developed capabilities to use the existing analog cellular phone network to transmit data in digital form. A standard called Cellular Digital Packet Data (CDPD) takes advantage of pauses in voice conversations during idle air time to send packets of data.

Portable computers can be linked to cellular telephone services using internal and external wireless cellular modems or devices that interface between ordinary modems and cellular telephones. Small, low-power radio modems can fit into card slots for the transmission devices used in wireless data and cellular networks.

Companies are starting to build new kinds of microcellular digital networks called **personal communications services (PCSs).** PCS technology is similar to cellular technology but uses low-power, high-frequency radio waves. Compared with conventional cellular networks, PCSs use smaller, closely spaced microcells that require lower-powered radio transmitters and phones. Where a city might have a dozen cellular stations, a PCS system might have hundreds. PCS phones are smaller and less expensive than cellular phones because they don't need to be as powerful. And they can be used in many more locations than cellular telephones—from inside office buildings, elevators, tunnels, trains, and subway platforms. Some people believe PCS networks will be as much as 20 times more efficient than existing analog cellular systems, with vastly better service and quality.

Personal communications services (PCSs)
Systems for wireless transmission of voice and data sending low-power, high-frequency radio waves to closely spaced microcells.

PCS transmission is entirely digital, designed for sending data as well as voice. It can work with a **personal digital assistant (PDA),** a pen-based, hand-held computer with built-in communication and organizational capabilities. For instance, Apple's 1-pound Newton MessagePad can serve as an electronic scheduler, calendar, and notepad. Equipped with a special modem card, it can also transmit E-mail, send documents to printers, fax machines, or PCs, or connect to the Internet or an intranet. The Newton recognizes notes penned on its glass screen with a special stylus, using intelligent software that not only executes but that also anticipates some common commands.

Personal digital assistant (PDA)
Pen-based, handheld computer with built-in communication and organizational capabilities.

The Federal Communications Commission (FCC) has allocated a huge spectrum of network air space for these wireless personal communications services, which could eventually challenge local telephone systems. The slice of frequencies is wider than for cellular communications. Since PCSs operate at higher frequencies than cellular systems, where the spectrum isn't so crowded, PCSs will be able to offer a wider range of services, including video and multimedia communication.

A hierarchy of wireless networks is taking shape. The most deluxe wireless networks will be the satellite networks (as shown in Figure 7.11), which can provide global wireless phone, data, and fax service by bouncing signals off low-orbit satellites. Low-orbit satellites are close enough to the earth to pick up signals from weak transmitters, they consume less power, and they are less expensive to launch than conventional communications satellites. For example, Iridium, a \$3.4 billion project sponsored by Motorola, Sony, and Sprint, will beam calls from a small hand-held set from any one point in the world to any other using a system of 66 low-orbit satellites encircling the globe. The Teledesic Corporation, a joint venture of McCaw Cellular Communications and Microsoft Corporation, is working on a \$9 billion system using 840 small satellites to create a high-capacity wireless network capable of

FIGURE 7.11

Sky Phones

Several companies plan to use satellites to help calls travel over vast regions, such as mountains, deserts, and oceans, that are not served by cellular systems. Satellite phones will also help international travelers stay in contact where local cellular technology is not compatible with their phones from home.

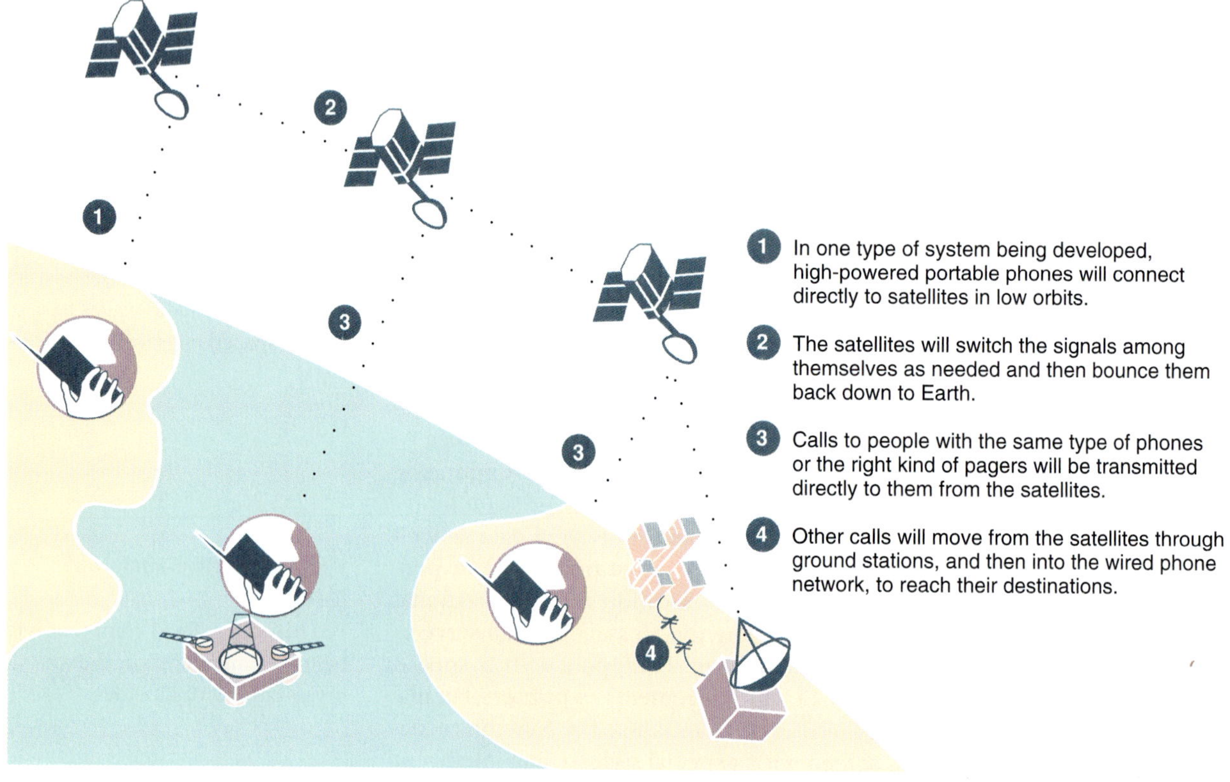

transmitting telephone calls, high-resolution computer images, and two-way video conferences to virtually any spot on the planet. Wireless satellite networks will be most useful for organizations wishing to bypass inadequate communications in underdeveloped or rural areas or for traveling business executives who cannot use cellular phones easily when they travel abroad.

1 In one type of system being developed, high-powered portable phones will connect directly to satellites in low orbits.
2 The satellites will switch the signals among themselves as needed and then bounce them back down to Earth.
3 Calls to people with the same type of phones or the right kind of pagers will be transmitted directly to them from the satellites.
4 Other calls will move from the satellites through ground stations, and then into the wired phone network, to reach their destinations.

While wireless networks hold great promise, they have several limitations. At present, transmission speeds are practical for short messages. Wireless transmission has a high incidence of errors because it is susceptible to many kinds of interference, especially when transmission occurs from moving vehicles. Elaborate error-correcting features, which reduce the actual throughput of wireless networks, are required. Data may have to be transmitted repeatedly until the entire message is received. Many wireless modems that work with ARDIS can't work with Ram or cellular networks. Different cellular systems use incompatible transmission standards. To make wireless communication as easy to use as the wired telephone system will require complex software that lets incompatible networks and technologies work seamlessly together.[3]

SUMMARY

- Telecommunications can be defined as communication by electronic means, usually over some distance.
- Asynchronous transmission and synchronous transmission are two conventions for determining where a character begins or ends when data are transmitted from one computer to another.
- Three different transmission modes govern the direction of data flow over a telecommunications medium: simplex transmission, half-duplex transmission, and full-duplex transmission.
- Two types of signals are used in telecommunications systems: analog and digital. Analog signals are used primarily for voice transmission, whereas digital signals are used for data transmission and some voice transmission. A modem can be used to convert digital signals to analog form and vice versa.
- The essential components of a telecommunications network are computers, terminals or other input/output devices, communications channels, communications processors (such as modems, multiplexers, and front-end processors), and telecommunications software.
- Different components of a telecommunications network, which typically use a wide array of hardware and software technology, can communicate with each other using a common set of rules called protocols.
- The principal telecommunications transmission media are twisted wire, coaxial cable, fiber-optic cable, microwave, and satellite.
- Telecommunications transmission rate is measured in bits per second. The transmission capacity of a particular telecommunications medium is determined by its bandwidth, the range of frequencies that the medium can accommodate.
- The three common network topologies are the star network, the bus network, and the ring network.
- Local area networks (LANs) and private branch exchanges (PBXs) are used for local, short-range office and building systems. A PBX is a central, private switchboard that can be used for digital transmission among computers and office devices as well as for voice transmission. A LAN typically consists of a group of PCs linked together. LANs are useful for large-volume, high-speed communications among computers, whereas PBXs are most useful for mixed voice and data traffic involving low volume and lower speed.
- Client/server computing divides processing work between client computers on a network and servers, with each function assigned to the machine best suited to perform it. Client/server networks are starting to replace centralized mainframes.
- Wide area networks (WANs) cover large geographical areas and are provided by common carriers but managed by the customer.
- Value-added networks (VANs) are privately owned and managed networks that carry digital information over long distances. In addition to providing baseline communications, VANs also provide editing, storage, and redistribution of information for a firm.

- Standards are required in order to link different hardware, software, and network components together to transfer information from one computer to another. Transmission Control Protocol/Internet Protocol (TCP/IP) and Integrated Services Digital Network (ISDN) are important standards.
- Electronic mail, voice mail, fax, teleconferencing, videoconferencing, and electronic data interchange (EDI) are widely used telecommunications applications.
- Six factors to consider when designing a communications network are response time, reliability, cost, security, standards, and ethics.
- New forms of wireless communication are being provided by mobile data networks, cellular telephones, paging systems, personal communications services, and satellite telephone services.

KEY TERMS

Analog signal
Digital signal
Modulation
Demodulation
Modem
Asynchronous transmission
Synchronous transmission
Simplex transmission
Half-duplex transmission
Full-duplex transmission
Channel
Front-end processor
Host computer
Multiplexer
Concentrator
Controller
Protocol
Twisted wire
Coaxial cable
Fiber optics
Microwave
Communications satellite
Baud
Bandwidth
Network topology
Star network
Bus network
Ring network
Private branch exchange (PBX)
Local area network (LAN)
Server
Network gateway
Wide area network (WAN)
Value-added network (VAN)
Packet switching
Frame relay
Client/server computing
Transmission Control Protocol/ Internet Protocol (TCP/IP)
Integrated Services Digital Network (ISDN)
Asynchronous Transfer Mode (ATM)
Electronic mail
Voice mail
Facsimile (fax)
Teleconferencing
Videoconferencing
Electronic data interchange (EDI)
Mobile data networks
Paging systems
Cellular telephones
Personal communications services (PCSs)
Personal digital assistant (PDA)

REVIEW QUESTIONS

1. Name and briefly describe the principal functions of telecommunications systems.
2. What is the difference between an analog signal and a digital signal?
3. What is the difference between synchronous and asynchronous transmission? How do half-duplex, full-duplex, and simplex transmission differ?
4. Name and briefly describe the components of a telecommunications network.
5. How do a modem, a concentrator, and a controller differ?
6. What are the five principal telecommunications transmission media? Compare them in terms of speed and cost.
7. What are the measures of telecommunications transmission speed? What is the relationship between the bandwidth and the transmission capacity of a channel?
8. Name and briefly describe the three principal network topologies.
9. What is the difference between a local area network and a private branch exchange? Between a wide area network and a value-added network?
10. What is client/server computing?
11. Name and describe two important telecommunications standards.
12. What is the difference between electronic mail and electronic data interchange (EDI)?
13. Distinguish between teleconferencing and videoconferencing.
14. Name and describe the major wireless communication technologies.

DISCUSSION QUESTIONS

1. What type of transmission medium is most suitable for the following situations? Why?

   a. *USA Today* uses a network to relay each day's newspaper layout to 31 print locations around the world.

   b. The law firm of Sidley & Austin wants to link 1,000 PCs used for legal document preparation and to send electronic mail between the firm's primary offices in Chicago and its branches in New York, Los Angeles, and Washington, D.C.

   c. Lloyd's of London wants to link all of its 1,000 underwriters, located in the same building in corporate headquarters.

2. Nathan Kaplan is a prominent obstetrician-gynecologist in Fairfield County, Connecticut, who is starting to use PCs in his busy office. His office staff includes one receptionist, one secretary, and one nurse. The office uses an IBM PC for writing letters, simple office accounting (payroll, accounts payable, PC billing), and maintaining patient files. Business has grown to the point where one PC is not enough. Kaplan wants to purchase another so that

one PC can be used by the receptionist in the front office and one by the secretary in the back room. Both need access to the same data and files. What networking options should Kaplan consider? What factors should be taken into account in the final selection?

PROBLEM-SOLVING EXERCISES

1. *Group exercise:* Newton's is a discount appliance and electronics retail chain with outlets in more than 50 locations throughout the Northeast. Its inventory and other major application systems are processed by a minicomputer in corporate headquarters in Hartford, Connecticut. If an outlet runs out of a popular item, such as large air conditioners, it can obtain that item from another outlet or from the firm's central warehouse. Newton's currently has no way to maintain up-to-date data on inventory. Outlets collect purchase transactions at the checkout counter and mail them to corporate headquarters. Customer complaints have mounted because customers are frequently told that an item is in inventory when it has been sold out for the season.

   Newton's is afraid it will lose market share unless it develops an online, point-of-sale system with up-to-date inventory for each outlet and for its central warehouse. Divide into groups. Each group should write a proposal for an online, real-time point-of-sale system using telecommunications technology. The group should include a diagram of the proposed network and an analysis of appropriate hardware, transmission, media, and network topology. The analysis should include reasons for the group's recommendations. Each group should present its findings to the class.

2. Using Table 7.2 for reference, calculate approximately how long it would take to transmit this chapter over the following media: twisted wire, coaxial cable, fiber-optic cable, and satellite.

3. *Hands-on exercise:* If your college or university computers are linked to the Internet and have an account that can be used by students, send a brief (one- or two-paragraph) electronic mail message via the Internet to the President (president@whitehouse.gov) explaining your position on whether the federal government should pass additional legislation to protect E-mail privacy. If your school has no Internet connection, use an online service such as CompuServe, Prodigy, or America Online to send the E-mail message. Be sure to consult your instructor and your school's technical support staff before sending the message.

4. *Internet problem-solving exercise:* Your 1995 Chevrolet Cavalier LS tires are worn out. You would like to buy tires that have a long life and also good traction in the snow because you live in St. Paul, Minnesota (ZIP code 55117). You would like to find out whether Goodyear Tire & Rubber Company has any tires that meet those requirements. Use the tire selector on Goodyear's Web site to determine the tire you should purchase, including tire size, and locate the name and address of your nearest Goodyear dealer.

NOTES

1. Bruce Caldwell, "Client-Server: Can It Be Saved?" *Information Week,* April 8, 1996, and Alok Sinha, "Client-Server Computing," *Communications of the ACM* 35, no. 6 (June 1992).
2. Ellis Booker, "ATM Faces High Expectations," *Computerworld,* January 24, 1994.
3. Quentin Hardy, "Iridium Creates New Plan for Global Cellular Service," *The Wall Street Journal,* August 18, 1997, and G. Christian-Hill, "Look! No Wires!" *The Wall Street Journal,* February 11, 1994.

PROBLEM-SOLVING CASE

CAN NETWORKS PROTECT PRIVACY?

The widespread use of networks and the Internet has raised new ethical questions for information systems. New software tools allow supervisors to electronically check on employees in a number of ways. A supervisor can use these tools to check an employee's performance by tracking the number of keystrokes per minute, the number of mistakes made, and the total time spent at the computer. Such electronic monitoring is routinely used in airline reservation sales, insurance companies, mail-order houses, and telephone companies to check on employees. The telephone system technology in most large business firms can record the time, length, and destination of employees' telephone calls or listen in on employees' telephone conversations with customers.

While such devices can be used to monitor employee communications, employers note that there are legitimate reasons for using them. They believe that computer monitoring is a valuable quality-control technique. Covert monitoring is accepted for many jobs classified by the government or a company, and it is the responsibility of the information systems department to inform workers that they will be monitored and to be sure that the monitoring devices are not used maliciously.

Many companies contend that they have a right to monitor the electronic mail of their employees because they own the facilities and expect their use to be for business purposes only. In some instances—when there is evidence of safety violations, illegal activity, racial discrimination, or sexual impropriety—it may be appropriate for employers to monitor E-mail. Companies may also need to access business information, whether it is kept in an employee's file cabinet, desk, or E-mail system. Clear policies on E-mail use and administration must be established to prevent misunderstandings that can cause ill will and lead to litigation. The issues of privacy and property relating to E-mail are complex. Jerry Berman, director of the Information Technology Project for the American Civil Liberties Union, says they will be decided by the courts, Congress, and the institutions developing a culture around these technologies.

At present, the only federal law to cover E-mail privacy is the Electronic Communications Privacy Act of 1986. This law prohibits interception or disclosure of E-mail messages by parties outside the company where the messages were sent unless a warrant is obtained by law-enforcement agents. The act does not cover the interception of messages within a company.

Some employers, such as Federal Express, Nordstrom, Eastman Kodak, and the Bank of Boston, have issued policy statements informing employees of the company's right to intercept and read their E-mail messages. These firms contend that the E-mail system is company property and its use should be for company business only. Other firms, such as General Motors and Hallmark Cards, have policies that give their employees greater privacy.

Regardless of their decision regarding E-mail privacy, employers can greatly reduce misunderstandings and legal actions by taking the time to develop internal policies that explicitly outline company rules and responsibilities regarding employee monitoring. Employees should be notified if a company decides to monitor electronic messages. Companies can add policy messages to screen menus, place stickers on equipment, or even require employees to sign affidavits indicating that they understand the rights and responsibilities of using corporate E-mail systems.

The Internet poses additional privacy challenges, especially through the growing use of the World Wide Web. Sites on the World Wide Web can be programmed to track not only the number of times the sites were accessed by other computers but also the location of the computers that accessed them. Marketers using the Web can determine, without your knowledge or permission, the domain portion of your E-mail address, which can indicate whether you reached the Web site through a corporate connection or a consumer online service such as America Online. This information helps marketers target their ads.

Even more controversial are "cookies," a technology that allows Web sites to track individual users. A Web site can place a tiny file on a computer that accesses that site. The file contains the name of the Web site, an identification code unique to the file, and some other data. When you use your computer to access a Web site, the site can check your cookie file to see whether you've been there before and act accordingly. Although the cookie doesn't provide the Web site owners with your name or E-mail address, it does know that your computer represents a distinct user. The Web site can track some of your actions, including other Web sites you have accessed, and then use a previously deposited cookie to link the data to your name and address. Some Web site owners could then sell the information (product descriptions you have viewed on the Web, products you purchased via the Web) to other companies for advertising and marketing.

Technology and consumer pressure can help thwart the cookie monster. Web browsing software such as Netscape Navigator and Microsoft Internet Explorer can be set to notify you when a Web site wants to deposit a cookie, leaving you the option of whether to take it or not. CommerceNet, a business consortium promoting Internet commerce, and the Electronic Frontier Foundation, an advocacy group, have established an organization called eTrust to rate privacy policies of Web sites.

SOURCES: Stephen H. Wildstrom, "Privacy and the Cookie Monster," *Business Week*, December 16, 1996; Thomas E. Weber, "Browsers Beware: The Web Is Watching," *The Wall Street Journal*, June 17, 1996; "Does E-Mail Mean Everyone's Mail?" *Information Week*, January 3, 1994; and David Bjerklie, "E-Mail: The Boss Is Watching," *Technology Review*, April 1993.

CASE STUDY QUESTIONS

1. Should businesses have the right to monitor employees using networks? Why or why not?

2. Should E-mail privacy be protected by law? Why or why not?

3. If companies can obtain information about consumers through ATM machines, credit cards, and checkout scanners, should they be allowed to obtain consumer information from people accessing Web sites? Why or why not?

4. Develop a company privacy policy regarding workplace monitoring, E-mail, and the gathering of personal information from the Internet.

Chapter

EIGHT

THE INTERNET

CHAPTER OUTLINE

Opening Vignette: Electric Minds

8.1 The Internet and the Information Superhighway

- What Is the Internet?
- History of the Internet
- The Technology behind the Internet
- Internet Tools and Capabilities

8.2 The World Wide Web

- Web Technology
- Searching for Information on the Web
- Intranets

8.3 The Role of the Internet in Problem Solving

- Expediting Access to Information
- Enhancing Communication and Collaboration
- Accelerating the Distribution of New Knowledge and the Pace of Scientific Discovery
- Facilitating Electronic Commerce

8.4. The Challenge of the Internet

- Technology Issues
- Organizational and Social Issues
- People Issues

LEARNING OBJECTIVES

After reading and studying this chapter, you will

1. Understand how the Internet works and how it is designed.
2. Be familiar with the major Internet tools for communicating and accessing information.
3. Know the capabilities and benefits provided by the World Wide Web and Internet technology, including the use of intranets.
4. Understand the role of the Internet in problem solving.
5. Be aware of the major people, organization, and technology challenges posed by the Internet.

ELECTRIC MINDS

What is a community? It can be a group of people with common interests and needs who want to be together in a village, town, university, or other organization. Today, thanks to the Internet and networked information systems, new kinds of communities are springing up in cyberspace, bringing together people who otherwise might not meet because of their widely scattered physical locations.

By providing a place where people with common interests can share information and experiences, regardless of where they live, these virtual communities are satisfying important social needs. They can also create new opportunities for business. In November 1996, Howard Rheingold created an Internet community called Electric Minds specifically to serve both purposes.

Electric Minds is a community—and a business—built around the exchange of ideas about technology and what it means. In the month after it was launched, more than 10,000 people from various countries, including Japan and Sweden, registered. The Electric Minds staff publishes interviews, articles, and essays spun off from the discussions about technology, culture, and community as well as topics suggested by members. The Electric Minds World Wide Web site is studded with commentary from leading humanists, technologists, and futurists to encourage other people to create insightful content that could attract more visitors. Electric Minds hopes to branch out into other media, including a magazine, books, and segments for Ziff-Davis Publishing Company's ZDTV site on the MSNBC network.

Electric Minds is supported by advertising and sponsorships from companies that expect to benefit from their association with this community of ideas. It sells "participatory sponsorships," where vendors can purchase banner ads on its Web site. These banners might jump to an interview with a representative of the company or link to a discussion forum where visitors can register to ask questions of the sponsor or provide opinions about its products or services. The banners might link to the sponsor's commercial site on the World Wide Web. By interacting with the electronic community and inviting discussion, businesses can develop closer relationships with potential and existing customers. Electronic communities can provide businesses with new concentrated channels to target their marketing efforts by bringing together groups of people with similar interests who benefit from sharing information and advice, such as doctors, lawyers, scientists, and teachers.

SOURCE: Heath Row, "Social Studies," *Webmaster,* February 1997.

Electric Minds is both a new kind of community and a new kind of business based on bringing people together online to exchange ideas. These are just some of the exciting new uses of information systems propelled by the Internet. The Internet is transforming the way people exchange ideas and information throughout the world, widening and enriching the role of computers in business, government, education, and everyday life.

The Internet is a set of technologies, but it also represents a new mindset and a new culture in the information systems world, as well as a new role for information technology in organizations. In this chapter we describe the technology and capabilities of the Internet, exploring their impact and role in problem solving.

8.1 THE INTERNET AND THE INFORMATION SUPERHIGHWAY

The Internet has been the focus of so much attention because it is the single largest and fastest-growing implementation of an information superhighway. The term **information superhighway** refers to high-speed telecommunications networks that are national or international in scope and that offer open access (with or without a fee) to the general public. The Internet is having a massive impact on the business world, on university and government communities, and on many individuals as well. As you shall see in later sections, this impact arises from the Internet's ability to virtually eliminate many of the barriers of time and place and to do so inexpensively.

Information superhighway
High-speed telecommunications networks that are national or international in scope and that offer open access to the general public.

WHAT IS THE INTERNET?

The Internet is, without question, the world's largest computer network. It is actually a global, seamless network of hundreds of thousands of other local, regional, and national networks. Most people access it through their networks at work or school, although increasing numbers of individuals and small businesses now access it through commercial online services such as Compuserve, America Online, and Prodigy, and through commercial Internet service providers (ISPs). An **Internet service provider (ISP)** is an organization with a permanent connection to the Internet that sells temporary connections to subscribers.

Internet Service Provider (ISP)
A company with a permanent connection to the Internet that offers Internet access to subscribers.

The Internet (or simply the "Net") is confusing to many people partly because it has no owner. Of course, the constituent networks are all owned by some organization—government, business, or not-for-profit—but not the Internet itself. It also has no central management and no centrally offered services. Any decisions that need to be made, such as technology standards, are made by a voluntary membership organization known as the Internet Society (or ISOC), which any individual or organization may join.

HISTORY OF THE INTERNET

The origins of the Internet are found in ARPANET, a single network created in 1969 by the U.S. Defense Department's Advanced Research Projects Agency (ARPA) to enable data sharing and to create an electronic mail (E-mail) system. The decentralization of the Net was purposeful—the Defense Department wanted to make ARPANET less vulnerable to attack by a foreign power or by terrorists. ARPANET was designed so that all computers on the network would have equal ability to communicate with other computers on the network.

By the mid-1980s, the U.S. Department of Energy and the National Aeronautic and Space Administration (NASA) were both connected to the Net, with ARPANET acting as the backbone. In 1986, the U.S. National Science Foundation (NSF) created a national network to connect university computer science departments; it quickly evolved into NSFNET, a backbone network linking university researchers and scientists. When ARPANET and NSFNET were linked, the modern Internet was born, and the phenomenal growth began. Scientific and educational networks began hooking up as the Net became a way for scientists and educators from around the world to converse daily, to share their work, to collaborate regardless of distance, and to gather information. Business use of the Net began slowly in the late 1980s but exploded since 1993 with the advent of the World Wide Web.

In 1990 ARPANET ceased to exist, leaving NSFNET as the sole backbone. Finally, in the spring of 1995, the Internet backbone function was transferred to a series of interconnected, mainly commercial networks, and NSFNET reverted back to its original role as a research network. These regional backbone networks are privately owned, profit-making companies that charge a connection fee to organizations. Organizations that cannot afford to connect directly to one of these regional networks can access the Net the same way individuals do—through a commercial Internet provider. Government and university organizations remain as major presences on the Internet.

The size and impact of the Internet can be seen by highlighting a very few of the organizations that consider it valuable enough to use on an ongoing basis. The United States Supreme Court, the White House, and both houses of Congress are on the Internet, as are most large U.S. government agencies and most of the states within the United States. The United Nations,

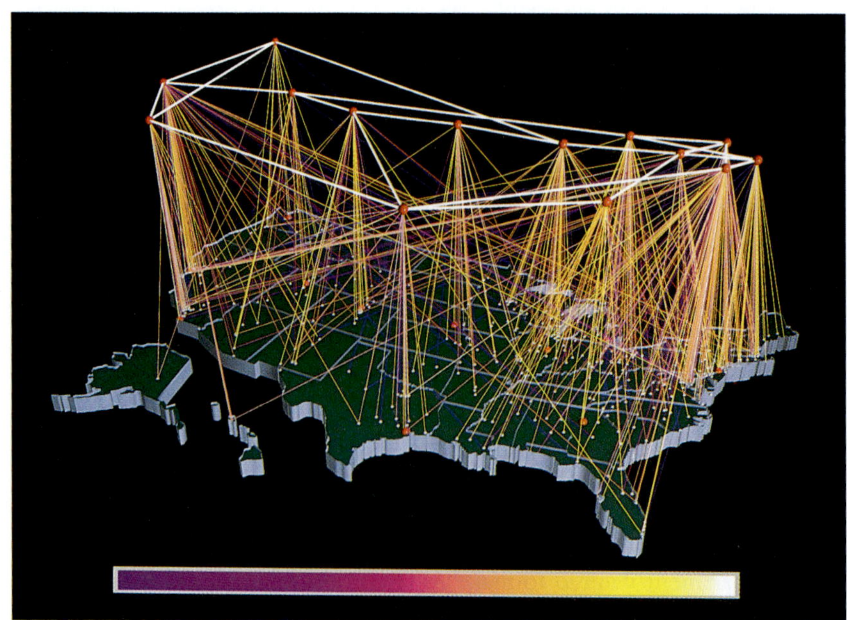

The Internet is the world's largest implementation of the information superhighway, linking a vast web of electronic networks. Businesses, universities, government agencies, and individuals can use the Internet to instantly access information from anywhere in the world.

SOURCE: Courtesy of the National Science Foundation.

the North Atlantic Treaty Organization (NATO), the Japanese prime minister, and the treasury of the United Kingdom are all online, as is the World Bank. One startling observation that demonstrates the reach and power of the Net is that, according to Internet Society Executive Director Anthony-Michael Rutkowski, "It's asserted that 80 percent of all the scientists who ever lived are on the Internet today!"[1] The number of known commercial organizations on the Internet is in the millions and growing daily.

THE TECHNOLOGY BEHIND THE INTERNET

The Internet is valued because it enables people to communicate easily, quickly, and inexpensively with others almost anywhere on earth—it virtually eliminates the barriers of time and place. The technology that makes all of this possible includes networks, client/server computing, telecommunications standards, and hypertext and hypermedia.

Networks are the Net's underlying technology. As with other networks, everything that travels through the Net—E-mail, files of data, graphics, sound—are all simply a series of electronic messages. When two networks are linked, the external network is seen by the local network as just another network node. A **node** is a component device in a network. A message being sent to a computer anywhere else in the world originates on a node on a local network and is first transmitted to a regional backbone network. From there, a routing table determines the route to the destination network, and the message is sent on its way. The message traverses as many regional backbone networks as needed until it reaches the regional backbone to which the destination local network is attached. The message is then transmitted to that local network and then on to the specific destination node (see Figure 8.1).

Node
A device connected to a network.

Client/server technology is a related technology that is key to the Net. User computers act as clients, whereas Net-connected computers all over the world that contain information of interest to others are configured as servers. Even organizational network computers that receive and store your E-mail, waiting for you to retrieve it, are servers.

To make this communication possible, users of the Internet do have to agree to a *telecommunications standard.* The standard for the Internet is TCP/IP (Transmission Control Protocol/Internet Protocol), which we introduced in Chapter 7. TCP/IP is a set of protocols that allows communication between almost every type of computer and network. The protocols define how information can be transmitted between different computers and how any machine on the network can be identified with a unique address. Data (which might consist of a document, an E-mail message, or a chart) are broken down into packets and transmitted via packet switching (see Chapter 7) from network to network until they reach their destination, where they are reassembled into the original message. Each packet contains the data and Internet address of the sending and receiving computer. Every host computer on the Internet has a unique address called an *IP (Internet protocol) address.*

Hypertext and *hypermedia,* first described in Chapter 6, is another technology that has helped make the Internet so popular. On a screen that employs hypertext, users can click on any highlighted word, phrase, or graphic to bring up another set of screens with more detailed information or

FIGURE 8.1

The Internet: An Interconnected Network of Networks

A high-speed communications link called a backbone connects major Internet host computers. The host computers provide Internet access to local networks and links to other host computers.

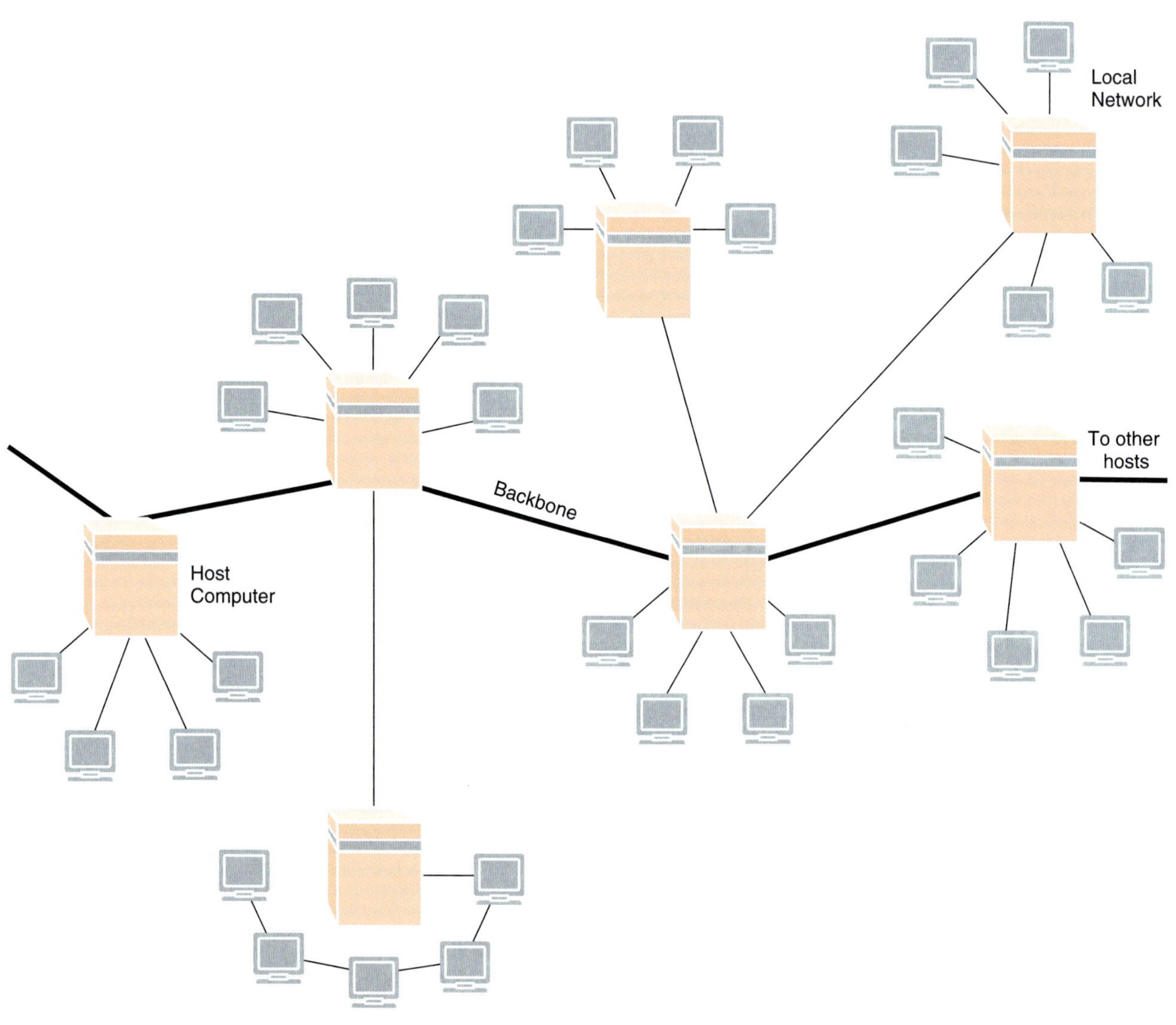

Hyperlink

A built-in link to other related documents or Web pages that enables the user to jump directly from one document or Web page to another.

information on a related topic. Internet hypertext can contain not only built-in links, or **hyperlinks,** to specific text within the same file or computer, but it can contain hyperlinks to text and files located on other computers at different locations. For example, if you were online looking up Lincoln in a file located at the University of California, Berkeley's library, it might contain a highlighted hyperlink to information on the Civil War that is actually stored in the University of Virginia's library. You need not know where the Civil War information is stored. You only need click on that highlighted item, and the information on the Civil War would appear—your computer would have jumped to the specific text in a file stored on the University of Virginia computer. Thus, moving from site to site can be extremely easy on the Net.

Most of this Internet technology is low in cost, another major factor in the Internet's growth. Mail messages are sent at local telephone rates and are multiplexed to make maximum use of bandwidth. Costs are also low because the Net itself owns nothing and has almost no costs to offset. Organizations with networks, of course, must pay for their own networks, including their costs of connection to the Internet, but most of these costs are generated independently of that connection. Organizations that establish a connection to the Internet must also agree to forward one another's traffic at no charge, but their messages in turn are forwarded by all other users, similar to the way international mail is delivered.

Before examining the problems the Internet solves, we need to discuss some key Internet tools.

INTERNET TOOLS AND CAPABILITIES

Users of the Internet rely on many tools. The most important are E-mail, Usenet newsgroups, LISTSERVs, online chatting, Telnet (for logging on to a remote computer), file transfer protocol (FTP), Archie, Gophers, Veronica, and the World Wide Web.

E-mail We previously introduced E-mail as a telecommunications function. E-mail has been the most widely used function on the Net today, with many millions of messages exchanged daily throughout the world. The cost of E-mail communication is usually far lower than the equivalent postal, voice, or overnight delivery expense and is becoming ever more popular partly for that reason. Also, E-mail communications are essentially instantaneous. Other E-mail capabilities that contribute to its popularity include the ability to

- Broadcast a message to a predefined group of any size.
- Store messages electronically (no file cabinets using up large amounts of floor space).
- Forward messages to other interested parties with a few clicks of a mouse.
- Reply without re-entering the address or the body of the received message.
- Maintain an easy-to-use address book of E-mail partners.
- Transmit word processing, graphics, or other types of data as attached files.

Students will find it helpful to understand the construction of an E-mail address. To explain it, we will use Figure 8.2 and a fictional address that might have been used by Princeton University physicist Albert Einstein:

aeinstein@princeton.edu

The portion of the address to the left of the @ symbol is the personal identifier selected by (or for) the individual recipient, in this case, *aeinstein*

FIGURE 8.2

Anatomy of an Internet E-mail Address

Internet addresses are classified according to domains. This E-mail address signifies that Albert Einstein is the user whose E-mail is stored on the host computer Princeton in the top-level education domain.

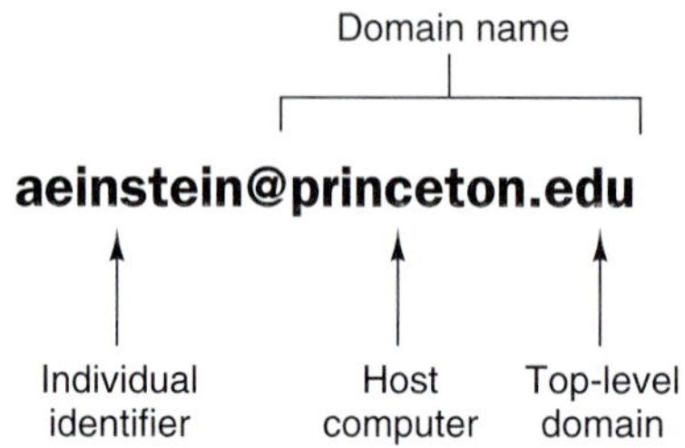

Domain name
The unique name of a collection of computers connected to the Internet.

(Albert Einstein). To the right of the @ symbol is the domain name. The **domain name** is the unique name of a collection of computers connected to the Internet. The domain contains subdomains, each separated from the other by a period. The domain that is farthest to the right is the top-level domain, and each domain to the left helps further define the domain by network, department, and even specific computer. In this case, *edu,* the top-level domain, indicates that the address is an educational institution, while *princeton* (in this case, Princeton University in New Jersey) indicates the specific location of the host computer. Many other top domain names exist, including "com" for commercial and "gov" for government. Table 8.1 lists common domain name categories.

Because the Internet began in the United States, no national domain indicator is used at the end of the Einstein address—the absence of a country indicator at the end of an address indicates that the address is located in the United States. However, if the address is in any other country, the address must end with a country domain name, such as *jp* for Japan or *ca* for Canada. For instance, if Einstein had moved to the University of Tokyo, his E-mail address might have been:

aeinstein@tokyou.edu.jp

Usenet
Internet news and discussion groups in which people share information and ideas on a defined topic through large electronic bulletin boards.

Usenet Newsgroups **Usenet** newsgroups are public forums, ongoing conversations over a period of days, weeks, months or more, carried on through

TABLE 8.1

Top-Level Domain Names

Domain Code	Description
com	Commercial organization
gov	Government agency
edu	Educational institution
org	Private organization
mil	Military site
net	Network resource

The Internet can be used as a vast online research service, delivering library catalogues, articles, books, and other information from all over the world to a desktop computer.

SOURCE: Tony Stone Images, Inc. © Stewart Cohen.

the Net with a group of individuals located anywhere in the world. Discussions are organized by topics, and messages are stored on electronic bulletin boards where any member of a given group can post messages for others to read. Discussion groups can be restricted to specific individuals, but most are kept open. All members of the group can also reply to messages on the board or post notes on new topics within the larger theme. Figure 8.3 illustrates some of the newsgroups that were available on the subject of textiles.

LISTSERVs A second type of public forum, **LISTSERVs,** are also discussion groups, but they use E-mail instead of bulletin boards for communication. If you find a LISTSERV topic you are interested in, you may subscribe, and from then on, through your E-mail, you will receive all messages sent by others. You can, in turn, send a message to your LISTSERV mailing list server and it will automatically be broadcast to the other subscribers. Tens of thousands of LISTERV groups exist, discussing every conceivable topic.

LISTSERVs
Online discussion groups that use E-mail instead of bulletin boards for communications.

Chatting **Chatting** is yet a third type of person-to-person communication through the Internet. Chat forums enable live, interactive conversations through the Net. However, the participants must be online simultaneously, a major drawback. Of course, if two or more people make an appointment to chat at a given time, it can be a most useful business or organizational tool. Another drawback to this approach is that other messages are not saved—no record exists for others to read later if they were not "there" at the appropriate time unless chat software with capabilities for recording and logging messages is utilized.

Chatting
Live, interactive conversations conducted over the Intert by typing messages on a keyboard while reading responses on a screen.

A major drawback of all three forms of discussion groups is that anyone can join and say anything—no restraints or prior censorship exists. Any user must be careful about relying on information received through these groups. They are also not appropriate forums in which to discuss confidential information.

FIGURE 8.3

Usenet Groups

Here are some of the Internet discussion groups that are available on the subject of textiles.

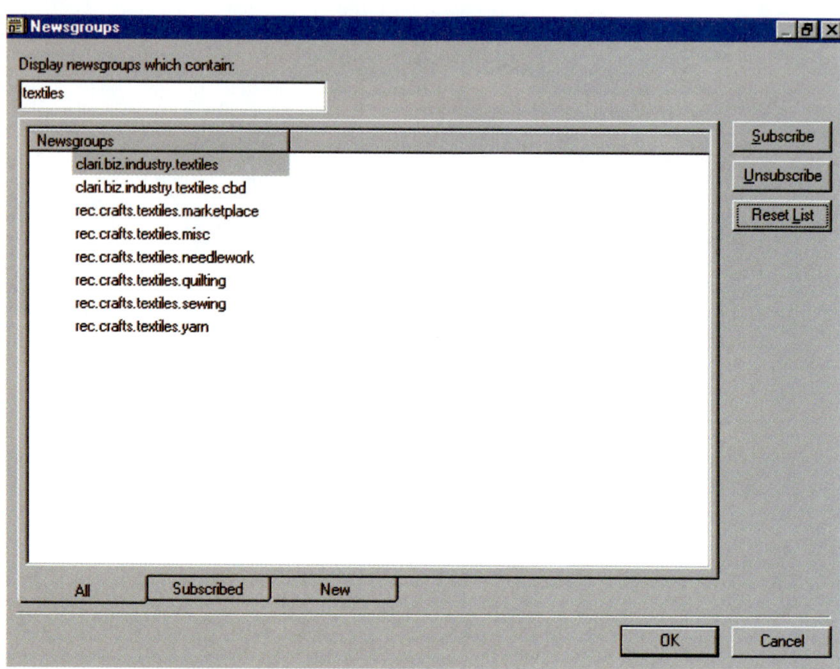

Telnet
A network tool that allows a person to log on to one computer system and access its files from a remote computer.

Telnet: Logging in to Remote Computers Using a facility called **Telnet** run on the Internet, you can work on a remote computer by typing or clicking commands on the computer in front of you as if you were actually sitting in front of the remote computer. Telnet sets up a rapid, error-free link between the local computer and the remote computer. Thus, you can log in to your work computer from home or while on a trip. You are able to run programs, retrieve mail, or perform any other functions you could perform if you were sitting right in front of the remote computer. You can also use this facility to log on to a number of third-party computers that are open to the public for specified limited purposes, such as searching university or government libraries.

File transfer protocol (FTP)
An Internet tool for transferring and retrieving files to and from a remote computer.

File Transfer Protocol (FTP), Gophers, and Other Information Retrieval Tools The Internet is widely used to retrieve information. Many thousands of organizations of all types—such as universities, corporations, public interest groups, governments, and political organizations—now make information available to others via the Internet. The amount of information available via the Net is overwhelming—millions upon millions of files containing textual information of all types, as well as programs, graphics, videos, and sound.

The underlying tool for information retrieval is **file transfer protocol (FTP).** Using it you can gain access to any computer in the world that is on the Internet and that allows FTP access. Once in the computer, you can

FIGURE 8.4

Gopher Menus

This figure illustrates the first two levels of the Gopher menus at the University of Minnesota's Gopher server. Panel b shows the menu that appears when the user selects the Pacific directory from the main menu.

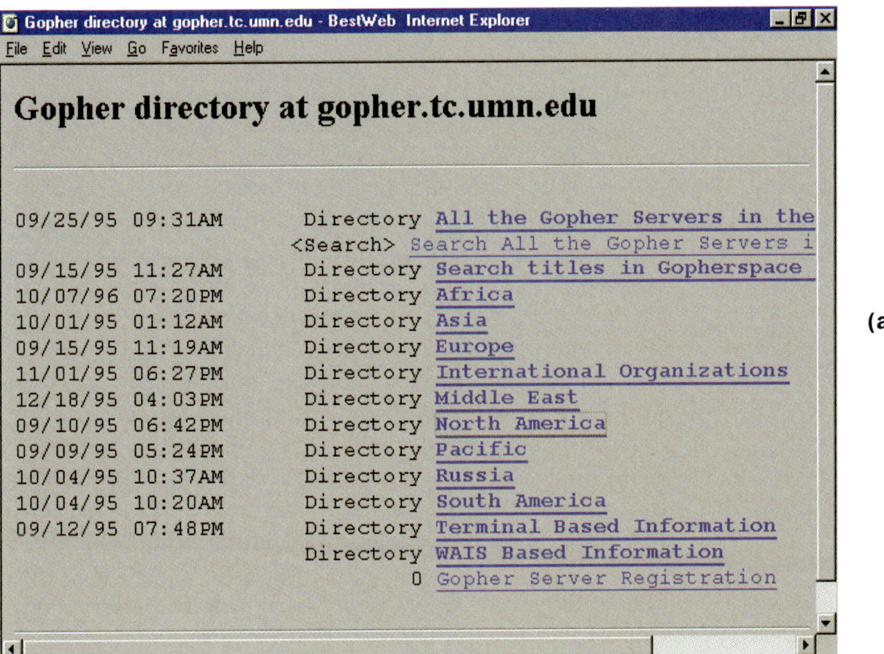

(a)

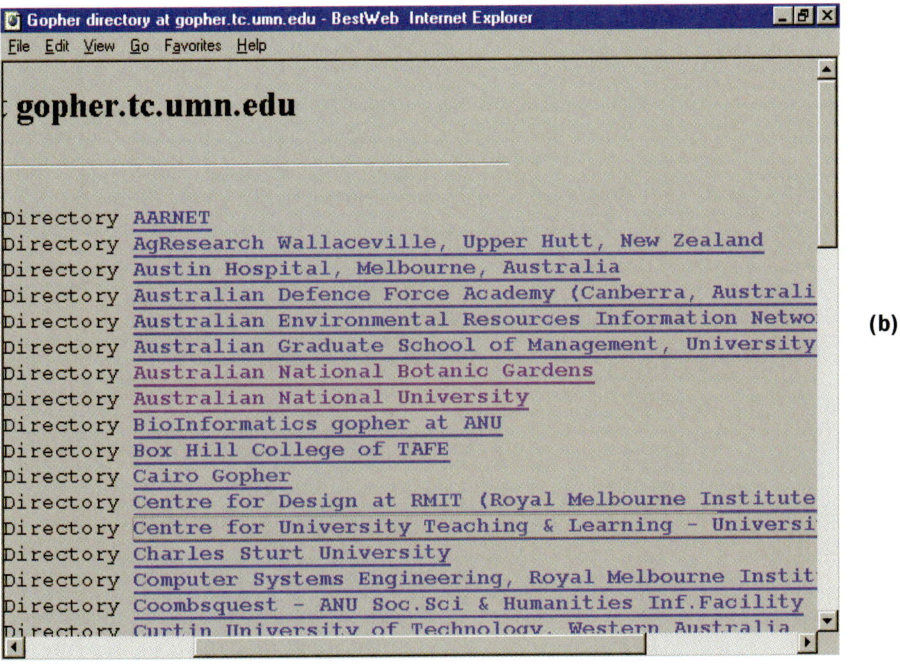

(b)

browse all directories that have been made open to FTP access and download any files you select to your own computer. You need to know the FTP address of the computer to retrieve any files, however, and because many tens of thousands of computers around the world allow FTP access, locating an FTP address can be a daunting task.

Archie
A tool for locating FTP files on the Internet that performs keyword searches on an actual database of documents, software, and data files available for downloading from servers around the world.

Archie is a tool that can be used to search the files at FTP sites. It monitors hundreds of FTP sites regularly and updates a database called an Archie server. Archie can locate files whose names match a keyword that you enter. For example, if you entered the keyword *pollution,* you would receive a list of sites that contain files on that topic.

Gopher
A tool that enables the user to locate information stored on Internet servers through a series of easy-to-use, hierarchical menus.

Gophers are Internet client tools that consolidate the retrieval and search of information through descriptive menus. Most files and digital information that are accessible through FTP are also available through Gophers. *Gopher sites* (computer sites open to and organized for Gopher access) have two features that make them easier to use. First, they are menu driven, which means you can search through a hierarchical easy-to-use series of menus to find the files that interest you (see Figure 8.4). A second feature of Gopher sites is that their menus include listings that are actually hyperlinked to other Gopher sites containing collections of files on the topics described. To move to the other site, all you need do is select the appropriate menu item and click. For example, if you were doing research on a specific steel alloy, you would start with your own local Gopher site, find a topic as closely related as possible (perhaps "metals" would be the best you could do), and then jump to another site with that topic listed in the Gopher menu. At that site, you would again search the menu for the closest listing to your topic. You would keep jumping from Gopher site to Gopher site in this manner until you zeroed in on a site that contained files on your specific topic. With descriptive menu listings that are actually hyperlinks to other Gopher sites, you do not need to know in advance where relevant files are stored or the FTP address of a specific computer.

Veronica
An Internet capability for searching gopher directories for files about a specific subject by using keywords.

A tool called **Veronica,** which stands for Very Easy Rodent-Oriented Netwide Index to Computer Archives, searches Gopher sites more quickly to locate specific files and directories. When the user enters a key word, Veronica searches through thousands of Gopher sites to find titles that contain your keyword. It then places these files onto a temporary menu on your own local server so that you can browse through them, making file retrieval by topic relatively painless.

8.2 THE WORLD WIDE WEB

World Wide Web
A system and set of standards for storing, retrieving, formatting, and displaying information in a networked environment using graphical user interfaces and dynamic links to other documents.

The surging popularity and business use of the Internet can be tied directly to the **World Wide Web** (also known as the Web or WWW). Through the Web, Net users can design captivating, informative presentations combining text, sound, graphics, and video that are easy to use and even entertaining. Web sites can be interactive so that users can obtain information and also interact with the owner of the Web site (see the Focus on Technology). Many Web sites even enable visitors to modify and enhance those sites. One reason for Web popularity is that the technology behind Web sites is simple enough that people who are not trained, experienced programmers can easily access information from the Web and even create sites themselves—hundreds of thousands, if not millions, of personal Web sites already exist.

WEB TECHNOLOGY

Web sites are located on Web servers attached to a local network that is, in turn, connected to the Internet. Such a server may be devoted exclusively to one Web site, but it can just as easily be a multiple-purpose server that might contain multiple Web sites, Gopher sites, and even non-Net related files. The person in charge of an organization's Web site is called a **Webmaster.**

Webmaster
The person in charge of an organization's Web site.

Home page
The text and graphical screen display that welcomes a visitor to a Web site.

A Web site visit begins with a **home page,** a display that might contain text, graphics, and/or sound. The home page welcomes visitors and usually offers information on the organization or individual who has established the site. Unless the site is simple, with only one page, the visitor will find links to other pages within the same site. Many sites also contain links to other sites of interest and a point-and-click E-mail facility for contacting the site owner.

Hypertext, with its embedded hyperlinks, is another key to the success of the Web. Hyperlinks enable users to point and click to be automatically transported to another Web site anywhere in the world rather than typing complex commands. Because the hyperlink address is embedded in the hypertext, users can jump to other sites without knowing their addresses.

URL
The address of a specific resource on the Internet; short for uniform resource locator.

Web pages can be accessed by using a **uniform resource locator (URL),** which points to a specific resource on the Internet. For example, the actual URL for the White House, the residence of the President of the United States and the seat of the executive branch of the United States government, is

http://www.whitehouse.gov

http: is the access method—hypertext transport protocol—the communications standard used to transfer pages on the Web. *www.whitehouse.gov* is the domain name identifying the Web server storing the Web pages.

Hypertext markup language (HTML)
A programming tool for creating Web pages that uses hypertext to establish dynamic links to other documents stored in the same or in remote computers.

A worldwide standard language for Web site programming enables all Web navigation tools to display a Web site regardless of which site the user navigated to. The language is known as **Hypertext Markup Language (HTML).** Recent releases of the top word processing software packages such as Microsoft Word or WordPerfect have capabilities for creating HTML documents that can be used as the foundation of Web pages. More sophisticated and powerful authoring tools for creating, editing, and publishing Web pages are also available, such as Microsoft FrontPage and Claris Home Page.

We introduced Web browser software in Chapter 5. A browser must support hypertext and URLs and be able to display graphics as well as text and handle sound and video. The first Web browser, Mosaic, was developed at the National Center for Supercomputing Applications at the University of Illinois, Champaign-Urbana. Mosaic had an enormous impact on the growth of the Web because it made navigating (*surfing*) the Web easy and properly handled the display of Web sites. Netscape Navigator and Microsoft's Internet Explorer have eclipsed Mosaic as the leading Web browsers used today.

MULTIMEDIA MULTIPLE CHOICE

While both the World Wide Web and CD-ROMs enjoy widespread, effective use as reference tools, a large segment of the population values them first and foremost for their entertainment value. The driving forces behind this appeal are the multimedia capabilities available with Web applications and CD-ROMs. Watching video clips, listening to sound clips, playing games with spectacular graphics and sound, or taking virtual vacations, all at the click of a mouse button, fascinate computer users sufficiently to keep software companies very busy.

Businesses are using the entertainment value of multimedia to develop applications on both CD-ROM and the World Wide Web to educate employees, solicit customers, and even let both groups play with products online. For example, Altia, Inc. created a Web-based prototype of the Advantix camera for its customer, Eastman Kodak. (Altia provides prototyping software that allows companies to create animated interactive prototypes where customers can experience and evaluate new products prior to production.) Visitors to Altia's

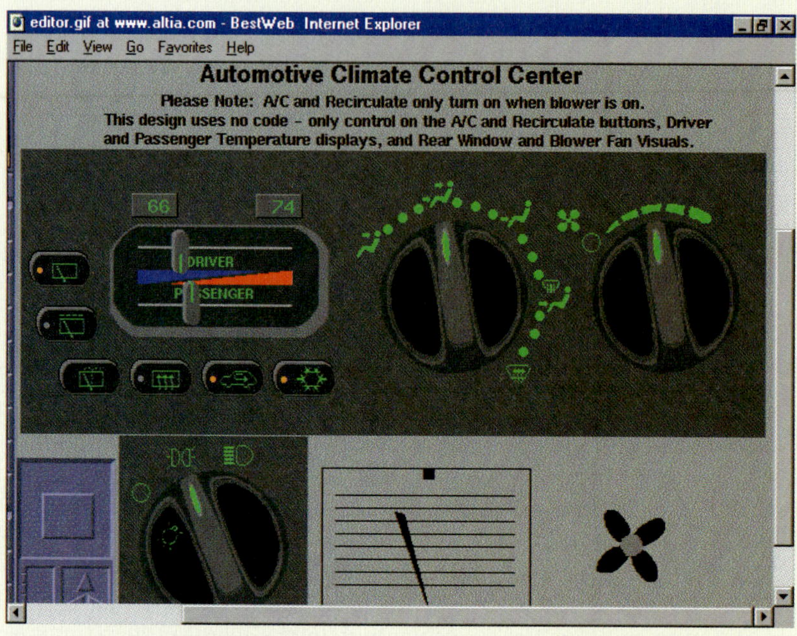

Altia's Web site contains demos of interactive prototypes that enable customers to experience proposed product features before the products are actually constructed. One of its projects was automobile dashboard prototyping.

SEARCHING FOR INFORMATION ON THE WEB

The explosive growth of Web sites has created a vast sea of information resources. Locating and keeping track of specific sites of interest among millions of Web sites could be an impossible task for an individual. No comprehensive catalog of Web sites exists (any more than does a worldwide centralized telephone yellow pages directory). The principal methods of locating information on the Web are Web site directories, search engines, and broadcast, or push, technology.

Web Directories and Search Engines Several companies have created directories of Web sites and their addresses, providing search tools for locating information on specified topics. Yahoo! is an example. People or organizations submit sites of interest, which the managers of Yahoo! then classify. To search the directory, you enter one or more keywords and will quickly see a list of categories and sites with those keywords in their titles (see Figure 8.5).

Web site can virtually open, load, and "shoot." Such prototypes can also be used to educate customers about complex products or to test designs before products are released.

Corporate Express, a $2.4 billion company providing corporations worldwide with low-cost round-the-clock delivery of supplies and services, enhanced its Web site with animations that show how charges can build up by using wasteful procurement practices. Animations lead customers through a typical procurement process for one pencil. Person one needs a pencil, person two approves the pencil purchase, person three orders the pencil, and so on. With each step, a counter visually adds up the dollars, showing why the average cost to procure a pencil in a large company amounts to $150. Another section of Corporate Express's Web site interactively demonstrates an ergonomically correct office. Visitors to the online office can adjust a chair, keyboard, monitor, or wrist rest to healthful positions. A voice-over talks users through the process. This portion of the Web site helps build customer relationships by acting as an information resource, and it promotes Corporate Express's office furniture products as well.

Employee training delivered through multimedia can significantly reduce what can be a very large expense. The bulk of training costs comes from travel expenses incurred by sending staff members to remote training sites or from fees paid to on-site instructors. Allowing workers to learn at their PCs or workstations improves matters greatly. Most people view the Web as the better method for distributing training programs because CD-ROMs cost more and they cannot be updated as readily. On the other hand, using multimedia tools in a Web format is a relatively new science that has not yet been perfected. Overall performance, including sound and picture quality, can be better guaranteed for now by a CD-ROM.

To reconcile these differences, some companies have hoped that the Internet and CD-ROMs can work in concert. Motorola Inc.'s training division, Motorola University, contracted an engineering training course on CD-ROM and then had a scaled-down version programmed onto the Web. Motorola originally envisioned using the Web version as an enticement for the engineers to purchase the full CD version. However, if it proves to be successful, the Web may become the sole provider of training material and exercises. Its flexibility gives it a tremendous advantage.

FOCUS Questions:
What kind of problems can be solved by using the multimedia capabilities of Web and CD-ROM technology? What are the advantages and disadvantages of each technology?

SOURCE: Lynda Radosevich, "Sizzle and Steak," *Webmaster,* November 1996.

Other search tools do not require Web sites to be preclassified and will search Web pages on their own, automatically. Such tools, called **search engines,** can find Web sites that people might not know about. They contain software that looks for Web pages containing one or more of the search terms entered by the user and then displays matches ranked by a method that usually involves the location and frequency of the search terms. These search engines do not display information about every site on the Web; rather, they create indexes of the Web pages they visit. The search engine software then locates Web pages of interest by searching through these indexes. AltaVista, Lycos, and Infoseek are examples of these search engines. Some are more comprehensive or current than others, depending on how their components are tuned. Many of these search tools also organize Web sites into categories. Table 8.2 lists and describes the principal Web Directories and Search Engines.

Search engine
A tool for locating specific sites or information on the Internet. Primarily used to search the World Wide Web.

Tools called **bookmarks** (or *hot lists*) have been integrated into Web browsers to enable users to store Web site names and addresses for future

Bookmark
A Web browser tool for keeping personal lists of favorite Web sites and their addresses.

FIGURE 8.5

Yahoo! Web Site Directory

Yahoo! combines a search tool with a directory of Web sites. One can locate information by exploring the various categories or by entering a search term.

use with just a click of a mouse. To return to a site, the user need only click on the specific listing within the bookmark file.

Push technology
A method of obtaining relevant information on the Internet by having a computer broadcast information directly to the user based on prespecified interests.

Broadcast and Push Technology Instead of spending hours scouring the Web, you can have the information you are interested in delivered automatically to your desktop through **push technology.** A computer broadcasts information of interest directly to you, rather than having you "pull" content from Web sites.

TABLE 8.2

Web Directories and Search Engines

Name	Description	Web Address
Yahoo!	Directory of Web sites	www.yahoo.com
AltaVista	Power searching by keywords or by words linked by AND, NOT, or OR; can search for phrases or find Java applets	www.altavista.digital.com
Lycos	Can search for multimedia as well as text content	www.lycos.com
Infoseek	Searches Web or Usenet for words or phrases	www.infoseek.com
Web Crawler	Natural language search tool; concentrates on limited number of key sites	www.webcrawler.com
Excite	Allows searches by keyword or concept, searching and search grouping by subject; automatically generates abstract summaries	www.excite.com

"Push" comes from *server push*, a term used to describe the streaming of Web page contents from a Web server to a Web browser. When you register for a push delivery service, you download client software on your computer. You can customize its interface to deliver only certain channels, or categories of information, offered by content providers such as news, sports, financial data, and so forth. You also specify how often you want this information updated. A profile is submitted to the push delivery service and stored on a database. Special software programs monitor Web sites and other information sources. The push client software runs in the background of your computer while you use it for other tasks. Upon finding information of interest to you, the push programs serve the information to the push client, notifying you through E-mail, by playing a sound, by displaying an icon on the desktop, by sending full articles or Web pages, or by displaying headlines on a screen saver. When you click for more details, you might be launched into the Web sites of interest.

Some of the leading push delivery systems include PointCast, BackWeb, Marimba Castanet, and Intermind Communicator. BackWeb and Marimba Castanet feature richer multimedia capabilities, with Castanet capable of delivering Java software and applications.

The audience for push technology is not limited to individual users. Companies are using push technology to set up their own channels to broadcast important internal information. For example, Amoco and Fruit of

FIGURE 8.6

PointCast Push Delivery

PointCast uses push technology to deliver information on specific subjects preselected by the user on channels of interest.

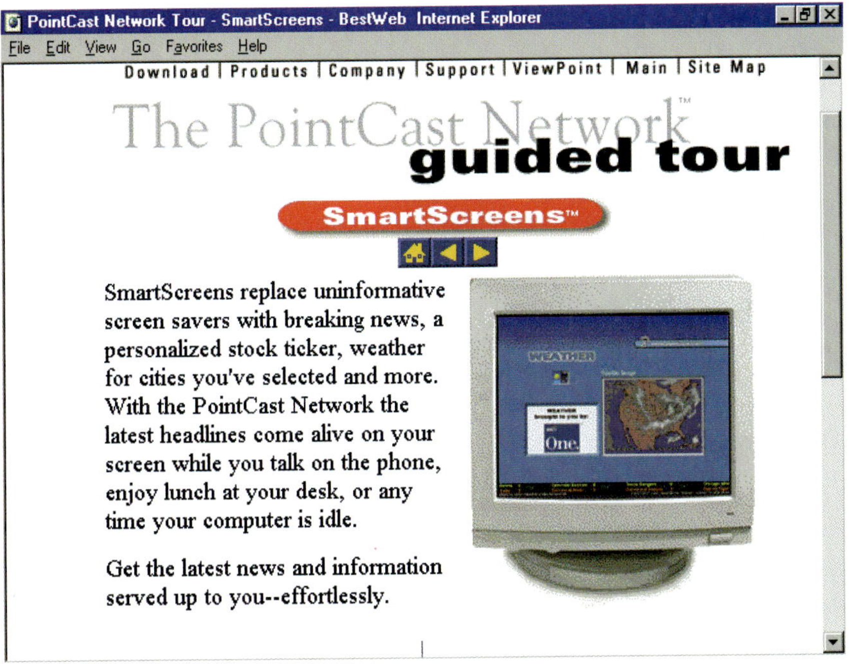

the Loom are using this mechanism to deliver industry news and other data to employee desktops. Direct marketers are using it to send promotions or animated ads directly to the desktops of targeted customers. Some are concerned about this technology's potential threat to privacy because push delivery services have information on your personal preferences and can track what you click on for more detail.[2]

INTRANETS

Intranet
An internal private network based on Internet and Web technology.

Firewall
Specialized hardware and software used to prevent outsiders from invading private networks.

Internet technology can be used to distribute and share information inside the organization as well as to connect to the outside. Many organizations are starting to build internal networks called intranets based on Internet technology. An **intranet** is an internal organizational network that is modeled on the Web. It uses the existing company network infrastructure, Internet communication standards, and the software developed for the World Wide Web. By applying Internet technology to their own business applications, companies can communicate and distribute information across the enterprise while keeping unauthorized users out.

While the Web is open to anyone, an intranet is private and is protected from public visits by **firewalls**—security systems with specialized software to prevent outsiders from invading private networks. The firewall consists of hardware and software placed between an organization's internal network and an external network, including the Internet. The firewall is programmed to intercept each message packet passing between the two networks, examine its characteristics, and reject unauthorized messages or access attempts. Intranets have spread very rapidly in the past few years and may very well become the most popular use of the Web in business.

Intranet Technology Intranets require no special hardware and so are run using any existing network infrastructure. Intranet software technology is the same as that of the World Wide Web. Intranets use HTML hypertext language to program Web pages and to establish dynamic, point-and-click hypertext links to other sites. The intranet Web browsers are the same as those used on the Web; even the Web server software is the same. Figure 8.7 shows that a simple intranet can be created by linking a client computer with a Web browser to a computer with Web server software via a TCP/IP network.

Intranets are becoming popular because they are inexpensive to build, easy to use, and compatible with diverse computing platforms. Because Web browsers run on any type of computer, the same electronic information can be viewed by any employee, regardless of the type of computer being used. This overcomes a major obstacle to organization-wide information sharing in most companies—employees using different brands of hardware and software being unable to communicate with one another electronically. Web browser software presents users with a uniform interface, reducing the user training requirements. Companies can connect their intranet to company databases just as they connect to the Web. Programming Web pages is quick and easy; some employees are fashioning their own Web pages with personal Web page authoring software.

FIGURE 8.7

Anatomy of an Intranet

In its most basic form, an intranet consists of a client computer with a Web browser linked to a computer with Web server software via a TCP/IP network. A firewall keeps unwanted visitors out.

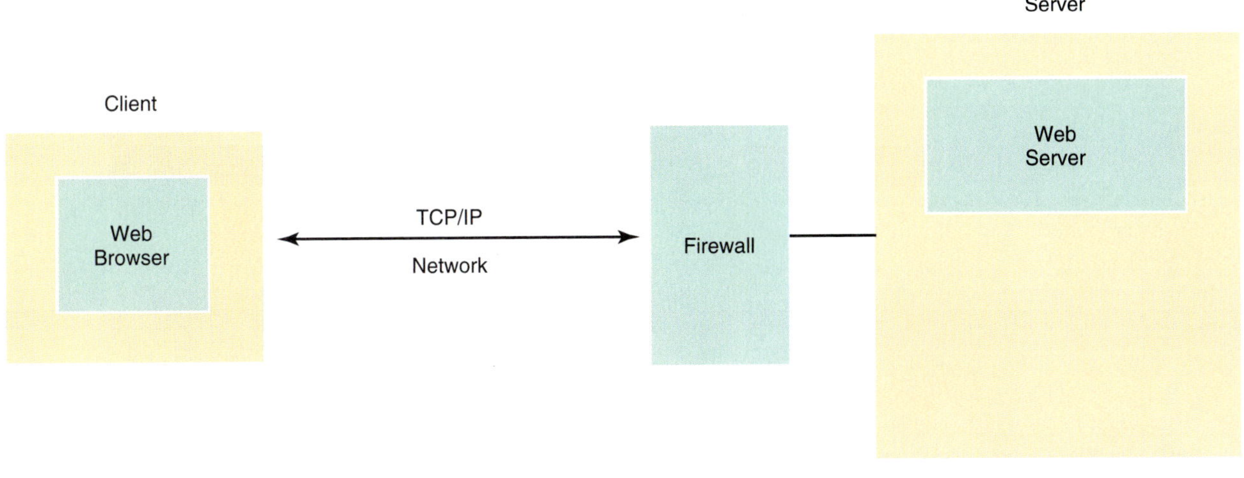

How Organizations Are Using Intranets One of the most popular uses for intranets is to distribute important corporate information. Companies are making all sorts of documents—customer profiles, product inventories, policy manuals, training materials, job postings, and company telephone directories—available as electronic Web applications to their employees. Made available this way, these documents are always up to date, eliminating paper, printing, and distributing costs. For example, General Electric is saving $240,000 per year in printing costs by publishing its directory of company information on an intranet. Silicon Graphics uses an intranet to enable its 7,200 employees to create reports from corporate databases using easy point-and-click technology. In addition to documents, the intranet delivers video and audio material to employees. Some companies are even using their intranets for virtual conferencing (see Chapter 14).

Intranets can also provide some of the same group collaboration and support functions as groupware (see Chapter 14). If properly designed, an intranet can help specific work groups or everyone in the company share resources, update information, teach, learn, and keep in touch with colleagues in faraway locations. With personal Web-page authoring tools, users can publish product proposals, project schedules, product plans, quarterly objectives, or information about competitors in electronic form to place on the intranet Web server to share with other colleagues. These "documents" can include text, tables, images, links to other documents, and even animation.

Human Genome Sciences, a genetics research firm in Rockville, Maryland, uses an intranet to process and transfer information about DNA sequencing. Approximately 250 employees use Netscape Navigator Web browser software to obtain genetic information from a database of DNA samples, using the intranet to share lab notes and test results.[3]

FOCUS ON ORGANIZATIONS

CANADA'S FINANCIAL COMMUNITY CONNECTS UP

Timely information is vital in today's fast-paced financial world. Canadian financial institutions, including banks, brokerages, and insurance firms, have found a way to exchange information using an intranet called FIN/net.

Before FIN/net was set up, Canada's financial community lacked an efficient means of communication. There were many instances where member organizations were not sharing information electronically or by any other means. Reports were mailed, faxed, or discussed "over lunch." Electronic communication was limited to costly private networks that were described as "a mess of telephone circuits." These networks were wasteful, operating with duplicate transmission capacity, networking equipment, and management costs, and their disparate technologies made them difficult to connect. Each organization, vendor, and application required new connections.

The Canadian financial institutions were on the lookout for less expensive and complicated ways of sharing information. FIN/net Inc., a Toronto company formed from a business unit of Solect Technology Group (a partner of Sun Microsystems), seized the opportunity. It created an intranet initially composed of four member firms: CIBC Wood Gunay, Midland Walwyn, Nessbitt Burns, and Scotia McLeod. To attract more members, FIN/net launched itself as an Internet service provider (ISP) focused exclusively on financial services. Once members joined, they gained access to FIN/net's other services. More than a dozen financial institutions, information providers, and investment management firms subsequently signed up.

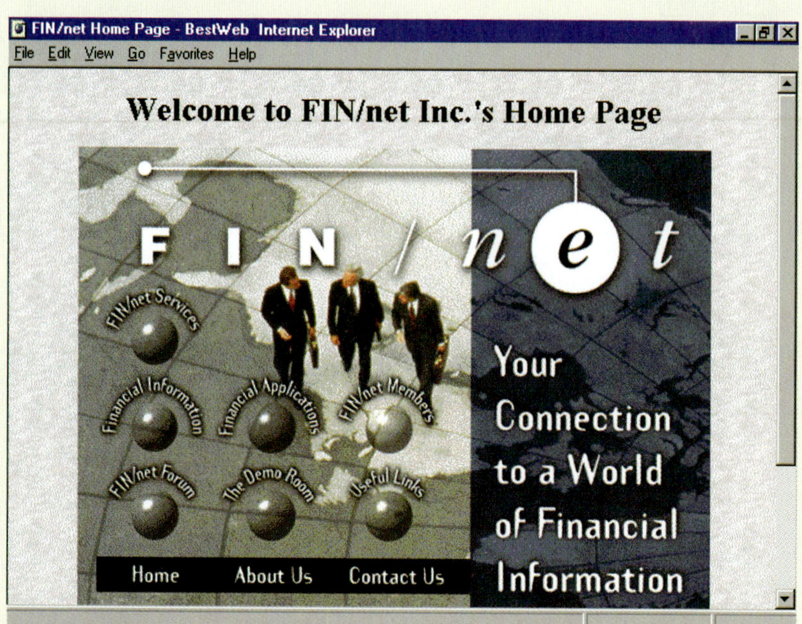

FIN/net is a specialized intranet set up exclusively for the Canadian financial community and its clients. It provides quick and easy access to a variety of information sources, including real-time stock quotes.

FIN/net was built using Sun Microsystems technology, and Sun hardware was integral to the system. Members are free to choose any networking supplier, but most have followed FIN/net's recommendation of Sun servers and firewalls. Sun had previously developed a strong track record as a technology provider to critical business environments such as financial trading floors.

Members can access FIN/net from local area networks using dial-up ISDN or a dedicated ATM link, or they can link via a modem and a standalone PC. Applications that consolidate data from different sources and make them available to member firms are being developed based on Netscape Navigator Web browser technology. One FIN/net application saves money managers from wading through piles of their clients' buy/sell lists that were delivered by fax each morning. Now these lists are distributed over FIN/net, and the money manager's Web browser can gather and organize the information immediately online as it is received.

FOCUS Questions: What problems were solved by using Internet technology to build FIN/net? What people, organization, and technology factors should be considered when building an intranet or extranet?

SOURCE: "Well Connected," *Open Finance*, Autumn 1996.

TABLE 8.3

Examples of Intranets

Organization	Intranet Application
Rockwell International	Check status, tolerances, and output of computer-controlled machine tools
Babson College	Provide electronic grading and online course registration
Home Box Office	Distribute sales data and promotional video clips to eight remote locations
First Union Bank, Charlotte, North Carolina	Provide online telephone directory linked to organization charts and information about employee job experience
Mayo Clinic	Provide clinical, research, and medical training materials

SOURCE: Teri Robinson, "The 25 Most Innovative Intranets," *Information Week,* November 18, 1996.

Expanded Intranets and Extranets Some firms are allowing limited outside access to their internal intranets. For example, the customers of a brokerage firm might be able to access a portion of its intranet from the public Internet to obtain information about their portfolios. Private intranets that are accessible to select outsiders are sometimes called **extranets.** The brokerage firm can use firewalls to ensure that access to its internal data is limited and remains secure.

Extranet
A private intranet that provides access to select outsiders.

Extranets are especially useful for linking organizations with customers or business partners, with many used for providing product availability, pricing, and shipment data. For example, Geffen Records, an audio and video producer in West Hollywood, California, allows its distributors as well as its own staff to access retail sales figures from its Web server. The Focus on Organizations provides another example of an extranet used for similar purposes.

Potential applications for intranets are endless. Table 8.3 illustrates some of the diverse uses for intranets.

8.3 THE ROLE OF THE INTERNET IN PROBLEM SOLVING

Many organizations and individuals are using the Internet to help solve a wide range of problems. In this section, we describe some of the more important of these uses.

EXPEDITING ACCESS TO INFORMATION

The Internet provides instant access to a wealth of information resources that previously might have taken days or months to locate. One can search many thousands of databases for information in areas such as medicine, agriculture, molecular biology, foreign trade, or ZIP codes. Advanced Network and Services (ANS) claims that patent research using the Net is 40 percent faster than previous methods while also reducing search and legal costs related to patents. Business strategists at J. P. Morgan, the New York-based bank, research the latest business forecasts and theories through Internet connections with university economics departments around the world. Their mortgage-backed securities analysts use the Net weekly to obtain the latest government census data to help them analyze trends in such relevant areas as property values. Access to information can also come via E-mail and Usenet groups.

Hasan Rizvi, a Pakistani physicist, tells of a 2.5-ton dump of toxic material inside the crowded city of Karachi that scientists did not know how to clean up. Through the Association for Progress of Conservation, an Internet grouping that includes Greenet, Econet, and the U.S. Environmental Protection Agency, the Pakistanis were quickly flooded with electronic mail and faxes filled with advice that enabled them to solve their problem rapidly.

ENHANCING COMMUNICATION AND COLLABORATION

Many companies are finding that the Internet is very important in facilitating communication among different locations and coordinating the work of geographically dispersed business units.

Cole & Weber Inc., a Seattle, Washington, advertising agency, found E-mail to be an extremely popular and valuable tool for communicating with its many clients. However, at first the company had to deal with using multiple E-mail packages that would connect to their clients' differing E-mail systems. It did not take long for them to turn to the Net, enabling them to send E-mail to all of their clients through only one internal E-mail system. Today, documents that previously arrived overnight now arrive in minutes, while printing and delivery service costs have been reduced.

Northern Telecom (Nortel) originally turned to the Internet to enable its scientists to communicate with university research scientists and to enable its employees to participate in technical industry forums in areas related to its telecommunications businesses. In 1993 the company began to use the Internet to make it easier for its own programmers and technologists to communicate with one another. Next, Nortel's advertising departments began to use the Net to distribute reports and advertisements internally. Eventually, the company put its companywide directory online. Today, 40,000 Nortel employees have access to the Internet and to easy internal communications. Similarly, J. P Morgan has ended up using the Net for internal communication, making it accessible to every employee. The company even puts its telephone book on the Web so that all employees have access to it. The advantage? Given that the book is electronic, Morgan is able to update it weekly while saving the cost of printing and distributing it.

Many people find the Net ideal for collaboration. Computer scientist Dr. Brendan McKay in Australia is half a world away from Dr. Stanislaw Radziszowsky in New York, yet the two exchanged more than 1,000 messages in three years, allowing them to work almost as if they were at the same site.[4]

Internet tools for communication are actually creating new social forms. People are using Internet technology to create online communities where they can exchange ideas and opinions with people who have similar interests in different locations. The nonprofit Hazeldon Foundation in Center

In the control room for the Woods Hole Oceanographic Institution network, powerful workstations help scientists relay oceanographic research data over the Internet to anxiously awaiting scientists.

SOURCE: Photo by Thomas Kleindinst. © The Jason Foundation and the Corporation of the City of Hamilton. Courtesy of Woods Hole Oceanographic Institution.

City, Minnesota, has helped people with chemical dependencies since 1949, counting more than 100,000 alumni of its treatment programs. It set up a Web site as an outreach to people, who can use its interactive chat rooms to meet people from all over the country and share experiences.

Electric Minds, described in the chapter-opening vignette, a cyberspace community for people interested in technology and culture, spawned a business where advertisers can target pockets of potential customers. Companies such as GeoCities and Tripod are others that use advertising revenue to support online communities. Geocities is organized into "neighborhoods" such as "Wall Street," "Motor City" (for vehicle enthusiasts), and "Area 51" (for science-fiction buffs). It provides members with tools to set up a Web page quickly and with free server space. New members pick a neighborhood based on their interests and set up a Web page as a "cyberhome" (see Figure 8.8).

ACCELERATING THE DISTRIBUTION OF NEW KNOWLEDGE AND THE PACE OF SCIENTIFIC DISCOVERY

The Net has become a major source in accelerating the distribution of new knowledge. NASA now makes images gathered by satellites available on the Net within minutes after it receives the pictures. A robot from the Woods Hole Oceanographic Institution has been exploring the black ocean floor in the Gulf of California. When the data the robot collects are transmitted by tether to the surface ship, they are immediately transmitted to a satellite, where they are broadcast by network to waiting scientists all over the world. At Los Alamos, New Mexico, the Genbank collects DNA research data from around the world. In the past, the data were released to the world through printed books, a process that took 13 months to complete. Now those data are released electronically via the Net with a total turnaround time of 48 hours.

FIGURE 8.8

Internet Communities

Geocities is an Internet community organized into "neighborhoods" for people of similar interests. The "neighborhood" illustrated here would appeal to outdoor recreation enthusiasts.

Evidence of how much scientists have come to rely upon instant publication of data has emerged recently in the form of a fight being waged by some venerable scientific journals, such as the *New England Journal of Medicine*, to remain a source of original publication. Traditional publishing through scientific journals can take months as articles are submitted, sent out for peer review, revised, submitted again in final form, scheduled for publication, and finally published. Scientists are turning to the Internet as a faster, cheaper alternative. By simply posting to a community bulletin board on the Net, many scientists and academics are trying to form their own journals and information communities. Publishing on the Internet is instantaneous, albeit often without prior peer review. The Focus on People explores this controversy.

FACILITATING ELECTRONIC COMMERCE

Electronic commerce
The process of buying and selling goods electronically through computerized business transactions.

One of the fastest-growing uses of the Internet is for electronic commerce. **Electronic commerce** is the process of buying and selling goods electronically. By computerizing purchase and sale transactions, businesses can reduce their manual and paper-based procedures and speed up ordering, delivery, and payment for goods and services. The Part 2 illustrated case is dedicated to electronic commerce because it is becoming such an important new way of doing business.

SCIENTIFIC JOURNALS ON THE INTERNET

Traditionally, scientists publish their findings in printed journals, the preeminent forum for the presentation and discussion of scientific research. Some members of the scientific community are trying to change all that. The Internet, which grew out of its military beginnings into an academic haven, is threatening the very existence of the time-honored print journal.

Researchers who laud the Internet, such as Stevan Harnad, director of the cognitive studies center at the University of Southampton in Great Britain, would like to see a complete transition from print journals to electronic journals as the primary medium for publishing scientific research. Harnad and others reason that the old method of publication takes too much time. They do not insist that print journals be put to death, but they do support the idea that publication should take place on the Internet first. Critics of this stance foresee serious consequences should the electronically inclined triumph.

Publications such as the *New England Journal of Medicine* and *Science* apply strict evaluation procedures to articles that they receive as submissions. This process keeps approximately 90 percent of the submissions from being published. Scientists are disturbed by the notion that articles being placed directly on the Web do not undergo such scrutiny. The possibility of inaccuracies and misinformation being passed off as conclusive scientific discovery concerns them greatly. In response to that fear, some journal editors are choosing to continue as though nothing had changed, in some senses ignoring the Internet and its influence. Jerome P. Kassirer of the *New England Journal of Medicine* has declared that his organization's standards for publication will remain as they always were, which essentially means that any document that has already appeared on the Net will not appear in the journal because it does not print previously published material.

While some may admire Kassirer's fortitude, practicality may dictate the final outcome. Internet technology has dealt a significant blow to the traditional scientific publishing industry already. Economic factors heavily favor electronic publishing, which does away with many of the expenses related to printing and distribution. Plenty of scientific titles exist exclusively on the Internet, while many more can be found in both formats. Other scientific publishers may be forced to go to the Web eventually. *Science* magazine has even entered the realm of the Web with its own site.

The resistance to scientific publishing on the Internet is not to distributing research electronically but to publishing articles that have not been evaluated using high academic standards. The Internet contains numerous sites dedicated to posting new ideas and fresh essays that have not yet been reviewed. Visitors to these sites extol the virtues of being able to exchange data so quickly and widely. They also assert that they, themselves, scrutinize the work of their peers with as much effectiveness as a journal review, possibly more. Although the future of the scientific journal remains in question, scientific debate seems to have lost no momentum.

FOCUS Questions: What role do scholarly standards play in the debate over print journals versus electronic journals? What are some of the advantages of electronic publishing? The disadvantages?

SOURCES: Robert Frank, "A Stodgy Publisher Is Turning Electronic," *The Wall Street Journal,* August 11, 1997, and Joan O'C. Hamilton and Heidi Dawley, "Darwinism and the Internet," *Business Week*, June 26, 1995.

Buying and Selling Goods on the Web For certain kinds of businesses, the Internet has opened up new channels for marketing, buying, and selling goods and services. The greatest boost to electronic commerce has come from the Web because it provides such a rich medium for displaying colorful electronic brochures and for creating interactive electronic storefronts.

Many retailers maintain their own virtual storefronts on the Web, such as Virtual Vineyards, described in Chapter 1, or Amazon.com, a cyberbookstore that offers over 2 million titles for sale online (see Chapter 13). Others offer products through electronic shopping malls, such as the Internet Mall, where thousands of electronic "shops" sell food, furniture, clothing, sporting goods, computers, gifts, books, and automotive products. Customers can locate products in this mall by either the type of product or the shop they seek.

Many more companies, such as EPM (see the Chapter 1 opening vignette) do not actually sell over the Web but use their Web sites primarily as electronic brochures and catalogs. The Web sites describe their wares using text, illustrations, animation, or video, but customers must do their actual ordering via telephone.

The Web is especially beneficial to small companies, giving them access to faraway markets that previously could be tapped only by larger companies that had more resources. EPM, a two-person company, has been able to use the Web to sell gaskets from all over the world. The Document Center of Belmont, California, sells engineering documents (specifications) for all types of products. It competes with Global Engineering Documents of Denver, Colorado, a company more than ten times its size ($1.2 million versus $15 million in annual sales). Global uses various electronic media to distribute its documents, including satellite broadcast for immediate delivery. The Document Center cannot afford such distribution methods but flourishes by underpricing Global and selling to smaller companies around the world that need its lower prices. The company solved its problem of reaching customers in Eastern Europe, Africa, and other distant places at an affordable price by establishing a Web site that includes an interactive database of product standards. Customers can ask questions through the site as well as place orders. Since establishing the Web site, the company has seen its business rise by 10-15 percent.

Customer Service Many companies have found that they can use the Net to improve customer service while lowering their costs. Federal Express customers are now able to use the package tracing facilities at FedEx's Web site to check the status of their shipments online without having to call FedEx. Customers like it because they are able to get a full report without having to wait in a telephone queue. However, for FedEx, which delivers more than 2 million overnight packages per day, it meant 90,000 fewer inquiries for the month of May 1995 alone, enabling FedEx to reduce its customer service staff and save $8 per telephone call.

GE Plastics, the Pittsfield, Massachusetts, subsidiary of General Electric, has made over 1,500 pages of technical product data available through the Web, enabling customers to obtain needed technical information within minutes instead of the days it would take if the information were requested by telephone and sent by mail. Hewlett-Packard of Palo Alto, California, uses its Web site to distribute to its customers updates to its operating systems and other software.[5]

The Focus on Problem Solving describes other companies that are using the Web for customer support.

FOCUS ON PROBLEM SOLVING

SUPPORTING CUSTOMERS ON THE WEB

One reason behind many companies' entries to the World Wide Web is the ability to use their Web site as a help desk for customers.

Many companies start by installing help-desk software that contains easy-to-locate solutions to many problems customers have. Once the help desk software is running, the companies then link the help desk to their Web sites. Others simply connect data currently on their computers directly to their Web sites so that customers can retrieve it themselves without the help-desk software. What internal problems are such companies solving in this way? According to Cypress Semiconductor applications engineer Todd Melnick, his company put its help desk online for two reasons. First, it wanted "to help reduce the support load for the applications engineers." And second, it wanted "to give our customers faster answers." These are the two reasons cited by most companies for connecting a help function to their Web sites.

Actually, Cypress, a producer of computer chips, not only combines its Web site and its help-desk application but also adds E-mail to the mix in order to offer its customers support. The customer service department claims that "about 20 percent of all . . . incidents that are logged with us are either through E-mail or the Web now." While the company has not been able to free up existing support staff, it does claim that it has not added new staff as quickly as it had expected. As for the customer perspective, Bill Kirkwood, director of customer service, claims that his department is speeding delivery of answers to problem inquiries.

Broderbund Software is another company that has found success using help desks linked to its Web site. Broderbund claims that the number of help calls is not decreasing. However, the company has seen a decrease in calls that ask easy questions. The result is that Broderbund's highly skilled help-desk staff is able to focus on dealing with the more difficult problems. According to Mason Woodbury, vice-president of marketing services, "Our productivity has gone up and our customers are happier."

The experience of American Airlines has been different. While the airline's Web site originally contained only the kind of corporate information stockholders might wish to see, American has slowly been converting it into a real customer support function. John Samuel, director of distribution planning (meaning ticket sales), wanted a Web site that the customers would find useful while also reducing the airline's customer service costs. The company maintains a toll-free customer service line that costs millions of dollars every year to keep staffed. A large percentage of the calls are not related to booking a flight and, therefore, produce no income. Rather, customers call with such questions as how to reach a particular airport, how to travel with a pet, or how to carry skis. Samuel believed that many customers would rather get the answers to such questions themselves if they could get them quickly and easily. So the American Airlines Web site has undergone a slow metamorphosis. First it posted information that answered common travel-related questions such as those about airport logistics, in-flight movies, and even seating charts. Then they added departure and arrival times—updated every 30 seconds. Then American gave its frequent flier program members the ability to check the status of their own accounts as well as see a list of rewards. Finally American added online booking and electronic ticketing. Samuel claims that the sites are used by many customers. As evidence, he cites a 40 percent increase in the usage of the Web site during the heavy snow blizzards of 1996. (Actually, flight schedule checks increased 400 percent during those same blizzards.) When the airline offered discount fares later that year, it found that usage of the site exploded. All this Web site usage offered a great deal of relief to American Airlines telephone and support staff.

FOCUS Questions: What problems do help-desk software combined with the World Wide Web solve? What are the limitations of this approach for the company? For the customer? Suggest other uses for this combination of software and the Web.

SOURCES: Patricia B. Seybold, "Don't Let PR Control Your Web Site!" *Computerworld*, April 8, 1996, and Sarah Varney, "Link Your Help Desk to the Web," *Datamation*, May 15, 1996.

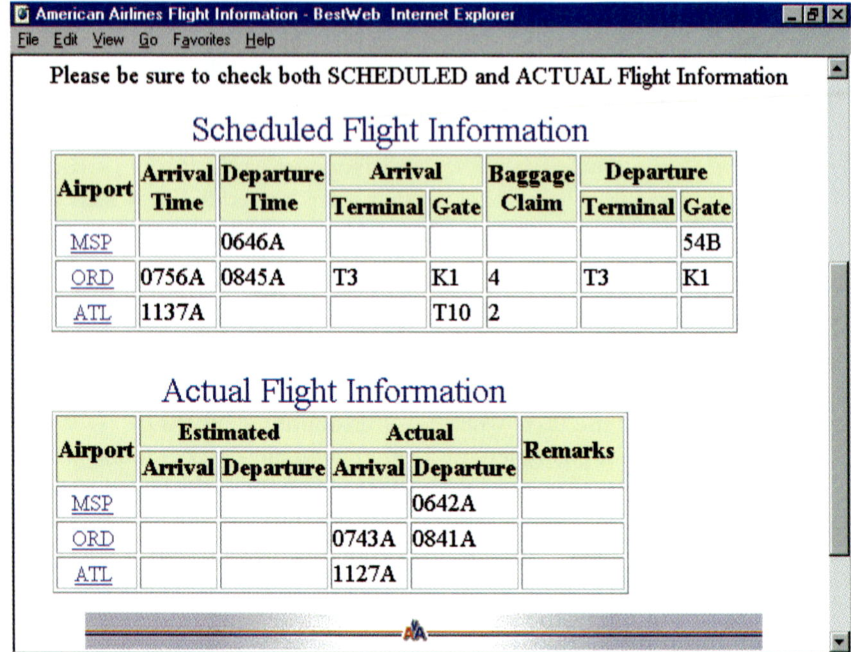

Scheduled Flight Information

Airport	Arrival Time	Departure Time	Arrival		Baggage Claim	Departure	
			Terminal	Gate		Terminal	Gate
MSP		0646A					54B
ORD	0756A	0845A	T3	K1	4	T3	K1
ATL	1137A			T10	2		

Actual Flight Information

Airport	Estimated		Actual		Remarks
	Arrival	Departure	Arrival	Departure	
MSP				0642A	
ORD			0743A	0841A	
ATL			1127A		

American Airlines is one of many companies using the Web for customer support. This screen shows both scheduled and actual arrival, departure, and gate information for American Airlines flight 574 from Minneapolis to Chicago on August 31, 1997.

8.4 THE CHALLENGE OF THE INTERNET

The Internet has created new challenges and problems as it has gained popularity. In this section, we describe the major people, technology, and organizational challenges that it now poses and their social and economic impact.

TECHNOLOGY ISSUES

Internet security is one obvious issue. When the Net was only a data highway for the free exchange of ideas among scientists and educators, security was not a major issue—most users wanted others to read what they wrote. However, with increased business usage, the transmission of proprietary or sensitive data in such areas as product development, manufacturing processes, and marketing plans needs to be protected from prying competitors. Companies offering products for sale on the Net and their customers are also concerned about theft of credit card information. Retail sales have not mushroomed on the Net as quickly as many had hoped, and the inability of people to trust security over the Net is one major reason why. We discuss these security issues in greater detail in the Part 2 illustrated case and in Chapter 12.

Another security problem on the Net is unauthorized access to connected computers. The Internet has proven vulnerable to scoundrels intent on creating trouble because it was designed to be easily accessible. Security experts are concluding that current password protection systems are no longer adequate. Internet security issues are discussed in detail in Chapter 12.

Bandwidth is another major technology issue. With the success of the Web, sound, graphics, and even full-motion video are now an important aspect of the Net. Yet these all require immense quantities of data, greatly slowing down transmission and the downloading of screens. Some Web servers become overloaded with servicing requests and may be impossible to connect to during busy periods. The Focus on Technology in Chapter 10 explores the Internet bandwidth issue in greater detail.

Transmission via ISDN is, by its nature, many times faster than transmission over traditional, modulated telephone lines. ISDN is slowly spreading, offering more and more Net users a way to greatly reduce the bandwidth problem. Additional technology is now available to enable the Internet to be brought into homes and offices using cable TV lines and a cable modem. This approach promises transmission speeds of up to 1,000 times faster than current methods, essentially downloading Web pages almost instantly. This solution will be available only when cable companies begin to offer this service.

ORGANIZATIONAL AND SOCIAL ISSUES

The culture of the Internet has been an area of controversy. The original body of Net users, scientists and educators, view the network as an electronic vehicle for free speech. They have created a culture that abhors traditional advertising or electronic junk mail. Already overburdened, even overwhelmed, by E-mail messages and other information they are seeking, users do not want to be deluged with unwanted advertising.

On the other hand, few seem to object to quiet commercial use, such as employees communicating with each other via E-mail or a company Web site. Some E-mail systems can automatically screen all incoming messages, rejecting those that do not meet certain criteria established by an individual user. Recently a consensus seems to have been reached that advertising is acceptable if handled properly. Many Web sites do contain advertising, but the viewer must choose to come to the site (unless he or she is using push technology).

The social and cultural impact of the Internet is another issue of great concern for many. It is obvious that the Net breaks geographic barriers, that physical isolation no longer need imply intellectual isolation, as the McKay-Radziszowsky collaboration illustrates so well. With the Internet, the world is truly becoming smaller. But the Net does have other potential cultural impacts.

Observers point out that while more people than ever have easier access to data worldwide, such access requires expensive technology that only a relatively small elite can afford. The cost leaves the individuals and countries who most need the technology without the ability to participate in this equalizing revolution. Some believe that while the knowledgeable elite is becoming larger, the gulf between that elite and the rest of the world is widening and becoming ever more difficult to bridge. The world is being permanently divided between a small, technologically based group of haves and a vast majority who are becoming a permanent underclass of have-nots.

The inability to control access to information is creating difficulties in some countries. We have already seen how important the Net has become to both business and science. In the long run, countries that are trying to grow their economies or support their scientists have no choice but to allow or even enable links to the Internet. Many governments try to control what their citizens read and see, but this is a nearly impossible task once people are connected to the Net.

PEOPLE ISSUES

Information overload is yet another problem for Net users. The Internet is so large that an inquiry often leads to more responses than the recipient can handle. Some people have stopped using the Internet because they get 500 messages a day. Mitch Kapor, founder of the Lotus Development Corporation, equates the Net to a library in which all the books are dumped on the floor in no particular order. How can human beings possibly sort through and handle all this data? How can we locate what is there and make intelligent choices as to what we want to access? Broadcast technology and information filtering devices are only of partial help.

SUMMARY

- The Internet is a worldwide network of networks that originated as a Defense Department network that could withstand foreign attack, connecting scientists and researchers. All computers have an equal ability to communicate with other computers on the Internet. The Internet has no central management.
- The technologies used in the Internet include networks, client/server computing, TCP/IP protocols, and hypertext and hypermedia.
- Major Internet capabilities include E-mail, Usenet, chatting, LISTSERVs, Telnet, file transfer protocol (FTP), Archie, Gophers, Veronica, and the World Wide Web.
- The World Wide Web is a system and set of standards for storing and accessing information in a networked environment, including text, graphics, sound, and video, using hypertext and hypermedia. Web pages are created using hypertext markup language (HTML) and can be linked to other Web pages on the same Web site or on other Web sites using hyperlinks.
- Each Web site has a unique address indicated by its URL. Information can be located on the Web using Web site directories, search engines, or push technology.
- Organizations can use Web technology to create internal private networks called intranets. Firewalls are used to prevent unauthorized outsiders from accessing these networks.
- The Internet and the Web have helped organizations and individuals solve problems by reducing communication costs, making it easier for businesses to coordinate organizational activities and communicate with employees. Researchers and knowledge workers are finding the Internet a quick, low-cost way to both gather and disperse knowledge. The Internet facilitates

electronic commerce, creating new opportunities for marketing, sales, and customer support.

• The Internet poses people, technology, and organizational challenges. Much of its technology is relatively new. Security is difficult because the Net offers spies, thieves, and hackers out to do damage many potential entry points. The rapid growth of Net popularity and the rapid expansion of the transmission of data-intensive graphics, sound, and video applications has created inadequate bandwidth. Use of the Internet is exacerbating social and economic inequality among individuals and nations. No adequate system has yet developed to allow individuals to effortlessly search on the Internet through immense amounts of data located anywhere in the world. The culture of the Internet is still evolving, with opinion divided on the suitability of the Internet for commercial use.

KEY TERMS

Information superhighway
Internet service provider (ISP)
Node
Hyperlink
Domain name
Usenet
LISTSERV
Chatting
Telnet
File transfer protocol (FTP)
Archie
Gopher
Veronica
World Wide Web
Webmaster
Home page
URL
Hypertext markup language (HTML)
Search engine
Bookmark
Push technology
Intranet
Firewall
Extranet
Electronic commerce

REVIEW QUESTIONS

1. What is the Internet? How can it be accessed by individuals or organizations?
2. How does the history of the Internet help explain its design and organization?
3. What technologies are used in the Internet? Describe the role of each.
4. What are the principal Internet tools for communicating? Describe how each of them works.
5. What are the principal Internet tools for accessing information? Describe how each of them works.

6. What is the World Wide Web? Why is it so useful? What technologies does it include?
7. Describe and compare the various ways of locating information on the Web.
8. Define and describe intranets. What technologies do they require?
9. How can intranets and extranets benefit organizations?
10. Describe some of the ways organizations can use the Internet to improve communication and coordination.
11. Describe some of the ways scientists and businesses can use the Internet to distribute and exchange knowledge.
12. What is electronic commerce? How is it facilitated by the Internet?
13. What technology issues does the Internet raise?
14. What social and organizational issues does the Internet raise?
15. What people issues does the Internet raise?

DISCUSSION QUESTIONS

1. Should everyone use the Internet? Why or why not?
2. What aspects of everyday life and business is the Internet changing?
3. The Internet is fundamentally transforming the way information systems are being used by people and businesses. Do you agree? Why or why not?

PROBLEM-SOLVING EXERCISES

1. *Group exercise:* With pornography and offensive, even harmful, material so easily available on the Internet, should it be censored? Divide into groups to debate this issue. Each side should research the issue by visiting relevant Web sites and defend its position before the class.

2. Select a Web site being used by a business. A list of suggestions can be found at this textbook's Web site, or you can choose another site in which you are interested. Analyze the site in terms of how it is being used to help that business. Some of the questions you should answer are: What can you learn about this company by examining its Web site? How is this company benefiting from using this Web site? Has the Web changed the way this company conducts its business? What new ideas can you learn from this site? Are there any ways for the company to obtain more benefits from the Internet? How would you improve this Web site?

3. *Hands-on exercise:* Team Jackets is a small firm manufacturing sports jackets with local team logos. It receives its fabric, trim, and other materials from various suppliers. The company's receiving department opens each package from suppliers and records the contents in a receiving log. Download the file for this receiving log from the Laudon & Laudon Web site. Use

appropriate software to total the number of pieces shipped, and save the completed log.

4. *Internet problem-solving exercise:* You are doing research on sport utility vehicles and would like to gather statistics and other information available on the Web. Use two different tools for locating information on the Web, such as Yahoo!, Alta Vista, or Lycos. Compare the volume and quality of information you found with each tool.

NOTES

1. Anthony-Michael Rutkowski, "Bottom-Up Information Infrastructure and the Internet," Keynote Address, Founder's Day Symposium, University of Pittsburgh, February 27, 1995.
2. Amy D. Wohl, "The Internet Learns to Push," *Beyond Computing,* July–August 1997.
3. Teri Robinson, "The Revolution Is Here," *Information Week,* November 18, 1996, and Elisabeth Horwitt, "Intranet Intricacies," *Computerworld Client/Server Journal,* February 1996.
4. William J. Broad, "Doing Science on the Network: a Long Way from Gutenberg," *The New York Times,* May 18, 1993, and John Markett, "A Web of Networks, an Abundance of Services," *The New York Times,* February 21, 1993.
5. Mark Halper, "Meet the New Middleman," *Computerworld E-Commerce,* April 28, 1997, and Sarah E. Varney and Vance McCarthy, "E-Commerce: Wired for Profits," *Datamation,* October 1996.

PROBLEM-SOLVING CASE

THE INTRANET ARRIVES IN SILICON VALLEY

California's Santa Clara County is truly one of the great high-tech centers in the world today. For many years, each of Santa Clara's more than 50 departments and agencies created its own, isolated computer systems without regard to countywide standards or needs and with no thought given to communicating with the other departments. The isolated departmental information systems were based on all kinds of technology—some were Macintosh based, others PC based, and still others UNIX client/server systems. Each had its own, isolated E-mail system—altogether using six different E-mail technologies. Examples of the effects of its lack of communications abound. The Valley Medical Center (the county hospital) and the Social Services division were unable to communicate electronically, even though they had to do a great deal of work together. In fact, the many members of the Social Services staff who work in the medical center were even unable to access their own systems from the hospital and had to rely instead on phone, fax and mail when they wanted information about clients from their own database. The county supervisors found that coordinating legislative analyses and reports among themselves was very difficult. "The only way we could do it, was to try to catch all six of us when we were in [California state capital] Sacramento at the same time," claimed Frank Lockfeld, director of the county's Center for Urban Analysis. The lack of telecommunications systems affected the county work in other ways, also.

Too many paper processes slowed down the everyday work, seriously impacting productivity.

The difficulties became too great to ignore any longer, and so in 1990, county deputy executive George Newell led a committee of technology and agency executives in drawing up plans to correct the problems. The project that was eventually established had a series of goals, including the following:

- Provide the framework and standards for integration and communication throughout the county;
- Link 40 major county agencies and departments;
- Link the existing 100 LANs;
- Connect the various departments to the Internet, including to the World Wide Web;
- Use the Internet to connect all users via E-mail, regardless of the E-mail system their own department was currently using;
- Share data among co-workers and departments; and
- Reduce redundant work and thereby increase productivity.

In addition, cost and effort were major concerns. The committee insisted that any solution it settled upon would need to accomplish all of this through an architecture that would encompass all existing systems. The county did not want to be forced to replace any of the existing systems. The committee also hoped to implement a system that would not require a great deal of expensive and time-consuming support. Finally, it wanted to limit the costs of such a project.

The only solution possible became a county government intranet. An intranet would run on top of existing systems and could easily be used to extract data from those systems. It would not only meet the above requirements but would have added advantages as well. Once the intranet was established, it would be easy to connect the users of the intranet to the Internet to further enhance the productivity of the county workers. Moreover, once the county was on the Net, it could give the public access to a great deal of county information through a county World Wide Web site. Cost and time projections of $4.3 million over a three-year period were considered acceptable for achieving all these goals.

The first deployment of the new intranet, dubbed Claranet, was completed in December 1993, linking the Valley Medical Center, the Social Services department, the General Services Agency data center, and the county administrative offices. When Phase One was completed in 1995, 32 networks at 17 sites had been connected, cross-agency E-mail capabilities had been added, as had file transfer and remote access capabilities. All users had been given access to the Internet. Phase Two was completed in May 1996, adding 15 additional sites, including the sheriff's department, the municipal and superior courts, the registrar of voters, and the agricultural department. Phase Three, completed in mid-1997, added the remaining major departments, including the district attorney's office, the public defender's office, and the parks department.

The intranet used a TCP/IP network and the Netscape Navigator Web browser.

While some new systems were built, most of the development time and cost was to make existing data from the multitude of systems more widely available. One system enables users to track the progress of bills through the California legislature. Another enables users to access welfare-recipient histories. Users can now view the minutes of the meetings of the county supervisors. Those who need the information now can access the county budget system and the county accounting systems. And, of course, users can access all this data from any site—yes, Social Service department workers can now access all the data they need while working at the Valley Medical Center site, and hospital workers can also access the social service data if necessary. For example, social workers are able to help incoming hospital patients sign up for emergency medical insurance when the patients arrive at the hospital.

The public has been given access to a broad selection of information in the county through Santa Clara's new World Wide Web site. County workers and the public can, for example, search medical libraries, access programs and procedures of the county General Services Agency, view injury reports from the county Emergency Services departments, obtain information about the county senior centers, access the county library catalog system, review zoning permits, learn more about their elected officials, check bus schedules, and review the county board meeting schedules and agendas.

How has the project fared? During the first year (Phase One had not yet been completed), Claranet saved the county an estimated $731,000 in communications and hardware costs. Moreover, some departments reported an increase in worker productivity. For example, the Employee Services department, with a staff of 140, reported an 11 percent rise in productivity rates. Based on these first-year results, estimates are that the county will gain a threefold return on its investment as early as the end of 1998.

SOURCE: Bronwyn Fryer, "Silicon Valley Gets Wired," *Information Week*, June 17, 1996.

CASE STUDY QUESTIONS

1. What problems did Santa Clara County systems have? In what ways were these problems serious?

2. Analyze the people, organization, and technology problems faced by Santa Clara County that caused it to develop Claranet. Why do you think the county had not faced these problems earlier?

3. How did the Internet and Internet technology help Santa Clara County to solve its technical, organizational, and people problems?

4. How much connectivity does an organization like Santa Clara County need in order to conduct its business? Do you think this project was important? Why? In what other ways might connectivity be useful to the county and its various departments?

ILLUSTRATED CASE

ELECTRONIC COMMERCE ARRIVES

A mechanic working for a major airline at New York's JFK Airport discovers a worn wheel assembly part in a Boeing 747 that is scheduled to fly to Europe the next day. Time is critical—a grounding or a delay will cost the airline up to $40,000 per minute. The mechanic does not know the part number, but using her computer, she immediately accesses Boeing's online catalogue (containing more than 2 million parts). She quickly identifies the part by its location on the plane and immediately orders it online from the closest warehouse to JFK. She will then monitor its shipment and delivery through the same Boeing system. When the mechanic arrives home that night, she turns to managing her own investments. Using a home computer, she connects to her broker's computer, where she obtains the latest quotes on her investments and on stocks she is monitoring. She then enters a transaction to sell shares of a mutual fund, using the funds to purchase two new stocks through two other online transactions.

Our mechanic has located and ordered a key airplane part and has managed her investments using a collection of technologies known as electronic commerce. Electronic commerce is a potential tidal wave that is revolutionizing the way both organizations and individuals buy and sell goods and services.

WHAT IS ELECTRONIC COMMERCE?

Electronic commerce (e-commerce) is the use of information technology such as computers and telecommunications to automate the buying and selling of goods and services. To better understand why e-commerce is such a revolution, let us first follow a traditional bill payment and then the same payment as an electronic transaction.

TRADITIONAL AND ELECTRONIC TRANSACTIONS COMPARED

In traditional bill payment, the seller prints a bill and mails it to the buyer, who opens the bill, reads it, writes a check, and mails it back to the seller. The seller opens the payment envelope, records the payment, and deposits the check. The bank codes the check, credits the seller's account, and forwards the canceled check to the buyer's bank. The buyer's bank debits the buyer's account, and at the end of the month both buyer and seller receive updated account information in their monthly bank statements.

Let us view the same transaction processed electronically. The bill is electronically sent to the buyer, who pays the bill online through his bank with only a couple of computer clicks. The bank electronically transfers the funds to the seller's bank, and both banks electronically adjust the relevant accounts. The only paper that changes hands is the monthly bank statement (which may be eliminated in time).

Of course, the same transaction also generates other documents that change hands either manually or electronically, including a shipment notification, a bill of lading airbill, and an invoice. Ultimately, only the shipment of the product must be handled manually.

BENEFITS OF USING ELECTRONIC COMMERCE

While electronic commerce does present important problems, it delivers many benefits.

Paper. The problem is simple. We are being swamped by paper and all the clerical work that accompanies it. For example, Pacific Bell (a regional telephone company) receives bill payments of about $1 billion per month, all by mail, all small payments. The printing, postage, processing, and handling costs related to these bills costs billions of dollars per year. Americans actually pay an astounding 18 billion bills per year, almost all of which are paid through the mail and are handled manually at key points. The solution to the problem is to bill customers electronically and have them, in turn, pay electronically. Bills would be sent electronically to the individual customers' home computers, perhaps via the Internet. Customers would then be able to have the bank pay with one simple

Companies can locate and order airplane parts from Boeing's online catalogue.

point-and-click operation. Banks, credit card companies, and other companies are beginning to offer some electronic billing, but it is still in its infancy.

Time. Transaction time is often a significant factor, and electronic transactions can save valuable time. The airline mechanic was able to use an up-to-date online catalogue to locate the needed part very rapidly. She then placed her order instantly and was even able to specify the closest warehouse as the source of shipment to speed delivery. Bill payment and check clearance can also be sped up this way.

Distance. Networks such as the Internet can instantly transform a local business into a global distributor. The Web is already full of examples of small local businesses, such as book stores and florists, that have grown dramatically by making use of electronic commerce to reach new customers at greater distances. EPM Inc. and Virtual Vineyards, described in Chapter 1, are other examples.

Staff costs. Paper-based buying and selling often requires large clerical staffs. Envelopes need to be opened, payments received need to be entered into the computer, bank deposits need to be prepared, and errors (a side effect of manual processing) need to be corrected. Organizations can achieve major clerical staff reduction by automating billing and bill payment.

Significant staff savings can also be achieved in many other ways through the use of electronic methods. For example, sales and support staff can be reduced when customers are able to obtain information online (a method that is often quicker for the customer as well) rather than via telephone inquiries. Staff for printing and mailing catalogues can also be eliminated when paper catalogues are converted to online versions. Orders entered online rather than via a telephone conversation require less staff time while generating fewer errors.

Customer relations. Electronic commerce often results in much closer relationships among companies and their customers and suppliers. For example, Boeing gave its customers direct access to its own computers, helping them to do their job better and causing those customers to want to remain with Boeing. Mechanics using the Boeing system are also able to see not only the inventory at all Boeing warehouses but also the inventory of Boeing's parts suppliers. In this way the mechanic is able to locate the closest source for a critical part. Thus, both customer and supplier are better served.

Ease of use and improved control. Many customers are turning to online financial markets trading because they have more control over their own funds as well as because these systems are so easy to use compared with placing telephone orders. Charles Schwab and many other firms now support stock, bond, futures, and options trading with direct dial-in to their computers, offering deep discounts for those who trade in this way. Some even offer deeper discounts for trading on their Internet sites. Many traders prefer electronic trading because orders can be entered at any time, 24 hours a day, with confirmations arriving almost immediately. Investors can also check their account status at any time and do not have to wait for monthly statements.

ELECTRONIC COMMERCE TECHNOLOGIES

E-commerce relies upon a wide range of technologies. Here we examine the more vital technologies for electronic commerce.

Networks. The telecommunications network is a fundamental building block of interorganizational electronic commerce. (Network technology and its capabilities are explored in Chapters 7 and 8.) Two main types of networks are used for e-commerce.

Currently, much online commerce is being handled through private EDI networks, usually run over VANs (value-added networks). VANs have traditionally been used for e-commerce because they are secure, are reliable, and offer additional desirable functions such as network auditing and communications tracking. However, because they have to be privately maintained and run on high-speed private lines, VANs are expensive, easily costing a company $100,000 per month. They are also inflexible, being connected to only a limited number of sites and companies. As a result, the Internet is emerging as the network technology of choice. The Net makes it easier and cheaper for a company's customers and suppliers to become involved with e-commerce. With many companies, all the customer or supplier needs in order to participate in e-commerce on the Net is a PC, a Web browser, and access to the Net. The Net is also much more flexible because its low cost makes it easy for any company or individual to participate. However, many companies, particularly financial organizations such as Citibank and Charles Schwab, continue to use private networks because the security and reliability of the Internet does not yet meet their strict standards.

E-mail. E-mail is vital to e-commerce because it makes communication so immediate and inexpensive. Buyers and sellers use E-mail to negotiate agreements, companies use it to advertise products, and customers use it to make inquiries about products. One growing use is subscriptions to online newsletters. For example, many companies now sell stock market analyses and recommendations that are delivered online through E-mail.

The World Wide Web. The Web is emerging as a major delivery system for electronic commerce. For example, many magazines and newspapers are now available on the Web. Some, like *The New York Times*, offer the same content as the printed product but are organized so that users can easily bring up items that interest them. Others, such as *The Wall Street Journal*, offer enhanced features such as online research on listed companies and the facility for subscribers to track their own portfolios. Some journals exist only online.

The Web is also being used for online catalogues. Electronic catalogues are easily kept up to date on price and product, they are easy and quick to search, and they can even be used for ordering online. They not only reduce the cost of paper publishing, but they also reduce the size of the staff needed to take orders over the telephone. In addition, they lower telecommunications costs and even lower processing costs as transactions become more automated. AMP, Inc. publishes about 400 catalogues per year with average life spans of 24 months. They cost $8–$10 million per year and yet are outdated as soon as they are printed. The company now hopes to reap major savings by use of catalogues that are accessible on the Web and can always be up to date.

Retail organizations are beginning to use the Web to market products, and they are even beginning to sell through the Web as transactions become more secure. For example, The Limited and Tower Records have established Web sites. The Price Club (the San Diego-based national chain of warehouse-style retail stores) has established Price OnLine to offer thousands of goods and travel services at discounts. One reason for establishing such sites is that new technology enables the customer to simply point at the product and click once to complete a sale. Cover Girl, the Procter & Gamble cosmetic product line, offers a site that answers a number of customer questions. The customer enters the color of different parts of her body (including skin tone, skin type, underarm skin tone, and hair color); and the site tells the user her color classification and specific makeup colors she should use, including eyeliner, blush, and mascara colors.

Some Web sites can actually deliver the product or service online as well as process orders if the product or service is digital. For example, PhotoDisc Inc. sells stock photos online over the Web to designers and Web site developers. Customers can search for photos based

The Internet Mall is a virtual mall that exists only on the Web. It merges thousands of retail Web sites under a single "roof." Visitors to the mall can link directly to these sites to purchase a diverse array of products and services, including books, computers, music CDs, automotive products, and gourmet foods.

on criteria such as color or subject matter and download the images they purchase directly from the Web site. Companies such as Cybersource and Online Interactive sell and deliver software over the Net.

The insurance industry is beginning to make use of the Web—650,000 insurance agents in the United States traditionally sell insurance policies via face-to-face calls on prospective clients. However, because prospective buyers often do not want to give up four or five evenings to insurance salespersons but do want to shop around, some companies, such as InsureMarket, are now offering Web sites where potential customers can gather information and obtain quotes without a single home visit. Blue Cross/Blue Shield of Massachusetts enables its customers to choose or change their health care options online either from kiosks placed in strategic places or from the privacy of their own home. Table 1 lists examples of different types of Web sites used for electronic commerce.

ISSUES RAISED BY ELECTRONIC COMMERCE

The explosive growth of electronic commerce has raised or accentuated a number of fundamental issues, which we examine here.

Online Security. The need for online security is the most pervasive of the fundamental issues raised by electronic commerce. Not only must security problems be solved, but both individuals and businesses must believe that these problems are solved before the use of e-commerce can begin to reach its full potential. Until then, both retail and business-to-business e-commerce will be held back.

The underlying problem is the vulnerability of networks and telecommunications to snoopers and those seeking to do mischief or harm. Large public networks are vulnerable because they are open to virtually anyone and because they are so huge that when abuses do occur, they can have an enormously widespread impact.

Many people have the skill and technology to intercept and spy upon streams of electronic information that flow through the Internet and all other open networks. For example, a simple E-mail message, as it works its way through the Net, passes through many points, sometimes hundreds of them. It can be intercepted at any of these points along the route. Valuable data that might be intercepted include credit card numbers and names, private personnel data, secret business plans, negotiations between companies, and a wide range of data that might be of value to

Cover Girl's interactive Web site provides visitors with personalized recommendations for make-up products based on information they provide.

competition. Neither businesses nor private individuals can afford to have confidential information stolen.

Encryption is a key technology for addressing these problems. Encryption is the coding and scrambling of messages to prevent unauthorized access to data being transmitted over networks. It is vital to e-commerce that commerce-related data of buyers and sellers be kept private when they are transmitted electronically. The data being transmitted must be protected against purposeful alteration by someone other than the sender so that, for example, stock market execution orders or product orders accurately represent the wishes of the buyer and seller.

Secure payment systems for electronic commerce are being developed. Electronic cash (e-cash) is money represented in electronic form that moves outside the normal network of money (paper currency, coins, checks, credit cards) and (for now) is not under the purview of the Federal Reserve system within the United States. Users are supplied with client software and can exchange money with another e-cash user over the Internet. When someone makes an online purchase, the e-cash software creates a "coin" in an amount specified by the user and sends it to the user's bank wrapped in a virtual "envelope." The bank withdraws the amount requested from the user's account, puts a stamp on the "envelope" to validate the coin's value, and returns it to the user. When the user receives the envelope back, he or she can spend the coin. This process is illustrated in Figure 1.

Electronic cash offers many advantages. It is convenient because it can be used to buy anything, anywhere. It enables instant payment all over the world because it can bypass banks and the entire banking system. It is very inexpensive to use because it does not rely upon printing paper money or printing and mailing checks. It is very flexible because it is software and so can be programmed to do whatever the user wants. For example, it can be programmed to be spent only at certain stores, enabling a parent to send money to a child in college while restricting the funds to be used only for tuition or books.

E-cash does present some security problems. It can be stolen by electronic thieves whenever it is transmitted across a public network. In addition, if it were stored on a computer hard disk and that disk suffered a crash, all the electronic cash stored on it would be lost forever. Just like regular cash, lost e-cash cannot be recovered. When networks are truly secure, e-cash transmission will also be secure.

Another alternative is to bypass the public network for private data, transmitting such data as a credit card number over a secure, private network. For example, First Virtual Holdings Inc. in San Diego has estab-

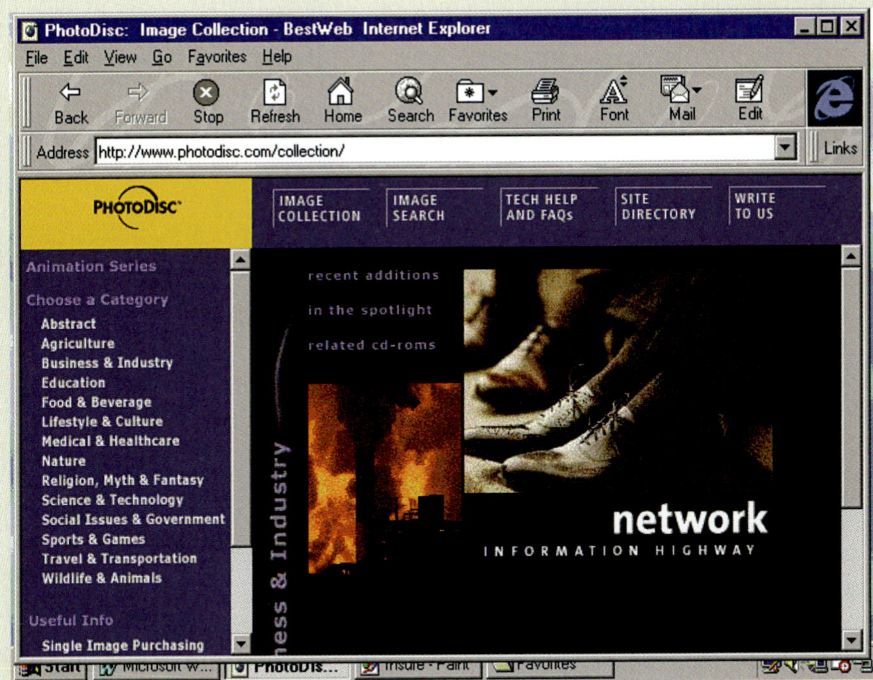

Visitors can search for images, purchase them, and download them directly from PhotoDisc's Web site.

lished an electronic payment service that maintains the customer's credit card information on its private network for a $2 annual fee per customer. The customer is assigned an identification number and a PIN (personal identification number) similar to those used with bank ATM machines. The PIN is stored with the user's credit card number offline on a secure computer. When a customer makes a purchase over the Internet, all that travels on the Internet is the customer First Virtual Holdings PIN number. The vendor submits this to First Virtual over its private network, which in turn transmits the credit card data to the vendor.

Some companies, such as Boeing, create a level of security by requiring user registration and passwords, allowing access to their databases only to those the company decides to admit.

Authentication—the ability of each party to know that the other parties are who they claim to be—is another problem that must be solved. In the non-electronic world, we use our signatures. Bank-by-mail systems avoid the need for signatures on checks they issue for their customers by using well-protected private networks where the source of the request for payment is recorded and can be proven. Experts are currently working on methods that involve encryption for creating agreed-upon certified digital signatures. One issue related to authentication is *message nonrepudiation.* No party to a transaction must be able to deny the existence of that transaction once it has been agreed upon. Again, the solution appears to be certified signatures.

Message integrity is the ability to be certain that the message that is sent arrives without being copied or changed. Modern encryption methods may yet be the solution. They are expected to be mathematically so complex that it becomes almost impossible to change a message and have the resulting message be understandable.

Costs. It is not expensive to set up simple Web sites for advertising a company's products, but most are primarily "electronic brochures" with no capabilities for processing actual transactions. Full-function electronic commerce sites are much more costly. Forrester Research in Cambridge, Massachusetts, reported that the start-up and first-year costs for sites delivering financial services over the Internet could run from $5 million to $23 million per site, depending on the services offered.

Telecommunications remains expensive. High bandwidth is necessary to be able to transmit the immense amounts of data needed for graphics, sound, and video. Yet sales literature, catalogues, and pictures of products are all vital for the success of purchasing products online. Projections are that in time, more

TABLE 1

Examples of Electronic Commerce Web Sites

Web Site	Example
Virtual Vineyards	Sell wine directly online through a "virtual storefront"
Internet Mall	On-line mall providing a central point of access to many "stores" selling products online
EPM Inc.	Provide online product catalogue
Travelocity	Online travel service. Users can book hotel, airline, and car rental reservations online
E*Trade	Online securities trading
PhotoDisc	Online sale and delivery of a digital product
Wall Street Journal Interactive	Provide online content
Boeing Corporation	Automate company-to-company purchases

bandwidth will be made available at lower prices as competition continues to grow and technological advances continue. Also, newer methods of data compression are being developed so that some transmission will not require as much bandwidth.

As these issues are resolved, electronic commerce will grow and have a major effect on the way we do business.

Sources: "Sticker Shock on the Internet," *The New York Times*, June 15, 1997; Eva Freeman, "How to Move E-Cash," *Datamation*, October 1996; Saul Hansell, "Paying Bills without Any Litter," *The New York Times*, July 5, 1996; Sarah E. Varney and Vance McCarthy, "E-Commerce: Wired for Profits," *Datamation*, October 1996; Heath Row, "The Electric Handshake," *CIO Magazine*; and Mark Glaser, "Selling Online: Electronic Storefronts that Work," *New Media*, October 28, 1996.

CASE QUESTIONS

1. What is electronic commerce? What technologies does it require?
2. What role can the Internet play in electronic commerce?
3. If you were going to set up a Web site to sell children's books, what people, organization, and technology issues would you address?
4. Evaluate one of the electronic commerce Web sites described here. What functions does it perform? How easy is it to use? What business activities does it support? How would you improve it?

FIGURE 1

The Future of Electronic Commerce over the Internet

The future of Internet commerce will involve some form of e-cash for digital transfers of payments between computers. Such systems will most likely deploy security procedures such as encryption/decryption and the use of public/private keys.

SOURCE: James Martin, *Cybercorp* (American Management Association, 1996), as reprinted in *Datamation*, October 1996.

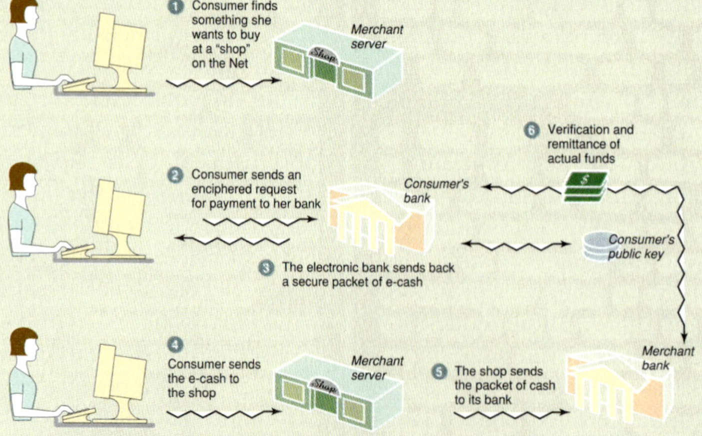

Part 3

PROBLEM SOLVING WITH INFORMATION SYSTEMS

Chapter

→ NINE ←

PROBLEM ANALYSIS: CRITICAL THINKING SKILLS

CHAPTER OUTLINE

LEARNING OBJECTIVES

After reading and studying this chapter, you will

1. Know how to solve problems using a simple five-step model.
2. Know how to develop your critical thinking skills.
3. Understand the three major factors to consider when approaching a business problem.
4. Be able to design logical and physical system solutions for a business.
5. Be familiar with the three major factors to consider when implementing a system solution.

CAN AEROFLOT FLY WITH THE COMPETITION?

Aeroflot, the former state-run airline of the Soviet Union, used to be known for its sullen service, lax safety, and overcrowded planes. Its reservation system was primitive at best. In 1990 Aeroflot reportedly had to turn away 30 percent of its ticketed passengers because there were no seats. The company had no way of tracking the seats it had sold. Tickets were only sold at downtown locations in Moscow and other cities. In those days, having a ticket merely meant that a traveler was allowed to stand in line at the airport. There, seats were given first to VIPs, then to foreigners, and then to everyone else on a first-come, first-served basis. The concept of advance reservations, seat assignments, and boarding passes was nonexistent. Russian air travel was a morass of endless lines, lost reservations, and canceled flights. But Aeroflot always had passengers because Soviet citizens had no other choice. It was a state-run monopoly subsidized by the government.

After the breakup of the Soviet Union in 1991 and the introduction of free market enterprise, Aeroflot started to become privatized. It changed its name to Aeroflot Russian International Airlines. The company had to start earning profits the hard way, by competing with other carriers for passengers. Its rivals include Western airline companies and Transaero, a private Russian-owned startup.

In a few respects, Aeroflot has benefited from its legacy of monopoly. As Russia's flagship carrier, it enjoys the pick of gate slots at Russian airports. Smaller domestic airlines that had been spun off from Aeroflot after privatization were stuck with money-losing domestic routes, while Aeroflot won almost all the international routes. Aeroflot still carries nearly two-thirds of Russia's international traffic, with service to 94 countries around the world.

Treatment of passengers has dramatically improved on Aeroflot's international routes. Flight attendants have been trained to smile and tend to passengers. In place of leathery gray chicken legs, Aeroflot offers a choice of meals, including kosher and vegetarian selections. Aeroflot instituted a customer complaint telephone line. But service is still not polished enough for business travelers. For example, Aeroflot still won't deliver delayed baggage to passengers' homes or hotels. Delays, bad food, and surly service still plague domestic Aeroflot flights within the former Soviet Union.

Aeroflot contracted with Société Internationale de Telecommunications Aeronautiques (SITA) to install a modern computerized passenger reservation system. This system is not yet set up to make it easy to purchase tickets outside of Russia. Inside Russia, customers must stand in line for reservations at Aeroflot's Moscow office and then queue up again to pay a cashier.

Aeroflot's safety record is considered quite respectable, but a number of highly publicized accidents have strained public trust. Most of these accidents involved smaller local airlines that had split off from Aeroflot after privatization.

Foreign carriers have used this opportunity to expand their business in Russia. Lufthansa now has more than 250 flights a week to and from ten former Soviet republics, looking more and more like Russia's main national carrier. Transaero lures millions of passengers annually with superior service. Most Russian and foreign business travelers book with Transaero or with Western competitors.

Aeroflot's only competitive advantage, the ability to offer lower-priced tickets, is eroding in the face of soaring fuel costs. Within a few years, a round-trip economy ticket from Moscow to New York jumped from $700 to $1,137, nearly $400 less than on Delta Airlines, the only U.S. carrier with flights to Russia. But FinnAir charges only $984 for the same flight. Industry experts believe that hidden subsidies allowed Aeroflot to break even in 1995, but mounting fuel costs and competition put the company in the red the following year. In 1996 the airline reported a small after-tax profit of $24.5 million.

Yevgeny Shaposhnikov, Aeroflot's CEO until March 1997, inherited a bloated workforce of 14,000 from the Soviet era and an aged fleet of fuel-guzzling aircraft. He started to purchase more efficient equipment from the West, buying ten new Boeing 737s for Aeroflot's European routes and leasing Boeing 767s and Airbus A310s for longer flights to the United States and Asia. Boeing 767s on Aeroflot's transatlantic flights use 40 percent less fuel than Soviet-made Ilyushin-62 aircraft while carrying one-third more people. Shaposhnikov also purchased Pratt & Whitney engines and Rockwell International avionics equipment for 20 new long-haul Russian-made Ilyushin-96 planes. But by bucking Russia's ingrown aviation manufacturing lobby, he created another public relations crisis because these moves suggested a lack of confidence in Russia's own aviation industry. Cutting staff is difficult because the Russian government owns 51 percent of Aeroflot stock and is opposed to large-scale layoffs.

Shaposhnikov had some allies in the Kremlin and the government who supplied him with new forward-looking members of his management team. Then he was replaced by Valery Olarlov, a former Aeroflot navigator, in March 1997. Olarlov's wife Yetera is the eldest daughter of Russian president Boris Yeltsin. If Olarlov can continue improving the airline while reining in costs, Aeroflot could prosper in a growing market for foreign travel. But can Aeroflot compete on a global basis? The solution is neither clear nor simple.

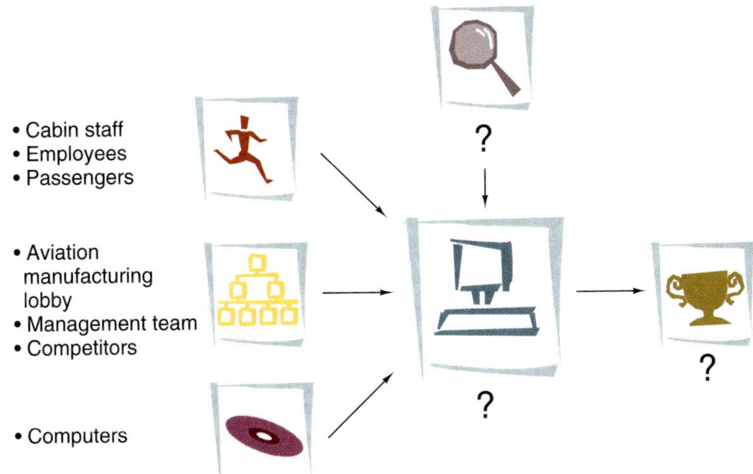

SOURCES: Alessandra Stanley, "Hold the Jokes, Please: Aeroflot Buffs Its Image," *The New York Times,* June 29, 1997; Carol Matlack, "Aeroflot Gets in the Game," *Business Week,* December 23, 1996; and Victoria Pope, "The Gray Chicken Is Definitely Out," *U.S. News & World Report,* October 28, 1996.

The difficulties facing Aeroflot are typical of many companies struggling with changes unleashed by a harsher, more competitive business environment. The problems these firms face are multifaceted and the potential solutions complex. Although technology offers a partial answer in many cases, experience shows that changes in organization and people are also required to save business firms like Aeroflot. Where would you start looking for solutions? Learning how to solve these and simpler problems is the subject of the next four chapters.

In this chapter you will learn some very important concepts about problem solving that can be applied in virtually all business settings. In Chapter 10 these conceptual skills will be applied to real-world cases. This conceptual framework is not tied to technology, although, as you will see, information technology can be useful in solving some business problems.

9.1 INTRODUCTION: CONCEPTS

At first glance problem solving in daily life seems to be perfectly straightforward: A machine breaks down, parts and oil spill all over the floor, and obviously, somebody has to do something about it. So, of course, you find a tool around the shop and start repairing the machine. After a cleanup and proper inspection of other parts, you start the machine, and production resumes.

No doubt some problems are this straightforward. But few problems are this simple, and, in general, when they are, they are not very interesting. Most real-world problems are considerably more complex. In real-world organizations, a number of major factors are simultaneously involved in problems. These major factors can be grouped into three categories: technology, organization, and people. When a problem occurs, it is usually not a simple technology or machine problem but some mixture of organization, people, and technology problems. In other words, a whole set of problems is usually involved. Even establishing the existence of a problem, or declaring that a problem exists, can be controversial in a business or other organization. Why is this so?

DEFINING THE PROBLEM

Contrary to popular conception, problems are not like basketballs on a court just waiting to be picked up by some "objective" problem solver. There are an infinite number of solutions in the world, each with its own advocates. Choosing the right solutions in an organization depends on the ability of key organization members to define the problem correctly.

Before problems can be solved, there must be agreement in an organization that a problem exists, about what the problem is, about what its causes are, and about what can be done about the problem given the limited resources of the organization. Problems have to be properly defined by people in an organization before they can be solved. Once you understand this critical fact, you can start to solve problems creatively.

In the case of Aeroflot, different people have defined the problem in different ways. Depending on how one defines Aeroflot's problem, different courses of further research and action can be recommended. If, for instance, one defines Aeroflot's problem as one of trying to compete using inadequate technologies, then Aeroflot would be wise to start focusing on improving its reservation system with the ultimate goal of increasing sales. Alternatively, Aeroflot's problem could be defined as a cultural problem of failing to come to grips with behaviors and attitudes inherited from the past. Proponents of this view would advocate putting more emphasis on educating staff members to provide better service. Aeroflot's problem could additionally be described as a bureaucratic and political problem. Interest groups, including employees inherited from the Soviet era and the Russian aviation industry, have opposed the company's efforts to downsize and upgrade its fleet. Has Aeroflot's management defined the problem broadly enough to devise a solution addressing all of these issues?

Our point here is that the "problems" facing all companies are usually subject to complex and often controversial interpretation. These problems are not objective objects but, rather, subjective interpretations involving competing views of the world by powerful actors both inside and outside the company.

THE PROBLEM-SOLVING FUNNEL OF REAL-WORLD DECISION MAKING

The example of Aeroflot can be used as a starting point to illustrate the typical stages problem solving goes through. Real-life problem solving can be seen as a kind of funnel (see Figure 9.1) with five stages.[1] The model begins

FIGURE 9.1

The Five Stages in the Problem-Solving Process

We can think of problem solving as a five-step process. The first task is to define the problem. Various people in an organization may have various ideas about what the exact problem is. The second step is to gather and analyze information, helping us to understand the problem better. Third is the decision-making stage, in which we look at possible solutions and select the best one. Next comes the process of designing the solution, and last is solution implementation, during which the solution is tested and refined.

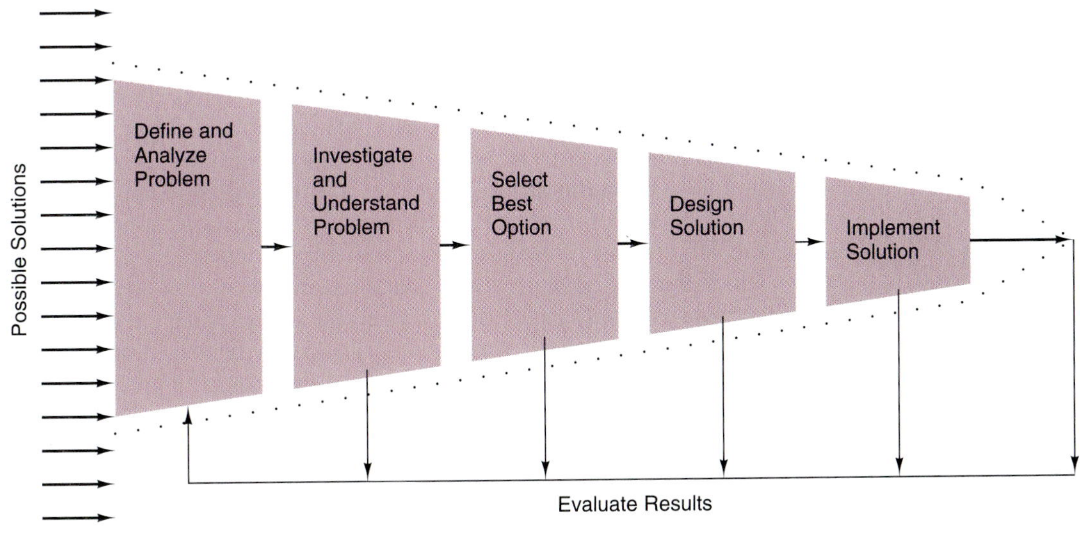

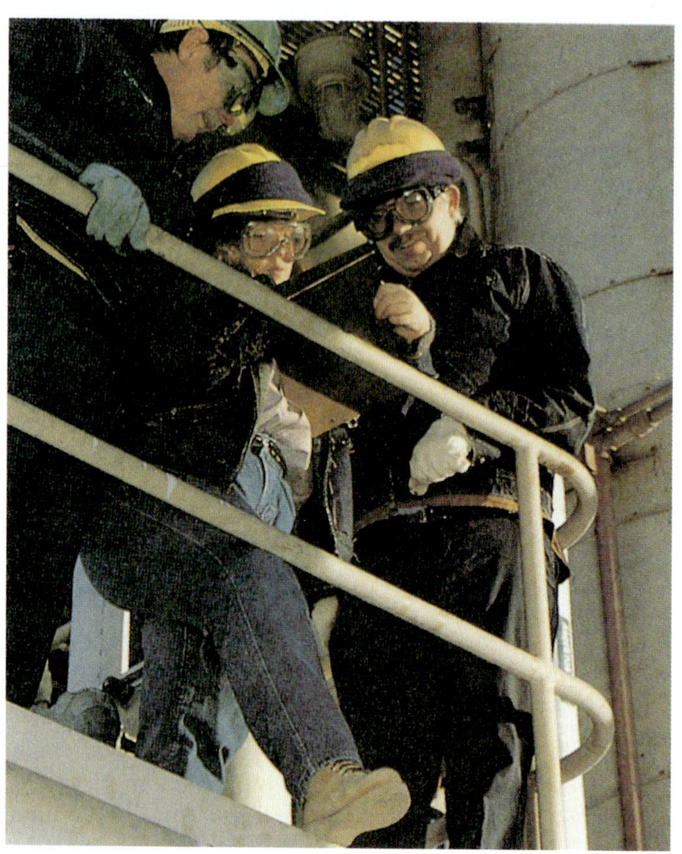

By investigating, analyzing, and defining problems, people can design and implement effective solutions. To solve a problem with the production of chemicals, Dow Corning manufacturing engineer Sue Jacob and her team studied procedures and analyzed production data. Their solution was an operating guideline that, when implemented, exposed a new problem: lack of communication between machine operators and supervisors. Their solution to the second problem included clarifying the manufacturing process to operators and supervisors to improve communications and training for operators.

Source: Courtesy of Dow Corning Corporation.

Problem analysis
The consideration of the dimensions of a problem to determine what kind of problem it is and what general kinds of solutions may be appropriate; the first step in problem solving.

Problem understanding
The investigation—fact gathering and analysis—of a problem to gain better understanding; the second step of problem solving.

Decision making
The process of debating objectives and feasible solutions and choosing the best option; the third step of problem solving.

Solutions design
The development of a solution to a problem, including both logical and physical design; the fourth step of problem solving.

Implementation
The process of putting the solution of a problem into effect and evaluating the results in order to make improvements; the fifth step of problem solving.

by recognizing that there are a large number of solutions in the environment; our goal is to capture the correct solution from the many possibilities. A first step in problem solving typically involves the search for a consensus on what—in very general terms—the problem is and what general kinds of solutions might be appropriate. This is a critical period of **problem analysis** and definition in which the definition of the problem is narrowed considerably. The second stage is **problem understanding;** this is a period of investigation—fact gathering and more analysis—with the goal of better understanding. Next comes a period of **decision making,** when objectives and feasible solutions are debated and the best option is chosen. Fourth, once options are identified, the process of **solution design** can begin. Note that each stage in the model has narrowed the possible solutions down to a smaller number. Finally, a period of **implementation** is entered, during which theoretical designs and concepts are tested in the real world and final changes are made in the design based on field experience. Evaluating the results and performance of this solution helps the firm to improve and refine it. As the business environment changes, feedback may signal that it is time to go through the decision-making process again.

We will use this real-world view of decision making later as the basis for a five-step model of how you can solve problems. First, however, we need to examine the early process of problem solving a little more closely.

CRITICAL THINKING

It is amazingly easy to accept someone else's definition of a problem or to adopt the opinions of some authoritative group that has "objectively" analyzed the problem and offers quick solutions. You should try to resist this tendency to accept existing definitions of any problem. Through the natural flow of decision making, it is essential that you try to maintain some distance from any specific solution until you are sure you have properly identified the problem, developed understanding, and analyzed alternatives. Otherwise, you may leap off in the wrong direction, solve the wrong problem, and waste resources. You will have to engage in some critical thinking exercises.

Critical thinking can be briefly defined as the sustained suspension of judgment with an awareness of multiple perspectives and alternatives. It involves at least four elements:

Critical thinking
The sustained suspension of judgment with an awareness of multiple perspectives and alternatives.

- Maintaining doubt and suspending judgment.
- Being aware of different perspectives.
- Testing alternatives and letting experience guide.
- Being aware of organizational and personal limitations.

Simply following a rote pattern of decision making, or a model, does not guarantee a correct solution. The best protection against incorrect results is to engage in critical thinking throughout the problem-solving process.

First, maintain doubt and suspend judgment. Perhaps the most frequent error in problem solving is to arrive prematurely at a judgment about the nature of the problem. By doubting all solutions at first and refusing to rush to a judgment, you create the necessary mental conditions to take a fresh, creative look at problems, and you keep open the chance to make a creative contribution. Second, recognize that all interesting business problems have many dimensions and that the same problem can be viewed from different perspectives.

Technology perspective
A way of viewing a problem that emphasizes information technology hardware, software, telecommunications, and database as sources of business problems and the ways in which they can contribute to a solution.

Organization perspective
A way of viewing a problem that emphasizes the firm's formal rules and procedures, production process, management, politics, bureaucracy, and culture as sources of its problems and the ways in which they can contribute to a solution.

People perspective
A way of viewing a problem that emphasizes the firm's employees as individuals and their interrelationships as sources of its problems and the ways in which they can contribute to a solution.

In this text we have emphasized the usefulness of three perspectives on business problems: technology, organizations, and people. Within each of these very broad perspectives are many subperspectives or views. The **technology perspective,** for instance, includes a consideration of a firm's hardware, software, telecommunications, and database. The **organization perspective** includes a consideration of a firm's formal rules and procedures, culture, management, business processes, and politics. The **people perspective** includes consideration of the firm's employees as individuals and their interrelationships in work groups.

You will have to decide for yourself which major perspectives are useful for viewing a given problem. The ultimate criterion here is usefulness: Does adopting a certain perspective tell you something more about the problem that is useful for solving the problem? If not, reject that perspective as being not meaningful in this situation, and look for other perspectives.

The third element of critical thinking involves testing alternatives, or model solutions to problems, letting experience be the guide. Not all contingencies can be known in advance, and much can be learned through experience. The story of Perfect Courier, described in the Focus on Organizations,

FOCUS ON ORGANIZATIONS

PERFECT COURIER SUCCEEDS BY TRIAL AND ERROR

Perfect Courier, recognized three times as one of *Inc.* magazine's top 500 companies, started out in 1979 in the messenger-service business. It was a highly competitive industry with between 300 and 400 messenger companies in New York City alone. The only way Perfect Courier could make sales was by lowering its prices—to the point where the company couldn't survive.

One day, Norm Brodsky, the company's owner, was pitching its service to the manager of a large advertising agency called Scali-McCabe Sloves. The agency wasn't very receptive until Brodsky found out that it had trouble matching up its delivery bills with its customers. Scali-McCabe charged the cost of a delivery back to the client on whose behalf it was made. Whenever people from the agency called for a messenger, they were supposed to provide an account code to note on the delivery ticket. The messenger company then batched delivery tickets together and included them with the bill it sent to the agency. The agency's accounting department had to sort out the tickets and calculate the total charges for each account.

Perfect Courier volunteered to use its IBM-32 computer to solve the problem for the agency. It created a prototype bill by hand from 50 delivery tickets with the individual charges grouped according to the agency's account codes. Brodsky's staff designed about 20 versions on their typewriter before they were satisfied. Scali-McCabe was delighted. Brodsky's programmers then wrote software to program the company's computer to produce the bills. Perfect Courier won the Scali-McCabe account, boosting sales from $10,000 to $35,000 a month.

The new billing system became Perfect Courier's competitive advantage. It was one thing they had that rival messenger firms couldn't offer. By the time the others caught up, Perfect Courier had a foothold in the market and a reputation for providing that service. The company used this additional service to redefine its business. It determined who its customers were, how much Perfect Courier could charge, and how it went about selling. Technically, it was still a messenger company, but what it really sold was its ability to use information systems to solve clients' chargeback problems. To solve the problem of how to survive and prosper, Perfect Courier had become a different company.

FOCUS Question: Describe how Perfect Courier used the problem-solving process to develop a successful business.

SOURCE: Norm Brodsky, "A Niche in Time," *Inc.,* February 1997.

is a good example of how a firm may have to test several alternatives before it arrives at a solution.

Perfect Courier ended up with quite a different solution than it originally anticipated. Not all organizations have to redefine themselves to solve their problems as Perfect Courier had to do, but solutions often require companies to be flexible and open minded.

The fourth and final element of critical thinking involves an awareness of the limits on the human and organizational resources at your command. Remember, there is a difference between what an organization "should do" and what it "can do." And there is a difference between an "optimal" solution and a "satisfactory" solution. Some solutions may be so expensive that the organization would go bankrupt if it adopted them (creating a whole new set of problems). An awareness of the feasibility of a solution—whether it is actually doable—will not only help you choose the right solution to problems, but will also help you save time and money by avoiding solutions that are beyond your organization's resources.

9.2 A FIVE-STEP MODEL OF PROBLEM SOLVING

As we noted in Figure 9.1, real-world decision making can be summarized in a simple five-stage model of problem solving that is applicable to personal problems as well as to business decisions. In the world of information systems, the first three stages are usually called systems analysis, and the last two stages are called systems design. Thus, "systems analysis and design" is another term for problem solving.

STEP 1: PROBLEM ANALYSIS

Problem analysis is somewhat analogous to "ball parking"—that is, estimating the dimensions of a problem. The most important question answered in this step is, "What kind of problem is it?"

Lantech Inc., a manufacturer of industrial packaging equipment, discovered this when it set out to increase its sales. The Lantech plant assembles machines that stretch plastic wrap around items so that they are held together as a single package. Lantech's standard response to competitive pressures was to install ever more powerful computers to accelerate the mass production process. But in 1989 Lantech lost a key design patent and its lead in the wrapping-machine market. New competitors entered the field with aggressive pricing tactics.

What kind of problem did Lantech have? Was it a people or labor problem related to poor worker attitudes or poor training? Was it a technology problem that more powerful computers could solve? Or was it an organizational problem related to outdated procedures? Pat Lancaster, Lantech's founder and chairman, decided that the problem was not one of insufficient technology but one of organizational procedures. Lantech had organized its work around traditional mass production methods, where division of labor requires workers to toil away at a single task.

Lancaster decided to adopt the Japanese-style system of "lean production," based on generalization of labor, where workers are organized into integrated teams that oversee the entire production process from start to finish. Productivity is achieved not by reducing costs per part but by lowering costs for the production cycle as a whole, from design to manufacture to sales.

Lantech teams redesigned every aspect of its production process. The company replaced its "hurry up and wait" pattern, in which inventory was moved in batches from one part of the factory to another, to a system where production cells are responsible for all of the processes—sawing, welding, electrical wiring—that were once spread throughout the factory. The new production process cut down on excess inventory and production delays because it made it possible for each component moving through production to correspond to a specific customer order. Under the old system, Lantech produced parts in lots and batches specified by projections.

Lantech backed away from computer technology because it was too expensive to redesign its information systems to support lean production methods. Many of Lantech's procedures are now manual. Managers use simple visual aids such as strips of tape to show the direction of production flow or cue cards to signal when to order new supplies. Since changing its procedures, Lantech's productivity has risen almost 100 percent and production defects have been cut in half. The company can complete orders in 12 hours instead of five weeks and is competitive once again.[2]

STEP 2: PROBLEM UNDERSTANDING

What causes the problem? Why is it still around? Why wasn't it solved long ago? These are some of the questions that must be asked in the second step of problem solving. Finding the answers involves some detailed detective work, some fact gathering, and some history writing. Facts may be gathered through personal interviews with people involved in the problem, analysis of quantitative and written documents, or attitude questionnaires. Generally, the more different kinds of data you have, the better understanding you will achieve.

At the end of this second step, you should be able to give a rather precise, brief account of what the problem is, how it was caused, and which major factors are sustaining it.

STEP 3: DECISION MAKING

Once a problem is analyzed and a sense of understanding is developed, it is possible to make some decisions about what should and can be done. We emphasize these two aspects of decision making because they are quite different.

What should be done has to do with objectives; these are the goals that the business hopes to attain. Is the firm's objective short-term profit maximization, intermediate-term growth, or long-term survival? Sometimes, to

Interviews and surveys can be used to gather facts about a problem or to verify satisfaction.

SOURCE: © Owen Franken, Stock, Boston.

your surprise, you may find out that no one has ever asked that question. It is your job to understand precisely what the firm's objectives are.

Second, whatever the firm's objectives may be, it has resources to pursue only selected options. Your job is to understand what can be feasibly done within the resources of the business. Generally, a business cannot hire a whole new labor force, develop new products overnight, or enter entire new markets in the short run. All these may be things the firm should do but cannot do in the short run because of resource limits.

STEP 4: SOLUTIONS DESIGN

Most people think that once a decision is made to pursue a given option, the process is over. Actually, only the beginning is over. Solutions have to be designed and planned. In the process, the solutions will continue to be modified and changed. As we describe in Section 9.5, a design may be logical or physical. In a **logical design,** the general level of resources, the general operational process, and the nature of outputs that the solution should require are described. A **physical design** involves a more detailed description of equipment, buildings, personnel, and inventories than the logical design provides.

Logical design
The part of a solutions design that provides a description of the general level of resources, the operational process, and the nature of outputs that the solution should require; it describes what the solution will do, not how it will physically work.

Physical design
The part of a solutions design that translates the abstract logical system model into specifications for equipment, hardware, software, and other physical resources.

STEP 5: IMPLEMENTATION

Once a solution is designed, the last step in problem solving is implementation. The world's best solutions do not implement themselves. Virtually all real-world business solutions require a planned implementation strategy in order to work properly. You will have to consider when and how to introduce the solution, how to explain the solution to your employees, how to modify the planned solution to account for field experience, how to change existing business procedures so the solution can work, and how to evaluate the solution so you know it is working.

Figure 9.2 summarizes the five-step model of business problem solving described here. It is a very general model that can be used in a variety of business or personal settings. But we also need to be more specific in describing the problems businesses typically face. In the next section, we look at the first two steps and three major sources of business problems and their related solutions. In the next chapter, we describe logical and physical designs of solutions and illustrate some charting tools used to depict solutions graphically.

When this problem-solving methodology is applied specifically to information system-related problems, it is called systems analysis and design. **Systems analysis** is the study and analysis of problems of existing information systems; it involves both identifying the organization's objectives and determining what must be done to solve its problems. While systems analysis shows what the problems are and what has to be done about them, **systems design** shows how this should be realized. The systems design is the model or blueprint for an information system solution that shows in detail how the technical (hardware, software), organizational (procedures, data), and people (training, end-user interfaces) components will fit together. Sometimes a problem will not require an information system solution but an adjustment in management or existing procedures. Even so, systems analysis may be required to arrive at the proper solution.

Systems analysis
The study and analysis of problems of existing information systems; it includes identifying both the organization's objectives and its requirements for the solution of the problems.

Systems design
A model or blueprint for an information system solution to a problem; it shows in detail how the technical, organizational, and people components of the system will fit together.

FIGURE 9.2

Systems Analysis and Design

Systems analysis includes the first three stages in our five-step model, during which we identify the problem, gather information about it, and make a decision about the best solution. The final two steps encompass systems design: designing the logical and physical specifications of the solution and implementing this solution. Feedback from each step, and from the postimplementation evaluation, helps us judge the effectiveness of the solution.

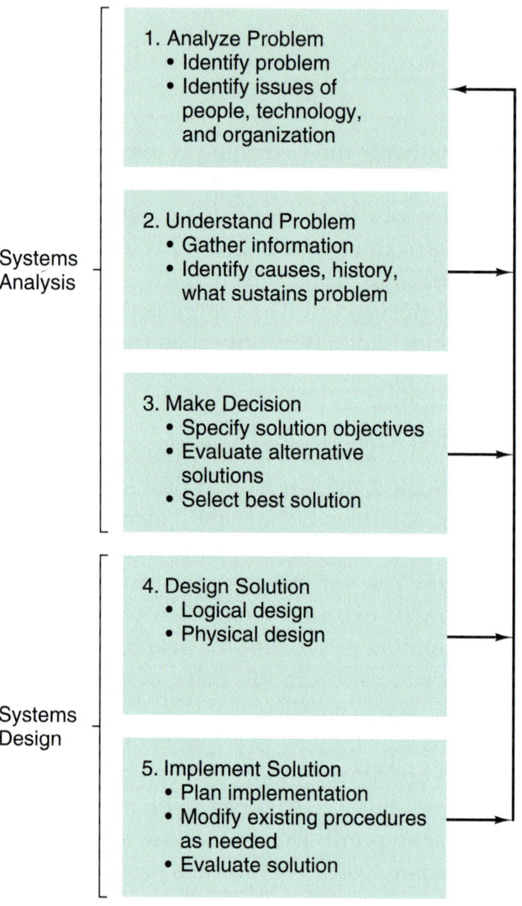

9.3 TYPICAL BUSINESS PROBLEMS: ANALYSIS AND UNDERSTANDING

We have suggested throughout this book that all problems (and solutions) can be seen as some combination of technology, organization, and people issues. These three perspectives can be applied throughout the problem-solving process. They are especially helpful in the first two steps of problem solving—problem analysis (what kind of problem are we facing?) and problem understanding (where did the problem come from and why does it persist?)—but they can be valuable in the decision-making and implementation steps.

Table 9.1 shows the matrix of perspectives we use throughout the book to guide the problem-solving process and lists the real-world examples in this chapter along with the particular perspective each illustrates.

TECHNOLOGY PERSPECTIVES

Problems—and solutions—are rarely technology problems *per se.* However, information technology is often one of the major sources of organizational problems. There are several kinds of technology problems, as shown in Figure 9.3. In general, when problem solving, you should ask yourself, "What changes in information technology hardware, software, telecommunications, and database are required to solve this problem?"

For all types of technology, the most common hardware problems are capacity, compatibility, and change. You can usually tell when computer capacity is exceeded by looking at response time: When response times approach 30 seconds to a minute, you know a capacity problem exists. Expanding capacity is not as simple as it sounds. Often, a firm will want to change from one generation of computer to another to take advantage of new technology. But this may necessitate a change in software. What begins as a simple hardware upgrade may eventually require an expensive rewriting of all the organization's software. Compatibility issues must be considered as well: Will the new computer be compatible with all the older computers and related equipment, such as printers and communication networks?

The experience of Credit Suisse First Boston Corp. is typical. Its old mainframe computer could not handle the company's rapidly expanding computational needs. This multibillion-dollar securities business required a system that could handle in eight hours more than 1,000 transactions linking traders representing companies waiting to sell short-term securities with

TABLE 9.1

Problem-Solving Perspectives and Examples in This Chapter That Illustrate Them

Perspective	Example
Technology	
Hardware	Credit Suisse First Boston
Software	TSI
Telecommunications	
Database	
Organization	
Culture	Aeroflot
Management	Aeroflot, Lantech
Politics	Aeroflot
Bureaucracy	Aeroflot, Lantech
Resources	Aeroflot, Perfect Courier, TSI
Turbulence	Aeroflot, Lantech
Complexity	
People	
Ergonomics	
Evaluation and Monitoring	
Training	
Employee Attitudes and Involvement	Aeroflot
Legal and Regulatory Compliance	

FIGURE 9.3

Looking at Problems from a Technology Perspective

Information technology can often contribute to organizational problems. The most common technology issues are capacity (is the system overloaded?), compatibility (can the system's various components "talk" to each other?), and change (is the system still meeting organizational needs?). These issues affect hardware, software, databases, and telecommunications. It is wise to look at all of these aspects before ruling out technical problems.

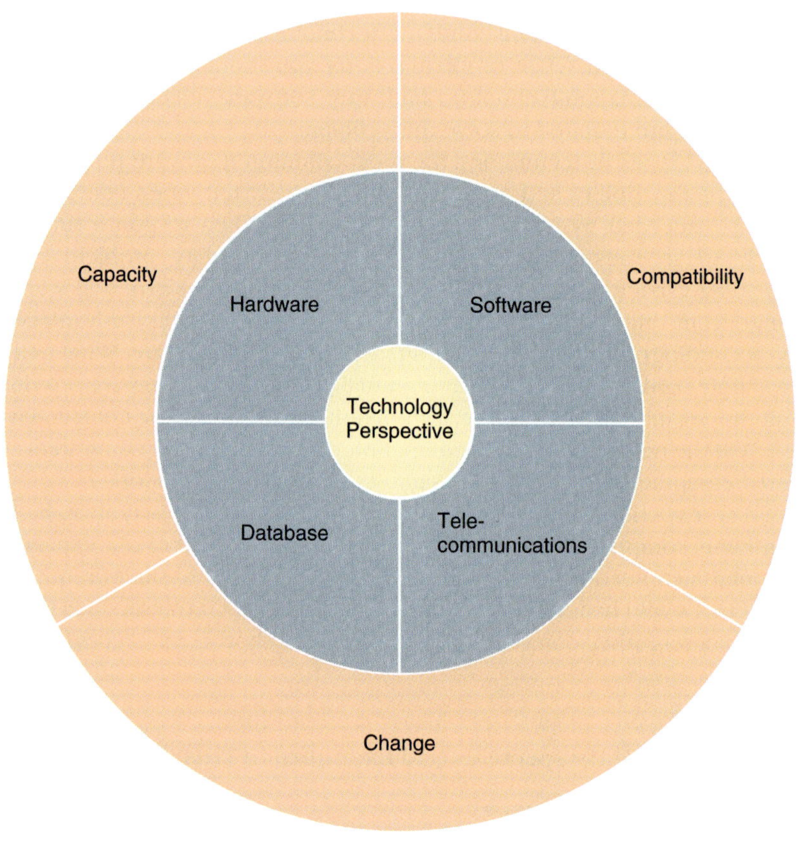

salespeople who sell them to investors. It took several minutes to over half an hour to assemble a list of offerings from a trader to investors. Only a few users could access the old system at one time; otherwise, the system would slow to a crawl. The slow computer performance was bad for business. Investors were frustrated because it took too long for them to buy what they wanted. Traders lost money because they could complete only a limited number of transactions and sales.

To alleviate these problems, Credit Suisse First Boston replaced its worn-out mainframe system with a new client/server application called CP-Trade that runs on a Sun server networked to Sun workstations. The new system, which can generate a list of 50 offerings of interest to an investor in half a second, will help First Boston increase its securities business, since sales staff can assist seven investors in the time it previously took them to help just one. Service for each customer has markedly improved.

Credit Suisse First Boston is creating other client/server applications, which have further reduced its dependence on mainframes. The company was able to retire one of its mainframes in its Princeton, New Jersey, computer center by distributing processing to servers and workstations.[3]

Software often presents a problem when an organization wants to do something new or to accomplish traditional tasks in a new way. Existing software will have to be replaced with new software when the organization changes, develops new products, institutes new organizational structures, or initiates new procedures.

The most common software issues involve the creation of interfaces with existing software, management of cost and projects, and personnel. Organizations build large libraries of software applications over many years. New software typically will require inputs from the old software and may be required to output information to the old systems. Generally, software interfaces have to be built. This is a time-consuming, expensive, and difficult process. It is no secret that the typical software project is 50 to 100 percent over budget and behind schedule. What looks like a six-month project costing $200,000 can quickly turn into a year-long extravaganza costing $500,000 or more.

Part of the problem with the management of software projects involves personnel. Typically, organizations do not have in-house personnel trained in the techniques of building new software. Most of the existing staff is involved in maintaining the old software, not in writing new software. Hence, organizations must often hire outside consultants to write new software, and the outsiders may take many months to master the complexities of the organization.

Telecommunications has recently become a major source of problems for organizations because of the need to network large numbers of desktop computers and the desire to develop integrated systems that can link mainframes, minicomputers, and PCs into single networks. Typically, telecommunications issues involve standards (compatibility) and capacity planning.

Different brands of computers, such as Apple and IBM PCs, cannot easily exchange data or programs with each other, nor can PCs easily communicate with minicomputers or mainframes. Overcoming these incompatibilities and developing standards to link disparate pieces of hardware and software have posed major problems for organizations.

The Internet has solved some of these connectivity problems because it uses a networking standard that can link all types of computers. However, not all information system applications are appropriate for the Internet, so organizations using networks will continue to be faced with the standards problem.

Capacity planning remains a guessing game. It is extremely difficult to predict the demand on a communications network. Like improved highways that attract new traffic, when communications networks are made user friendly, the message traffic often skyrockets. The Focus on Technology in Chapter 10 describes how surging use is creating slowdowns on the Internet.

A final technology area that causes problems for organizations is the database. A firm often learns that it has a database problem when it discovers that needed information is located somewhere in the organization's computers but cannot easily be found or used. A second indicator of a database problem is an inability to write new software because the organization has no central repository or library showing what information is stored and where it is located.

ONE STEP AT A TIME

Tom Smith bought his company, a molder of thermoplastic material based in Englewood, Ohio, in 1981. He lasted until 1989 before he finally gave in to acquiring more modern technology. Until that time, Smith ran an old-fashioned, and marginally efficient, ship. It produced massive quantities of predesigned molded plastic products with what amounted to a cookie-cutter process. The advantage to operating in this manner was that Tom Smith Industries (TSI) could easily beat its competitors' bids for contracts. However, the downside to producing millions of units at a reasonable cost was that the products returned only a moderate profit. While the company certainly was not floundering, it by no means flourished. The profit margins on its products were just too low.

In order to ensure profitable longevity for his company, Smith decided to change TSI's orientation. Smith, who holds an electrical engineering degree, reasoned that TSI could take over some of the design and engineering responsibilities from its clients. He could pool his knowledge of engineering and plastics to help manufacturers substitute plastic parts for more expensive metal ones. It was an ambitious plan, one that involved much more attention to detail and specialized work than had the previous incarnation of TSI. At the same time, it would give TSI an undeniable advantage over its competitors in the molding business, in effect creating a new class of operation. Thus began Tom Smith's quest for information systems technology.

From the very beginning, TSI approached computer technology cautiously. The company's first attempt at automating its internal-management systems failed because the chosen software did not mesh with the company's established business practices. For example, the billing department could not use the system to calculate price breaks for large orders—those still had to be figured manually. In 1992, Smith purchased an IBM AS/400 minicomputer to run a manufacturing resource planning (MRP) system to integrate the company's major administrative tasks. The manufacturing resource planning software reduced duplicate effort by allowing staff members in different de-

Frequently, organizations inherit outmoded file structures that cannot adequately meet contemporary demands. Sometimes, organizations have thousands of application files but no real integrated database. Other organizations may have an integrated database, but it is an older hierarchical system that cannot easily be changed.

Solutions to these database problems are expensive. Typically, the database has to be completely redesigned. This requires a major and fundamental software effort.

Although technology problems are usually not the sole cause of an organization's difficulties, and they certainly are not the only solution, information technology is increasingly playing a larger role in problem solution. In large part, this is because what organizations want to do in terms of new products, new methods of manufacture, new organizational designs, and new methods of product delivery often directly involves information technology. But you should remember that information technology is only the servant of larger organizational purposes and issues.

Solutions requiring technology need not necessarily use the most leading-edge system that is available. The technology selected should be one that is appropriate for the organization and for the nature of the problem to be solved. The Focus on Technology reinforces this point.

partments (billing, production scheduling, and shipping) to refer to the same order information in a single database. A PC linked to customers receives their orders and sends back information on shipping and billing. The orders received by the PC are keyed into the AS/400, which produces work orders for the manufacturing department, setting in motion processes for purchasing raw materials, scheduling for pressing, and billing once the order is shipped. If production falls behind schedule anywhere along the line, the system issues an alert. If a delivery date needs to be changed, the system reworks the schedule. It can even run simulations to determine how the completion of other orders will be affected by the change. Because the system eliminates tasks such as redundant data entry and paper processing, it reduces the possibility of error.

The technology TSI uses is far from state-of-the-art. The company operates only eight PCs, and its AS/400 minicomputer centralizes computing tasks—an older approach compared with what's possible using client/server computing. Smith, though, feels no need to rush out to buy the latest technology. His PCs still operate on Windows 3.1, even though some might consider it antiquated. Many of TSI's customers still use programs that will not run properly on Windows 95. They would not be able to exchange engineering and administrative files if Smith moved to the newer operating system. Smith views not upgrading too fast as simply a wise business decision. The company has been introducing computer-aided design (CAD) software and computer-driven metal-cutting tools gradually, letting its tool designers and machinists figure out on their own how they want to use the new technology. The technology he has implemented has enhanced his business, but has not taken it over. The combination of patient growth and continued precision in manual functions has led to much success. TSI's design and production capabilities have earned it contracts with five major auto manufacturers, and Smith is now looking to expand his company by absorbing others.

FOCUS Questions: What problems might the gradual installation of an information system cause an organization? What problems might it solve?

SOURCE: Jeffrey Zygmont, "When Slow and Steady Wins the Race," *Inc. Technology,* 1996, No. 4.

ORGANIZATIONAL PERSPECTIVES

As Figure 9.4 shows, the organizational perspective on problem solving can be divided into internal institutional areas and external environmental areas (see Chapter 2). Let's look at some internal sources of problems first.

Internal Institutional Perspectives At the most general level, organizational problems should be related to an organization's culture, management, policies, and bureaucracy. Organizational culture refers to the rarely questioned bedrock assumptions and publicly espoused values that most members of the organization freely accept. For example, at Aeroflot it was simply assumed (until recently) that employees need not care about customer service. Job security was guaranteed. But times change, and old cultural assumptions often become outdated and even dangerous. When looking at an organization, you should ask, "Are the cultural assumptions of the organization still valid; that is, can the firm still survive by doing what it always did in the past?" Can the business survive with its traditional values, or are new public statements of its purpose needed?

How can an organization change its culture? Think again about Aeroflot. The answer is that cultures change over long periods of time, with great difficulty, and largely through experimentation. Strong leadership from both

FIGURE 9.4

Looking at Problems from an Organizational Perspective

The organizational perspective requires a multifaceted approach. Factors in the internal environment that can play a role include the organization's culture, management, company politics, and bureaucratic structure. Forces in the external environment must also be considered: resources that are available to the firm, the turbulence or rate of change in such important areas as technology and prices, and the complexity in inputs and products with which the firm must cope.

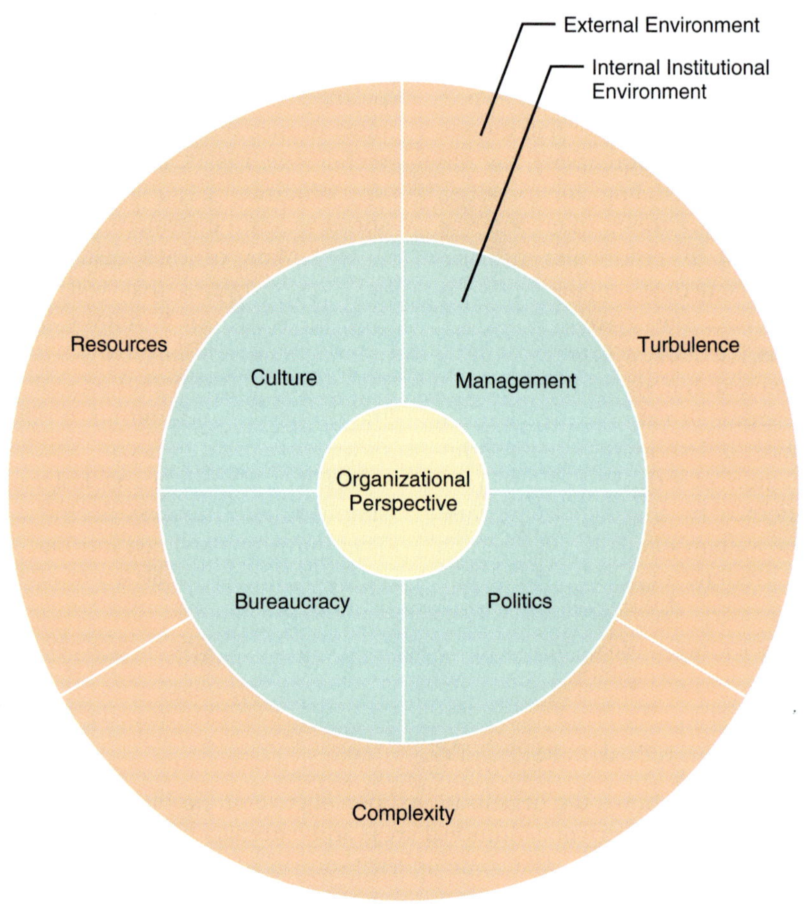

management and employees is required. Many businesses cannot survive extensive cultural changes.

Management is expected to both control the existing organization and guide it into the future. Management problems become obvious when unexpected events happen and the business seems out of control. For instance, when profits fall due to cost overruns on major products, you will know there is a management problem. And although all managements have a strategic plan that purports to guide the future activities of the organization (this is a skill taught in business school), not all plans work or are appropriate. Therefore, you should question strategic plans in terms of their ability to meet the challenges of a changing environment. When problem solving, ask

Aeroflot is struggling to remain competitive as a private company. Its problems can be analyzed using organization, technology, and people perspectives. Aeroflot needs to find a solution that can address all of these issues.

yourself, "Can this management team control the business and, in addition, adequately plan for the future?"

Whatever organizations in fact do is often the result of a political struggle among major organizational players. One of the questions to ask when problem solving in an organization is, "Will the political struggles in this organization impede the adoption of suitable solutions?" If the answer is yes, you will have to devise ways to change the political landscape or tilt the balance in the political competition. You will have to choose sides and work for the side you believe in.

A last, very broad feature to consider when problem solving is business bureaucracy. Bureaucracy simply refers to the fact that all successful, large organizations develop specialized subunits (structures) over time that do most of the work; these specialized units, in turn, develop finely tuned procedures to get the work done in an acceptable manner. These standard operating procedures are difficult to change. In general, whatever a large organization does is an output of its bureaucratic subunits and their standard operating procedures.

When problem solving, you should ask yourself, "Are changes in bureaucratic structure or procedure required in order to solve the problem?" If the answer is yes, you will have to develop new, highly trained specialized groups to accomplish the solution and new bureaucratic procedures. The example of Lantech illustrates how changes in procedure can do wonders.

External Environment Once you have examined these internal organizational issues, you should look further at the external constraints facing an organization. The most powerful environmental dimensions are resources, turbulence, and complexity.

All businesses need financial, political, cultural, and other resources from the environment. Some environments are rich with support for certain business firms but poor for other firms. For instance, the proliferation of dual-career families in the United States has created a rich environment for fast-food restaurants, take-out stores, and other service businesses. A rich environment does not guarantee success, but poorly managed firms may be able to survive in a rich, forgiving environment.

When you examine an organization in trouble and are looking for solutions, you should ask, "Is this firm in a rich or poor environment? Is its market growing or declining?" Often firms fall into financial difficulty not simply because they are poorly managed but because they are in declining markets and have failed to identify areas of growth in which to invest. Obviously, if a firm is starved for funds, the solutions it ultimately chooses will have to be inexpensive and will have to show a return on investment in the very short run (one year). In a cash-rich environment, a firm has many more options and can afford to take a longer-term view (three to five years).

Turbulence refers to rates of environmental change in such areas as production technologies, sales, and prices. While computer manufacturers in general have benefited from expanding demand for their products (resource richness), they have been subject to incredible change in production technologies—that is, a turbulent environment. One result is a high level of failure among computer manufacturers. Having become competent in one set of production technologies, most firms find it difficult to adopt new techniques. Young, new firms built around the new technologies quickly rise to dominate older firms.

When you examine a problem at an organization, ask yourself, "Is this problem related in any way to broad environmental changes in production technology, sales, or prices?" If the answer is yes, you will have to consider ways in which the organization might respond.

Complexity refers to the number of inputs and products that a firm has as well as the geographical diversity of its production. Firms operating in a complex environment have many suppliers, a vast array of products, and widely distributed production facilities. The automobile industry and the petrochemical industry are typically identified as complex: They have a large number of suppliers, widely distributed production facilities, and a vast array of products and niche markets. A chain of hamburger stands is marvelously uniform and not complex: A limited menu is served worldwide, and each store is a carbon copy of the others.

In complex industries, administrative overhead is high, and decision making is difficult. Complex firms tend to have very large bureaucracies, with layer upon layer of middle management whose job it is to control the complex organization. Profits and return on investment tend to be lower in complex industries than in "simpler" industries.

When you begin the analysis of an organization or seek better understanding, you should ask yourself, "To what extent are the problems visible here the result of a complex environment?" If environmental complexity is a problem, what solution might reduce that complexity?

PEOPLE PERSPECTIVES: STRATEGIC HUMAN RESOURCES ISSUES

One of the major findings of research on information systems in the past ten years is that systems frequently do not achieve hoped-for productivity gains because insufficient attention has been paid to the "people" perspective, or human resources issues. Because business organizations are made up of people, just about any problem in a business is a "people" problem. Research has identified five strategic human resources issues (see Figure 9.5). By "strategic" we mean simply those issues that must be accounted for or dealt with to assure success in problem solving.[4]

Ergonomics is the science of designing machines, operations, systems, and work environments in general so that they best meet the needs of the human beings involved and optimize economic returns. This broad field encompasses the study of the physical design of hardware and furniture, the design of jobs, health issues, and the user/software interface design (e.g., the software logic and its presentation on the screen). Some typical ergonomic issues raised by information systems are VDT screen radiation and its potential to harm; the height of terminals above the floor, which can contribute to back strain and fatigue; the collection of too many (or too few) tasks into jobs, which can lead to fatigue and high absenteeism; and the way in which screens display information (software interface), which can also produce fatigue, monotony, and boredom. In addition, ergonomics has expanded its concerns to include the social psychology and physical results of screen

FIGURE 9.5

Looking at Problems from a People Perspective: Strategic Human Resource Issues

Five key areas are especially important for identifying problems related to people in an organization. They are ergonomics, or the design of effective work environments to meet the needs of the human beings involved; evaluating and monitoring employees' work, which can backfire because it creates pressure and resentment; training employees, which is vital but all too often ignored; employee involvement, a controversial issue in many firms that can affect productivity; and legal and regulatory compliance, or assuring that the organization protects its employees' legal rights.

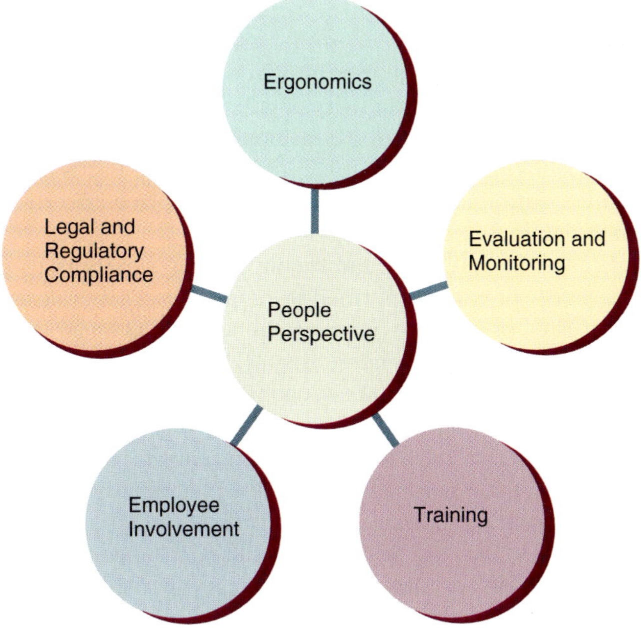

FIGURE 9.6

Some Physical Ergonomic Considerations in Designing a Computer System

Making computer systems more comfortable to use pays off in higher employee morale and productivity and lower absenteeism. Such features as screen angle, viewing angle, and viewing distance can make the difference between comfortable viewing and eye strain. The correct knee angle, seat back angle, and back support can greatly reduce the possibility of back strain.

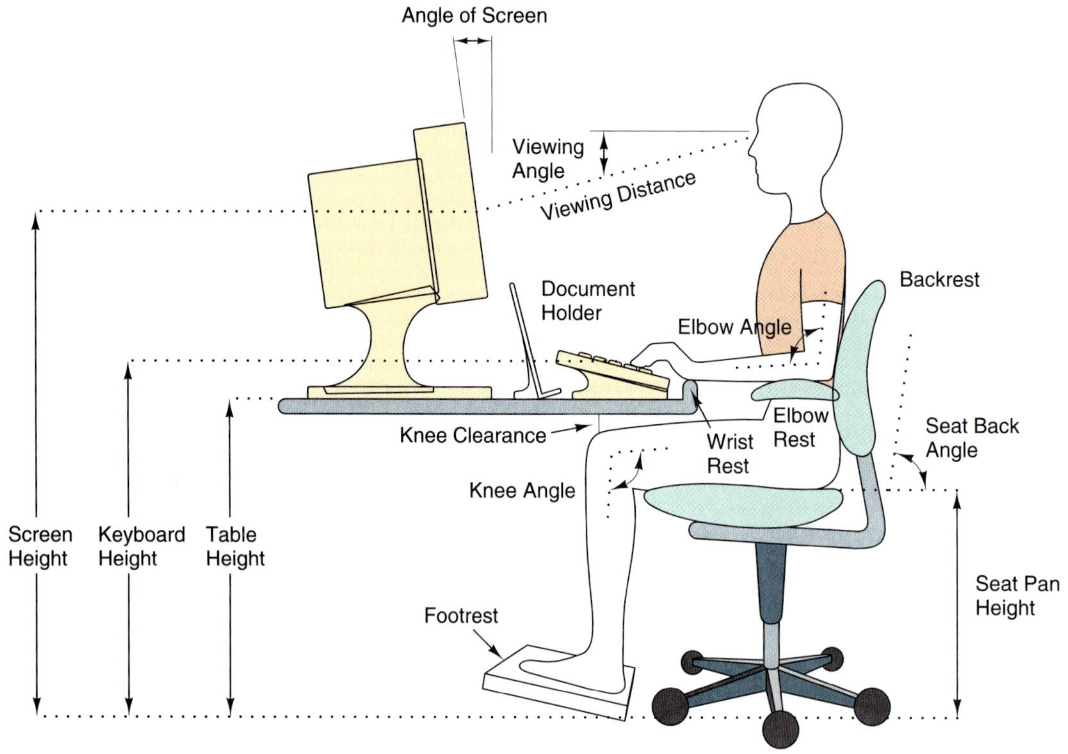

design and software design. The user interface that the software creates has an important effect on the productivity of information technology. Figure 9.6 illustrates many of the physical relationships that have to be taken into account when designing human-machine interfaces. The Focus on People explores whether commercial products in the marketplace effectively address these ergonomic issues.

All jobs involve evaluation and monitoring by superiors to gauge the quality and quantity of work performed by employees. This evaluation can be fair and unobtrusive, or it can be perceived by workers as unfair and intrusive. Computers permit much closer monitoring of the output of workers than the traditional means of monitoring and evaluating work, but they may be resented by workers. Computer monitoring may at first appear to be a "solution" to a productivity problem, but it can backfire into a human relations disaster.

It is obvious that training employees is a vital part of a successful human relations program. Training involves an investment of resources, however, and although many employers are willing to spend a great deal of money and time to ensure that employees are properly trained, many businesses and government agencies view formal training as an unnecessary expense. It is often the first budget to be cut when fortunes turn down.

Corporate chief executives learn how to use notebook computers in intensive training sessions at a technology "boot camp." Training is a key factor in successful information systems.

SOURCE: San Diego *Union Tribune*/ Charles Newman.

Inadequate training is a major source of information system failure, or at least disappointment.

Traditionally, American management has adopted a hostile attitude toward employee involvement, participation, and feedback. Since the turn of the century, a dominant attitude on the part of management has been that employees should follow orders, and if they disagree, they should resign. With very few exceptions, employment law allows employers great discretion in determining whom to hire, how the job will be done, and whom to terminate.

But these old attitudes are changing for many reasons. In a knowledge- and information-driven economy, skilled employees are in short supply and their views must be heeded. Hence, many managers are encouraging employee feedback, reducing the social distance between senior and middle management and promoting a family-like atmosphere. Still other managers have adopted Swedish- and European-style employee participation schemes in which employees operate in teams with less direct supervision. Finally, a number of federal and state laws have been enacted that have established a body of employee rights (described below).

When examining an organizational problem, you should ask yourself, "To what extent is this problem a result of poor employee attitudes related to lack of involvement, participation, and communication?" If this seems a problem, try to find solutions in this area.

A last human resources issue to consider is legal and regulatory compliance. Because the American public is concerned about the welfare of all working people, since the 1930s both the federal government and most states have enacted legislation establishing a number of employee rights. The following are the most important:

- The right to join a union.
- The right to "no fault" worker compensation for injury on the job.

FOCUS ON PEOPLE

ERGONOMIC PRODUCTS: REAL SOLUTIONS OR COSTLY GIMMICKS?

As more and more individuals use computers in their work, vendors find there is money to be made in ergonomic products such as wrist rests, gloves, keypads, chairs, and software that cues users to stretch and tells them what stretches to do. But do these products really help computer users avoid injury or reduce pain?

Upper extremity disorders such as carpal tunnel disease (CTD) and repetitive stress injury (RSI) are on the rise. The increasing incidence of CTD and RSI are costly to organizations that must pay not only workers' compensation but also in other, less direct expenses such as overtime and training for individuals who must step in for the injured worker.

But "at least 90 percent" of the vendors of ergonomic products have no objective scientific proof to support claims that their products will help, according to Michael Gauf, co-owner of the *CTD News,* a Haverford, Pennsylvania, monthly newsletter that tracks upper extremity disorder issues. Much of the available research is funded by the vendors themselves, Gauf says, thereby reducing credibility. In addition, "Some products are certified as ergonomically correct by manufacturers themselves," says Bill Yeazrian, a volunteer at Compensation Alert, a non-profit organization in Santa Rosa, California, that assists injured workers.

Part of the problem is that the market is so new, there is no stan-

An ergonomically designed keyboard may help reduce or eliminate some computer-related work disorders.

SOURCE: Courtesy of Alps Electric.

- The right to equal employment opportunity regardless of race, gender, or ethnicity.
- The right to a safe and healthy workplace.
- The right to have a pension and to have it protected.
- The right to freedom from reprisal for reporting violations of federal public-protection laws.
- The right of access to selected management information concerning toxic chemicals in the workplace.

dard set for ergonomic products. Since vendors aren't promising cures for existing conditions, they don't need approval from the Food and Drug Administration.

Some say the industry doesn't want a standard put in place. Many in the RSI-support community contend that big business lobbied Congress to kill a national ergonomics standard that the Occupational Safety and Health Administration (OSHA) tried to introduce in 1995. But others, such as Richard Marklin, an assistant professor in the department of mechanical and industrial engineering at Marquette University in Milwaukee, think that OSHA's efforts to develop an ergonomic standard failed because there still isn't enough quantitative scientific data on which to base an industry standard.

Marklin and his colleague, Marquette assistant professor Guy Simoneau, are independently testing five keyboards with the help of a two-year grant from the National Institute for Occupational Safety and Health (NIOSH) to determine whether the keyboards let users hold wrists and forearms in a better posture than conventional keyboards do. But their study cannot determine whether using an alternative keyboard will prevent CTD and other upper extremity musculoskeletal disorders because the causes are still not fully understood.

Braces and supports, although employed by many computer users, are now considered more of a hindrance than a help, according to Kate Montgomery, a licensed holistic health practitioner in San Diego who specializes in treating CTD cases. Such products only stabilize the wrist, which further atrophies the muscles, she says, and when the supports are removed, the wrists hurt even more. Instead, Montgomery recommends stretching and strengthening the muscles after they are in proper alignment.

Correct posture is the key, according to Roger Dennis, a chiropractor and partner in the ergonomics consulting firm Robinson, Dennis & Associates in Ventura, California. Frances Pisano, corporate and ergonomics manager at Polaroid Corp. in Cambridge, Massachusetts, agrees. Polaroid has spent over three years developing an ergonomics program and now recommends three types of chairs that contribute to correct posture.

Both Dennis and Pisano also believe that combining regular stretching and strengthening with correct posture can be effective in avoiding upper extremity disorders. Add massage therapy, and even better results can be obtained, according to Carl Rood, health resources manager at Sauder Woodworking Co. In Archibold, Ohio. After instituting a preventive program, Sauder cut workers' compensation costs by 62 percent, from an average of nearly $700,000 annually between 1990 and 1992 to $265,000 a year between 1993 and 1995. "This is a maintenance program for our workers," says Rood. "People don't wait 'til their machinery breaks down before fixing it, but for years they've done that for workers, one of their most costly investments."

FOCUS Question:
To what extent can ergonomic problems in the workplace be solved?

SOURCE: Richard Adhikari, "Do Vendors Feel Your Pain?," *Ergonomics,* March 4, 1996.

Some states have also enacted laws that protect workers from arbitrary termination; under these laws, fired workers are entitled to a due process hearing.

These rights are often a source of organizational problems as well as part of the solution. The growth of information technology, the development of new systems, and their use by organizations have raised legal issues in health areas (as we explained earlier in the discussion of ergonomics), in matters related to employees' access to corporate information, and in the equal opportunity area. Briefly, the growth in management information made possible by computers has led employee groups and courts to subpoena information from the firm to support litigation against the firm. Women and minorities, for instance, who believe they have been discriminated against may demand that corporations release management and statistical information on employment practices. Likewise, workers who believe they have been illegally exposed to toxic chemicals can demand corporate management information on product composition, exposure levels, and internal reports. Employers cannot use the defense of claiming they did not or could not collect and analyze the information: Statutes and court decisions make clear that, in this information age, it is the responsibility of employers to maintain complete employee data for periods of up to 60 years.

Usually, it will be obvious if legal and regulatory issues are a cause of the problems facing an organization. Generally, unions or groups of employees bring suits against the corporation for alleged violations of rights. Rather than waiting for suits to arise, however, wise managers periodically review their organization's compliance with existing regulations.

If employees were fearful of using VDTs, how could you resolve some of their fears? If employees believed they had been unfairly compensated for their work with information systems, how could you address this concern? If minorities and women claimed that they were unfairly relegated to low-level data entry jobs or were not receiving promotions as rapidly as others, how could you address their complaints?

9.4 PROBLEM SOLVING: MAKING DECISIONS

If you have done a good job of analysis and understanding, the next step of the problem-solving process will be to choose among several alternative solutions. This should be a relatively simple process if you are properly prepared. What at first seemed like a hopelessly complex problem should at this point appear much clearer. The number of potential "solutions" or options should now be reduced to a manageable number—a few that stand some chance of working. In choosing among them, what criteria should be foremost? Figure 9.7 illustrates the three major steps involved in making a good decision.

ESTABLISH OBJECTIVES

The process of establishing objectives may be the most complicated part of decision making if only because many people in a firm have different perspectives. Nevertheless, in a firm, objectives must be carefully chosen and agreed on in a group process; otherwise, people will not be committed to a common course of action. One way to begin is to consider the overall corporate objectives as well as the major divisional or subunit objectives. The following might be a firm's overall corporate goals:

- Long-term survival.
- Meeting a competitive challenge at any cost.
- Improving productivity.
- Increasing employee morale and loyalty.

FIGURE 9.7

What's Involved in Step Three: Making Decisions

To make an effective decision, first be sure that everyone agrees on the organization's objectives, both the broad corporate goals and the more focused subunit goals. Then determine the feasibility of each proposed solution, considering both internal and external constraints. Perform a cost-benefit analysis to determine the most appropriate solution for your firm. Remember to consider intangible benefits as well as tangible gains.

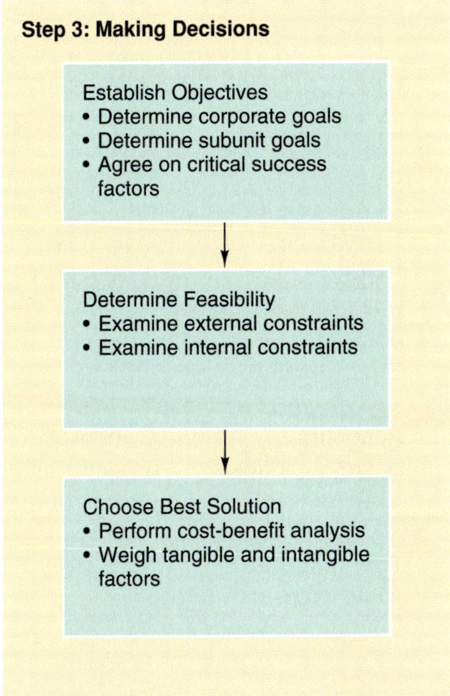

Step 3: Making Decisions
Establish Objectives
• Determine corporate goals
• Determine subunit goals
• Agree on critical success factors
Determine Feasibility
• Examine external constraints
• Examine internal constraints
Choose Best Solution
• Perform cost-benefit analysis
• Weigh tangible and intangible factors

Subunit goals might include the following:

- The introduction of new products.
- More effective marketing.
- Lower administrative costs.
- Lower manufacturing costs.
- Better financing terms.

Because a firm can pursue several objectives, you may want to list the goals in order of importance or establish the critical success factors that are absolutely essential for the firm to attain.

It is very important that problem solvers agree on a time frame over which a solution can and should be put in place. This entails deciding whether a short-term solution (starting this week) or a long-term solution (a program that lasts for several years) is appropriate. Some solutions can be staged: A short-term emergency action can head off imminent disaster while a long-term program is undertaken.

PLANNING FOR THE WEB

Businesses are facing difficult decisions about how they will harness Web technology so that it will be most beneficial to them. With more and more at stake due to increased competition, creating a business-related Web site without first establishing well-defined goals is dangerous.

The person who organizes a company's Web goals and maintains them wears the title of business strategist. The business strategist first defines the company's Internet goals and ranks them in order of their importance to the company's mission. Then the business strategist creates a plan that promises early, basic success, allows for future growth of more complex projects, and never loses sight of the company's overall mission. Next, the business strategist selects an initial objective for the Web site. This step can prove complicated because the Web offers so many opportunities to different areas of the firm—sales and marketing, human resources, technical support. Various departments will undoubtedly view themselves as most fit to take advantage of the Web as a medium. Criteria that the strategist may consider in selecting one Web application over others include competitive forces, value to the company's operation, likelihood of financial payback, and time constraints. It is advised that the number of objectives be limited to three.

Sometimes the business strategist must consider more specific details. For example, a sales department would obviously want its company's Web site to exist for the purpose of online order transactions. That, however, would encompass other elements of the overall operation. If the inventory, order processing, and accounting systems do not have the capabilities to handle the added electronic activity, a significant amount of restructuring might have to be done just to accommodate the sales department's hopes.

Another problem that the business strategist must face involves budget constraints. While a company may provide a substantial budget for information technology or marketing, the piece of that budget earmarked for the Web may not be that generous. If the project has more than one focus, money problems can be a source of even greater strain.

Perhaps the greatest challenge to Web business plans emanates from the dynamic nature of the technology. Strategists can exert little control over an industry that changes so quickly at times that even highly skilled experts have difficulty keeping pace. It would be disastrous to incorporate technology into a Web project and then have it become obsolete. As it turns out, the best way to ground a Web business plan firmly is to create it with flexibility in mind. Therefore, maintenance of the plan and the site acquires at least as much importance as conception and implementation.

Technology is available to help Web strategists monitor how well their plans are being accomplished. Tracking and analysis tools can log and categorize all of the activity at a particular Web site to determine how many people are visiting the site and what they are interested in. The strategist can use this information to make adjustments in content, resource distribution, or any other strategic area.

The final key to establishing goals for conducting business on the Web is the person behind the business strategist title. The role has gained increased importance; managers occupy it with more and more frequency. Eventually, Web activities will likely be transformed from sideline business processes to core business processes, and the status of Web strategist will rise accordingly.

FOCUS Question:
What people, organization, and technology issues should be addressed when developing a Web business plan?

SOURCE: Matthew Cutler, "Goal Keepers," *WebMaster,* December 1996.

Setting objectives is essential for solutions based on the Internet as well as other information system technology. To take maximum advantage of the World Wide Web, organizations need to determine how their Web sites contribute toward their overall goals. The Focus on Problem Solving explores this topic.

ESTABLISH FEASIBILITY

By now the number of possible solutions should have been pared down to a handful of options. At this point, you must decide which of the remaining solutions are doable given your firm's resources. Here you should consider both the external and internal constraints on your organization.

As we noted earlier, external constraints include the following:

- Financial resources.
- Legal/regulatory demands.
- The action of competitors.
- Suppliers.
- Customers.

You must consider how each of the proposed solutions is affected by these factors. For instance, it may be financially feasible to install a network of personal computers in your customers' order rooms (thus assuring customers they have easy access to your products), but you may fear the reprisals of competitors, which may lead to an unending technology war for customers.

Internal constraints are equally important. Can the subunits in the organization carry out the solution? Is the solution compatible with your company's culture? Are there major opposition groups that will try to scuttle your solution?

CHOOSE COST-EFFECTIVE SOLUTIONS

In the end, you will be left with a very small number of realistic solutions. Realistic solutions are those that meet your firm's objectives and are feasible. The last question is, "What solution is best in a financial sense?" In other words, you must try to determine the **cost effectiveness** of a solution, or whether it is economical in terms of providing sufficient benefits for the cost.

Cost effectiveness
The degree to which benefits exceed costs; measured by cost-benefit analysis.

The answer to this question can be estimated by conducting a cost-benefit analysis. Cost-benefit analysis involves adding up all the costs of a project and dividing by all its benefits. You will arrive at a ratio of costs to benefits. Ideally, you should choose the option or solution that is the least costly for a given amount of benefit.

For instance, if you had two options, one that delivered $2.00 in benefit for each $1.00 in cost and the other that delivered only $1.50 in benefit for each $1.00 in cost, you would choose the first option.

But adding up all the costs and benefits of feasible solutions is not easy, especially with large projects. Many factors, such as "speed of decision making," cannot be assigned a monetary value. These factors are called intangible, as opposed to tangible, factors. If a bank can process a loan in one hour instead of in three days, how much is that "worth" to the bank in terms of increased loan activity from enthusiastic customers and decreased clerical cost? Here, only "guesstimates" can be obtained. But good guesses are usually better than no estimate at all.

9.5 PROBLEM SOLVING: DESIGNING SOLUTIONS

Just because you have arrived at a solution that has broad support in your organization does not mean you have "solved" the problem. Once you have arrived at a feasible option, you will have to design the solution. At first, in the problem-solving process, solutions and options are only vaguely understood, even though many organizational actors pretend they understand precisely what is involved. When you get down to the nuts and bolts of specific solutions, however, you almost always discover new aspects of the solution—and the problem.

A design is a detailed description of a proposed solution in the form of a document. The document includes both textual description and graphs, charts, lists, and figures. As we mentioned earlier, there are two aspects to the design document: logical and physical design (see Figure 9.8).

MAKING A LOGICAL DESIGN

The most critical steps in problem solving take place before the hardware or software for an application is considered. Unless the requirements for solving a problem are clearly understood beforehand, they can become obscured or even overshadowed by concerns with programming languages or hardware, and the result is an incorrect solution.

FIGURE 9.8

The Two Stages in Step Four: Designing Solutions

There are two parts to the process of designing a solution: creating a logical design and translating it into a physical design. The logical design phase comes first; it involves developing a conceptual model for the system showing what the system will do rather than how it will work. The physical design translates the logical model into design specifications for hardware, software, manual procedures, and other physical considerations.

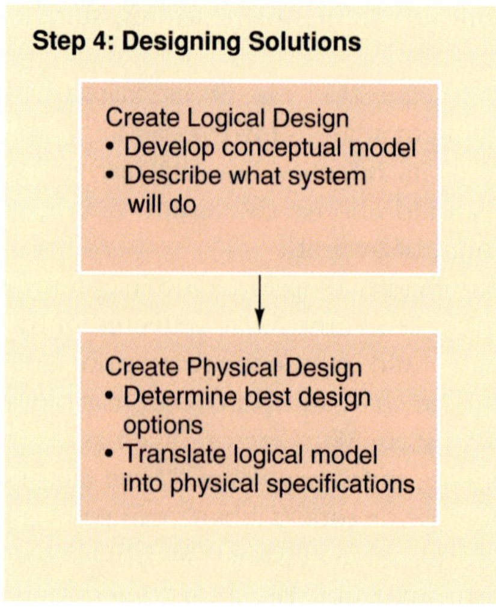

Therefore, in order to develop an information system application, a logical design, or model, of the proposed system is needed. This model must be built and understood in logical or conceptual terms before it can be translated into a specific, detailed system solution. The logical design presents the functional, or business, requirements of the proposed application solution as opposed to the technical requirements. It describes what the solution will do, not how it will work physically. The following are the basic components of a logical design (see Figure 9.9):

- **Outputs:** The information to be produced by the system. This includes reports, files, and online displays. The model must consider what pieces of output information are required and how they are to be organized and displayed.
- **Inputs:** The data required to be input into the system in order to create the desired output. The model must consider what pieces of data must be input and how they can best be arranged.
- **Processing:** The activities, both manual and automated, required to transform input data into output. The model must consider what kinds of decision rules, calculations, and modeling are required in order to perform the required manipulations on data.
- **Database:** The method of organizing and storing information in the system, through either computerized or manual means. The model must consider what pieces of data to store, when and how to update them, the relationships among them, and how they should be arranged.
- **Procedures:** The activities that must be performed by end users and operations staff to run and use the system. The model must consider manual activities required to produce the desired information, business policies, and rules governing these activities, as well as the sequence of the activities.
- **Controls:** The manual and automated processes and procedures that ensure that the system is accurate, secure, and performing as required. The model must consider tests and measures for ensuring that the information produced is accurate and secure.

These components may be arranged in a number of ways. In problems in which one alternative is an information system application, the application itself can have alternative design solutions.

Although it may seem rather easy to determine what outputs a system should have (e.g., what reports should be produced, what screens of information are needed, and the like), in many cases the users themselves do not know or are not very good at describing what they want from their software. On the other hand, people are quite definite in their desires and tastes once they see a product. Many companies have developed software development systems that permit software engineers to build a mock-up or model of the software product before actual programs are written. Users can critique the prototype before large investments are made, and the result is a more useful piece of software.

The process of logical design provides an opportunity to examine the way the organization itself works and to change management, jobs, and procedures to make it more efficient. Procedures may need to be streamlined, jobs rearranged, and functional areas combined to maximize the advantages

FIGURE 9.9

Scope of the Logical Design

The logical design is a document that specifies a system's functional business requirements. Input procedures must take into account the content, format, and source of the input data as well as the volume, frequency, and timing with which it enters the system. The design must also include controls to ensure the system's security, accuracy, and validity and must allow adequate supervision to maintain it on an ongoing basis. These logical considerations are independent of specific types of hardware and software.

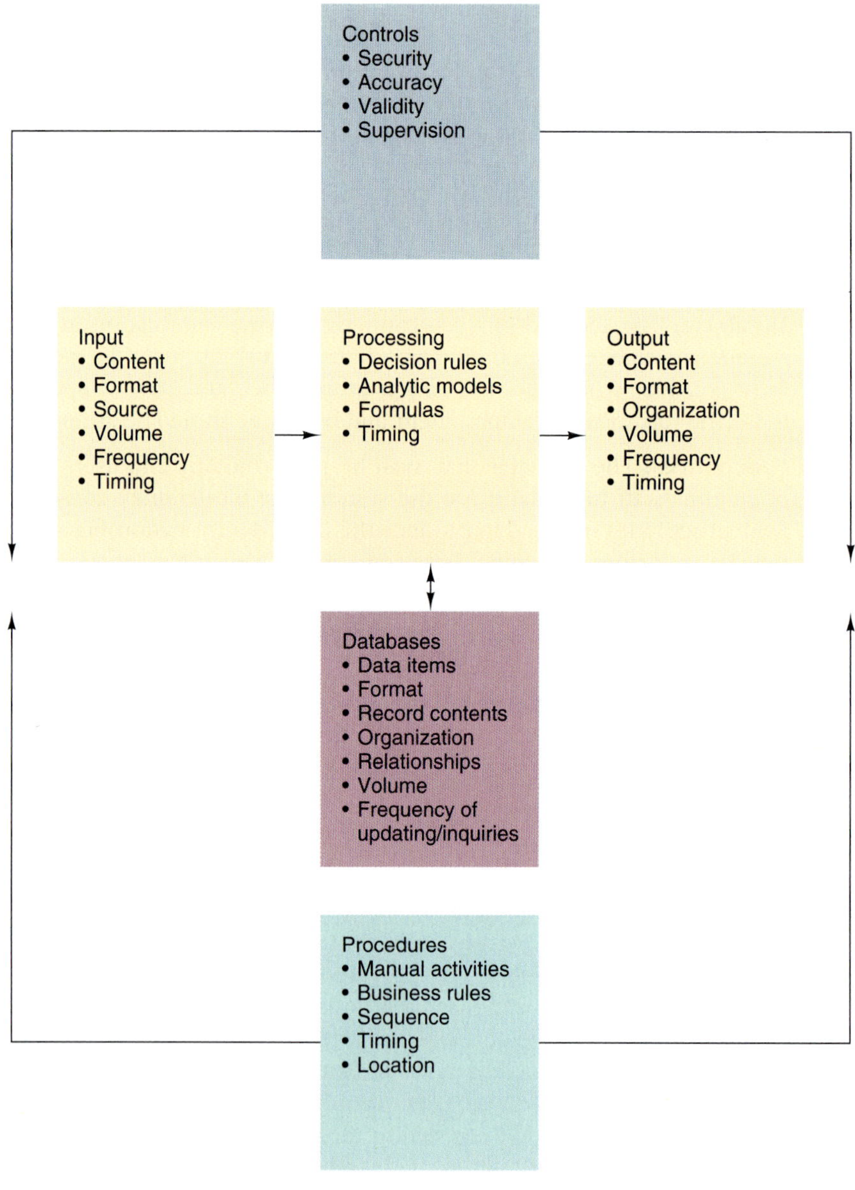

of computerization. Sometimes the best solution will call for only minor changes to procedures, but in many cases, more extensive organizational change will be required. Chapter 3 introduced the concept of reengineering, whereby an entire business process is redesigned to reorganize the flow of work, eliminate repetitive steps, cut waste, and consolidate job responsibilities. The solution may call for such reengineering—rethinking and redesigning the way an entire organizational process works (review Section 3.4).

MAKING A PHYSICAL DESIGN

During the physical design process, the abstract, logical system model is translated into specifications for hardware, software, processing logic, input/output methods and media, manual procedures, and controls. The following are some of the detailed specifications that must be addressed by physical design (see Figure 9.10):

FIGURE 9.10

Physical Design Specifications

There are many options for translating a logical design into a physical system. The physical design chooses among these possibilities to create the most effective design to meet business needs. Note that the physical design, like its logical counterpart, also includes specifications for procedures and controls.

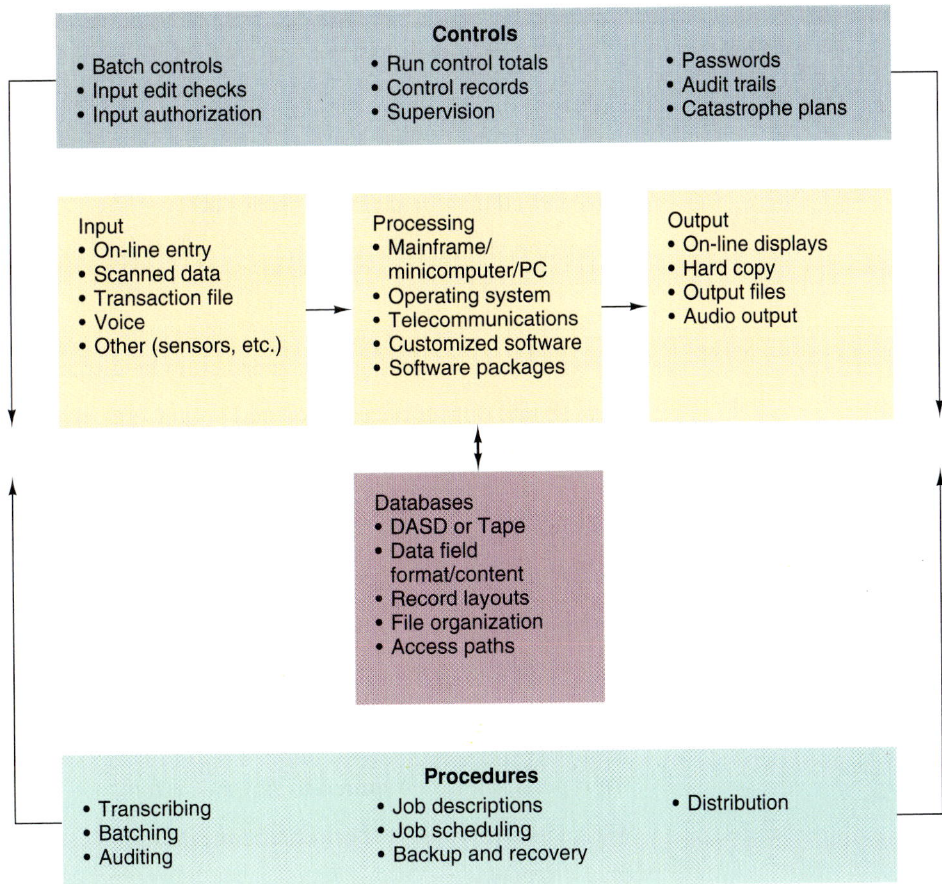

- **Databases:**

  What are the relationships among data items?

  What is the file and record layout?

  How much storage capacity is required?

  Through what path will data be accessed?

  How often will data be accessed or updated?

- **Software:**

  Is much complex logic required to transform input data into output?

  Do large files and lists need to be combined and manipulated?

  Does the application require modeling and mathematical formulas among interrelated pieces of data?

- **Hardware:**

  What hardware is already available?

  What processing power is required?

  Does the application require a special environment, such as a telecommunications network?

- **Input:**

  On what media should input data be collected?

  How should data be collected for input?

  How often should data be input?

- **Output:**

  On what media should output information be displayed?

  How should output be arranged and organized?

  How often should output be produced?

- **Controls:**

  What technology and procedures will make the system secure?

  How can the accuracy and integrity of data be ensured?

  How will the system be supervised?

- **Procedures:**

  What personnel are required to run the system?

  What activities must be performed for input, processing, and output?

  Where will these activities be performed?

As with the logical design, there may be physical design alternatives. Some applications could be implemented on a personal computer or a mainframe; with software packages or custom programs; on a traditional file or a database; and using online data entry through a keyboard or scanner. The physical design options are myriad. But clearly, the nature of the application plus the solution constraints will determine which design options are the most desirable.

9.6 PROBLEM SOLVING: IMPLEMENTING SOLUTIONS

In the final step of problem solving, the solution must be implemented. Often firms arrive at correct decisions, but their implementation is a failure. Effectively implementing solutions and decisions is a complex topic involving questions of psychology, organizational design, sociology, and finance. Here we present only a summary of the steps needed for effective implementation. (See Figure 9.11.)

STEPS IN THE IMPLEMENTATION OF A SYSTEM SOLUTION

If the problem called for an application solution, the following activities would be performed:

- **Software development:** Software would be developed to perform any processing that had to be automated. Custom programs might be written, or the software might be based on an application package, on a personal computer spreadsheet or database management system, or on a Web site design product.
- **Hardware selection and acquisition:** Appropriate hardware would be selected for the application and purchased if it was not immediately available.
- **Testing:** Each component of the system would be thoroughly tested to ensure that the system produced the right results. The testing process requires detailed testing of individual computer programs and of the entire system as a whole, including manual procedures. The process of testing each program in a system individually is called unit testing. System testing tests whether all the components of a system (program modules, hardware, and manual procedures) function together properly.
- **Training and documentation:** End users and technical specialists would be trained in using the new application. Detailed documentation generated during the development process for end users and technical systems specialists would be finalized for use in training and everyday operations. Without proper documentation, it would be impossible to run or use an information system. The importance of technical and user documentation cannot be overemphasized.

FIGURE 9.11

A Close-up of Step Five: Implementing Solutions

Four procedures make up the final step in the systems development process. First, we must develop software for the new system, whether it means writing totally new software or modifying existing programs. Second, we must select the right hardware to run the software we've written. In the testing phase, we run the programs and try out the hardware and manual procedures to ensure that everything is working properly. Finally, users must be trained to use the new system, and documentation must be written for it.

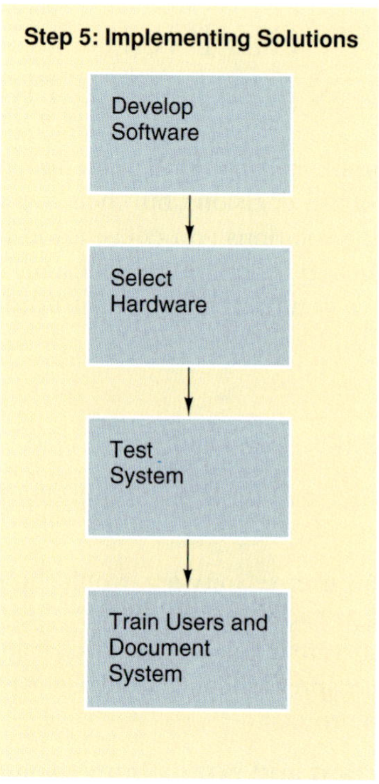

Conversion strategies
Plans and methods for changing from an old system to a new system; they include parallel conversion, direct cutover, pilot study, and the phased approach.

Parallel conversion
A conversion strategy in which the old system and the new system run in tandem until it is clear that the new system is working correctly.

CONVERSION STRATEGIES

A final matter to consider is the strategy used to convert from the old system to the new system. In complicated systems, this will involve changes in personnel, procedures, databases, processing, inputs, and outputs. Such changes cannot be accomplished overnight and must be planned carefully beforehand.

The following are the most important **conversion strategies:**

- **Parallel conversion:** The old system and the new system are run in tandem until it is clear that the new system works correctly. The old system can serve as a backup if errors are found, but additional work is required to run the extra system.

- **Direct cutover:** The old system is replaced entirely with the new system on an appointed day. This carries the risk that no system is available to fall back on if errors are discovered.
- **Pilot study:** The new system is introduced to a limited part of the organization, such as a single department. Once the pilot is considered safe, the system is installed in the rest of the organization.
- **Phased approach:** The new system is introduced in steps. For example, a new payroll system could be phased in by introducing the modules for paying clerical employees first and managerial employees later.

Direct cutover
A conversion strategy in which the old system is replaced entirely with the new system on an appointed day; no backup system is available if the new system fails.

Pilot study
A conversion strategy in which a new system is introduced to only a limited part of an organization; if the system is effective there, it is installed throughout the rest of the organization.

Phased approach
A conversion strategy in which a new system is introduced in steps.

In complicated projects, in which you expect that the solution will change as you gather field experience, the safest strategies are a pilot study or a phased approach. They will enable the solution to be deployed slowly over time. Direct cutover strategies are suitable for simple substitutions (when one kind of machine replaces another) and when human and social organizational changes are minimal. Perhaps the safest strategy is to run both the old system and the new system in parallel for a short period of time. In case the new system collapses, you will always have the old system to fall back on. The disadvantage of this strategy is that it is expensive.

CHANGE MANAGEMENT

The introduction of a new business solution is an organizational change that affects the way various individuals and groups perform and interact in the firm. Different groups and individuals in organizations have varying objectives, goals, and levels of power. People typically resist new business procedures, job relationships, and technologies because they are uncertain of how they will be affected. A very well-designed solution may not work unless it is carefully planned and prepared for. The process of planning change in an organization so that it is designed and implemented in an orderly and controlled manner is called **change management.** The design of any business solution needs to take change management into account.

Change management
The process of planning changes within an organization to ensure that the changes are implemented in an orderly and controlled manner.

How can the change process be managed? In addition to determining people, organization, and technology factors that cause problems, one must determine the people, organization, and technology impacts of proposed solutions. Encouraging affected parties to participate in the development of a particular solution can make people more committed to realizing the solution and reduce their fears of change as well. People are more likely to accept a solution if they have had proper training and if the solution is supported by top management.

Individuals involved in developing solutions can act as change agents, working to win acceptance of their solutions among all parties involved. If an organization has successfully created an atmosphere that encourages creativity, innovation, and teamwork, new business solutions will be much easier to implement.[5]

RUNNING CASE PART 3

WHAT HAPPENED AT MACY'S?

During the 1980s Macy's was bought by its management and once again became a privately held company. To buy the company back at a cost of $3.7 billion and to pay for new acquisitions such as I. Magnin and the Bullock's retail chain, Macy's management borrowed heavily at very high interest rates. The debt was to be repaid from Macy's earnings.

The plan didn't work. By the late 1980s Macy's was losing money. In late 1991 Edward S. Finkelstein, Macy's chief executive officer, announced that he would increase television advertising by 25 percent, spending an unprecedented $150 million. The spending seemed outrageous, given Macy's deteriorating sales and staggering debt. Nevertheless, Finkelstein believed there was no reason to worry about Macy's financial obligations.

Macy's was known as a hierarchical, backbiting organization that was dominated by its imperious, if talented, chief executive. While management was preoccupied with financial affairs, Macy's could not keep pace with changes in the retail industry. It began losing younger customers to small, specialized stores, such as Benetton and The Gap. Customers interested in standard goods such as pants, shirts, and shoes flocked to large discounters such as Kmart and Wal-Mart.

Macy's completed its fiscal year ending August 1, 1992, with a $1.25 billion loss on sales of $6.4 billion and with sales falling 3.7 percent at stores open a year or more. Suppliers refused to deliver goods, fearing they would not be paid. Macy's lenders demanded their money. By 1992, Macy's filed for bankruptcy, and Finkelstein was out of a job.

That year, Macy's conducted its first customer survey in 25 years, surveying 8,000 shoppers. The survey indicated that Macy's customers often left the stores empty-handed because they couldn't find what they wanted in stock. They were also dissatisfied with Macy's service, complaining that there weren't enough sales associates to help them in departments such as high fashion, where they expected heavy attention. Customers also mentioned that it took too long to pay for Macy's purchases.

Kurt Salmon Associates, the consulting and research firm that conducted the survey, estimated that Macy's could increase sales by 17 percent simply by carrying the right stock. But Macy's had little or no idea of what merchandise was selling and what wasn't until weeks after the sales took place. Frequently, store shelves would be empty of items that sold quickly and filled with unpopular items that would have to be marked down.

SOURCES: Laura Zinn, "Prudence on 34th Street," *Business Week*, November 16, 1992, and Stephanie Strom, "A Key for Macy Comeback," *The New York Times*, November 1, 1992.

RUNNING CASE Questions:

1. Use the three perspectives of people, organization, and technology to analyze and categorize Macy's problems. Rank the problems in order from most significant to least significant. How serious were these problems?
2. What steps would you take to better understand the problems you identified?

SUMMARY

- Problem solving in business involves a number of conceptual steps and is rarely a simple process. An infinite number of solutions exists: The right solution depends on defining the problem correctly.
- Problems are not simply objective situations but depend greatly on how organizations and people define matters. Solutions depend on how problems are defined.
- Critical thinking is an important attribute of wise decision making. You should suspend judgment and sustain a skeptical attitude until you become convinced of the true nature of a problem.
- Problem solving involves five steps: analysis, understanding, decision making, solutions design, and implementation.
- Systems analysis is the study and analysis of problems of existing information systems and the identification of requirements for their solution. Systems design provides the blueprint for the information system solution.
- Most organizational problems involve a mix of technological, organizational, and people problems.
- Designing solutions requires both a logical and a physical design. A logical design describes the functional performance of a solution—what it is supposed to do—and a physical design describes how the solution actually works.
- Logical design presents the functional or business requirements of an application solution independent of technical considerations. It presents a model for solving a problem from an end-user or business standpoint. An information system will not be successful unless this business model is clearly visualized before technical factors (such as hardware and software) are considered.
- Physical design consists of detailed specifications for hardware, software, processing logic, input/output methods and media, manual procedures, and controls. Physical design will be shaped by the requirements of the logical business design and existing technical, economic, or operational constraints.
- Solution implementation involves four steps: software development, hardware selection, testing, and training. Four conversion strategies for implementing a solution are parallel conversion, direct cutover, pilot study, and a phased approach.
- Change management facilitates the implementation of business solutions.

KEY TERMS

Problem analysis
Problem understanding
Decision making
Solutions design
Implementation
Critical thinking
Technology perspective
Organization perspective

People perspective
Logical design
Physical design
Systems analysis
Systems design
Cost effectiveness
Conversion strategies
Parallel conversion
Direct cutover
Pilot study
Phased approach
Change management

REVIEW QUESTIONS

1. In what sense are problems "not like basketballs on a court"? Does this mean problems are not real?
2. What is the problem-solving funnel? Do all problems go through these stages?
3. What is meant by critical thinking?
4. What are the five steps involved in problem solving?
5. How are systems analysis and design related to the general model of problem solving presented in this chapter?
6. What is a technology perspective on problems? What makes technology problems easy (or difficult) to solve? Give some examples.
7. What is an organizational perspective on problems? What makes organizational problems difficult to solve? Give some examples.
8. What is a people perspective on problems? Give some examples.
9. What are the three facets of decision making that are required in order to arrive at a specific solution?
10. What is the difference between a logical design and a physical design?
11. What are the key features of the logical design of an information system?
12. What are the key features of the physical design of an information system?
13. Describe the steps involved in implementing a system solution. What factors should be taken into account when implementing a solution?
14. Name and describe the most important conversion strategies.
15. What is change management? Why is it important for business problem solving?

DISCUSSION QUESTIONS

1. Review the Aeroflot opening vignette. With a group of students, make a list of the company's possible problems. Then make a list of solutions for each problem you identify. If you were an Aeroflot senior executive, which solutions (and problems) would you prefer?

2. With a group of students, identify a problem at your college or university that you all agree is indeed a problem. Next, identify the technology, organizational, and people features of this problem. Last, identify some feasible solutions.

3. Calculate the costs and benefits of each of the solutions you identified in Question 2. What does this tell you about establishing the cost-effectiveness of solutions?

PROBLEM-SOLVING EXERCISES

1. *Group exercise:* Divide into groups. In *Business Week, Fortune, The Wall Street Journal,* or some other business publications, each group should find a story about a business failure or mistake. The group should write a short paper describing the situation and the errors made in the problem-solving process. Each group should tell the class how it might have improved on the problem-solving process.

2. Locate a small business firm in your neighborhood and interview the owner. Make a list of the five most important problems identified by the owner and a list of the solutions (if any) the owner currently uses to "solve" or cope with the problems. Write a short paper analyzing how well the owner's solutions fit the problems. Can you suggest better solutions?

3. *Hands-on exercise:* One of the principal activities of a financial planner is to recommend appropriate investment strategies to clients. Individuals can invest in stocks, bonds, and short-term instruments such as money market funds and bank certificates of deposit (CDs). Each has a different rate of return and a different risk. Stocks are considered to pay the highest rate of return in the long run but have the greatest short-term risk. Bonds promise a fixed rate of return, but their value can fluctuate, depending on prevailing interest rates. Short-term instruments have a lower fixed rate of return than bonds, but their value is stable. The financial planner will recommend portfolios that represent a mix of each of these instruments, depending on the client's tolerance for risk and their time perspective. For instance, retirees who need to live off of their investments immediately and cannot afford to risk losing their original investment are recommended to have 50 percent of their investment in short-term instruments, 20 percent in stocks, and 30 percent in bonds. Individuals who do not need to draw on their investment for at least five years are recommended to have 40 percent in stocks, 40 percent in bonds, and 20 percent in short-term instruments. The adviser might use a worksheet like the following to analyze the client's assets.

	Market Value	**Percentage of Total**
Stocks	________	________ %
Bonds	________	________ %
Short-term	________	________ %

Doris Heinrich has enlisted the services of financial planner Marlene Jamison to help her allocate her investments. She is retiring in three months. Over the years she has accumulated $19,000 in stocks, $35,000 in bonds, and $17,000 in money market funds and bank deposits. Use appropriate software to develop an application that Marlene can use to help Doris revise her investment portfolio. Use the software to create a portfolio that would meet Doris's needs.

4. *Internet problem-solving exercise:* You are a small manufacturer of plastic molding and would like to expand your business in Australia. Your first step in problem investigation is to locate companies to help you determine whether there is a market for your product and companies that could help you sell your product in Australia. You would also like to see whether there are any local competitors. Use Cowley's Consultant's Register to research this information, and write up your findings.

NOTES

1. We do not argue that all real-world decision making follows this sequence in lockstep fashion, but rather that it is useful to conceive of problem solving with this sequence. Some real-world problem solving follows this sequence; other sequences are possible, even likely. See Michael D. Cohen, James G. March, and Johan P. Olsen, "A Garbage Can Model of Decision-making," *Administrative Science Quarterly* 17 (1972). See also Karl E. Weick, "Educational Organizations as Loosely Coupled Systems," *Administrative Science Quarterly* 21 (March 1976), and James G. March and Zur Shapira, "Managerial Perspectives on Risk and Risk Taking," *Management Science* 33 (November 1987).
2. Fred Hapgood, "Keeping It Simple," *Inc. Technology,* March 19, 1996.
3. Robert Sales, "New CS First Boston CIO Speaks Out," *Wall Street and Technology,* August 1996, and Mike Ricciuti, "The Best in Client/Server Computing," *Datamation,* March 1, 1994.
4. An excellent description of "strategic human resource issues" can be found in Alan F. Westin, et al., *The Changing Workplace: A Guide to Managing the People, Organizational, and Regulatory Aspects of Office Technology* (White Plains, N.Y.: Knowledge Industry Publications, 1985).
5. M. Lynne Markus and Robert I. Benjamin, "The Magic Bullet Theory in IT—Enabled Transformation," *Sloan Management Review*, Winter 1997, and Michael Beer, Russell A. Eisenstat, and Bert Spector, "Why Change Programs Don't Produce Change," *Harvard Business Review,* November-December 1990.

PROBLEM-SOLVING CASE

A STATE-OF-THE-ART AIRPORT CAN'T GET OFF THE GROUND

Denver's Stapleton Airport has been the sixth busiest airport in the United States, with 1,600 takeoffs and landings per day. But the airport, built in the 1920s, was clearly no longer capable of meeting Denver's needs. Mayor Federico Peña (later Secretary of Transportation in the Clinton administration) decided that the airport needed to be replaced, and the project to build the Denver International Airport began in the late 1980s.

As the first new major airport to be built since the Dallas-Fort Worth airport opened in 1974, Denver International was clearly designed for the future. Its 53 square miles makes it the largest airport in the United States. The voice and data networks for the airport campus are almost exclusively fiber optic and can operate at 100 megabits per second. An even higher-speed network—2.4 gigabytes per second—has been installed specifically for use by video security cameras, allowing the airlines to monitor such areas as gates and jetways. The airport traffic control tower is the tallest in the United States and contains the most modern electronic technology. It is supported by not just one, but two surface detection systems (which locate plane positions while they are on the ground); three systems are planned for the future. The airport construction plans were approved at a budgeted cost of a little over $2 billion and with a completion date of October 1993.

Each functional unit of the airport, including facilities, security, heating and ventilation, and the airline operations themselves, has its own computer systems operated by subcontractors. One of the airport's most advanced features is its automated luggage handling system, which is designed to carry 700 bags per minute (the modern United Airlines system at San Francisco airport handles only 100 per minute). The system is controlled by a network of desktop computers that processes millions of messages per second. All bags are tagged with a bar-coded route/destination label and then placed on a conveyor belt, much as they are in other airports. Every bag is automatically placed in a fiberglass baggage cart, and the bar-coded tag is read by a laser device. Each baggage cart has a small radio transmitter mounted on it. Every 150 to 200 feet the cart transmits to the computer system its location and the bar-code information on the luggage it is carrying. When a bag reaches the conveyor belt that will carry it to the appropriate airplane or baggage claim area, the cart flips the bag onto that conveyor belt. The belts and carts are propelled by over 10,000 motors and travel at 17 miles per hour. The designers claim that the system is so fast that in many cases the bag will reach the airplane before the passenger reaches the boarding gate. Like the other distributed systems serving the airport, the baggage system operates outside the control of the airport's information systems department.

Denver's system is the first automated baggage system to serve an entire airport. It is also the first where baggage carts do not stop, but only slow down to drop off and pick up bags; the first to be run by networked desktop computers rather than a mainframe; the first to use radio links; and the first to handle oversize bags (in Denver, usually for skis). The system can quickly reroute bags for last-minute gate changes or send them to special inspection stations.

Troubles developed prior to the scheduled opening of the airport. Budget overruns exceeded $1 billion. When problems with the baggage-handling system appeared, the opening of the airport was delayed until March 1994. The system, which is owned by the city of Denver, was described as "the spine of the airport." Government officials insisted that the baggage-handling system be operable before the airport would be allowed to open. The system was being built by BAE Automated Systems of Carrollton, Texas. BAE president Gene Di Fonso wanted his company to be hired directly by the city to construct the system, but instead BAE became a subcontractor of a maintenance company that was hired by a consortium of airlines leasing the system from the Denver city government. BAE also lost its bid to operate and maintain the system once it was built. BAE had built similar systems elsewhere, but they were all much smaller and operated at one-third the speed. When construction of the baggage system began in mid-1992, airport construction work was already well under way, and Di Fonso was forced to accept an accelerated schedule. He agreed to the tight schedule but only with the provision that no changes be made to the plans. Di Fonso claims that in the following months city officials repeatedly made changes. City officials deny the charge.

The baggage system problems did not surface until the first test in September 1993, just a month before the airport was initially scheduled to open. Tested under realistic conditions, the system generated unexpected power surges that tripped the electrical circuit breakers, automatically shutting down the motors. The city of Denver, United Airlines, and BAE all hired their own consultants. Special filters that could maintain an even power supply were needed to repair the problem, but the city delayed in ordering them. As a result, the original airport opening was postponed until March 1994.

Although electrical glitches were the main reason for postponing the opening of the airport at that time, Di Fonso said that too little testing had been done to establish the reliability of the system. On March 9, 1994, with the surge problem corrected, a second full system test took place with hordes of reporters, photographers, and TV crews in attendance. When the system ran at full speed, bags flew everywhere, and many fell and broke open. About two-thirds of the bags were shunted to the hand-sorting area because the bar codes on the tags were too smudged to be read by the computer. The test was a dramatic failure, and the opening was again postponed.

Other problems added to the complications caused by the snarled baggage system. Television monitors that flash flight information were not ready. A sign directing passengers to the baggage claim area led instead to a concrete wall. In the meantime, the new airport cost Denver $500,000 each day it remained closed.

The airport did not open officially until February 28, 1995. The delay of 16 months and the need to correct its baggage-handling problems put overall costs at $5 billion, nearly $3 billion more than originally projected. Airport authorities decided to operate the baggage system on a small scale at first, moving only 30 to 60 bags per minute, well below the rate of 700 bags per minute estimated for a fully operational system.

A year later, the Denver airport reported very few problems, emerging as the most efficient cold-weather airport in the United States. It ranks only after Honolulu and Las Vegas, Nevada, for the fewest flight delays. Statistics show that baggage loss and damage in Denver falls well below the national average.

SOURCES: James Brooke, "Denver Airport Nestles into Its Lair," *The New York Times,* March 6, 1996; Allen R. Meyerson, "Automation Off Course in Denver," *The New York Times,* March 18, 1994; Dirk Johnson, "Spilled Luggage Grounds Denver's New Airport," *The New York Times,* March 2, 1994; and Ellis Booker, "Airport Prepares for a Takeoff," *Computerworld,* January 10, 1994.

CASE STUDY QUESTIONS

1. Peter G. Neumann, the founder and manager of *Risks Digest,* an Internet forum on computer reliability and security, observed that an accidental glitch at an airport such as Denver's new airport could have a dramatic effect on air traffic around the country. Do you agree? Why?

2. Use the three perspectives outlined in the chapter—technology, organization, and people—to analyze and categorize the problems in the Denver International Airport construction project. Describe some of the possible interrelationships. Rank the problems in order from the most significant to the least significant.

3. What steps would you take to obtain a better understanding of the problems you identified in Question 2?

4. Take the project back in time to 1991, and in a short (three- to five-page) paper, design a plan that would have avoided the problems encountered.

Chapter

TEN

DESIGNING INFORMATION SYSTEM SOLUTIONS

CHAPTER OUTLINE

LEARNING OBJECTIVES

After reading and studying this chapter, you will

1. Be able to apply the five problem-solving steps to systems analysis and design.
2. Be able to devise and evaluate alternative systems solutions.
3. Be able to determine when a solution requires an information system application.
4. Understand the functional requirements of an information system application solution.
5. Be able to translate a logical or conceptual system design into a physical system design.
6. Understand how to use data flow diagrams, system flowcharts, and data dictionaries as tools for solution design.

U.S. BANK OVERHAULS ITS WEB SITE

U.S. Bank, headquartered in Portland, Oregon, is a full-service banking institution operating hundreds of branches in six states in the northwestern United States—Oregon, Washington, Idaho, California, Utah, and Nevada. Its UBank division focuses on convenience banking, consisting of a variety of self-service banking services such as ATMs, debit cards, interactive video kiosks, and online banking using America Online and the Internet. U.S. Bank hopes to stay on top in a highly competitive industry by taking advantage of the latest trends in financial services, one of which is to allow customers to interact with the bank without making a physical trip to a branch office. To keep up with other banks going into Internet banking, UBank needed to develop an interactive, transaction-based service that would allow customers to conduct self-service banking over the Internet.

The bank launched its first Web site in mid-1995 with that strategy in mind. This first Web initiative was a piecemeal effort. The bank's management did not yet understand the business potential of the World Wide Web. An advertising agency provided some graphics and a rough design, and U.S. Bank's information systems staff did the programming.

U.S. Bank's first-generation home page lacked personality. It looked like little more than a small image map on a repeating logo background. The writing and images, which came from many sources, were not well integrated. Some pages were graphics intensive, while others had no graphics at all. Users had trouble navigating through the Web site. For example, there was no easy way to access an E-mail response area on the site. To send an E-mail message, users had to go to a section called "About Us" and then into a section called "How to Reach Us." U.S. Bank's Web site had good functionality and content, but it was confusing to use and didn't effectively convey the message that UBank was an efficient banking resource and a reliable Internet banking service. Customers needed to get into and out of the home page and into the virtual bank branch more easily.

U.S. Bank solved its problem by redesigning its Web site to be more supportive of Internet banking and its marketing campaign, which emphasizes northwestern ideals—a "pioneering spirit" and appreciation of the unique quality of life in that region. Since the refurbished site was launched on December 2, 1996, U.S. Bank estimates that its Web site traffic has increased as much as 50 percent. We show how U.S. Bank arrived at this solution later in the chapter.

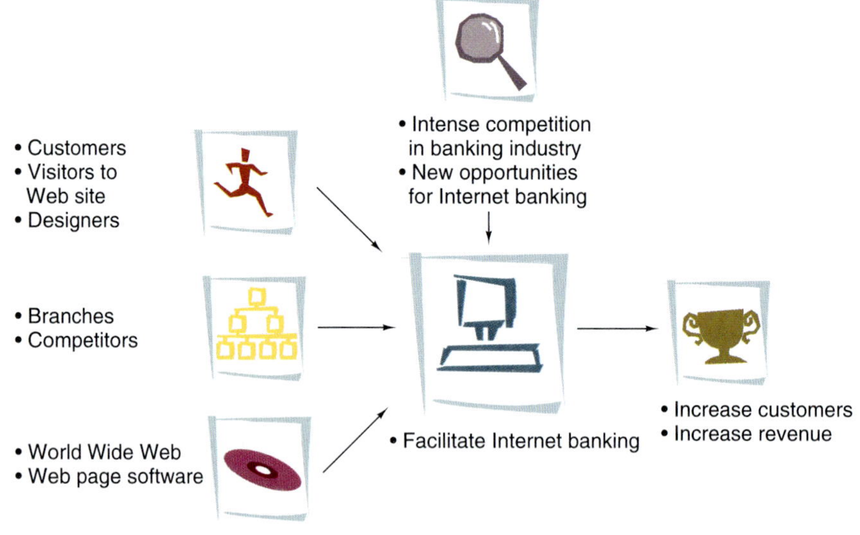

SOURCE: Lori Piquet, "The Virtual World," *ZD Internet*, March 1997.

The experience of U.S. Bank and other examples in this chapter illustrate how the problem-solving methodology can be applied more specifically to the analysis of information system-related problems and the development of information system solutions. The critical thinking skills you have learned in earlier chapters can be applied to a variety of situations. They can be used to analyze everyday business problems for which the answer lies in better procedures or better management. The skills can also be applied for building new information systems or improving existing ones. They may even be used to help redesign organizations.

In many instances, the solution to a problem will be a "system solution." Indeed, this problem-solving framework lies at the heart of the analysis and design of information systems. No matter what hardware, software, and systems development methodology you use, you must first be able to understand a problem, describe it, and design a solution. Thus, this process lays the groundwork for all subsequent systems development activities. Unless it is performed properly, the result can be major errors in a new system or even total failure.

Alternative systems-building approaches are discussed in subsequent chapters. The purpose of this chapter is to illustrate the core problem-solving methodology that is the foundation for all approaches, traditional or alternative.

10.1 PROBLEM SOLVING IN ACTION: DATABASE APPLICATION

Throughout this chapter, we use real-world cases to illustrate how problem solving and systems analysis and design actually work, step by step. Our purpose is to focus on the process of analyzing a problem and visualizing the right business solution. Accordingly, we have simplified these cases for instructional purposes; their actual analysis and solution required many more details than can be presented here.

Let's start by looking at a fairly simple problem, one of a small start-up business grappling with a heavy load of record keeping and paperwork. For this case, as well as for all the other cases in this chapter, we need to answer the following questions:

1. What exactly was the problem?
2. What were its causes, and what was its scope?
3. What was the solution objective?
4. What alternative solutions were available?
5. What were the constraints on these solutions?
6. Why was a particular solution chosen?

THE PATIENT BILLING SYSTEM

Mark and Evelyn Springer are two up-and-coming child psychologists. After working in clinics for a decade, they decided to form their own private practice in Norwalk, Connecticut, an area with no therapists who could handle child disorders. Because of their excellent credentials and expertise with children, their practice is flourishing, and they have had to open a second office in nearby Bridgeport. But this leaves them with virtually no time for office record keeping.

Both psychologists must maintain detailed records of therapy sessions and periodic patient evaluations. They must also prepare a biweekly bill for each patient and keep records of payments. The Springers charge $95 per session, and most patients have sessions once or twice a week. Each patient's session is scheduled for the same day and time every week. The Springers find that they barely have time to maintain their patient evaluations, let alone send bills. Because they are still in a start-up situation, they do not have the resources to hire secretarial help.

In addition to patient charts, the Springers maintain patient records with the patient's social security number, name, address, and outstanding balance. Do the Springers have a problem? If so, how can it be solved?

APPLYING THE METHODOLOGY

Step 1: Problem Analysis The preceding discussion serves as our fact-finding results.

Step 2: Problem Understanding We apply our problem-solving matrix and find that the Springers' problem involves mainly organizational factors.

Technology	Organization	People
Hardware	Culture	Ergonomics
Software	Management	Evaluation
Telecommunications	Politics	Training
Database	✓ Bureaucracy	Employee Attitudes
	✓ Environment	Legal Compliance

The Problem

The Springers do not have time to maintain adequate billing records or perform all the other record keeping required for a therapy practice.

Problem Dimensions

The Springers' problem has both external and internal dimensions:

- **External:** There is an enormous demand for child therapy services in the Springers' area, so they are very busy.
- **Internal:** The Springers are in a start-up situation with very little capital or resources for a permanent clerical employee. They have heavy record-keeping requirements. In addition to patient billings, very detailed patient charts and evaluations must be maintained. Higher priority is placed on patient charts and evaluations because they are critical to the treatment process. No systematic way exists to ensure that patient billing records are kept up to date.

Step 3: Decision Making The solution objective would be to reduce the time and effort required to maintain patient records and send out bills. But we must also consider certain economic and operational constraints: The Springers cannot afford a full-time secretary or bookkeeper. In addition, they must maintain the patient evaluation records themselves and do not have any time left for other kinds of record keeping.

Given these constraints, the Springers have three solution alternatives: (1) hire an office temporary to do the billing every two weeks; (2) develop an automated patient record-keeping and billing system; or (3) automate patient evaluations.

The most time-saving alternative would be an automated patient billing and record-keeping system. This would consist of a simple file with patient name, social security number, address, amount due, amount paid, and outstanding balance. Automating patient evaluations by using word processing would not save as much time as automating the billing process. Hiring a temporary to prepare bills would have little impact because the Springers themselves would still have to keep track of payments on an ongoing basis.

Step 4: Solution Design The logical design for a patient billing and record-keeping system might look like this:

Inputs

Basic patient data: Patient name, social security number, address

Payment transaction data: Date paid and amount paid

Processing

Create and maintain patient records.

Calculate amount owed by each patient every two weeks.

Accumulate and total payment transactions for each patient every two weeks or on request.

Adjust balance due every two weeks.

Outputs

Semimonthly bill for each patient

Payment transaction listing that shows payment amounts and dates over each two-week period

Amount of bill and payment

Listing of patients with overdue balances

Mailing labels

Database

(a) A simple patient file with all of the fields for basic patient data

(b) A payment transaction file showing patient name, payment amount, and payment date

(c) A service file showing the date and cost of each client therapy session

A relational database design would allow the Springers to combine data from these three files (tables) for various reports and queries.

Procedures

Input basic patient data when patient starts therapy.

Update patient data for address changes or therapy session changes.

Input payment data whenever a payment is received.

Generate bills and mailing labels once every two weeks.

Generate payment transaction listing on request.

Controls

Reconcile checks with transaction listing report.

Several physical design options are possible. The Springers could use a time-sharing service (a commercial firm that allows other firms to use its hardware and software for a fee on a time-sharing basis). A printer and terminal networked to the time-sharing company's mainframe or minicomputer could be installed in their office, but this would be too costly for such a small business with simple processing needs. The Springers require a very elementary application with small files that could be easily and inexpensively developed on a PC using database software. Patient bills could be calculated with spreadsheet software, but the advantage of database software is that it can generate individual patient invoices and many kinds of reports. The application requires flexibility and file management capabilities that are more readily available with database software. The PC could also be used for word processing and other office tasks.

Figure 10.1 illustrates the physical design for the new system: the patient (client) file (a), the payment file (b), and the service file (c). The designs were created on a PC using Microsoft Access database software.

FIGURE 10.1

Patient Billing and Record Keeping

This figure illustrates the physical design for the patient billing system implemented in Microsoft Access. The data are organized into three tables.

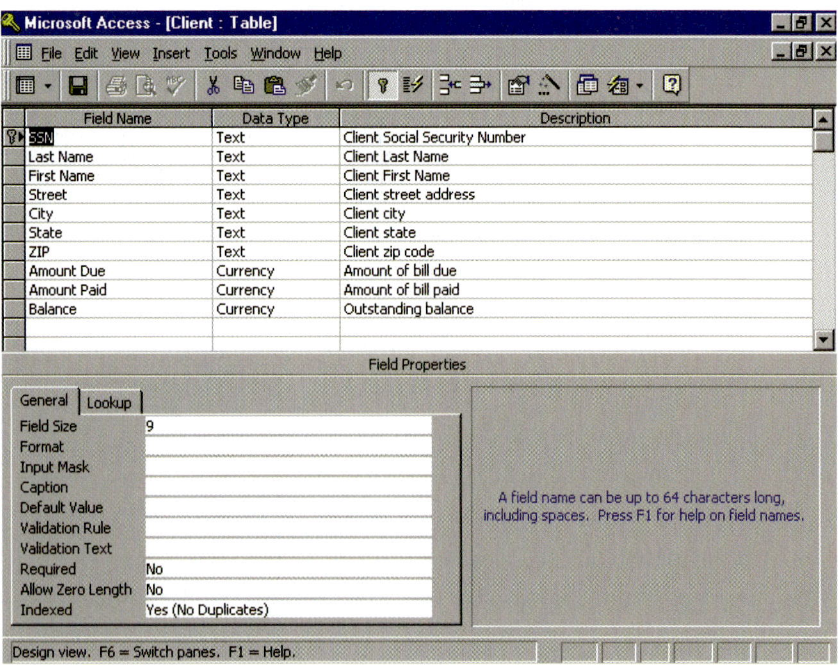

(a) Client Table

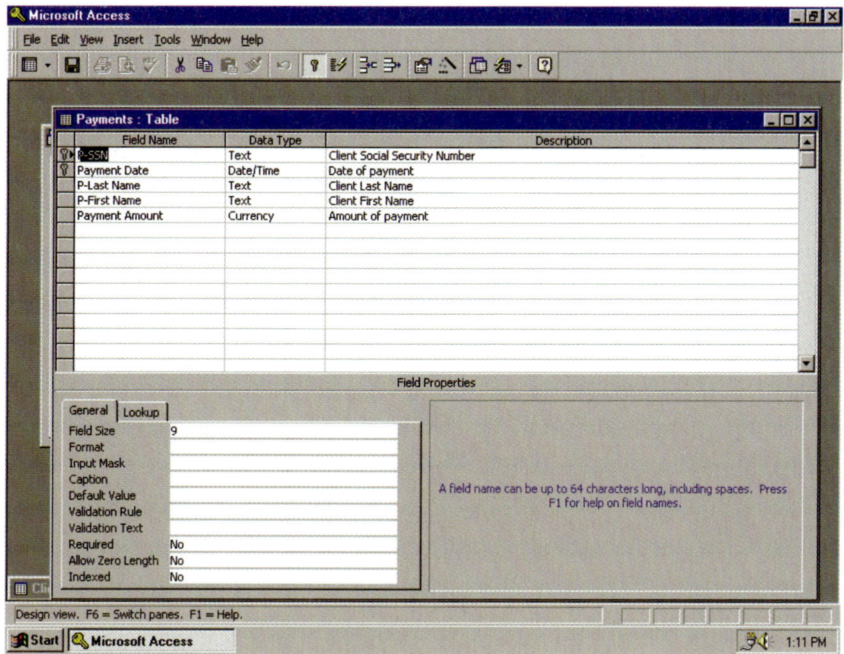

(b) Payments Table

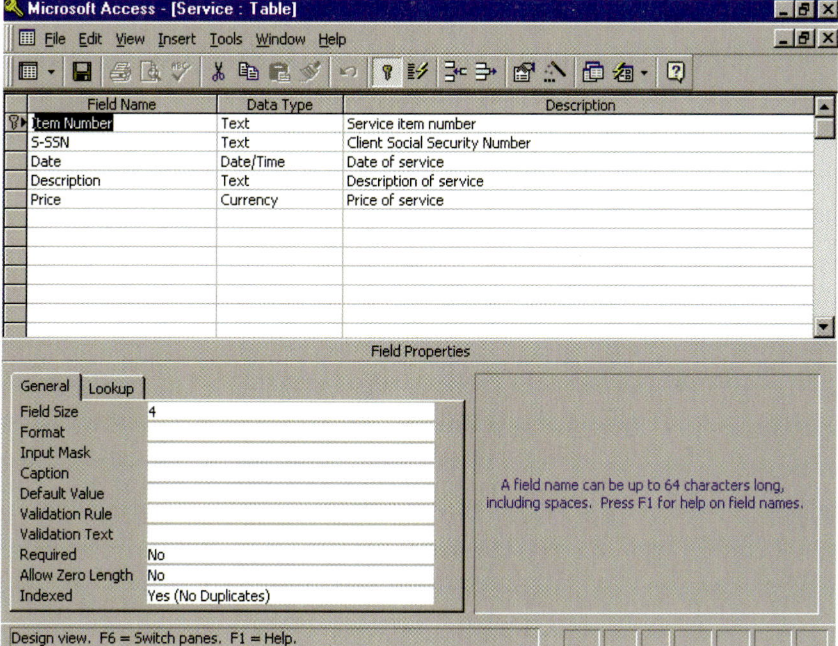

(c) Service Table

FOCUS ON ORGANIZATIONS

SEARS CANADA USES ITS DATABASE TO COMPETE

Sears Roebuck & Co.'s catalog business may have faltered in the United States, but it is still going strong in Canada. Two thirds of Sears Canada Inc.'s customers still make some or all of their purchases through the Sears catalogs. But the Canadian Sears retailers face the same competitive pressures as their U.S. counterparts, including competition from discount retailers and specialty catalogs that overwhelmed the Sears catalog in the United States. Sears Canada was losing 5 percent of its catalog customer base each year, even when it purchased external mailing lists to locate new customers.

One reason for declining sales performance was that Sears Canada's mainframe-based catalog marketing system was not up to the task. Customers who didn't buy anything for a year were dropped from Sears Canada's database. Sears marketers couldn't use the database to find out what people had actually bought from its various catalogs. A query on sales of Levi jeans, for example, couldn't examine past sales data—it could only collect data going forward. Fred Hagerman, the customer list manager for Sears Canada's catalog division in Toronto, likened the database to "a black box that we couldn't see into."

The catalog unit fought back by performing a merchandising makeover to widen selection and lower pricing. It also installed a new state-of-the-art customer analysis system. The new system, called Prophet, uses a DB2 relational DBMS, an IBM RS/6000 UNIX server, custom-built catalog management software, and a retail analysis tool called Archer, made by Retail Target Marketing Systems Inc. in Waukesha, Wisconsin.

The database is designed to enable Sears Canada to query deeper into customer behavior. Marketing staff and others can use Archer to analyze sales data in DB2 and then import the results into spreadsheets to predict and track catalog performance. The database is set up to make data from 1994 to the present available, and Sears Canada plans to keep five years' worth of sales data available for analysis. The company can then use this information to target catalog mailings more precisely, reducing costs and increasing profits. It can also put together marketing campaigns to keep customers from straying to other retailers. Sears Canada's catalog sales have started to turn around and are projected to grow 5 percent in 1997 alone.

FOCUS Question:
How was database design linked to the sales performance of Sears Canada?

SOURCE: Craig Stedman, "Sears Canada Catalog Gains," *Computerworld,* April 7, 1997.

Step 5: Implementation The Springers would have to transfer required patient data from their manual records to the database. They could hire a PC consultant to develop and test the database software programs for printing the patient bills, mailing labels, lists of overdue payments, and payment transaction logs and for calculating payments due. Finally, they would have to change procedures for updating their patient files when they received payments or address changes and for generating patient bills.

In the Springers' case, a simple relational database with three tables was sufficient to solve their problem. An illustration of the Springers' patient billing and record-keeping system is shown later in the chapter.

A well-designed database is an important element of an application solution, as the Focus on Organizations describes.

10.2 PROBLEM SOLVING IN ACTION: SPREADSHEET APPLICATION

This case shows how a simple spreadsheet application can cut through a complex web of procedures and red tape in a firm with several hundred employees.

PARTNERSHIP ALLOCATION AT HASKELL, SIMPSON, AND PORTER

Haskell, Simpson, and Porter is a medium-sized New York City law firm specializing in trusts and corporate law. Its 35 partners and 150 associates generate annual revenues of over $25 million, with $5 million in total assets.

Haskell, Simpson, and Porter's accounting department consists of a controller, assistant controller, and ten staff members. At the end of each fiscal year, one of the major public accounting firms audits Haskell, Simpson, and Porter's books, determines the accuracy of its financial statements, and approves the figure for net income.

In addition to a fixed salary, the 35 partners receive shares in the net income of the partnership. The percentage of each partner's share is determined by seniority and the amount of partnership revenue generated by the partner. Once the auditor approves the firm's net income, the accounting

With user-friendly software and application development tools, PCs provide low-cost solutions to small businesses seeking to automate their record keeping.

SOURCE: Courtesy of International Business Machines Corporation.

department allocates partnership income. At year end, the law firm's accounting department also summarizes tax information for each partner, a task that requires numerous calculations of each partner's income and deductions.

The public accounting firm issues a first draft of financial statements during the first week in January, and then Haskell, Simpson, and Porter's accounting department finalizes the partnership income allocations. The auditing firm typically revises the bottom line of the drafted financial statements several times before the final version is approved.

Each time a change is made, the accounting department must prepare a new allocation of each partner's income. Each calculation is performed manually, including those for allocated partnership income, total income, unincorporated business tax, nondeductible insurance (which must be treated as additional income for tax purposes), retirement plan contributions, charitable contributions, and financial statement income.

Total income consists of each partner's fixed salary plus his or her allocated partnership income. (Total income is reported as ordinary income from the partnership on the federal income tax form 1040 Schedule E.) Each partner takes 6 percent of total salary for nontaxable retirement plan deductions, 0.3 percent of total salary for charitable contributions, 4.16 percent of total income for New York City unincorporated business tax (the law firm is a partnership), and 0.5 percent of total income for nondeductible insurance. Financial statement income consists of total income minus unincorporated business tax. It is reported as net earnings from self-employment on federal income tax form 1040 Schedule SE.

Mathematical errors are common, and the process of correcting them is tedious and even more time consuming. For example, if the sum of the individual partners' allocations for an insurance deduction does not equal the partnership's total for that deduction, the assistant controller is forced to recalculate each number until the error is located.

In addition, the accounting department must prepare a tax letter for each partner, listing his or her share of the firm's taxable income and deductions. This letter is required for individual record keeping and for preparation of the partners' federal, New York State, and New York City income tax returns.

Partners continually pressure the accounting department to complete their income allocation calculations and tax letters. During the past few years, several changes were made to the bottom line of the firm's income statement after the allocation calculations were completed. Since all the calculations are based on this figure, all the partnership allocation calculations had to be performed again, which took an extra three days. Let's analyze this problem.

APPLYING THE METHODOLOGY

Step 1: Problem Analysis Again, we can use the facts from the preceding discussion.

Step 2: Problem Understanding Using our matrix, we find that this law firm's problem has both organizational and people dimensions.

Technology	Organization	People
Hardware	Culture	Ergonomics
Software	Management	Evaluation
Telecommunications	✓ Politics	Training
Database	✓ Bureaucracy	Employee Attitudes
	✓ Environment	Legal Compliance

The Problem

Partnership allocations and tax calculations cannot be performed in a timely manner.

Problem Dimension

The problem has both external and internal dimensions:

- **External:** The law firm is dependent on an external auditing firm for finalizing its bottom-line financial statement figures. It must base all of its partnership allocation calculations on input from an external source and work within a very narrow time frame to complete tax letters and income distribution for partners.
- **Internal:** Calculations for partnership allocations are complex and variable and require special approvals and bureaucratic procedures. The controller's office operates with primarily manual tools and technology and resists efforts to automate.

Step 3: Decision Making The objectives here are to expedite and increase the accuracy of partnership allocations and tax calculations. At the same time, several constraints must be considered: The time frame for finalizing partnership allocations and tax calculations will remain very narrow because business rules require that the firm use an external auditor. The firm's internal accounting department is very resistant to extensive automation.

Given these constraints, the law firm appears to have two solution alternatives: (1) hire extra staff for the controller's office to perform the calculations manually once figures have been finalized, or (2) develop an automated model for partner income allocation that can be easily revised when bottom-line figures are changed.

The first alternative is not very desirable since this process leads to mathematical errors and repetition of effort. The second alternative is feasible, provided that it can be done with minimum disruption to the accounting department.

Step 4: Solution Design A system model for partnership income allocation would incorporate these requirements in a logical design:

Inputs

Final bottom-line figure for net income

Each partner's percentage

Each partner's fixed salary

Unincorporated business tax percentage

Nondeductible insurance percentage

Retirement plan contribution percentage

Charitable contributions percentage

Processing

Compute each partner's gross partnership income allocation.

Compute each partner's total income.

Compute unincorporated business tax.

Compute nondeductible insurance.

Compute retirement plan contribution (deduction).

FIGURE 10.2

Using Spreadsheets at Haskell, Simpson, and Porter: The Physical Design and Sample Output

Panel a is the worksheet that was developed for the partnership allocation system. The calculation factors are grouped at the lower left and are referenced by the formulas. The factor entitled "firm's net income" is the bottom-line figure, supplied by the auditor, that drives the rest of the calculations. Panel b shows a sample of the output, which displays the figures for each partner.

(a) Physical Design for Spreadsheet

PARTNER	PARTNERSHIP PERCENT	FIXED SALARY	ALLOCATED INCOME	TOTAL INCOME	UNINCORPORATED BUSINESS TAX
Donaldson, Paul	2.52%	48000	+$B5*$C$20	+$C5+$D5	+$E5*$C$21
Grover, Pauline	1.81%	48000	+$B6*$C$20	+$C6+$D6	+$E6*$C$21
Haskell, Thomas	3.83%	46000	+$B7*$C$20	+$C7+$D7	+$E7*$C$21
Porter, Arnold	4.42%	48000	+$B8*$C$20	+$C8+$D8	+$E8*$C$21
Simpson, Jeffry	2.76%	41000	+$B9*$C$20	+$C9+$D9	+$E9*$C$21
Thomas, Linda	3.12%	48000	+$B10*$C$20	+$C10+$D10	+$E10*$C$21
Westheimer, Charles	6.61%	55000	+$B11*$C$20	+$C11+$D11	+$E11*$C$21
TOTALS		@SUM ($C5 . . $C11)	@SUM ($D5 . . $D11)	@SUM ($E5 . . $E11)	@SUM ($F5 . . $F11)

CALCULATION FACTORS

FIRM'S NET INCOME	$5,125,000
UNINCORPORATED BUSINESS TAX	4.16%
RETIREMENT PLAN CONTRIBUTION	6.00%
NON-DEDUCTIBLE INSURANCE	0.50%
CHARITABLE CONTRIBUTION	0.30%

(b) Sample Output

PARTNER	PARTNERSHIP PERCENT	FIXED SALARY	ALLOCATED INCOME	TOTAL INCOME	UNINCORPORATED BUSINESS TAX
Donaldson, Paul	2.52%	$48,000	$129,150	$177,150.00	$7,369.44
Grover, Pauline	1.81%	$48,000	$92,763	$140,762.50	$5,855.72
Haskell, Thomas	3.83%	$46,000	$196,288	$242,287.50	$10,079.16
Porter, Arnold	4.42%	$48,000	$226,525	$274,525.00	$11,420.24
Simpson, Jeffry	2.76%	$41,000	$141,450	$182,450.00	$7,589.92
Thomas, Linda	3.12%	$48,000	$159,900	$207,900.00	$8,648.64
Westheimer, Charles	6.61%	$55,000	$338,763	$393,762.50	$16,380.52
		$334,000.00	$1,284,837.50	$1,618,837.50	$67,343.64

Compute charitable contributions deduction.

Compute financial statement income.

Compute firm totals for each of the above.

Outputs

Schedule of partner allocations

Individual tax letters

Database

A record must be kept for each partner with the following fields:

Partner's name

Partner's fixed salary amount

Percentage of net income

Amount of net income allocation

Total income

(a) Physical Design for Spreadsheet

RETIREMENT PLAN CONTRIB.	NON-DEDUCT INSURANCE	CHARITABLE CONTRIBUTION	FINANCIAL STAT INCOME
+$E5*$C$22	+$E5*$C$23	+$E5*$C$24	+$E5–$F5
+$E6*$C$22	+$E6*$C$23	+$E6*$C$24	+$E6–$F6
+$E7*$C$22	+$E7*$C$23	+$E7*$C$24	+$E7–$F7
+$E8*$C$22	+$E8*$C$23	+$E8*$C$24	+$E8–$F8
+$E9*$C$22	+$E9*$C$23	+$E9*$C$24	+$E9–$F9
+$E10*$C$22	+$E10*$C$23	+$E10*$C$24	+$E10–$F10
+$E11*$C$22	+$E11*$C$23	+$E11*$C$24	+$E11–$F11
@SUM ($G5 . . $G11)	@SUM ($H5 . . $H11)	@SUM ($I5 . . $I11)	@SUM ($J5 . . $J11)

(b) Sample Output

RETIREMENT PLAN CONTRIB.	NONDEDUCT INSURANCE	CHARITABLE CONTRIBUTION	FINANCIAL STAT INCOME
$10,629.00	$885.75	$531.45	$169,780.56
$8,445.75	$703.81	$422.29	$139,906.78
$14,537.25	$1,211.44	$726.86	$232,208.34
$16,471.50	$1,372.63	$823.58	$263,104.76
$10,947.00	$912.25	$547.35	$174,860.08
$12,474.00	$1,039.50	$623.70	$199,251.36
$23,625.75	$1,968.81	$1,181.29	$377,381.86
$97,130.25	$8,094.19	$4,856.51	$1,551,493.86

Unincorporated business tax amount

Nondeductible insurance amount

Retirement plan contribution amount

Charitable contribution amount

Financial statement reporting income amount

Procedures

Input the net income figures after approval by the auditor and management.

Mail tax letters and partnership income allocation statements to each partner.

Controls

Require management's as well as the auditor's authorization of the final net income figure before it is input for partner income calculations.

Total all partners' shares of income and reconcile this total with the firm's net income figure used as input.

The physical design requires a very small file, with records on only 35 partners. Since the law firm does not need to have its own mainframe or minicomputer, the application could be farmed out to a time-sharing service. But the application is so small that it is most appropriate and cost effective on a PC, which could also be used for word processing and other office tasks. This application requires many calculations that are interrelated in a very small file. Spreadsheet software would be preferable to database software in this instance because spreadsheet software handles such problems more easily.

The Web site maintained by HomeBuyer Internet Real Estate Service allows visitors to search for homes according to price, location, size, and other criteria. The results of the search display photos and detailed descriptions of the properties along with information on how to contact local real estate agents.

FOCUS ON **PEOPLE**

WILL THE INTERNET REPLACE REAL ESTATE AGENTS?

Real estate has always been an information-driven business, based on informing customers about homes that fit their budgets and tastes. The function of providing this information to prospective home buyers was traditionally performed by the real estate agent, who was paid for providing information to customers so that they could make a purchasing decision. Now, multimedia, the Internet, and other information technology enable consumers to bypass agents and shop on their own.

Technology can furnish customers with much of the same information formerly provided by real estate agents. In some locations, consumers can already obtain data to view houses from a CD-ROM disk or from an online information service or the Internet using their home computers.

Real estate sites have sprung up on the World Wide Web. Real estate listings on the Web can include pictures and floor plans as well as descriptive information. These Web sites typically charge the seller a small fee, as little as $15 per month, for the listing. Buyers view listings for free. Some sites, such as the HomeBuyer Internet Real Estate Service, include listings from anywhere and rely on powerful search engines to help visitors locate what they want. Others focus on real estate listings for a specific area. For example, Real Estate On-line provides residential and commercial real estate listings for the New York metropolitan area. HomeBuyer Internet Real Estate Service provides an array of services and offers real estate listings, mortgage and home buyer information, photographs, classified listings, and mortgage and insurance information. This Web site even has a search facility to locate local real estate agents to represent property hunters once they have located an area or listing that interests them. The more traditional real estate firms, such as Coldwell Banker, are also establishing a presence on the Web, trying to capture part of the cyberspace business. However, they still charge the seller a commission, often 6 percent of the sale price ($12,000 on a $200,000 home), a powerful incentive for sellers to seek other avenues in which to advertise their properties.

According to many industry analysts, such products will "fundamentally redefine" the role of the real estate broker. The National Association of Realtors (NAR) will probably lose its monopoly on the distribution and use of home listings. In time, customers will use CD-ROM technology or the Web to locate home listings entirely on their own. Real estate agents will be needed only to show the homes and negotiate the deal. On the other hand, observes Harley E. Rouda, a Columbus, Ohio, real estate agent who served as NAR president in 1991, the current network of real estate agents is too well established to be quickly supplanted by a more public, centralized source for real estate data. Information systems are helping real estate agencies to become a source of one-stop shopping for homes, where buyers can obtain listings, secure mortgages, initiate title searches, find insurance, buy homes, and even locate movers.

FOCUS Questions: What problems are solved by using information system technology in the real estate industry? How much will the Internet change the role of real estate agents?

SOURCES: E. B. Baatz, "Will the Web Cut Your Job?" *Webmaster,* May/June 1996, and Chuck Appleby, "Real Estate Gets Real," *Information Week,* March 2, 1994.

Figure 10.2 shows the physical design of the partnership allocation worksheet and a sample of the output. Panel a displays the organization of the worksheet, cell relationships, and calculation formulas. Panel b is a printout of the partnership allocation report. Data are extracted from the partnership allocation report for the tax letter sent to each partner, so the letters can be created much faster than before.

Step 5: Implementation The firm would have to purchase a PC and printer and compatible spreadsheet software. With the spreadsheet software, a template could be developed to produce the required partnership allocation calculations. Data formerly maintained manually (such as all of the partners' names and fixed income) would have to be entered into the template. The accuracy of the template would be tested by comparison with the same calculations performed manually. Procedures would have to be modified so that the calculations were performed on the template rather than by hand. The accounting department would have to be trained to use the PC and spreadsheet software.

In addition to spreadsheet and database applications, multimedia systems and the Internet are gaining use as application solutions. The Focus on People describes one such solution and the effect it is having on real estate agents' jobs and the entire real estate industry.

10.3 PROBLEM SOLVING IN ACTION: USER INTERFACE DESIGN FOR THE WORLD WIDE WEB

Sometimes a solution does not call for a completely new system but requires only the redesign of its user interface. This problem focuses on redesigning Web sites to improve the input part of an existing information system.

U.S. BANK'S WEB SITE

U.S. Bank's Web site provided the user interface for a self-service banking information system. Clients with proper security could visit the Web site to access account information, transfer money between different accounts, and send E-mail inquiries to the customer service group. Behind the Web site was a system to process these transactions and update customers' account records. This portion of the system worked fine, but U.S. Bank decided to improve its user interface. How and why did U.S. Bank decide to redesign its Web site? Let's put our problem-solving methodology to work again.

APPLYING THE METHODOLOGY

Step 1: Problem Analysis The chapter-opening description of U.S. Bank provides sufficient facts for our investigation.

Step 2: Problem Understanding Again we apply our matrix to find that U.S. Bank's problem had both people and organizational dimensions.

Technology	Organization	People
Hardware	Culture	✓ Ergonomics
Software	✓ Management	Evaluation and Monitoring
Telecommunications	Politics	Training
Database	Bureaucracy	Employee Attitudes
	✓ Environment	Legal Compliance

The Problem

U.S. Bank was not gaining customers because of a poorly designed user interface on its Web site for Internet banking.

Problem Dimensions

U.S. Bank's problem had both external and internal dimensions:

- **External:** U.S. Bank is facing increasing competition from other banks providing online banking services. The Internet is creating new opportunities for online banking.
- **Internal:** U.S. Bank's business strategy is to emphasize self-service banking. Management initially did not understand the potential of the Internet for providing such services. The user interface of the first Web site was poorly designed and difficult to use for Internet banking, discouraging customers from using the site and even turning away potential new customers (see Figure 10.3).

Step 3: Decision Making The objective is to ensure that U.S. Bank's Web site is designed to maximize ease of use and to promote its marketing message. U.S. Bank had three alternatives. (1) It could leave the existing Web site as is, (2) it could abandon its Web efforts in favor of a private online banking network, or (3) it could redesign its Web site to make it more efficient and user friendly.

Step 4: Solution Design The third alternative was selected. U.S. Bank did not change any of the processing for its underlying customer account systems. It did change the user interface for its Web site. U.S. Bank hired a professional Web site design team to direct the facelift. The logical design for this solution primarily involves changes in Web pages used for input and output and for information displays.

FIGURE 10.3

U.S. Bank's Web Site—Before

U.S. Bank's first Web site was confusing and difficult to use. Many pages had no graphics at all and were very dull.

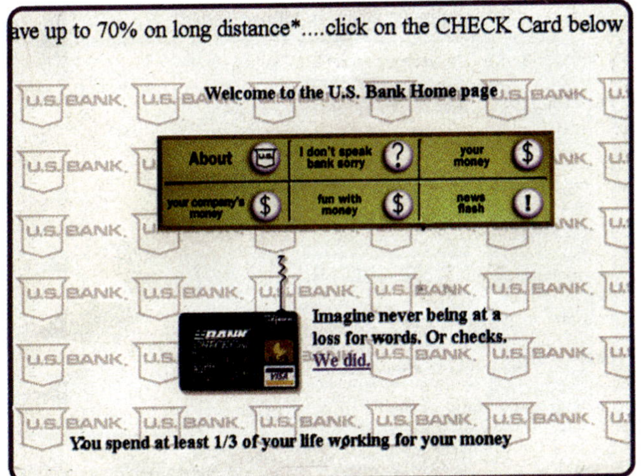

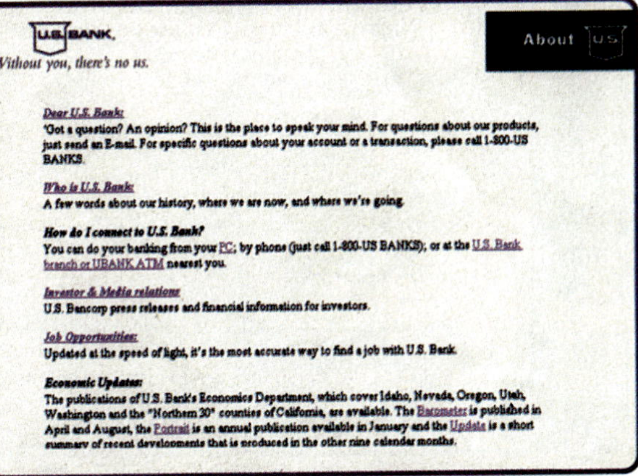

Input and Output

The team redesigned U.S. Bank's Web pages to incorporate photographic imagery and icons evoking a Northwest motif.

Navigation paths between Web pages were streamlined and redesigned so that users can go to and from anywhere in the site from wherever they are.

Visitors can use the E-mail user response capability from any level in the site.

An interactive loan calculation form that calculates the amount of a loan that a customer might afford was moved to the Personal Solutions area, which contains related material.

Processing

Unchanged

Database

Unchanged

Procedures

Unchanged

Controls

Unchanged

U.S. Bank did not have to make any physical design changes in existing hardware or databases for its Web-based self-service banking system. It did have to change the design and programming of Web pages and the navigation paths among them so that the Web site was easier to use. Figure 10.4 shows some of the redesigned Web pages.

FIGURE 10.4

U.S. Bank's Web Site—After

U.S. Bank redesigned its Web site to give it more personality and interest. Graphics and text are thoughtfully arranged. High-priority areas are immediately available.

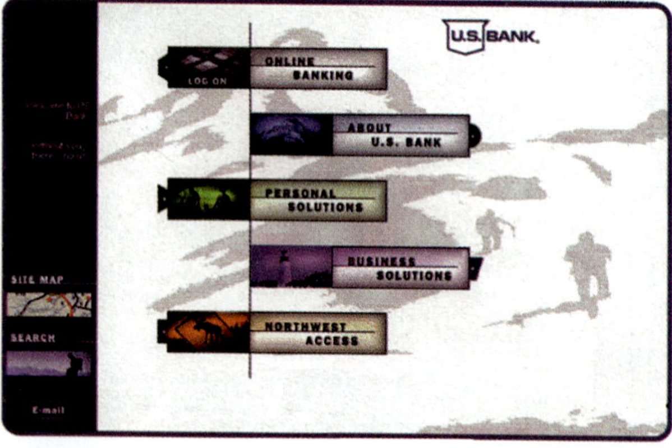

FOCUS ON **PROBLEM SOLVING**

THE ROYAL BANK OF CANADA GRAPPLES WITH APPLICATION STANDARDS

The user interface for systems is supposed to be easy to use. But if users have to learn seven different types of menus, if tapping the D key means "Delete" in one application but "Down" in another, many advantages of graphical user interfaces and so called user-friendly software are lost. Users have to spend too much time learning how to make each application work. If all applications had the same user interface, users would be more productive and less frustrated. Moreover, programmers would not have to start from scratch each time they developed a new application. A standard interface would have a template for how the screen should look and operate, how users could browse a menu, and other elements.

The Royal Bank of Canada tried to create a standard graphical user interface for its applications in 1993 but had trouble keeping it updated, writing reusable code, and getting programmers to actually use the template. The bank wanted to reduce the amount of training and relearning necessary in order to use its applications. It developed successful working models of the standard screens but encountered resistance when it tried to get its software developers to use the standard rather than to create screens from scratch.

One way the bank is surmounting this hurdle is by using Java and Internet technology. Royal Bank of Canada became the first business to use American Management Systems AMS/Web Access, a letter-of-credit application written in Java. This application is the foundation for Royal Bank's Import Direct service, launched in the spring of 1997. Import Direct lets chief financial officers, corporate treasurers, and other financial professionals access Royal Bank's AMS TradeLine back-office applications using a standard Java-enabled Web browser.

Using Java and standard Web browsers, the Royal Bank will be able to deliver letters of credit just as easily to Indonesia as to Toronto. The service will be available on the bank's Web site. Users can work with the system using the same software they use to access the Web. They are already familiar with the workings of the interface of their Web browsers, so no new training should be required. Java also creates robust, sophisticated-looking products that can run on any type of computer.

According to Patricia McGinnis, a technology analyst at the Tower Group, a financial service consulting firm in Newton, Massachusetts, Web-based applications are appropriate in many other areas of banking, including cash management, corporate treasury functions, and foreign exchange.

FOCUS Questions:

Royal Bank's letters of credit application may be only the beginning of Java-enabled financial applications provided by large commercial banks. Why? How do the World Wide Web and Java help solve user interface and other standards problems?

SOURCES: Clinton Wilder, "Java in the Bank," *Information Week,* December 9, 1996, and Mitch Betts, "Standard GUIs Make Sense," *Computerworld,* March 14, 1994.

Step 5: Implementation To produce the new Web pages for Internet banking, U.S. Bank had to modify and test the programming for its Web pages and also had to test how the new Web site interacted with its underlying customer account systems. No special training or documentation was required for this modification since the Web site was designed to be self-explanatory. To determine whether the solution is achieving its objectives, UBank is collecting statistics on site usage and monitoring user reaction to the revamped Web site.

The Royal Bank of Canada is using Java and the Web for international trade applications that can run on computers all over the world.

Another source of user interface problems is conflicting standards for data input or display screens used in application software. The Focus on Problem Solving describes how the Royal Bank of Canada dealt with these problems.

10.4 PROBLEM SOLVING IN ACTION: REENGINEERING

Sometimes the solution to a problem requires not merely changes in procedures or technology but a fundamental rethinking of the organization's goals and the best means to achieve them. The next case illustrates a problem that was solved by redesigning some of the core processes of the organization.

AGWAY

Two straight years of business losses convinced management that Agway, the giant farm supply cooperative in the Northeast, was in serious trouble. Agway's 600 stores sold everything from cattle feed to garden trowels. The business, which operated like a retail chain, was supported by 18 warehouses and feed mills, a system that could no longer meet the needs of Agway's changing customer base. One of eight farms in the Northeast disappeared during the 1980s, and surviving farms were primarily large, sophisticated agricultural businesses whose owners and managers wanted more expertise than store personnel could provide. Although Agway shipped many orders directly from its mills and warehouses, the farmers placed their orders at the stores. The stores then submitted the orders to the appropriate mill, plant, or warehouse. The net result was a costly tangle of bills and records. Agway's retail, manufacturing, and distribution facilities ordered from and billed one another—all to serve the same customer. Customers with billing problems had to talk to one, two, or three people to find an answer. A complaint might take several weeks to resolve.

Discount retailers such as Wal-Mart started to take away general merchandise sales from Agway stores. Agway's ability to respond was hampered by its need to serve commercial farmers. Let's analyze Agway's problem.

APPLYING THE METHODOLOGY

Step 1: Problem Analysis The description of Agway above provides sufficient facts for our investigation.

Step 2: Problem Understanding Again we apply our matrix to find that Agway's problem is primarily organizational.

Technology	Organization	People
Hardware	Culture	Ergonomics
Software	Management	Evaluation
Telecommunications	Politics	Training
Database	✓ Bureaucracy	Employee Attitudes
	✓ Environment	Legal Compliance

The Problem

Agway is losing money because of a shrinking customer base, new competition, and an inability to service its traditional customers in an efficient and cost-effective manner.

Problem Dimensions

The problem has both external and internal dimensions.

- **External:** Agway's business environment is changing. There are fewer and fewer small farmers because changes in the farming industry favor large agribusinesses. These large agricultural businesses are willing to buy from Agway, but they require more service and efficiency. They do not want to take the trouble to visit stores to order.
- **Internal:** Agway has inefficient ordering and customer service processes with considerable duplication of paperwork and manual effort.

Step 3: Decision Making The solution objective was to make Agway more attractive to customers and more profitable. Agway must be able to sell general merchandise at prices competitive with discounters such as Wal-Mart, yet many of its customers are commercial farmers with specialized product needs. Agway had three alternatives: (1) Increase the number of store sales staff and customer service representatives helping farmers; (2) lower prices and focus on winning back customers from Wal-Mart; or (3) reorganize the business to differentiate more clearly between farm and nonfarm customers and to lower operational costs.

Agway selected the third alternative. Agway's senior managers carefully reviewed its business strategy and decided to separate the retail and commercial farming businesses because the needs of these businesses were too different to be served in the same way. They decided to reengineer the ordering process used for sales to farmers to make Agway's farm business more efficient and responsive to customers. Agway redesigned its organization so that farmers ordering farm supplies no longer had to go to the retail outlets. Instead, farmers could order all feed, crop, and seed supplies directly from regional service centers by calling (800) GO-AGWAY. It consolidated the number of ordering points to 15 regional customer service centers. Agway created an information system based on data collected from the point-of-sale system used in its retail stores. Customer service specialists can use PCs and terminals to access information on customer histories, credit information, and other data that are stored locally at the service centers and on Agway's Amdahl mainframe computer.

Step 4: Solution Design To implement the third alternative, Agway simplified the ordering process. It eliminated the step requiring farmers to place their orders at retail stores. Instead, farmers can place orders directly over the telephone. The regional service centers receive the telephone calls and transmit the orders directly to Agway's mills and warehouses, which then ship the goods to the farmers. Figure 10.5 compares Agway's old and new ordering processes.

The solution also called for new information systems to support these changes. Agway did not build all the systems it needed at once. It installed an interim computer system for customer service that connects an older system previously used by Agway's consumer group with two that had been used by its agricultural group. The result is an inefficient conglomeration of systems. For instance, Agway's customer service staff members can serve customers more knowledgeably by accessing background information on farmers' purchases, such as the kind of feed bought in the past. However, the system can access only the farmers' five previous orders. Some large farms put in five orders in only a week's time, so the system can't maintain enough order history data on them to be helpful. Although the customers are satisfied with the new ordering process, Agway realizes that it needs new systems that will more fully support the use of regional service centers in the ordering process.

The logical design for this interim system looks like this:

Inputs

Orders (name or customer identification number, items ordered, order date)

Customer data (name, address, credit terms)

Payment data (name, order, amount of payment)

Processing

Verify customer credit.

FIGURE 10.5

Agway's Reengineered Ordering Process

This figure illustrates Agway's ordering process before and after reengineering. The redesigned ordering process eliminated the need for farmers to visit retail outlets to place orders. Now farmers place their orders over the telephone.

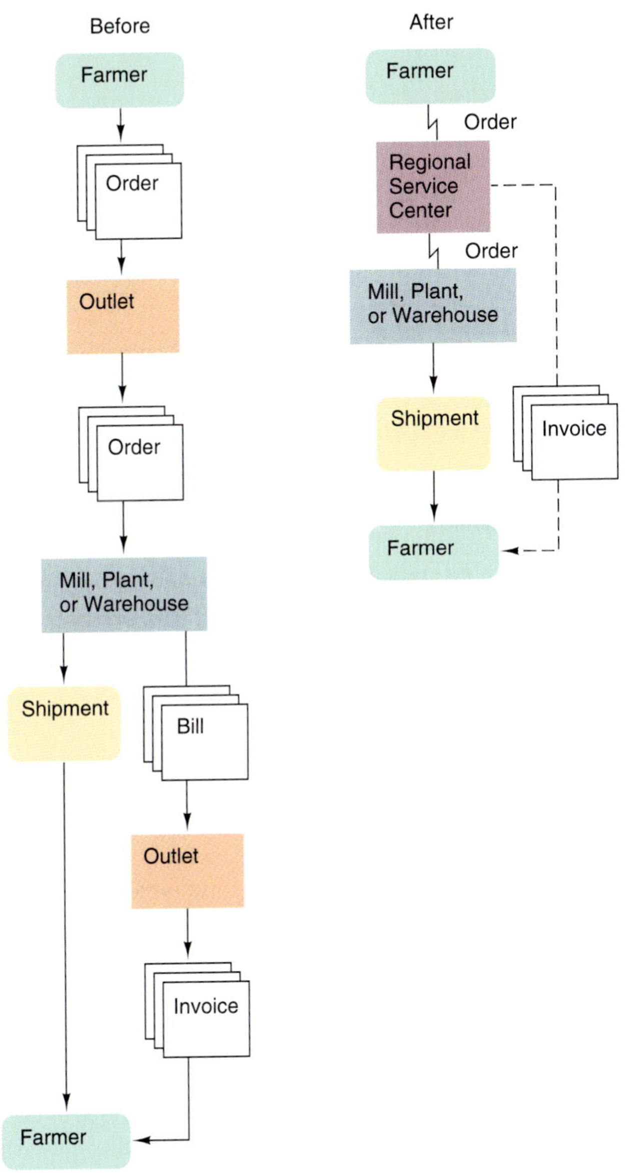

Calculate order amount and outstanding account balance.

Transmit order to mill or warehouse.

Update customer database with order and payment data.

Outputs

Order invoice

Order transaction listing

Order status information

Billing status information

Database

Customer database with customer data and order history data

Order file

Procedures

Input orders online at regional service centers when farmers call them in.

Assign the same employee to respond to customer inquiries about the status of orders or problems with bills.

Input payment data whenever it is received.

Controls

Reconcile payment checks with order amounts.

The physical design uses Agway's central mainframe computer linked to PCs and terminals at its regional service centers. Agway's customer database is replicated at the regional service centers and at the company's central mainframe.

Step 5: Implementation After Agway reengineered, employees had to undergo extensive training. Agway eliminated the jobs of many clerks in its retail outlets and reassigned employees to the regional customer service centers. The firm retrained them as customer service representatives. These employees need continued training as new functions are added to their information system. Although the retraining process has been largely successful, Agway has had problems changing employee attitudes. Some employees cannot understand the need for change.

The Focus on Technology explains why solutions based on networks, such as Agway's, or on the Internet should take transmission speed and capacity into account.

Most problems you will encounter in the real world will be more complex than the preceding examples. Their solutions will require in-depth research, analysis, and consideration of other factors, such as organizational culture or conflicting interest groups, that were not addressed here. In these cases, information system solutions were deliberately kept very simple so that we could focus on the problem-solving process itself.

What stands out in all these cases is the importance of analyzing all the dimensions of a problem in order to derive the right solution. If an information systems application is called for, these cases demonstrate that the solution must be visualized first in business terms, as a business solution or

FOCUS ON TECHNOLOGY

INTERNET TRAFFIC JAMS

If you are one of the people (and there are more than you think) who have given up surfing the Web because of the time it takes to "get" anywhere in the Web, you might soon have plenty of company: According to experts, the popularity of the Internet may be leading straight to its downfall. The arteries that carry the blood of the Internet have become so clogged that a full cardiac arrest has become more than just a possibility. Some refer to the phenomenon that has been called the "World Wide Wait," the time it can take to receive the information you requested, as evidence that traffic on the Internet has become too dense for its byways to handle.

The Internet was created as a means for academics to share information. It was not intended to carry the photos, images, movie clips, and sound files that now flow freely from computer to computer. Only a few years ago, Web pages numbered in the thousands. That number has quickly jumped to over 50 million.

The Internet contains several constructions whose functions or limitations can lead to slowdowns, and that perhaps one day will cause a major shutdown. The principal Internet operators pass electronic data to one another at intersections called "interconnects." At times, an operator's own lines are too busy to accept more data from other operators, and this results in congestion. Some of the large companies that offer Internet service will deal only with other operators who have a certain number of high-speed lines. Intercontinental lines can carry extremely high fees.

Internet service providers (ISPs) cannot keep up with the demand for their services. Service failures such as the November 1996 loss of nearly 200,000 E-mail messages by AT&T WorldNet Service and America Online's 19-hour service blackout in August 1996 are likely to increase. Logjams are starting to appear in the telephone systems that subscribers use to access their service providers. Current telephone systems were designed and priced so that 10 percent of all phones could be in use at any one time, with the average voice call lasting three to four minutes and the average phone line used less than one hour per day. The average Internet session lasts 22 minutes, and many people stay connected for hours.

Kinks in the Web come from a variety of sources. A software error can shut down online service for hours. The computers responsible for storing and delivering Web pages, called servers, sometimes run into situations where they simply cannot respond to all the requests they receive. Routers, the machines that ensure data heads down the correct pathway, experience more critical problems when they lose track of data packets. Packets that form part of the same message do not always travel the same route to arrive at their destination, making the system vulnerable to mistakes. To add to the complications, lost packets are constantly sent again, augmenting the stress on the routers.

Two schools of thought have emerged in regard to handling the saturation of the Internet. One side says to do nothing, insisting that every time people have foreseen the doom of the Internet throughout its history, it has survived. The other side believes that the technology has been pushed to its threshold and that it is growing faster than developers can possibly create methods to contain it.

One hope is that the trend of companies setting up their own private intranets will ease some of the strain on the Internet. If nothing is done to improve the flow of traffic on the Web, many more people may get frustrated and simply abandon it.

FOCUS Questions: How have changes in the Internet affected its use and effectiveness? How might Internet transmission capacity affect a solution design?

SOURCES: Cary Lu, "Make Room for Data," *Inc. Technology,* March 18, 1997, and Bart Ziegler, "Slow Crawl on the Internet," *The Wall Street Journal,* August 23, 1996.

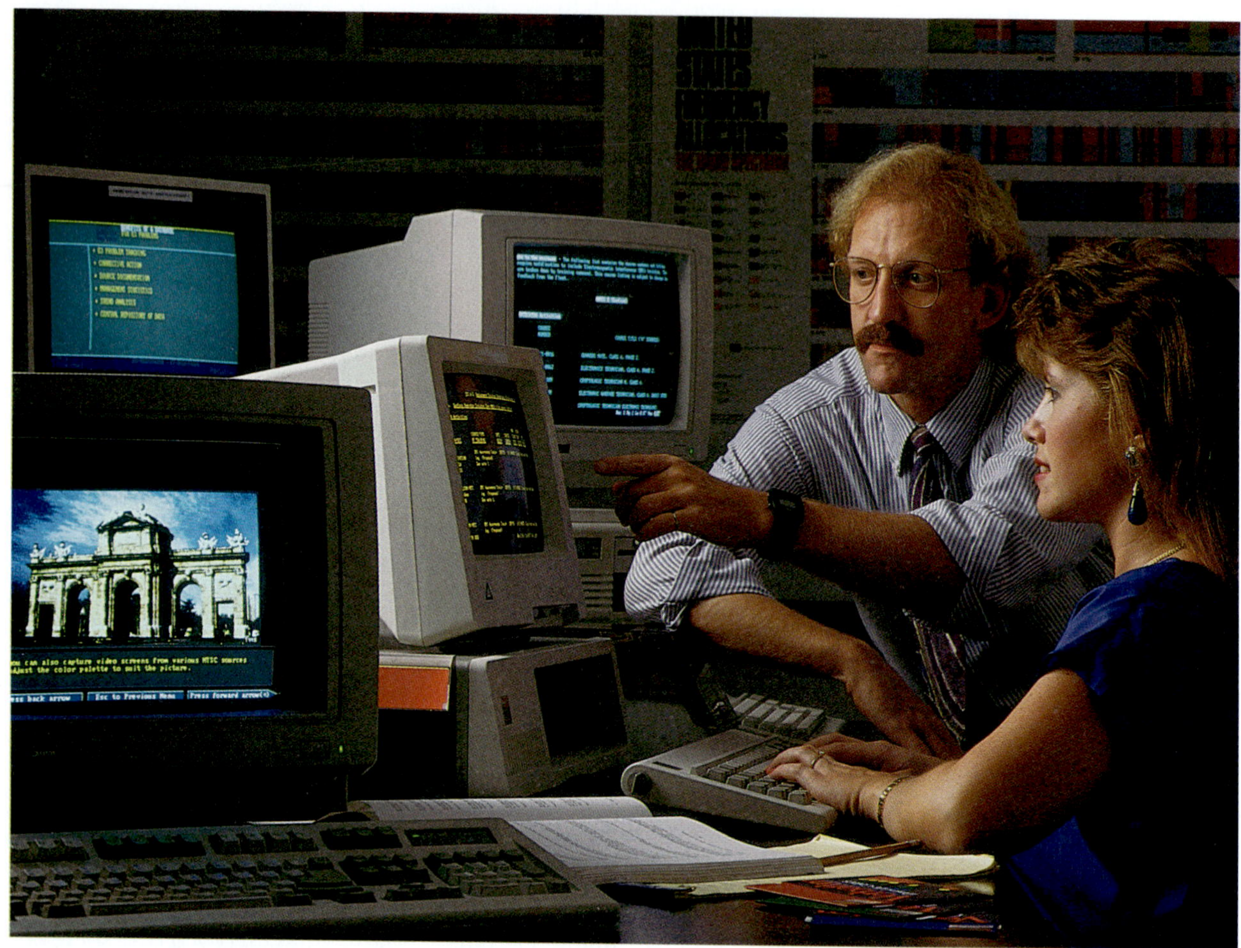

Many companies conduct programs and workshops for employees that emphasize customer service. Employee training—whether in customer service or systems procedures—will often solve business problems and prevent new ones.

SOURCE: © Matthew Borkoski, Stock, Boston.

logical systems model, before any details concerning computer hardware or software are addressed.

10.5 SYSTEMS-BUILDING TOOLS AND METHODOLOGIES

A number of tools and methodologies have been developed to document various aspects of the systems-building process. The most widely used are data flow diagrams, data dictionaries, and system flowcharts. These can be used during analysis of a problem to document an existing system or during solution design to help visualize a new solution. They are most useful for describing large, complex information systems. Simple, PC-based applications are often developed without these tools, especially if they involve only a limited number of data elements and one or two basic processes.

DATA FLOW DIAGRAMS

Data flow diagrams are useful for documenting the logical design of an information system. They show how data flow to, from, and within an information system and the various processes that transform those data. Data flow diagrams divide a system into manageable levels of detail so that it can be visualized first at a very general or abstract level and then gradually in greater and greater detail.

Data flow diagram
A graphic design that shows both how data flow to, from, and within an information system and the various processes that transform the data; used for documenting the logical design of an information system.

Basic data flow diagram symbols are shown in Figure 10.6. The arrow depicts the flow of data. The rounded box (sometimes a "bubble" or circle is used) is the process symbol; it signifies any process, computerized or manual, that transforms data. The open rectangle is the data store symbol; it indicates a file or repository in which data are stored. A rectangle or square is the external entity symbol; it indicates a source or receiver of data that is outside the boundaries of a system.

Data flows can consist of a single data element or of multiple data elements grouped together. The name or contents of each data flow are listed beside the arrow. Data flows can be manual or automated and can consist of documents, reports, or data from a computer file.

Data flow
The movement of data within an information system; it can consist of a single data element or multiple data elements grouped together and can be manual or automated.

Data flow diagrams can break a complex process into successive layers of detail by depicting the system in various levels. For example, Figure 10.7 shows a general picture of the patient billing and record-keeping system described earlier in this chapter. It is called a context diagram. The context diagram depicts an information system at the most general level, as a single process with its major inputs and outputs. Subsequent diagrams then break

FIGURE 10.6

Data Flow Diagram Symbols

Data flow diagrams can be constructed using only four basic symbols. Arrows represent the flow of data in a system. A box with rounded edges represents a process that changes input data into output. The open rectangle symbolizes a data store, a collection of data such as a file or database. Finally, a rectangle or square is an external entity that lies outside the system and serves as a source or destination of data.

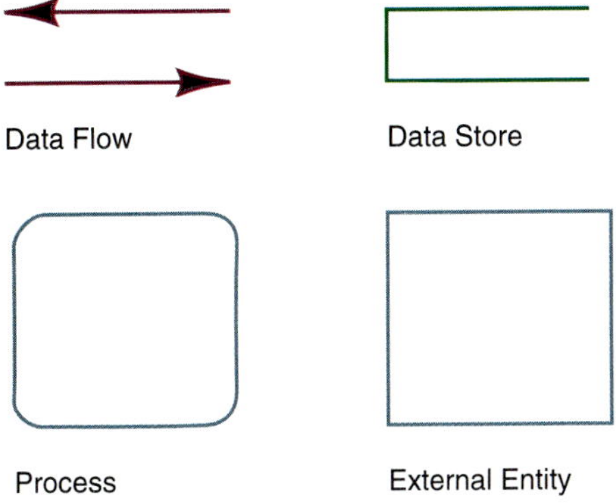

FIGURE 10.7

A Context Diagram of a Patient Billing System

A context diagram is a data flow diagram that gives a broad picture of a system: a single process with its principal inputs and outputs. The process in this case is the patient billing and record-keeping system discussed earlier in the chapter. The patient and the therapist are the principal external entities; the arrows depict the data flowing between the external entities and the system.

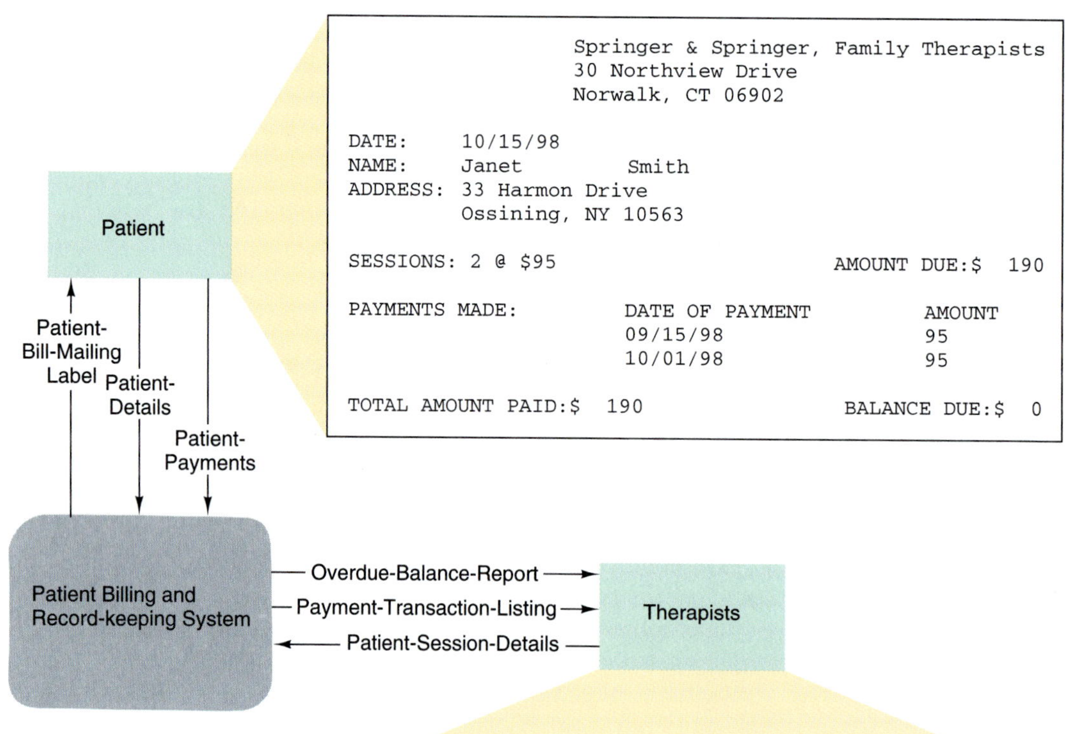

Springer & Springer, Family Therapists
30 Northview Drive
Norwalk, CT 06902
DATE: 10/15/98
NAME: Janet Smith
ADDRESS: 33 Harmon Drive
Ossining, NY 10563
SESSIONS: 2 @ $95
AMOUNT DUE:$ 190
PAYMENTS MADE:
DATE OF PAYMENT
09/15/98
10/01/98
AMOUNT
95
95
TOTAL AMOUNT PAID:$ 190
BALANCE DUE:$ 0
Patient
Patient-Bill-Mailing Label
Patient-Details
Patient-Payments
Patient Billing and Record-keeping System
Overdue-Balance-Report
Payment-Transaction-Listing
Patient-Session-Details
Therapists

Page No. 1
10/15/98

PAYMENT TRANSACTION LISTING REPORT

P-LAST NAME	P-FIRST NAME	PAYMENT DATE	PAYMENT AMOUNT
Harrison			
	Thomas	09/15/98	$0.00
SUM			$0.00
Smith			
	Janet	09/15/98	$95.00
	Janet	10/01/98	$95.00
SUM			$190.00
GRAND TOTAL			$190.00

FIGURE 10.8

Zero-Level and First-Level Data Flow Diagrams and Process Specifications

Data flow diagrams can be "exploded" into greater levels of detail. Panel a shows a zero-level data flow diagram, the next step in detail after the context diagram from Figure 10.7. Here the patient billing system includes three major processes: Capture Patient Details, Track Payments, and Prepare Bills and Reports. Panel b is a first-level data flow diagram that explodes process 3.0 into the next level of detail. We see that this process itself consists of three processes: Calculate Balance Due, Generate Bills and Reports, and Generate Mailing Labels. Panel c illustrates process specifications for process 3.3.

(a)

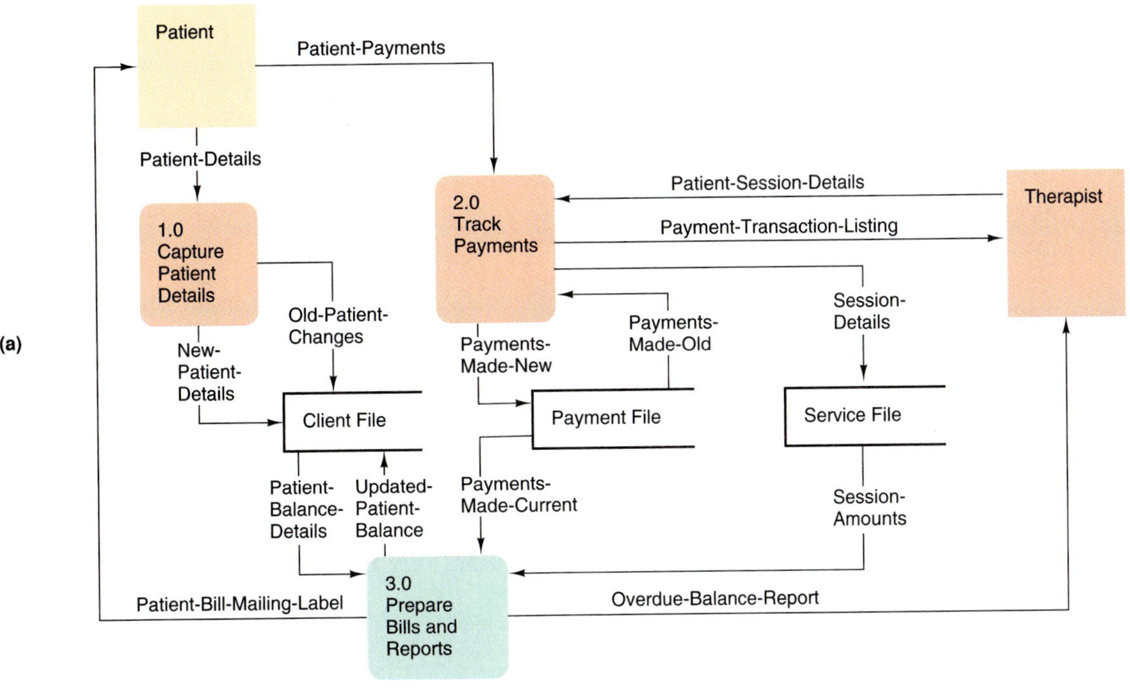

(b)

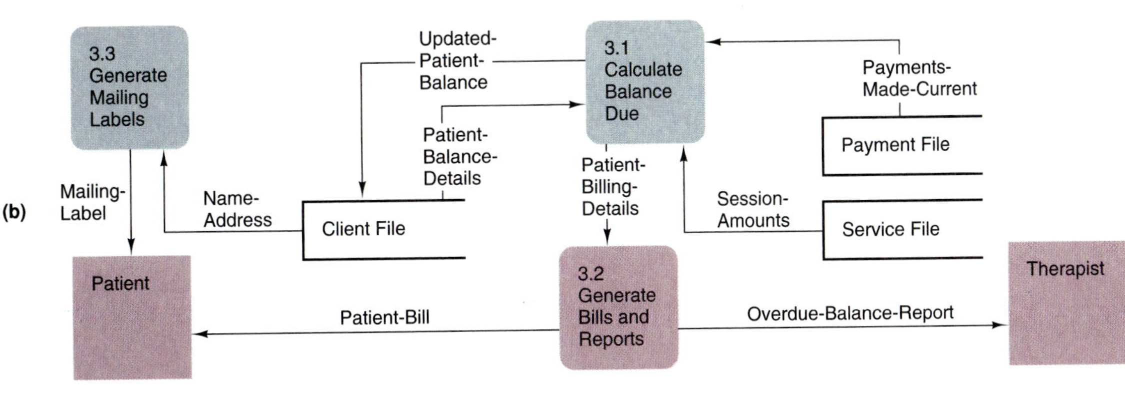

(c)

```
Generate Mailing Labels

For each patient in the client file do the following:
    IF the amount due is greater than 0,
        Print client's first name, last name, street,
        city, state, and zip code on mailing label report.
```

down the system into greater levels of detail. Panel a of Figure 10.8, which is called a zero-level data flow diagram, shows the same system at the next level of detail. It explodes the context diagram into multiple processes that are the major processes of the system: capturing patient details; tracking payments; and producing bills, mailing labels, patient listings, and other reports. Panel b is a first-level data flow diagram; it shows more specific detail about process 3.0, "Prepare Bills and Reports." If necessary, lower-level data flow diagrams can be used to break this process and others into even greater detail.

Accompanying the data flow diagrams is additional documentation with more detail about the data in the data flows and the logical steps in each process. For example, panel c illustrates the **process specifications** (the logical sequence of steps for performing a process) for process 3.3, "Generate Mailing Labels," in our first-level data flow diagram.

Process specifications
The logical steps for performing a process; they appear in documents accompanying lower-level data flow diagrams to show the various steps by which data are transformed.

THE DATA DICTIONARY

Details about each piece of data and the data groupings used in the data flows are maintained in a data dictionary. The data dictionary contains information about each data element, such as its name, meaning, size, format, and the processes in which it is used. Figure 10.9 shows sample data dictionary entries for our patient billing and record-keeping system. Panel a is a sample

FIGURE 10.9

Two Data Dictionary Entries for the Patient Billing System

A data dictionary "defines" each data element in a system by giving information such as its meaning, size, format, and the processes in which it is used. Panel a defines a data element called "Last-Name," which represents the patient's last name in the patient file. Panel b is an entry that defines a data flow, a group of elements that "travel" together through the system. This particular group is called "Payments-Made-Current."

(a)

Data Elements

NAME:	Last-Name
DEFINITION:	Designates the patient's last name
TYPE:	Character
LENGTH:	15 positions
ALIASES:	P-Last-Name
FILE WHERE FOUND:	Client Payment
PROCESSES WHERE USED:	1.0: Capture Patient Details 2.0: Track Payments 3.0: Prepare Bills and Reports 3.1: Calculate Balance Due 3.2: Generate Bills and Reports 3.3: Generate Mailing Labels

(b)

Data Flow

NAME:	Payments-Made-Current
DESCRIPTION:	Patient's payment transaction
CONTENTS:	Last-Name First-Name Payment-Amount Payment-Date Social-Security-Number
PROCESSES WHERE USED:	3.0: Prepare Bills and Reports 3.1: Calculate Balance Due

FIGURE 10.10

Basic System Flowchart Symbols

System flowcharts document the sequence of information flow and processing steps within a system. Notice that more symbols are involved in building a system flowchart than in drawing a data flow diagram.

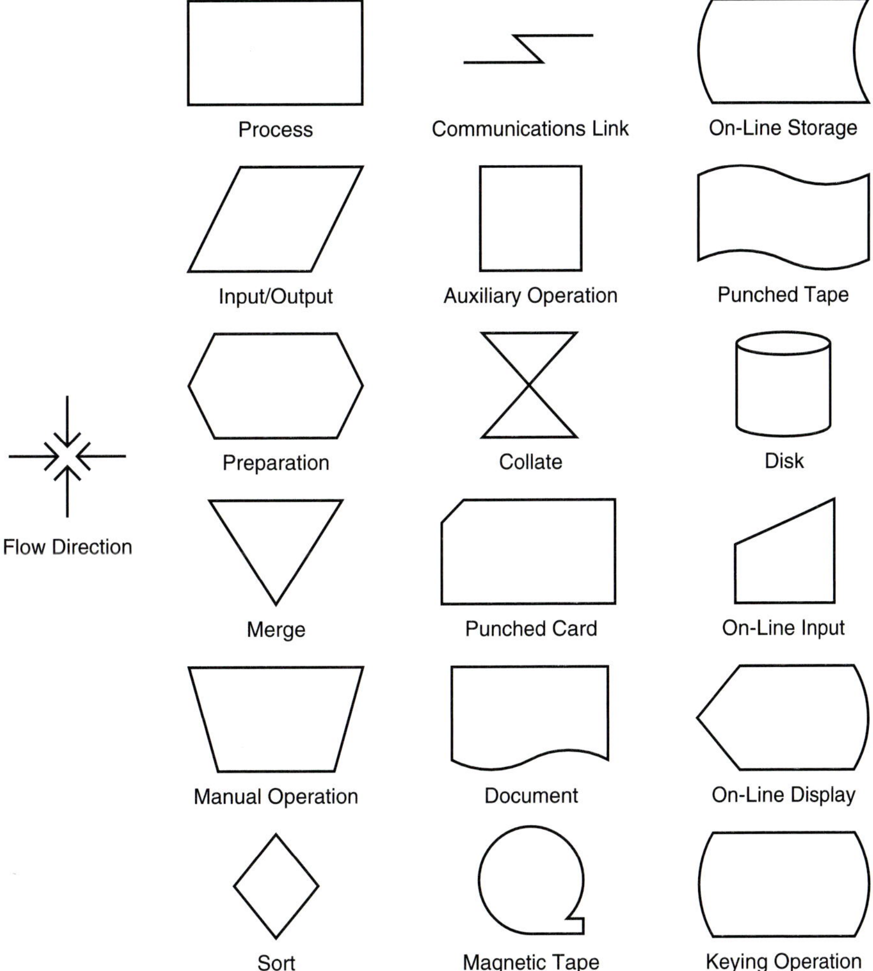

description of an individual data element from the patient file, the patient's last name. Panel b is a dictionary entry for a group of data elements traveling together as the data flow called Payments-Made-Current.

The data dictionary can be in paper and pencil form, but it is often automated since a large or medium-sized information system application must keep track of many pieces of data, processes, and interrelationships. Data dictionaries are not used only when a new system is being developed. They can also be used to help an organization keep track of all the data and groupings of data it maintains in existing systems. As discussed in Chapter 6, the data dictionary is a key component of a database management system. Data dictionaries thus provide a multipurpose data management tool for a business.

SYSTEM FLOWCHARTS

System flowchart
A diagram that documents the sequence of processing steps that take place in an entire system; most useful for physical design, in which such diagrams show the sequence of processing events and the files used by each processing step.

System flowcharts document the sequence of processing steps that take place in an entire system. They show the sequence of the flow of data and the files used by each processing step.

Figure 10.10 shows the basic symbols for system flowcharting. The most important are the plain rectangle, representing a computer processing function; the flow lines, which show the sequence of processing steps; and the arrows, which show the direction of information flow. Figure 10.11 illustrates how our patient billing and record-keeping system would be represented as a system flowchart.

System flowcharts differ from data flow diagrams in that more attention is paid to the sequence of processing events and the physical media used in processing. Data flow diagrams, in contrast, are a more logical and abstract way of representing a system. Data flow diagrams do not show the physical characteristics of the system or the exact timing of steps taken during processing.

FIGURE 10.11

A System Flowchart Depicting the Patient Billing System

This system flowchart illustrates the major steps involved in the patient billing system discussed earlier in this chapter. Note that this flowchart is more specific than a data flow diagram about the sequence and physical characteristics of processes, inputs, and outputs in this system.

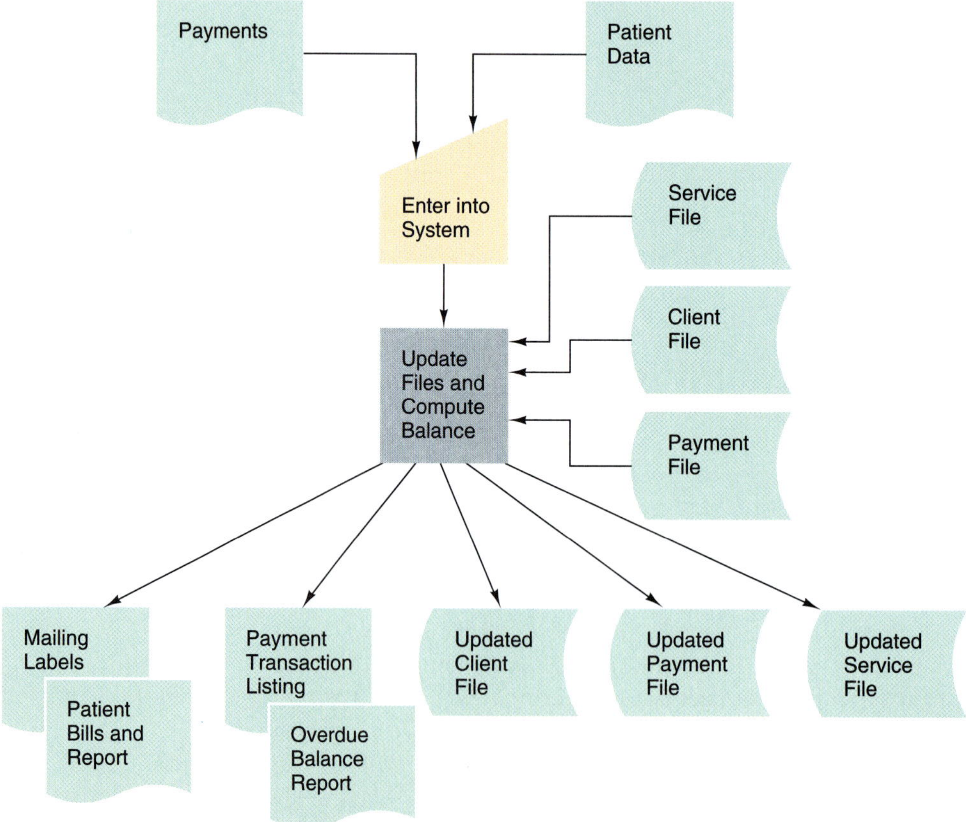

FIGURE 10.12

A Structure Chart for an Order Processing Program

A structure chart is a tool for documenting levels and relationships within a computer program. Each box represents a module, a logical subdivision that performs one task or a few related tasks. We can see that the basic functions of this program are to input orders, update the inventory, and produce order reports as output.

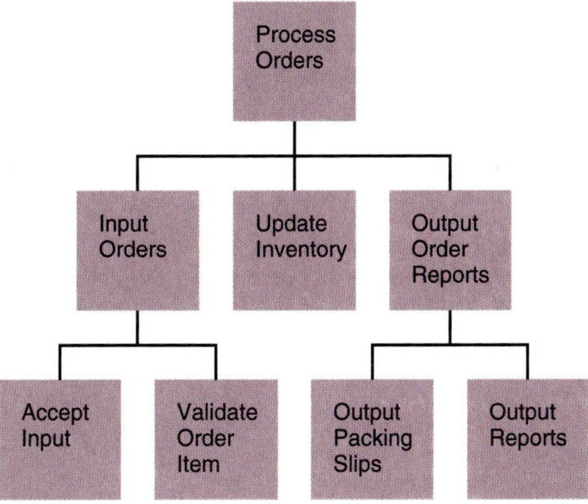

STRUCTURED DESIGN AND PROGRAMMING

To develop good software, developers must carefully think out and design the programs. In the earliest days of computing, programmers wrote software according to their own whims, with the result that programs were often confusing and difficult to work with. Software today is expected to follow recognized design principles. The prevailing design standards are structured design and structured programming.

Structured Design According to **structured design** principles, a program should be designed from the top down as a hierarchical series of modules. A **module** is a logical way of partitioning or subdividing a program so that each module performs one or a small number of related tasks. In **top-down design,** one should first consider the program's main functions, subdivide each function into component modules, and then subdivide each component module until the lowest level of detail has been reached.

The structured design is documented in a structure chart showing each level of the design and its relationship to other levels. Structure charts resemble corporate organizational charts, but each box represents a program module. The chart shows how modules relate to each other but does not depict the details of the program instructions in each module.

Figure 10.12 shows a structure chart for a simple order processing program. There are three high-level program modules for the major functions of the program: inputting orders, updating inventory, and generating appropriate output documents. The structure chart shows that the modules for "Input Orders" and "Output Order Reports" can be further broken down into

Structured design
A software design principle according to which a program is supposed to be designed from the top down as a hierarchical series of modules with each module performing a limited number of functions.

Module
A logical way of partitioning or subdividing a program so that each component (i.e., module) performs a limited number of related tasks.

Top-down design
A principle of software design according to which the design should first consider the program's main functions, subdivide these functions into component modules, and then subdivide each component module until the lowest level of detail has been reached.

Structured programming
A way of writing program code that simplifies control paths so that programs can be easily understood and modified by others; it relies on three basic control constructs—the sequence construct, the selection construct, and the iteration construct.

Sequence construct
A series of statements that are executed in the order in which they appear, with control passing unconditionally from one statement to the next; one of three basic control constructs in structured programming.

Selection construct
A series of statements that tests a condition; depending on whether the results of the test are true or false, one of two alternative instructions will be executed; one of three basic control constructs in structured programming.

Iteration construct
A series of statements that repeats an instruction as long as the results of a conditional test are true; one of three basic control constructs in structured programming.

another level of detail. The "Input Orders" module has subsidiary modules for accepting input and validating orders. The "Output Order Reports" module has subsidiary modules for generating packing slips and various reports.

Structured Programming **Structured programming** is a way of writing program code that simplifies control paths so that programs can be easily understood and modified by others. A structured program uses only three basic control constructs, or patterns, for executing instructions: the sequence construct, the selection construct, and the iteration construct (see Figure 10.13).

The **sequence construct** consists of a series of statements that are executed in the order in which they appear, with control passing unconditionally from one statement to the next. Panel a of Figure 10.13 shows a sequence construct in which a program executes statement A and then statement B.

The **selection construct** tests a condition. Depending on whether the results of that test are true or false, one of two alternative instructions is executed. In panel b of Figure 10.13, a selection construct tests condition D. If D is true, statement E is executed. If D is false, statement F is executed. Control then passes to the next program statement.

The **iteration construct** repeats an instruction as long as the results of a conditional test are true. In panel c of Figure 10.13, statement H will be executed as long as condition G is true. Once G is found false, H is skipped, and control passes to the next program statement.

Proponents of structured programming claim that any program can be written using one or a combination of these control constructs. Each construct has a single entry and exit point so that the path of the program logic remains clear.

Structured analysis and design embody a more traditional approach to developing software, which treats data and procedures as independent components. A separate procedure must be written each time someone wants to take an action on a particular piece of data. Newer approaches to designing

FIGURE 10.13

The Three Constructs of Structured Programming: Sequence, Selection, and Iteration

These three constructs, or patterns for executing instructions, are the building blocks of structured computer programs. Panel a shows the sequence construct, a series of statements that are executed in the order in which they occur. Panel b is the selection construct, which tests a given condition and then branches to one of two possible alternatives ("true" or "false"), depending on the outcome of the test. The iteration construct, panel c, repeats an instruction as long as the outcome of a test is "true."

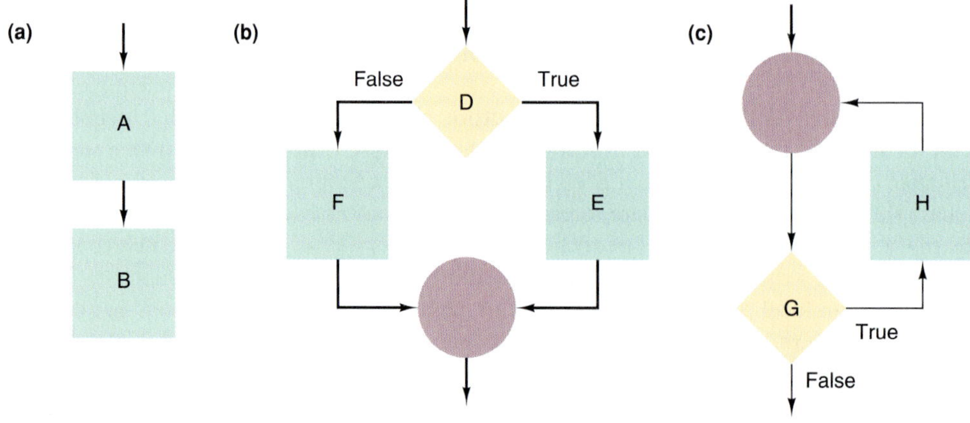

FIGURE 10.14

Program Flowchart Symbols

Program flowcharts graphically document the steps that are followed in a specific computer program (as opposed to system flowcharts, which depict an entire information system). Structured program flowcharts are drawn using the three control structures of structured programming—sequence, selection, and iteration.

Process

Represents a group of instructions performing a processing function.

Predefined Process

Designates program instructions not detailed in the flowchart.

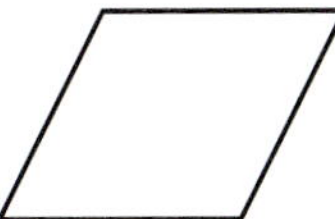

Input/Output

Designates movement of data into or out of a program's processing flow.

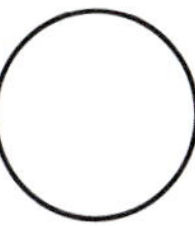

Connector

Links portions of a flowchart on the same page or separate pages.

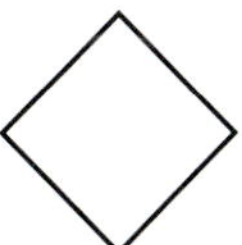

Decision

Designates a point in a program where the decision construct is used and the program flow can take one of two alternative paths.

Terminal

Indicates the beginning or end of a program.

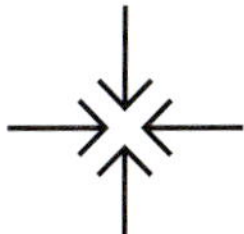

Flow Lines

Show the direction of the flow of program logic.

software, such as object-oriented programming, do not make such distinctions between data and procedures (see Chapter 6).

Documenting Program Logic Two popular methods of documenting the logic followed by program instructions are structured program flowcharts and pseudocode. **Structured program flowcharts** use graphic symbols to depict the steps that processing must take in a specific program, using the three control structures of structured programming. Figure 10.14 explains the flowcharting symbols. The left portion of panel a of Figure 10.15 shows a structured program flowchart for a program that reads student records and prints out each record. The right portion of panel a is a second flowchart that details the steps involved in the predefined process "Process Records Routine."

Structured program flowchart
A method of documenting the logic followed by program instructions; uses graphic symbols to depict the steps that processing must take in a specific program, using the three control constructs of structured programming.

FIGURE 10.15

Program Flowcharts and Pseudocode for a Program That Reads and Prints Student Records

Panel a illustrates the program flowchart, showing the sequence of instructions for a program that reads student records and then prints them out. Notice the predefined process, "Process Records Routine." To the right is another flowchart that represents the steps followed in "Process Records Routine." Panel b shows the pseudocode statements that describe the logic in the first flowchart.

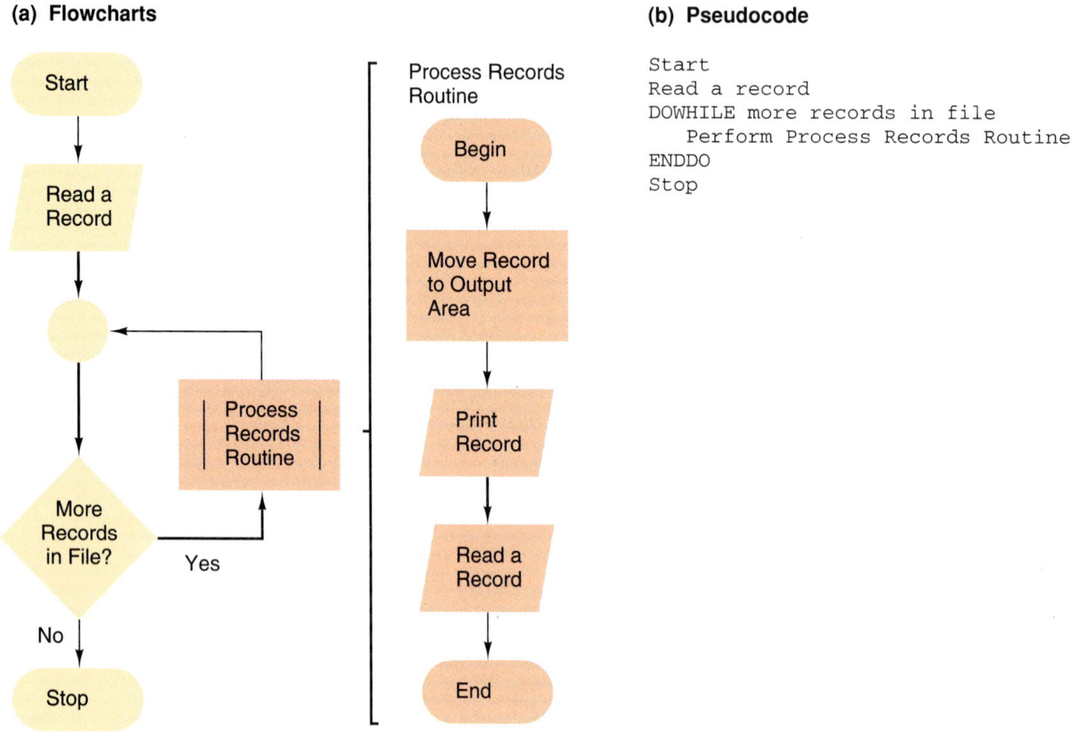

(b) Pseudocode

```
Start
Read a record
DOWHILE more records in file
   Perform Process Records Routine
ENDDO
Stop
```

Pseudocode
A method of documenting the logic followed by program instructions in which English-like statements are used to describe processing steps and logic.

Pseudocode uses plain English-like statements rather than graphic symbols or programming language to describe processing steps and logic. Once the outline for processing has been established, pseudocode can easily be translated into a programming language. Pseudocode uses the same control structures as structured programming. Panel b of Figure 10.15 shows the pseudocode for the first flowchart in panel a.

COMPUTER-AIDED SOFTWARE ENGINEERING

Special software has been developed to automate the generation of data flow diagrams, system flowcharts, data dictionaries, program code, and other tasks in the systems development process so that systems can be fashioned much more rapidly and efficiently. The automation of methodologies for software and systems development is called computer-aided software engineering, or CASE. Many different kinds of CASE tools are commercially available. The most sophisticated integrate multiple tasks, such as linking a description of a data element in a data dictionary to all data flow diagrams or process specifications that use this piece of data. The illustrated case concluding Part 3 describes the myriad capabilities of CASE tools.

SUMMARY

- You cannot successfully build an information system without first understanding a problem, describing it, and designing a solution using the five-step approach to problem solving introduced in the text.
- Even if a problem does not involve an information system application, the implementation of the solution will still require changes in the procedures, management, or personnel.
- Data flow diagrams are most useful for documenting the logical design of an information system. They show how data flow to, from, and within an information system and the various processes that transform those data.
- A data dictionary is used in solution design to define and describe each piece of data and the data groupings used in an information system.
- System flowcharts document the sequence of processing steps that take place in an entire system. They are most useful for physical design, in which they show the sequence of the flow of data and the files used by each processing step.
- Structured design and structured programming are software design principles that promote software with a simple, clear structure that is easy to follow and maintain.
- Structured design organizes a program into a hierarchy of modules from the top down, with each module performing a limited number of functions.
- Structured programming is a method of writing programs using only three basic control constructs: sequence, selection, and iteration.

KEY TERMS

Data flow diagram
Data flow
Process specification
System flowchart
Structured design
Module
Top-down design
Structured programming
Sequence construct
Selection construct
Iteration construct
Structured program flowchart
Pseudocode

REVIEW QUESTIONS

1. Why should the solution to an application problem be worked out before hardware and software are considered?
2. How can you distinguish between a problem that requires an information system application solution and one that does not?
3. What is a data flow diagram? How is it used in systems analysis and design?
4. What is a data dictionary? How is it used in systems analysis and design?
5. What is a system flowchart? How is it used in systems analysis and design?
6. Define structured design and structured programming. How do they contribute to software design?
7. Name and describe the three basic control structures in structured programming.
8. Describe how each of the following is used in software development: structure charts, structured program flowcharts, and pseudocode.

DISCUSSION QUESTIONS

1. How would you decide whether an information system application should be processed on a PC? How would you decide whether an application should be processed with spreadsheet or database software?
2. Why is programming such a small part of the development of an information system?
3. Why must procedures be considered in solution design as well as hardware and software?

PROBLEM-SOLVING EXERCISES

1. *Group exercise:* Divide into groups. Each group should use several levels of data flow diagrams and a system flowchart to document the solution design for partnership allocation at Haskell, Simpson, and Porter.
2. Create a data dictionary for the data elements used in the solution design for Haskell, Simpson, and Porter.
3. *Hands-on exercise:* Use a structured program flowchart to document a program that reads a student file and outputs a report of names of students qualifying for the dean's list. To qualify, students must have a grade point average of at least 3.5. Then, document the same program using pseudocode. Use appropriate software to either write the program or develop an application that performs these functions. You can use the following list of students to test your solution:

ID	Name	Grade Average
323442373	Stephen Turkell	2.8
693920485	Carla Burton	3.6
405828451	Angela Myers	3.4
684092346	Timothy Shaw	3.5
583023988	Andrew Lund	1.9

4. *Internet problem-solving exercise: Buying a Home*

You are thinking of relocating to another part of the country and want to check out the price and availability of a home. Before you start traveling around, you can use HomeBuyer Internet Real Estate Service to help you with your research. Use the Home Search feature. Select a county and state where you might want to live, and check out the listings for homes priced under $100,000. (A list of suggestions is posted on the Web site for this text.) Once you locate a listing you like, calculate the monthly payment cost for owning this home. Assume that the mortgage interest rate will be 9.5 percent, the length of the mortgage will be 30 years, and the amount of the mortgage will be $80,000. Write a brief description of your findings, including the location, price, number of bedrooms, annual taxes, and monthly payment costs for the home.

PROBLEM-SOLVING CASES: SOLUTION DESIGN PROJECTS

RIVER EDGE SUPERMARKET

Profit margins in the supermarket business are only 1 to 2 percent of gross sales. The River Edge Supermarket in Peekskill, New York, is fighting stiff competition from new Shoprite and Food Emporium markets several miles away. It has been able to survive on much lower sales volumes than its competitors by keeping operating costs to a bare minimum and specializing in fresh fruits, vegetables, baked goods, and natural beef for an upscale local village clientele.

Most products, with the exception of fresh produce, are marked with a price tag. The price of fruits and vegetables is calculated by weighing them and multiplying the weight by the cost per pound of each item. The cost of fresh produce changes daily and is posted above each cash register on a chart. However, some produce items, such as Idaho potatoes, are marked with a product code number, such as 547. The cashier at the checkout counter must consult the produce chart for the price of code 547. Sometimes the cashier rings up $5.47 instead. River Edge recently modernized its store facilities to attract more customers, and lines have been growing longer.

What is River Edge Supermarket's problem? How can it be solved?

THE OFF-CAMPUS HOUSING OFFICE

Finger Lakes University in upstate New York does not have sufficient dormitory space to house all its liberal arts, agricultural school, and graduate students. It uses a lottery system to determine which students can live in dorm rooms and which must find housing elsewhere. About half of Finger Lakes' students seek off-campus housing.

The ultimate responsibility for locating suitable housing rests with each student, but Finger Lakes offers assistance through its Off-Campus Housing Office (OCHO). OCHO maintains bulletin board listings of available housing and provides legal counseling services for students and landlords with questions about their leases.

Only 10 percent of OCHO's resources are devoted to legal services. Its most critical function is listing available housing in the surrounding area. Some landlords advertise in local newspapers, but virtually all openings flow through OCHO.

Landlords fill out an OCHO card describing the type of lodging they have available. This card is then placed on a bulletin board. Students review the bulletin board listings and copy down those of greatest interest. Then they call the landlords for appointments to view the lodgings.

Cards are often put up haphazardly on the wrong bulletin board. Occasionally, a student will pull a card off to prevent other students from learning of the opening. Both students and landlords complain that listings remain posted several months after they have been filled. OCHO has no idea how many students actually use its services or the amount of student housing available. It does know, however, that around the time of the on-campus dormitory lottery, its office is jammed to capacity, to the point of being dangerously overcrowded, and students have difficulty seeing the bulletin board.

What is the problem at OCHO? How can it be solved? If an application solution is required, develop a logical model for the solution and determine whether it is a PC, mainframe, or Internet application. If the application can be developed on a PC, develop the application using spreadsheet or database software. Justify your design and your decision. Document your solution design using data flow diagrams, the data dictionary, and a system flowchart. For this case, you might want to consider how the Internet could be used in addition to a PC software tool.

MADISON BED AND BREAKFAST HOUSE

The Madison Bed and Breakfast House in the historic Connecticut River Valley rents rooms to overnight guests. The house is a restored Victorian mansion, decorated in period furnishings, with a sunshine-filled breakfast and sitting room. The room charge covers the cost of an overnight stay and breakfast. Overnight guests can choose among seven rooms, each with its own personality, such as the dark wood-paneled "Library" or the "Honeymoon Suite" with Jacuzzi. Room charges range from $85 per night for the smallest room to $165 per night for the Honeymoon Suite.

Sylvia Norton, the owner and sole proprietor of Madison Bed and Breakfast House, keeps records of guests in a fat, loose-leaf notebook. When a guest calls to make a reservation or checks in, Sylvia enters the name, permanent address, telephone number, credit card number, arrival date, departure date, and name of the room onto a piece of paper and files it in the notebook. At the end of a guest's stay, she calculates the total cost with a calculator and enters it into the notebook as well. To total room revenues for the week or for the year, she must go through all her notebook entries again and use her calculator again. Sometimes she has trouble locating a guest's record if the pages have been misfiled.

Sylvia would like to increase her occupancy rate. She has no way of knowing where most of her guests come from, whether guests are more interested in renting rooms because of their decor or their price, and the occupancy rates at different times of the year. Sylvia feels that if she had this information, she might learn how to improve her services or advertising to attract more guests. She would also like to be able to quickly calculate her total room revenues for the week or for the year.

Sylvia's advertising budget is very small. Most of her guests learn about the house through word of mouth, travel magazines, or regional travel guides.

Analyze the problem at Madison Bed and Breakfast House. If an application solution is required, develop a logical model for the solution and determine whether it is a spreadsheet, database, mainframe, or Internet application. If the application can be developed on a PC, develop the application using spreadsheet or database software. Justify your design and your decision. Document your solution design using data flow diagrams, a data dictionary, and a system flowchart. For this case, you might want to consider how the Internet could be used in addition to one of the PC software tools.

VIDEO-SAVE MAIL-ORDER CASSETTES

James and Susan Branson found that they could make money in their own home by selling videocassette tapes through the mail at discount prices. They can sell a cassette that would normally retail for $29.95 at the video store for $10.00 less because they have almost no overhead expenses. Their inventory is stored in their garage and family room, and Susan Branson uses a home office with a WATS line to answer telephone orders. Many orders are placed by mail as well.

The Bransons started out by advertising in several popular television and movie magazines. Now that they have a customer base of over 3,000, they would like to change their marketing strategy. Video-Save has an inventory of over 500 titles. Its full-color catalog with a description of each tape initially cost $15,000 to print and mail. The Bransons would like to find a more inexpensive way to contact customers, such as with an occasional announcement of new releases or a special mailing directed to a special interest group—for example, purchasers of "self-help" tapes. They want to avoid expensive catalog mailings that do not bring in sales.

The Bransons recently purchased a PC and printer with word processing, spreadsheet, and database software, but they are not sure what to do next. They do not need an elaborate accounts receivable system because all orders must be prepaid. Video-Save receives approximately 18 orders each day. Mrs. Branson uses preprinted invoice forms and types out the customer's name, address, credit card number, product number, quantity, title (product description), unit cost, shipping cost, and total cost of each order. The product numbers consist of five characters, with the first character designating the type of video: A designates adult-only videos;

C, children's videos; S, sports videos; H, self-help videos; F, foreign films; and G, dramas or comedies of general interest. The Bransons maintain their customer list on index cards and have used a direct mail service to generate mailing labels for their catalogs and announcements.

Analyze the problem(s) at Video-Save. If an application solution is required, develop a logical model for the solution and determine whether it is a PC spreadsheet, PC database, Internet, or mainframe application. If the application can be developed on a PC, develop the application using spreadsheet or database software, whichever is more appropriate. Justify your design and your decision. Document your solution design using data flow diagrams, a data dictionary, and a system flowchart. For this case, you might want to consider how the Internet could be used in addition to one of the PC software tools.

H. V. CONSTRUCTION COMPANY

Real estate development is a high-risk method of investment but one in which rewards can be substantial. In addition to a strong vision of a project, correct timing and accurate profit calculations are essential. Moreover, without adequate bank financing at supportable interest rates, a project will never be built.

The real estate boom of the past decade left the market highly volatile. Costs of building materials and land spiraled upward, while an uncertain economy and high levels of consumer debt made the demand for housing much less predictable.

Under such conditions, the H. V. Construction Company, a small general contracting firm, has been moving into development of residential townhouse complexes. H. V. hopes to combine its track record for quality construction with competitive pricing. To do this, the company tries to minimize overhead by subcontracting most of the construction work and maintaining a small office with a skeleton staff. The permanent staff consists of only the owner, a secretary, a carpenter/superintendent, an additional carpenter, a general utility man, and a laborer.

H. V.'s owner, Harold Larson, feels that this is the only way his company can compete with the development giants. But he finds himself overwhelmed since he must find prospective properties, complete all financial calculations, prepare all proposal and correspondence documents, and shop around various banks for project financing. At present, he prepares all his project estimates with a handheld calculator. Any changes in relevant costs that alter the profitability of a project, such as interest rates, must be changed manually and retabulated.

Larson also knows that preparing a good bid is critical for survival. A sound estimate has double objectives: It must be low and solid enough that the construction company will be awarded the job yet provide enough extra that the construction company can make a profit from the contract. If the bid fails on one or the other count, the company will soon be out of business. There is no margin for error. In bidding a job, there is no prize for second place. The company is either awarded the contract or isn't.

The formula for a successful bid requires many ingredients: labor requirements, current labor rates, materials required and material costs, and total labor-hours anticipated. The cost of each component constantly shifts. When labor rates and prices from suppliers are volatile, the longer a company can wait before submitting its estimate, the better its chances are of being the low bidder.

The following cost components must be considered:

- Up-front fixed costs: architect, developed lot, and legal and accounting fees
- Sales and marketing
- Total number of units
- Cost of building materials per unit
- Estimated labor cost per unit
- Financing costs: loan principal, interest rate, and financing period
- Profit margin

The company has a PC and printer. H. V. uses it primarily for word processing, and it has been a very cost-effective tool for generating correspondence and proposals.

Analyze the problem(s) at H. V. Construction Company. If an application solution is required, develop a logical model for the solution and determine whether it is a PC spreadsheet, PC database, Internet, or mainframe application. If the application can be developed on a PC, develop the application using spreadsheet or database software, whichever is more appropriate. Justify your design and your decision. Document your solution design using data flow diagrams, a data dictionary, and a system flowchart.

Chapter

ELEVEN

ALTERNATIVE APPROACHES TO INFORMATION SYSTEM SOLUTIONS

CHAPTER OUTLINE

LEARNING OBJECTIVES

After reading and studying this chapter, you will

1. Be able to apply the most important approaches for designing information system solutions: the traditional systems life cycle, prototyping, the use of software packages, fourth-generation development, and outsourcing.
2. Understand the relationship of each approach to the core problem-solving process.
3. Know the steps and processes of each design method.
4. Be aware of the kinds of problems for which each design method is most appropriate.
5. Know the roles assigned to end users and technical specialists in each system-building approach.
6. Understand the strengths and limitations of each system-building approach.

PFIZER'S SHERLOCK SLEUTHS FOR SOLUTIONS

Pressures to contain health-care costs have impacted the pharmaceutical industry as well as physicians and hospitals. The average sales call for prescription drugs has been reduced from 15 minutes to less than five. With less "face time" to spend with doctors, pharmaceutical sales representatives need to pack the most precise and effective information into a tightly organized sales pitch.

Pfizer Inc. responded to this challenge by building a new sales automation system called Sherlock, which consolidates the information from three previously separate territory management systems into a single platform. By pooling the knowledge of 2,700 sales representatives about physicians' prescription patterns, managed care organizations, and company sales promotion programs, the new system helps Pfizer's sales representatives assemble critical information much faster to customize their sales pitches.

To design Sherlock, Pfizer first developed a prototype database using Microsoft Access database management software. The prototype was used to design a pilot program that was tested in several Pfizer sales districts. Pfizer then used the feedback from those trials to develop its full-blown sales automation system. Since Pfizer did not have the in-house staff to develop or support the new system, it outsourced these tasks to Dendrite International, a developer of pharmaceuticals sales territory management systems based in Morristown, New Jersey.

Dendrite used PowerBuilder software from Powersoft Corporation in Concord, Massachusetts, to develop database, territory management, travel and expense, sales activity, call reporting, and E-mail applications. Dendrite also created a "shared fields" application that lets sales representatives and managers exchange notes about doctors and managed care plans. Sales representatives store the information in Sybase SQL Anywhere databases stored on 4.3 pound Toshiba 486 notebook computers. When the representatives dial into Pfizer's central system using modems, their shared-fields information is added to Pfizer's main Oracle database. The representatives can simultaneously download information from this database that others have entered. For instance, if different sales representatives meet with the same doctor, the other representatives should know who was there and what they discussed. Dendrite developed special software to handle the synchronization between the Oracle database and the SQL Anywhere databases on the sales representative's laptops.

The year Sherlock was implemented, Pfizer reported a sales increase of 26 percent, followed by promising gains in sales the next year. These gains in large measure came from strong sales of new drugs such as Norvasc, a high blood-pressure treatment, and Zoloft, an antidepressant rival to Eli Lilly's Prozac. Sherlock's developers don't claim credit for all this growth but believe that team selling was a factor. The new system provides a better understanding of Pfizer's sales environment and its customers.

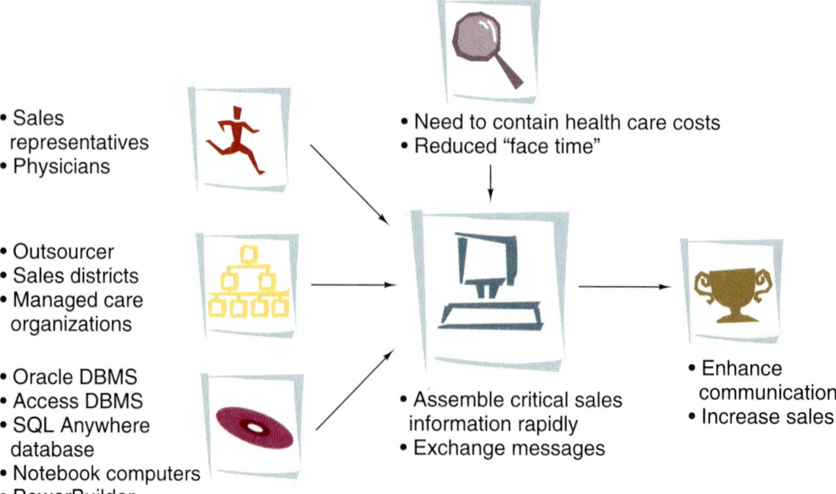

SOURCE: Jill Gambon, "Sales Sleuths Find Solutions," *Information Week,* July 2, 1996.

To implement the Sherlock sales automation system, Pfizer turned to an external contractor. This approach to developing system solutions is called outsourcing. Pfizer also used another approach called prototyping to design a preliminary version of the system. Outsourcing and prototyping are two alternative methods for creating information system solutions. Others include the use of application software packages, end-user development, and in-house custom development using the traditional systems life cycle. Different problems call for different rules, procedures, and philosophies for building information systems. In this chapter we describe and compare these alternative approaches.

11.1 INTRODUCTION

The actual development of an information system solution can take many paths. The solution may require a large central mainframe connecting 20,000 people or a laptop personal computer, elaborate programming and testing or a simple word processing and graphics package. The problem to be solved may be fully structured or only semistructured. A structured problem is one for which the solution is repetitive, routine, and involves a definite procedure that can be used each time the same problem is encountered. For a semistructured problem, only parts of the problem have a clear-cut answer, provided by a definite procedure. Depending on the size, scope, complexity, and characteristics of the firm, different kinds of systems require different approaches to put them in place.

Some methods entail a more formal approach to solution design than others. Some call for clearly demarcated roles of end users and technical specialists; others blur this distinction. What is common to all of them is the core problem-solving methodology described in preceding chapters.

11.2 THE TRADITIONAL SYSTEMS LIFE CYCLE

The oldest methodology for building an information system is called the **traditional systems life cycle.** This method of developing systems is still the predominant method for building large and medium mainframe-based systems today.

Traditional systems life cycle
The oldest methodology for building an information system; consists of six stages (project definition, systems study, design, programming, installation, and postimplementation) that must be completed sequentially.

The "life cycle" metaphor partitions the development of a system into a formal set of stages, in much the same way as the life cycle of a human being or other organism can be divided into stages—a beginning, middle, and end. The systems life cycle has six stages:

1. Project definition
2. Systems study
3. Design

4. Programming
5. Installation
6. Postimplementation

Each stage is assigned activities that must be completed before the next stage can begin. Thus, the system must be developed sequentially, stage by stage. Formal sign-offs, or agreements between technical staff and business specialists, are required in order to mark the completion of each stage.

Another characteristic of life cycle methodology is its clear-cut, formal division of labor between business specialists and technical specialists. Much of the solution design is relegated to technical staff such as professional systems analysts and programmers. Systems analysts are responsible for the analysis of problems in existing systems and for solution design specifications. Programmers are responsible for coding and testing a system's software components. Both analysts and programmers use information and feedback provided by business specialists to guide their work, but the business specialists play a relatively passive role.

THE RELATIONSHIP OF THE LIFE CYCLE TO PROBLEM SOLVING

The stages of the life cycle correspond to some degree to the steps in our problem-solving methodology. Figure 11.1 illustrates the stages of the life cycle, the corresponding steps in problem solving, and the appropriate division of labor between end users and technical specialists throughout the cycle. Notice that there is not always a one-to-one correlation between stages in problem solving and the systems life cycle, but they follow a similar process. The **project definition** stage of the life cycle investigates whether a problem actually exists and whether it requires further analysis and research. If so, a formal project to build a new information system or modify an existing system will be initiated. Thus, this stage incorporates some aspects of our first step in problem solving.

Project definition
The process of investigating a perceived problem to determine whether a problem actually exists and, if so, whether it requires further analysis and research; the first stage of the traditional systems life cycle.

Systems study
The process of describing and analyzing problems of existing systems, specifying solution objectives, describing potential solutions, and evaluating various solution alternatives; the second stage of the traditional systems life cycle.

The **systems study** stage incorporates some of the first step of problem analysis as well as the next two steps. Activities during this stage focus on describing and analyzing problems of existing systems, specifying solution objectives, describing potential solutions, and evaluating various solution alternatives. Constraints on solutions and the feasibility of each alternative are examined.

All of the information gathered from studying existing systems and interviewing business specialists will be used to specify information requirements. A systems solution must identify who needs what information, where, when, and how. The requirements must be specified in detail, down to the last piece of data, and must consider organizational procedures and constraints as well as hardware, software, and data.

It is important to emphasize that an information system solution will not work unless it is built around the correct set of requirements. If it is not, the system will have to be revised or discarded, often with a great waste of time and money. Capturing requirements accurately is perhaps the most difficult aspect of system building.

Once requirements have been captured, the *design* stage can proceed. At this point, logical design specifications are generated. Design and documentation tools such as the data flow diagram, data dictionary, and system

FIGURE 11.1

The Systems Development Life Cycle

The systems development life cycle divides the process into a series of stages similar to the life cycle of a human being. These stages correspond to the steps in the five-step problem-solving process discussed in earlier chapters. As this diagram shows, the systems life cycle can be a very formal process where end users play a relatively passive role.

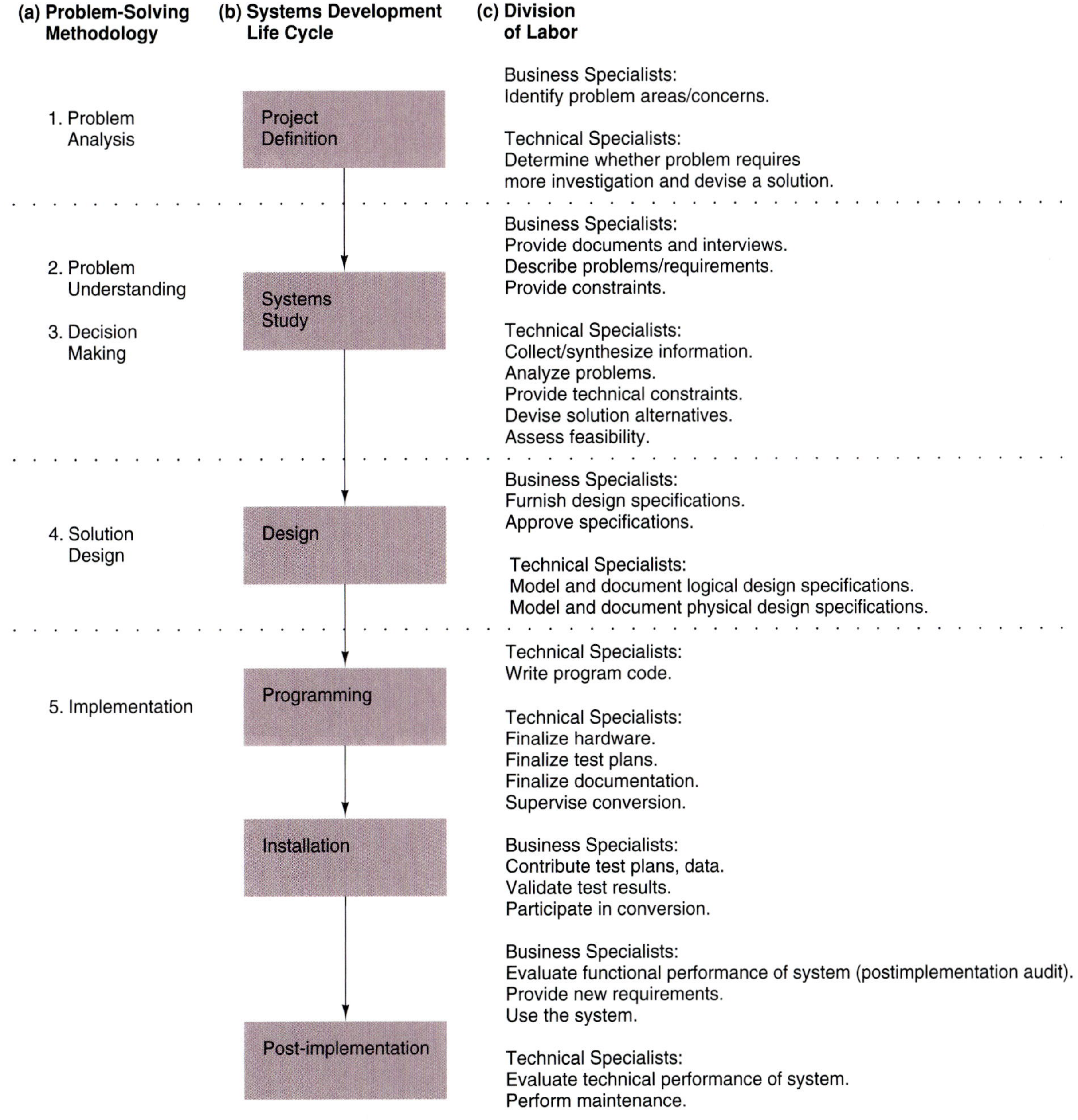
(a) Problem-Solving Methodology
(b) Systems Development Life Cycle
(c) Division of Labor
1. Problem Analysis
Project Definition
Business Specialists:
Identify problem areas/concerns.
Technical Specialists:
Determine whether problem requires more investigation and devise a solution.
2. Problem Understanding
3. Decision Making
Systems Study
Business Specialists:
Provide documents and interviews.
Describe problems/requirements.
Provide constraints.
Technical Specialists:
Collect/synthesize information.
Analyze problems.
Provide technical constraints.
Devise solution alternatives.
Assess feasibility.
4. Solution Design
Design
Business Specialists:
Furnish design specifications.
Approve specifications.
Technical Specialists:
Model and document logical design specifications.
Model and document physical design specifications.
5. Implementation
Programming
Technical Specialists:
Write program code.
Technical Specialists:
Finalize hardware.
Finalize test plans.
Finalize documentation.
Supervise conversion.
Installation
Business Specialists:
Contribute test plans, data.
Validate test results.
Participate in conversion.
Post-implementation
Business Specialists:
Evaluate functional performance of system (postimplementation audit).
Provide new requirements.
Use the system.
Technical Specialists:
Evaluate technical performance of system.
Perform maintenance.

flowchart introduced in Chapter 10 are likely to be employed because the life cycle puts so much emphasis on detailed specifications and paperwork. Business specialists and technical staff must review and approve these documents before physical design and programming can begin.

The bulk of time and resources needed to build an information system is not spent in programming. When William M. Mercer, Inc., was hired by Bechtel Group, Inc., one of the world's largest multinational engineering firms, to evaluate its employee benefits program, the team analyzed and evaluated existing benefits and alternatives; obtained management's opinion on cost and administrative concerns and employees' reaction to the existing plan; and designed several alternative plans, using a computer system to project costs and administration. After Bechtel selected its final plan, Mercer used its enrollment and administration computer system to implement it.

SOURCE: © Steve Chenn/Westlight.

During the *programming* stage, detailed design specifications for files, processes, reports, and input transactions are translated into software for the proposed information system. Technical specialists will write customized program code using a conventional programming language, such as COBOL, FORTRAN, or a high-level fourth-generation language.

During the *installation* stage, the software is tested to be sure it performs properly from both a technical and functional, or business, standpoint, and the old system is converted to the new one. Business and technical specialists are trained to use the new system. The activities surrounding programming, testing, conversion, and training correspond to the fifth and last step of our problem-solving methodology.

The systems life cycle also includes a stage for using and evaluating a system after it is installed. This is called the **postimplementation** stage. When a system is actually used on a day-to-day basis as the system of record, it is in production. At this point, it is evaluated by both business and technical specialists to determine whether the solution objectives specified earlier have been met. This formal evaluation is called the postimplementation audit.

The results of the audit may call for changes in hardware, software, procedures, or documentation to fine-tune the system. In addition, systems may have to be modified over the years to meet new information requirements or increase processing efficiency. Such changes to systems after they are in production are called maintenance. As time goes on, an information system may require increasing amounts of maintenance to continue meeting solution objectives. When maintenance becomes overwhelming, the system is usually considered to have come to the end of its useful lifespan. The problem-solving process initiates a call for a completely new system.

PROBLEMS WITH THE LIFE CYCLE

Large mainframe- or complex client/server systems and systems with highly complex technical requirements will continue to use the traditional life cycle methodology. But 90 percent of today's applications will be based on workstations and PCs. Generating the paperwork and voluminous specifications and sign-off documents for life cycle methodology is very time-consuming and costly and may delay a system's installation for several years.

The life cycle methodology is rather rigid and inflexible. Volumes of new documents must be generated and steps repeated if requirements and specifications have to be revised. Consequently, the methodology encourages freezing of specifications early in the development process. Changes can be made later, but at that point they become very costly. If a system solution cannot be visualized immediately—as is often the case with decision-oriented applications (see Chapter 16)—this methodology will not help.

ALTERNATIVES TO THE LIFE CYCLE

Postimplementation

The use and evaluation of a new system after it is installed; the last stage of the traditional systems life cycle.

Other ways of building information systems can overcome some of the limitations of the life cycle. They, too, are founded on the problem-solving methodology we have outlined. However, the means of establishing requirements, developing software, and finalizing the system solution differ from those of the traditional life cycle, and business specialists play a much larger role in the solution design process. The most important alternatives to the traditional life cycle are prototyping, the use of software packages, fourth-generation development, and outsourcing.

Prototyping entails building an experimental system or part of a system quickly and cheaply so that end users can evaluate it. As users interact with this prototype, they get a better idea of what their needs are, and the features of the final system can be adapted accordingly.

Prototyping
Building an experimental, or preliminary, system or part of a system for business specialists to try out and evaluate.

Application software packages are an alternative to writing software programs and developing custom systems within a firm. Instead, the firm can buy a software package in which all of the programs have already been written and tested. Software packages are most appropriate when the information system solution is one required by many organizations and when software packages to meet such needs are on the market.

Fourth-generation development promotes the development of information systems with little or no formal assistance from technical specialists. This approach is useful for smaller information systems and for personal computer applications such as desktop file management or graphics applications. Much of the solution design process can be performed by end users themselves. When users understand the requirements, they can design their own information system solutions with user-friendly fourth-generation software tools.

Fourth-generation development
The construction of information systems with little or no formal assistance from technical specialists; useful for smaller information systems and personal computer applications.

Outsourcing involves using an external vendor to develop (or operate) an organization's information systems. The organization develops an application solution using the resources of the vendor instead of its own internal information system staff. This approach is useful when the organization lacks the financial or technical resources to develop systems on its own.

Outsourcing
Using an external vendor of computer services to develop or operate an organization's information systems.

11.3 THE PROTOTYPING ALTERNATIVE

A prototype is a preliminary model of a system (or part of a system, such as data input screens) solution for end users to interact with and analyze. The prototype is constructed quickly and cheaply, within days or weeks, using PC software or fourth-generation software tools. End users try out the experimental model to see how well it meets their requirements. In the process, they may discover new requirements they overlooked, or they may suggest areas for improvement. The prototype is then modified, turned over to end users again, and enhanced over and over until it conforms exactly to their needs.

With prototyping, solution design is less formal than with the life cycle methodology. Instead of investigating and analyzing a problem in detail, prototyping quickly generates a solution design, assuming an application solution is called for. Requirements are determined dynamically as the prototype is constructed. Problem analysis, problem understanding, decision making, and solution design are rolled into one.

The prototyping approach is more explicitly iterative than traditional life cycle methodology. The steps to develop a solution can be repeated over and over again. Unlike the traditional life cycle, which must capture the correct version of a system the first time around, prototyping encourages experimentation and repeated design changes. Prototyping is also highly interactive, with end users working directly with solution designs at a much earlier stage of the development process.

Compared with the traditional life cycle, prototyping calls for more intensive involvement of business specialists in the problem-solving process. Business specialists must be in close contact with the technical specialists who fashion the prototype. With fourth-generation or PC-based software tools, end users may actually design the prototype themselves. They will also have to make frequent decisions about further improvements each time the prototype is revised.

STEPS IN PROTOTYPING

As Figure 11.2 illustrates, prototyping involves four steps, which incorporate the steps of our problem-solving methodology:

1. **Identify preliminary requirements:** A technical specialist or analyst works briefly with the business specialist to capture a basic solution model and information needs. The process is more rapid and less formal

CA-OpenROAD is a graphical development environment that can rapidly create information system applications.

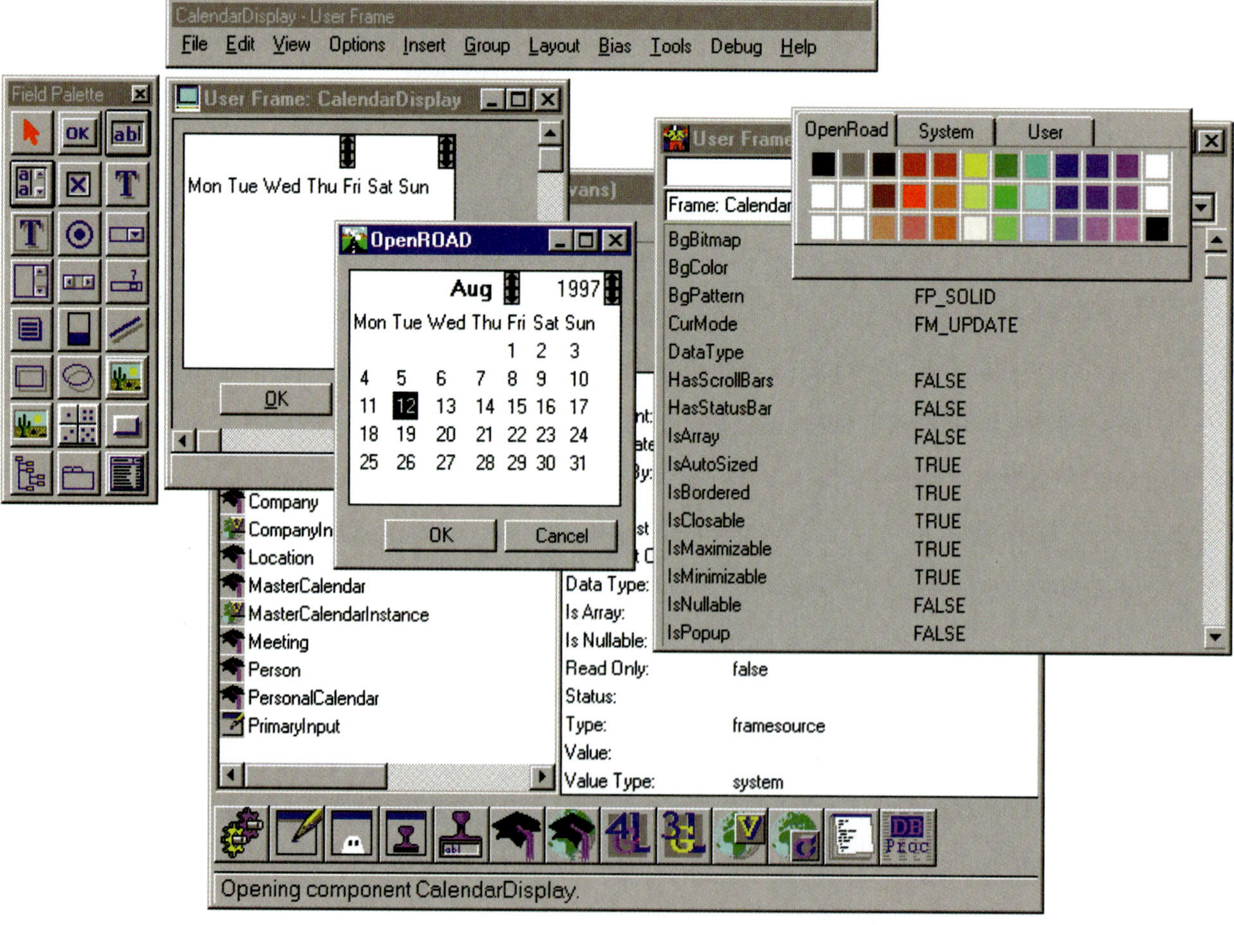

FIGURE 11.2

Prototyping: A Quicker Way to Develop a System

Prototyping involves constructing a prototype, or preliminary model, of a system aimed at meeting users' needs. The end users then try out this model and suggest ways to refine it. The technical specialists enhance the prototype, and the users try it again. This process continues—as shown by the iterative construct in this diagram—until the prototype is acceptable. Only then is the final version produced.

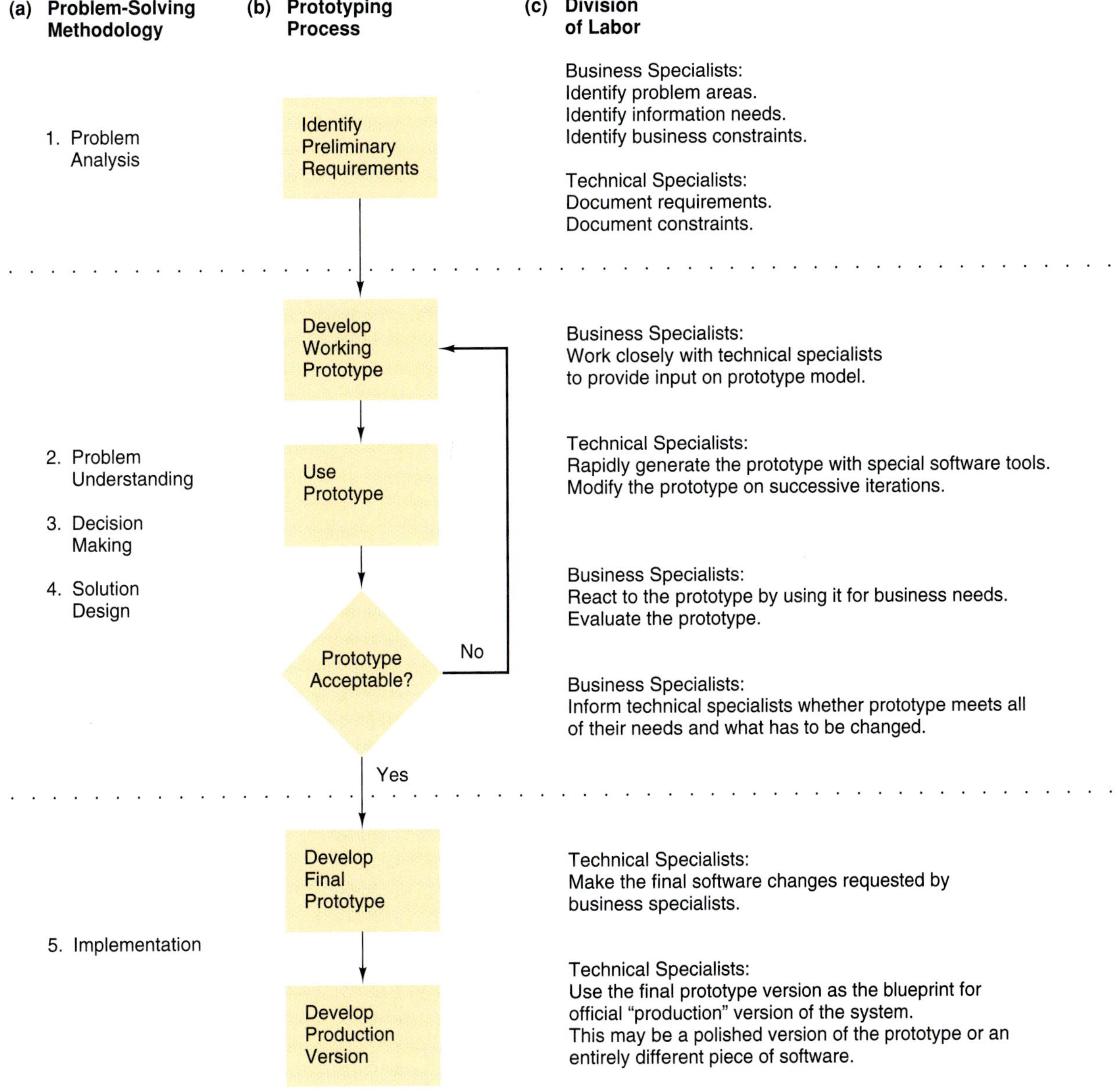
(a) Problem-Solving Methodology
(b) Prototyping Process
(c) Division of Labor
1. Problem Analysis
Identify Preliminary Requirements
Business Specialists:
Identify problem areas.
Identify information needs.
Identify business constraints.
Technical Specialists:
Document requirements.
Document constraints.
Develop Working Prototype
Business Specialists:
Work closely with technical specialists to provide input on prototype model.
2. Problem Understanding
3. Decision Making
4. Solution Design
Use Prototype
Technical Specialists:
Rapidly generate the prototype with special software tools.
Modify the prototype on successive iterations.
Business Specialists:
React to the prototype by using it for business needs.
Evaluate the prototype.
Prototype Acceptable?
No
Yes
Business Specialists:
Inform technical specialists whether prototype meets all of their needs and what has to be changed.
Develop Final Prototype
Technical Specialists:
Make the final software changes requested by business specialists.
5. Implementation
Develop Production Version
Technical Specialists:
Use the final prototype version as the blueprint for official "production" version of the system.
This may be a polished version of the prototype or an entirely different piece of software.

than in life cycle methodology. Several steps of solution design are consolidated into one.

2. **Develop a working prototype:** A functioning prototype is created rapidly. It may consist of only online screens or reports for a proposed system, or it might be an entire system with very small files of data.

3. **Use the prototype:** The end user works with the prototype to see how well it meets his or her needs. The user is encouraged to make recommendations for improving the prototype.
4. **Revise and enhance the prototype:** On the basis of end-user recommendations, the technical specialist or analyst revises the prototype. The cycle then returns to Step 3. Steps 2, 3, and 4 are repeated over and over again until the user is completely satisfied. The approved prototype furnishes the final specifications for the information system solution. Sometimes the prototype itself becomes the final version of the system.

WHEN TO USE PROTOTYPING

Prototyping is most effective when user requirements are unclear. This is characteristic of many decision-oriented systems. Often the final system cannot be clearly visualized because the decision process itself has not been fully worked out. For example, TRW, Inc. has used prototyping to accommodate both users who think "intuitively" and those who think "systematically." The intuitive thinkers typically prefer graphs, charts, and trend lines, whereas the systematic thinkers generally want information displayed quantitatively as dates, numbers, and places. The advantage of working with a prototype is that business specialists can use a working system as a mechanism for clarifying the problem-solving process, which helps them arrive at a solution rapidly.

End-user interface
The parts of an information system with which end users must interact—for example, online data entry screens or reports.

Prototyping is also useful for testing the **end-user interface** of an information system—those parts of the system that end users must interact with, such as online transaction screens or reports. The prototype enables users to react immediately to the parts of the system they will use.

LIMITATIONS OF PROTOTYPING

Some studies have shown that prototypes that fully meet user requirements can be created in 10 to 20 percent of the time estimated for conventional development. However, prototyping is not suitable for certain types of information systems.

Prototyping is most effective for smaller applications. It cannot be applied easily to massive, mainframe-based systems with complex processing instructions and calculations; in those cases, the traditional life cycle methodology is more appropriate.

In addition, prototyping is not a substitute for all of the detailed research and analysis required in order to build an information system. Large systems will still necessitate thorough problem investigation, analysis, and requirements specification before prototyping can begin.

Often, critical activities such as testing and documentation are glossed over because it is so easy to create a prototype. Sometimes a prototype system will be immediately converted into a production system. Yet, under real business circumstances, it may not be able to accommodate large numbers of users, process numerous transactions, and maintain large numbers of records.[1]

The Focus on Technology explores these strengths and limitations of prototyping as it explores the use of prototyping for rapid application development.

RAPID APPLICATION DEVELOPMENT: BIGGER, BETTER, FASTER?

In their never-ending quest to design software applications with greater speed, companies have begun entertaining the concept of rapid application development (RAD). The concept of rapid application development replaces the more traditional method of programming known as the waterfall model. The waterfall model requires a conservative approach in which programmers must conclude each phase of development before embarking on the following one. Many companies believe they can no longer afford to spend six months gathering new system requirements.

In contrast, RAD allows developers to code on the fly, completing their jobs without worrying about every detail of the full-scale application. According to Burt Rubenstein, vice-president of technology services at Cambridge Technology Partners in Cambridge, Massachusetts, a project that takes longer than half a year risks losing the interest of the user or becoming obsolete due to changes in the business process. RAD supporters subscribe to the theory that putting a functional product out as quickly as possible is the best answer because they can always upgrade software later if the demand arises. They also believe that the sooner end users see a result, the more relaxed they can be about the application they are expecting.

RAD development has benefited from the proliferation of visual point-and-click programming tools, which enable users to develop graphical user interfaces very rapidly. In fact, RAD is most widely used for building user interfaces. Left unsettled is the matter of whether RAD should be employed only for coding or for the entire development process. Adage Systems International of Westport, Connecticut, believes the latter. Dave Phelan, director of Adage, says: "Our methodology includes RAD techniques in the analysis and design phases as well as in the construction or development phase." In systems design, Adage uses RAD to rapidly prototype the database. Adage then uses RAD for coding the user interface and for the first level of testing, stepping the user through the application to refine the user interface. Adage uses CA-Open Road, a graphical tool from Computer Associates International, for its Windows graphical user interface development.

Some software developers insist that RAD does not belong in all stages of the development process because software designed in pieces does not always add up to a fully functioning whole. George Cagliuso, founder of Visible Systems Corp. in Waltham, Massachusetts, states that RAD loses its effectiveness if traditional analysis and design do not precede it. Cagliuso believes, simply put, that users will not receive the system for which they asked. Other critics point out that companies may not be able to significantly reduce development time and cost unless RAD tools are combined with a methodology of reusing programming code. The methodology should define how software modules are developed, named, and documented, describe how different software modules communicate, and establish frameworks for their reuse. This strategy will prove most effective if the systems within an organization are similar.

FOCUS Question: What people, organizational, and technology factors should be addressed when considering whether to use rapid application development (RAD)?

SOURCES: Rich Levin, "Design for Reuse," *Information Week,* October 7, 1996, and Mary Hanna, "Farewell to Waterfalls?" *Software Magazine,* May 1995.

11.4 DEVELOPING SOLUTIONS WITH SOFTWARE PACKAGES

Chapter 5 introduced the topic of software packages—prewritten, precoded, commercially available programs that eliminate the need for writing software programs when an information system is developed. More and more systems today are being built with such packages because some problems encountered by many organizations require the same or very similar information system solutions. For example, payroll, accounts payable, accounts receivable, and order processing are standard needs for almost all businesses.

ADVANTAGES OF PACKAGES

Packages offer a number of advantages, especially for firms that do not have a large staff of technical systems personnel or whose staff lack the requisite technical skills for developing a particular application. Leading package vendors maintain their own technical support staff to furnish customers with expert advice after the system has been installed. Thus, a firm that buys packaged software has less need to maintain its own internal specialists.

A related advantage is the cost savings that organizations may achieve by purchasing packaged software rather than developing their own. Packages also eliminate some of the need to work and rework the specifications for a system because users must accept the package as it is. Many features of the design solution have already been worked out, so the purchaser knows precisely what the capabilities of the system are.

PACKAGES AND THE SOLUTION DESIGN PROCESS

How do packages fit into our solution design methodology? As Figure 11.3 shows, even when considering a package, system builders still have to investigate and analyze the problem, specify solution objectives, consider con-

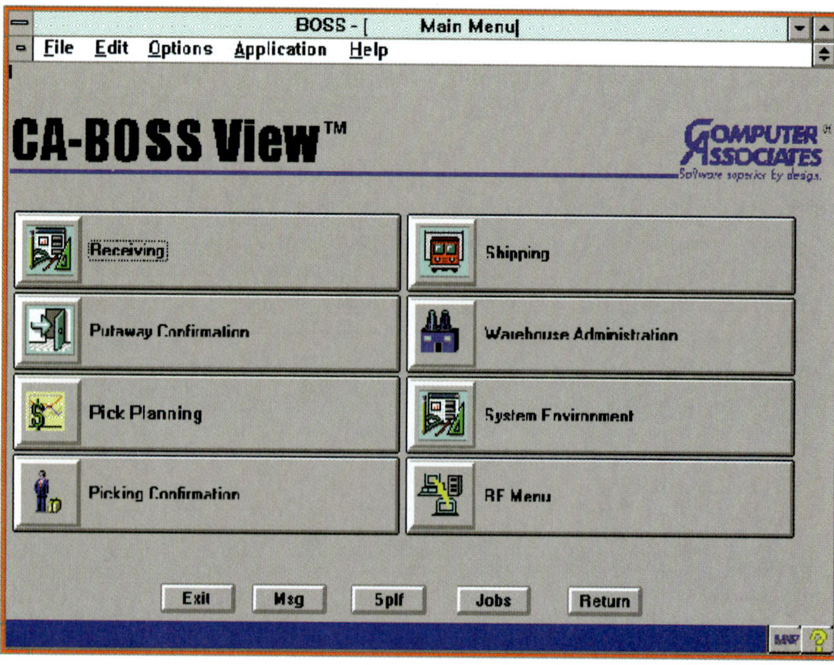

Computer Associates' CA Warehouse-BOSS is an application software package that provides a complete warehouse management system to control all operational aspects of a warehouse, including receiving, locating, putaway, order pool management, picking, replenishment, and shipping.

FIGURE 11.3

Prewritten Software Packages

Even if a firm is considering basing a system on a software package, it should still follow the step-by-step solution design process. This diagram shows that system builders should still analyze the problem and evaluate alternative solutions.

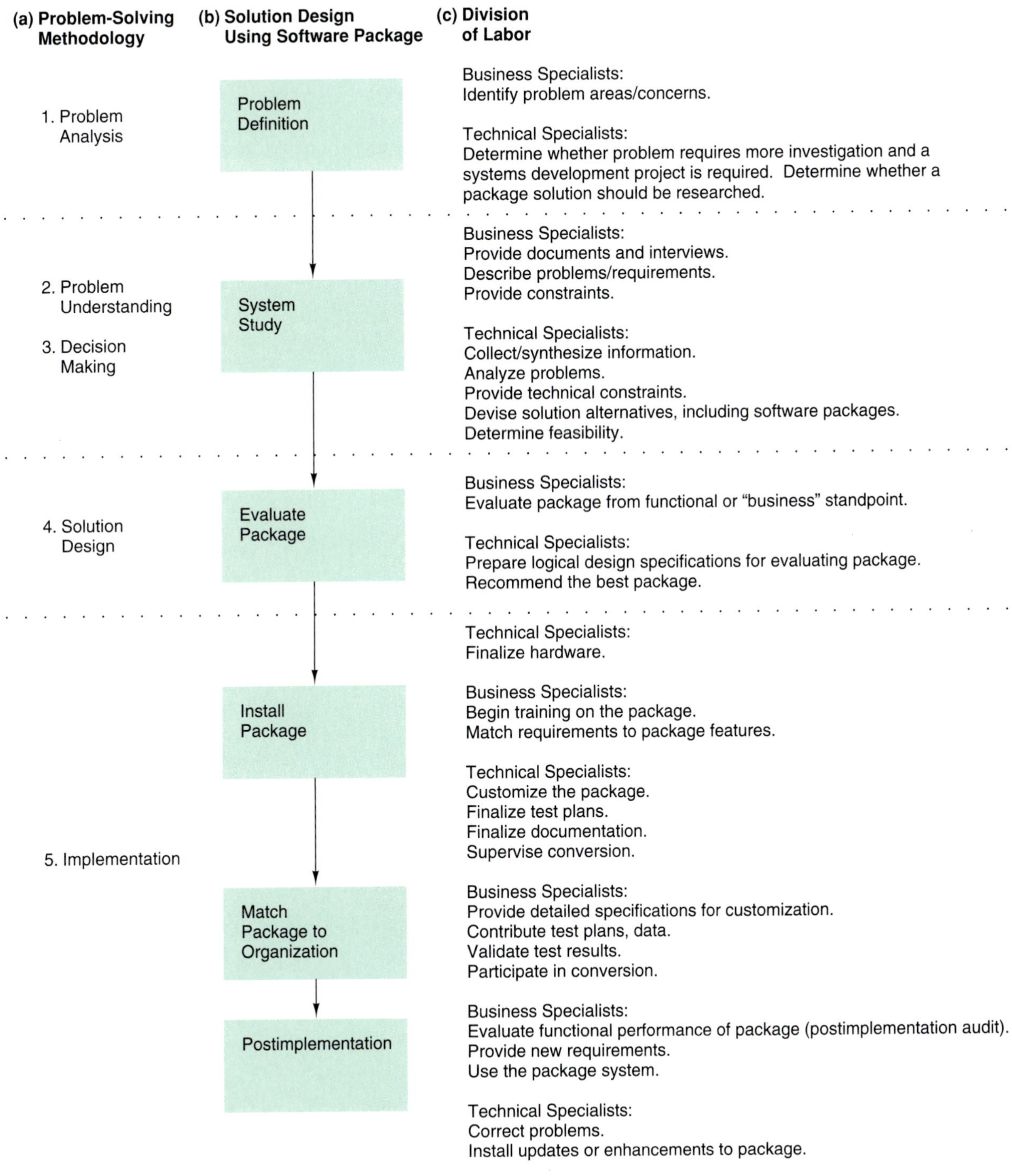

(a) Problem-Solving Methodology
(b) Solution Design Using Software Package
(c) Division of Labor
1. Problem Analysis
Problem Definition
Business Specialists:
Identify problem areas/concerns.
Technical Specialists:
Determine whether problem requires more investigation and a systems development project is required. Determine whether a package solution should be researched.
2. Problem Understanding
3. Decision Making
System Study
Business Specialists:
Provide documents and interviews.
Describe problems/requirements.
Provide constraints.
Technical Specialists:
Collect/synthesize information.
Analyze problems.
Provide technical constraints.
Devise solution alternatives, including software packages.
Determine feasibility.
4. Solution Design
Evaluate Package
Business Specialists:
Evaluate package from functional or "business" standpoint.
Technical Specialists:
Prepare logical design specifications for evaluating package.
Recommend the best package.
5. Implementation
Install Package
Technical Specialists:
Finalize hardware.
Business Specialists:
Begin training on the package.
Match requirements to package features.
Technical Specialists:
Customize the package.
Finalize test plans.
Finalize documentation.
Supervise conversion.
Match Package to Organization
Business Specialists:
Provide detailed specifications for customization.
Contribute test plans, data.
Validate test results.
Participate in conversion.
Postimplementation
Business Specialists:
Evaluate functional performance of package (postimplementation audit).
Provide new requirements.
Use the package system.
Technical Specialists:
Correct problems.
Install updates or enhancements to package.

FOCUS ON **PROBLEM SOLVING**

AT WHAT COST?

Keeping track of one's personal finances can be a daunting task. How many times have you heard a friend or relative complain about the challenges posed by balancing a checkbook? Now imagine the complexity involved in managing the finances of a business. Not every business has room in its budget for a full-time accountant. Thus, the need for accounting software systems becomes apparent. In some cases, it is not a question of finding the right package but of making the best use of the one you have. Sharon Fullen, who keeps the books for Hoodoo Ski Area in Sisters, Oregon, encountered this exact situation.

Hoodoo Ski Area runs 15 campgrounds during the summer months in conjunction with the United States Forest Service. In the past, Fullen had tallied the accounts payable and accounts receivable for the operation on her own and then kept track of them by plugging them into her accounting software, BusinessWorks. This method proved to be inefficient and marginally useful. Looking to improve her ability to report on Hoodoo's finances, Fullen augmented her system with the BusinessWorks job-costing application. Job costing refers to the process of analyzing the expenses and profits of any individual task. Construction companies use the job-costing technique to follow the progress of a job from the moment they begin bidding on it, but job costing can also be used for tasks such as writing a magazine article or creating an advertising brochure. Fullen recognized that this approach would be effective for her organization. Instead of having a general grasp on the funds of the whole organization, she could characterize each campsite as a job. The software would then enable her to manage both expenditures and earnings for each campground, taking into account factors such as maintenance and labor.

With the new system in place, Fullen has become much more efficient. Her reports detail specific information with organized, hard numbers. Such data allows Hoodoo to conduct the business of each campground, as well as that of the entire organization, with more precision.

Jim Osmundson applies job-costing software to his Yacolt, Washington, graphic design company in a different way. Osmundson's company, Sierra Information Services, logs both the time spent and the software employed for every project it undertakes. Different projects might require different pieces of graphics design software, which may need to be replaced or updated as new features become available. An annual summary details exactly how many hours were billed for each graphics program used. If the report shows that the company billed fewer than 50 hours during the year using a particular software package, Osmundson doesn't bother to upgrade it. Unless a software program is used frequently, it probably isn't worth the time and money that Sierra would have to spend to purchase and learn the upgraded software. Sierra Information Services uses the job-costing tools that come with Intuit's QuickBooks Pro accounting package for this purpose.

Organizations intent on improving their business usually focus on cutting costs and saving time. The issue of how to accomplish these goals can be a complicated one. Job-costing software can be one part of the solution.

FOCUS Question: What changes did both these companies have to make to use the job-costing features of their accounting software packages?

SOURCE: Ellen DePasquale, "Ledger-demain," *Inc. Technology* no. 2, 1996.

straints, and evaluate solution alternatives. During these processes, they can determine whether a package solution alternative will meet information requirements. Then, when they evaluate solution alternatives, they can weigh the feasibility of a package solution against other solution options.

The package evaluation process is often based on the results of a **request for proposal (RFP).** The RFP is a detailed list of questions submitted to vendors of packaged software. The questions are designed to measure the extent to which each package meets the requirements specified during the solution design process.

Request for proposal (RFP)
A detailed list of questions for software vendors to answer as part of the process of evaluating a software package; the questions are designed to determine the extent to which the software package meets the requirements specified during the solution design process.

If a package solution is selected, the solution design step of problem solving is carried out around the package. In particular, logical and physical design do not proceed from scratch, tailored to the requirements and specifications generated first. Instead, the design work focuses on adjusting user requirements and specifications to meet the characteristics of the package. In other words, instead of end users designing their own payroll register, the payroll register report provided by a payroll package is used. In this sense, the organization and end users have less control over the shape and design of solution outcome.

The Focus on Problem Solving shows how this process might work for small businesses using the job-costing features of accounting software packages. The organizations described had to adjust their definition of "jobs" to use the job-costing software to analyze expenses for activities that might not traditionally be considered "jobs."

DISADVANTAGES OF PACKAGES

The main disadvantage of software packages is that they often are unable to meet all of an organization's requirements. Each organization treats even a standard function such as payroll a little differently from other organizations.

FIGURE 11.4

A Customized Software Package

These diagrams show three possible organizational structures that could be created by customizing a large payroll/personnel system package. The package enables each customer to organize employees into groups for reporting and control purposes. Data can be gathered and calculated for each organizational level defined. Each of these examples lists the highest level of the organization first.

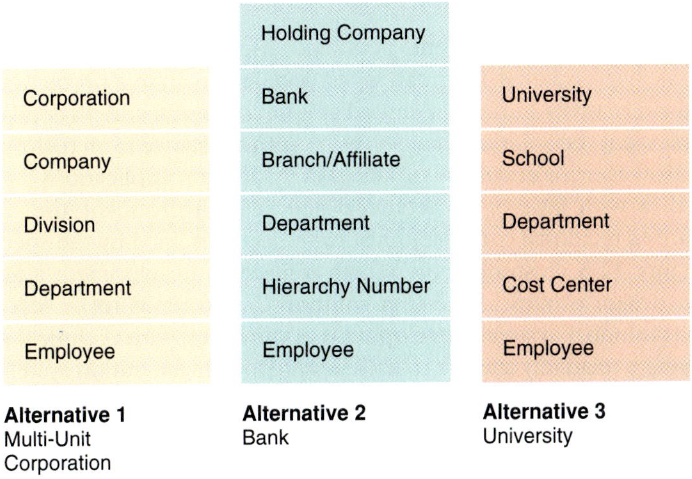

Alternative 1 Multi-Unit Corporation	Alternative 2 Bank	Alternative 3 University
	Holding Company	
Corporation	Bank	University
Company	Branch/Affiliate	School
Division	Department	Department
Department	Hierarchy Number	Cost Center
Employee	Employee	Employee

Consequently, many instances may occur in which a package is not able to meet 100 percent of a firm's solution requirements.

Customization
The modification of a software package to meet a firm's unique requirements.

Package vendors try to address this problem through **customization;** that is, the package includes features that allow it to be modified without destroying the integrity of the software. For example, the package may include areas in its files or databases where a firm can add and maintain its own pieces of data.

Figure 11.4 shows how a major payroll software package can be customized to accommodate different organizational reporting structures. This package allows firms to define different types of organizational structures, such as a corporation, a bank, or a university.

Even with customization features, there are limits to how much packages can be changed. If the package cannot be modified to meet a firm's unique needs, the firm will have to change its procedures and ways of doing business to conform to the package.

11.5 FOURTH-GENERATION DEVELOPMENT

Many information systems can be developed by end users with little or no formal assistance from technical specialists. This approach is called fourth-generation development. It incorporates some of the software tools introduced in Chapter 5, such as fourth-generation languages, personal computer tools (including Web page authoring tools), and graphics languages, which make it possible for end users to perform tasks that previously required trained information systems specialists. (As you may recall, fourth-generation languages are programming languages that are not only less procedural than conventional languages but also contain more English-language commands; consequently, they are easier for nontechnical specialists to use.)

FOURTH-GENERATION SOLUTION DESIGN

Fourth-generation development puts end users more in control of the problem-solving process. They can investigate and analyze a problem, specify solution alternatives, perform a limited amount of logical and physical design, and implement the solution themselves or with assistance from technical specialists. However, for end users to successfully develop applications using corporate data with little or no technical specialist involvement, the database (preferably a relational database) must have been designed by the specialists.

Figure 11.5 illustrates how fourth-generation development affects the solution design process. Note that solution design tends to be less formal than in traditional systems development approaches, with technical specialists playing a relatively smaller role. Generally, fourth-generation systems tend to be quite simple and can be completed more rapidly than those using conventional life cycle methodology.

With fourth-generation development, the solution design process may actually be facilitated because end users are in charge of problem analysis

FIGURE 11.5

Fourth-Generation Development

Fourth-generation development enables end users to do much of the development work themselves with easy-to-use software such as query languages and PC packages. The users are responsible for identifying problems, designing and implementing solutions, and evaluating the results. Technical specialists take on a consulting role.

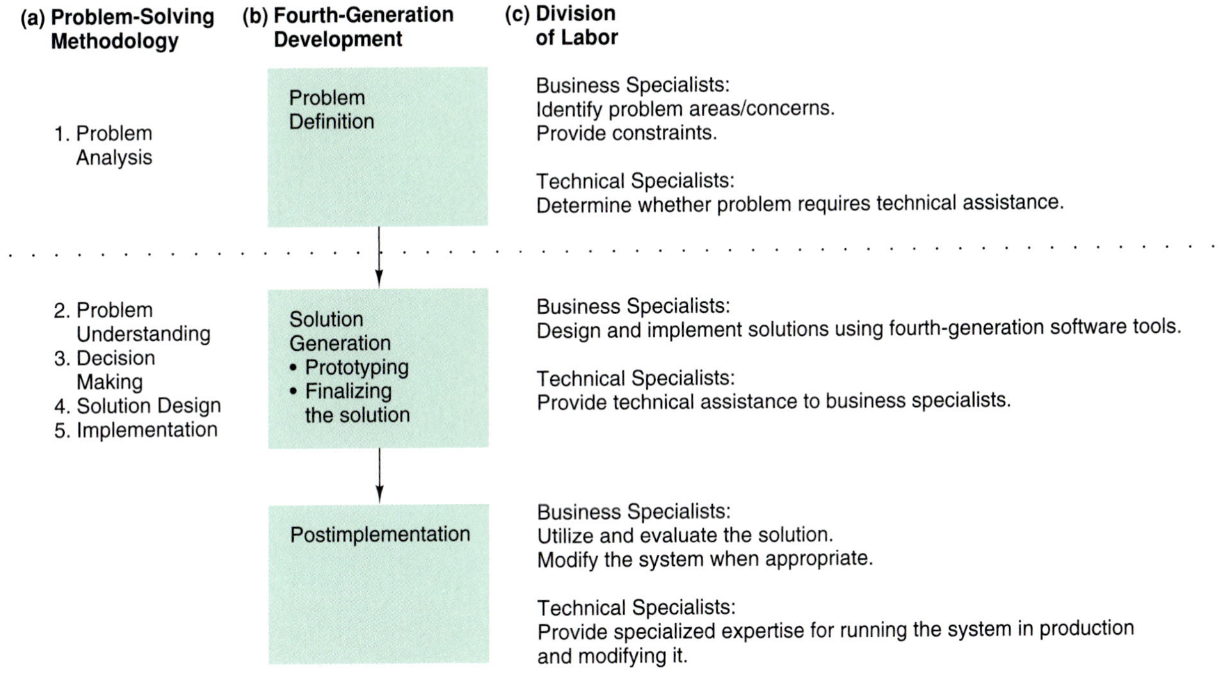
(a) Problem-Solving Methodology
(b) Fourth-Generation Development
(c) Division of Labor
1. Problem Analysis
Problem Definition
Business Specialists:
Identify problem areas/concerns.
Provide constraints.
Technical Specialists:
Determine whether problem requires technical assistance.
2. Problem Understanding
3. Decision Making
4. Solution Design
5. Implementation
Solution Generation
• Prototyping
• Finalizing the solution
Business Specialists:
Design and implement solutions using fourth-generation software tools.
Technical Specialists:
Provide technical assistance to business specialists.
Postimplementation
Business Specialists:
Utilize and evaluate the solution.
Modify the system when appropriate.
Technical Specialists:
Provide specialized expertise for running the system in production and modifying it.

and requirements specification. Since end users are in the best position to understand their own problems, there is less chance of issues being misunderstood, which often occurs when the problem-solving process is dominated by technical specialists.

FOURTH-GENERATION SOFTWARE TOOLS

Fourth-generation development requires easy-to-use software tools that can be employed by end users alone or by technical specialists as productivity aids. The following are usually considered the major types of software tools for end users:

1. Personal computer tools
2. Query languages and report generators
3. Graphics languages
4. Application generators
5. Very-high-level programming languages
6. Application software packages

FIGURE 11.6

Fourth-Generation Solution Design Tools

The term *fourth-generation tools* actually describes a broad range of products, as is evident here. It includes software such as Lotus 1-2-3 and query languages such as SQL, which are suitable for simpler problems. Other tools, such as very-high-level programming languages and application software packages, can address more technically sophisticated situations.

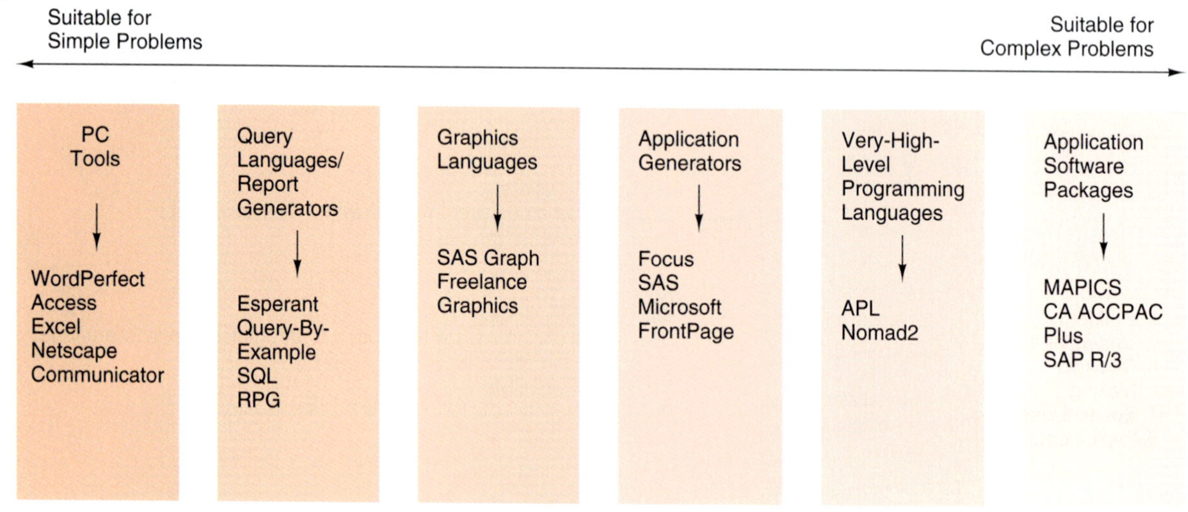

Figure 11.6 lists some representative, commercially available tools in each category and indicates the applications for which they are most appropriate.

Personal computer tools consist of the PC software described throughout this book: spreadsheet, database management, graphics, word processing, Web browsers, Web page authoring tools, and communications software. PC software is especially well suited to end-user development because it was designed for end users rather than technical specialists and because personal computer operating systems are relatively simple.

Query languages, graphics languages, report generators, application generators, and very-high-level programming languages were introduced in Section 5.3. Query languages are easy-to-use, fourth-generation languages used for accessing data stored in databases or files. Report generators extract data from files or databases to create customized reports. With an application generator, an entire information system application (including a Web application) can be generated without customized programming; the end user specifies the tasks that need to be done, and the generator creates the appropriate program code. Very-high-level programming languages produce program code with far fewer instructions than are required by conventional languages.

Application software packages can serve as fourth-generation computing tools if they are simple and can be installed by end users. An example might be a mailing label or client database that can be installed by an end user on a personal computer without any special programming or customization.

In recent years, fourth-generation development tool functionality has expanded so much that it will soon be difficult to categorize these tools in this traditional manner. Many database management systems (Chapter 6) now have end-user application generator tools, including query languages and report generators. Query languages and report generators are often capable of accessing other databases in addition to their own. Many application software packages now come with user-controlled report generators, graphics languages, and Internet tools.

DISADVANTAGES OF FOURTH-GENERATION DEVELOPMENT

Although fourth-generation development offers many advantages, it can be used to solve problems only when the information system solution is relatively simple and easily understood by users. Fourth-generation languages and other end-user computing tools tend to work best with small files and simple processing procedures. Because these languages are heavily nonprocedural, they cannot easily handle applications that require complex procedural logic. Information systems to support, for example, production scheduling or nuclear reactor design still require the use of conventional languages.

Another disadvantage of fourth-generation development is the organization's potential loss of control over the solution design process and its information resources. Fourth-generation systems are developed much more informally than those using traditional methods. Consequently, no professional programmers or systems analysts may be involved to assist with problem analysis, evaluation of solution alternatives, and solution design. In addition, standards for ensuring data quality, security, or conformity with the information requirements of the firm as a whole may never be applied.

The Focus on People illustrates both the strengths and weaknesses of end-user development as enhancements to popular personal computer tools give millions of people the capability of developing Web pages on their own.

INFORMATION CENTERS

Some companies manage fourth-generation development and maximize its benefits through **information centers.** An information center is a facility that provides training and support for end-user computing. Its objective is to provide business specialists with tools to access computerized data and solve problems themselves. An information center furnishes computer hardware, software, and technical specialists, all of which are geared to fourth-generation systems development. The technical specialists serve as teachers and consultants; their primary goal is to train business specialists in the computing tools they will use, but specialists may also assist in the analysis, design, and programming of complex applications.

Information center
A facility that provides training, tools, standards, and expert support for solution design by end users.

An information center may offer users access to mainframes and minicomputers as well as PCs, although some information centers contain only PCs. Information centers support the solution design process at many stages. Their staffs are prepared to work intensively to help end users understand their problems and solve them as much as possible on their own. The services provided by an information center can be summarized as follows:

- Referring business specialists to existing information system applications that may help solve their problems.

FOCUS ON PEOPLE

WHEN USERS DESIGN FOR THE WEB

A Web site for every desktop? It could easily happen because even computing novices can create their own Web pages. Popular desktop software tools such as word processors and spreadsheets have been enhanced with features that let them work on the Internet. Nearly all new versions of the major desktop applications include some capability to output files in the Web's HTML (hypertext markup language) page-formatting language. Users can save documents in HTML format, download HTML pages, or embed hypertext links in documents. For instance, all the applications in Microsoft Office 97 and Lotus SmartSuite 97 are able to save their data as HTML documents and publish directly to a Web site. Autodesk Inc. enhanced its AudoCAD computer-aided design software to let users publish engineering drawings on the Web.

Before these enhancements, creating HTML documents was much more difficult. The effort required laborious hand coding or special software such as Quarterdeck's WebAuthor to convert output from word processors to HTML. This meant that users had to learn a new skill or tool. Furthermore, the conversion tools typically didn't work with spreadsheet, database, or presentation graphics packages. In contrast, Internet enhancements to existing word processing or spreadsheet software are geared to users' existing skills. Harriet Donnelly, president of Technovative Marketing, a marketing communications firm in Berkeley Heights, New Jersey, notes that it is easier for her to use a package with which she is familiar: "If I'm spending the time to create a document, I don't want to have to recreate the same information in another application." Donnelly developed pages for NetChannel, the Web site for Oracle's Network Computer, using Lotus Development's WordPro and Freelance graphics software.

Internet extensions to the popular desktop applications are expected to fuel the growth of intranets because they provide many more people with tools to publish information and locate the data they need. But if people aren't careful, they will exacerbate information overload. In companies with thousands of employees, everyone publishing information on the Web could create serious data management problems. Moreover, if people don't keep their Web pages up to date, old news is never removed. Companies must vigilantly monitor the flood of new data, or users won't be able to find what they want.

FOCUS Questions: Should users create their own Web pages? Why or why not?

SOURCE: Andy Patrizio, "From the Desktop to the Web Site," *Information Week,* December 2, 1996.

- Providing technical assistance by suggesting appropriate hardware, software, and methodologies for solving a particular problem.
- Training business specialists in the tools supported by the information center.
- Providing documentation and reference materials for information center resources.
- Generating prototypes for business specialists to evaluate.
- Evaluating new pieces of hardware and software.
- Giving staff access to terminals, PCs, associated software, and databases.

Another advantage of information centers is that they can establish standards for hardware and software so that end users do not introduce too many incompatible pieces of equipment or data into a firm. Typically, an information center works with a firm's information systems department to establish standards and guidelines for hardware and software acquisitions by the firm; then, the information center provides assistance with only those brands of equipment and software.

For example, an information center may provide training only on Microsoft Word as opposed to other word processing packages because Word is the company standard. Otherwise, its staff would have to learn several different types of word processing software, each of which would be used by only a small number of people. Such a policy also contributes to the efficient use of information in an organization. Files created by one kind of word

Information centers provide computers, software tools, and training classes to help employees access data or create applications on their own.

SOURCE: Courtesy of International Business Machines Corporation.

processing software cannot always automatically be used by another, which restricts transportability of data across the organization. Information centers are declining in popularity because so many end users today have computing skills, but they are useful in organizations concerned with managing end-user development.

11.6 OUTSOURCING

In recent years, more organizations have concluded that they no longer want to maintain the internal resources needed for the development and operation of some or all of their information systems. They turn instead to outsourcing, the strategy of handing over to external vendors some or all of an organization's information systems functions. Outsourcing firms provide a variety of services, including the following:

- Staffing and managing a company's computer center;
- Operating some or all of a company's computer systems at the outsourcing firm's computer center;
- Developing applications for an organization; and
- Operating an organization's telecommunications networks.

Companies such as the Toronto Stock Exchange, described in the Focus on Organizations, often turn to outsourcing when they lack the expertise to develop the correct system solution internally. But selecting the right outsourcing vendor takes skill. The vendor must have both technical and application skills. If you planned to outsource the development of a chemical plant's process control system, you would want a vendor who is not only skilled in applications development but who also understands chemical processing controls. Figure 11.7 shows how the solution design process can be accomplished with outsourcing.

ADVANTAGES OF OUTSOURCING

Companies turn to outsourcing for a variety of reasons, the most common of which is economic. Outsourcing companies are specialists in the services they provide and therefore are able to provide those services at either a lower cost or with higher quality for the same cost. In addition, outsourcing vendors sell their services to multiple clients and thus can generate economies of scale that their clients cannot. Savings of 15 to 30 percent are not uncommon.

Outsourcing can often reduce costs by turning fixed costs into variable costs. For many transaction-driven systems, such as payroll or accounts payable, the outsourcing vendor agrees to charge by the transaction (in these examples, an issued check) so that if the number of transactions (checks) drops, systems costs also drop. The alternative, maintaining these systems internally, results in a fixed cost to support each system.

FIGURE 11.7

Developing a System through Outsourcing

When a system is developed through outsourcing, the final design and implementation of the solution is assigned to an external vendor of information services. Outsourcing can be useful if an organization lacks the internal resources to develop a solution entirely on its own.

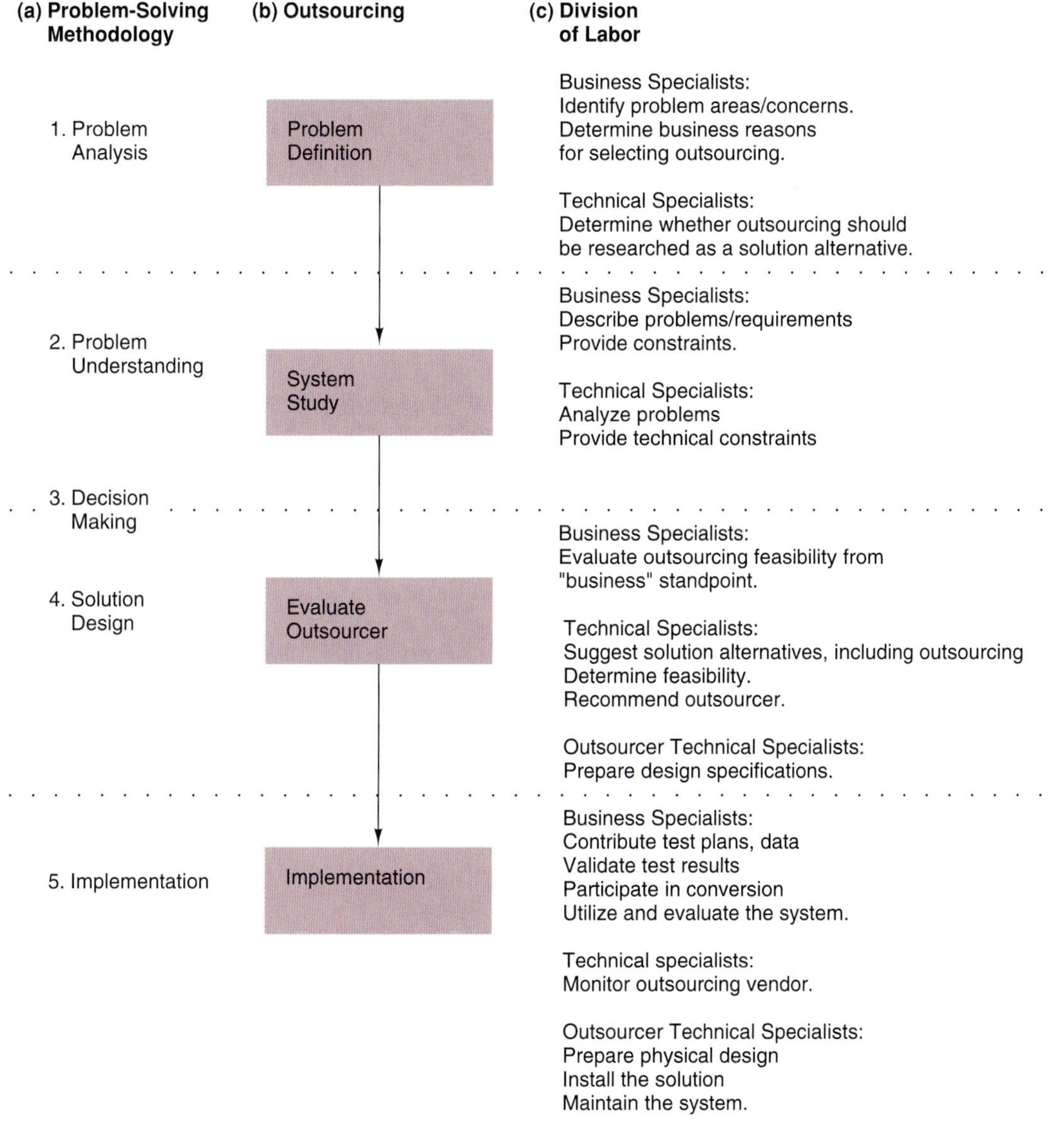

(a) Problem-Solving Methodology
(b) Outsourcing
(c) Division of Labor
1. Problem Analysis
Problem Definition
Business Specialists:
Identify problem areas/concerns.
Determine business reasons for selecting outsourcing.
Technical Specialists:
Determine whether outsourcing should be researched as a solution alternative.
2. Problem Understanding
System Study
Business Specialists:
Describe problems/requirements
Provide constraints.
Technical Specialists:
Analyze problems
Provide technical constraints
3. Decision Making
4. Solution Design
Evaluate Outsourcer
Business Specialists:
Evaluate outsourcing feasibility from "business" standpoint.
Technical Specialists:
Suggest solution alternatives, including outsourcing
Determine feasibility.
Recommend outsourcer.
Outsourcer Technical Specialists:
Prepare design specifications.
5. Implementation
Implementation
Business Specialists:
Contribute test plans, data
Validate test results
Participate in conversion
Utilize and evaluate the system.
Technical specialists:
Monitor outsourcing vendor.
Outsourcer Technical Specialists:
Prepare physical design
Install the solution
Maintain the system.

Outsourcing contracts offer still another economic advantage, that of predictability. The systems development process is notorious for cost overruns of 100 percent or more. Through outsourcing, the company can often negotiate a fixed price for the system. Care must be taken, of course, to specify system performance to be certain that the vendor does not cut costs by taking shortcuts.

Organizations with a limited number of IS professionals often use outsourcing as a way to free up talented IS staff for critical projects. Using staff to develop or maintain routine systems can be a waste of talent. Able analysts, for example, offer more benefit to their companies by developing new production-related systems than by maintaining a routine payroll system.

DISADVANTAGES OF OUTSOURCING

Outsourcing is not a solution for all companies or in all situations. First, gains will not be realized unless the company effectively manages outsourcing.

FOCUS ON ORGANIZATIONS

TORONTO STOCK EXCHANGE OUTSOURCES ITS VIRTUAL TRADING FLOOR

When the Toronto Stock Exchange decided to create a virtual trading floor that would eventually replace its physical trading floor, using in-house resources for the project seemed to make sense. After all, the Stock Exchange had its own information services division and had developed the Canadian Automated Trading System (CATS), which had been in place since the 1970s. Four years, $35 million, and multiple failures later, something had to change.

Adhering to the telling comment of senior vice-president of information systems and trading systems Brian Harding that "we're a stock exchange, not a software factory," the exchange began to seek outside help. The Toronto Stock Exchange contracted Reuters Information Services Ltd. to configure trading workstations as the first step toward purchasing its virtual trading floor. Next, the exchange looked to France, buying a trading system from the Paris Bourse for $2 million. In an odd twist of fate, the French system is actually a reworked version of CATS, which Toronto originally sold to Paris in the 1980s.

The upside to the Toronto Exchange's technical problems was that they delayed the building process long enough so that the exchange no longer had to rely on itself to build a system. It could buy the expertise and technology for the new system from outsiders instead of building it. What, exactly, mired the exchange's internal effort to produce an electronic trading floor? A variety of problems put the project out of sorts, including unrealistic scheduling expectations, client/server technology glitches, and message format inconsistencies. The latter left the system unable to communicate with some trading firms. When Rowland Fleming took over as president of the exchange, he evaluated the situation and elected to take the new direction.

Trading on the Toronto Stock Exchange was supposed to convert to an entirely virtual format by 1995. However, as the exchange grew (it is the second most active in North America), daily activities demanded more and more attention, and the virtual project suffered as a result. The final blow arrived in the form of consultants' conclusions that the new system would not even work as well as the old one. At that point, Fleming decided it was time to cut the exchange's losses. CATS will be temporarily reengineered until the Paris system can be fully installed at the end of 1997. Once it takes its place, it will run in COBOL rather than in CATS' assembly language. Executives at securities firms in Toronto are relieved that the problem has been solved, having endured delays in implementing their own trading systems while the Stock Exchange figured out its debacle.

FOCUS Questions: What was the motivation behind the Toronto Stock Exchange's decision to outsource? What people, organization, and technology factors would you consider in deciding whether to use outsourcing for a large company?

SOURCE: Frank Hayes, "Toronto Stock Exchange: Going, Going, Gone," *Computerworld,* July 22, 1996.

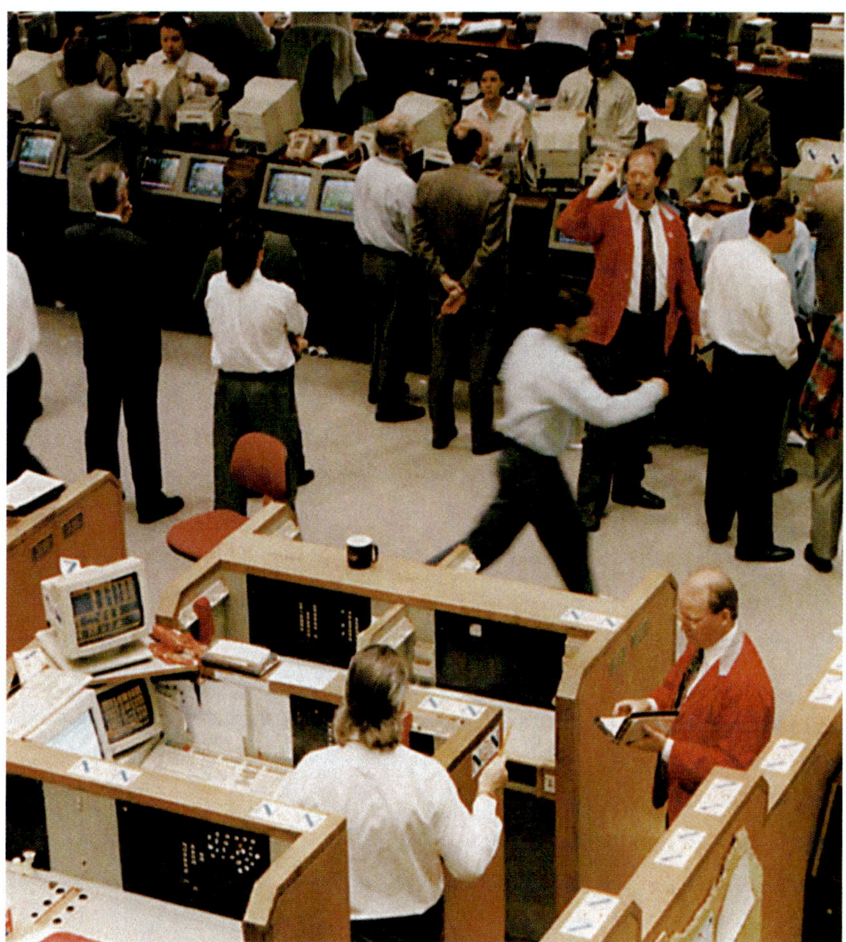

The Toronto Stock Exchange turned to external vendors to develop its electronic trading floor. Outsourcing is useful when organizations lack the technical expertise or resources to develop a system solution on their own.

SOURCE: AP/Wide World Photos.

Outsourcing can be costly and harmful if potential functions for outsourcing are not evaluated carefully. It is risky for a company to outsource applications on which its competitiveness depends. For example, because excellent performance of reservation systems is critical to the success of hotel chains and airlines, these systems probably should be managed internally. On the other hand, these same companies could probably outsource their medical claims systems because they will lose little if claims processing is occasionally interrupted. The same cannot be said of major health insurance providers, for whom the medical claims system is pivotal. For them, occasional medical processing problems could be disastrous and could even threaten their survival. Thus, they would be wise to retain direct control of medical claims themselves.

Companies must guard against loss of control that can be the result of outsourcing. Firms sometimes find they have become overreliant on the vendor; in fact, the vendor may be the firm's only alternative for providing the outsourced service. In that unacceptable situation, the vendor is free to exploit the contract by raising fees and reducing the level of service. Overreliance also leaves a company vulnerable should the vendor develop financial difficulties or actually close down.[2]

SUMMARY

- The traditional systems life cycle is the oldest methodology for building information systems solutions. It consists of a formal set of stages that must proceed sequentially, clearly demarcating the responsibilities of business and technical specialists.
- The six stages of the traditional systems life cycle are project definition, systems study, design, programming, installation, and postimplementation.
- The traditional life cycle is considered a very rigid and costly way to develop a systems solution. Moreover, it is not well suited for simpler, less structured applications for which requirements cannot easily be visualized.
- The most important alternatives to traditional life cycle methodology are prototyping, the use of software packages, fourth-generation development, and outsourcing.
- Prototyping entails building an experimental system or part of a system rapidly for business specialists to interact with and evaluate. The process is highly interactive and iterative.
- Prototyping involves four steps: identifying preliminary requirements; developing a working prototype; using the prototype; and refining and enhancing the prototype.
- Prototyping is most useful for simple, less-structured applications for which solution requirements are vague. When the system solution is massive and complex, prototyping cannot substitute for comprehensive requirements analysis and careful programming, testing, and documentation.
- Software packages are commercially marketed, prewritten software that can considerably reduce system development costs if they meet solution requirements. Solution design using application software packages focuses on package evaluation and fitting the solution design to package characteristics.
- If a package does not meet an organization's unique requirements, it must be customized, or modified. However, extensive customization can elevate development costs to the point that a package solution is no longer feasible.
- Using fourth-generation development techniques, business specialists can construct information system solutions with minimal assistance from technical specialists. This is possible because of the productivity and ease of use provided by fourth-generation development tools: personal computer tools, query languages, graphics languages, report generators, application generators, very-high-level programming languages, and application software packages.
- Fourth-generation-developed solutions are most appropriate for applications with small files and relatively simple processing procedures. Potential problems from fourth-generation development include loss of organizational control and standards for solution design.
- Information centers can help control fourth-generation development by providing training, tools, standards, and expert support for solution design.
- Organizations can benefit by outsourcing applications development to an external vendor if such an arrangement reduces costs and allows the organization to control the solution design process.

KEY TERMS

Traditional systems life cycle
Project definition
Systems study
Postimplementation
Prototyping
Fourth-generation development
Outsourcing
End-user interface
Request for proposal (RFP)
Customization
Information center

REVIEW QUESTIONS

1. Why is the oldest methodology for building an information system called the "systems life cycle"?
2. List and define each stage in the systems life cycle.
3. Why is it important to conduct a postimplementation audit of an information system?
4. What are the strengths and limitations of life cycle methodology?
5. What are the most important alternatives to conventional systems-building methodology?
6. Define information system prototyping.
7. What kinds of situations benefit most from prototyping the solution?
8. What are the four steps in prototyping?
9. What are the limitations of prototyping?
10. What kinds of situations benefit from using software packages to develop a solution?
11. Describe two advantages and two disadvantages of software packages.
12. What is customization? Why is it an important feature to consider in a software package?
13. What is fourth-generation development? Name the major kinds of software tools employed with this approach.
14. What problems are associated with fourth-generation development?
15. Define an information center. How can information centers solve some of the problems introduced by fourth-generation development?
16. What is outsourcing? What are its advantages and disadvantages as a solution design approach?

DISCUSSION QUESTIONS

1. Discuss how the problem-solving methodology presented in this text is applied in the traditional systems life cycle, prototyping, software package-based development, fourth-generation development, and outsourcing.

2. Describe the roles of business specialists and technical specialists in each of the approaches to information systems solutions presented in this chapter.

3. Application software packages and fourth-generation computing tools eliminate the need for professional programmers. Discuss.

4. It is impossible to develop a good solution design the first time around. Discuss the alternatives.

PROBLEM-SOLVING EXERCISES

1. *Group exercise:* Divide into groups. Each group should obtain product information about a personal computer application software package, such as Quicken, Microsoft Profit for Windows, or DacEasy Accounting, and then write an analysis of the package selected. What are its strengths and limitations? Under what circumstances could it be used for a system solution?

2. What kind of approach (methodology) would you choose for the following application solutions? Justify your decision.

   a. A system for tracking job applicants at six different branches of a nationwide retail chain.

   b. A money market account system for a major regional bank.

   c. A system to evaluate the financial and tax consequences of purchasing rental property.

   d. A medical and dental claims administration and payment system for 14,000 employees of a major corporation.

3. *Hands-on exercise:* Use appropriate application software to create a prototype of a simple student record-keeping system for a university. The system should maintain data on the student's name, address, age, sex, marital status, high school attended, citizenship, and grade point average. If possible, use your software tool to create an online data entry screen for inputting the data. Then modify the prototype to capture these additional data elements: student's social security number, parent's name, parent's address, and date of high school graduation. Present the first version of the prototype and the revision to your instructor.

4. *Internet problem-solving exercise:* You run a small business and want to try out some shareware for sending out bills. Access a shareware Web site such as Jumbo Shareware, Freeware Favorites, or Shareware, and locate all the available shareware packages for billing. Try to answer the following questions for shareware software packages you select:

   What does the package do? Describe the functions it performs.

   What are the operating system and hard disk storage requirements?

   What documentation is provided?

NOTES

1. Maryann Alari, "An Assessment of the Prototyping Approach to Information System Development," *Communications of the ACM* 27, No. 6 (June 1984).
2. Lawrence Loh and N. Venkatraman, "Determinants of Information Technology Outsourcing," *Journal of Management Information Systems* 9, No. 1 (Summer 1992), and Michael J. Earl, "The Risks of Outsourcing IT," *Sloan Management Review* (Spring 1996).

PROBLEM-SOLVING CASE

UNIFYING COMMUNICATIONS IN ALASKA

The Telecommunications Act of 1996 broke up the monopoly held by the major long-distance telephone services, allowing smaller companies to offer both local and long-distance service to their customers. General Communications Inc. of Anchorage, Alaska, used this development as the impetus to revamp its operations. General Communications accounts for nearly half of all the long-distance customers in Alaska, a state with a population of just over half a million. The company sensed a future in which all communications services could be streamlined together, simplifying all aspects of communication for the customer. In this vision, most customers would opt to have a single carrier provide all their communications services. With the threat of competition for long-distance agreements suddenly increased, the time to begin the move toward the future had arrived.

General's plan called for unifying services for telephone, cable television, mobile communications, and satellite communications, providing customers with one-stop shopping. Utilities such as electricity and water were even factored into the equation. The task of redesigning General's billing service so that each type of communications service would appear on one comprehensive bill received top priority. Consolidating this information would be complicated because all of General's billing information was already contained in a 20-year-old system. Discarding that system and starting over simply was not feasible.

Ed Spradling, vice-president of management information systems and administration, and David Oglesby, director of MIS, turned to Cincom Systems for a solution to the problem. Cincom offered an object-oriented development and execution environment called Total FrameWork that provided Spradling and Oglesby with exactly what they needed: the ability to convert their old billing system into a form that would eventually fit into the new comprehensive system.

General's first step consisted of producing a billing system that combined their telephone and cable TV services. To do this, they updated their old system using object code. Eventually, they will use Cincom's object-oriented programming to create an entirely new billing system that includes all of their communications services. Oglesby realized that his company was fortunate to come across Total FrameWork. He knew that customers would appreciate a comprehensive bill and that any company that offered one would have great appeal. The business of providing one, however, had the potential to overwhelm General, both financially and time-wise. Early estimates indicated that the process of moving from an outdated Wang minicomputer to the desired technology would require three years and $85 million, a full 65 percent of the company's annual revenue. FrameWork reduced the time frame to 20 months and the initial cost to $1 million, with additional costs not approaching anywhere near $85 million.

FrameWork's value lies in its high-level language capability, which saves General's employees from having to learn the complexities of writing object code. Its advantage over other similar products stems from the ease with which it manipulates object code and legacy systems such as the one General was using in the same environment. Oglesby also found a nontechnical advantage to employing Cincom software. The developers demonstrated genuine enthusiasm for acquiring General's business by ignoring the hardships of visiting a frigid Alaska during the winter months. Other software companies showed up only when it was convenient for them.

General did seek the help of other companies to assist them with some of the other problematic steps. The new billing system would be housed on IBM RS/6000 multiprocessors. The task of translating the old Wang COBOL programs to a form compatible with the RS/6000 went to Unicon Conversion Technologies Inc., a known specialist in that area. Objective Communications Software Inc. tackled the problem of allowing a Wang programming language to run on UNIX, General's operating system of choice. Finally, General needed to alter the structure of its data for the system, moving from indexed and sequential files to a relational structure. Leverage Technologists and Objective Communications completed this job.

The first new bill combined long-distance telephone usage with bills from three cable companies that General acquired in March 1996. Subsequent bills will incorporate local telephone and personal communication service charges. General will be able to make these billing changes by reusing the object that calculates the cost of long-distance calls and modifying it to handle personal communication service rates. The object-oriented environment will let General implement new pricing plans more quickly, beating out competitors.

Obviously, the process of streamlining its billing services proved to be a lot of work for General Communications. However, customers benefit from receiving one bill for local and long-distance telephone service, cellular usage, Internet access, and entertainment. General expects to create an advanced customer service program with FrameWork's workflow mechanisms. Spradling asserts that flexibility in billing is the key to beating the competition.

SOURCE: Emily Andren, "Freezing Out Competitors," *Information Week,* June 24, 1996.

CASE STUDY QUESTIONS

1. What people, organization, and technology problems did General Communications face that required it to build a new system?

2. Was the solution development approach appropriate for the problem? What other alternatives might the developers have employed?

3. What were the technology and people problems General Communications encountered in implementing the new system? How did they overcome them?

4. What were the benefits of the solution chosen? What were its drawbacks?

Chapter TWELVE

SAFEGUARDING INFORMATION SYSTEMS

CHAPTER OUTLINE

LEARNING OBJECTIVES

After reading and studying this chapter, you will

1. Be aware of the major threats to computer-based information systems, including computer crime, hackers, computer viruses, and information system quality problems.
2. Be able to describe the role of general and application controls in safeguarding information systems.
3. Be able to describe the most important techniques for promoting information system security.
4. Be able to assess software and data quality problems.

INTERNET SABOTAGE

In September 1996 Public Access Networks, or Panix, a New York Internet service provider, reported a new type of sabotage. The company was virtually shut down for days when a computer hacker started bombarding its computers with requests to send or receive information. The requests contained fake Internet addresses, which Panix's computers had to sort out before discarding. But the computers had to spend so much time sorting out the flood of bogus requests—up to 150 per second—that they could not handle legitimate requests for access to the World Wide Web sites that Panix hosts.

Recipes for conducting the attack were recently published in two underground computer publications, *2600* and *Phrack.* The attacks spread to a dozen other World Wide Web sites around the United States.

Alexis Rosen, a co-founder of Panix, said that if the attacks kept up, the company could be out of business in a week. Three years earlier Panix had undergone another attack when an intruder penetrated its computers and stole passwords of Panix subscribers that could be used to access other computer networks.

A recent probe of World Wide Web sites by security expert Dan Farmer found that nearly two-thirds of the most popular commercial and government Web sites are wide open to penetration and abuse. Farmer is a co-developer of SATAN (Security Analysis Tool for Auditing Networks), a software package that probes networks of UNIX computers, searching for security flaws. It reports information about poorly configured network services and bugs in system or network utilities such as file transfer protocol, sendmail, and the network file system. Although recognized as a valuable diagnostic tool, SATAN could also be used by hackers to help them figure out ways of illicitly penetrating networks.

In a controversial move, Farmer used SATAN to surreptitiously probe 1,735 Web sites for security flaws. Farmer didn't exploit the security flaws to actually break into the Web sites but used SATAN merely to assess their vulnerability. SATAN's probe showed that 68 percent of bank Web sites, 62 percent of U.S. government Web sites, and 70 percent of newspaper Web sites were vulnerable. Farmer found only three sites that appeared to detect the probes. Farmer's findings were borne out when hackers penetrated the U.S. Air Force's main Web site, defacing the home page with bloody images and obscene pictures. Other surveys have found Web site vandalism on the rise.

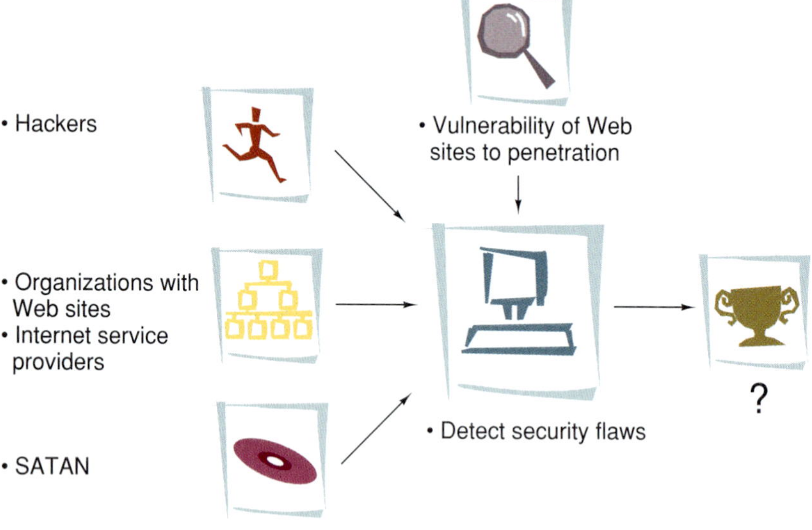

SOURCES: Gary H. Anthes, "Don't Call It a Safety 'Net,'" *Computerworld,* January 6, 1997; Bart Ziegler, "Savvy Hacker Tangles Web for Net Host," *The Wall Street Journal,* September 12, 1996; and John Markoff, "A New Method of Internet Sabotage is Spreading," *The New York Times,* September 19, 1996.

This story illustrates how vulnerable computerized systems are to theft, damage, disruption, or misuse. It also shows that the proper use and operation of information systems depend on the behavior of people as well as on technical, organizational, and design factors. The critical role played by automated information systems in business, government, and daily life requires special steps to protect them and to ensure that they are accurate and reliable. In this chapter we describe the considerations that must be taken into account when designing information system solutions to ensure that systems serve the purposes for which they were intended.

12.1 THE VULNERABILITY OF INFORMATION SYSTEMS

Although computer-based information systems can help solve a firm's problems, they are vulnerable to many more kinds of threats than manual systems. Events such as a fire or electrical power failure can cause massive damage because so much of a firm's information resources are concentrated in one place. Valuable data can be destroyed if computer hardware malfunctions or if individuals tamper with computerized files. Businesses such as banks, airlines, or credit card companies could lose millions of dollars every hour their systems are not operational. For example, a brokerage firm could lose $5-7 million for every hour that its systems were not working.[1]

THE MAJOR THREATS TO COMPUTERIZED INFORMATION SYSTEMS

The major threats to computerized information systems are disasters, such as fire or electrical failure, hardware malfunctions, software errors, user errors, and computer crime and abuse. These threats and their effects are summarized in Table 12.1.

Online information systems and those based on telecommunications networks are especially vulnerable because they link information systems in many different locations. As a result, unauthorized access or abuse can occur

TABLE 12.1

Major Threats to Computerized Information Systems

Threat	Effect
Fire	Computer hardware, files, and manual records may be destroyed.
Electrical power failure	All computer processing is halted; hardware may be damaged, and "disk crashes" or telecommunications disruptions may occur.
Hardware malfunction	Data are not processed accurately or completely.
Software errors	Computer programs do not process data accurately, completely, or according to user requirements.
User errors	Errors inadvertently introduced by users during transmission, input, validation, processing, distribution, and other points of the information processing cycle destroy data, disrupt processing, or produce flawed output.
Computer crime	Illegal use of computer hardware, software, or data results in monetary theft or destruction of valuable data or services.
Computer abuse	Computer systems are used for unethical purposes.

FIGURE 12.1

A Telecommunications Network Is Vulnerable at a Number of Points

Potential security problems—unauthorized access or abuse of the system—can occur at many points in a telecommunications network. Unauthorized access and illegal connections can occur at the input stage. It is also possible to "tap" communications lines and illegally intercept data. Within the CPU itself, either the hardware or software can fail, and stored files can be accessed illegally, copied, or stolen. Telecommunications systems linked by satellite are even more vulnerable because transmissions can be intercepted without using a physically attached device.

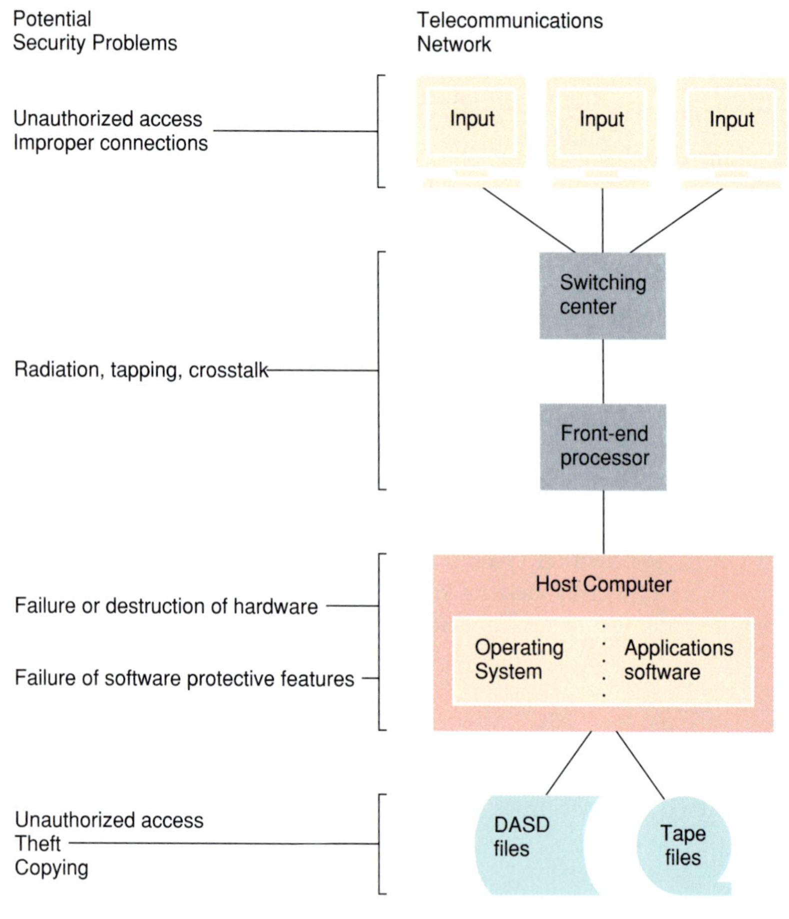

at a multitude of access points. Figure 12.1 illustrates the vulnerabilities of a generic telecommunications network. New network technologies and computing patterns magnify these vulnerabilities. Wireless data networks are easily penetrated since wireless data transfer uses devices that are essentially radio transmitters. Anyone with the right receiver can tune into a voice or data transmission. Client/server networks are especially difficult to safeguard because there are even more points at which the system can be accessed, which allow more opportunities to tamper with information. Local area networks (LANs) lack many of the backup and security features that are found in mainframe systems and are easily disrupted. Many things can go wrong, including server crashes, faulty hard disks, problems with network operating systems, or application errors. Applications using the Internet are highly vulnerable because the Internet's TCP/IP networking environment is easily accessible by unauthorized users.[2]

COMPUTER CRIME, HACKERS, AND COMPUTER VIRUSES

Of special concern to information system designers and users are the issues of security and computer crime. **Security** refers to all the policies, procedures, and technical tools used for safeguarding information systems from unauthorized access, alteration, theft, and physical damage. As organizations continue to store critical data on networks, the problems of unauthorized penetration are growing.

Security
All the policies, procedures, and technical tools used to safeguard information systems from unauthorized access, alteration, theft, and physical damage.

Although the greatest threats to computer systems come from accidents and human error, a major objective of computer security is to prevent **computer crime** (which includes the deliberate theft or criminal destruction of computerized data or services, the use of computer hardware or software to illegally alter or destroy data, and the application of computer technology to perpetrate a crime) and to prevent legal but unauthorized access to computer systems.

Computer crime
The deliberate theft or criminal destruction of computerized data or services; the use of computer hardware, software, or data for illegal activities; or the illegal use of computers.

Sources and Types of Computer Crime Computer crime can range from a teenage prank to international espionage. Although monetary theft is the most common form of computer crime, it can also involve theft of services, information, or computer programs; alteration of data; damage to software; and trespassing. Here are some examples:

Computers are highly vulnerable to floods or other threats posed by natural disasters. Special measures are required to protect and safeguard computerized information systems.

SOURCE: AP/Wide World Photos.

- Ivy James Lay, a technician in the Greensboro facilities of MCI Communications Corp., programmed an MCI PC to capture more than 50,000 credit card numbers. Before he was apprehended in September 1996, Lay had sold the numbers to a network of dealers, resulting in over $50 million in fraudulent charges.
- In the summer of 1994, Vladimir Levin, a mathematician in St. Petersburg, Russia, penetrated Citibank's cash management system, a network that allows corporate customers to transfer money to any bank account in the world. Levin had found a way to obtain valid user IDs and passwords of other banks for this purpose. Before being apprehended, Levin and his accomplices had transferred $10 million to various bank accounts around the world. Citibank was able to recover all but $400,000 of the illegal cash transfers.
- Three technicians at AT&T's British headquarters in London set up their own company in 1992, assigned it a 900 number, and programmed AT&T computers to dial the number often. AT&T lost close to $500,000 before the fraud was accidentally detected.[3]

Losses from computer crime are difficult to quantify because many computer crimes go undetected and corporations are reluctant to publicize such problems. Computer crime has been estimated to cost over $1 billion in the United States, billions more if cellular and corporate telephone theft are included. The concentration of assets in computer form makes computer crime a high-loss, high-risk proposition for a business firm. Even if the crime does not involve major theft, it can severely damage a business's operations or record keeping. For example, USPA, Inc., and IRA, Inc., two branches of an insurance and brokerage firm based in Fort Worth, Texas, could not pay 550 employees for several weeks when a former programmer wiped out 168,000 payroll records.

The vast majority of computer crimes are committed by authorized insiders (see the Focus on People). The National Center for Computer Crime Data in Los Angeles, California, estimated that 70 percent of reported computer crimes were perpetrated by people inside the organization.

Hacker
A person who gains unauthorized access to a computer network for profit, criminal mischief, or personal reasons.

Hackers Nevertheless, loss and damage from **hackers** attempting to penetrate information systems from the outside cannot be dismissed. The press has reported numerous incidents of inventive teenagers who invade computer networks for profit, criminal mischief, or personal thrills. Sophisticated personal computer users are becoming increasingly adept at connecting their personal computers to the nation's telephone network to eavesdrop, charge calls to another person's bill, destroy data, disrupt telephone switching services, or penetrate computer systems linked via telecommunications.[4]

Among the most notorious of these hackers is Kevin Mitnick, who was finally apprehended by the FBI in February 1995. Mitnick had been breaking into computer systems for more than a decade. Between 1992 and 1995 alone, he had stolen thousands of data files and software programs and at least 20,000 credit card numbers from computer systems around the United States. Mitnick frequently used the Internet and other online services to gain access to systems and to store his stolen software and data.

Computer virus
A rogue software program that spreads rampantly through computer systems, destroying data or causing the systems to become congested and malfunction.

Computer Viruses Alarm has risen over hackers propagating **computer viruses**, rogue software programs that spread rampantly (like viruses) from

FOCUS ON PEOPLE

COMPUTER FRAUD AT THE SOCIAL SECURITY ADMINISTRATION

In November 1996, federal law enforcement officials arrested six workers at the Social Security Administration, charging them with the distribution of confidential personal data to credit card thieves. A total of ten federal employees have now been charged with this crime since an investigation began in February of the same year. The information to which the employees had access allowed the thieves to use newly issued credit cards they had stolen from the mail without suspicion until Citibank's record of fraudulent charges showed an unusually high number of instances in which customers never received the card on which the charges had been made.

This case brings up serious issues regarding the security of information systems. Breaches of security threaten to endanger the livelihood of every person whose personal profile has ever been entered into an electronic system. Most banks and credit card companies provide safeguards for their customers by asking for a password such as their mother's maiden name in order to activate an account or proceed with a transaction. When the system is compromised by unscrupulous workers who sell the information to criminals, as in this case, then one can only hope that other plans are in place to detect illegal activity.

Fortunately, the Social Security Administration monitors its employees' requests for data files. Investigators found that one worker had unlawfully accessed personal files more than 20 times, selling the files to scam artists who activated and used other people's credit cards thanks to the social security information. In an ironic twist of fate, the government worker then "sold out" other agency employees by passing on information about their illegal activities to the government. In total, the violators, all from the Brooklyn, New York, Social Security office, infringed on the privacy of approximately 1,000 people. As a result of their actions, Citibank, Visa, and Mastercard lost a combined $10 million due to fraud.

Brian F. Gimlett, the Secret Service's top special agent in New York, revealed that the government had arrested nine people for actually stealing and using the credit cards. They abused them in many ways, including making purchases and withdrawals from automatic teller machines. In almost all cases, the thieves did not work together, nor were they part of any crime organization. They turned to workers at the Social Security Administration because they already possessed social security numbers, which can be easily obtained from universities, hospitals, and other public institutions such as the Department of Motor Vehicles. Many states use the numbers as driver's license identification numbers. The thieves needed only the final piece of the puzzle, such as a person's mother's maiden name. For a fee sometimes as low as $10, some government employees were willing to hand over the information.

According to Mr. Gimlett, "This is another example of greedy people finding new ways to compromise the security systems to financially gain from credit card fraud and other types of fraud." The danger to the security of information systems cannot be ignored. Even though these government workers face prison terms and heavy fines for bribery and misuse of government property, they surely will not be the last to take advantage of the technology.

FOCUS Question:
What people, organization, and technology factors allowed this crime to take place?

SOURCE: Lynda Richardson, "Social Security Workers Held In Frauds Using Credit Cards," *The New York Times,* November 21, 1996.

system to system. Information systems become congested and malfunction as the viruses endlessly replicate themselves. Depending on the intent of the creator, the virus might flash a harmless message such as "Merry Christmas!" on computer terminals, or it might systematically destroy all the data in the computer's memory.

The most notorious computer virus epidemic occurred in November 1988, when a brilliant computer science student introduced a program that spread uncontrollably throughout a nationwide Department of Defense data network. Created by Robert Tappan Morris, the son of one of the U.S. government's most respected computer security experts, the virus program rapidly reproduced itself throughout ARPANET (Advanced Research Projects Agency Network), which links research centers, universities, and military bases.

Computer security experts concluded that this virus contained no harmful hidden features and left data files unharmed, but it did clog the ARPANET computers and eventually caused the network to shut down. More than 6,000 computers were infected. The Defense Department asserted that it was impossible for classified military networks that manage nuclear weapons systems and store vital secrets to be penetrated in this manner.

Incidents such as this continue to occur on a smaller scale because personal computers are plentiful and their networking software and equipment are relatively easy to use. The following measures have been recommended for combating software viruses; taking these measures will decrease but never eliminate the problem:

1. Make backup copies as soon as you open a new software package, and store the copies offsite.
2. Quarantine each new piece of software or data file on an isolated computer, and review it carefully before installing it, especially if it was obtained via a network or the Internet.
3. Restrict access to programs and data on a "need-to-use" basis.
4. Check all programs regularly for changes in size, which could be a sign of tampering or virus infiltration.
5. Be especially cautious with "shareware" and "freeware" programs, which are a prime entry point for viruses.
6. Institute a plan for immediate removal of all copies of suspicious programs and backup of related data.
7. Be sure all purchased software is in its original shrinkwrapping or sealed disk containers.

Corporate Espionage In addition to hacking and computer crime, the vulnerabilities of contemporary systems have opened new opportunities for committing commercial espionage. Corporations are storing more and more of their confidential information on computers, including strategic plans, sales data, production formulas, and even confidential memos and E-mail exchanges. This information is very valuable to competitors. Such valuable, confidential data are potentially more accessible because the growing use of telecommunications has dramatically expanded the number of points at which commercial spies are able to access a firm's system.

INFORMATION SYSTEM QUALITY PROBLEMS: SOFTWARE AND DATA QUALITY

While computer disasters such as fire, espionage, and viruses grab the headlines, software and data quality problems are a larger and more constant threat to computer operations. **Software bugs** (errors or defects in the code of a program), which can cause untold amounts of damage and losses in productivity, are everywhere. Developing high-quality software presents particularly difficult problems.

Software bug
An error or defect in the code of a software program.

Software Quality Problems Total quality management and "zero defects" are popular business concepts today. They were pioneered by the Japanese, and the rest of the business world began to pay attention when the quality of Japanese products improved sharply and consumers began to demand Japanese goods. Zero defects is an appropriate target for most goods and is absolutely essential for some products (think of the results of failed heart valves or airplane engines). Computer software, however, is different. Programs with zero defects cannot be achieved with current technology. Let's look at why.

In writing any but the simplest of computer programs, bugs cannot be avoided. The main technique used in most computer programs is making decisions based on a given set of choices. For example, a simplified version of part of an income tax program might contain lines like the following:

```
IF NET-INCOME IS LESS THAN 12,000
   THEN TAX-OWED EQUALS 0
   PERFORM PRINT-RETURN-ROUTINE
ELSE IF NET-INCOME IS EQUAL TO OR GREATER THAN 12,000 AND LESS
   THAN 24,000
   THEN TAX-OWED EQUALS (NET-INCOME MINUS 12,000) TIMES 0.14.
CALCULATE NET-TAX-OWED EQUALS TAX-OWED MINUS TAX-PAID.
IF NEXT-TAX-PAID IS GREATER THAN ZERO
   THEN PERFORM OWES-TAX-ROUTINE
ELSE IF NET-TAX-PAID IS LESS THAN ZERO
   THEN PERFORM REFUND-DUE-ROUTINE
ELSE PERFORM TAXES-EVEN-ROUTINE.
```

The code would continue with all the many tax possibilities and the accompanying mathematical formulas and actions. Most choices include a series of steps that contain further choices and steps, creating many complex paths. A program of several hundred lines will have many tens of such choices and paths. Important programs within an organization will have thousands or even millions of lines as well as hundreds or thousands of decision points. An ordinary payroll system for a large corporation, for example, may have hundreds of programs, each of which will require thousands or tens of thousands of lines of instructions.

With so many lines of code and so many decision points, a large number of errors will creep in. Errors occur for a number of reasons: typing errors, improper use of a complex programming technique to code a tricky passage, lack of clarity in program specifications, even misunderstandings by the end users concerning the actions needed under every possible combination of circumstances. The only way to make certain no errors exist within a program is to test every line of code, making certain that every possible path is executed through to its end and that every kind of data error can be handled.

However, studies indicate that testing every possible choice and line within a large system (such as a payroll, manufacturing control, or hotel reservation system) would require a minimum of thousands of years, even with the most powerful computers now available. Thus, complete testing of larger systems is a complete impossibility.

Worse yet, once testing has been "completed," no one can estimate with any accuracy how many bugs are left or what their effect might be. Hidden bugs will surface only when the lines of code that contain them are executed, triggered by an unusual combination of conditions. A hidden bug recently surfaced in a New York City-area bank that caused the bank to deduct $2 from each customer's account for every dollar the customer withdrew through the bank's ATM. The cost to the bank was enormous, not only in work to correct the bug and reinstate the funds in customers' accounts, but also in negative public relations. Imagine the havoc and tragedy a hidden bug could cause in a railroad signal control system, an onboard airplane navigation system, or even an automobile brake control system.

Ultimately, the goal for most companies in relation to information systems bugs is not one of zero defects, but rather one of reducing the number and seriousness of bugs as much as possible within an acceptable time and cost framework, thus producing systems of as high a quality as is reasonably feasible.

One enormous issue faced by computer software users is that of system maintenance. The maintenance phase of a system begins once a system goes into production, and it lasts for as many years as the system continues to be used. To many, maintenance refers to keeping the system running. However, maintenance also includes the need to keep the system up to date so that it supports the changing needs of the organization. If the business grows, a sales system might have to be modified to support added sales offices or additional products. It might also have to be enhanced so that it can be accessed via a network in order to serve a more dispersed sales staff. A changing legal environment might require modifications to a payroll system or an environmental monitoring system. Increased cost pressures might cause a company to modify its manufacturing process, which in turn might require changes in production control systems. Maintenance is an ongoing need for most large systems and in many companies costs much more than does the development of new systems.

Data Quality Problems The most common source of information systems failure, however, is not software quality but problems that result from inaccurate, outdated, or incomplete data. According to a recent study, 69 percent of corporate executives surveyed said that their corporate data had an unacceptable level of corruption. Corrupted data can wreak havoc. A tiny error in a percentage figure can cost a bank millions of dollars. But a single data error is not the most significant problem. Rather, the largest problem is the many bits of inaccurate data in massive numbers of records, from name and address errors in customer lists to mistakes made in individual accounts payable records. Credit histories of individuals, used to establish eligibility for all kinds of loans and credit cards, were so fraught with errors that the United States government forced the credit bureaus to give customers access to their credit histories in order to improve credit record quality.

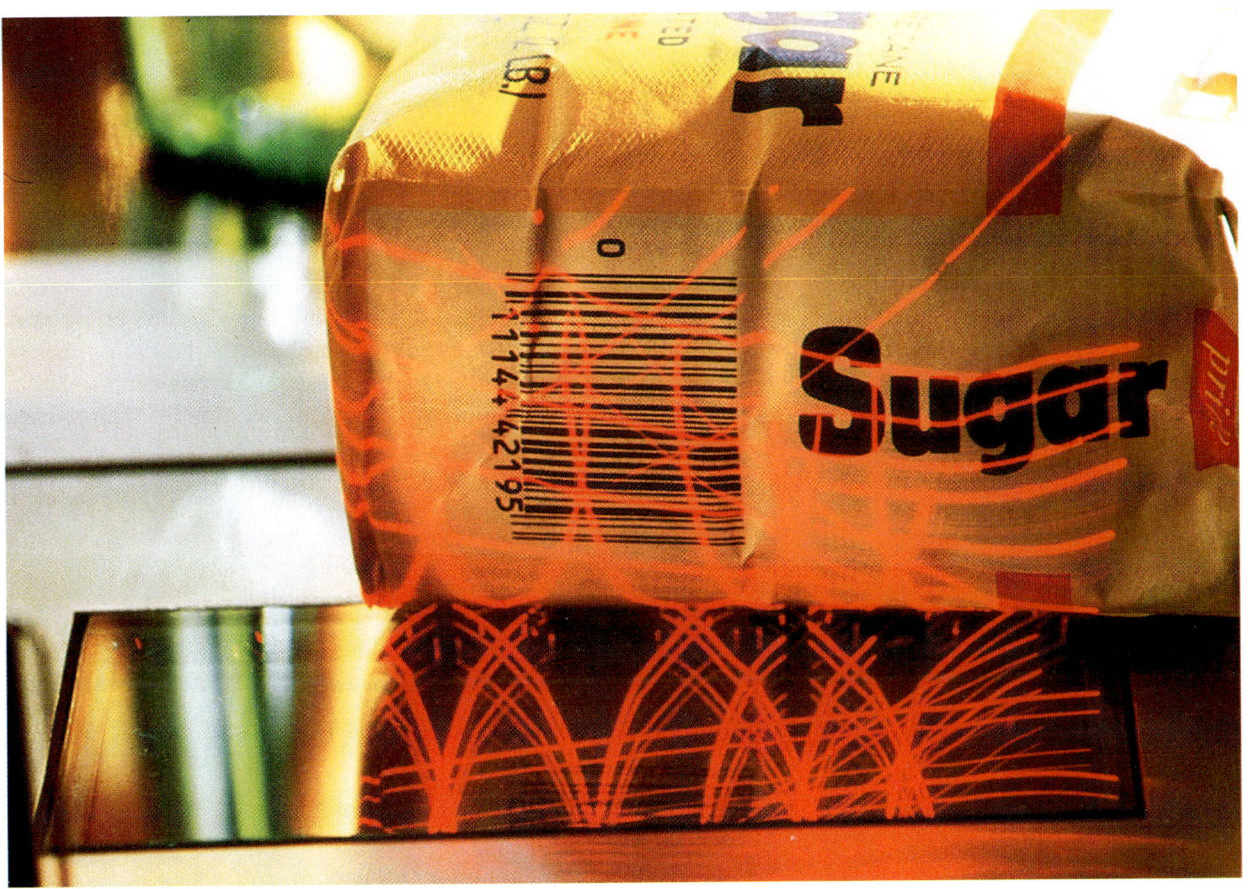

Between 5 and 10 percent of all bar code sales in supermarkets and merchandise chains are erroneous, resulting in many customers being overcharged for their purchases. Poor data quality is the single largest cause of information system problems.

SOURCE: Courtesy of International Business Machines Corporation.

Following are some other examples of data quality problems:

- For months an airline had aircraft take off carrying only half the number of passengers listed for each flight because it had corrupted its database of passenger reservations while installing new software.
- J. P. Morgan, the New York investment bank, discovered that 40 percent of the data in its credit risk management database was incomplete and had to be double-checked by users.
- Several studies have documented that 5–12 percent of prices on bar codes at supermarkets and retail stores are erroneous and that the ratio of overcharges to undercharges runs 4:1. The problem stems mainly from human error in keeping shelf prices accurate.[5]

When bad data go unnoticed, they can lead to product recalls, bad decisions, and financial losses. In the following sections we examine how organizations can address these problems and the other threats to their systems.

12.2 DEVELOPING CONTROLS FOR SYSTEMS

Controls
The specific technology, policies, and manual procedures used to protect assets, accuracy, and reliability of information systems.

General controls
Organization-wide controls, both manual and automated, that affect overall activities of computerized information systems.

Application controls
Manual and automated procedures to ensure that the data processed by a particular application remain accurate, complete, and valid throughout the processing cycle.

As the preceding section shows, safeguarding computer information systems can no longer be treated as an afterthought but must be integral to the system design. Effective business problem analysis and solution design include considerations of how the information system can be protected and controlled.

The specific technology, policies, and manual procedures for protecting assets, accuracy, and reliability of information systems are called **controls.** There are two types of controls: **general controls,** which can be applied to the overall business and computing environment of an organization, and specific **application controls,** which govern individual information system applications.

GENERAL CONTROLS

General controls are all the organization-wide controls, both manual and automated, that affect the overall activities of computerized information systems. In other words, they provide an umbrella for all information systems in the firm. General controls ensure the following:

- The security and reliability of computer hardware.
- The security and reliability of software.
- The security of data files.
- Consistent and correct computer operations.
- Proper management of systems development.

TABLE 12.2

General Controls for Information Systems

Control	Example
Hardware	Restricting access to machines/terminals; checking for equipment malfunction.
Software	Requiring logs of operating system activities; restricting unauthorized access to software programs.
Data security	Using passwords; restricting access to terminals to limit access to data files.
Operations	Establishing procedures for running computer jobs correctly; establishing backup and recovery procedures for abnormal or disrupted processing.
Systems development	Requiring management review and audit of each new information system project for conformity with budget, solution requirements, and quality standards; requiring appropriate technical and business documentation for each system.
Management	Establishing formal written policies and procedures; segregating job functions to minimize error and fraud; providing supervision and accountability.

A supervisor works with an online reservation agent at an airline reservation center. Ongoing management supervision and accountability are essential for ensuring that all the controls for an information system work properly.

SOURCE: © Jon Feingersh, Stock, Boston.

They also include **management controls,** which provide appropriate management supervision and accountability for information systems. Table 12.2 presents examples of general controls in each area.

Documentation is a critical but often overlooked element of information system control. It is critical because information systems will not work properly unless clear-cut explanations of how they work from both end-user and technical standpoints are available. Each information system solution requires three levels of documentation: system documentation, user documentation, and operational documentation.

Management controls
A type of general control that provides appropriate management supervision and accountability for information systems (e.g., establishing formal written policies and procedures and segregating job functions in order to minimize error and fraud).

Documentation
A control that involves establishing and maintaining a clear-cut explanation of how an information system works from both an end-user and a technical standpoint; includes system, user, and operational documentation.

TABLE 12.3

Examples of Information System Documentation

System Documentation
System flowcharts
Structure charts
File and record layouts
Program listings

User Documentation
Functional or business description of system
Data input instructions
Transaction authorizations
Sample data input forms or online input screens
Report distribution lists
Output report samples
Error correction procedures

Operational Documentation
Computer job setups
Run control procedures
Backup and recovery procedures
Hardware and operating system requirements
Disaster recovery plan

FIGURE 12.2

Application Controls and General Controls Work Together to Promote System Security and Accuracy

General controls govern the security and accuracy of the overall computing environment. They include such safeguards as data security measures, routine error checks in hardware, restriction of access to programs, and standards for system development. Application controls govern individual system applications. There are three types of application controls, corresponding to the three basic steps in computing: input, processing, and output.

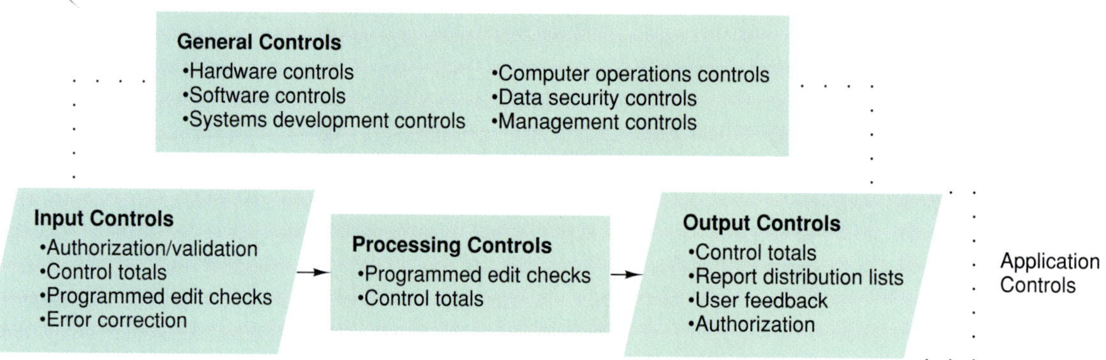

System documentation describes the design, structure, and software features of an information system solution. User documentation details manual procedures and how an information system solution is used from an end-user standpoint. Operational documentation describes the steps for running and operating a system, or for backup and recovery, that would be used in a corporate data center. Table 12.3 provides examples of all three kinds of documentation.

APPLICATION CONTROLS

So far we have looked at general controls that monitor the firm's overall computing environment. In addition to these broad general controls, there are specific controls, called application controls, that govern individual information system applications. Application controls consist of both manual and automated procedures to ensure that the data processed by a particular application remain accurate, complete, and valid throughout the processing cycle. There are three types of application controls: input controls, processing controls, and output controls (see Figure 12.2).

Input controls
Application controls that ensure the accuracy and completeness of data entering the information system.

Processing controls
Application controls that ensure that the accuracy and completeness of data during updating.

Output controls
Application controls that ensure that the results of computer processing are accurate, complete, and properly distributed.

Input controls ensure the accuracy and completeness of data when the data enter an information system. **Processing controls** ensure the accuracy and completeness of data during updating, and **output controls** ensure that the results of computer processing are accurate, complete, and properly distributed. Some of the most important application control techniques are procedures for authorizing and validating input and output, programmed edit checks, and control totals.

An organization can establish formal procedures that allow only selected individuals to authorize input of transactions into a system or to review system output to ensure that it is complete and accurate. These are known as authorization and validation procedures. For example, the signature of the head of the payroll department might be required in order to authorize corrections to employee time cards before such transactions are entered into the payroll system. The payroll department head might likewise be required to "sign off" on the results of each payroll processing run, indicating that he or she has reviewed the results and that they are complete and processed properly.

Programmed edit checks are a common technique for checking input data for errors before the data are processed. Transactions that fail to meet the criteria established in computerized edit routines will be rejected. For example, an order processing system might check the product codes on the order transaction to ensure they are valid by matching them against the product codes in an inventory master file. If a product code does not conform to any existing product codes, the order transaction is rejected. If the transaction passes this test, the program might then check the product price on the order to determine that it is accurate (if the item has a fixed price), appropriate (if the price may vary depending on quantity ordered), or reasonable (falling within present appropriate limits if the salesperson has discretion in setting the price). Sometimes preprogrammed edit checks are used as a processing control as well. Figure 12.3 describes some of the most important techniques for programmed edit checks.

Programmed edit check
An application control technique for checking input data for errors before the data are processed; it uses a computerized checking procedure.

Control totals are used at all points in the processing cycle to ensure completeness and some level of accuracy. An information system can make a manual or automated count of the number of transactions processed during input, processing, or output or of total critical quantities, such as order amounts. These totals can then be compared manually or by computer; any discrepancies will signal potential errors. Table 12.4 summarizes the major types of control totals—record counts, quantitative totals, hash totals, and run-to-run control totals.

Control totals
A manual or automated count of the number of transactions processed during input, processing, or output, or of critical quantities, such as order amounts; this count is then compared manually or by computer with a second count; discrepancies in the counts signal errors.

TABLE 12.4

Major Types of Control Totals

Control	Description	Example
Record counts	Counts the total source input documents and compares this total to the number of records at other stages of input preparation.	Number of order forms should match the total number of order input transactions for a batch order entry system.
Quantitative totals	Totals a quantitative field such as total sales or total orders for a batch of transactions and compares this number with a manual total established for this group of transactions.	Total order amount should match the order total for a batch of order transactions in a batch order entry system.
Hash totals	Totals nonquantitative data fields for control purposes and compares them with a total manually established for a group of transactions.	Total product code numbers should match a total established manually for a batch order entry system.
Run-to-run controls	Totals can be generated during processing to compare the number of input transactions with the number of transactions that have updated a file or with output totals. The totals can represent total transactions processed or totals for critical quantities.	Total number of time cards input should equal the total number of employees updated on the payroll master file during processing and the total number of employees with paychecks generated.

FIGURE 12.3

Programmed Edit Checks Are a Valuable Application Control Technique

Programmed edit checks can be used in both the input and processing phases to ensure data accuracy. Special edit check programs read input transactions and scan their data fields for accuracy. Transactions that do not meet the criteria of these checks are rejected and reported. The transactions must be corrected to pass the edit criteria before they can become part of the updated files.

Programmed Edit Checks

Technique	Description
1. Format check	The system checks the contents, size, and sign of individual data fields. Example: A telephone long distance code should be a 3-position numeric field.
2. Existence check	The system checks for valid codes by comparing input data fields to tables or master files. Example: State code should be one of the valid state codes on a state code table.
3. Reasonableness check	The system checks to see if selected fields fall within specified limits. Example: An employee's gross pay can't exceed six figures.
4. Check digit	The check digit is an extra reference number added to an identification code bearing a mathematical relationship to the other digits. The check digit is input with the other data, recomputed by the computer, and compared with the one input. Example: The check digit for vendor code 29743 is 9. The vendor code with appended check digit would be 297439.

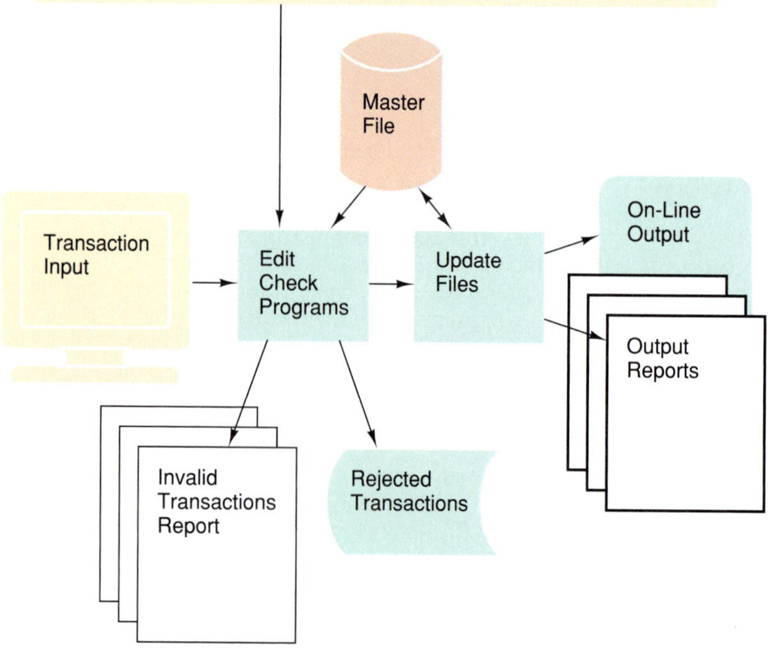

PROBLEM SOLVING WITH CONTROLS

An integral part of solution design is being sure an information system has the proper controls. It is essential that vulnerabilities be identified during problem analysis and that solution alternatives consider different options for

FIGURE 12.4

Control Issues Must Be Considered at Each Step of the Systems Development Process

This diagram illustrates that at each step in the problem-solving process, crucial control issues must be considered. From the beginning of the systems development process, criteria should be established for both general and application controls.

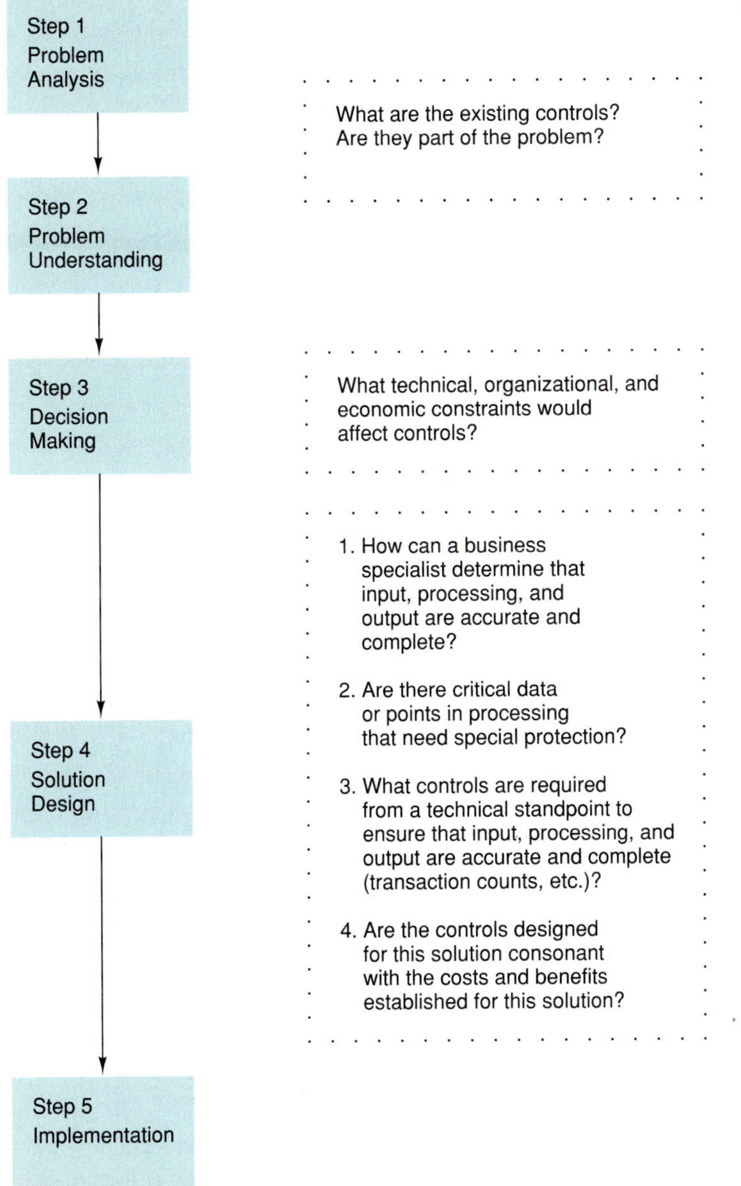
Step 1
Problem
Analysis
What are the existing controls?
Are they part of the problem?
Step 2
Problem
Understanding
Step 3
Decision
Making
What technical, organizational, and
economic constraints would
affect controls?
1. How can a business
specialist determine that
input, processing, and
output are accurate and
complete?
2. Are there critical data
or points in processing
that need special protection?
3. What controls are required
from a technical standpoint to
ensure that input, processing, and
output are accurate and complete
(transaction counts, etc.)?
4. Are the controls designed
for this solution consonant
with the costs and benefits
established for this solution?
Step 4
Solution
Design
Step 5
Implementation

controls. We can apply our people, technology, and organizational framework to control issues.

Technology	Organization	People
Hardware malfunction	Management supervision	Insider crime
Software errors	Segregation of functions	Training
Program security	External pressure (privacy laws, need to distribute systems and data)	Ease of use of controls
Telecommunications security		User errors
Database security		

The logical and physical design of an information system solution should establish the criteria for ensuring completeness and accuracy of input, processing, and output. Figure 12.4 illustrates how analysis and design of controls fit into the problem-solving process. At each step in the problem-solving process, specific control issues must be addressed.

Not all information systems use application controls to the same degree, nor do they all need to. Much depends on the nature of the application and how critical its data are. We can expect major banking and financial systems to use more controls than other systems because so much money and credibility is at stake.

Safeguarding information systems can be a costly and complicated process. Moreover, a system that has too many controls—one that is "overcontrolled"—can be so unwieldy and difficult to use that people may be discouraged from using it at all. The problem-solving process must weigh the benefits of each control or safeguard against financial costs and ease of use to determine the right mix for each application.

12.3 SECURING INFORMATION SYSTEMS

Securing information systems includes securing computers from disruption and unauthorized use and programs and data from unauthorized modification. Three important aspects of security are ensuring data security, safeguarding PCs and networks, and developing recovery plans for disasters affecting information systems. All of these areas require more attention now than ever before because of the growing reliance on networking and the Internet.

DATA SECURITY

Data security
A control aimed at preventing the unauthorized use of data and ensuring that data are not accidentally altered or destroyed.

Data security entails both preventing unauthorized use of data and ensuring that data are not accidentally altered or destroyed. Data security must be provided for both data storage and data usage in both online and batch systems. In doing so, the organization needs to determine what data are stored in its systems, how they are used, and who is allowed to access and update the data. A fundamental data security policy is to restrict access on a "need-to-know" basis—in other words, allow individuals to access only the kind of data they need to do their jobs. Especially sensitive data, such as salaries or medical histories, may need a very strict definition of "need-to-know."

Data security must be especially tight for online information systems since they can be accessed more easily by nontechnical specialists than batch systems can. A principal data security technique is the use of passwords, or secret words or codes giving individuals authority to access specific portions of an information system or systems. A password may be required to log on to a system, to access data and files, to change data in the system, and to view sensitive data fields.

Data security is often multilayered, with passwords for logging on tied to overall operating system software and additional passwords and security restrictions established by data security features of specific applications. Figure 12.5 illustrates the multilevel data security system for a mortgage loan system. User identification and authorization are checked at the system software level when a staff member first logs on. A former employee whose password has been deleted would be unable to access the system at all. The

FIGURE 12.5

A Data Security System

This figure illustrates a multilevel data security approach for a mortgage loan system that requires all employees to provide an authorized password when logging on. Staff must supply an additional password to access customer mortgage account files. A former employee whose password has been deleted would be unable to access the system at all; a clerk would be able to access the system but not the mortgage account files. A banking specialist could access mortgage account data but would be restricted from viewing the Annual Income field. A loan officer, however, would be able to view all the data.

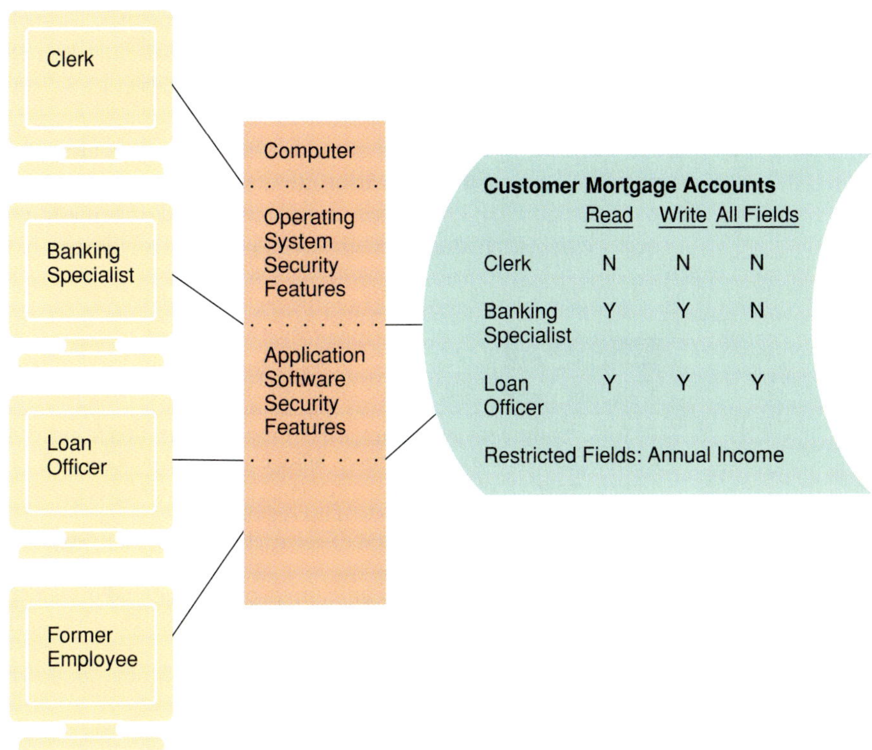

banking specialist and loan officer must then provide a password to access customer mortgage account files; a clerk would be unable to access these files. At the individual data field level, only the loan officer would be allowed access to annual income data. The banking specialist would not be allowed to view this sensitive information.

One problem with passwords is that they are not guarded carefully enough. Unauthorized individuals can easily discover another person's password if he or she writes it down on a piece of paper and carelessly leaves it by a desk or terminal. Yet individuals cannot be expected to memorize all their passwords, especially if they need a different password for each application or if the passwords are periodically changed. Passwords must also be guarded when used on a network.

Encryption
The process of encoding data into unreadable form to prevent unauthorized access.

As a result of the increased use of telecommunications and the Internet, organizations have turned to an additional data security safeguard in the form of data **encryption**. Data are scrambled into a coded form before transmission on a telecommunications network and then decoded on arrival. An authorized user enters a unique, secret key that is not stored anywhere on the system to trigger the encoding process. The Problem-Solving Case at the end of the chapter raises some issues related to data encryption.

SAFEGUARDING PCS AND NETWORKS

Stand-alone PC systems have tended to have less formal and stringent controls than those that are mainframe or minicomputer based. Control requirements change, however, when PCs are networked or linked to mainframes and other computers for cooperative processing. As applications formerly relegated to mainframes are downsized to PCs, they, too, will require serious controls if they make use of critical data. Safeguarding PCs raises special problems and requires a special approach. Table 12.5 lists some considerations for PC security.

Providing security is more difficult when PCs are networked into LANs or when the organization uses client/server computing or the Internet. The wide distribution of and easy access to critical information in networks open new channels through which users can alter or destroy data and intruders

TABLE 12.5

A PC Security Checklist

1. Is PC equipment stored in a locked room or attached firmly to work areas?
2. Are disks locked in drawers or filing cabinets? Are disks with critical data stored in a fireproof place?
3. Are data on hard disks backed up regularly?
4. Have individuals authorized to use each machine and application been formally identified?
5. Does each PC application have input, processing, and output controls?
6. Have a procedure and individual been authorized for verifying the data in each application?
7. Are there standards, passwords, and other precautions for downloading data from networks?
8. Are individuals using PCs held accountable for security?
9. Have training and formal documentation for PC security been instituted?

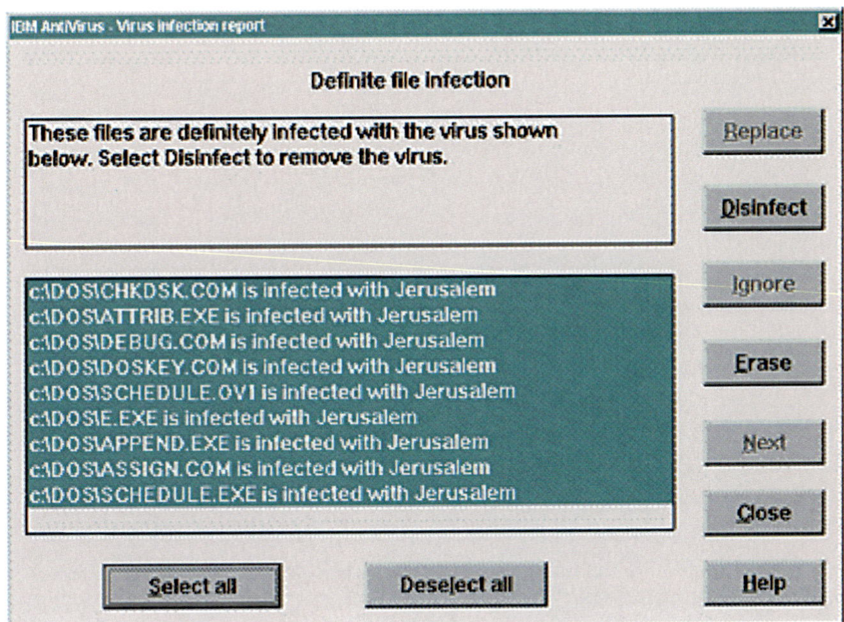
IBM AntiVirus - Virus infection report
Definite file infection
These files are definitely infected with the virus shown below. Select Disinfect to remove the virus.
c:\DOS\CHKDSK.COM is infected with Jerusalem
c:\DOS\ATTRIB.EXE is infected with Jerusalem
c:\DOS\DEBUG.COM is infected with Jerusalem
c:\DOS\DOSKEY.COM is infected with Jerusalem
c:\DOS\SCHEDULE.OV1 is infected with Jerusalem
c:\DOS\E.EXE is infected with Jerusalem
c:\DOS\APPEND.EXE is infected with Jerusalem
c:\DOS\ASSIGN.COM is infected with Jerusalem
c:\DOS\SCHEDULE.EXE is infected with Jerusalem
Replace
Disinfect
Ignore
Erase
Next
Close
Help
Select all
Deselect all

IBM Anti Virus is a leading antivirus software package. Antivirus software can detect and eradicate computer viruses and should be used along with other protective measures.

can gain access. Many of the tools that are available for mainframe and minicomputer security are not available for networked environments.

Special steps must be taken to address network security as information system solutions are being designed. They include the following:

- **Backing up critical data.** Critical data should be copied to a variety of media so that data can be restored if a hardware failure occurs or the data are corrupted or destroyed.
- **Providing redundant servers or disk drives.** Redundant servers and disk drives should be included in the design so that the system can keep working if one piece of hardware breaks. The organization should keep a supply of spare server, workstation, and disk drive components on hand for such emergencies.
- **Controlling access to workstations.** Physical access to networked workstations should be restricted and protected.
- **Classifying network users.** Network users should be carefully classified and assigned a level of security appropriate to their jobs. Users who need system data to perform their jobs should have fairly easy access, while users who do not need such data should have little or no access.
- **Documentation.** Procedures for restoring parts of the network and the telephone numbers of key technical specialists should be thoroughly documented for use during emergencies.
- **Antivirus software.** Special software for detecting and eradicating computer viruses can be installed to limit the risk of virus damage.

The Focus on Problem Solving describes special steps that can be taken to safeguard Web sites.

FOCUS ON PROBLEM SOLVING

PROTECTING YOUR WEB SITE

John Wylder, senior vice-president for information technology at Sun Trust Service, one of Atlanta's largest banks, was presented with a typical Web puzzle: How do you transform a Web site from a simple point-and-click advertising brochure to one supporting customer interaction and electronic commerce? While a business manager might think of this as a trivial change, Wylder knew it posed major security problems. The enhanced Web site would be more accessible to outsiders and would also have to be made more secure to support purchase and sale transactions.

In the search for the solution, Wylder had to answer a question facing many companies: How much security is enough for dealing with the Internet? A wide array of security technologies is available, including firewalls, encryption, and even retinal scanners. The key is not knowing the features of these products but precisely understanding the kinds of threats posed by different types of Internet use and matching the right products to those threats.

Wylder joined a special task force of Open User Recommended Solutions (OURS), a Chicago-based consortium of 60 leading companies, including Bellcore, Pacific Gas & Electric, and Phillips Petroleum. The task force developed general guidelines for Web security, consisting of three basic steps:

1. Identify how the Web application is being used. OURS broke down Web applications into three basic categories: advertising, secure Internet/intranet, and electronic commerce. Some Web sites represent all three of these categories. Companies should base their security around their most vulnerable publicly accessible Web applications.

2. Identify the most serious threats to the Web site. OURS developed a list of nine basic threats to Web sites, which can be found in Table 12.6. The most serious threats to Web sites include unauthorized access to either read or update the contents of a Web site, interception of data, and efforts to undermine electronic commerce.

3. Apply appropriate protection technologies and organizational procedures to combat these threats. Technologies for authenticating user identification, ascertaining authorized users, encryption, message authentication, and establishing responsibility and ownership of Web actions are the most useful. Measures such as installing fault tolerance and backup/recovery also need to be taken to ensure that a Web site is always available to people who want to use it.

Wylder found this third step especially valuable in developing the security plan for Sun Trust because he could see which product categories (such as firewalls, user IDs, etc.) would best address his concerns. Information systems specialists kept touting encryption as the best way to create a secure link. But while encryption can prevent unauthorized interception of data, it does not protect against destruction of data, interference, or inadvertent misuse.

FOCUS Question: What people, organization, and technology issues should be addressed when planning the security for a World Wide Web site?

SOURCE: Vance McCarthy, "Web Security: How Much Is Enough?" *Datamation*, January 1997.

DISASTER RECOVERY PLANNING

Disaster recovery plan
A plan detailing how an organization can resume operations after disasters have disrupted its computer processing.

A wise step for firms that are highly dependent on computerized information systems is to develop a **disaster recovery plan.** Such a plan describes how firms can resume operations after disasters such as fires, floods, power disruptions, or sabotage have disrupted their computer processing. A disaster recovery plan typically provides for immediate access to alternative computer hardware and restoration of software programs, data, and telecommunications facilities. The following are key elements of a disaster recovery plan:

TABLE 12.6

The Nine Basic Threats to Web Sites

The Open User Recommended Solutions (OURS) consortium has identified nine basic threats to Web-based applications. The risks that these threats pose depend on the Web application being considered. Basically, Web applications can be grouped into three main categories: advertising, secure Internet/intranet, and electronic commerce.

1. **Data destruction**—Loss of data on a Web site (through accident or malice) and the interception of traffic (unencrypted or encrypted) going to or coming from the Web site.
2. **Interference**—The intentional rerouting of traffic or the flooding of a local Web server with inappropriate traffic in an attempt to cripple or crash the server.
3. **Modification/replacement**—Altering of data on either the send or receive side of a Web transmission. The changes, whether they are accidental or not, can be difficult to detect in large transmissions.
4. **Misrepresentation/false use of data**—Offering false credentials, passwords, or other data. Also included is a person's posting of a bogus or counterfeit home page to intercept or attract traffic away from the intended destination.
5. **Repudiation**—An after-the-fact denial that an online order or transaction took place.
6. **Inadvertent misuse**—Accidental but inappropriate actions by approved users.
7. **Unauthorized altering/downloading**—Any writing, updating, copying, etc. performed by a person that has not been granted permission to conduct such activity.
8. **Unauthorized transactions**—Any use by a nonapproved party.
9. **Unauthorized disclosure**—Viewing of Web information by an individual not given explicit permission to have access to this information.

SOURCE: Vance McCarthy, "Web Security: How Much Is Enough?" *Datamation*, January 1997.

- Identifying the most critical business functions and their vulnerabilities.
- Knowing what hardware, software, files, and human resources are required in order to resume processing of critical applications.
- Training personnel to follow the recovery plan correctly.
- Having a step-by-step course of action for implementing the plan.

A key component of disaster recovery is backing up and restoring data for critical applications. Disaster recovery plans must also be sensitive to how much of these data flow through PCs and telecommunications links and how much reside in mainframes. Firms can use either internal or external disaster recovery facilities.

For example, the Beneficial Data Processing Corp., the data processing subsidiary of Beneficial Corp. in Peapack, New Jersey, relies on its own distributed processing facilities for disaster recovery. It has distributed processing to local branches so that the branches can operate for several days if the main computer center is lost. The Elkay Corp. split its applications between two mainframe computers, one in Oak Brook, Illinois, and the other in Broadview, Illinois. The mainframes are connected to each other and to remote sites via dedicated data lines. Each mainframe can back up the other.

Sungard Disaster Recovery Services and Comdisco Disaster Recovery Services are specialized external disaster recovery services. They provide fully operational data processing and telecommunications backup facilities to subscribers on less than 24 hours notice. These facilities include computer hardware and software for a firm to run its applications when needed, plus technical assistance in disaster planning testing and use of recovery centers.

The Focus on Organizations examines the resurgence of interest in disaster planning and some special problems that need to be addressed.

FOCUS ON ORGANIZATIONS

DISASTER HEADLINES ENCOURAGE DISASTER PLANNING

Major disasters have been front page news in recent years—the 1990 and 1993 California earthquakes, Hurricane Andrew in Florida, the Chicago and midwestern floods, the World Trade Center bombing. Until recently, information system disaster recovery has not been taken seriously by many organizations. Although disasters have severely affected the information system facilities (and hence the operational abilities) of many companies, only about 40 percent of large organizations even have disaster recovery plans. Not surprisingly, concern over planning for possible disaster has grown as disaster headlines have multiplied.

Some disasters have affected many companies simultaneously (see Figure 12.6). For example, the Chicago flood of April 1992 caused extensive power and telecommunications outages and water damage that crippled major banks, retail stores, and government centers. Billions of dollars were lost. The management of many organizations has been forced to recognize the obvious fact that disasters are unpredictable; it is too late to prepare for them after they occur.

Many organizational leaders have concluded that the cost of a disaster can no longer be measured only in terms of the cost of repair and the immediate business lost. The larger, if more nebulous, loss is the customers who go elsewhere for more reliable service.

Today's disaster planners must think about a disaster's effect on their staff as well as their customers. When a widespread disaster occurs, an organization will naturally find many staff members more concerned with caring for their families than their computers. At the University of Miami, for example, officials had difficulty persuading staff to operate their systems after Hurricane Andrew hit. Plans must take this people factor into consideration. Disaster planners need to work with end-user staff to evaluate the risks in each department and the costs of protecting data.

Methods of planning for disasters are also changing. Today a company can purchase a software package designed to aid the complex disaster-planning process. For example, the American Automobile Association, based in Heathrow, Florida, uses the PC-based Total Recovery Planning System from Chi/Cor Information Management, Inc. of Chicago. New ways of dealing with disaster backup are also being developed. The University of Miami has developed a partnership with a northern Florida company whereby each organization performs a weekly backup of the other's data. In this way an offsite (and out-of-area) backup occurs at no charge for both organizations.

The biggest change in disaster planning, however, is the result of the changing configuration of computers. Traditional disaster planning focused on the data center, an approach that was adequate for centralized mainframe systems but that today leaves vital networks unprotected. Organizations that have had disaster plans for years may find themselves vulnerable as they decentralize their information systems. Because disasters tend to be localized, wide area networks actually have some disaster protection inherent in them. That is, a disaster in one location will leave the hardware at other locations untouched. Nonetheless, because software and data for all locations will usually be affected when even one key node is hit by disaster, the entire system will probably stop. Planning to operate a key widespread network after a disaster hits one site is a complex matter and must be planned carefully, possibly using software designed to support network disaster planning. Traditional hot-site services emphasize mainframe use in case of disaster. But today, operating the mainframe without being able to operate the networks can cripple a company. Because organizations need hot sites for networks as well as mainframes, Sungard, IBM, Hewlett-Packard, and a number of other companies have begun to offer network hot-site services; Comdisco is redesigning its sites to provide client/server recovery capabilities.

FOCUS Questions:

How would you justify the expense of disaster planning to your company? What people, organization, and technology issues should a disaster recovery plan address?

SOURCES: "Worst-Case Scenario Need Not Be Staged," *Information Week,* July 15, 1996; Joseph C. Panettieri with Chuck Appleby, "Survival of the Fittest," *Information Week,* January 10, 1994; and Bob Francis, "Recovery from Distributed Disasters," *Datamation,* December 1, 1993.

FIGURE 12.6

Days of Infamy

The ten worst U.S. information technology disasters.

Incident	Date	Data Centers Hit
1. Nationwide Internet virus	May 16, 1988	500+
2. Chicago flood	April 1992	400
3. New York power outage	August 13, 1990	320
4. Chicago/Hinsdale fire	May 8, 1988	175
5. Hurricane Andrew	September 1992	150
6. Nationwide Pakistani virus.	May 11, 1988	90+
7. San Francisco earthquake	October 17, 1989	90
8. Seattle power outage	August 31, 1988	75
9. Chicage flood	August 13, 1987	64
*10. East coast blizzard	March 1993	50
Los Angeles riot	April/May 1992	50

*Tie

12.4 SOLVING SYSTEM QUALITY PROBLEMS

While zero-defect computer systems may not be possible, system and data quality can be improved dramatically if developers draw on the knowledge and skills in system building gained over the past three decades.

ENHANCING SOFTWARE QUALITY

Software quality is a major ongoing issue for information systems professionals. Although progress is being made, no magic bullet exists that can improve the quality of software. Moreover, as indicated above, problems cannot be totally solved with today's technology. However, software quality can be improved by considering the problem from a number of angles.

Development methodology
A proven method of accomplishing the tasks of systems development to provide standards for guiding the activities of a systems development project.

Development Methodologies Any good-quality program should begin with the adoption of a **development methodology.** The primary function of a development methodology is to provide discipline to the whole development process. A good methodology is based on proven methods of accomplishing all the standard tasks that are part of the development process. It establishes an organization-wide standard approach for gathering specifications and designing, programming, and testing the new system. In addition, the methodology usually indicates the appropriate tools acceptable within the company for performing these tasks. By standardizing the building of systems in this way, a methodology makes systems easier to develop, test, audit, and maintain.

A sound development methodology includes methods and tools for controlling the development project itself. Planned testing tasks by business and technical staff, which help ensure that the system will be adequately tested, should also be included in the methodology. Such an approach results in projects that are more likely to stay within budget, be completed on time, and satisfy the users.

Quality Measurements People do not automatically recognize quality or agree on its definition, although what quality is and how it is defined are often assumed in application development projects. Measurement of quality requires careful planning, including agreements in advance as to what quality is and how it is to be measured. Those party to the agreements must include all who have a major stake in the project, including analysts, programmers, end users, and auditors. Quality measurements must reflect the organizational goals established by the users and must also consider the limits of technology and the cost of achieving certain goals (e.g., improving online response time may cost more than it is worth to the organization). Issues of quality, from a business perspective, include interface ease of learning and use; computer response time; systems hours of availability; location and hours of service of telecommunication connections; number of bugs per 1,000 lines of programming code; and any other elements the users require.

Programming Standards Traditional programming code was aptly nicknamed "spaghetti" code because it was so tangled that its logic was often impossible to follow. Programs could not be reviewed by other programmers to ensure quality while they were being written. Once the system was implemented, finding and fixing bugs was a lengthy, expensive, and frequently impossible task. Today, structured programming standards produce programs that are written in English-like language (e.g., a data name might be "gross-income" rather than the more mysterious name "GI1") and that are modularized (review the discussion of structured programming in Chapter 10). Other programmers, and often even end users, can follow the code and review it for correctness. When bugs do appear, they are more easily isolated and corrected. If necessary, whole sections (modules) can be changed without affecting the basic logic of the program. Such code will contain fewer bugs and be more easily maintained.

Testing Testing standards are critical to improving system quality. Testing is also a skill with tried-and-true methodologies and useful tools. Test cases must be developed for each specification and test banks developed so that the data for testing will be reliable. Testing must take place at all phases, including specification and design, and not just after programs are completed. Adequate time must be allocated for testing, and its importance must be stressed by project management.

Development Tools Many automated tools are available to support the developer while improving the quality of the software. Some tools that can assist in improving the quality of application systems development were designed for use in general areas, such as project management and graphics software. Other tools were designed specifically for use in developing software, such as the CASE tools described in the Part 3 Illustrated Case. For example, code-generating tools can be used to generate a large portion of the program code of many systems. These generators produce structured, easy-to-follow code. Fewer bugs are produced by using a generator, and the tool can save a great deal of time. Experience shows that while development tools cannot take over most development work, their appropriate use improves the quality of the final system.

ENSURING DATA QUALITY

Data quality can be improved in a number of ways. Data can be edited when they are first entered into a system so that obviously bad data are rejected. For example, a stock price can be automatically checked to ensure that it is all numeric and that it falls within a certain range. A stock that normally ranges in price from $20 to $50 might be rejected and brought to the attention of a monitor if it were entered at more than $100. The trained monitor would then check the price to see whether it had jumped that high. If so, the monitor would change the editing parameters; if not, the monitor would trace the source of the error and correct it. By using computer security procedures, data can also be protected so that only designated programs or persons are authorized to add, delete, or modify them. If others who have access to the data attempt (accidentally or otherwise) to alter them, such activity will be blocked.

Data quality is also being improved through the growing use of DBMS, which we discussed in Chapter 6. A DBMS centralizes the data and stores them separately from the processing programs. One piece of data can be stored in only one place instead of in many files, thereby reducing data redundancy and eliminating most of the data integrity problems that accompany data redundancy. Moreover, a DBMS makes the editing of data input relatively easy so that more input errors can be caught before they corrupt the data. Most important, however, DBMS make the data easily accessible for use in reporting and analysis while securing them from unauthorized updating. Set up properly, for example, a DBMS would be able to support the security pattern illustrated in Figure 12.5, which allows a bank's loan officer to view and update all mortgage data while restricting access by other bank employees.

Setting up a data warehouse creates a new set of standards for measuring data quality and new opportunities to improve the organization's data, as described in the Focus on Technology.

FOCUS ON TECHNOLOGY

TOOLS TO SCRUB DIRTY DATA

Not even the most elaborate data warehouse can deliver the information decision makers need if the data are bad. Sometimes the data that flow into data warehouses are faulty. In other cases, the data may be acceptable for operational databases but unusable in data warehouses for decision making. A survey of Digital Consulting Inc.'s Data Warehousing Conference in February 1996 found that the leading challenge for data warehouses was data quality, followed by data scrubbing, or cleansing. Data cleansing is required in order to eliminate redundant or extraneous data that piles up because of faulty processes.

Automated tools have been developed for data quality improvement and for data cleansing. Data quality analysis and audit tools analyze data against a set of business rules to discover inconsistencies. For example, QDB/Analyze software from QDB Solutions detects and measures data quality problems such as invalid values, incomplete data, inconsistent data, and duplicate records. The tool also monitors the quality of source data prior to its migration to the data warehouse and allows users to assign a cost for each error type to assess the financial impact of low-quality data. However, automated audit tools can only analyze conformance with the company's business rules. They cannot determine that a specific value, such as a particular employee's birth date, is correct.

Automated data cleansing products are helpful when data from disparate systems are consolidated into a single database in a data warehouse. These tools analyze and standardize data, identify duplicate data, and transform data into what are most likely the correct values. For example, DB Star's Migration Architect analyzes data from different data sources and discovers the rules used for processing the data, data elements with multiple names, and other useful information. It can even derive a relational data model from the analyzed data. Other data cleansing tools are more specialized. Group 1 Software's toolset cleans, structures, and standardizes name and address data, allowing users to check and correct new records during data entry.

Of course, the best way to ensure data quality is to prevent corrupted data from entering the database in the first place. Error prevention products can scrutinize data as they are input. For instance, Postalsoft provides libraries of software programs to correct and standardize addresses and to check geographic codes, gender codes, and titles. Its Merge/Purge Library identifies all of the data records for an individual customer, consolidating and cleansing them before they are placed in the data warehouse database.

FOCUS Question: What people, organization, and technology issues should be addressed when developing a plan to improve data quality?

Source: Larry P. English, "Help for Data Quality Problems," *Information Week,* October 7, 1996.

Data quality audits
Surveys of data in information systems to ascertain their level of accuracy and completeness.

Data quality audits are also important in improving the quality of data. By regularly scheduling such audits, business units can spot emerging data quality problems and take early corrective action. Such audits can be done in several ways: by interviewing end users to determine their perceptions of problems with the data, or by actually checking data or data samples manually or with auditing software. The Social Security Administration has established a regular audit procedure that checks 20,000 sample beneficiary records each month.

SUMMARY

- Computer information systems are more vulnerable to destruction, error, abuse, and crime than manual systems because data are concentrated in an electronic form in which they can be more easily accessed, altered, or destroyed. Networked systems are especially vulnerable, including those using the Internet.

- The major threats to computerized information systems are disasters, such as fire or electrical failure, user errors, hardware malfunction, software errors, and computer crime.

- Computer crime involves using software and hardware to alter or destroy data or applying computer technology to perpetrate a crime. The major types of computer crime are monetary theft; theft of services, information, or computer programs; alteration of data; damage to software; and trespassing. The vast majority of computer crimes are committed by insiders.

- Hackers and computer viruses are growing threats to information systems because of the upsurge in networked computing.

- Information system quality problems caused by software errors and data that are inaccurate, outdated, or incomplete are major causes of malfunctioning information systems.

- Controls refer to the specific technology, policies, and manual procedures for protecting the assets, accuracy, and reliability of information systems. General controls govern the overall business and computing environment of a firm, and specific application controls govern individual information system applications.

- General controls consist of hardware controls, software controls, data security controls, systems development controls, computer operations controls, and management controls. Complete user, system, and operational documentation are essential for maintaining a sound general control environment.

- Application controls consist of input, processing, and output controls. Principal application control techniques include control totals, programmed edit checks, and procedures for authorizing and validating input and output.

- Analysis and design of information system controls must be included at various stages of the problem-solving process. A solution design must consider the costs and benefits of each control as well as ease of use.

- Security encompasses all the policies, procedures, and technical tools for safeguarding information systems from unauthorized access, alteration, theft, and physical damage. Three important aspects of security are data security, safeguarding PCs and networks, and disaster recovery planning.

- Data security, which involves restricting access to data in computer information systems, is essential, especially in online information systems. Two important techniques for promoting data security are the use of passwords and encryption.

- A disaster recovery plan is a plan for restoring critical information system operations after physical disasters or sabotage have disrupted computer processing. It provides access to alternative computer hardware and tools and procedures for restoring software programs, data, and telecommunications capabilities.

- Software quality problems can be solved or minimized by using appropriate software development methodologies and standards, development tools, and careful testing. Data quality can be improved by carefully editing input data, using database management systems, and performing regular data quality audits.

KEY TERMS

Security
Computer crime
Hacker
Computer virus
Software bugs
Data quality problems
Controls
General controls
Application controls
Management controls
Documentation
Input controls
Processing controls
Output controls
Programmed edit check
Control totals
Data security
Encryption
Disaster recovery plan
Development methodology
Data quality audits

REVIEW QUESTIONS

1. Why are computer information systems more vulnerable than manual systems? What kinds of computer information systems are the most vulnerable?
2. List the major threats to computer information systems.
3. What is computer crime? Name various types of computer crime.
4. What is security? What is its relationship to computer crime? To hackers?
5. What is a computer virus? How can computer virus attacks be prevented?
6. Describe the major quality problems that prevent information systems from functioning properly.
7. What are controls? Distinguish between general controls and application controls.
8. List and describe each of the general controls required for computer information systems.
9. Why is documentation so important for safeguarding and controlling information systems?

10. What are the three types of application controls? Describe the techniques that are used for each.
11. What kinds of techniques can be used for promoting data security?
12. Describe some steps that can be taken to safeguard PCs.
13. Describe some steps that can be taken to safeguard networked systems.
14. What is a disaster recovery plan? What are some of the key elements of such a plan?
15. What steps can be taken to improve software quality?
16. How can data quality be improved?

DISCUSSION QUESTIONS

1. There is no such thing as a totally secure system. Discuss.

2. If you were designing an information system, how would you determine which controls to use?

PROBLEM-SOLVING EXERCISES

1. *Group exercise:* With three or four classmates, select a system described in one of the Focus boxes or chapter-ending cases in this text. Use the information supplied in this text to write a description of what the general and application controls might be. Present your findings to the class.

2. Write an analysis of what might happen if each of the general controls for computer information systems were not in place.

3. *Hands-on exercise:* Using appropriate software, develop an application to help security specialists analyze the data provided in Figure 12.6. Your application should be able to provide reports that can answer the following questions:

   How many IT disasters were caused by power outages?

   Which major IT disaster caused by viruses took place in 1988?

   How many IT disasters involving more than 100 data centers occurred after 1991?

4. *Internet problem-solving exercise:* You often send and receive Microsoft Word word processing files over the Internet attached to E-mail messages. You are concerned about macro viruses and want to find out how to identify and eradicate them. Use the search capability of the Virus encyclopedia at the Anti Virus Center of Trend Micro Incorporated to find this information. Then use the other capabilities of this Web site to find additional information.

NOTES

1. David Simpson, "A UNIX Server Is No Mainframe," *Datamation,* December 15, 1995.
2. Lynn Haber, "TCP/IP: Is It Safe?" *Information Week,* April 29, 1996, and Katherine Jones, "Castle Internet Under Attack," *Client/Server Computing,* April 1995.
3. Michael Meyer, "Stop! Cyberthief!" *Newsweek,* Feburary 6, 1995.
4. Wade Roush, "Hackers: Taking a Byte Out of Computer Crime," *Technology Review,* April 1995.
5. John Foley, "Data Warehouse Pitfalls," *Information Week,* May 19, 1997, and Catherine Yang with Willy Stern, "Maybe They Should Call Them 'Scammers'," *Business Week,* January 16, 1995.

PROBLEM-SOLVING CASE

THE CLIPPER CHIP: GOVERNMENT INTRUSION OR CITIZEN PROTECTION?

A hot debate is raging over the Clipper chip. Is it a tool for "Big Brother" to use in spying on United States citizens? Or is it a necessary weapon for the U.S. government to use in protecting its citizens against criminals and terrorists?

As the industrialized economies have globalized, cross-country and around-the-world data movement have become essential: Telephone calls, faxes, orders, shipping information, product research, product specifications, strategic plans, marketing plans, sales results, personal medical records, and electronic meetings are necessary in order to conduct business. Organizations and individuals must protect confidential data from commercial or military espionage, and encryption has long been the favored method of doing so.

Encryption software today has become so sophisticated that codes are virtually unbreakable. At the same time, encryption has become easy to use. When using encryption, the sender and receiver must agree upon a "key" to encode and decipher the communication. Encryption software automatically and instantaneously encodes the voice and/or data communication at the sender's end and deciphers it at the receiver's end. Anyone trying to steal the communications finds that without the key, garbage will be the only prize. In recent years, widespread reports of hackers breaking into corporate and government computers, the stealing of passwords on the Internet, and increased commercial espionage have caused a dramatic growth of interest in encryption.

Governments have long used wiretapping and other devices to "eavesdrop" on telephone conversations in order to break up criminal conspiracies and to gain evidence for criminal prosecutions. Court-approved wiretaps in the United States have played a key role in the conviction of many organized crime leaders, spies, and terrorists. As telephone communication is gradually digitized and the use of E-mail expands rapidly, the encryption of more and more communications is possible. U.S. government officials believe that without the ability to break these unbreakable codes, they will lose the ability to wiretap, a valuable weapon in the fight against crime, spying, and terrorism. John Markoff, technology reporter for *The New York Times,* summed up the problem this way: "How to preserve the right of businesses and citizens to use codes to protect all sorts of digital communications without letting criminals and terrorists conspire."

The Clipper chip is the U.S. government's proposed answer to the conflict between the need to encrypt and the government's need to eavesdrop. It is a microprocessor chip that contains software for encrypting any telecommunications in unbreakable codes. Connected to a telephone or data terminal, it will scramble communications as any other contemporary encryption device does. When two people want to secure their communications, they activate their encryption devices to exchange secret numerical keys, using the Clipper chip to encode and decode their data. However, the Clipper chip has an added feature, a so-called "back door" that under certain circumstances would allow U.S. federal agents to unscramble communications. The federal government would have a key to the Clipper chip. To protect communications privacy, the plan is to split the key into two parts, storing one part at the Commerce Department's National Institute of Standards and Technology and the other part in the Treasury Department. Use of the keys would require both halves, so no individual could act on his or her own. As with any wiretap today, use would require a court order. Anyone using the back door key without a court order would be subject to severe criminal penalties. Figure 12.7 shows a diagram of how the security would work.

On February 4, 1996, the Clinton administration announced the formal adoption of the Clipper chip encryption standard. This means that the federal government is requiring the use of the Clipper chip in all the computers and data terminals it purchases. Given that the federal government is the largest single purchaser of such equipment in the world, this requirement could create the Clipper chip as a standard within the United States. In addition, the government plans to require all encrypted communications with its departments to be done with the Clipper chip. Just two departments, the Internal Revenue Service and the Department of Defense, could involve millions of ordinary citizens in this way. Finally, the administration has made it illegal to export very powerful encryption devices. Moreover, users will be required to make encryption keys available to law enforcement if asked.

This issue involves more than the Clipper chip, however. The Digital Telephony and Communications Privacy Improvement Act of 1994 requires telecommunications companies to use specified technology that would enable the interception of telecommunications. The law also requires phone companies to collect and make available "setup" information—who is phoning whom—for each call made. The law-enforcement value of this technology came to public notice in early 1994 when it was used to solve the case of the attack against Olympic figure skater Nancy Kerrigan.

Organized, vocal opposition has arisen from many quarters. Opponents paint a picture of a spying Big Brother trampling on citizens' right to privacy in a free society. The ultimate fear is the loss of privacy and freedom at the hands of an overly powerful government. Critics contend that the technology will enable the government not only to listen to the contents of conversations, but also to monitor transactions and so learn a great deal of personal information about private citizens, including their

FIGURE 12.7

Putting Privacy in Escrow

1 **Electronic Fingerprint** When Clipper chips are activated to encode a call, they exchange a packet of information called a Law Enforcement Access Field, or LEAF. It includes a newly generated "session key" (used to encode the rest of the call) and the chips' serial numbers. The FBI has a universal "family key" that can decode the serial numbers but not the session key.

Conversation (encrypted with session key)

LEAF (parts encrypted only with family key)

Clipper-equipped phone "A123456"

Another Clipper-equipped phone

2 **Eavesdropping** FBI agents armed with a warrant for a wiretap record the call and extract from the LEAF the serial numbers of the Clipper chips being used.

LEAF $#@&%*$* &*%##'©T%$=ø &&#© A123456

3 **Request** Once they have the serial number for the phone being tapped, FBI agents contact the custodial agencies that hold parts of the unique numeric keys for each chip made. They need not get keys for the chips on both ends; one chip's key will do.

Custodian No. 1

Custodian No. 2

4 **Matching Halves** Each custodial agency looks up the serial number supplied by the FBI and provides the FBI with its part of the key for the specified Clipper chip. The custodial agencies do not know whose phone has the chip with that serial number.

Chip key part No. 1

A123456

Chip key part No. 2

5 **Decoding** Combining the two parts allows the FBI to decode the session key in the LEAF, which it then uses to decode the encrypted call. Session keys for other calls involving the same phone can also be decoded using the same chip key.

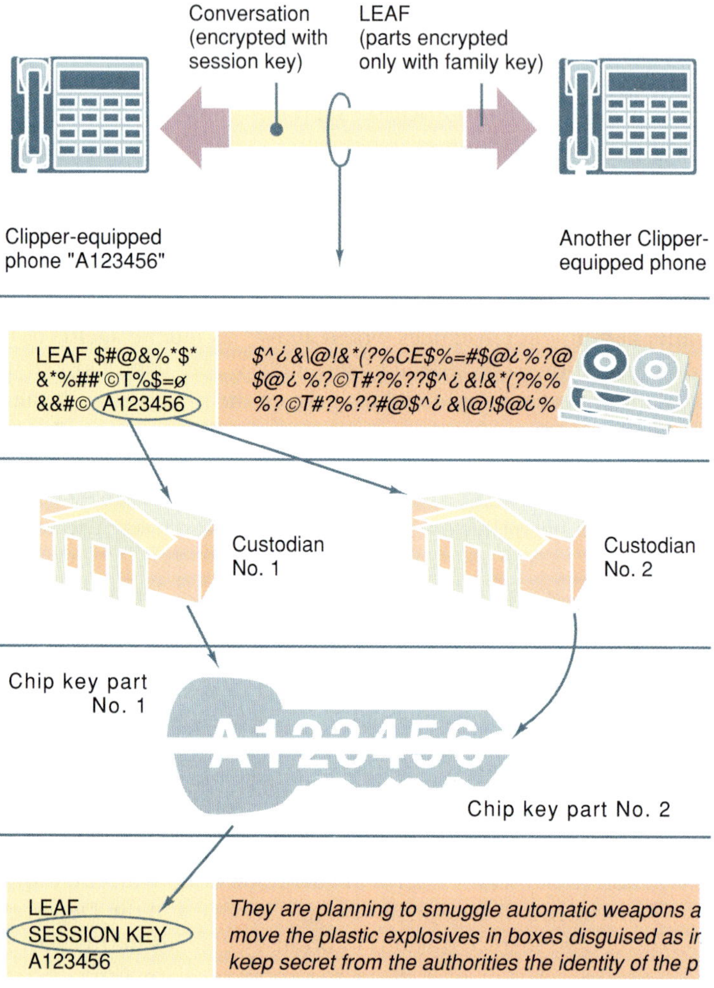

LEAF SESSION KEY A123456

They are planning to smuggle automatic weapons a move the plastic explosives in boxes disguised as ir keep secret from the authorities the identity of the p

spending habits (credit card transactions), their network of friends, their locations, even their sexual preferences.

What about the protection afforded by the split key and the need for a court order? NSA expert James Bamford points out that one court that issues wiretap warrants, the Foreign Intelligence Surveillance Court, is a little-known court that publishes almost no public documents. In its entire 20-year history, Bamford claims, the court has never turned down a wiretap request, so it affords little protection. Supporters claim that the 8,000 wiretaps that were authorized in the decade prior to 1994 resulted in about 22,000 convictions. FBI director Louis J. Freeh points to the World Trade Center bombing in 1993—and its $5 billion estimated damages—as an example of why the FBI needs this authority, but critics counter that telecommunications played no role in breaking that case.

In addition, many critics believe that officials with access to the electronic key could be bribed; enough money could jeopardize the system. Others fear that hackers could break into government computers and steal the codes. Still others believe the government's approach is unnecessary. A 1993 study by the Computer Professionals for Social Responsibility claims they could find no instances in recent years in which FBI agents were unable to wiretap due to technological problems. The FBI, however, claims that hundreds of such cases exist.

Major opposition to the Clipper chip centers on the argument that foreign companies and governments will not trust and thus will be unwilling to adopt an encryption device for which the United States government holds a key. A recent count showed that hundreds of competing encryption products are available around the world. If the U.S. standard is not adopted abroad, critics believe it will result in a great loss of business to U.S. firms. The CEOs of such software giants as Microsoft, Lotus, and Novell told Vice-President Al Gore that tight encryption export controls had already cost the U.S. software industry the loss of some $9 billion per year in encryption software sales and in sales of other software that integrates encryption capability. The financial services industry might not be able to compete in a global economy if U.S. companies cannot be part of an internationally accepted standard.

Critics of the Clipper chip further point out that besides being a bad idea, it doesn't work as advertised. Matthew Blaze, a computer scientist at AT&T Bell Laboratories, discovered a basic flaw in the chip's design that would allow someone with sufficient computer skills to encode messages that could not be cracked by the government. Two people could then have secret conversations that law enforcement officials could not unscramble. The Clipper chip then would be no more useful to the government than existing encryption technology on the market.

SOURCES: Barb Cole, "Encryption Connip-tion," *Computerworld,* January 6, 1997; Center for Democracy and Technology, "Clipper Chip II Archive," December 2, 1996; John Markoff, "Flaw Discovered in Federal Plan for Wiretapping," *The New York Times,* June 2, 1994; Peter H. Lewis, "Of Privacy and Security: The Clipper Chip Debate," *The New York Times,* April 24, 1994; John Carey, "Big Brother Could Hobble High Tech," *Business Week,* March 21, 1994; James Daly, "Security Pros, Clinton Clash Over Encryption Standards," *Computerworld,* January 31, 1994; John Markoff, "A Push for Surveil-lance Software," *The New York Times,* February 28, 1994; and "U.S. Code Agency Is Jostling for Civilian Turf," *The New York Times,* January 24, 1994.

CASE STUDY QUESTIONS

1. Use the three perspectives of technology, organization, and people to categorize and analyze the problems the U.S. government is attempting to solve with the Clipper chip.

2. Given the strong opposition to the Clipper chip, why do you think the government persists in supporting it?

3. As a member of the U.S. Congress, would you support the Clipper chip and accompanying legislation and policy? Why or why not?

4. Taking into consideration the needs of the FBI, the NSA, business organizations, and citizen privacy, suggest any compromises or other approaches that might meet most of the needs of all sides in the dispute.

Part 3

→ ILLUSTRATED CASE ←

AUTOMATED SOLUTIONS WITH COMPUTER-AIDED SOFTWARE ENGINEERING (CASE)

As Chapters 9–12 have shown, designing information systems to solve an organization's problems can be a complex, multifaceted process. When a proposed solution requires a system with many inputs, outputs, and processing steps, information systems specialists and users must work closely together. The solution will need to be described using both narrative and graphics. Considerable time and effort are required in order to generate, revise, and refine these descriptions and then translate them into software code.

Through computer-aided software engineering (CASE), some of the repetitive work of developing system solutions can be automated, freeing time for the more creative aspects of problem solving. For example, CASE can automatically produce charts and diagrams, create prototypes of screens and reports, generate program code, analyze and check design specifications, and generate documents in standard formats.

Some CASE tools focus on the early stages of problem understanding, decision making, and solution design. These CASE tools automatically produce data flow diagrams, structure charts, systems flowcharts, data dictionaries, diagrams of business processes and work flows, and other documentation. Other types of CASE tools primarily support the implementation step of problem solving and some aspects of solution design. They focus on coding, testing, and maintenance activities. Such tools include testing facilities, code generators (which generate modules of source code from higher-level specifications), and application generators. A number of CASE products allow system designers to model desired data entry screens and report layouts or menu paths through a system without writing complex formatting specifications or programming.

Many CASE tools contain a central information repository, which serves as an "encyclopedia" for storing all types of information related to a specific project: data descriptions, screen and report layouts, diagrams, project schedules, and other documentation. The people working on the project can easily look up the information, share it, and reuse it to solve other problems. Information is especially easy to share with CASE tools that run on PCs in local area networks. Thus, not only do CASE tools help system designers create clear documentation, they also help coordinate group problem-solving activities.

CASE products such as Andersen Consulting's FOUNDATION attempt to support the entire problem-solving process. They contain design and analysis tools that can be integrated with tools for generating program code and for managing systems development. For instance, the DESIGN/1 component of FOUNDATION enables users to perform word processing, design data entry screens and report layouts, diagram the flow of data through a system, generate structure charts, design databases, and prototype the flow of online screens.

DESIGN/1 tools are integrated through a shared repository. Problem solvers can define relationships among various design components, combine text and graphics within a single design component, and move or copy material from one component to another. For example, one can establish relationships between a process in a data flow diagram and the data elements used in that process, using text to describe the process or to add personal notes. The components of the repository are cross-referenced (see Figure 1). As information is changed in one diagram (for instance, the addition or deletion of a data flow), the CASE software ensures that the information will be automatically changed in related diagrams and other design components. DESIGN/1 also enables the user to review and revise design data for completeness, accuracy, and consistency. The design components stored in the DESIGN/1 repository provide specifications for generating program code.

FIGURE 1

The DESIGN/1 Repository

Through extensive cross-referencing capabilities, users can quickly identify the impact of change across all design elements stored in the DESIGN/1 repository.

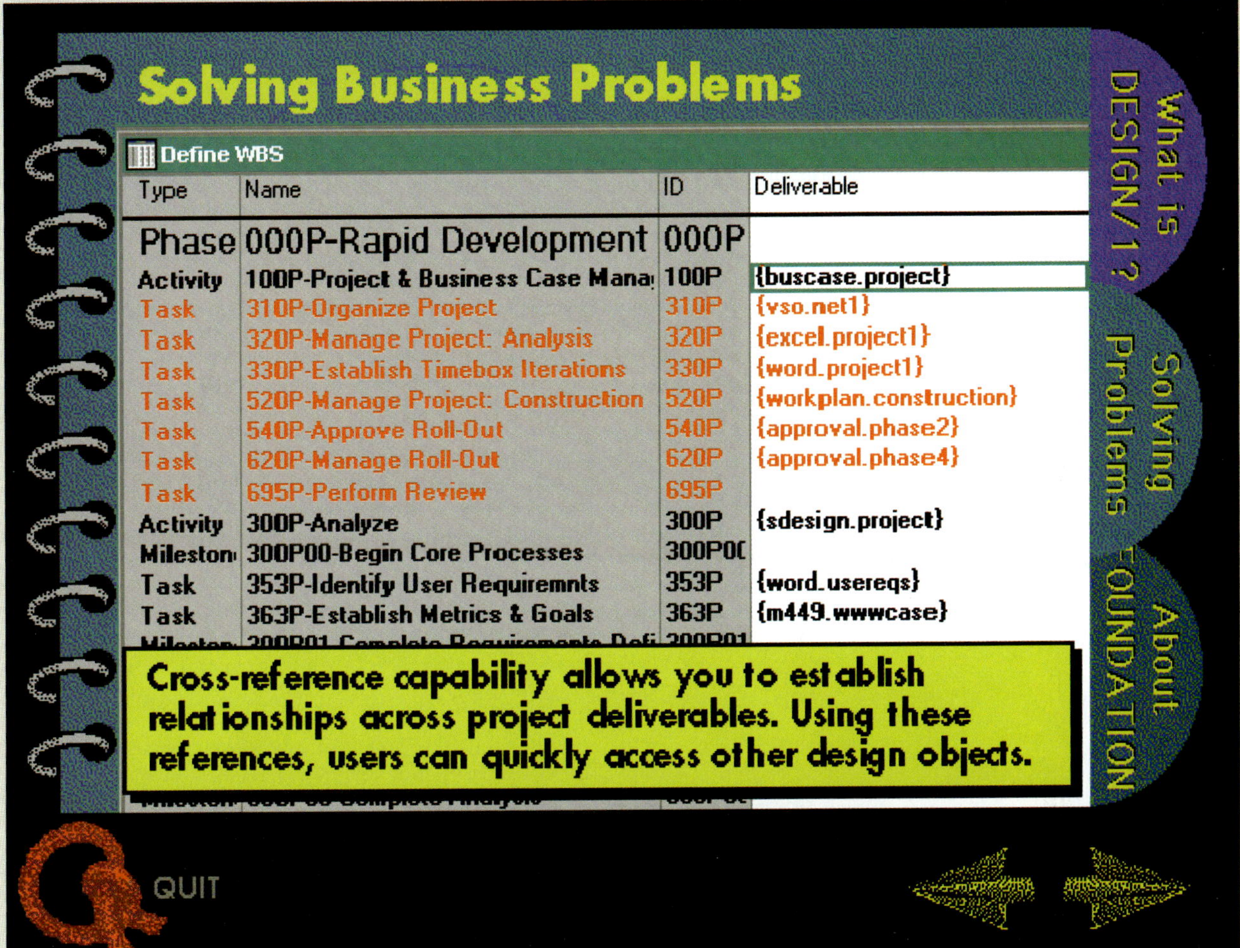

Another useful component of FOUNDATION is METHOD/1, which provides a comprehensive methodology plus automated tools to support various approaches to systems development, including client/server development, traditional host or mainframe-based development, rapid development, development based on software packages, and object-oriented development. System builders using METHOD/1 acquire a common view of the tasks and activities required to build and support an information system as well as tools to help them plan and manage these tasks (see Figure 2). Automated project management tools with estimation, planning, and scheduling capabilities are provided. METHOD/1 can be used for both large and small projects and for supporting business process reengineering projects.

To use CASE tools effectively, members of a problem-solving team must adhere to common standards for diagramming and common conventions for naming data flows, data elements, or program modules. The team must also stick to an agreed-upon solution design discipline. If each system builder were to cling to his or her own way of developing systems, the incompatibility between old approaches and new tools could create confusion. Educating users and technical specialists in how to use these tools effectively is an intricate process of change management.

FIGURE 2

METHOD/1 Automated Systems Development Methodology

METHOD/1 provides guidelines outlining the steps for specific activities for the entire systems development cycle.

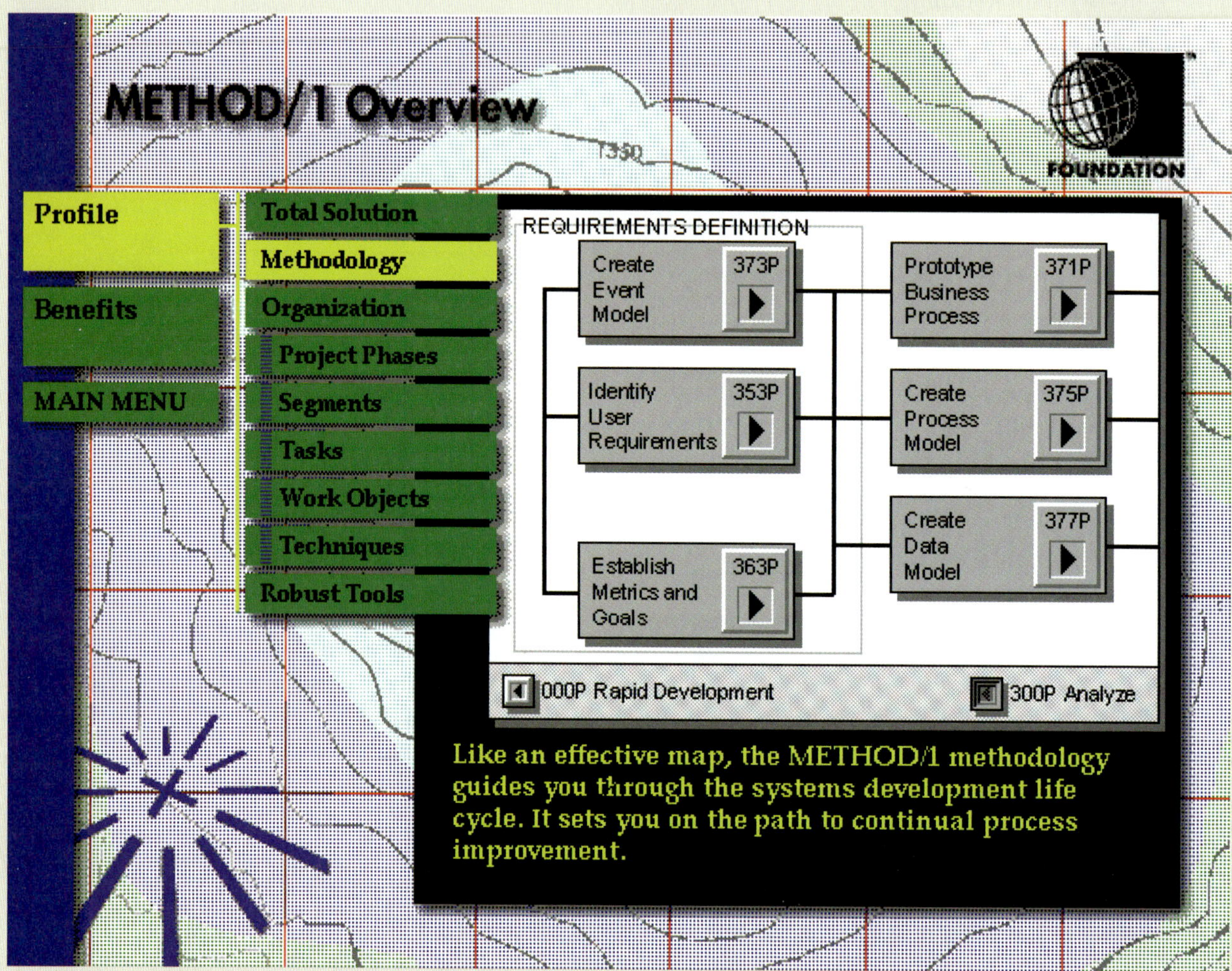

Creating a welcome environment for CASE tools can take a long time—in some cases, up to two years—so companies must be committed to adequate planning and training for CASE. Employees sometimes fear that CASE tools will rob them of their creativity or eliminate their jobs. They need to be told that they'll be able to be creative and continue in their jobs but that instead of figuring out the best way to write program code, they'll be learning how to solve business problems.

CASE QUESTIONS

1. How useful are CASE tools for developing information system solutions? What aspects of problem solving cannot be addressed by CASE tools?

2. What people, organization, and technology factors must be addressed when using CASE tools to design information system solutions?

3. It has been observed that firms that use CASE tools as a quick, low-cost path to creating new systems often lose money on their investment. Why?

Part 4

OVERVIEW OF INFORMATION SYSTEM APPLICATIONS

Chapter
THIRTEEN

BASIC BUSINESS SYSTEMS

CHAPTER OUTLINE

LEARNING OBJECTIVES

After reading and studying this chapter, you will

1. Be able to describe the distinguishing features of basic business systems.
2. Be aware of the kinds of problems that basic business systems help to solve.
3. Understand the purpose of fault-tolerant computers.
4. Know how basic business systems can support each of the major functional areas of a firm: manufacturing and production, sales and marketing, accounting and finance, and human resources.

KENDALL-JACKSON STREAMLINES ITS WAREHOUSE

Since corking its first bottle in 1982, Kendall-Jackson Winery and Vineyards has garnered many awards and has become noted for its blended chardonnays. But wine is a commodity, with many competitors, and mass-market retailers don't care as much about brands as about being able to put bottles on their shelves whenever they need them. Being able to say "We can have that for you at noon" means that Kendall-Jackson wines are stocked instead of one of its competitors.

Until recently, Kendall-Jackson could not provide retailers with that kind of rapid response. It used an old IBM AS/400 system connected to several dozen PCs for inventory management, but none of these computers could generate the details the company needed to track and manage its inventory. Kendall-Jackson had to use manual processes to manage its eight warehouses. It had to shut down for two days each month while employees counted cases of wine. Instead of focusing on selling wine, the company was bogged down in the mechanics of distribution.

In the summer of 1996, Kendall-Jackson replaced its old software with modular integrated enterprise software called ApplicationPlus, which has inventory management and planning capabilities. ApplicationPlus allows Kendall-Jackson employees to retrieve inventory data automatically and tallies units of inventory by wine variety every 14 days. For example, the company can now automatically count all of its cabernet wines. The running count of units in inventory has cut down on the rate of errors, which was much higher when inventory was counted by hand.

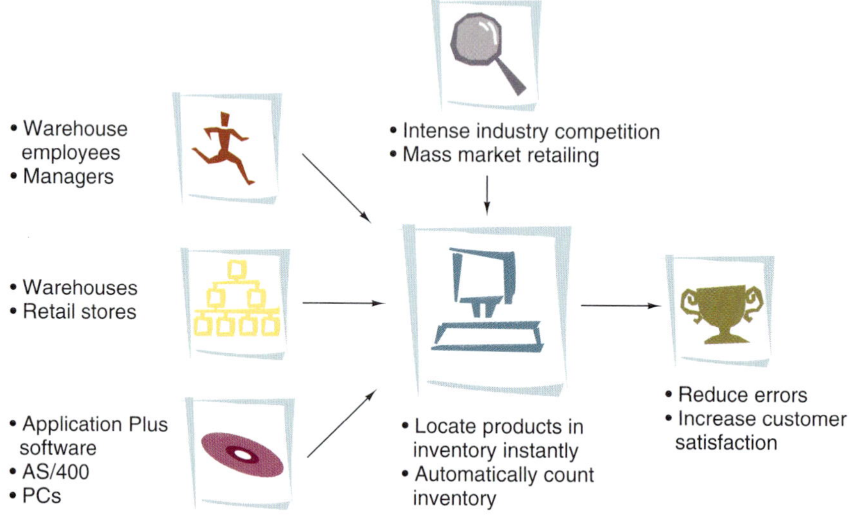

SOURCE: Deborah Ashbrand, "Squeeze Out Excess Costs with Supply-Chain Solutions," *Datamation,* March 1997.

Kendall-Jackson had to develop a more powerful information system to make the process of tracking products in inventory more accurate and efficient. Its inventory control system is an example of a basic business system that monitors, records, and performs the essential day-to-day activities of firms. This chapter describes how basic business systems work and the role that they play in organizations.

13.1 INTRODUCTION: BASIC BUSINESS SYSTEMS

Basic business system
A system that serves the most elementary day-to-day activities of an organization; it supports the operational level of the business and also supplies data for higher-level management decisions.

Transaction
A record of an event to which a business must respond.

At the most elementary level, information systems keep track of the day-to-day activities of a business, such as sales, receipts, cash deposits, credit decisions, and the flow of materials in a factory. These **basic business systems** perform and record the routine transactions necessary in order to conduct the business.

A **transaction** is a record of an event to which the business must respond. For example, data about an order that has just been recorded constitute a transaction. The company responds to this transaction by filling the order, adjusting its inventory to account for the items used to fill the order, generating a packing slip, packaging and shipping the order, and billing the customer. The transaction thus triggers a whole series of events that eventually update the firm's business records and produce appropriate documents. Another name for these basic business systems that use transactions to update company records is **transaction processing systems (TPS).**

Transaction processing system (TPS)
A basic business system that keeps track of the transactions necessary to conduct a business and uses these transactions to update the firm's records. Another name for a basic business system.

Many organizations, especially those in banking or financial services, could not survive for more than a day if their basic business systems ceased to function. For example, MasterCard cannot even afford a few minutes' disruption to its system, which processes billions of credit card transactions each day from all over the world. MasterCard employs multiple backup power supply systems for its World Data Center in St. Louis, which is the clearing center for all credit transactions. The First Interstate Bank of California in Los Angeles, which handles from $3 billion to $5 billion of securities trading transactions daily, continually reviews and tests its disaster recovery plan.

13.2 FEATURES OF BASIC BUSINESS SYSTEMS

Basic business systems serve the most elementary level of an organization by processing data about the operations of that enterprise. Such systems keep records of routine business activities—bank deposits, long-distance calls and charges, tax returns, payrolls, and university grades and transcripts. They support the functions of recording, monitoring, and evaluating the basic activities of the business. These systems are important suppliers of data to the operational level of a business and to higher levels of the firm as well. Much of their output is critical to the day-to-day survival of the firm.

THE FUNCTIONS OF BASIC BUSINESS SYSTEMS

The principal purpose of basic business systems is to answer routine questions and to track the flow of transactions through the organization. How many parts are in inventory? What happened to Mrs. Talbert's payment? How many employees were paid this month? The kinds of problems solved by such systems involve very short-term issues. Information for their solution is structured and based on the firm's routine standard operating procedures.

Basic business systems support lower levels of the firm, where tasks and resources are predefined and highly structured. For example, the decision to pay an active employee is based on two predefined criteria: Is the employee on the company's payroll, and did the employee work that week? Such a decision does not require much management deliberation. All that must be determined is whether the employee meets those criteria. Consequently, these systems are used primarily by people with little or no management responsibility—payroll clerks, order entry clerks, or shop floor stewards. The systems require few, if any, decisions from the people who operate them.

Basic business systems enable organizations to perform their most essential activities more efficiently (see the Focus on Organizations). Business firms need them to function on a day-to-day basis, but often the systems have far-reaching strategic consequences that make them valuable for more than

FOCUS ON ORGANIZATIONS

BENETTON BENEFITS FROM ELECTRONIC COMMERCE

Every morning, when Asuncion Henry arrives at her office at Fideta, in the heart of the garment-buying district on Paris's Right Bank, she first logs on to her network. The network is a value-added network operated by General Electric Information Services (GEIS) for Benetton Group SpA, the world-famous Italian clothing manufacturer and retailer. Henry is an office manager at Benetton's Fideta office, which manages more than 300 Benetton clothing stores throughout France. She uses the network to forward a new batch of orders to company headquarters in Ponzano, Italy, or to download information from Benetton.

From a small family clothing company in northern Italy, Benetton has grown into a global fashion merchandising and manufacturing giant. It operates more than 6,500 retail outlets in over 100 countries. The network is a vital link between Benetton and its offices and trading partners in 30 countries, handling more than 8 million transactions per year for the firm.

Whenever Benetton introduces a new fashion collection, it adds the new clothing items in the collection to its master file of product items and revises its price list. Benetton transmits its item master file and price lists over the network. Its country agents, such as Asuncion Henry, use the network to transmit orders back to Benetton. The agents can connect directly through the network to Benetton's IBM 3090 mainframe in Ponzano to obtain up-to-the-minute information online about the state of an order and its transport or about customer credit. Agents can also review Benetton's master file and price lists online.

The network connects the country agents to Benetton's factories in France, Brazil, Spain, Italy, and Argentina. Benetton maintains separate production agencies in Italy: Benetton for sweaters, Benetton Undercollar for underwear, Azimut for shirts, SAP for accessories, and Divarese for shoes. The country agents can use the network to contact the production agencies as well.

After a country agent places an order, an orders management program analyzes the order transaction before it is sent to Benetton. The software compares the agent's identification number and item numbers in the order to Benetton's database of product codes. When it encounters a discrepancy, it generates a "wait file" that lists the client number and the problem with the item. For instance, the item ordered might be the wrong color or size, or the agent might not have ordered the minimum number of items required. After the agent corrects the problem and re-enters the data, the system assigns an order number to the transaction. Each day, after order numbers have been generated for each agent's transactions, they are grouped together in batches and transmitted on the network to Benetton's main computer. Benetton's system groups the order transactions by country and sends them to the appropriate production agency. The production agencies extract orders from the system three times daily.

Benetton ships finished garments from its factories to customs agents in the appropriate country. It uses the network to send importation documents for these garments to one of 13 independent transport firms in 11 countries. The transport agency forwards the importation documents electronically on another network to customs agents. The import documents arrive before the boxes of garments, cutting the time for customs processing by three to five days.

FOCUS Questions: How important is Benetton's network for its business? What transactions does it process? What problems does it solve? Draw a diagram of how Benetton processes order transactions.

SOURCES: Elisabeth Horwitt and Ron Condon, "Right Here, Right Now," *Computerworld/Network World,* September 9, 1996, and Marsha Johnston, "Electronic Commerce Speeds Benetton Business Dealings," *Software Magazine,* January 1994.

operational efficiency alone. The SABRE and Apollo systems for processing airline reservations gave American and United Airlines a lead in the computerized airline reservation market and helped them promote their flights over those of competitors.

Although much of the information in basic business systems comes from inside the firm, these systems must also deal with customers, suppliers, and factors external to the firm. For example, an order processing system will contain customer data; a purchasing system will contain supplier data; a human resources system must incorporate government regulations concerning occupational safety, unemployment, and benefits accounting practices; a payroll system must incorporate changes in federal, state, and local tax laws. Thus, basic business systems help solve problems concerning the firm's relationship with its external environment.

Most basic business systems are in constant use because they are the underpinnings of the day-to-day activities that drive the business. Many (although not all) of these systems take a high volume of input and produce a high volume of output. A large firm may process thousands or millions of transactions daily. Input data can come from several sources: data entry, punched cards, scanning devices, audio input, or computerized files. The outputs may consist of finished pieces of goods or documents such as paychecks, packing slips, or purchase orders (see Figure 13.1).

Another form of output supplied by basic business systems is the data they provide for other systems used by managers. The basic business systems are the primary suppliers of data for information systems that support

FIGURE 13.1

The Concept of Transaction Processing in Basic Business Systems

A transaction processing system is the mainstay of a company because it performs the basic procedures that keep the firm in business. The system accepts input related to a transaction event, processes it, and produces output that enables the firm to continue functioning.

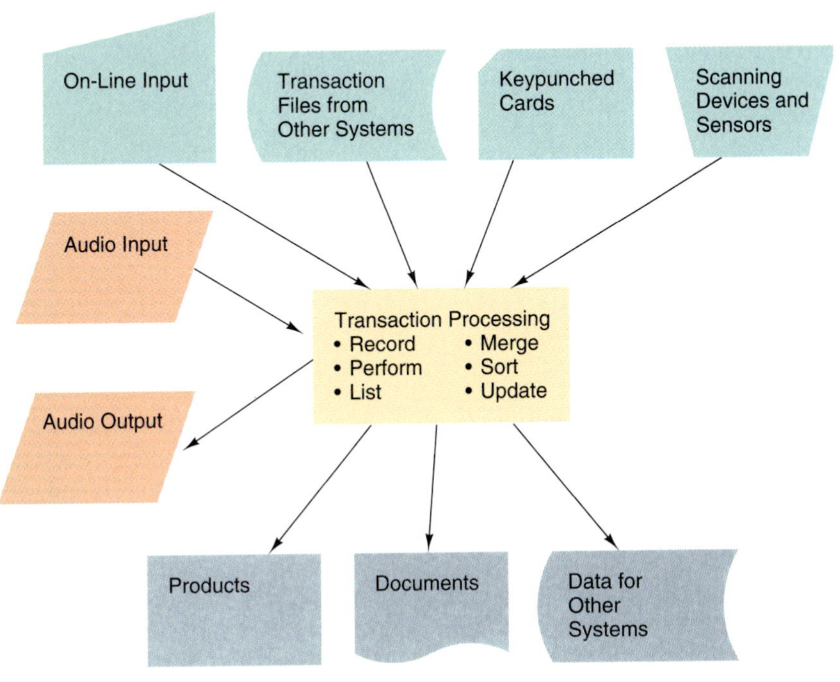

Online transaction processing (OLTP)
A transaction processing mode in which transactions entered online are immediately processed by the CPU.

Fault-tolerant computer systems
Systems with extra hardware, software, and power as backups against system failure.

mid-level managers, who use summaries of transaction data for monitoring and controlling the firm's performance. For example, a typical report for a middle manager in a firm's sales department would be a summary of sales transactions by each sales region for a month or a year. In many instances, the basic transaction data and summarization of that data for management control will be produced by the same system. Systems specifically serving managers are discussed in Chapter 16.

FAULT-TOLERANT SYSTEMS

Imagine the consequences to American Airlines if its reservation system were "down" for more than a few minutes or if a bank's customers were deprived of their automated teller machines. Such firms have heavy **online transaction processing (OLTP)** requirements, with multitudinous requests for information and changes to files occurring each instant. Their online transaction processing systems, in which massive numbers of transactions are processed instantly by the CPU, can create major business disruptions if they break down.

To forestall such calamities, many firms with heavy OLTP requirements rely on **fault-tolerant computer systems** with extra hardware, software, and power supply as backups against system failure. Fault-tolerant computers contain extra processors, memory chips, and disk storage. They can use software routines or self-checking logic built into their circuitry to detect hardware failures and automatically switch to a backup device. Parts can be removed or repaired without disrupting the computer system.

About half of the systems of the Securities Industry Automation Corp., the computing trading arm for both the New York and American Stock Exchanges, are fault tolerant. Major airline and hotel reservation systems also depend on fault-tolerant technology. Fault-tolerant systems are typically one and one-half to two times more expensive than traditional minicomputers or mainframes, but their reliability makes the extra costs worthwhile for certain critical applications.

With computerized inventory control systems, businesses can automatically locate items in inventory, reorder items that are running low, and calculate the size of their inventory. These basic manufacturing systems can reduce inventory costs and improve performance in shipping orders to customer specifications.

SOURCE: Courtesy of International Business Machines Corporation.

13.3 EXAMPLES OF BASIC BUSINESS SYSTEMS

A typical firm has basic business systems for all its major functional areas: manufacturing and production, sales and marketing, finance and accounting, and human resources. Depending on the nature of the firm's goods and services, these basic business systems are more prominent in some functional areas than in others. For example, a bank or brokerage house may have only a small production system since it primarily deals in financial services, but it will have extensive financial systems. Conversely, a firm that manufactures carburetors will put more weight on manufacturing systems; its financial systems will be less important.

TABLE 13.1

Standard Manufacturing Systems

Application	Purpose
Purchasing	Enter, process, and track purchases.
Receiving	Track the receipt of purchased items.
Shipping	Track shipments to inventory and to customers.
Materials	Catalog usage of materials in production processes.
Labor costing	Track the cost of labor as a production cost.
Equipment	Track the cost of equipment and facilities as production costs.
Quality control	Monitor production processes to identify variance from quality control standards.
Process control	Monitor ongoing physical production processes.
Numerical control (machine)	Control actions of machines.
Robotics	Use programmed intelligence to control actions of machines.
Inventory systems	Record the number, cost, and location of items in stock.

BASIC MANUFACTURING AND PRODUCTION SYSTEMS

Information systems support basic manufacturing and production functions by supplying the data to operate, monitor, and control the production process. They collect data and produce reports concerning the status of production tasks, inventories, purchases, and the flow of goods and services. Such manufacturing and production systems are not limited to manufacturing firms. Other businesses such as wholesalers, retail stores, financial institutions, and service companies use manufacturing and production systems to monitor and control inventories, goods, and services. Table 13.1 lists typical basic manufacturing and production systems.

Purchasing systems maintain data on materials purchased for the manufacturing process, such as files on vendors, prices of purchased items, and items on order. Receiving systems maintain data on purchased goods that have been received and their delivery dates and supply this information to the production, inventory, and accounts payable functions (see the Focus on Problem Solving). Shipping systems track the placement of finished products into inventory and shipments to customers; this information is then passed on to inventory and accounts receivable. Inventory systems track inventory levels, stock-out conditions, and the location and distribution of stock in the organization.

Materials systems track the usage of materials in the production process. The bill-of-materials system described in Chapter 2 inventories the raw materials and component parts needed to fashion a specific product. Labor-costing systems track the usage of personnel resources in the production process, and equipment systems track the costs of equipment and facilities for production.

Quality control systems collect data using shop floor data collection devices, such as counters, assembly-line data entry terminals, or process control sensors. The latter might be used to monitor the gauge of metal as it is fabricated into sheets, bars, or wire. If the system detects any variance, signifying that an item fails to meet established standards, it notifies supervisory

Quality control systems
Manufacturing and production systems that monitor the production process to identify variances from established standards so that defects can be corrected.

FOCUS ON PROBLEM SOLVING

BOB'S STORES STREAMLINES WAREHOUSE MANAGEMENT

Two years ago, Bob's Stores—one of several retailing divisions of the Melville Corporation in Rye, New York, was projected to more than triple its revenue to $1 billion by 1998 and double its casual clothing retail stores to 40 stores in the northeast. But some of its newer stores didn't take off as quickly as expected. Sales grew, but the costs of expansion left Bob's Stores with profit margins that were only "marginal," according to David A. Poneman, a retailing analyst at Stanford C. Bernstein & Co. in New York.

Bruce Fetter, vice-president of logistics at Bob's, decided to scrap plans to build a new high-tech distribution center in Cheshire, Connecticut, and instead decided to focus on automating the manual-intensive operations at Bob's already existing facility in Meriden, Connecticut. The distribution center was supposed to use high-speed carton-sorting systems to help Bob's handle an annual volume of 31 million units of Reebok sneakers and other goods for its retail outlets.

Bob's had ordered a warehouse management information system from Optum Software in Costa Mesa, California, that was based on the requirements of the new Cheshire distribution center. But the company could not install it right away because its Meriden warehouse facility was much less sophisticated. According to Fetter, the new system would have been "a Mercedes where a Chevy would have done just fine." Fetter and his staff decided that what Bob's really needed first was to improve the manual-intensive operations at the Meriden facility.

The warehouse management system in Meriden required that status reports on inbound inventory be entered into a homegrown PC-based system. The reports were then printed and delivered to merchandising managers. The merchandising managers had to wait until 3:00 P.M. each day to receive this information. Using this system, it took nearly two days to dispatch 80 percent of Bob's merchandise.

The Optum warehouse management software provided the push to make this process more efficient. Merchandisers can now check incoming product shipments on a continuous basis. Knowing the number of cartons of Reebok sneakers that will arrive at Dock No. 4 at 10:00 A.M. will help receiving managers more accurately forecast the number of workers needed to unload the goods. By having shipping and receiving information more readily available to managers, the system will streamline the flow of inbound merchandise. The new system and software are expected to cut overhead costs and help managers reorder faster-moving merchandise. It is expected that the new system will allow Bob's Stores to process 100 percent of its goods in 24 hours.

The RS/6000, 25 new PCs, and radio-frequency-based handheld scanners will cost in the low "seven figure" range, according to Fetter, and are expected to reduce Bob's Stores operating costs by 17 percent over the next two years.

FOCUS Question:
Why did focusing on the automation of manual-intensive operations make more sense for Bob's than building a brand-new high-tech distribution center?

SOURCE: Thomas Hoffman, "Retailer Takes Stock of Distribution Center," *Computerworld,* September 23, 1996.

Process control systems
Manufacturing and production systems that use computers to monitor the ongoing physical production processes.

personnel. **Process control systems** use computers to monitor an ongoing physical process, such as the production of paper, food products, or chemicals. Figure 13.2 illustrates some sample output for a process control system used by Elco Industries in Rockford, Illinois, a producer of fasteners and precision metal components. The system helps Elco ensure that its products have precise dimensions.

Numerical control systems, also called machine control systems, use computers to control the actions of machines, such as machine tools in fac-

FIGURE 13.2

Sample Output from the Elco Statistical Process Control System

Elco's statistical process control system provides information to help the company ensure that its products have accurate dimensions. This system calculates average measurements for groups of sample products in a production run. Output from the system includes charts, histograms, and bell curves. Also shown are measurements for the samples and acceptable limits.

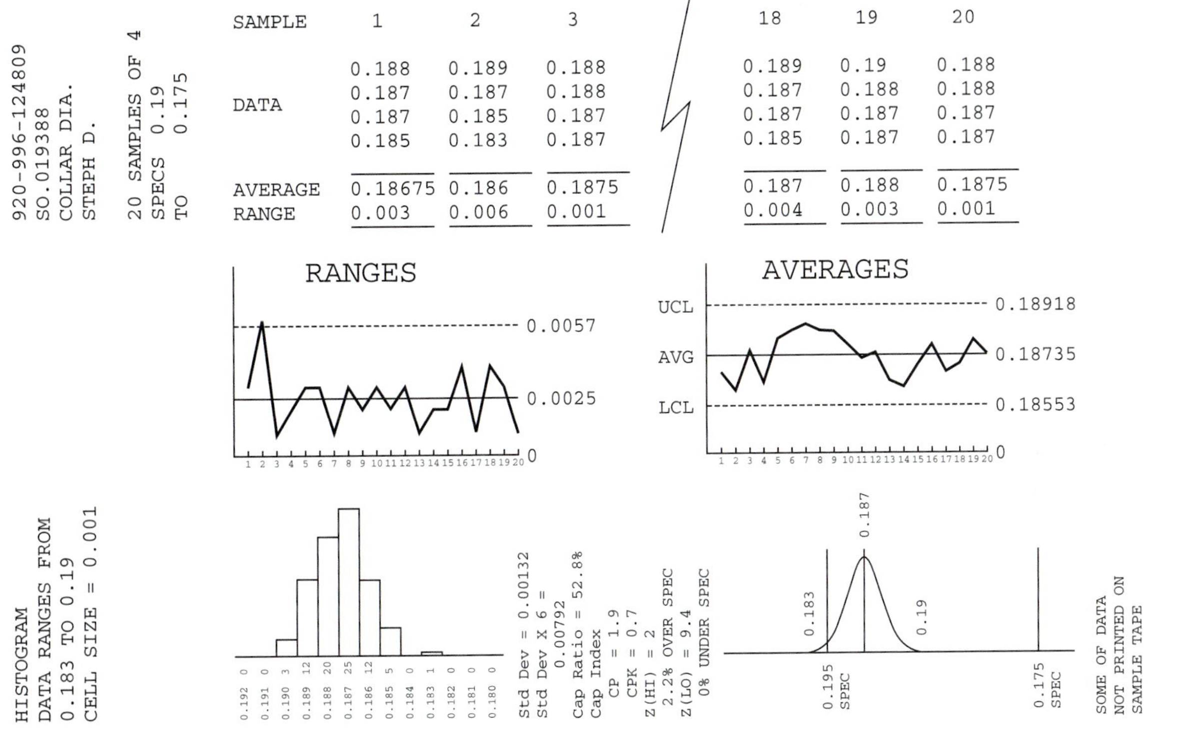

tories or typesetting machines. Numerical control programs for machine tools convert design specifications and machining instructions into commands that control the action of the machinery.

Robotics is a more intelligent version of machine control. Robotic devices are machines with built-in intelligence and computer-controlled, humanlike capabilities (such as movement or vision) that can control their own activities. For example, a robot might be used in automobile manufacturing to pick up heavy parts or to paint doors.

Robotics
The use of devices with built-in intelligence and computer-controlled, humanlike capabilities that can control their own activities.

In addition to performing these tasks, manufacturing and production systems are important sources of data for other systems. They interact with the firm's inventory, order processing, and accounting systems and supply data for systems serving mid- and higher-level management, such as capacity planning, production scheduling, and facilities planning.

Significant economies, efficiencies, and competitive advantages have resulted from integrating basic manufacturing and production systems. Many firms have implemented manufacturing resource planning systems, which coordinate materials requirements planning, process control, inventory management, and capacity planning and exchange data automatically with the firm's financial accounting systems. Computer-integrated manufacturing

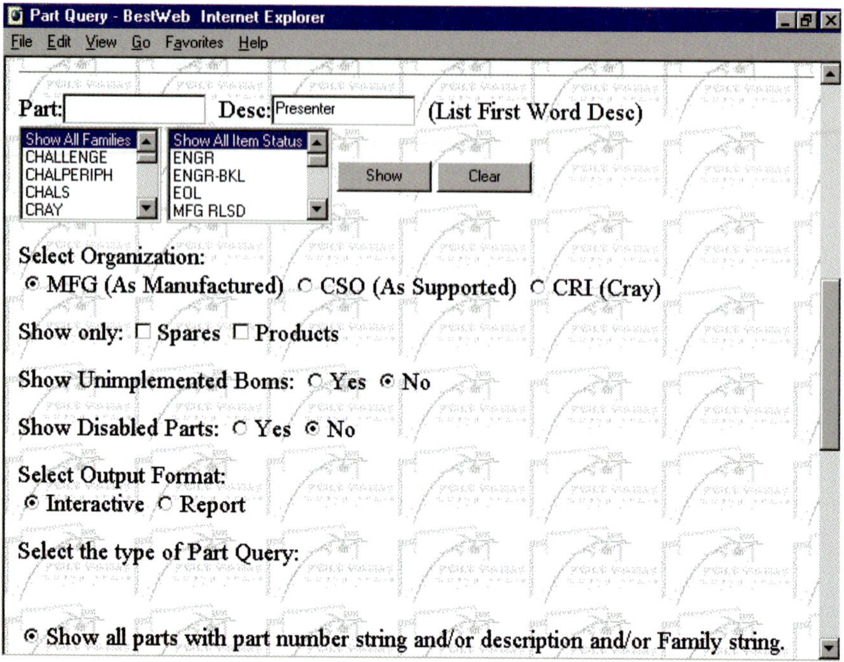

This Web page displays a sample of the types of information available to users of Silicon Graphics' Pole Vault system. The Part Query option enables users to find parts by part number or part description.

(CIM) systems tie together all the computer systems used in manufacturing—computer-aided design, computer-aided manufacturing, computer-aided engineering, and manufacturing resources planning, replacing uncoordinated islands of automation with seamless integration and control.

The Focus on Technology shows how basic manufacturing systems are starting to be built using intranets.

Bayer Chemical's container tracking system, which is described next, illustrates key features of basic manufacturing systems. As you read this case study, ask yourself, "Where does a basic manufacturing system obtain its data? What does it actually do with the data? What business problems does a manufacturing system solve? What difference does this manufacturing system make for the firm?"

A Typical Manufacturing and Production System: Container Tracking at Bayer Chemical Bayer Chemical in Kansas City, Missouri, manufactures crop protection products and specialty chemicals for controlling weeds, insects, and diseases. Some of its products are shipped in returnable containers. Bayer must track individual containers for several reasons. First, the company must be sure that hazardous agricultural chemicals are carefully handled according to federal and state regulations. Second, customers place a deposit on each container and want their deposits reimbursed when the containers are returned. Third, to extend the lifetime of the container, each container is always filled with the same product. When a container is returned, Bayer must know exactly what it held before.

Here's how Bayer's container tracking system works. When a container is first purchased, it is labeled with a bar-coded pressure-sensitive polyester label supplied by Intermec, a company specializing in bar-coding systems. After being labeled, the container is filled and placed on a pallet with its own bar-coded label. Bayer prints these pallet labels in-house using an Intermec

440 thermal-transfer printer. The bar-coded labels track data such as product, container identification, pallet identification, and fill date and time.

Full pallets are placed in inventory. The pallet's label is scanned again to track its journey from inventory through shipment by a common carrier into a remote warehouse. When it is received at the warehouse, it is scanned once more. From there, the container is sold and delivered to a customer. Returned containers are rescanned. Usually these returned containers are empty, but sometimes customers return containers that are unused or damaged. Additional fees are charged if the container is damaged or not returned.

The system was recently enhanced to run in a client/server environment and provides managers from various departments with new capabilities to access data. At any time, a supervisor, operator, or marketing employee can log in to the system, enter transactions, or generate a report. For example, a manufacturing production operator could enter data for a container identification number or access data such as the number of containers processed per batch, containers scanned per pallet, and any bad scans. Warehouse operators could manually update records or obtain accurate

FOCUS ON TECHNOLOGY

INTRANETS FOR MANUFACTURING

Intranets are becoming widespread in human resources, sales, and customer service, but only recently have they been used for manufacturing. Manufacturing systems are somewhat more complex, with changing relationships and costs, time-sensitive data, and heavier use of graphics than other business functional areas. Companies have been somewhat hesitant about introducing intranets to the factory floor or opening up complex systems to a wider audience.

A pioneer in this area is Silicon Graphics Inc., a manufacturer of high-performance workstations. The company used to keep different types of data used in manufacturing, such as CAD documents, materials requirements, routine data, and control data, in different systems, each with its own interface. In 1996, Bob Zalusky, a senior analyst in the manufacturing information systems office, wrote a program called Pole Vault, which provides a common interface to all of those disparate manufacturing databases through Silicon Graphics' intranet. A casual user can enter a part number (or even part of a part number) and retrieve related data on stock, sales history, purchase orders, work orders, and quality drawings—without any special training.

Silicon Graphics' manufacturing center in Cortaillod, Switzerland, uses board assemblies routed through its factory in Mountain View, California. Production and materials staff in Cortaillod can use Pole Vault to determine the status of deliveries to them from California. To help forecast delivery schedules, they can view their pending sales orders against inventory levels in California.

Silicon Graphics lets approved vendors use Pole Vault to access the latest revisions of parts drawings. The company saves hundreds of hours in labor and expedites the delivery of information to its partners.

Silicon Graphics' intranet is also used to document and process inventory requisitions, part-number requests, and time cards. The site includes a daily revenue page updated every 15 minutes, where senior managers can view the firm's financial performance.

FOCUS Questions: What problems were solved by using an intranet for manufacturing? What is the relationship between Silicon Graphics' intranet and its TPS?

SOURCE: Fred Hapgood, "Taking the Floor," *Webmaster,* March 1997.

FIGURE 13.3

Bayer's Container Tracking System

Bayer's container tracking system tracks bar-coded chemical containers as they move in and out of the company's plant and warehouse. The transaction data are stored in a database, where they can be accessed by various departments for reports.

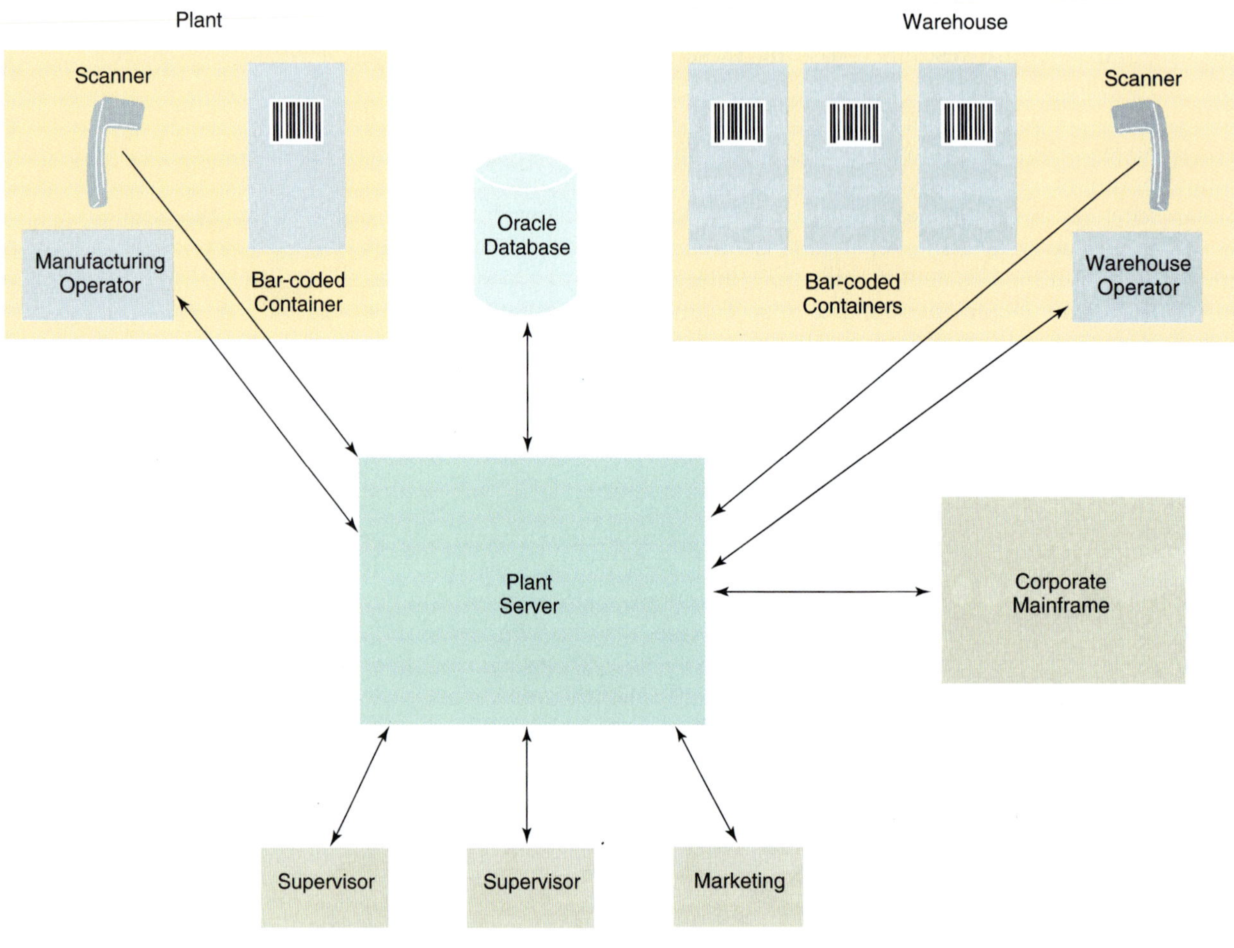

counts of containers and pallets. Marketing personnel would use the system to process container returns and credit each customer with the appropriate deposit. They also refer to information about containers, pallets, batches, and lots to identify which containers belong to each batch/lot. The system generates a daily report sent to Bayer's corporate mainframe in Pittsburgh.[1] Figure 13.3 illustrates the system.

Let's return now to the questions that we raised at the beginning of the case study.

- **Where does a basic manufacturing system obtain its data?** Bayer's container tracking system obtains its data primarily from bar-coded container identification data scanned into the system. However, manufacturing, production, and warehouse operators occasionally enter container identification data.

- **What does a manufacturing system actually do with the data?** The system can locate a container at any point in the distribution process. It tracks the location of containers as they move from inventory through shipment to customers and as they are returned to the company. It also identifies returned containers and automatically generates a credit to customers who made deposits on the containers. The system produces summary reports such as counts of the number of containers in the warehouse or on a specific pallet and an overall summary report for corporate management.
- **What business problems does a manufacturing system solve?** This system helps the company monitor the shipment of hazardous chemicals, enabling it to comply with government regulations. It also reduces inventory and handling costs by providing precise information on where containers are located, what the containers held, which containers have been returned, or the number of containers in the warehouse.
- **What difference does this manufacturing system make for the firm?** The system allows the company to operate efficiently while complying with government regulations concerning handling hazardous chemicals. It reduces inventory and handling costs and allows the company to keep down the cost of purchasing new containers by providing precise information on container history and container contents. It increases customer satisfaction by quickly refunding deposits to customers who have returned undamaged containers.

BASIC SALES AND MARKETING SYSTEMS

At the most elemental level, information systems support the sales and marketing function by facilitating the movement of goods and services from producers to consumers. These systems collect and process routine, repetitive data concerning locating customers, offering goods and services, processing sales and orders, and authorizing customer purchases. Table 13.2 lists typical sales and marketing information processing systems.

Sales support systems help sales staff identify potential customers, make customer contacts, and follow up on a sale. These systems record and

TABLE 13.2

Standard Sales and Marketing Systems

Application	Purpose
Sales support	Track customer contacts and prospective customers.
Telemarketing	Track the use of the telephone to make contacts, offer products, and follow up on sales.
Order processing	Enter, process, and track orders.
Point-of-sale systems	Record sales data.
Customer credit authorization	Inform sales staff about a customer's maximum allowable credit.

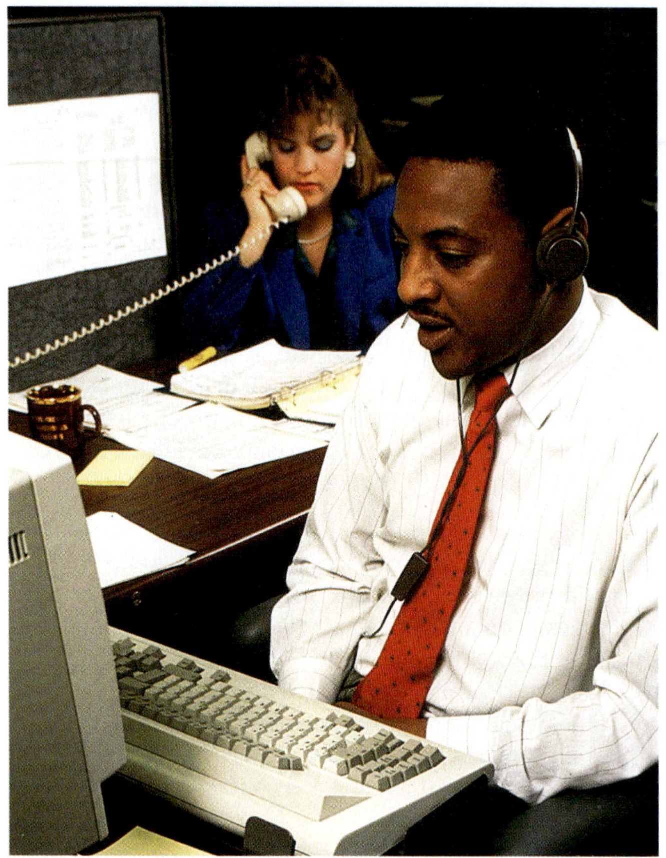

Many firms use telecommunications-based telemarketing systems to locate prospective customers, offer products for sale, and provide customer support.

SOURCE: © Bob Daemmrich, Stock, Boston.

keep track of prospective customers and customer contacts. They may include information such as the prospect or contact's name, address, and product preferences. **Telemarketing systems** track the use of the telephone for contacting customers, offering products, and following up on sales.

Telemarketing systems
Sales and marketing systems that track the use of the telephone for contacting customers, offering products, and following up sales.

Order processing systems
Sales and marketing systems that record and process sales orders, track the status of orders, produce invoices, and often produce data for sales analysis and inventory control.

Point-of-sale systems
Sales and marketing systems that capture sales data at the actual point of sale through the cash register or handheld scanners.

Order processing systems record and process sales orders by tracking the status of orders, producing invoices, and often producing data for sales analysis and inventory control. **Point-of-sale systems,** which were described more fully in Chapter 2, capture sales data at the actual point of sale through the cash register or handheld scanners.

Customer credit information systems provide sales representatives or credit managers with information concerning the maximum credit to be granted to a customer; they may also contain credit history information. These systems are often integrated with the firm's order processing and accounting systems.

Like other basic business systems, sales and marketing transaction systems supply data to other systems. Data from order processing and point-of-sale systems, for example, are used not only to track sales but also in sales management information systems to help sales managers evaluate sales performance or to shape sales targets. Sales systems are also linked with information systems from other functional areas, such as purchasing systems and accounts receivable systems.

Amazon.com, a virtual storefront selling books on the Internet, is an example of a leading-edge sales system. As you read this case study, ask yourself, "Where does a basic sales and marketing system obtain its data? What does it actually do with the data? What business problems does this system solve? What difference does this system make for the firm?"

Amazon.com: An Internet-Based Sales System Amazon.com bills itself as the world's largest bookstore, offering 2.5 million titles for sale. It is a virtual bookstore whose storefront is a site on the World Wide Web. (In comparison, a physical superstore can stock 175,000 titles at most.) Amazon offers almost everything you can find in *Books in Print* and does almost no advertising.

Amazon's nerve center is a 17,000-square-foot warehouse in an industrial section of Seattle. The company has several hundred employees, no expensive furnishings, and no sales staff. It is open for business 24 hours a day and has customers in 70 countries. Amazon stocks about 300 best-selling titles in its own warehouse but relies on a variety of distributors for order fulfillment.

The appeal of this virtual bookstore lies in its wide selection and its on-line search capabilities that help customers find books they want, including obscure titles, from their desktops. For the titles that it stocks, Amazon provides reviews by other readers, book authors, or Amazon editors. An intelligent agent feature called Eyes allows customers to tell Amazon which writers or subjects they like. Amazon will then alert them to new books on these topics or authors via E-mail.

Here's how Amazon's ordering system works. Visitors access the amazon.com Web site, where they can search for books they are interested in by author, title, and subject, or browse through books featured in 23 subject

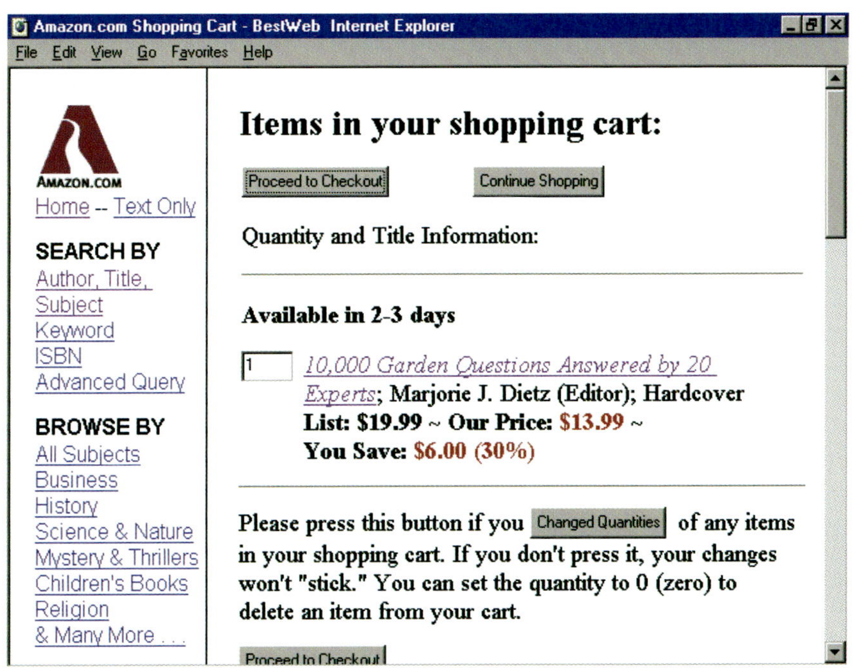

As a customer selects books, Amazon.com's electronic commerce software displays each selection, indicating its availability and offering the option of adding the title to the customer's order transaction.

categories. Their query on the Web is directed to Amazon's Oracle database with over 2 million titles. If the title is found, a Web page displays a description of the book and reviews. (Visitors can submit their own reviews via E-mail if they wish.) To order the book, a customer clicks on the button labeled "Add This Book to Your Shopping Cart" that can be found on the Web page describing the book. This places the book title in an electronic "shopping cart." Other titles the customer orders are placed in the shopping cart as well. When the customer is finished ordering, he or she can view the shopping cart to display the titles that have been ordered and then check out. The customer checks the order to verify that items and quantities are correct and then provides credit card information, name, address, shipping option, E-mail address, and password. Credit card information is stored in a separate computer via a secure network. Customers have the option of entering only the last five digits of their credit card number and providing the remainder of the number over the telephone. The customer clicks on a button to submit the order. The system then displays an order summary listing the customer's E-mail address, shipment option, shipping address, telephone number, items ordered, and total amount due.

Once customers enter their name address, and credit card number, they do not have to enter them again to make a purchase from Amazon. Amazon stores this information on its database. The company estimates that 35 to 40 percent of its orders are from repeat customers.

The Web site transmits the order transactions to Amazon's order database. The system sends the customer an E-mail message confirming the order. If the titles are among the best-sellers stocked in Amazon's Seattle warehouse, the order is shipped to the customer immediately. For other titles, the order information is transmitted to the southern Oregon warehouse of Ingraham Book Co., the country's largest book distributor, for fulfillment.[2] Figure 13.4 illustrates this system.

Let's return to our list of questions to examine more carefully what a sales and marketing system does.

- **Where does a basic sales system obtain its data?** The raw data come from actual customer online order transactions entered through Amazon's Web site. Each time a customer adds a book title to his or her shopping cart, the system records this purchase. These sales transactions are recorded, grouped, and totaled in the customer's electronic shopping cart for that particular online session. Shipping fees are added to the order amount data.
- **What does a basic sales and marketing system actually do with the data?** Like other basic business systems, this system primarily records transaction events—that is, the purchase of each item. The system groups the order transactions for each customer, adds shipping charges, and displays this information online for the customer to review. These order data are placed in a sales database and transmitted to Amazon's warehouse or to Ingraham's warehouse for fulfillment. The warehouse ships the order to the customer, along with a packing slip.
- **What business problems does this system solve?** This system solves the problem of how to record individual purchase transactions and how to supply customers with their purchases. These are very rou-

FIGURE 13.4

The Amazon.com Order Processing System

Amazon.com uses the Internet to capture orders for books. When a customer orders a book through Amazon's Web site, the order transaction updates an order database. A transaction to ship the book is sent to Amazon's own warehouse or the warehouse of Ingraham Book Company.

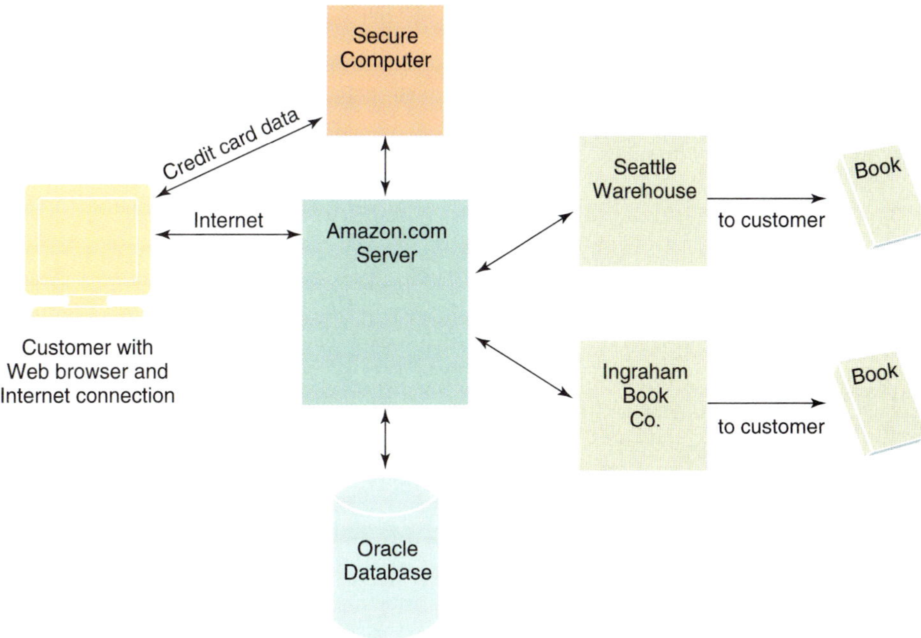

tine, repetitive, unstructured problems that require no decision making: If a customer purchases a book (and has the means to pay for it), he or she must receive the book unless it is out of stock. In addition, customer purchase transactions from this system feed a database of customer purchase records. This information can be used by Amazon to target E-mail to customers about other books to purchase.

- **What difference does this sales system make for the firm?** Amazon.com's online sales system expedites the purchase process, but it does much more. It is actually the lifeline of the firm because Amazon has no physical storefront. The only way people can shop at Amazon is through its Web site. Amazon's system creates a strategic advantage because it enables people to look for and purchase books without leaving their homes and provides additional value through its reviews and customized services.

BASIC ACCOUNTING AND FINANCIAL SYSTEMS

Some of the earliest computer systems automated accounting and financial functions. Accounting systems maintain records concerning the flow of funds in the firm and produce financial statements, such as balance sheets

TABLE 13.3

Standard Accounting and Financial Systems

Application	Purpose
Accounting	
Accounts receivable	Track money owed the firm; issue bills.
Accounts payable	Track money the firm owes.
General ledger	Summarize business accounts used to prepare balance sheets and income statements.
Payroll	Manage payroll records and produce paychecks.
Finance	
Cash management	Track the firm's receipts and disbursements.
Loan processing	Track transactions for consumer and commercial loans and credit card transactions; calculate interest and issue billing statements.
Check processing	Track checking account deposits and payments; issue statements of checking account activity and balances.
Securities trading	Track buying and selling of stocks, bonds, options, and other securities.

and income statements. Financial systems keep records concerning the firm's use and management of funds. Table 13.3 lists the basic accounting and financial systems.

Accounts receivable systems keep records of amounts owed by customers and credit information, based on customer invoice and payment data. **Accounts payable systems,** in contrast, keep track of amounts owed to the firm's creditors. They generate checks for outstanding invoices and report payment transactions.

Accounts receivable systems Accounting systems that keep track of amounts owed to the firm.

Accounts payable systems Accounting systems that keep track of amounts owed by a firm to its creditors.

General ledger systems use data from the accounts receivable, payroll, accounts payable, and other accounting systems to record the firm's income and expenses. They produce the income statements, balance sheets, general ledger trial balance, and other reports.

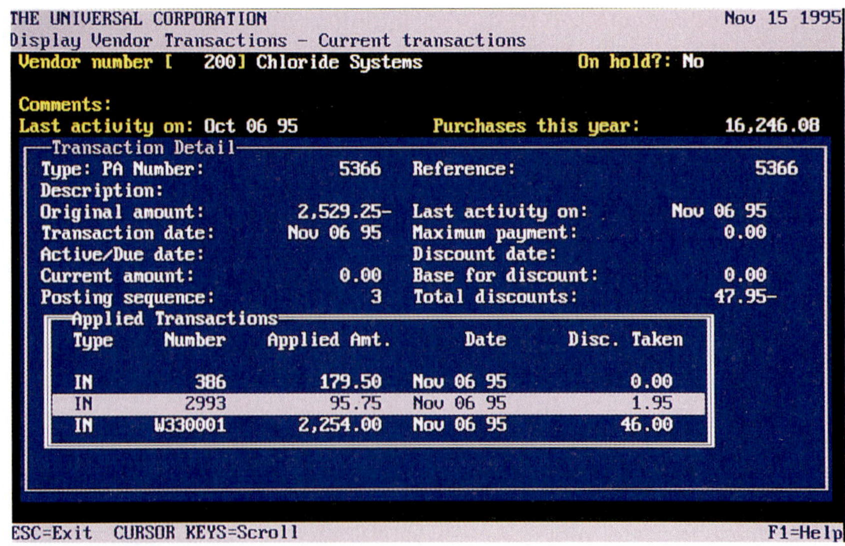

ACCPAC Plus Accounting provides multiuser accounting software for medium-sized businesses and divisions of large corporations that have sophisticated accounting requirements and large transaction volumes. The system has 14 different modules for functions such as accounts payable, accounts receivable, payroll, and general ledger. The various modules can be operated independently or integrated to share data.

SOURCE: Courtesy of Computer Associates International, Inc.

Payroll systems are sometimes treated as human resources systems, but they also perform important accounting functions. They calculate and produce employee paychecks, earning statements for the Internal Revenue Service and state and local taxing authorities, and payroll reports.

Cash management systems track receipts and disbursements of cash. Firms use this information to identify excess funds that can be deposited or invested to generate additional income. Cash management systems may also produce cash flow forecasts that managers can use for planning and development of alternative investment strategies.

Cash management systems Financial systems that keep track of the receipt and disbursement of cash by a firm; they may also forecast the firm's cash flow.

The accounting and financial systems described above are found in virtually all firms, whereas loan processing, check processing, and securities trading systems are industry specific, serving primarily the banking and securities industries. Loan processing systems are used by banks to record transactions that initiate and pay for consumer and commercial loans and credit card transactions. Such systems keep track of principal and interest and issue customer billing statements. Banks use check processing systems to track deposits and payments in checking accounts and to produce customer statements of account activity. Securities trading systems are used by the New York and American Stock Exchanges to track the purchase and sale of stocks, bonds, options, and other securities.

Accounting and financial TPS have created efficiencies for organizations, but they are not always perceived as being useful or beneficial. The Focus on People explores this issue as it examines the U.S. government's system for automating social security benefit payments.

The transaction processing system for credit card payments described in the next section is an example of a financial system that is shared by multiple companies. Visa's credit card payment system acts as an accounts receivable and billing system for the merchants and stores whose customers charge their purchases using the Visa credit card. The system is also an industry-specific system, a source of revenue for participating banks and the principal source of revenue for the Visa Corp. The description of Visa's system can help us understand the workings of basic financial systems if we keep in mind the following questions: Where does a basic financial system obtain its data? What does it actually do with the data? What business problems does the system solve? What difference does this system make for the firm?

A Basic Financial System: Visa's Credit Card Payment System About 10 million merchants worldwide accept Visa and MasterCard credit cards. Visa and MasterCard's credit card networks represent two of the most massive transaction processing systems in the world. Let's examine Visa's credit card payment system, which processes 20 million transactions a day. Figure 13.5 shows how the system works.

When a customer makes a purchase of, say, $100 using a Visa card, the merchant or clerk swipes the card through a special electronic terminal connected by telephone lines to the computer network linking the merchant's bank, Visa, and the cardholder's bank. About 20,000 banks worldwide belong to this network. The credit card machine records the customer's credit card number, expiration date, and purchase amount and dials a number at the store's bank (1).

FOCUS ON **PEOPLE**

AUTOMATIC FOR THE PEOPLE?

Since its inception, electronic data interchange (EDI—see Chapter 7) and electronic payment systems have played an increasingly larger role in daily business operations. Businesses use the technology to directly deposit their employees' salaries, to pay bills, and to transfer money. Essentially, the technology exists to provide convenient methods of handling money. The United States government, with 250 million "customers," has found making payments electronically to be both convenient and cost efficient. With over three quarters of a billion separate payments to make each year, it is no wonder that the federal government would want to avoid using actual checks whenever possible. Currently, the government makes slightly less than half of its total payments with paper checks at a cost of 42 cents each. The remaining transactions, completed electronically, carry a fee of only 2 cents per payment. With this knowledge in hand, the Treasury Department has decided to phase out paper checks almost entirely. The move has angered some citizens who believe the government should not force a system on the public that is not necessarily beneficial to all.

In April 1996, Congress finalized a budget law that included provisions to eliminate postage and printing costs, thereby cutting half a billion dollars from the budget over a five-year period. Thus, the conversion to electronic payments, with the exception of tax refunds, scheduled to be completed by 1999, is bound by law. The problem with the law is that between 10 and 20 percent of the individuals that receive benefit payments from the government do not have bank accounts, many by choice. Forcing them to open accounts seems to conflict with their freedom of choice. Furthermore, the change has the potential to hurt check-cashing stores that do a significant portion of their business with recipients of government checks who do not have bank accounts.

The government is taking one step at a time in dealing with the logistics of the switch. The first phase of the budget law requires that all new recipients of government payments use direct deposit. To make the transition smooth, some government agencies such as the Social Security Administration have discontinued the use of a form to initiate direct deposit. Social security checks can be deposited electronically with only a phone call or visit to the bank.

Displeasure over having no choice in method of payment is not the only problem the government has to overcome. While its agencies are supposed to make electronic payments to companies with which they deal, many of the agencies and the businesses are not yet equipped to handle such transactions. So some sectors will definitely benefit from the government's new policy—namely, companies that install the software needed to comply with the government's demands.

The government does realize that additional steps need to be taken to make its plans functional. The Treasury Department has approached banks about the idea of creating simple accounts solely for the purpose of direct deposit. Customers would use a debit card to make purchases using the account or to withdraw from it at an ATM. Should banks choose not to become involved, the government might distribute its own cards that could be used to receive social security and other benefits electronically. Some check-cashing businesses have taken their own initiative by acquiring ATMs in order to turn a potentially harmful situation into an opportunity that could be profitable. A number of these services hope that ATM network operators will allow benefits recipients to use debit cards in their stores without installing a machine.

Until all institutions that handle government money, from small banks to utility companies, have the means to accept direct deposits, the transition to that strategy promises to be rough. More importantly, accommodating the individuals affected by the move will continue to be an issue that demands to be addressed.

FOCUS Question: What people, organizational, and technology factors need to be addressed regarding the U.S. government's decision to eliminate paper checks?

SOURCE: Saul Hansell, "U.S. Shifting Its Payments to Direct Deposit," *The New York Times,* November 18, 1996.

FIGURE 13.5

Visa's Plan to Reduce Errors and Fraud

In Visa's credit card payment system, a charge transaction goes through several steps involving the cardholder, the merchant, the merchant's bank, the bank issuing the credit card, and Visa itself.

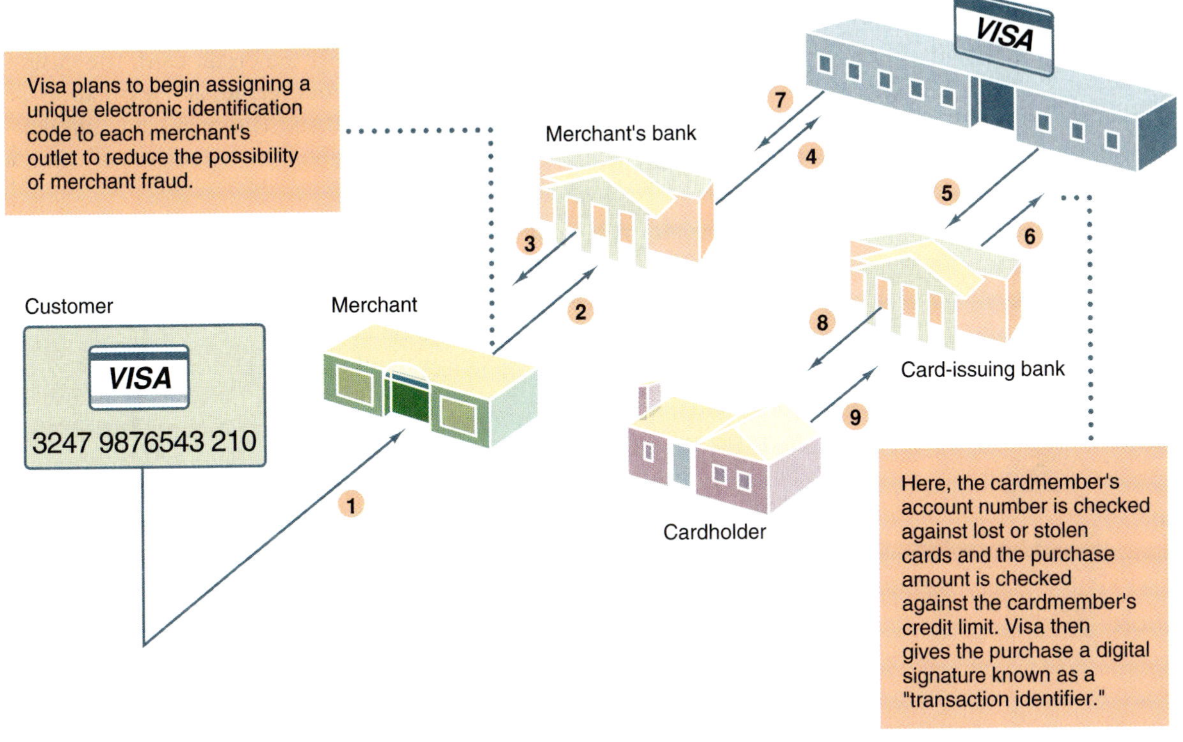

The merchant's bank is linked via Visa's network to the bank that issued the credit card. The card-issuing bank approves the charge. Then the merchant submits the charge to the store's bank (2). The bank subtracts an average fee of 1.9 percent and pays the rest to the merchant (3). For a purchase of $100, the merchant would usually receive $98.10.

The merchant's bank submits the charge to Visa (4), which charges the amount of the purchase to the bank that issued the Visa card (5). The cardmember's account number is checked against those of lost or stolen cards. The purchase amount is checked against the cardmember's credit limit. To reduce error and fraud, Visa assigns a special digital signature called a "transaction identifier" to the transaction. This identifier remains attached to the purchase transaction until everyone is paid. The card-issuing bank subtracts an interchange fee of approximately 1.3 percent (6) from the purchase amount and pays the rest ($98.70) to Visa, which then pays the merchant's bank (7). (The merchant's bank paid the merchant only $98.10 and gets to keep the 60-cent difference.) Both the issuing bank and the merchant's bank then pay small fees to Visa.

The card-issuing bank bills the customer for the original amount of $100 (8). When the customer pays the bill, the bank will either receive $100 immediately or $100 plus interest over time (9).[3]

Now let's return to the questions we posed earlier:

- **Where does a basic financial system obtain its information?** The Visa credit card payment system obtains its information initially from the merchant and the customer holding the credit card. The customer supplies his or her credit card number, name, and expiration date, which help identify the card-issuing bank. The merchant supplies the purchase amount and data identifying the merchant and the merchant's bank for the system.

- **What does a basic financial system actually do with the data?** The credit card payment system tracks purchase transactions, authorizes these transactions, and issues payments to the merchant, the bank issuing the credit card, the merchant's bank, and Visa. It also provides a bill for the purchase to the cardholder.

- **What problems does this system solve?** The credit card payment system provides a relatively simple and instant way for merchants to receive payment for their sales. Merchants do not have to set up their own accounts receivable and billing systems or administer them. Visa does all the work. Additionally, the credit card payment system encourages consumers to buy more by providing nearly instant credit all over the world at little or no extra cost to them. The various banks involved profit from the transaction fees and interest. The system is Visa's core source of revenue since it receives about 5 cents to process each credit card transaction.

- **What difference does this basic financial system make for the firm?** The Visa credit card payment system actually represents two types of financial systems. For the merchant, it represents a variant of an accounts receivable system, instantaneously granting credit to customers, tracking money owed, and issuing bills. For the merchant's bank, the card-issuing bank, and the Visa Corp., the system is an industry-specific one that provides an essential service to subscribers and an important source of revenue.

BASIC HUMAN RESOURCES SYSTEMS

At the most elementary level, human resources information systems deal with the recruitment, placement, performance evaluation, compensation, and career development of a firm's employees. Basic human resources systems collect data concerning employees and support repetitive, routine tasks such as tracking new hires, promotions, transfers, and terminations and maintaining records of employee benefits and beneficiaries.

Table 13.4 lists the most important basic human resources systems. In addition to the systems listed, some firms treat payroll systems as human resources systems because they maintain employee data that is used by the human resources function. Others consider payroll primarily an accounting function.

TABLE 13.4

Standard Human Resources Systems

Application	Purpose
Personnel record keeping	Maintain employee records.
Applicant tracking	Maintain data about job applicants.
Positions	Track positions in the firm.
Training and skills	Maintain employee training and skills inventory records.
Benefits	Maintain records of employee benefits and perform benefits accounting.

Personnel record-keeping systems maintain basic employee data such as name, address, marital status, dependents, age, Equal Employment Opportunity (EEO) category, and job performance appraisals, and they also record hiring, termination, transfer, promotion, and performance evaluation transactions. **Applicant tracking systems** maintain data about applicants for jobs and provide reports to satisfy federal, state, and local employment regulations.

Positions systems, by contrast, do not maintain information on employees but on the positions in the firm. A position can be defined as a slot in the firm's organizational chart. Positions systems maintain data about filled and unfilled positions and track transactions concerning changes in positions and job assignments.

Training and skills systems maintain records of employees' training and work experience, interests, and special skills and proficiencies. Such systems can identify employees with appropriate skills for special assignments or job requirements.

Benefits systems maintain data about employees' life insurance, health insurance, pensions, and other benefits and track transactions such as changes in beneficiaries and benefits coverage.

Basic human resources systems may also provide data for managers or supply data to other systems specifically serving management. For example, positions systems are used for management analysis of turnover problems and recruitment strategies as well as for succession planning.

Traditionally, the basic business systems in large firms have been based on mainframes and minicomputers. Today, with powerful PCs and workstations, many high-volume transaction processing tasks can be performed using these smaller machines or client/server networks. Compaq Computer's Employee Self-Service Personnel System is an example of how transaction processing can be accomplished with client/server technology. Again, as you read the following account, keep our list of questions in mind: Where does a basic human resources system obtain its data? What does it actually do with the data? What business problems does this system solve? What difference does this system make for the firm?

Applicant tracking systems Human resources systems that maintain data about applicants for jobs at a firm and provide reports to satisfy federal, state, and local employment regulations.

Positions systems Human resources systems that maintain information about positions (slots in a firm's organizational chart); they maintain data about filled and unfilled positions and track changes in positions and job assignments.

Training and skills systems Human resources systems that maintain records of employees' training and work experience so that employees with appropriate skills for special assignments or job requirements can be identified.

Benefits systems Human resources systems that maintain data about employees' life insurance, health insurance, pensions, and other benefits, including changes in beneficiaries and benefits coverage.

A Basic Human Resources System: Compaq Computer's Employee Self-Service Personnel System The trend in human resources, as in all business functions, is to have fewer people handle benefits, pay raises, pension plans, vacations, and related administrative functions. Yet many human resources systems, even those that are online and networked, still rely on employees to

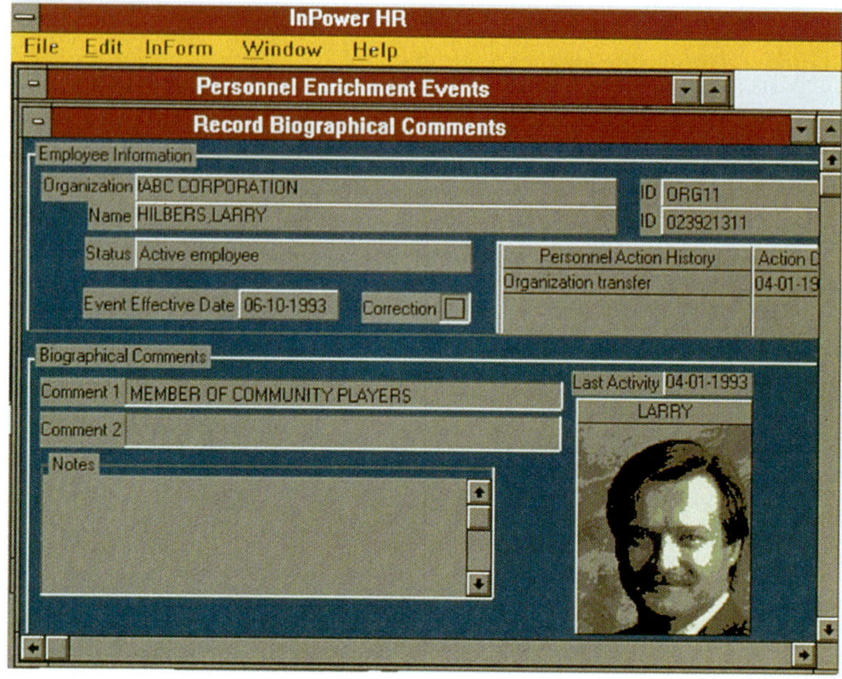

Integral Systems' InPower HR human resource management system operates in a client/server environment on a variety of database management systems and server operating systems. It can display employee records and related information using a graphical user interface.

SOURCE: Courtesy of Integral Systems, Inc.

send in paper forms for processing. The forms are keyed into the system by a central data entry staff. At Compaq Computers, it might take as many as 31 steps involving multiple telephone calls and paper flows for a Compaq manager at a remote site to give an employee a pay raise.

To reduce some of the inefficiencies and expense associated with processing human resources transactions, Compaq developed a new online human resources system that turns over nearly all of the data entry and validation work to its 6,000 employees and their supervisors on its 800-acre corporate campus in Houston, Texas. The new system is expected to reduce the human resources staff from 300 to 90 people within two years and to produce $313,000 in annual savings.

We can see how the "employee self-service" strategy features of this system work by looking at how it handles the process of enrolling employees in a cafeteria-style flexible benefits program. In an effort to cut costs and improve service to employees, Compaq, like many large corporations, implemented a flexible benefits plan that lets employees choose from a menu of benefit options. This cafeteria approach provides employees a fixed number of dollars that can be spent any way they wish on medical or life insurance coverage. For instance, employees might have the option of two different medical plans—a conventional plan that reimburses them for medical care provided by a physician of their choice, or a less-expensive health maintenance organization plan in which they must use prespecified physicians and services. Employees can spend their dollars on either of the medical plans and use the rest for additional life or disability insurance.

Good benefits packages such as flexible or cafeteria-style benefits plans are an important way for organizations to attract and retain good employees and to offset spiraling health insurance costs. Instead of paying more and more each year for one standard health care or life insurance plan, companies can stabilize these costs by giving each employee a fixed amount to spend on benefits. Employees gain by having the ability to choose among many benefits options.

Compaq employees can interactively craft their own benefits plans using either a PC or a telephone. The PC prompts them for information about themselves and their dependents and guides them through a menu of health and life insurance choices. As the employee selects these options, the bottom of the display screen shows the number of their benefits dollars that have been allocated to the options they have selected and the number of dollars remaining. The employee's selections update the employee database. When the benefits allowance is exhausted, the system notifies the user of deductions that can be taken from the person's paycheck to pay for the benefits.

Alternatively, the employee can enroll in a flexible benefits plan using a TouchTone telephone with an automated voice response capability. This interface captures the employee's voice input, validates it, and reads back enrollment information to the employee. Employees can enroll at home by telephone and later check their enrollment data on a PC at work, or they can enter the data at work using the PC and later listen to the enrollment choices at home. In either case, the system creates deduction transactions and passes them to the firm's payroll system.[4] Figure 13.6 illustrates this system.

FIGURE 13.6

Compaq Computer's Online Human Resources System

In Compaq Computer's online human resources system, employees and their supervisors can enter benefits data directly into the system using either a PC or a telephone. Employee benefits plan selections update the employee database. The system then creates transactions for benefits plan contribution deductions to be taken from the employees' paychecks. These deduction transactions are passed to Compaq's payroll system. The system also displays the benefits plan options selected by each employee.

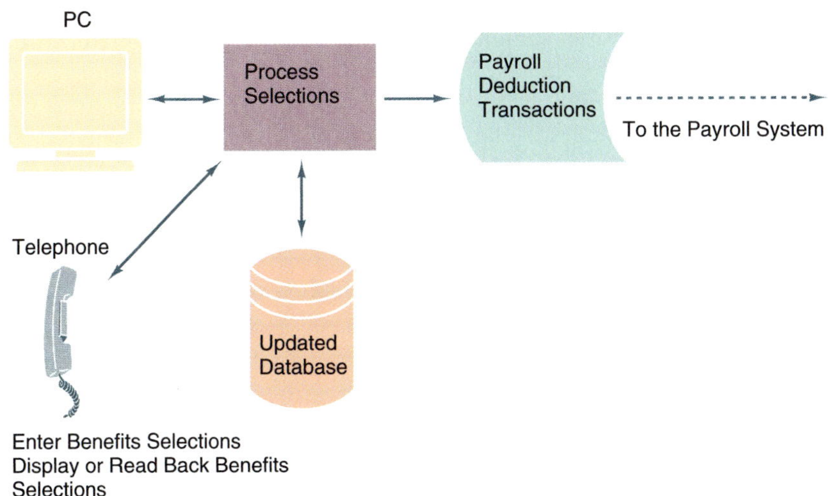

Once again, we return to the questions we raised at the beginning of the chapter:

- **Where does a basic human resources system obtain its information?** The human resources system obtains its data directly from employees and from their supervisors. Both can input transactions directly into the system. Supervisors can input transactions for pay increases or for hiring and terminating employees. Employees can input transactions to select their benefit plans, providing data such as their name, department, health and life insurance choices, and coverage amounts.

- **What does a basic human resources system actually do with the data?** Employee selections of health care and life insurance benefits plans and coverage amounts are the transactions for the benefits portion of the human resources system. These transactions create or update the employee records in the human resources database (which is stored on a server). Output consists of displays of benefits options; the number of dollars left in the employee's benefits allowance after choices have been made; and payroll deduction transactions passed to the payroll system.

- **What problems does this system solve?** To comply with both internal record-keeping and external legal requirements, all organizations must keep accurate records of employee participation in benefits plans and their payments to these plans through payroll deductions. This system solves the operational problem of determining which benefits options were selected by each employee, the amount of each employee's benefits allowance that has been spent, and who must have benefits plan payments deducted from their paychecks. The system automates this record keeping and the transactions that feed related business systems such as payroll.

- **What difference does this basic human resources system make for the firm?** The new human resources system has enabled the company to move to a more flexible yet more complex benefits program with no increase in administrative and support costs. In fact, the company has been able to sharply reduce the number of people and the expense of administering the human resources function. The system also helps the company strategically by providing a way to attract and maintain desirable employees. Flexible benefits programs are believed to increase employee satisfaction and motivation by giving employees choices in constructing their benefits plans.

The case study concluding this chapter shows how self-service personnel systems are starting to use the Internet.

SUMMARY

- Basic business systems keep track of the most elementary, day-to-day activities of the firm, dealing with routine, repetitive problems for which the solution is based on the firm's standard operating procedures. These systems support the operational level of the business but also supply data for management decisions at higher levels of the firm.
- A transaction is a record of an event to which a firm's system must respond. Basic business systems, which keep track of the elementary transactions necessary to conduct a business, are also called transaction processing systems.
- In online transaction processing (OLTP) systems, transactions are immediately processed by the CPU. Firms that have to process massive numbers of transactions online are turning to fault-tolerant computer systems with backup hardware, software, and power supply to forestall major business disruptions if their online transaction processing breaks down.
- Basic business systems are used primarily by people at lower levels of the firm who have little or no management responsibility.
- Basic business systems help solve internal operating problems and problems concerning transactions with the firm's external environment—customers, suppliers, and government regulations.
- Output from basic business systems may consist of finished goods, paychecks, other documents, or data supplied to other systems. Basic business systems supply data to higher-level systems in the same functional area (for example, an order entry system supplies data for a sales management system) or to systems in different business areas.
- The basic business systems support the manufacturing and production functions by supplying data to operate, monitor, and control the production process. Materials, purchasing, receiving, shipping, process control, numerical control, equipment, quality control, labor costing, and robotic systems are examples of basic manufacturing and production systems.
- The basic business systems support the sales and marketing function by collecting and processing routine, repetitive data concerning locating customers, offering goods and services, processing sales and orders, and authorizing purchases. Sales support, telemarketing, order processing, point of sale, and customer credit authorization systems are examples of basic sales and marketing systems.
- The basic business systems support the accounting and finance function by recording the flow of funds in the firm, by tracking the firm's use of funds, and by producing financial statements. There are also industry-specific financial systems for the banking and securities industries. Accounts receivable, accounts payable, general ledger, payroll, cash management, loan processing,

check processing, and securities trading are examples of basic accounting and financial systems.

- The basic business systems support the human resources function by tracking the recruitment, placement, performance evaluation, compensation, and career development of the firm's employees. Personnel record keeping, applicant tracking, positions, training and skills, and benefits systems are examples of basic human resources systems.

KEY TERMS

Basic business system
Transaction
Transaction processing system (TPS)
Online transaction processing (OLTP)
Fault-tolerant computer systems
Quality control systems
Process control systems
Robotics
Telemarketing systems
Order processing systems
Point-of-sale systems
Accounts receivable systems
Accounts payable systems
Cash management systems
Applicant tracking systems
Positions systems
Training and skills systems
Benefits systems

REVIEW QUESTIONS

1. Define a basic business system. What functions do basic business systems serve?
2. What is a transaction? Give examples of three transactions used by businesses.
3. What kinds of problems do basic business systems solve? What kinds of positions in the firm use basic business systems?
4. What are the outputs of basic business systems?
5. What are fault-tolerant systems? Why are they necessary?
6. How do basic business systems support the manufacturing and production function? List and describe five kinds of manufacturing and production systems.
7. How do basic business systems support the sales and marketing function? List and describe four kinds of sales and marketing systems.
8. How do basic business systems support the accounting and financial functions? List and describe three accounting systems and four financial systems.

9. How do basic business systems support the human resources function? List and describe three human resources systems.

DISCUSSION QUESTIONS

1. An important function of basic business systems is to produce information for other systems. Discuss.

2. Why can failure of basic business systems for a few hours or days lead to a business firm's failure?

3. To be most effective, sales and marketing systems should be closely coordinated with basic business systems from other functional areas, such as manufacturing and production, and accounts receivable systems. Discuss.

PROBLEM-SOLVING EXERCISES

1. *Group exercise:* As the director of Equal Economic Opportunity affairs for your firm, you are responsible for gathering the data concerning your firm's record in hiring and promoting women and minorities. How could you use human resources transaction processing systems for your work?

Divide into groups. Each group should develop two or three reports from the human resources systems described in this chapter that could assist the EEO director in this task. Each group should design a mock-up of each report, showing column headings, data fields required, and any kind of totals that would be useful. Each group should then present its reports to the class.

2. Herman's Hardware is a mom-and-pop business in a neighborhood that is becoming increasingly gentrified on New York City's Upper West Side. Store space is limited, and rents have doubled over the past five years. Consequently, Herman and Ida Stein, the owners, are under great pressure to use every square foot of space as profitably as possible.

The Steins have never kept detailed records of stock in inventory or of their sales. Stock items are automatically placed on shelves to be sold. Invoices from wholesalers are kept only for tax purposes. When an item is sold, the item number and price are rung up at the cash register. The Steins use their own judgment and observation in identifying stock items that are moving quickly and might need reordering. Many times, however, they are caught short and lose a sale.

How could the Steins use the information they already maintain to help their business? What data would these systems capture? What reports would these systems produce?

3. *Hands-on exercise:* Advanced Cartridges in Hayward, California, is a small manufacturer of cartridges for computer laser printers. Its quality control department prepared the following report of the number of defective cartridges per 1,000 cartridges produced between 1991 and 1997:

Defects per 1,000 Cartridges Manufactured

Year	Defects per 1,000
1991	1.89
1992	2.27
1993	2.72
1994	3.26
1995	3.17
1996	3.91
1997	4.23

The department would like to display this information graphically for management to determine whether new quality control measures should be instituted. Use appropriate software to create a graph showing the number of defects per 1,000 units produced each year. Print out your graph.

4. *Internet problem-solving exercise:* You are planning a business trip to Phoenix, Arizona, and would like to make a hotel reservation. You need a hotel that has a business center, restaurant, free parking, and rooms for less than $150 per night. Use the Hotel Database Search capability of TravelWeb to fine a suitable hotel. Then examine TravelWeb's hotel reservation capabilities. Write a brief description of TravelWeb as a sales TPS. What are its inputs and outputs? What is the value of this system for the company?

NOTES

1. "Weeding Out a Terrific Tracking System," *Automatic I.D. News,* November 1996.
2. Clinton Wilder, "Booksellers' Battles Head for the Web," *Information Week,* March 3, 1997; G. Bruce Knight, "How a Wall Street Whiz Found a Niche Selling Books on the Internet," *The Wall Street Journal,* May 16, 1996; and Mark Glaser, "Virtual Storefronts that Work," *New Media,* October 28, 1996.
3. Robert E. Calem, "Taking the Worry Out of Paying with Plastic," *The New York Times,* November 14, 1993.
4. Gary H. Anthes, "Compaq Empowers Employees," *Computerworld,* August 2, 1993.

PROBLEM-SOLVING CASE

YOUR SOURCE FOR HUMAN RESOURCES

The human resources department deals with many basic, everyday business activities of the organization—recruiting and hiring employees, maintaining health insurance and benefits plans, providing career development, and training. Because these activities involve all of an organization's employees, it is not surprising that HR departments would want to make their services as available and as easy to use as possible.

Many HR departments headed right to the cutting edge of information technology in redesigning their operations: Web applications. More specifically, many companies put up their own intranets, one of the best possible tools for sharing information. Web applications distribute data so effectively because they can present information on so many different platforms. Users can take advantage of the technology by visiting kiosks or workstations, or they can use their desktop PCs. It is a technology that can also prove cost effective in regard to both development and training.

Keeping the intranet simple seemed to be the pattern for early ventures made by HR departments. They posted items like job listings and information on company policy and benefits. However, as the technology continues to advance, the use of the intranet continues to expand. Many companies now offer their employees the opportunity to perform certain tasks online such as submitting electronic forms, checking their personal records, or experimenting with different benefits packages. One company that has enhanced its operations through the use of an intranet is Oracle.

As recently as 1995, Oracle conducted its HR department the old-fashioned way, with no computers. Then, Elizabeth Grover, the company's director of compensation and benefits, led a movement to put Oracle's flexible benefits enrollment program online. The process was completed by attaching a Web application to the program administrator's database. Initially, almost 25 percent of the staff, approximately 2,000 people, chose to try out the new system. A high percentage of those people responded favorably to it. Many found that the new method was far less complicated than the slow-going traditional way. They were particularly enthusiastic about the opportunity to test different plans. By entering different values for benefits allocations online, employees can project the costs of various options and then sign up for their best option immediately. They do not need to spend time calculating and comparing costs manually or filling out extra paperwork. The positive feedback has served as somewhat of an inspiration for Oracle's HR department. Under normal circumstances, its staff is not perceived as a ground breaker in systems development. Now HR has proven that its plans for the intranet are very ambitious and will accomplish much more than simply posting information.

One obstacle that Grover encountered in working with Web technology was the security concern. Linking to Web sites outside of Oracle's intranet could pose threats to the company's security. Gaining illegal access to other people's records within the system also presented a problem. Grover ironed out these concerns with the help of Oracle's Internal Data Center. They will continue to work together to ensure that links to Fidelity Investments' 401(k) Web site and to their health care provider's directory of primary care physicians do not endanger the welfare of the organization or its employees.

First Bank System Inc. also reworked its HR department to incorporate intranet technology. The company surmised that the change would add convenience and flexibility that its previous system did not have. First Bank System employees gained the ability to deal with their normal human resources-related activities through a system that responds to voice commands. However, according to the company's manager of human resources systems integration and support, Tim Bruzek, the results have been limited. The interactive voice response system functions only with a specified set of commands and scenarios. First Bank's employees cannot yet do more than conduct research with the service. Bruzek foresees the time when they will indeed be able to conduct their actual affairs with voice commands from desktops or kiosks.

Another organization in the midst of altering the way in which it conducts basic, day-to-day business activities is the semiconductor manufacturer Intel. Intel's human resources information services department began by combining 13 separate databases into one data source that all employees could access. Having transferred its HR logs to the Web, Intel set 1997 as the date to install applications to allow the company to hire employees online and for employees to enroll in health benefit programs and update their personal profiles in the HR department's compilation. This last feature again brings up the issue of privacy. The question of how to keep personal records safe from curiosity seekers is certainly a valid one. Many companies approach the matter using a model with which many of us are already familiar: personal identification numbers, much like the ones used for calling card or ATM transactions.

In addition to convenience and better service to employees, another reason companies are creating human resources intranets is their relatively low cost. Applications developed for a Web environment tend to cost less than applications developed with other technology, and applications that allow employees to help themselves can reduce the cost of basic human resources transactions. Merck & Co., Inc. found that having a human resources representative handle a transaction cost $16.96, whereas the same transaction handled by a self-service technology such as an interactive voice-response system or a kiosk cost only $2.32.

Nancy Heckman of Intel's HRIS division insists that taking HR functions to the Web does more than save money and simplify tasks. Before the move to online services, HR staff spent much of its time digesting forms and recording the information contained in them. The paperwork held back the staff from serving the organization to the best of its abilities. With the intranet taking over most of the tedious work, the HR staff can concentrate more on advising employees and orchestrating the growth of the company, resulting in something of a human resources renaissance. And since Web applications usually place fewer demands on support staff, the information systems and technology departments find themselves less overextended.

Of course, these advantages mean very little if employees do not use the systems. Many people in the workforce do not have an understanding of computers, much less the Web. Training those people takes on added importance. Equally as crucial is the presentation of the applications that workers will need for selecting benefits packages and exploring job possibilities. To that end, the inclusion of a very user-friendly interface, one that can prevent people from making detrimental errors, ranks as a high priority. Although some may be frustrated initially by having to adapt their method of doing personal business, using Web technology for HR purposes opens doors that will open many eyes.

SOURCE: Heath Row, "Personnel Best," *Webmaster*, September 1996.

CASE STUDY QUESTIONS

1. What kinds of basic business transactions are being handled by human resources intranets? Describe one type of transaction that an employee might use to enroll in a health benefits program. What pieces of data would it contain? Draw a diagram of how an intranet-based system for health benefits enrollment might work.

2. What problems are solved by using intranets for human resources transaction processing systems?

3. What people, organization, and technology factors must a business address to use Internet technology for human resources employee applications?

Chapter

FOURTEEN

KNOWLEDGE WORK: SYSTEMS FOR OFFICES AND PROFESSIONALS

CHAPTER OUTLINE

LEARNING OBJECTIVES

After reading and studying this chapter, you will

1. Know what is meant by an "information and knowledge" economy, knowledge workers, and data workers.
2. Be able to describe the role of the office in contemporary organizations and how it can be supported by information systems.
3. Understand the role knowledge work and knowledge workers play in the modern firm.
4. Understand the generic information requirements of knowledge work and how they can be supported by special knowledge work systems.

FINANCIAL SERVICE CREATES VIRTUAL CONFERENCE ROOMS

Financial Service Corporation, which distributes financial products and services, maintains a network of 1,400 independent field associates and 200 preferred business partners at 60 companies in the United States and Puerto Rico. FSC's ability to provide timely, relevant business information to its partners and associates is directly tied to its profits. Many of FSC's field associates, who are independent financial advisers and planners, work alone, often in isolated areas. FSC needed to enhance the way these associates and the rest of its network communicated.

FSC decided to use the World Wide Web, creating an intranet that would expedite the flow of business information and enable the field associates to network with one another. The intranet features a "field networking" database, where associates can find others with similar experiences, as well as chat areas where the associates can talk privately online. (FSC calls these chat areas "conference rooms.") In these virtual conference rooms, a field associate who is the only person in her small Southern town specializing in retirees can "talk" with other field associates doing the same kind of work in other geographic areas.

FSC believes its conference rooms have an advantage over telephone or face-to-face conversations. Instead of taking notes, the participants can print out transcripts of their online conversations and highlight the important parts.

While FSC does not consider the information exchanged through its intranet sensitive or confidential, its management still does not want the information circulating in public. It also believes that field associates are more likely to talk more candidly about their concerns knowing that their conversations are for internal consumption only.

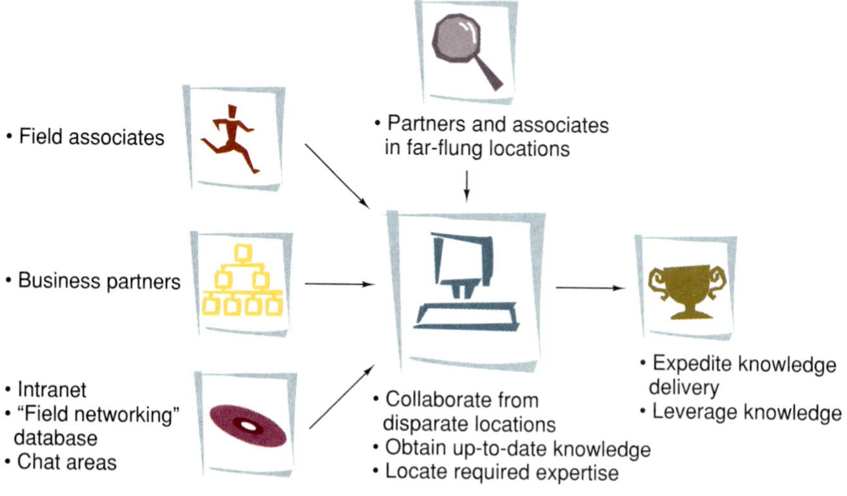

SOURCE: Anne Stuart, "By Invitation Only," *Webmaster,* October 1996.

Financial Service Corporation's intranet for electronic collaboration illustrates the growing need for information systems that can help organizations share and distribute knowledge. Information systems that help organizations create, coordinate, and distribute knowledge have become increasingly important as advanced industrial societies have shifted from industrial production to knowledge and information production as the primary basis of their wealth.

This chapter describes the role played by knowledge work and knowledge workers in contemporary organizations and shows how they can be supported by information systems applications for the creation and distribution of knowledge and information. We examine both office automation applications for clerical and managerial workers and knowledge work systems that support the work of highly trained professionals.

14.1 INFORMATION AND KNOWLEDGE WORK IN THE INFORMATION ECONOMY

Information work
Work that primarily involves the creation or processing of information.

What is information work, and what is an information worker? The Bureau of Labor Statistics defines **information work** as work that primarily involves the creation or processing of information. Information workers are, therefore, people who primarily create or process information. Advanced industrial countries such as the United States, Canada, and most European nations employ more information workers than workers who work with their hands. This shift toward information work and workers has profound implications for the kind of information systems found in organizations and the ways they are used.

At a conservative estimate, over half of the U.S. labor force consists of information workers. The productivity of the entire economy depends greatly on their productivity. Because information work and workers play such a large role in the American economy, scholars refer to our society and other economically advanced societies as **information and knowledge economies.** These can be defined as economies in which the majority of new wealth (gross domestic product) is produced by creating or processing information.

Information and knowledge economy
An economy in which the majority of new wealth (gross domestic product) is produced by creating or processing information.

THE TRANSFORMATION OF THE AMERICAN ECONOMY

Since 1900, the percentage of people who work in offices using information and knowledge to produce economic value (white-collar workers) has been rising, and the percentage of workers who work with their hands in factories or on farms (blue-collar workers) has been declining (see Figure 14.1). These employees are distinguished not by the color of their shirt collars, but rather by how they produce economic value through the use of knowledge and information.

FIGURE 14.1

The Growth of White-Collar Occupations Since 1900

Since the turn of the century, there has been a steady decline in the number of blue-collar workers, while the number of white-collar workers has risen. White-collar workers produce economic value through the use of knowledge and information. Since 1976 white-collar workers have outnumbered their blue-collar counterparts in the U.S. economy.

SOURCE: Vincent E. Giuliano, "The Mechanization of Office Work," *Scientific American,* September 1982, pp. 148–52.

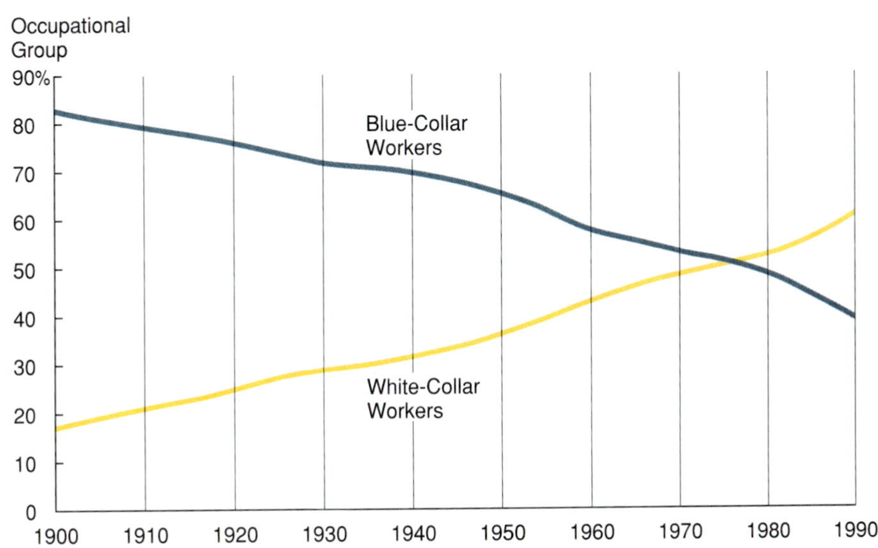

These trends appear to have accelerated since 1960 in the United States and to have spurred worldwide changes in production and consumption.

Knowledge- and information-intense products
Products that require a great deal of learning and knowledge to create and often require information technologies for delivery in a timely fashion.

Information and service industries produce **knowledge- and information-intense products,**[1] which are defined as products that require a great deal of learning and knowledge to create; often, information technologies are required in order to deliver these products in a timely fashion. Nintendo and other video games and all computer software are knowledge- and information-intense products because a great deal of knowledge and information is required in creating them, and specialized information technology is needed in order to produce and use them. The airline industry, which provides a service—transportation—requires a vast computer network simply to book its seats and make a profit. Hence, the airline reservation systems used in the United States are information-intense services. This is clearly less true of traditional industries such as mining and extraction, although even in these industries, information and knowledge are playing new roles, as we describe later.

The increased demand for information products and services has touched off a rapid shift in the demand for labor: More and more information and knowledge workers are required to produce the new goods and services. The airlines have had to hire many more computer specialists than pilots in the past 25 years. Even in traditional manufacturing businesses, more knowledge and information workers are being used to produce manufactured goods. The automobile industry, for example, has cut back on blue-collar production workers but has dramatically increased its hiring of designers, engineers, and computer specialists.

INFORMATION WORKERS: DATA VERSUS KNOWLEDGE WORKERS

The U.S. Department of Labor and the Bureau of the Census define information workers as all those people in the labor force who primarily create, work with, or disseminate information. The Department of Labor and the Bureau of the Census also distinguish two kinds of information workers: data workers and knowledge workers.

Knowledge work
Work whose primary emphasis is on the creation of new information or knowledge.

Data work
Work that primarily involves the process, use, or dissemination of information.

Knowledge workers are defined as those who create new information or knowledge; thus, **knowledge work** refers to work that primarily involves the creation of new information or knowledge. Data workers are defined as those who use, manipulate, or disseminate information; **data work,** then, is work that involves the use, manipulation, or dissemination of information, such as typing or filing.

Knowledge workers are distinguished by the amount of formal schooling required in order to perform their jobs and by a large creative component in their work. Knowledge workers—for example, architects, engineers, judges, scientists, and writers—are required to exercise independent judgment and creativity based on mastery of large knowledge bases. In general, knowledge workers must obtain a Ph.D., master's degree, or certificate of competence before they are accepted into the labor force. In contrast, data workers typically have less formal training and no advanced educational degrees. They also tend to process information rather than create it and have less discretion in the exercise of judgment than knowledge workers do. Examples of data workers include secretaries, bookkeepers, and data entry clerks.

Given these differences, it is not surprising that these two types of workers have different requirements. Data workers are primarily served by office automation systems (described in the following section). Knowledge workers,

FOCUS ON PEOPLE

CONSULTING AND AUDIT CANADA CREATES A VIRTUAL OFFICE

Faced with a rapidly expanding staff and orders to cut costs, Consulting and Audit Canada (CAC) decided to eliminate offices. It equipped its auditors and consultants with laptop computers that have networking capabilities so that they could work in the field several days per week. Each teleworker was given one telephone number through which he or she could be contacted no matter where he or she was working.

Where do you work if your office disappears? You work in a virtual office, wherever you happen to find yourself—at home, at a client's office, in your car, in hotel lobbies and airport terminals. But the virtual office concept still requires some sort of centralized work facility. The Canadian government agency is implementing a "hoteling" plan. Workers share desks and office space through an automated reservations system that assigns facilities on days when workers are not on the road. The new office site includes an informal drop-in center, portable filing units, and a formal meeting room. Since the teleworkers share desks, the facility has only one desk for every three workers. CAC hopes to save $234,000 in overhead, including an entire floor of office space, by implementing the telecommuting and hoteling concept.

Ernst & Young, the international accounting firm, moved their auditors from offices into a "hoteling" system because doing so reduced office space 15 to 18 percent and thereby reduced costs. Robert Cook, senior vice-president of Interior Architects Inc. in San Francisco, California, believes that one motivation for the VO is to force one's sales staff to spend more time with customers. Yet another possible explanation is the U.S. government's Clean Air Act, which requires companies with 200 or more employees in major metropolitan areas to reduce commuter automobile mileage 25 percent by 1996.

Whatever the reason, increasing numbers of people do not work in traditional offices. Most of them are independent consultants, contractors, or entrepreneurs rather than employed VO workers. However, one assertion is that telecommuting—the practice of having corporate employees work at home—has increased 40 percent in the past five years. Because the VO may be appropriate for as much as 40 percent of our workforce, we should expect to see it continue to grow.

Many employees are fearful of the VO. To some it sounds too much like downsizing, part-time work, or a "virtual" workforce of consultants. They are frightened for their jobs. Others respond poorly to the loss of daily social contact. A virtual office can be very lonely—there is no water cooler where employees can meet and chat. A Bell Telephone study done years ago on employees working from their homes found that their productivity and morale plunged precipitously unless they kept in close personal contact with the office. Some fear the breakdown of the separation between the refuge known as home and the pressure-cooker environment known as work. Paul Saffo of the Institute for the Future in California's Menlo Park sums up the conflict between having one's freedom in a VO and the loss of the work-home separation: "Heaven is the anywhere, anytime office. Hell is the everywhere, everytime office."

FOCUS Questions:
What do you think are the problems in managing people who work in VOs? If VO workers can be managed properly, does this hold any lessons for us on how to manage people who are in offices?

SOURCES: Mindy Blodgett, "Creative Use of Office Space Saves Time and Money," *Computerworld,* October 21, 1996, and Phil Patton, "The Virtual Office Becomes Reality," *The New York Times,* October 28, 1993.

FOCUS ON **PROBLEM SOLVING**

CAN COMPUTERS MAKE OFFICE WORKERS MORE PRODUCTIVE?

Beset by recession and intense competition, companies are beginning to apply to office workers what they did to factories—attempts to make office workers more productive. Are computers the solution? Not necessarily. Computers can speed up high-volume, assembly-line activities such as bill paying, check clearing, or claims processing. But using computers to bolster the productivity of knowledge workers can backfire. Personal computers, electronic mail systems, and multifunction telephones can actually generate more drafts, more memos, more spreadsheets, and more messages. According to Paul Strassman, former chief information officer for Xerox and the Defense Department, the United States for three decades used computers to speed up the kind of work that accentuates bureaucracy. Unless offices and service companies have a detailed plan when they automate, computers may end up being used for work that is trivial, peripheral, or downright counterproductive—sending and sorting through irrelevant E-mail or compiling electronic Rolodexes.

Stephen Roach, senior economist for Morgan Stanley, estimated that white-collar productivity increased an average of only 0.28 percent annually during the 1980s. Recently, service sector productivity accelerated, growing 3 percent annually by 1992. Roach and others believe that businesses started using computers to overhaul the way work is done in the office. Instead of blindly computerizing, firms such as Motorola, IBM, Security Pacific, and Corning Glass dramatically boosted white-collar productivity by reengineering office work. They realized that automating something that shouldn't have been done manually in the first place won't make workers more efficient. Instead, the firms have focused first on eliminating bottlenecks, improving customer service, and eliminating mistakes before introducing new technology.

Sea-Land Service, the largest containerized ocean shipping company in the United States, increased productivity by streamlining its business procedures in conjunction with the use of information technology. Customers do not like to wait for accurate bills of lading. If shippers send paperwork with mistakes, clerks are now empowered to call the shipper and correct the problem instead of going through a maze of bureaucratic procedures. For instance, if a shipper misclassified bamboo umbrellas as bamboo goods (which are shipped at a lower rate), the clerk calls the shipper and asks the shipper to reclassify them. In the past the clerk would have waited for the irritated consignee to call and ask for a revised bill of lading to be prepared at additional expense to Sea-Land. By getting the bills right the first time, Sea-Land has reduced the average cost of preparing the documents from around $22 to $14 each. The firm prepares 1.3 million bills of lading per year.

It used to take a corporate auditor at the Motorola Corp. an average of seven weeks to draft a report and deliver a final version to top management. The auditor would visit a plant to examine its books, return to corporate headquarters in Schaumburg, Illinois, write the first draft of the report in longhand, give it to a typist, make revisions, send the report to his or her supervisor, revise again, have the report retyped, remit the report to an audit manager, revise the report again, send the report to the auditee for comment, incorporate changes, and type up a final version. Now each auditor uses a personal computer to write the report in the field, shows it to the auditee, and incorporates comments from the auditee and an auditing department manager in the field. The entire process now takes just five days, a tenfold improvement in cycle time.

Nevertheless, the statistical evidence shows that computers have had relatively little impact on improving overall productivity, especially in the service sector. Computers have contributed to productivity and economic growth, they clearly have added value and quality to many goods and services of higher quality, but they have not demonstrated the robust productivity gains that many expected.

FOCUS Question: Why can't computers make office workers more productive?

SOURCES: Lawrence Zuckerman, "Do Computers Lift Productivity? It's Unclear, but Business is Sold," *The New York Times,* January 2, 1997, and Myron Magnet, "Good News for the Service Economy," *Fortune,* May 3, 1993.

although they certainly rely on and use office automation, also require much more powerful professional workstations (described in Section 14.3).

Although all persons in an organization depend on the office for support, information workers all work in offices. Or, to put it another way, all office workers are information workers of one kind or another. Sometimes the office is a "virtual office"—any place, such as a car, plane, train, or home, where an information worker can get work done (see the Focus on People). These virtual offices are possible because of information technology such as cellular telephones, fax machines, the Internet, and a host of other technologies.

A British Petroleum engineer studies a computer-generated view of Prudhoe Bay. Her analysis of the data and skill in interpreting it can lead to profits—or losses—for the company.

SOURCE: Courtesy of BP America.

THE PRODUCTIVITY CONNECTION: INFORMATION WORKERS AND OFFICES

With more than half the labor force now composed of information workers who predominantly work in offices, and with most of our fastest-growing industries being those that produce information- and knowledge-intense products that require high proportions of information workers, any overall advance in productivity for the advanced economies of the world will almost certainly depend on increasing the productivity of information and knowledge workers. For this reason, a massive increase has occurred in the capital investment in office workers and in systems to support information work.

Because of this, office automation systems and professional work systems were the fastest growing applications of information technology in the past decade and will continue to grow in the future. Thus, it is not an exaggeration to say that office and professional systems have come to symbolize computerization in American work life and the hope for future gains in productivity. But the extent to which computers have enhanced the productivity of information workers is still open to debate, as described in the Focus on Problem Solving.

14.2 OFFICE AUTOMATION: AUTOMATING INFORMATION WORK

Office automation is any application of information technology that is intended to increase the productivity of office information workers. The automation of specific office tasks accelerated in the nineteenth century with the first desktop mechanical calculators (1840) and desktop typewriters (1860), which were designed to semi-automate hand calculations and handwritten notes, respectively. With the digital revolution, much of this early electromechanical equipment was converted to digital machinery, including PCs and networks of desktop computers. Office automation used to refer primarily to document management and processing, but as hardware and software have improved, virtually all office activities—from sophisticated color graphics, to personal databases, to communications—can now be assisted by information technology. Before we describe office automation today, however, we must first look at the role of the office in the organization.

Office automation
The application of information technology to increase the productivity of office information workers.

THE THREE ROLES OF THE OFFICE IN ORGANIZATIONS

Office roles
The functions played by an office in an organization, consisting of (1) coordinating and managing people and work, (2) linking diverse organizational units and projects, and (3) coupling the organization to the external environment.

At least three primary **office roles** in organizational life can be discerned:

1. Coordinating the work of a diverse collection of business professionals who work together to achieve some common goal.
2. Geographically and functionally linking diverse parts and units of the business.
3. Spanning the boundary between the business and its external environment to connect the firm to its clients, suppliers, and other organizations.

You will discover a diverse array of professional, managerial, sales, and clerical employees who work in the office or who depend on the office in order to perform their daily jobs (see Figure 14.2). The office is a major tool for the coordination of diverse information work and the allocation of resources to projects; it also serves as a clearinghouse for information and knowledge. The centrality of offices to organizational life and work is a key feature of modern life.

In addition, the office plays a critical role in linking diverse functional areas and physically distant units of the firm. The office is a significant node that gathers information and knowledge and distributes it to other work groups and offices in the organization. The information and knowledge that the office decides to send up or down or across the hierarchy critically affect the fate of organizations.

Figure 14.3 illustrates the role of the office in linking a firm's functional areas as well as its third major role: the function of the office as the major link to the external environment. When you call an organization, you call an

FIGURE 14.2

Primary Role of the Office

Within an office are staff members from many organizational levels who perform a variety of information-intensive tasks. Office systems must therefore address various needs to help the office function more efficiently and coordinate the work of diverse groups of employees.

FIGURE 14.3

Two Other Major Roles of the Office

Offices connect the different functional areas of a firm. Each office gathers and distributes information according to its particular role in the organization. In addition, offices connect an organization to its external environment. Offices in the production area deal with the firm's suppliers of raw materials, while those in finance deal with outside auditors. Sales and marketing offices are the organization's link to its customers. The human resources office is responsible for ensuring that the firm meets government standards for fair employment practices. Offices in several of these functional areas may also be linked to databases, which provide businesses with pools of externally derived information.

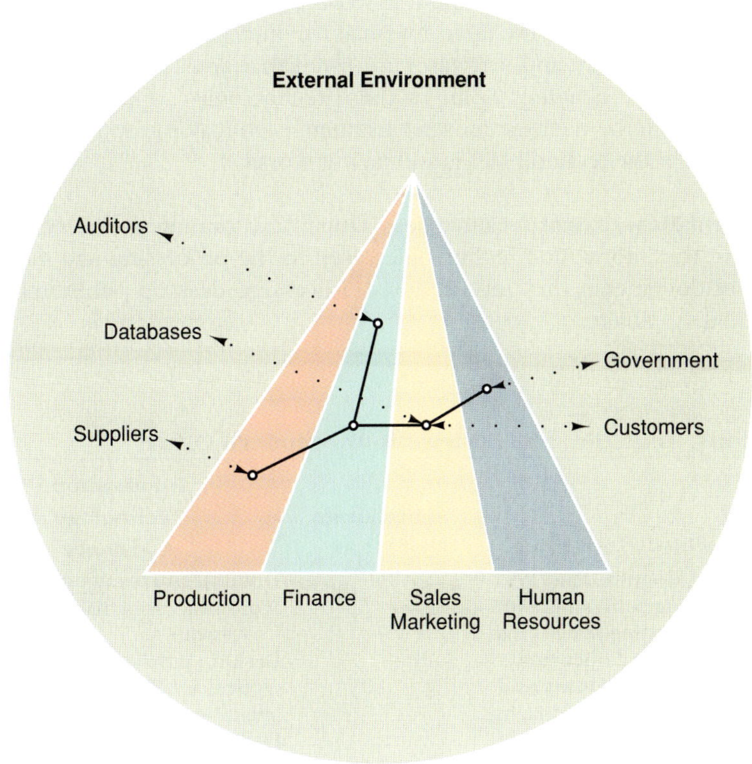

office. The office is where the sales staff reports, where records are kept on customers, and where clients are tracked. Offices are also key purchasing units of the organization and are linked directly to vendors and suppliers of materials and to outside auditors.

Viewing offices in terms of these three major roles can help you understand how and why businesses need to use information technology in the form of the office automation systems described below. At the same time, you should remember that all offices do not face the same problems. Some offices are swamped by paperwork. Other offices have telephones ringing off the hook and going unanswered. Still others routinely lose engineering drawings. Each of these problems has a different information systems solution.

Office activities
The activities performed by an office in an organization, consisting of (1) managing documents, (2) scheduling individuals and groups, (3) communicating with individuals and groups, (4) managing data on individuals and groups, and (5) managing projects.

Document management technology
Information technology that is used for producing and managing the flow of documents in an organization; includes word processing, desktop publishing, and optical disk storage.

ROLES, ACTIVITIES, AND SYSTEMS IN THE OFFICE

As Table 14.1 illustrates, the roles played by offices and the activities performed in them present different information challenges that can be met by various types of information technology. Table 14.1 identifies five major **office activities** that occur to some degree in every office: managing documents, scheduling, communicating, managing data, and managing projects. We have also provided an estimate—based on our own experience as office systems implementors and software writers—of the average percentage of office effort involved in each activity. For instance, managing documents typically involves about 40 percent of the total hours worked in an average office. Communicating involves another 30 percent of office time.

At the far right of the table, five major groups of information technologies (both hardware and software) are listed that are designed to support these five office activities. Some of these technologies support more than one activity. In the next sections, we examine each major group and explain what each of the technologies is and how it works.

Document Management Technologies **Document management technologies** are the information technologies used in the processing and management of documents; they include word processing, desktop publishing, and optical disk storage.

TABLE 14.1

Offices and Office Automation: Functions, Activities, and Systems in the Modern Office

General Functions of Offices	Activities in an Office	Percentage of Effort*	Information Technology Assistance
Coordinating and managing people and work **Linking** organizational units and projects **Connecting** the organization to outside groups and people	**Managing documents:** Creating, storing/retrieving, and communicating image (analog) and digital documents	40	**Document management** Word processing hardware and software Desktop publishing Optical and digital disk storage Digital local area networks
	Scheduling individuals and groups: Creating, managing, and communicating documents, plans, and calendars	10	**Digital calendars** Electronic calendars and schedules Electronic mail.
	Communicating with individuals and groups: Initiating, receiving, and managing voice and digital communications with diverse groups and individuals	30	**Communications** Private branch exchanges and digital phone equipment Voice mail Group work support software
	Managing data on individuals and groups: Entering and managing data to track external customers, clients, and vendors as well as internal individuals and groups	10	**Data management** Desktop database for client/customer tracking, project tracking, and calendar information
	Managing projects: Planning, initiating, evaluating, and monitoring projects; allocating resources; and making personnel decisions	10	**Project management** Desktop project management tools Critical path method (CPM) and program evaluation and review technique (PERT)

*Based on the authors' experience with office systems.

Word Processing

Word processing refers to the software (see Chapter 5) and hardware used to create, edit, format, store, and print documents. Word processing systems are the single most common application of information technology to office work, in part because producing documents is what offices are all about.

Word processing
Software and hardware that are used to create, edit, format, store, and print documents.

Desktop Publishing

The term **desktop publishing** refers to applications for producing documents that combine high-quality type, graphics, and a variety of layout options. Working on the computer screen, the user arranges words and graphics on pages. The user can type in words or charts and use an electronic scanner to scan in photographs and drawings, converting them into data that instruct the printer to generate a duplicate of the image by printing tiny dots. The system enables the user to enter commands for how the various elements are to be printed on the page. The user then sends the document to a laser printer, which produces the final output quickly and in excellent quality. If the user of such a system has good judgment in matters of design, he or she can use desktop publishing to single-handedly produce reports, advertisements, or other documents of a quality that closely approximates the work of professional typesetters and graphic designers.

Desktop publishing
Applications for producing documents that combine high-quality type and graphics with a variety of layout options, allowing users to produce professional-quality reports and documents.

Office Communications Technologies The most common office communications systems are local area networks (LANs), which are digital communications systems that connect digital devices such as computers, printers, fax machines, and storage devices (see also Chapter 7). A LAN usually operates in a small area of up to half a mile; after that, a more powerful network design is required. LANs are designed to integrate word processing and other PC-based or workstation projects (such as spreadsheets or database applications) into a single, coherent system that permits documents, pictures, and related graphics to be shared and communicated. With a LAN, for instance, only one laser printer is needed in an office because many workstations have access to it via the network.

Office Scheduling Technology Keeping track of appointments, activities, and meetings is an important job in the modern office. A variety of software tools, known collectively as **office scheduling technology,** is now available to coordinate individual and group calendars. A simple electronic calendar keeps track of personal appointments and activities.

More sophisticated software—sometimes referred to as **groupware**—tracks the calendars of related individuals, or all individuals, in an office and makes that calendar available to a central receptionist. In this way, for instance, if a customer calls and asks for an appointment with a specific salesperson who is out of the office, the receptionist can use an electronic group calendar to guide the customer to an available salesperson. Likewise, if a senior executive wants to meet with all his or her subordinates, a group calendar will show when all the subordinates are available. Other aspects of groupware are discussed in the following pages.

Office scheduling technology
Information technology used to coordinate individual and group calendars, such as electronic calendars.

Groupware
Software that attempts to expedite all the functions of a typical work group—for example, tracking the calendars of all or related individuals in an office, scheduling meetings, and sharing ideas and documents.

Office Data Management Technology Although business firms store basic transaction and client data in huge corporate databases on mainframes, the development of **office data management technology** has provided many

Office data management technology
Information technology that centers on desktop databases for client or customer tracking, project tracking, calendar information, and other information required for office jobs.

office workers the opportunity to develop their own client tracking systems, customer lists, and supplier and vendor lists using PCs. With contemporary database packages like Access, information workers can create their own databases on clients, customers, suppliers, and other data they need to do their jobs.

Most information workers do not create their own databases, however. In general, the PC database languages are still too difficult to use without special training. Instead, these workers turn to personal information managers (PIMs), software that is customized for specific positions such as salesperson, manager, real estate agent, stockbroker, and the like. Personal information managers are packaged database tools designed to support specific office tasks. They offer much greater flexibility than corporate databases and can easily be customized for individual preferences.

Project Management Technology Offices are hotbeds of individual projects. At the same time, they are central control points that coordinate the flow of resources to projects and evaluate the results. **Project management technology** is software that helps managers track and plan a multitude of projects.

Project management technology
Software that helps managers track and plan projects.

Project management software breaks down a complex project into simpler subtasks, each with its own completion date and resource requirements. Once a user knows what is needed, how much, and when, delivery schedules and resources can be provided precisely when needed. Some software provides suggestions about how resources should be allocated to tasks. Two traditional techniques of project management that most project managers use are CPM (critical path method) and PERT (project evaluation and review technique). These techniques can save thousands of dollars in inventory costs because users do not have to stockpile resources.

Figure 14.4 shows how these information technologies might be used in a single office, such as the branch office of a large national stock brokerage

FIGURE 14.4

Information Technologies Used by Employees in a Branch Office

In a branch office of a large stock brokerage firm, we would find several functional groups of employees, each group being served by certain information technologies. The clerical staff, including receptionists, for instance, would be likely to use document management software and electronic calendars to do their jobs and a PBX system to route telephone calls. All the staff would use a network to communicate with one another and with customers.

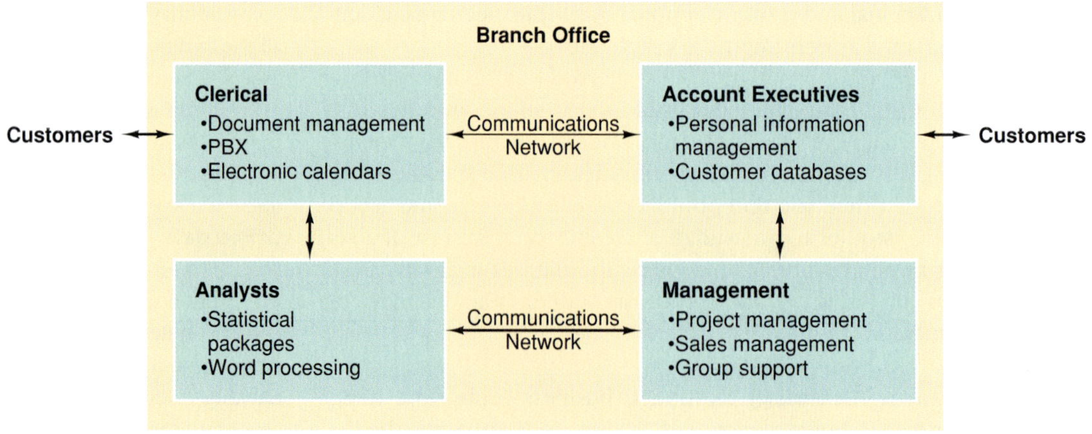

Consolidated Freightways' image processing system makes digitized document images immediately available online. Imaging systems can save companies time and money by reducing the number of steps required to process a document and by making documents easier to locate.

SOURCE: Courtesy of Consolidated Freightways, Inc.

firm. One would find in this office clerical workers, office managers, account executives (the sales force), and a small professional support staff of analysts. The clerical group would primarily use document management software to keep track of sales and manage the flow of documents. The receptionist(s) would route calls through a private branch exchange (a central private switchboard that handles a firm's voice and digital communications needs) and use electronic calendars to schedule clients' appointments with account executives. Account executives would rely on personal information management software and customer databases to assist their sales. The management group would use project management, sales management, and group support software to set sales goals and track progress. The analysts would use statistical packages to measure office performance or track new trends in industry sales. In addition, each of these different groups would use the office's communications network to communicate with one another and with customers.

IMAGING: STEMMING THE TIDE OF PAPER

Businesses today deal with mountains of paper—letters, reports, forms, sales literature, and vital records. Offices throughout the United States store more than 3 trillion documents, 95 percent of them in paper form. Can information technology help to stem the rising tide of paper? One promising approach is the use of imaging systems. **Imaging** is an umbrella term that incorporates a variety of systems and software tools. With modern imaging technology, a document can be digitized into a bit-mapped image that can be stored and made available within a database. The image can then be immediately retrieved and distributed if required.

Imaging
Systems and software that convert documents into digital form so that they can be stored, accessed, and manipulated by the computer.

The benefits of imaging include increased productivity, efficient use of physical storage space, and improved information management. Most important, imaging helps businesses quickly access information, eliminating extensive, exhaustive searches for documents and files that are often buried in traditional storage facilities.

The following components are typically found in complete imaging systems (see Figure 14.5):

- Scanners and optical character recognition software for digitizing hard-copy documents
- Workstations with high-resolution displays
- Software designed to manage document retrieval, work-flow automation, and communications functions
- High-capacity storage devices, especially optical disk
- Output devices such as printers

Optical storage media significantly reduce the amount of physical storage space for archival (long-term) storage and thereby reduce operating costs. The information contained in 20 file cabinets can be stored on a single 5-inch optical disk.

Documents are stored using optical or magnetic disks and can be retrieved online instantaneously, based on values in key fields. Compare this with waiting minutes or hours to retrieve a file from a file cabinet or even days to retrieve a file that has been archived in a warehouse. Files can also be accessed in different ways, such as by date, case number, or type, without

FIGURE 14.5

Components of a Typical Imaging System

Documents are scanned into the system. The scanner digitizes the document, creating an electronic image, which is compressed for storage and indexed for future retrieval. Compressed and indexed documents are stored either on magnetic or optical disks. The system controller moves images in and out of storage and routes them from one workstation to the next over a LAN, which can be limited to other departments or to a host computer. Workstations allow users to access the document index, view the documents only, or both view and edit them.

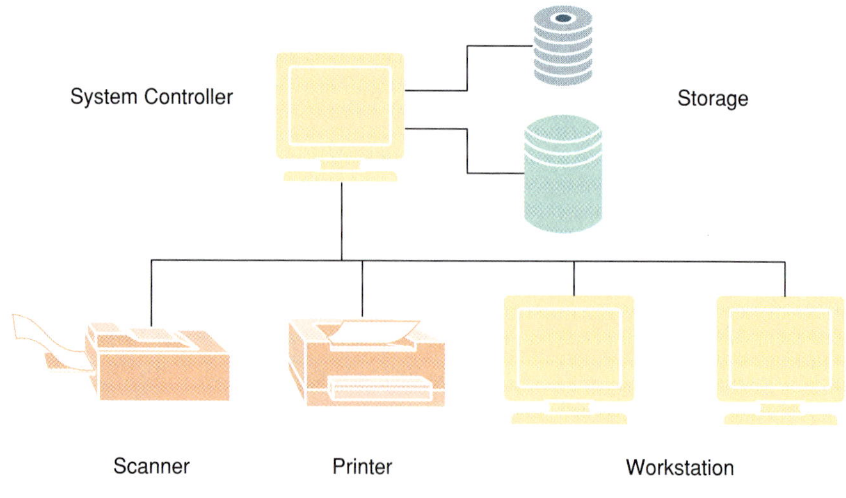

FIGURE 14.6

How Imaging Streamlines the Paper Trail

Consolidated Freightways, Inc., a major player in the freight transportation industry, streamlined its paper trail by converting the equivalent of a 75-mile-high stack of paper documents into 2,500 12-inch optical disks. Bills of lading and delivery receipts and attachments are electronically scanned into an information system. The electronic images are then transmitted to the main data center, where they are stored on optical disks. The day after a freight pickup or delivery, customers can access documents either through a telecommunications link or a phone call to their local image document service department. A hard copy of the requested document is sent to the customer's fax machine within minutes.

SOURCE: Courtesy of Consolidated Freightways.

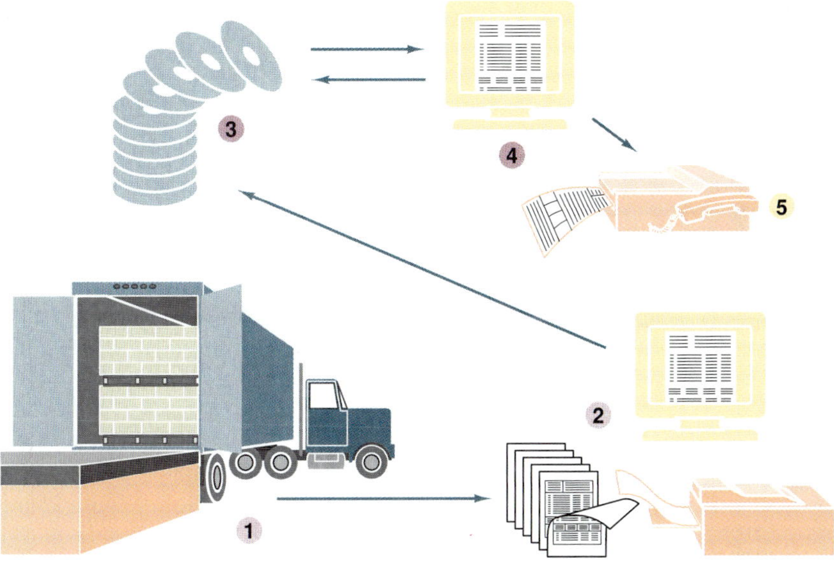

creating multiple copies. Because the electronic document is like any other computer record, it can be accessed by more than one person at a time.

Files stored electronically are less likely to get lost or physically damaged. It is also easy to create backups of electronic documents and store them in another location for added security. Fewer paper copies of documents are needed, and the physical space needed for paper storage is greatly reduced (see Figure 14.6).

Imaging has several functions. The first is document storage and filing and includes the ability to scan, store, and display documents online as digitized images. This is essentially an electronic replacement for the traditional file cabinet, except that the electronic file cabinet can be accessed by more than one user at the same time. The second function is work-flow automation. Imaging technology allows digitized documents to be electronically routed throughout the firm from one workstation to another, streamlining the entire work procedure. Processes such as approval cycles, schedules, productivity measurement, and report generation are automated as well. A third function integrates digitized documents with existing information system applications. Tools can collect all the information required for a specific purpose and deliver it to a specific user.

While the basic application of imaging technology in business is to store and retrieve images of documents, the biggest paycheck comes from using imaging to manage work flow. Work-flow automation actively routes documents through a system based on rules that reflect the decision criteria for processing the documents. This results in a streamlined processing and distribution of documents, with fewer people required to process documents. To maximize the effect of imaging, organizations must change their work procedures. If a firm automates only its current work flow, it cannot take full advantage of this tool.

The Focus on Organizations describes how companies are designing solutions to document management problems using the Internet as well as traditional technologies.

Management Recruiters International uses its Web site to cut down on paperwork. Candidates for jobs can submit resumes to MRI's database through the Web site, where they will be available to MRI's field offices.

FOCUS ON ORGANIZATIONS

THE INTERNET SLAYS THE PAPER DRAGON

Like many businesses, Management Recruiters International, a firm that recruits staff for managerial and technical positions, generates mountains of paper—letters, reports, forms, and vital records. Approximately 1.7 million documents are generated each month at headquarters and distributed by courier to its 650 franchises and directly owned offices.

MRI decided to take on the paper dragon by applying technology. It found it could reduce the $350,000 it spends annually on printing and courier services by 30 percent using high-speed Xerox multifunction output devices that handle printing, copying, document scanning, and networked fax services. MRI took the opportunity of its move to Cleveland in the spring of 1996 to replace its collection of mostly unconnected devices for sending, printing, and copying documents. The company linked Windows-based desktop machines and applications with a TCP/IP Ethernet LAN—10 Mbps, being upgraded to 100 Mbps.

MRI also installed seven document centers and hooked up its existing DocuTech 135 to handle bulk printing. A fax-on-demand system from FaxBack in Portland, Oregon, lets field offices have documents automatically faxed to them on request. MRI's new Web site will enable field offices to pull down documents such as training manuals, resumes, and job descriptions on demand. MRI can further reduce the mountain of paper it handles day to day by using Internet mail as an alternative delivery mechanism. The potential for cutting costs and speeding document delivery time is enormous.

Vince Agresti, director of information systems, plans to introduce Internet and intranet technology gradually at MRI. The intranet services will provide a way to post general information, accessible by dial-up connections from field offices. MRI's Web site will be extended to make it easier for job hunters to be alerted from the corporate site to suitable job vacancies. Agresti believes the firm's new intranet holds the most potential for reducing the size of MRI's paper mountain.

"The Internet is the ultimate document repository," said Priscilla Emery, senior vice-president of information products and services at the Association for Information and Image Management International (AIIM). "But we're still finding the same issues that we did in LAN-based document repositories, such as the need for search and retrieval, revision control and security." The ability of document management tools to effectively deal with the document repository problem involved in businesses' use of the Internet depends on the industry's ability to keep pace with the creative ways organizations are leveraging Internet and intranet technology to distribute electronic documents and manage high-value content.

J. D. Edwards & Co. (JDE), a Denver-based developer of financial and manufacturing applications, ran into trouble with its intranet pilot, which did not include a document management system. "We're finding it a maintenance and versioning nightmare to find out where the documents are and to manage them," said Ben Martin, manager of documents.

Dow Chemical Co. in Midland, Michigan, had a similar experience, finding that employees there were quick to generate home pages but didn't want to go back and refresh the information. Both companies solved the problems by extending their existing document management systems to the intranet. Dow became a beta site for the Accelera product from Documentum Inc. of Pleasanton, California. Dow had been using Documentum's Electronic Document Management System (EDMS) on a Sun Solaris server with an Oracle database. Accelera made it possible for every document put into Documentum to immediately be available through a Web browser.

J. D. Edwards also plans to use its existing document management system—the Interleaf Relational Document Manager (RDM) from Interleaf Inc. of Waltham, Massachusetts. JDE's Internet team decided it could leverage what it had already done and build the system using Interleaf's Business Web product.

FOCUS Questions:
How can the Internet help organizations with document management? What problems can it solve? What problems can't it solve?

SOURCE: Colleen Frye, "New Dimensions for Documents," *Software Magazine,* November, 1996; Jill Gambon, "From Paper to Web Page," *Information Week,* October 14, 1996; and Richard Adhikari, "Managing a Mountain of Paper," *Information Week,* October 14, 1996.

GROUP COLLABORATION: GROUPWARE AND THE INTERNET

Whereas early office automation systems focused on enhancing the productivity of individual workers, many important business activities depend on the effective functioning of small work groups. The productivity of work groups can be enhanced by using a specific type of software called groupware for supporting collaborative work. Groupware runs on networks and attempts to expedite all of the functions of a typical work group (we introduced one application of groupware in the discussion of scheduling technology).

Exactly how can information technology help small work groups? Think of what happens in work groups: Ideas develop, documents are shared for comment or modification, messages are sent, meetings are scheduled and held, and topics are discussed. Notice that these activities are similar to the five categories of office activities identified in Table 14.1. Groupware appropriate for each of these activities is available (see Table 14.2).

Groupware users define their own work groups, with separate groups being defined for separate functions. Employees frequently belong to a variety of groups. For example, the same employee may belong to her reporting work group, a special project development group, a group studying some new technology, a group of all employees that deal with a specific product line, and a company-wide group. Only those who belong to a specific group can access that group's groupware applications.

Price-Waterhouse, a major international accounting and consulting firm, uses Lotus Notes groupware to pool the expertise of its worldwide staff. Staff members can use the groupware to communicate via E-mail or access news articles on topics they have specified the computer to track. They could call up various bulletin boards dedicated to specific topics such as the firm's financial services business. If the bulletin board posted a request from a Miami manager seeking Spanish-speaking consultants for an assignment in Buenos Aires, staff members could send their recommendations via E-mail.

Lotus Notes from Lotus Development Corporation has been the leading commercial groupware product. However, commercial groupware products are in flux because the Internet can be used to support collaborative group work. In earlier chapters we described Internet capabilities for E-mail,

TABLE 14.2

Examples of Groupware and the Five Major Office Activities

Managing Documents
Group writing and commenting
Electronic mail distribution
Screen sharing

Scheduling
Team and project calendars
Office calendars and appointment books

Communicating
Electronic mail
Electronic meetings
Conversation structuring
Computer conferencing
Screen sharing

Managing Data
Shared data files and databases

Managing Projects
Shared time lines and plans
Project management software on networks

electronic discussion groups, and document sharing using the World Wide Web. Collaborators working on a common project from faraway locations can use the Web to display and exchange information, including text, graphics, and sound, using hyperlinks to link automatically to other documents. Many corporate intranets have been set up for this purpose.

For example, the Mitre Corporation in Bedford, Massachusetts, used Internet technology to create a multimedia group collaboration environment called the Collaborative Virtual Workspace. Software engineers can have virtual face-to-face meetings at their workstations with colleagues, participate in chat groups, receive news articles, and share documents and other information.[2]

Web browsers have been enhanced to incorporate groupware functions. Microsoft's Internet Explorer 4.0 and Netscape's Communicator include group collaboration tools, including videoconferencing, E-mail, and group scheduling and calendaring. However, Internet- and Web-based groupware tools lack some capabilities that can be found in commercial groupware products. Lotus Notes can easily synchronize different versions of the same document residing on different computers, so it can track revisions to a document when many contributors are working simultaneously. Lotus Notes also has stronger security provisions than the Web. It can limit information access to specific workers and is not easily shut down. (Web sites are more likely to crash or have their servers overloaded with many requests for data.)

Web capabilities for supporting group collaboration are continually improving. At the same time, Notes is being enhanced to link it to the Web. Domino, an Internet version of Notes, allows organizations to build Notes applications that can be accessed by Web browsers as well as by Notes software. Notes can act as a Web server, allowing Notes applications to be accessed by Web browsers, and it can function as a Web browser itself, allowing people to use it to access the World Wide Web. People using computers with Web browsers can create, edit and delete Notes documents.

Neither groupware nor the Internet can be used effectively to support group collaboration unless people are willing to share information. Organizations that encourage competition among employees may encounter resistance if employees do not feel it is in their interest to work cooperatively with their colleagues. Some employees may fear group collaboration tools because their use can make individual performance more visible, including the failure to meet deadlines. Group collaboration systems will be successful if they are compatible with the organization's goals and work practices.

14.3 KNOWLEDGE WORK: PROFESSIONAL WORK SYSTEMS

The information needs of highly skilled knowledge workers and professionals differ from those of data workers such as secretaries or file clerks. To understand the different information problems and requirements of knowledge workers, we need to understand more about knowledge work and the role of such workers in the business world.

FIGURE 14.7

Four Characteristics of Knowledge Work

Knowledge work has four characteristics: it is based on a codified body of information; it can be taught in a school as a collection of principles and procedures; proficiency in knowledge occupations is certified by the state or the school; and knowledge workers are regulated by independent professional associations that set standards for their work.

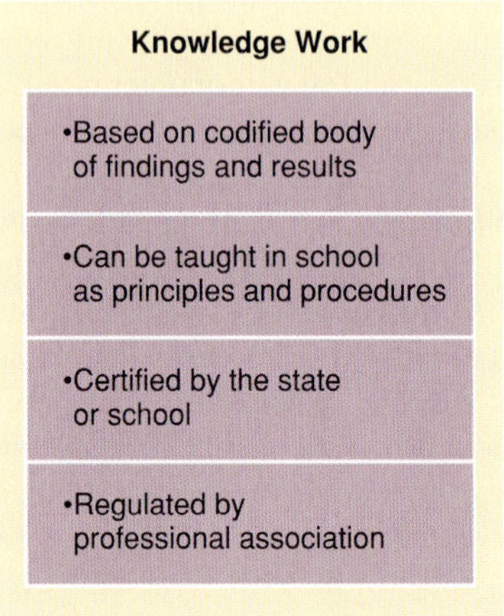

THE CHARACTERISTICS OF KNOWLEDGE WORK

Sociologists and economists who study occupations believe that four characteristics define knowledge work and knowledge workers (see Figure 14.7). This definition is accepted by the Bureau of the Census, the Bureau of Labor Statistics, and professional demographers. First, knowledge work is work that is supported by a body of knowledge, a collection of books, articles, and findings that are widely accepted as valid, can be tested, and are stored somewhere (usually a library). In other words, knowledge is codified.

Second, this body of knowledge must be capable of being taught at major universities rather than merely being passed on as experience. Thus, principles, procedures, and methods must exist independently of pure experience for work to be labeled as knowledge work.

Third, the people who learn the body of knowledge generally must be certified by the state (or university) to prove their mastery. Fourth, the field or profession must be regulated by independent professional bodies that maintain standards of admission and make independent judgments, based on their knowledge, of members' credentials as well as the social uses of their knowledge. At a minimum, these professional bodies maintain a published statement of ethics and educational or professional standards.

What kinds of work meet these qualifications? A list of knowledge workers would certainly include engineers, attorneys, physicians (to at least some extent), architects, biologists, scientists of all kinds, managers (to some extent), and even professors.

THE ROLE OF KNOWLEDGE WORK IN THE ORGANIZATION

It is becoming apparent that knowledge workers' roles in business firms are both unique and becoming more important (see Figure 14.8). Perhaps the most distinctive role of knowledge workers is to interpret the **external knowledge base** (which is always growing) for the organization. From the firm's point of view, a central purpose of hiring knowledge workers is to keep the business abreast of developments in science, technology, the arts, and social thought. Developments in these areas of knowledge often contain business opportunities. Consequently, knowledge workers are expected to refresh their skills and keep up to date so that the corporation may benefit from the latest development in a field. This means that knowledge workers must continually scan the environment and keep up with developments by participating in professional seminars and meetings.

External knowledge base
A knowledge base that is outside the organization, such as libraries of articles, collections of scientific or legal findings, and links to other professionals in universities or other organizations.

Second, knowledge workers are uniquely qualified to play the role of advisers and internal business consultants. Rather than merely writing reports, they are expected to use their expertise to play an active corporate role in advising managers.

Third, knowledge workers are change agents. They are expected to initiate, promote, and evaluate change projects that incorporate developments in science, the arts, and other areas into the corporation.

As this analysis of their roles suggests, knowledge workers are quite different from other information workers such as file clerks or secretaries and

FIGURE 14.8

Three Unique Roles of Knowledge Workers in a Business

One role of knowledge workers is to interpret the always-growing external knowledge base for the organization so that the firm can remain competitive. A second role is to serve as internal consultants and advisers for management. Third, knowledge workers often serve as change agents who develop and facilitate projects that bring new knowledge into the firm.

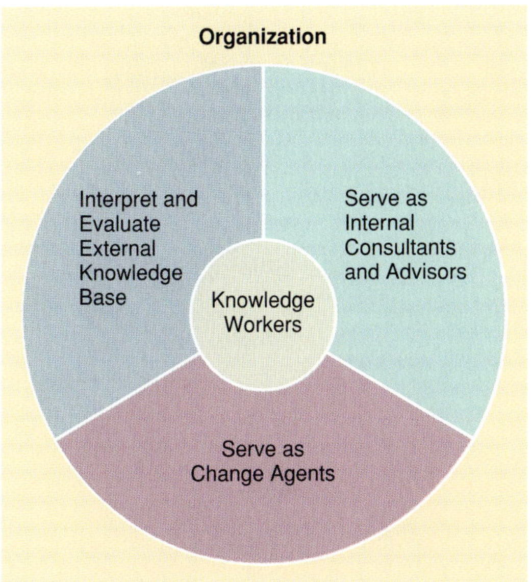

extremely different from lathe operators. Because their position depends on understanding a formal knowledge base, knowledge workers really cannot be told "what to do" and cannot be subject to the same kind of authority relationships that exist elsewhere in the firm. Knowledge workers often know more than the boss. Consequently, they tend to be independent and autonomous.

KNOWLEDGE WORK SYSTEMS

Due to their unique roles and setting in the firm, knowledge workers as a group have very different information requirements from data workers. As a result, a new class of systems has emerged—called knowledge work systems—that uses different hardware and software to serve knowledge workers. These systems must satisfy four requirements, as shown in Figure 14.9.

FIGURE 14.9

Four General Requirements of a Knowledge Work System

Four characteristics distinguish knowledge work systems from the more usual corporate workstations. First, knowledge work systems must provide easy access to an external knowledge base. Second, they must provide software that differs from the usual business software by offering greater capabilities for analysis, graphics, document management, and communications. Third, they need to support "computing-intense" applications that may require unusually large numbers of calculations and data manipulations. Finally, they should have a friendly, easy-to-use interface.

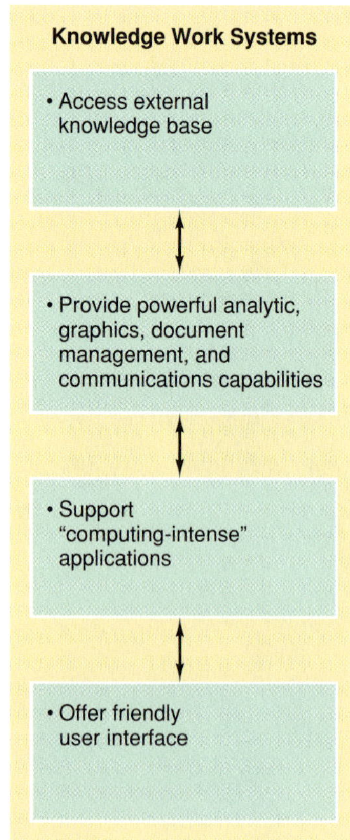

The first requirement is easy access to electronically stored knowledge bases external to the organization. These knowledge bases could be libraries of articles, collections of chemical or legal findings, or electronic mail links to other professionals working in universities or other businesses. Thus, one characteristic of knowledge work systems is that they are more directed toward external data and information than are typical corporate systems.

FOCUS ON TECHNOLOGY

A NEW INTERNET FOR KNOWLEDGE WORKERS

In mid-1995, Michael L. Norman, an astronomy professor at the University of Illinois at Champaign-Urbana, set out with his colleagues to simulate what would happen if our galaxy collided with its nearest neighbor, the Andromeda Galaxy. The work required three supercomputers in three different states linked to one another by high-capacity fiber optic telephone lines.

The scientists could easily transmit their numerical calculations over the Internet. But for their visualization of millions of stars moving through and past one another, all three supercomputers had to interact with one another at the same time. The Internet was clogged with too many users and limited in transmission capacity (it can carry 45 megabits of data per second) for this kind of work.

Fortunately, these scientists were able to use a much more powerful "second-generation" Internet that was created for scientists, engineers, and medical researchers. This new network is called the Very-High-Performance Backbone Network Service, and it will eventually be able to transmit 622 megabits per second, more than ten times the maximum capacity of the Internet. It is sponsored by the U.S. National Science Foundation and was built by MCI Communications using its existing fiber optic networks. U.S. military and energy laboratories will connect to the network with assistance from AT&T and Sprint. The high-performance network links the five academic supercomputer centers in the United States, including the three used for the galaxy collision simulations. At present, the high-performance network is being used only by scientists who work primarily in nonprofit institutions, although it may one day be open to the public.

In addition to being able to transmit more data, the new Internet differs from today's Internet in other ways. Users can be guaranteed links among two or more sites simultaneously, and the new network will be able to integrate video with online computing. For example, Lori Freitag, an assistant scientist at Argonne National Laboratory, will be able to use the network to transmit a visual model of how pollution control equipment will operate inside steam boilers at temperatures of 2,400 degrees Fahrenheit. Officials at Nalco Fuel Technology in Naperville, Illinois, who are funding the project, will be able to visualize how fluid, gas, and heat will react when the equipment is installed at various locations. By visualizing and manipulating the boiler's gas flow, technicians will be able to find the adjustments that will meet the required levels of nitrogen oxide emissions at the lowest cost to clients.

The high-performance network allows a team headed by Professor Oliver McBryan, computer scientist at the University of Colorado in Boulder, to transmit design changes to a model of an aircraft the team is developing. The model can interact over the network with a detailed air-flow model in computers at the National Center for Supercomputer Applications in Champaign-Urbana. Some of Professor McBryan's computations generate a terabyte of data in one run, enough data to fill 1,000 one-gigabyte hard drives on existing computers. At its 622-megabit-per-second transfer rate, the new network will be able to bring the data back in a few hours. It would take weeks for the existing Internet to pass along the data.

FOCUS Question: How does this "new Internet" support the requirements of knowledge workers?

SOURCES: Deborah Shapley, "Now Playing in Limited Release: Internet, the Next Generation," *The New York Times,* January 27, 1997.

Second, knowledge work systems typically require different software from other corporate systems. They need much more powerful analytic, graphics, document management, and communications capabilities than a typical PC can provide (see the Focus on Technology).

Knowledge work often requires much more computing power than typical information work. Some intensive simulations (called virtual reality) require very large and very fast supercomputers (see the "Leading-Edge Technology" description of virtual reality later in this chapter). Engineers may wish to run thousands of calculations before they are satisfied that a specific part is safe. Attorneys may want to scan thousands of legal findings before recommending a strategy. Designers using **computer-aided design (CAD)** systems to design a wide range of products from houses, to automobiles, to hand tools frequently need to use three-dimensional graphics software to fully visualize a model of a product. The computerized design can be easily modified, reducing both design time and expensive engineering changes once the production process begins.

Computer-aided design (CAD) Automation of the creation and revision of designs using sophisticated graphics software.

Finally, knowledge work systems should have a user-friendly interface so that professionals can gain access to knowledge and information without spending a great deal of time learning how to use the computer. A user-friendly interface is somewhat more critical for knowledge workers than for ordinary information workers because knowledge workers are more expensive. Wasting a knowledge worker's time is more costly than wasting a clerical worker's time.

The term *workstation* is typically used to describe the hardware platform on which knowledge work systems operate. As we saw in Chapter 4, workstations differ from simple PCs in both power and applications. PCs are designed to meet the general requirements of diverse groups ranging from

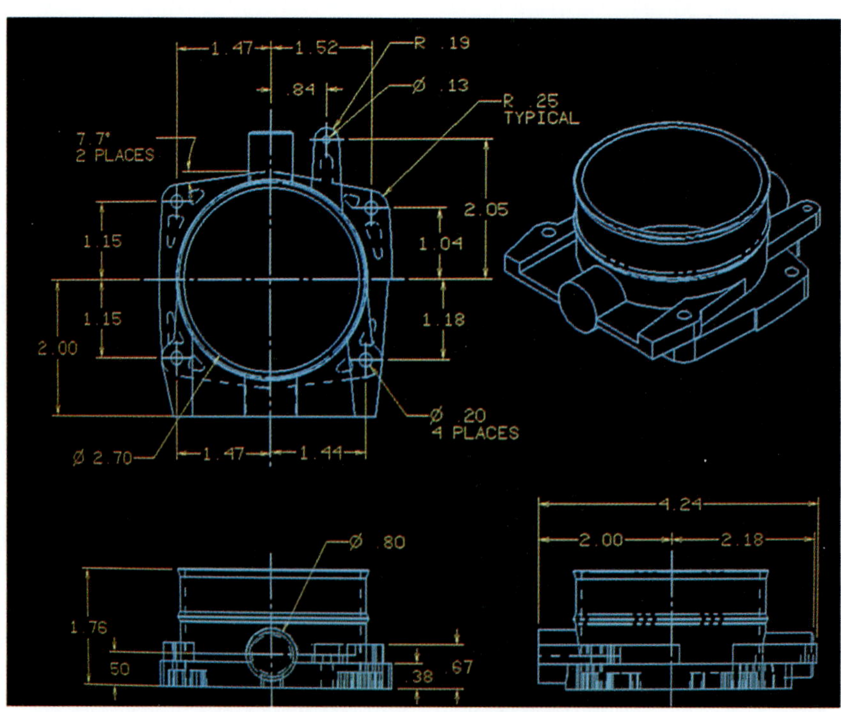

A tool design screen from a computer-aided design/computer-aided manufacturing (CAD/CAM) system. Because such systems provide high levels of design, manufacturing, and testing precision and efficiency, many companies are investing in them.

SOURCE: Courtesy of International Business Machines Corporation.

TABLE 14.3

Examples of Knowledge Workers and the Knowledge Workstations That Help Them Do Their Jobs

Specialized workstations involving unique hardware and software have been developed for many knowledge occupations. Architects can now use CAD (computer-aided design) software to design structures and test areas of stress to improve a structure's safety. Other knowledge workstations help scientists perform molecular modeling or help lawyers eliminate time-consuming legal research.

Architects	**CAD (computer-aided design):** Design building and floor plans
Engineers	**CAD/CAM (computer-aided design/computer-aided manufacturing):** Manage manufacturing operations and control machinery
Judges, Lawyers	**Legal research workstations:** Access legal databases, write legal briefs and opinions
Scientists	**Visualization workstations:** Perform three-dimensional modeling
Reporters	**Text publishing workstations:** Write news stories and translate into newspaper layout
Programmers	**Programmer workbench workstations:** Use CASE tools to produce software programs
Managers (some)	**Management workstations:** Access large databases, provide graphic displays, electronic mail, and word processing

secretaries to financial analysts. In contrast, a professional workstation—whether built for a sales manager or a chemist—must generally be fine-tuned and optimized for a particular occupation. Table 14.3 provides some examples of knowledge work occupations that rely on professional workstations.

The specific technology features of knowledge work systems depend on the profession supported. Designers want machines with powerful graphics displays, whereas lawyers may be more interested in the huge database storage capabilities provided by optical disks. Financial analysts typically desire a 600-megabyte optical disk, refreshed each week, with a complete listing of the financial data for all 4,000 public corporations.

LEADING-EDGE TECHNOLOGY: VIRTUAL REALITY

Virtual reality is a rapidly developing knowledge work technology that has turned fantasy into reality. Imagine that you are an aircraft designer designing a new, large, passenger aircraft. You would need to make certain that all parts of the aircraft would be accessible to the mechanic for maintenance. The mechanic may be 5 feet, 2 inches tall or may be 6 feet, 7 inches tall. In either case, he or she must be able to get the wrench to the correct place and be able to turn it as needed. The only way you can test your design for proper maintenance access is to build a mock-up of the craft, a slow, expensive process that may have to be repeated a number of times. You have designed the aircraft using CAD software. Think of the time and expense that could be saved if you could only enter and test that aircraft while it is still digitized data stored on a computer disk! You would want to be able to change your own height to test access for both a small and a large mechanic. You could reach into a tight spot on your left and then test to see whether both a left-

Virtual reality
Technology that creates computerized simulations that enable users to feel they are participating in "real-world" activities.

and a right-handed mechanic could turn a wrench. You could turn around to see whether you could access an area behind you. All this design testing could occur in an aircraft that doesn't yet exist. This is the fantasy world of virtual reality, and it is the technology being used today by Boeing Corp. to design its new model 777 jet aircraft.

Virtual reality technology allows the user to feel immersed in a computer-created "world" as if that world actually existed. How is this possible? The world—in this case, the aircraft—is first created in the computer. To "enter" that world, the user of virtual reality dons special clothing that contains sensors to record the user's movements and transmit that information to the computer. The user also wears a pair of special goggles that are really two tiny video screens. Audio attachments and "feeling" gloves can be included if such feedback is important to the application. The user will see the "virtual aircraft" in front of him. If he walks forward, the image will move closer. As he reaches out with his arm, he will see the arm reach out into the virtual aircraft. If he turns his head, his view of the aircraft will shift, exactly as it would in real life.

This technology is rather expensive because of the special clothing that is needed. Nonetheless, practical applications are in development. The most obvious application for this technology is related to architecture. The city of Berlin, Germany, is using virtual reality equipment to design a new subway system. Users can "walk" through the stations to critique the structures before they are ever built. Matsushita Electric has brought the fantasy world of virtual reality to the public through its retail department store chain. The department stores sell kitchen cabinets and appliances. To promote its products and make it easy for customers to make a purchase decision, Matsushita has created an application called Virtual Kitchen. Shop-

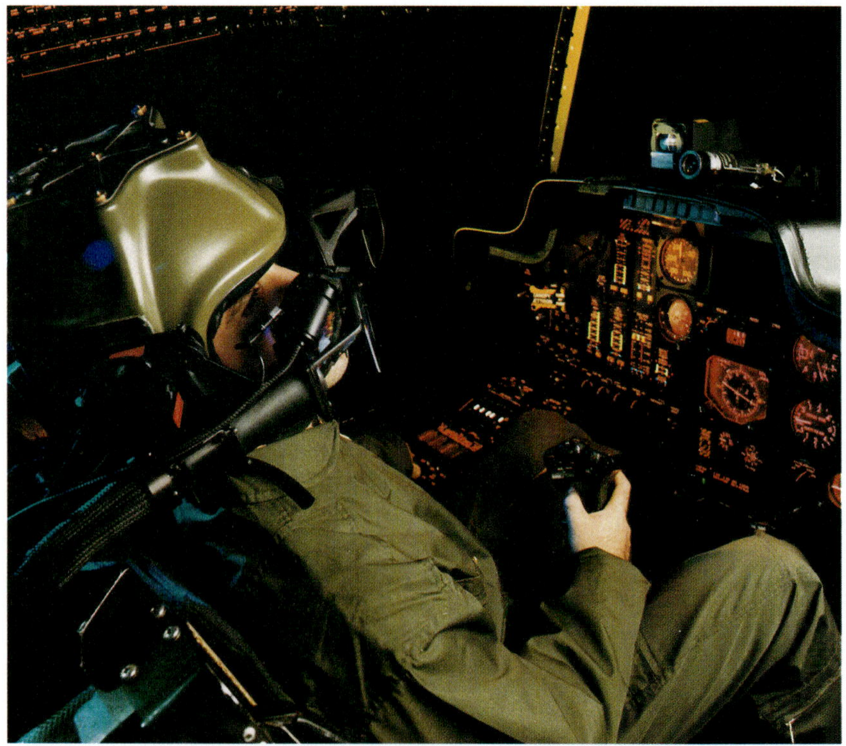

By donning special goggles and headsets and using instruments attached to sensors, pilots-in-training can be presented with computerized images that make them feel they are actually flying an aircraft. Flight simulation, medical training, product design, and interactive entertainment are but some of many applications for virtual reality.

SOURCE: Courtesy of CAE Electronic Ltd., Quebec. C. A. Barbier, Photographe.

pers give the trained staff their kitchen layout, which is entered into the computer. Shoppers also designate the cabinets and appliances to be purchased and their locations in the kitchen. Wearing the necessary special clothing, customers find themselves in their new kitchen. They can walk around (having already designated a location for their kitchen table) to feel the ambiance of their new kitchen. They can open cabinet doors and drawers to test them for proper height, size, and functionality. They can check for the convenience of left- or right-handed door openings. If something is wrong, they can move or substitute a piece of equipment. They can buy with higher-than-usual confidence that all will work properly. The store, in turn, benefits from making many more on-the-spot sales.

Using the high-performance network described in the Focus on Technology, people can walk around inside visualizations of "the CAVE" (Cave Automatic Virtual Environment), a three-dimensional virtual reality stage invented by Thomas A. DeFanti and Daniel J. Sandin at the University of Illinois at Chicago. Two SG Onyx computers might project a model of a complex interrelationship among molecules, such as a protein's effect on an antibody. Users stand inside a 10-square-foot virtual reality theater. With virtual reality headsets, they see a three-dimensional image of whatever is being modeled. They can manipulate the image using electric wands, thereby steering the computer's computations. A computer workstation coordinates integration of the huge quantities of data required to produce the simulations inside "the CAVE."

FMC Corp. set up a version of "the CAVE" at its Santa Clara, California, research center to develop deck structures that can withstand pounding waves when a ship is moved near oil production platforms. Simulated waves are set loose on make-believe vessels to test how well deck-mounted structures can withstand the battering. The simulations will help FMC design deck structures more rapidly and at lower cost. In another project, FMC used its virtual reality lab to test-drive models of aircraft cargo-loading vehicles. The only real-life parts are the driver's seat and accelerator pedal.

The medical world, not surprisingly, is beginning to find practical applications for this imaginative new technology. At General Electric's Research and Development Center in Schenectady, New York, GE scientists are working with a group of surgeons from Boston's Brigham and Women's Hospital to develop a virtual reality system that will allow a surgeon to have at her side a three-dimensional image of the relevant portion of a patient's body that she can consult during surgery. The ultimate goal of the project is to give the surgeon the ability to "walk through" a giant virtual image of the patient, approach the organ to be operated on (such as the liver), and perform the operation on the virtual image rather than on the patient. With such a large image, the surgeon will be able to be very precise in her cuts, preventing any damage to surrounding tissue. The computer would control the actual instruments performing the operation on the patient, duplicating the actions of the surgeon in a real-life, extremely precise operation. While achieving this goal is still far in the future, the project is already able to create three-dimensional images of a patient's brain and project them on the patient's head, allowing a brain surgeon to plan precise surgical pathways through the brain to the location where surgery is needed. The current virtual reality system can also create an image of that brain, rotate it, and peel off layers to expose the parts below, where the surgery is needed.[3]

Now let's review the questions we typically ask of information systems:

- **Where does a knowledge workstation obtain its information?** The systems described in this section obtain a great deal of information (and expertise) from external scientific, engineering, and legal databases, including databases available through the Internet. Some of this information must be internalized, or stored on local disks. Of course, much of the information is generated as a result of local knowledge workers' experiments and writing.
- **What does a knowledge workstation do to the information?** Knowledge workstations process far more information and data than typical transaction or management systems do. Generally, this occurs because knowledge work often requires the application of sophisticated mathematical routines and procedures in order to function. In the case of graphics systems, engineering CAD/CAM systems, and virtual reality applications, the amount of processing speed and power exceeds that of PCs and usually requires specialized workstations. Yet, as PCs become more powerful, they will be capable of performing more and more knowledge work.
- **What problems does a knowledge workstation solve?** How can business organizations interested in making a profit make use of basic science? This is the overall problem that knowledge work systems address. Obviously, businesses must first hire knowledge workers. But then, businesses must support these knowledge workers in order for them to be effective. Since World War II, science and business have moved much closer together. Knowledge work systems can provide a critical link between science and business by speeding up the dissemination of scientific findings to business. This, in turn, can make the realization of business goals (such as product development) more rapid. This is one of many ways in which knowledge work systems can have strategic impact.

SUMMARY

- Advanced economies such as those in the United States, Canada, and most European nations have been transformed from industrial economies, in which most wealth came from the production of goods and most employees worked in factories and assembled goods, to information economies, in which most wealth is derived from information and knowledge production and the majority of workers process and create information. This new type of economy is known as an "information and knowledge economy."
- As the economy becomes more dependent on information and knowledge to produce economic value, our productivity and wealth as a nation depend on the effective use of knowledge work systems.
- Information workers are those whose primary job is to create or process information. There are two kinds of information workers: knowledge workers, whose primary job is to create new information, and data workers, whose primary job is to process, use, or disseminate information.

- Office automation is any application of information technology that is intended to increase the productivity of information workers in the office.
- Offices coordinate work, link diverse groups in the business, and connect the firm to its external environment. Offices and office work are, therefore, central to the success of any modern business.
- The major office activities are document management, scheduling, communications, data management, and project management. Information technology can support all of these activities.
- Word processing and desktop publishing systems support the document management activities of the office. Systems based on local area networks support the communications activities of the office. Electronic calendar and groupware systems support the scheduling activities of the office. Desktop data management systems and customized personal information managers support the data management activities of the office. Project management systems break down complex projects into simpler subtasks, producing delivery schedules, allocating resources, and supporting the project management activities of the office. Imaging systems can help streamline organizational work flow.
- Group collaboration work can be supported by groupware software as well as by the Internet.
- Knowledge work systems are applications of information technology expressly designed to enhance the productivity of knowledge workers.
- Knowledge work is distinguished from other work by its reliance on a body of knowledge, its place in a university curriculum, its certification by the state, and the presence of professional societies with regulatory power. Knowledge worker roles include interpreting the body of knowledge to business managers and leaders, acting as internal consultants, and playing the role of change agents.
- Knowledge work systems require access to an external knowledge base, more powerful hardware, software, and communications capabilities than office systems, and a friendly user interface. Computer-aided design systems and virtual reality systems require powerful graphics and modeling capabilities.

KEY TERMS

Information work
Information and knowledge economy
Knowledge- and information-intense products
Knowledge work
Data work
Office automation
Office roles
Office activities
Document management technology
Word processing
Desktop publishing
Office scheduling technology
Groupware
Office data management technology
Project management technology
Imaging
External knowledge base
Computer-aided design (CAD)
Virtual reality

REVIEW QUESTIONS

1. What does the phrase "transformation of the economy toward an information economy" mean? When did this transformation begin?
2. What are knowledge- and information-intense products? Give some examples.
3. What is the difference between data work and knowledge work? Give some examples.
4. How is information work related to the productivity of a business?
5. Define office automation. How has office automation technology changed over time?
6. What are the three roles of offices in modern organizations?
7. What are the five major activities that occur in all offices? Give an example of how information technology supports each activity.
8. Describe the importance of imaging systems in organizations today.
9. What is groupware, and how does it differ from traditional office technology? How can the Internet support group collaboration activities?
10. What are the four distinguishing features of knowledge workers?
11. What role do knowledge workers play in an organization?
12. What are the generic elements of a knowledge work system?
13. Define and describe CAD and virtual reality.

DISCUSSION QUESTIONS

1. Some people argue that our country cannot survive as an information economy, that we need to produce manufactured goods as well, and that we should invest more money in factories and less money in offices. Divide into two groups, and debate this issue.

2. Why are knowledge work systems playing an increasingly important role in organizations? Do you expect that this trend will continue, or will it reach a plateau?

PROBLEM-SOLVING EXERCISES

1. *Group exercise:* Divide into groups. Each group should locate a small business firm in your neighborhood and write a short report that analyzes how the firm currently deals with office correspondence and publications—letters to customers, suppliers, sales force (if any), and the general public. Your group should identify where documents originate, how they are processed, and what communications technologies are used. Be sure to identify the people, hardware, and software separately. The report should trace the flow of example documents (e.g., letters to suppliers). The last page of the report should be a list of recommended improvements. Each group should present its findings to the class.

2. University students are knowledge workers in training. As such, they have unique workstation requirements. Write a description of what you think would be an ideal "student workstation."

3. *Hands-on exercise:* Consulting companies such as Price-Waterhouse need information systems that will allow them to easily access knowledge about the skills, background, and experience of highly trained employees. Choose appropriate software and develop a simple application that could be used by a firm such as Price-Waterhouse to maintain information about the experts on its staff. The information to be maintained by the system might include the employee's name, area(s) of expertise, work location, age, telephone number, and research interests.

4. *Internet problem-solving exercise:* You are in the research department for a company interested in expanding its line of sporting goods to include items made of carbon fiber. You would like to learn more about the properties of carbon fiber and find out what products made of carbon fiber are currently available. Use Internet search tools and online libraries to find this information. What did you learn?

NOTES

1. The phrases "knowledge-intensive organization" and "information-intensive organization" originated with Professor William Starbuck, Department of Management, Stern School of Business, New York University. The authors are indebted to him for several stimulating conversations about the issue. Doubtless, over the next years, a great deal of attention will be paid to the various kinds of knowledge and information organizations, their peculiar work forces, and unique management problems.
2. Lynda Radosevich, "Internet Plumbing Comes to Groupware," *Datamation,* May 15, 1996, and David Kirkpatrick, "Groupware Goes Boom," *Fortune,* December 27, 1993.
3. Deborah Shapley, "Now Playing in Limited Release: Internet, the Next Generation," *The New York Times,* January 27, 1997, and Gene Bylinsky, "To Create Products, Go into a CAVE," *Fortune,* February 5, 1996.

PROBLEM-SOLVING CASE

ROCKWELL'S RACE FOR THE SPACE SHUTTLE

As U.S. defense spending has been cut, aerospace companies have faced tougher competition in securing contracts for government work. Rockwell International Corporation, a major supplier for the National Aeronautics and Space Administration (NASA), was one of them. In the late 1980s the company lost a number of major contracts because of cost issues.

Rockwell's Space Systems Division had a $1.3 billion contract for NASA's space shuttle project. The shuttle has many thousands of parts, each of which requires engineering, manufacturing, assembly, and maintenance drawings. Often these drawings had to be modified through change orders, adding even more paper to the process. For this project alone, Rockwell had to deal with over 1 million drawings—a filing and maintenance nightmare.

It might take several days simply to locate and pull one document from piles of paperwork in a warehouse and deliver it to an engineer to review. Searching for many documents typically added weeks to the shuttle launch cycle, and it costs $1 million per day to keep the shuttle on the launching pad.

Almost everything was designed on paper and stored in print cribs at the Rockwell engineering department in Downey, California, the Johnson Space Center in Houston, and the Kennedy Space Center in Cape Canaveral, Florida. Due to the several-day wait to obtain a document from storage, design groups and manufacturing plants kept "shadow cribs"—private libraries of drawings that did not always contain the most recent changes. If a worker on the assembly line had a question about a component's design, he or she could either try to find something in the "shadow crib" or delay production until the correct drawing arrived by mail from the official print crib. This situation created a potential safety hazard as well as production delays.

The information management group in Rockwell's Space Systems Division (SSD) spent a year looking for ways to eliminate redundant and labor-intensive manual work from its production processes, especially in the way it created, used, and maintained the paperwork for its projects. It developed a document storage and retrieval system (DSRS) for electronically storing drawings and documents. All space shuttle project documents and drawings are now digitized and stored in Sun Microsystems file servers at all three sites—Downey, Kennedy Space Center, and Johnson Space Center. The documents are stored on an NKK Electronics optical jukebox (a device for storing and retrieving many optical disks), while a Sun SPARCserver 690 workstation manages the storage program. Several scanners are used to digitize paper documents and drawings for the system. Custom-written software handles drawing updates to the optical and database systems and synchronizes intersite updates. The application also uses an Oracle database and database management system.

The system went live in 1991, but, according to K. S. Radhakrishnan, director of SSD's information management division, the next few years "were an absolute nightmare." The development team seriously underestimated the volume of traffic on the network. The optical jukebox was not designed for the amount of storage it had to handle. Faced with mounting complaints, the team tried to make the system more modularized and flexible so that it would accept changes from users more easily. During the redesign in 1993 and 1994, the development team used prototyping to ensure that the system met users' needs, making user access to the system much simpler. Users can access the system from PCs or any platform running Windows, X Windows (a terminal emulation system), or a Web browser. If an engineer working on a PC makes an annotation to a drawing, a colleague working on a Sun workstation can see it. Any system user can obtain a drawing as soon as it is officially put into the system.

Rockwell's Space Systems Division saved about $1.3 million by closing its print cribs and eliminating the staff required to service them. The division estimates that it is saving $3.00 for every dollar spent on DSRS. One reason Rockwell was able to make modifications to the shuttle orbiter ahead of schedule and below estimated costs was because technicians could retrieve information about wiring, assembly sequences, and so forth by pulling up the drawings on PCs on the factory floor. The new system reduced the shuttle launch schedule from 6–8 weeks to 4–6 weeks, saving

NASA millions of dollars as well. Other NASA suppliers have asked to have their drawings put on DSRS. Rockwell has even expanded the system so that it can be used to retrieve financial reports from its Web server.

SOURCE: Carol Hildebrand, "Power Launch," *CIO*, February 1, 1996.

CASE STUDY QUESTIONS

1. What problems was Rockwell experiencing? What people, management, and technology factors were causing these problems?

2. What solution did Rockwell devise? What problems did it solve? What problems can't it solve? Was it an easy solution to implement?

3. Is the Internet an appropriate technology for Rockwell's situation? Why or why not?

Chapter

→ FIFTEEN ←

ARTIFICIAL INTELLIGENCE

CHAPTER OUTLINE

LEARNING OBJECTIVES

After reading and studying this chapter, you will

1. Know what artificial intelligence is and how it has evolved.
2. Be familiar with the many varieties of artificial intelligence.
3. Be able to define and describe expert systems.
4. Know what neural networks are and how they operate.
5. Understand what is meant by "intelligent" techniques such as fuzzy logic and genetic algorithms.
6. Know how and why organizations use artificial intelligence techniques.

NEURAL NETS SCAN FOR CREDIT CARD FRAUD

When you swipe your credit card through a card reader in a store, there is a strong chance that your action is being scrutinized by a computer to see whether you're making a valid purchase. Credit card companies such as MasterCard and Visa have installed neural network systems to counteract the rising tide of credit card fraud. The total combined losses from fraudulently used and counterfeit credit cards amounted to $1.3 billion in 1995 alone.

Here's how these neural net credit card fraud detection systems work. Suppose Jane Doe routinely uses her MasterCard only twice a month, once at a restaurant and once at a local department store. Suddenly she—or someone who has access to her card or card number—runs up four or five purchases in a day. The next time Doe's card is presented to a shopkeeper or used for a telephone order, the system matches the current buying patterns against Jane's charging history. The neural network was trained to detect patterns of activity in massive pools of data that a human being can't detect. By analyzing the type of transaction, amount spent, time of day, and other data, the neural network can make a fraud prediction in 45 seconds. It would either return a flat denial of credit or send the predictive score to a human analyst who would make the final decision on whether to request more identification.

Neural network systems saved the member companies of MasterCard more than $50 million in 18 months. MasterCard is now working with researchers at Los Alamos National Laboratory to use neural networks along with other artificial intelligence technologies such as fuzzy logic and genetic algorithms to create even more sophisticated fraud-fighting systems. Existing fraud detection systems deal with data the card issuer has about the customer, whereas these new systems will analyze credit card buying patterns at the merchant level, examining the potential for scams at particular stores.

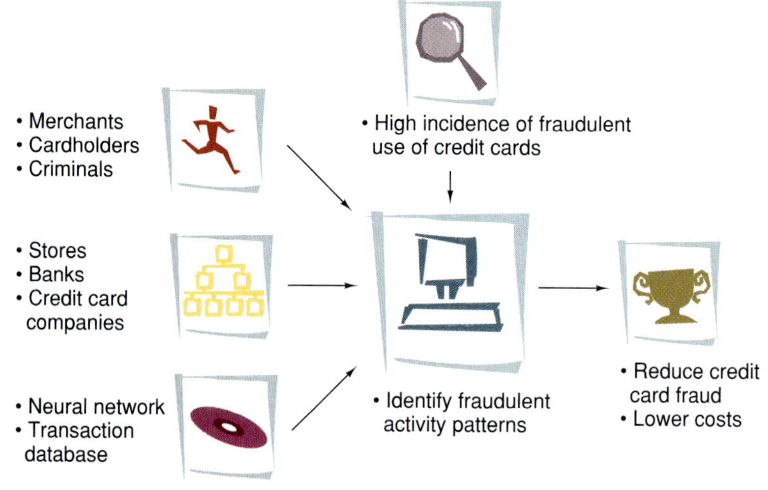

SOURCES: E. B. Baatz, "Making Brain Waves," *CIO,* January 15, 1996, and Otis Port, "Computers that Think Are Almost Here," *Business Week,* July 17, 1995.

The experience of credit card companies using fraud detection systems illustrates how powerful information systems can be if they display some intelligence. In many areas of business, science, and everyday life, from banks and credit card companies to medical laboratories and machine manufacturers, new kinds of information systems based on artificial intelligence technology are used to guide human experts, diagnose problems, and help managers make decisions. This chapter explains how expert systems, neural networks, and other artificial intelligence systems work and the kinds of problems they are now capable of solving.

15.1 INTRODUCTION

Imagine that someday you could go to a desktop computer in your room and in simple English speak into a microphone attached to the computer: "Summarize the major points of all articles dealing with artificial intelligence in computer magazines published since 1990. Then print the summaries on my printer and give me an oral report of no longer than 5 minutes." What would your desktop computer need in terms of hardware and software to be able to handle your request? Here are some requirements:

- Your desktop machine would have to understand and speak English.
- Your desktop machine would have to be linked to a main library collection of magazines or have access to a very large optical disk on your desktop.
- Your machine would have to know something about how to conduct research in order to summarize articles; that is, your software would need some real expertise.
- Your software would have to read and "understand" natural English-language statements found in articles and newspapers.

No machine or software yet in existence has these capabilities, but information scientists are working on building such machines and some with other capabilities as well. The Focus on People describes some of the progress that has been made with making computers closer to humans in the capacity to exhibit creative thinking.

THE NATURE OF ARTIFICIAL INTELLIGENCE

Put simply, **artificial intelligence (AI)** is the study and creation of machines that exhibit humanlike qualities, including the ability to reason. Even the seventeenth-century scientists and engineers who built the first calculators and mechanical robots that could play musical instruments may have dreamed of this goal, but none of these early machines had quite so ambitious a program as contemporary efforts in artificial intelligence. Experts in artificial intelligence believe that one day, computers will be able to learn natural languages such as English, perceive objects in the same way as humans do, and exhibit all the qualities that we think of as human reason—the ability to think, make judgments, arrive at conclusions, and make comparisons. These systems will not look like robots or R2-D2 in the film *Star Wars*. Instead, these systems will reside inside desktop computers, similar to the ones we now call personal computers. Artificial intelligence is also the stuff of military dreams in which AI machines fight future wars largely independent of human intervention.

Artificial intelligence
The study and creation of machines that exhibit humanlike qualities, including the ability to reason.

How would we know whether a machine possessed these qualities of intelligence? How could we tell that we had built a machine capable of conducting an autonomous war? One test was proposed by the British computer scientist Alan Turing in 1948. In the so-called **Turing test,** a human and a computer are placed in separate rooms connected by a communications link; if the person cannot tell whether he or she is talking to a machine or to another human, then the machine is intelligent.

Turing test
A test devised by Alan Turing to determine whether a machine is intelligent. A computer and a human are placed in separate rooms connected by a communications link; if the human is not aware that he or she is communicating with a machine, then the machine is intelligent.

So far, no machines have passed Turing's test, although the Focus on People describes how computers are coming closer. While computers are still a long way from behaving like humans, what has been accomplished is quite remarkable.

FOCUS ON PEOPLE

THE PROOF IS IN THE PROCESSOR

Scientists working with artificial intelligence have struggled for years trying to teach computers how to think like humans. For the most part, they have achieved success only when programming a computer to solve a specific problem, such as chess playing. Now, thanks to the work of Dr. William McCune of Argonne National Laboratory in Illinois, artificial intelligence has moved closer to effectively mimicking the human thought process. The field that opened the door for these strides to be made was that of mathematical proofs. Scientists have used computer programs to prove mathematical assumptions previously, but not in this fashion. The higher degree of human thinking that a computer can now mimic is the ability to reason.

The first step toward this accomplishment actually occurred about 60 years ago. Dr. Herbert Robbins, a professor of mathematics at Rutgers University, created an algebraic problem that he could not prove. He passed the problem along to many colleagues and students over the years. One of the many academics into whose lap it fell was Dr. Larry Wos, supervisor of the computer reasoning project at Argonne. Dr. Wos had been experimenting with automated reasoning since the 1960s, and when he learned of the Robbins problem in 1979, he introduced it to his staff of computer scientists. They would attempt to use their expertise to solve the same puzzle that mathematicians were addressing.

Dr. Wos's approach to automated reasoning differed from the general approach in that he did not wish to determine how humans reasoned and then program a computer to imitate the process. He based this approach on his belief that not even mathematicians themselves can describe how they go about proving a theorem. So, Dr. Wos and the other scientists at Argonne set about the task of describing a problem to a computer and then getting it to make logical conclusions about the problem when hypotheses were introduced. For a lengthy initial period, Argonne tested its programs with mathematical problems for which proofs had already been established. That way, if the computer failed to produce a proof, the testers knew their program contained an error.

After years of working with problems to which it already possessed the answers, the Argonne group finally tried a fresh problem in 1978. To the delight of Dr. Wos, they solved it using a computer. Not satisfied by conquering what he referred to as "a little baby problem," Dr. Wos and his colleagues continued to develop their programs by increasing the number of strategies the computer could employ in trying to prove a postulate. They discovered Dr. Robbins's problem in 1979 but could never crack it.

Dr. McCune arrived at Argonne in 1984 and found the challenge of the Robbins problem very inviting. Using his own automated reasoning program specifically designed to prove equations, McCune finally produced a proof in October 1996. After bettering the proof and having it checked by several experts, the proof was to be published in the *Journal of Automated Reasoning.* After 60 years, Dr. Robbins saw his problem solved by the creative reasoning of a computer.

According to Dr. Wos, mathematical research may have entered a new era in which mathematicians can concentrate solely on searching for new theorems while leaving the proofs to computers. Dr. Wos, however, does not want to confine the potential of automated reasoning to mathematics. He envisions a day when computers will thrive on their ability to reason creatively the way they currently do on their ability to calculate.

FOCUS Questions:

What do you think the computer is capable of doing in terms of thinking like humans? What is it not capable of doing well? What capabilities is a computer missing that would be needed in order for it to reason more like humans?

SOURCE: Gina Kolata, "With Major Math Proof, Brute Computers Show Flash of Reasoning Power," *The New York Times,* December 10, 1996.

FIGURE 15.1

Artificial Intelligence (AI) Involves Many Fields of Study

Artificial intelligence is not one discipline; it is many. Shown here are the major initiatives that AI currently includes: natural language, robotics, perceptive systems, expert systems, neural networks, and intelligent software. What do all these activities have in common? In brief, they are attempting to emulate human abilities.

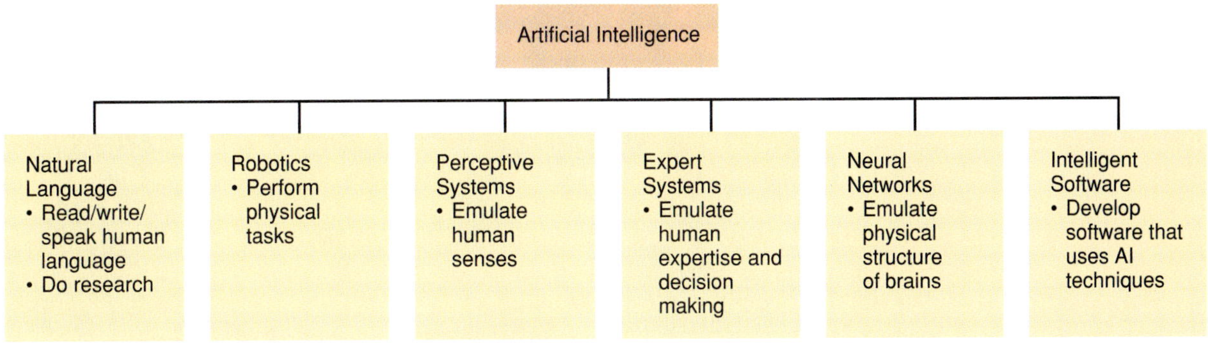

THE FAMILY OF ARTIFICIAL INTELLIGENCE TECHNIQUES

Artificial intelligence is not a single phenomenon but a family of sometimes related activities, each of which seeks to capture some aspect of human intelligence and being (see Figure 15.1). Computer scientists, electronic engineers, psychologists, linguists, physiologists, and biologists are all involved in that search, which leads them into research on natural language, robotics, perceptive systems, expert systems, neural networks, and intelligent software.

Natural Language **Natural language** focuses on computer speech recognition and speech generation. The basic goal is to build computer hardware and software that can recognize human speech and "read" text and that can speak and write as well. A related goal is to build software that can perform research requested by humans. The major impetus for this research began in the 1950s when the military attempted to develop computers that could automatically translate Soviet texts and speech for national security purposes. These early efforts largely failed: Machines have a very difficult time understanding idiomatic expressions or translating sentences such as "Jane took a swing at the ball." A computer would not know whether "swing" refers to a movement or an object and might produce a translation in which Jane used something like a porch swing. Nor would the computer know that "bat" is implicit in the sentence, even though just about every child knows that you swing at a ball with a bat.

Natural language
Languages, including idioms, that are used by humans (e.g., English, Swahili, French).

Robotics The goal of **robotics** research is to develop physical systems that can perform work normally done by humans, especially in hazardous or lethal environments. The origins of robotics lie in seventeenth-century clockworks, in which human forms mimicked human actions. Modern robotics is more concerned with the development of numerically controlled machine tools and industrial fabrication machines that are driven by CAM (computer-aided manufacturing) systems.

Robotics
The study of physical systems that can perform work normally done by humans, especially in hazardous or lethal environments.

Automobile manfacturers such as the Ford Motor Company use industrial robots in their automobile assembly lines. The robots perform tasks that are difficult or hazardous for humans, such as lifting and positioning heavy parts.

SOURCE: Courtesy of Ford Motor Company.

Perceptive Systems Like humans, robots need eyes and ears in order to orient their behavior. And humans who look for patterns in huge data streams need extensions of their own senses (see the visualization techniques described in Chapter 14). Since World War II, computer scientists and engineers have worked to develop **perceptive systems,** or sensing devices that can see and hear in the sense of recognizing patterns. This field of research, which is sometimes called "pattern recognition," has focused largely on military applications such as photo reconnaissance, submarine echo sounding, radar scanning, and missile control and navigation. Progress has been uneven because of problems teaching computers the differences between decoys and the real thing.

Perceptive systems
Sensing devices used in robots that can recognize patterns in streams of data.

Expert Systems **Expert systems** are relatively recent software applications that seek to capture expertise in limited domains of knowledge and experience and apply this expertise to solving problems. Media attention has perhaps focused more on expert systems than on any other member of the AI family. In part, this is because such systems can assist the decision making of managers and professionals when expertise is expensive or in short supply. These systems are described at greater length in Section 15.2.

Expert system
A software application that seeks to capture expertise in limited domains of knowledge and experience and to apply this expertise to solving problems.

Neural Networks People have always dreamed of building a computer that thinks, a "brain" modeled in some sense on the human brain. **Neural networks** are usually physical devices (although they can be simulated with software) that electronically emulate the physiology of animal or human brains. We describe in detail how these systems work in Section 15.3.

Neural network
Hardware or software that emulates the physiology of animal or human brains.

Intelligent Software Many products now on the market claim to use AI techniques or to be "intelligent." Later sections of this chapter describe some of these developments, including fuzzy logic for representing thought processes with some degree of ambiguity; genetic algorithms, which use genetic processes as models for solutions; and intelligent agents, which can perform specific tasks for individuals.

THE DEVELOPMENT OF ARTIFICIAL INTELLIGENCE

Research into artificial intelligence has actually been conducted in two directions, each of which has its own story.[1] One involves the history of efforts to develop **intelligent machines** that mimic what people at the time think is the way an animal or human brain works. This is called the **bottom-up approach;** it is essentially the effort to build a physical analog to the human brain. The second story involves the **top-down approach,** the effort to develop a logical analog to the way the brain works.

The effort to develop intelligent machines is hardly new. In fact, Charles Babbage, who invented a mechanical calculator in 1834, called his proposed calculating machine an "analytical engine," or thinking machine, and believed it would be able to play chess at some point. This was perhaps the first top-down intelligent device. Figure 15.2 illustrates major developments in the top-down and bottom-up methods over the past 50 years.

Intelligent machine
A physical device or computer that mimics the way people think.

Bottom-up approach
An approach to intelligent machines that concentrates on trying to build a physical analog to the human brain.

Top-down approach
An approach to intelligent machines that concentrates on trying to develop a logical analog to the human brain.

FIGURE 15.2

A Brief History of the Top-Down and Bottom-Up Approaches to AI

Since World War II there have been two main thrusts in AI research. The top-down approach seeks to develop a logical model of human intelligence and the workings of the human brain. The bottom-up school tries to build a physical analog to the human brain and thus reproduce human thought patterns. Both techniques have played an important role in current AI research.

(a) Top-Down Approach (Logic Analog)

Simon and Newell's
Logic Theorist

General Problem Solver

Pattern Recognition Software

Chess Playing Systems
Natural Language Software

Expert Systems

AI Shells
Parallel Processors

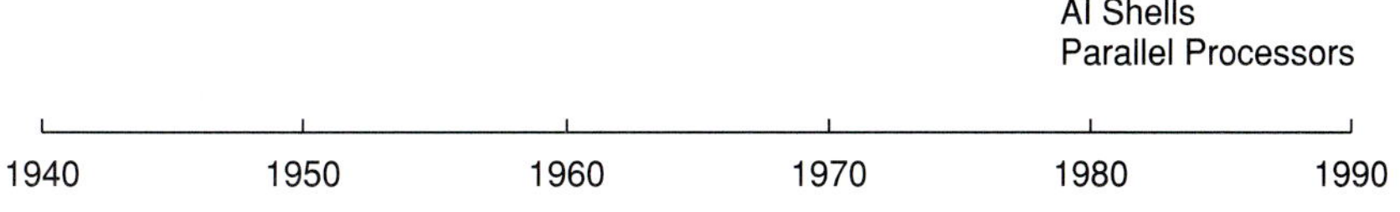

(b) Bottom-Up Approach (Physical Analog)

Image Recognition
Neural Network Simulation

Neural Chips

Word Recognition
Process Monitor

Neural Concepts
Discredited

Rosenblatt's
Perceptron

McCulloch and Pitt's
Neural Brain Theories

Wiener's "Feedback"
Machines

Feedback
The return to a machine of part of the machine's output; the machine then uses the input information to improve its performance.

Contemporary AI research can be traced to World War II and the concept of **feedback.** In feedback, part of a machine's output is returned to it as input, and the machine then uses the input information to improve its performance. Norbert Wiener, a scientist and mathematician at the Massachusetts Institute of Technology (MIT) in the 1940s, developed a method of radar control of antiaircraft guns for the U.S. Army in which the expected location of an aircraft was calculated based on new information—feedback—from radar. Wiener went on to propose in several books that feedback could explain how humans think and suggested that the principle could be applied to make machines think like humans.

Thus began the physiological, or bottom-up, approach to artificial intelligence. Warren McCulloch, a biologist interested in brain function, and Walter Pitts, a mathematician, used Wiener's idea of feedback to develop a theory of how the brain works. In this theory, a brain was composed of millions of neuron cells that both processed binary numbers (they were either "on" or "off") and were connected into a network that took in feedback or information from the environment. Learning was simply a matter of teaching the neurons in a brain how to respond to the environment.

Perceptron
A machine devised by Frank Rosenblatt that could perceive letters or shapes and could be taught, or corrected, when it made mistakes; an example of the bottom-up approach to artificial intelligence.

These ideas were taken further by Frank Rosenblatt, a Cornell psychologist and scientist, who in 1960 demonstrated a machine he called a **Perceptron.** This machine was composed of 400 photoelectric cells that could perceive letters or shapes and 512 neuronlike relays that conveyed information from the photoelectric cells to response units. The machine could recognize letters (as long as they were all of the same size and type) and could be taught: Operators would increase or decrease voltages in certain areas of the machine when mistakes were made. Interest in the bottom-up approach lagged for years, until the 1980s. The resurgence of interest in neural networks is discussed in Section 15.3.

Although machines like the Perceptron received considerable media attention, the theorists of the logical, top-down school of AI were also hard at work. This school has developed through three stages. In its earliest stage, the goal was to develop a general model of human intelligence. This was followed by a period in which the extraordinary power of third-generation computers—the machines of the 1960s—was applied to more limited problems, such as playing chess, or specialized areas, such as machine tool control. Finally, beginning in the 1970s, expert systems emerged in which the goals were scaled down to understanding knowledge in specific and highly limited areas.

Logic Theorist
Software developed by Herbert Simon and Alan Newell that mimicked deductive logic; that is, it selected correct rules and postulates to create a coherent logical chain from premises to conclusion.

In 1956 at the Dartmouth Summer Research Project on Artificial Intelligence, Herbert Simon (a Carnegie Mellon psychologist and scientist) and Alan Newell (a Rand Corp. scientist) announced they had developed a thinking machine, which they called a **Logic Theorist.** Its software could prove certain mathematical theorems found in the famous mathematical treatise *Principia Mathematica* by Alfred North Whitehead and Bertrand Russell. The software mimicked deductive logic; that is, it selected the correct rules and postulates to create a coherent logical chain from premises to conclusion.

Unfortunately, the Logic Theorist could not easily be adapted to other areas of life where deductive reasoning was used. The problem of following chains of "if a, then b" statements is that hundreds of thousands, or millions, of such rules are required for solving even simple real-world problems. In response to the difficulties of applying the Logic Theorist to real-world problems, Simon and Newell attempted in the late 1950s to discover the general principles of human problem solving. If a few principles could be found, then perhaps a few simple rules of thumb could be used to avoid a **combinatorial explosion,** the problem that arises when a computer must test more rules to solve a problem than it has the capacity to examine. Regrettably, no general or simple principles of human problem solving were discovered. The search for a general problem solver ended.

Combinatorial explosion
The difficulty that arises when a problem requires a computer to test a very large number of rules to reach a solution; even a very fast computer cannot search through all the possibilities in a reasonable amount of time.

In the 1960s advances in hardware offered some hope of coping with the combinatorial explosion. The newly developed third-generation computers—the first computers to use integrated circuits—made it possible to consider thousands of computations per second. Attention turned to pure "power" approaches: using the new machines to test out millions of rules, one at a time. But even a simple game such as chess contains 10^{120} possible moves, so ways had to be found to pare down the search tree to avoid a combinatorial explosion. An exhaustive search through all possibilities on a chess board would have quickly swamped all the computers known to exist in the 1960s. On the other hand, in restricted domains—such as chess—and with sufficient processing power, a number of problem-solving rules or strategies that are specific to the domain can be pursued and processed with some success, as evidenced by the defeat of world chess champion Garry Casparov by IBM's Deep Blue computer in the spring of 1997.

One result of these developments was the first expert system—a system of rules limited to a very specific domain of human expertise (such as chess). Unfortunately, the rules and strategies developed to play chess are not really applicable to any other area of life. Expert systems, which use heuristic, or rule-guided, searches, have helped solve some of these difficulties.

15.2 EXPERT SYSTEMS

Expert systems represent the latest evolution of top-down artificial intelligence thinking, in which the computer is used to assist or even replace human decision makers. Unlike robotics or perceptive systems, expert systems have a very wide potential application to many areas of human endeavor in which expertise is important.

THE NATURE OF EXPERT SYSTEMS

As we noted earlier, expert systems can be defined as systems that model human knowledge in limited areas or domains. Such systems are intended to solve problems as well as or better than human decision makers, to apply human knowledge to well-understood problems, and to be able to account for how they arrive at decisions. At the same time, it is important to recognize the limitations of expert systems: They do not draw analogies, they cannot reason from first principles (i.e., they have no understanding of the larger world beyond their expertise), and they are hard to teach. Briefly, expert systems lack common sense and for this reason may not be useful in some areas of business, such as general management, that require an open-ended search for solutions.

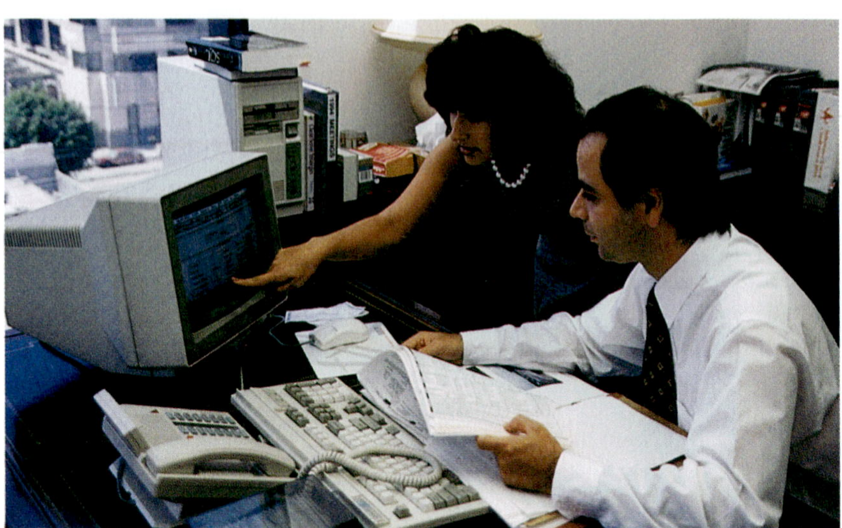

CLUES (Countrywide's Loan Underwriting Expert System) is a PC-based expert system designed to make preliminary decisions about the creditworthiness of loan applicants. The system contains about 400 rules that were provided by loan underwriters. The final decision for granting a loan is made by an underwriter, but CLUES can assist underwriters with their evaluations.

SOURCE: Courtesy of Countrywide Home Mortgage Loans.

THE COMPONENTS OF AN EXPERT SYSTEM

An expert system contains four major components: the knowledge domain, or base, in which one is building the system; the development team, which tries to capture relevant portions of the knowledge base; the shell, or programming environment, in which the system is programmed; and the user, who must interact with the system to guide it. Figure 15.3 illustrates these components.

The Knowledge Base What is human knowledge? Artificial intelligence developers sidestep this thorny issue by asking a slightly different question: How can human knowledge be modeled or represented so that a computer can deal with it? One way to represent human knowledge and expertise is with rules. These constitute the **knowledge base** in an expert system.

Knowledge base
A model of human knowledge used by artificial intelligence systems.

A standard programming construct (see Chapter 10) is the IF-THEN construct, in which a condition is evaluated and, if it is true, an action is taken. For instance:

IF

INCOME › $50,000 **(condition)**

PRINT NAME AND ADDRESS **(action)**

A series of these rules can be used to represent a knowledge base. Indeed, as you can easily see, virtually all traditional computer programs contain IF-THEN statements, and one can argue that these programs are intelligent. What, then, is the difference between an expert system and a traditional program?

AI programs can easily have 200 to 3,000 rules, far more than traditional programs, which may have 50 to 100 IF-THEN statements. Moreover, as Figure 15.4 indicates, in an AI program, the rules tend to be interconnected and nested to a far greater degree than in traditional programs.

FIGURE 15.3

The Four Basic Elements in an Expert System

Four major components combine to create an expert system. First, there is the knowledge base, the area of expertise for which the system is being built. Second, a development team composed of experts and knowledge engineers works to discover and develop the rules of thumb used by experts into a programmable and coherent whole. The third element consists of the development environment, which can either be a special-purpose AI language such as Lisp or PROLOG or a more user-friendly expert system shell. The final element is the user, who must guide the system with instructions, data input, and questions.

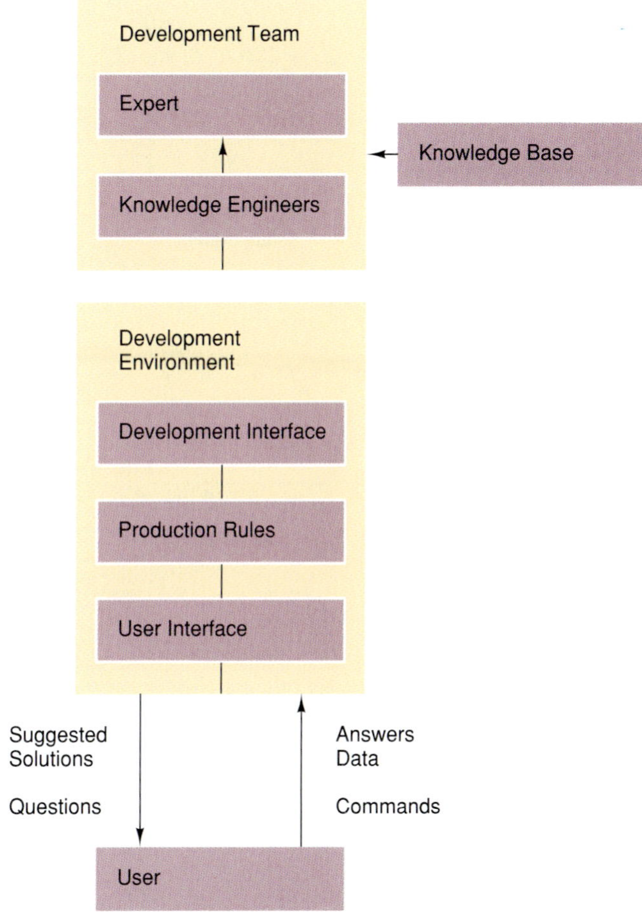

The order in which rules are searched depends in part on the information the system is given. There are multiple paths to the same result. If the system is given "F" in Figure 15.4, then "H" will be performed, and if the system is given "A", "H" will also be performed. The system is also nonsequential: If "H" occurs when rule #5 fires, then #3 will be fired on a second pass through the rule base.

Could you represent the knowledge in the *Encyclopaedia Britannica* this way? Probably not, because the rule base would be too large, and not all the knowledge in the encyclopedia can be represented in the form of

FIGURE 15.4

Production Rules in an Expert System

A simple credit-granting expert system contains a number of rules to be followed when interviewing applicants on the telephone. The rules themselves are interconnected, the number of outcomes is known in advance and is limited, there are multiple paths to the same outcome, and the system can consider multiple rules at the same time.

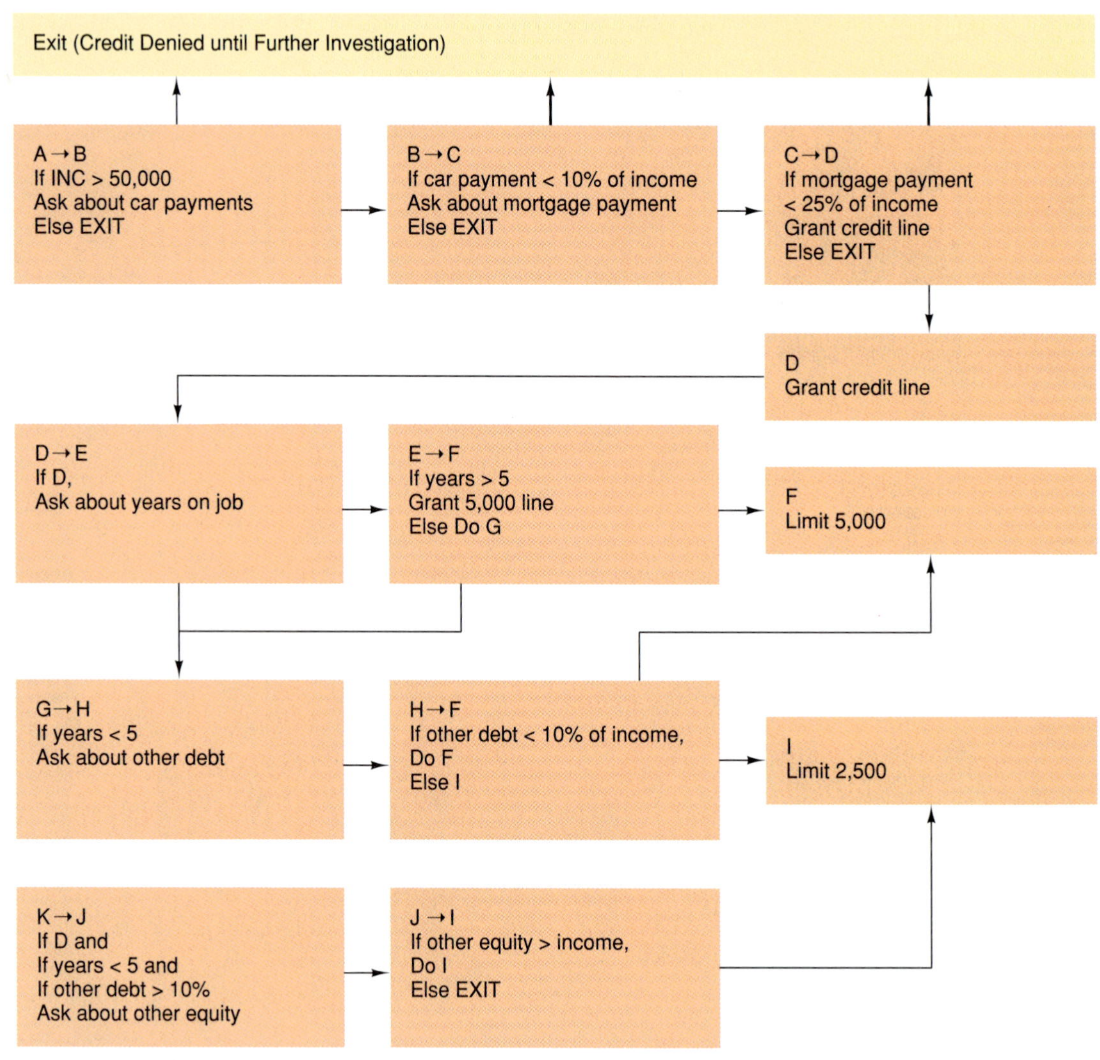
Exit (Credit Denied until Further Investigation)
A→B
If INC > 50,000
Ask about car payments
Else EXIT
B→C
If car payment < 10% of income
Ask about mortgage payment
Else EXIT
C→D
If mortgage payment
< 25% of income
Grant credit line
Else EXIT
D
Grant credit line
D→E
If D,
Ask about years on job
E→F
If years > 5
Grant 5,000 line
Else Do G
F
Limit 5,000
G→H
If years < 5
Ask about other debt
H→F
If other debt < 10% of income,
Do F
Else I
I
Limit 2,500
K→J
If D and
If years < 5 and
If other debt > 10%
Ask about other equity
J→I
If other equity > income,
Do I
Else EXIT

IF-THEN rules. In general, expert systems can be efficiently used only in situations in which the domain of knowledge is highly restricted (such as granting credit) and involves only a few thousand rules.

Knowledge engineer
Specialist trained in eliciting information and expertise from other professionals in order to translate the knowledge into a set of production rules.

The Development Team An expert system development team is composed of one or several "experts" who have a thorough command of the knowledge base and one or more **knowledge engineers** who can translate the knowledge (as described by the experts) into a set of production rules. A knowledge engineer is a specialist trained in eliciting information and expertise from other professionals. The knowledge engineer interviews the expert and determines the decision rules and knowledge that must be embedded into the system. Thus, the knowledge engineer works with the expert to refine and improve the system until a useful system has been created. While AI software continues to improve, the process of eliciting knowledge from an expert remains a major challenge. Because knowledge engineering requires some background in diverse fields (such as software design, clinical psychology, and anthropology) plus finely tuned communications skills, knowledge engineers are rare.

Indeed, according to many experts, the hard part of writing an expert system is knowledge engineering. Knowledge engineers have been described as "visitors to another culture they have not grown up in." At work they're much like anthropologists, who are trained to observe things they do not fully understand.

The Artificial Intelligence Shell The **artificial intelligence shell** is the programming environment of an expert system. Currently, expert systems can be developed in nearly any programming language, including BASIC, C, or Pascal. In the early years of expert systems, computer scientists developed specialized programming languages, such as Lisp and PROLOG, that could process lists of rules efficiently. Although these languages were efficient, they have proved difficult to standardize and even more difficult to integrate into a traditional business environment. Hence a growing number of expert systems today are developed using either C or, more commonly, AI shells, which are user-friendly development environments capable of quickly generating user interface screens, capturing the knowledge base quickly, and managing the strategies for searching the rule base. AI shells reduce the time and cost of expert system development and open up AI systems to nonexperts.

Artificial intelligence shell
The programming environment of an artificial intelligence system.

One of the most interesting aspects of the AI shell is the **inference engine;** this is simply the strategy used to search through the rule base. Two strategies are commonly used: forward reasoning and backward reasoning.

Inference engine
The strategy for searching through the rule base in an expert system; either a forward reasoning strategy or a backward reasoning strategy is used.

In **forward reasoning,** the inference engine begins with information entered by the user and searches the rules in a knowledge base to arrive at a conclusion. The strategy is to "fire," or carry out the action of the rule, when a condition is true. Figure 15.5 shows two sets of rules that enable a user to search a rule base in order to decide whether a client is a good prospect for a visit from an insurance sales representative. If the user enters the information that the client has an income greater than $100,000, the inference engine will fire all rules in sequence from left to right. If the user then enters the information that the same client owns real estate (panel b), another rule base will be searched again, and more rules will fire. The rule base can be searched each time the user enters new information. Processing continues until no more rules can be fired.

Forward reasoning
A strategy for searching the rules in a knowledge base in which the inference engine begins with information entered by the user and searches the rule base to arrive at a conclusion.

In **backward reasoning,** an expert system acts more like a problem solver who begins with a hypothesis and seeks out information to evaluate the hypothesis by asking questions. Thus, in Figure 15.5, the user might ask the question, "Should we add this person to the prospect database?" The inference engine begins on the right of the diagram and works toward the left. Thus, the person should be added to the database if a sales representative, term insurance brochure, or financial adviser will be sent to the client. But will these events take place? The answer is yes, if life insurance is recommended.

Backward reasoning
A strategy for searching the rules in a knowledge base in which the inference engine begins with a hypothesis and proceeds by asking the user questions about selected facts until the hypothesis is either confirmed or disproved.

FIGURE 15.5

How the Inference Engine Works

The inference engine is the strategy that has been programmed into an expert system to guide its search through the rule base. In forward reasoning, the inference engine takes its cue from the information entered by the user. In this example, if the user tells the machine that a certain client has an income greater than $100,000, the inference engine "fires," or carries out, a series of further rules based on additional information. If the user tells the machine that the same client owns real estate, this spurs a separate set of rules, some of which branch into the income rules. In backward reasoning, the engine would begin with the information at the right side of the diagram and reason "backward" through the same decision points.

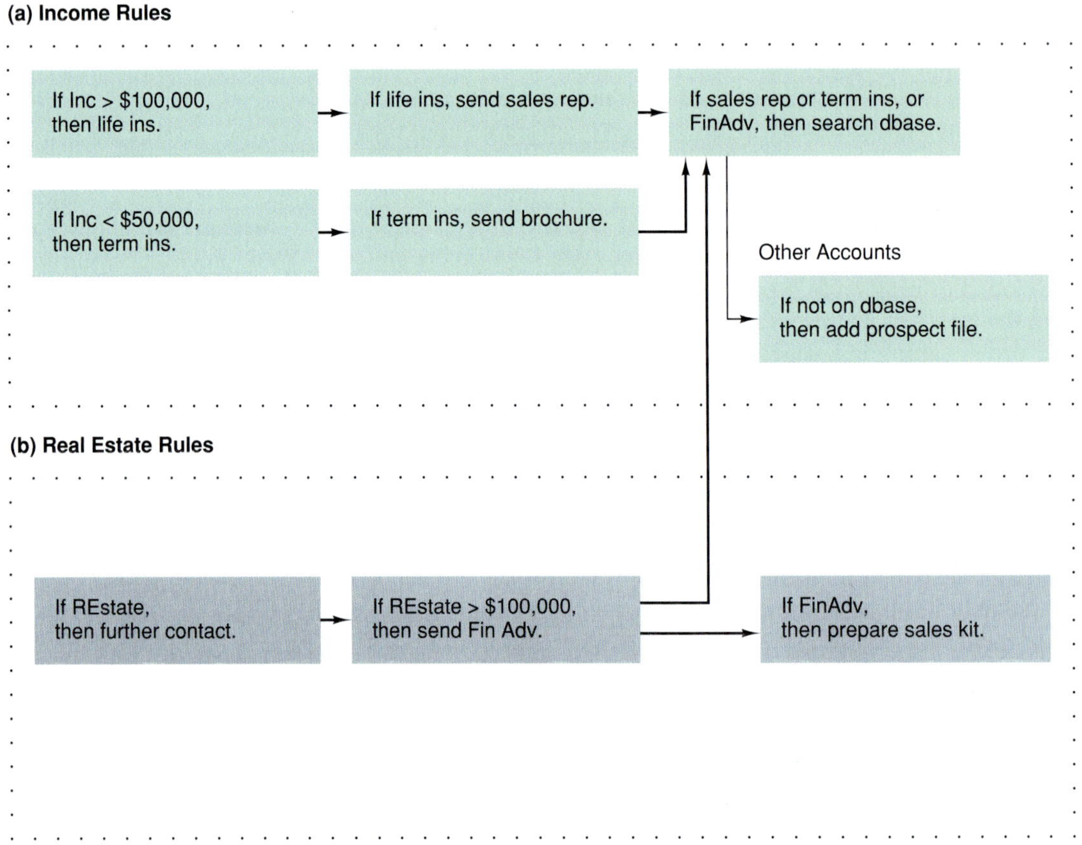

(a) Income Rules

If Inc > $100,000,
then life ins.

If life ins, send sales rep.

If sales rep or term ins, or
FinAdv, then search dbase.

If Inc < $50,000,
then term ins.

If term ins, send brochure.

Other Accounts

If not on dbase,
then add prospect file.

(b) Real Estate Rules

If REstate,
then further contact.

If REstate > $100,000,
then send Fin Adv.

If FinAdv,
then prepare sales kit.

The User The role of the user in an expert system is both to pose questions for the system and to enter relevant data to guide the system along. In most cases, the expert system will simply be an adviser to human experts and users, but on rare occasions, decision making may be turned over to the expert system entirely.

BUILDING EXPERT SYSTEMS

Building an expert system is basically similar to building any information system. A systems analyst (here a knowledge engineer) sits down with a user of the system (called an expert), and together they work out what the system should be able to do. They develop a preliminary version, which is tested and refined to produce the final expert system. Figure 15.6 depicts the process of expert system development.

Developing expert systems differs from building conventional systems in that expert systems rely much more heavily on experimental versions of the system and frequent, intense interactions with the user. Thus, as Figure 15.6 suggests, much time is spent on the preliminary version(s), testing, and improvement. One reason for this is that experts often discover that they cannot clearly articulate the rules they actually use when making decisions.

FIGURE 15.6

The Process of Developing an Expert System

The first step in developing an expert system is to capture the relevant information from the knowledge base. A knowledge engineer works with an expert in the knowledge base to determine what the system needs to know. Then they develop a preliminary version of the system, which is tested for accuracy and completeness. The final step involves implementing the finished system.

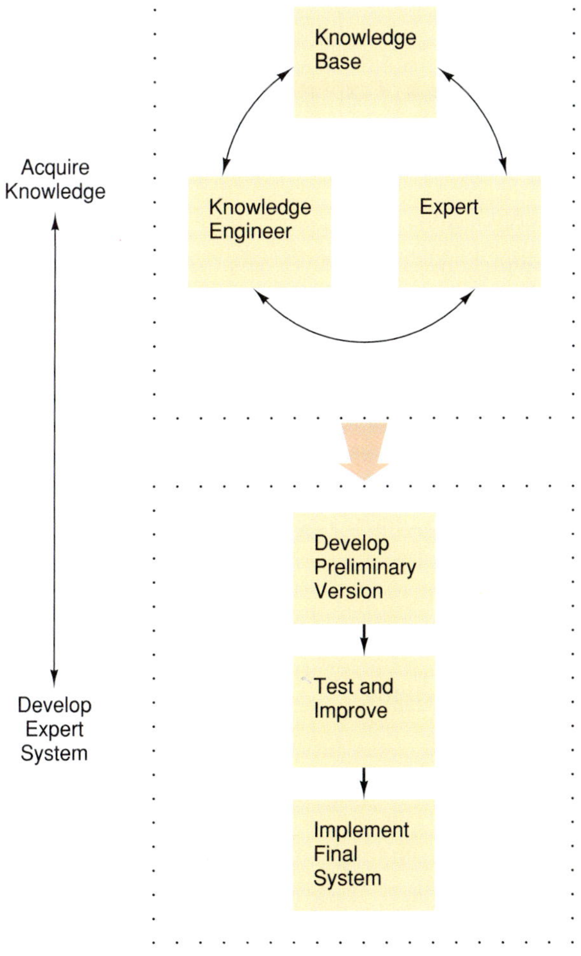

THE ROLE OF EXPERT SYSTEMS IN ORGANIZATIONS

Expert systems have proven useful for solving certain classes of problems where the solution can be arrived at by applying rules. Table 15.1 lists examples of expert systems that have been used in the commercial world. However, some limitations of expert systems are also becoming clear.[2]

First, it takes a very long time and a large commitment of resources to build interesting expert systems. Many institutions have found it cheaper to hire an expert than to hire a team of knowledge engineers to build an expert system. Although simple expert systems of up to 100 rules can be built quickly using one of several AI shells sold for personal computers, these applications tend not to be particularly important or powerful. Second, expert systems are brittle and cannot learn. They must be reprogrammed whenever knowledge changes in a field. Because knowledge does change often in an information society, expert systems' maintenance costs are considerable. Third, expert systems require that knowledge be organized in an IF-THEN format. This is appropriate for some knowledge and expertise, but much expertise cannot be organized in this fashion without producing erroneous results. Fourth, for all these reasons, expert systems are limited in application to taxonomy problems (i.e., problems in which the goal is to diagnose or assign objects to classes). Expert systems are not very good at typical management problems, which tend to be open ended, involve synthesis rather than deduction, require many kinds of expertise, and rely on expertise that is widely distributed in an organization.

CASE-BASED REASONING

Case-based reasoning
Artificial intelligence technology that represents knowledge as a series of cases stored in a database.

While the most widely used expert systems today are built on rules that experts follow in analyzing problems or making decisions, a newer type of expert system known as **case-based reasoning** (CBR) is fast gaining popularity. As we explained earlier, rule-based expert systems are actually a large number of IF-THEN-ELSE constructs used to evaluate specific conditions. The underlying technology of CBR is quite different. The fundamental unit of knowledge is not a rule but a case, a scenario, or an actual historical experience or occurrence. The cases are stored in a database for later retrieval when the user encounters a new case that has similar characteristics.

TABLE 15.1

Examples of Expert Systems

Expert System	Description
United Nations' Integrated Management Information System (IMIS)	Contains 350 rules for posting transactions to accounting systems. Checks financial transactions to ensure they follow the correct posting rule to prevent erroneous transactions reflecting conflicting policies.
American Express Authorizer's Assistant	Authorizes credit card transactions.
Digital Equipment Corporation's XCON	Helps configure VAX computer systems.
Ford Motor's Robot	Diagnoses sick robots.

The system searches for similar cases, finds the closest fit, and applies the solutions of the old case to the new case. Successful solutions are tagged to the new case and stored together in the knowledge base applied to the new case. Unsuccessful solutions are also appended to the new case, along with an explanation of why the solutions didn't work. In contrast to rule-based expert systems, the knowledge for CBR systems is continuously expanded and refined by users.

A popular use of CBR is as a help-desk tool to aid computer and technology company staffs in analyzing end-user problems. For example, to build a CBR system to analyze printer problems, the cases would be actual printer problems the help desk (or technical support staff or customer service department) has encountered—"The sheets came out blank," "The printing is smeared," "I press Print but nothing happens," "The printing is all there, but a black streak prints down the middle," "I didn't understand the error message," and so on. CBR systems are increasingly valued because their knowledge bases are continually updated as new data (cases) are received—the more experiences the knowledge base contains, the smarter the software. On the other hand, rule-based systems are changed only on occasion, when the business rules themselves are altered.

When the user is given a problem, he or she answers a series of general questions posed by the CBR system, which allows the software to use key words to narrow the search to a specific set of cases, eliminating all others. Then the software asks questions drawn from those selected cases. With each answer, every case within the set is assigned a weighting that depends on the answer given. When one (or several) case(s) achieves a high enough rating, it is selected, and solutions are displayed for the user. If no appropriate case can be found, a technician is assigned to analyze the problem, determine its cause and solution, and create a new case to be added to the CBR knowledge base, making it even "smarter" than before.

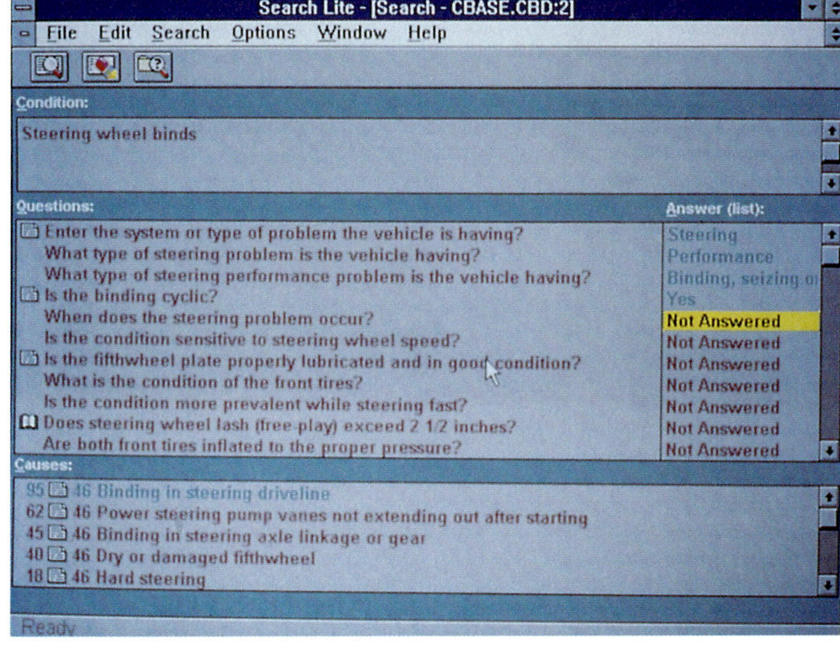

Case-based reasoning systems develop a solution by searching a database of cases. If a case in the database has characteristics similar to the problem being studied, its solutions will be applied to the new case.

Compaq Computers used CBR to create its automated help-desk system. When Compaq's management saw revenues and earnings declining in 1991, it increased Compaq's focus on customer service by establishing customer-support desks. A serious problem quickly surfaced: Studies showed that the technical staff assigned to support the help desk spent at least 50 percent of their time solving problems that had already been solved. Compaq's answer? Automate the help desk. Compaq turned to CBR Express from Inference Corp. in El Segundo, California. The system they developed, known as Smart (Support Management Automated Reasoning Technology), benefited Compaq in a number of ways. First, the time the technical staff devoted to solving customer problems was reduced. Second, help-desk staff training could be reduced while staff efficiency and effectiveness increased. Third, help-desk staff turnover at Compaq was no longer a problem because expert knowledge remained embedded in Smart rather than in the staff. Compaq now resolves 95 percent of its customer queries in ten minutes or less, a dramatic improvement for the customer and a major cost saving for Compaq. Figure 15.7 illustrates how Compaq's CBR system works.

FIGURE 15.7

A Case-Based Reasoning System

Case-based reasoning uses accumulated memories of past problems and solutions as a guide for solving current problems. While humans use it instinctively, computers need artificial intelligence software, called expert systems, to show them how. This figure shows a simplified example of how a case-based system works.

SOURCE: Sabra Chartrand, "Causing a Problem," *The New York Times,* August 4, 1993.

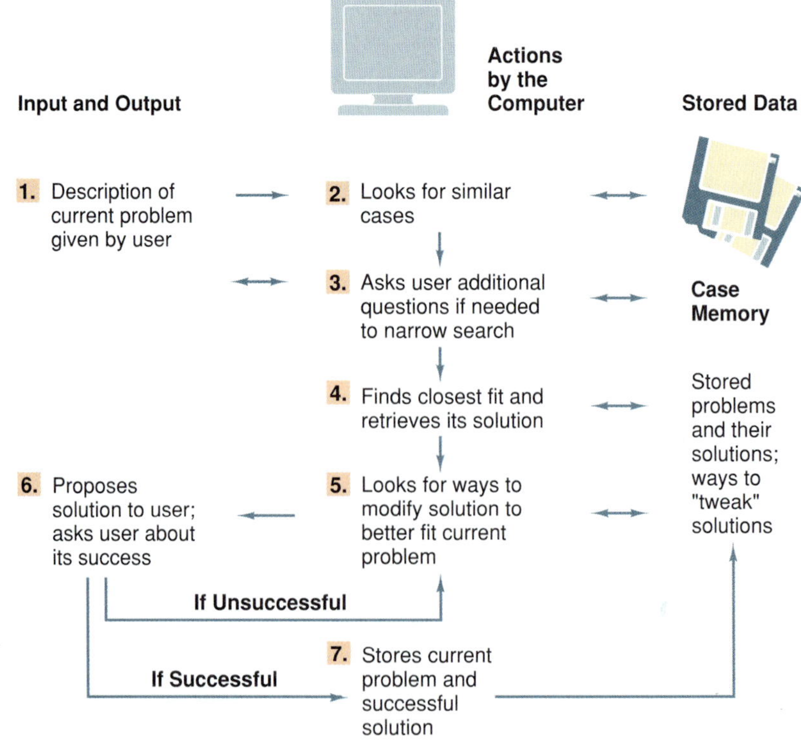

FOCUS ON **ORGANIZATIONS**

A CASE FOR CASE-BASED SYSTEMS

Although case-based reasoning has achieved its greatest popularity as a tool that benefits a customer or end user, its value to the organizations that utilize it cannot be overstated. Freightliner is one company that has found this to be true. Independent Freightliner dealers now make use of a client/server application called ServicePro to diagnose problems experienced by their big rigs. The application was generated at the company's headquarters in Portland, Oregon, with Microsoft serving as a consultant. The technical service staffs at Freightliner dealerships around the country have shown quite a bit of enthusiasm for the system.

The advantage of using ServicePro rests in its ability to save valuable time in solving problems. Its case-based logic system allows technicians to zero in on problems and their solutions quickly and efficiently. Before the client/server system, a driver having difficulty would bring the rig to the dealership, where the diagnosis would be performed manually. That process alone could take several hours. Now, drivers can call in from the road and describe the problem their truck has. A service person enters the information into the database, which uses case-based reasoning, to zero in on the problem. By the time the driver arrives at the dealership, the mechanic knows what has to be fixed without even having seen the truck. The time spent examining the vehicle is virtually eliminated.

Each dealership purchases the ServicePro application independently. Supplements to the database arrive on CD-ROM as Freightliner produces them. Dealers can also access information about warranties or parts from a mainframe in Portland. The company's director of technical service systems, David Vakoc, states that not all dealerships employed ServicePro immediately, but the distribution continues to progress at a solid rate. Chip Cliedman of the consulting firm Giga Information Group in Cambridge, Massachusetts, attests to the growing popularity of case-based systems such as Freightliner's. He points to a decrease in the supply of help as a cause of the need for more efficient troubleshooting methods. Using case-based logic permits technicians and mechanics to focus on the most crucial aspects of their jobs.

In addition to fine-tuning current operations, ServicePro will contribute to Freightliner's potential for growth. The company plans to increase the scope of its operations by incorporating school buses and fire engines into its lineup. Dealing with products that are initially unfamiliar and dealing with a larger total of products will demonstrate exactly how valuable a case-based reasoning system can be. Maximizing time and effort will become even more of a necessity.

FOCUS Questions:
What problems does cased-based reasoning technology solve? Why is it so important to service- and problem-solving-oriented industries?

SOURCE: April Jacobs, "Freightliner Tool Drives Employee Efficiency," *Computerworld,* June 17, 1996.

CBR is spreading to other areas besides customer service when organizations want to make knowledge gained from past experiences available to employees. For example, the oil industry uses CBR technology to rapidly classify the age of exploration drilling samples by fossil content. CBR is also widely used in medical fields and quality assurance. The Focus on Organizations describes how CBR is being used to diagnose vehicle repair problems.

15.3 OTHER INTELLIGENT TECHNIQUES

Although progress will continue to be made in expert systems, the development of other intelligent computing technologies is unleashing a host of new possibilities. Here we review briefly the intelligent computing techniques that stand the best chance of developing into major fields for applications today and in the future—neural networks, fuzzy logic, and genetic algorithms.

NEURAL NETWORKS

An exciting resurgence of interest has occurred in bottom-up approaches to artificial intelligence, in which machines are designed to imitate the physical thought process of the biological brain. Figure 15.8 illustrates the natural version—in this case, two neurons from the brain of a leech—and its man-made counterpart. In the leech's brain, the soma, or nerve cell, at the center acts like a switch, stimulating other neurons and being stimulated in turn. Emanating from the neuron is an axon, which is an electrically active link to the dendrites of other neurons. Axons and dendrites are the "wires" that electrically connect neurons to one another. The junction of the two is called a synapse. The synapse converts the activity from the axon into further electrical effects that either excite or inhibit activity in the adjoining neurons. This simple biological model is the metaphor for the development of neural networks.

The human brain has about 100 billion (10^{11}) neurons, each of which has about 1,000 dendrites, which form 100 trillion (10^{14}) synapses. The brain operates at about 100 Hz (each neuron can fire off a pulse 100 times per second)—very slow by computer standards. For example, an Intel Pentium II chip operates at over 200 megahertz, or millions of cycles, per second, executing one instruction at a time. But the brain's neurons operate in parallel, enabling the human brain to accomplish about 10 quadrillion (10^{16}) interconnections per second. This far exceeds the capacity of any known machine—or any machine now planned or ever likely to be built with current technology. The human brain weighs approximately 3 pounds and occupies about 0.15 square meters.

No technology now known can come close to these capabilities, but elementary neuron circuits can be built and studied, and far more complex networks of neurons—neural networks—have been simulated on computers. Figure 15.8 (b) shows an artificial electronic hardware equivalent of a biological neural cell. The transistors take the place of the nerve cells and act

FIGURE 15.8

Two Neural Networks: A Computer and a Leech

Neural networks are an area of research in artificial intelligence in which programmers attempt to emulate the processing patterns of the biological brain. Panel a illustrates part of an animal brain, that of a leech. Each neuron contains a soma, or nerve cell. Axons and dendrites are the branches by which it connects to other neurons; each connection point is called a synapse. Panel b represents the man-made version, in which each neuron becomes a switch or processing element. Axons and dendrites are wires, and the synapses are variable resistors that carry currents representing data.

SOURCE: Defense Advanced Research Project Agency (DARPA), "DARPA Neural Network Study, October 1987—February 1988," DARPA 1988.

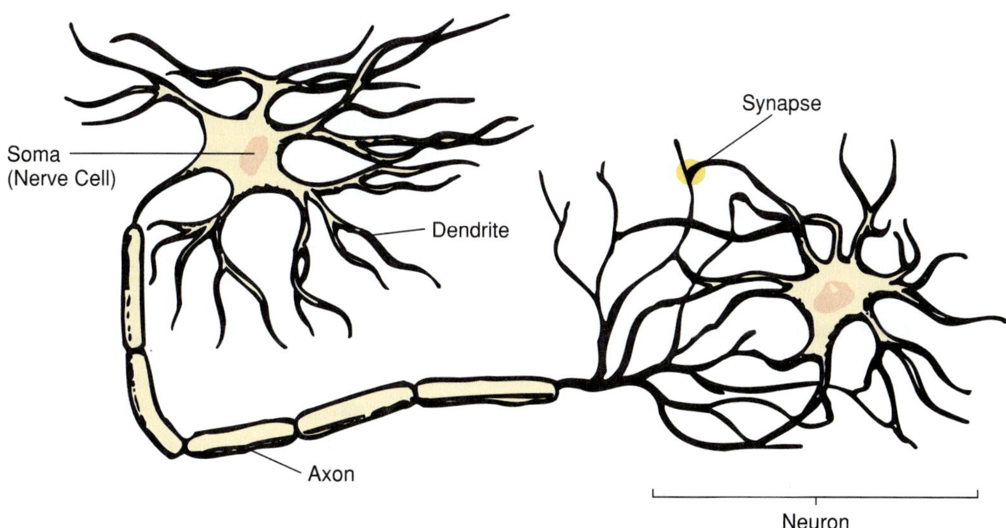

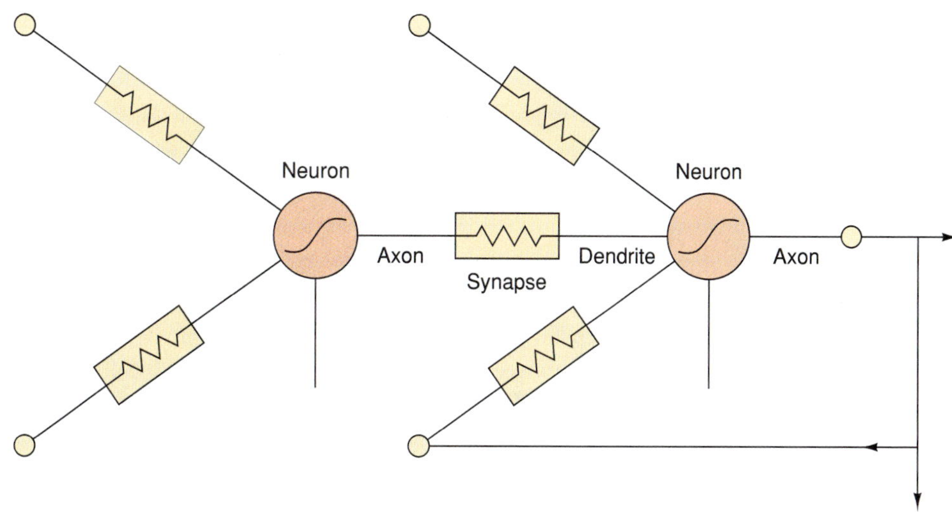

as switches. Wires replace the axons and connect one cell to another. Resistors take the place of synapses, the places where a decision is made as to whether the "firing" (the switching on) of one or more cells should cause the firing of other connected cells. Most neural networks are not built entirely from hardware switches because hardware-based neural networks are very expensive to construct. Instead, the patterns of hardware switching are emulated by software programs. Neural networks are quite different from expert systems, in which human expertise has to be modeled with rules. In neural networks, the physical machine emulates a human brain and can be taught from experience.

To explain how neural networks learn, let us examine one current application actually in use—spotting bad apples in a batch ("bad" here might mean spoiling or the wrong size or type of apple). First a color TV camera is connected to the neural network system. Then, as training examples, the net is shown apples one at a time and told whether each is good or bad. Soon the system begins to categorize them without prompting, although it makes many mistakes. Each time it makes a mistake, the "trainer" corrects it. Gradually it improves until ultimately it is accurate enough to be used. It can then be connected to a mechanical device that automatically sets aside bad apples based on instructions given it by the neural net.

Neural networks can be trained to recognize any number of patterns—letters, animal sizes and shapes, tanks, patterns in pictures, and patterns of credit charging by individual customers. They excel at pattern recognition. Generally, within a 24-hour period, a neural network can be taught to speak English when presented with text input or write text output when presented with speech input. Although today's neural networks can't begin to approximate the brain power of animals or humans, they can do some jobs better than humans.

Although there have been some impressive neural network applications, it is important to be aware of their limitations. These machines do not

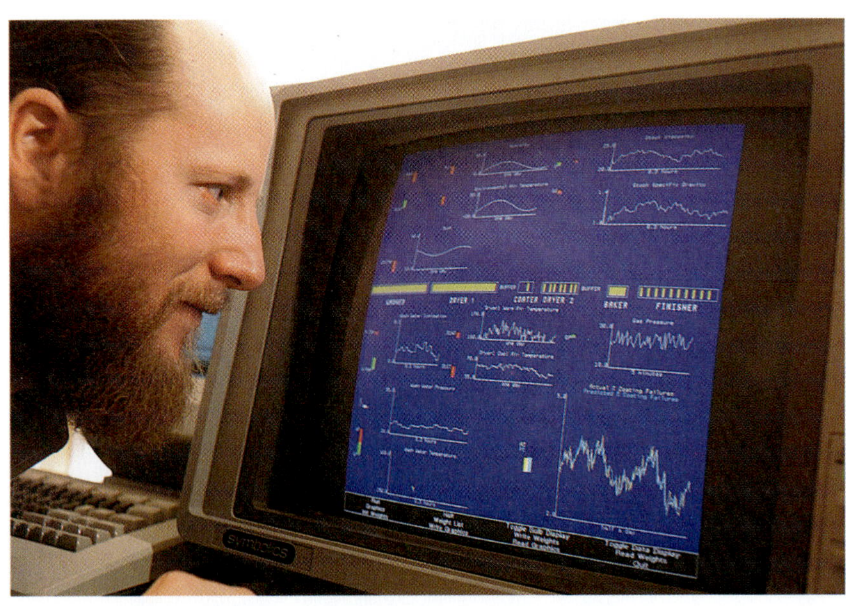

Neural net technology mimics the brain's network of neurons to solve a problem. GTE's neural network tracks variations in heat, pressure, and the chemicals used by Sylvania to make fluorescent light bulbs. This neural net will help reveal the best manufacturing conditions.

SOURCE: © Hank Morgan, Rainbow.

achieve generalizable intelligence that could be applied to many new situations. For instance, you could never ask an existing neural network to do anything it had never been trained to do, to synthesize the results of several research reports, or to write a term paper. Since a neural network is not "programmed" as an expert system is, no one knows how it works or understands the problem any better after building the network. Human judgment is still required in order to keep the networks running properly. In most current applications, neural networks are best used as aids to human decision makers instead of substitutes for them.

FUZZY LOGIC

Even expert system languages, which can capture very fine-grained logic for decision making, have limited ability to replicate human thought processes when a thought process can't be expressed in discrete IF-THEN rules. There are many instances in which a response depends on judgment and "shades of gray." For instance, what is a tall American male? If we use IF-THEN rules, we might define tall as being over 6 feet, 6 inches tall. But in real life, the range of heights considered tall is not well defined. Most people would recognize anyone over 7 feet in height as tall and anyone under 5 feet tall as short, but what about people who are 5 feet, 11 inches or 6 feet, 2 inches?

Until recently, computers had trouble handling situations that involved some imprecision and ambiguity. The traditional logic behind computers is based on things that can be categorized as true or false, yes or no, black or white.

Fuzzy logic, a relatively new, rule-based development in AI, is designed to overcome these limitations. Fuzzy logic consists of a variety of concepts and techniques for representing and inferring knowledge that is imprecise, uncertain, or unreliable. Fuzzy logic can create rules that use approximate or subjective values and incomplete or ambiguous data. By allowing expressions such as "tall," "very tall," and "extremely tall," fuzzy logic enables the computer to emulate the way people actually make decisions, as opposed to defining problems and solutions using restrictive IF-THEN rules.

Fuzzy logic
A variety of concepts and techniques in AI for using rules to represent knowledge that is imprecise, uncertain, or unreliable.

For instance, using traditional computer logic, a temperature controller on a room heater might react to 25° C as hot but 24.9° C as cold. Such a sharp boundary would cause abrupt changes in the heater's output. In contrast, fuzzy logic turns the hard-edged world of hot/cold, fast/slow into "soft" grades (warm/cool, moderately fast/somewhat slow). A temperature of 20° C can be both "warm" and "a little bit cool" at the same time. This is especially useful for heating systems or electric motors requiring smooth and continuous output.

Fuzzy logic is based on the concept of sets and the degree of membership in a set. In traditional computer logic, a set has rigid membership requirements—an object is either true or false, completely included or excluded. Fuzzy logic, on the other hand, allows "degrees" of truthfulness that measure the extent to which a given numeric value is included in a "fuzzy set." Terms (known as membership functions) are defined so that, for example, it might be 15 percent true that a 6-foot-tall man belongs to the "very tall" fuzzy set, 60 percent true that he belongs to the "tall" set, and 30 percent true that he belongs to the "medium height" set. (Since these "truth values"

ELECTRONIC DARWINISM

Anyone who worries that the world is moving too quickly toward becoming consumed with the development of technology while leaving behind the natural process of life can take comfort in a recent computer problem-solving trend. Software companies have joined with scientists to create programs for solving problems that use the problem-solving processes of the natural world as their model.

Genetic algorithms have found their way into computer software because scientists and developers have realized that the solutions to a number of their quandaries already exist in nature, especially those that pertain to genetics and natural selection. Thinking Tools Inc. of Monterey, California, is working with Texas Instruments to construct a system that would assist shipping companies' distribution of cargo to remote areas. Their model for the project is nothing other than the common salmon, who works out its best route to its destination, a spawning ground. The two companies envision equipping shipping crates with small display screens that would indicate their destinations and paths to workers. The units could also receive information from the shipping company's central computer so that they could alter their route in the event of a road closure.

FacePrints, created by Professor Victor S. Johnson of the psychology department at New Mexico State University, uses genetic algorithms to help witnesses describe and identify criminal suspects. Witnesses often can't describe a suspect's individual features, but they are much better at recognizing entire faces. FacePrints runs through random illustrations of faces on a computer screen, combining and recombining features until the best description emerges.

FacePrints consists of hundreds of individual features, such as a pug nose or a bushy eyebrow, each of which is represented as a digital string of computer code. The system enables the witness to a crime to select the most accurate picture of a suspect, a step closer to natural selection, from a group of 30 images composed of randomly chosen features. FacePrints then combines the best picture with 30 more randomly constructed faces and repeats the process over and over while eliminating the most unlikely features. Eventually, a very useful photo of the suspect evolves. "A particular face has one billion billion possibilities," notes Johnson, the FacePrints inventor. FacePrints can search an enormous "face space" very quickly.

refer to different sets, they don't have to add up to 100 percent.) The computer would combine the membership function readings in a weighted manner and, using all the rules, describe a measured height in a qualitative way—as very tall, tall, or medium—using English words.

Fuzzy logic has enabled AI to be applied to problems we could not have solved before. One important use has been in embedded controllers that allow a piece of equipment to make constant operating adjustments by calculating its reaction to current conditions. In Japan, the Sendai Metro subway system uses a Hitachi fuzzy control system that stops with much greater accuracy than a manual control system and accelerates and brakes so smoothly that passengers don't need handrails. Fuzzy control systems are frequently used for speed, fuel injection, and transmission control in automobiles. Many Japanese consumer products, such as air conditioners, washing

While a human might grow weary after a few dozen stabs at a problem, a genetic algorithm can keep on going, tirelessly trying out millions of solutions to reach an answer. Most will be instantly discarded. But thousands may be promising approaches no human ever thought of. For instance, when General Electric designers were asked to devise a more efficient fan blade for Boeing Co.'s 777 jet engines, they faced a bewildering number of choices. The factors affecting jet engine performance and cost amount to a number with 129 trios of zeroes! It would take a supercomputer performing billions of calculations per second billions of years to test every combination. Yet genetic algorithms supplementing an expert system solved the problem in less than a week.

The hybrid system, called Engeneous, starts with a pool of digital "chromosomes," each representing a design factor. These chromosomes combine to create dozens of hypothetical designs. The best models are allowed to "breed," to exchange "genes" and spawn a new generation of solutions, some of which are still better. The fittest are selected to breed again, and so forth, until good designs are produced. In only three days, Engeneous created a design that increased engine efficiency by 1 percent, a significant improvement in the jet engine field.

In another application, Engeneous increased the efficiency of a new fan for power-plant turbines by 5 percent. Surprisingly, the genetic algorithm violated some of the design rules that were used by the expert system. While humans tend to believe that what worked before is the best way to go, genetic algorithms have no such assumptions, so they can come up with solutions that humans would dismiss out of hand. Once people understand how the algorithm did this, they can capture the knowledge in new design rules.

Conceivably, genetic algorithms might even be able to find answers to problems too complex for people to define. Ordinary "intelligent" systems are based on some preconception of how to proceed, some type of model of the real world. But this model can be misleading, since people don't fully understand the forces that drive most complex real-world events. Genetic algorithms, like neural networks, look for solutions and patterns from the bottom up. Such "model-free" methods could lead to new avenues of understanding.

FOCUS Questions: How do genetic algorithms differ from expert systems logic? What problems are genetic algorithms useful for solving? Why? How have companies and individuals used genetic algorithms to improve their operations?

SOURCES: Gautam Naik, "In Sunlight and Cells Science Seeks Answers to High-Tech Puzzles," *The Wall Street Journal,* January 16, 1996, and Otis Port, "Computers That Think Are Almost Here, *Business Week,* July 17, 1995.

machines, televisions, camcorders, and auto-focusing cameras, also use the technology.

Fuzzy logic applications are beginning to appear in the United States, and experts predict that within the next few years, such applications are likely to expand significantly beyond the field of controllers. For example, fuzzy logic can be used in building applications in which there is uncertainty about the exact characteristics of the data to be retrieved, which might be the case for insurance and financial risk assessment applications. Users can ask about good and bad insurance risks without having to specify a plethora of IF-THEN rules. Recently a system has been developed to detect possible fraud in medical claims submitted by health care providers anywhere in the United States. Fuzzy logic technology is rapidly becoming a major factor in the AI field.

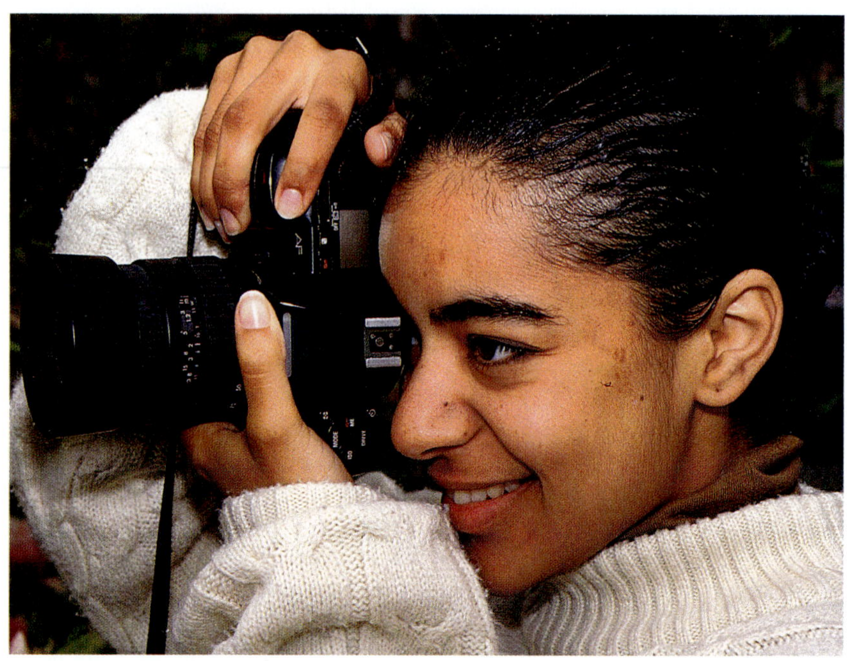

Auto-focusing cameras use fuzzy logic to determine the spot that has the highest probability of being the main focal point in a photograph.

SOURCE: © Oscar Palmquist, Lightwave.

GENETIC ALGORITHMS

Genetic algorithms
AI technology that "breeds" solutions to problems using the model of genetic processes such as reproduction, mutation, and natural selection.

Other artificial intelligence technologies are using problem-solving approaches found in nature. **Genetic algorithms** are one example. They consist of a variety of problem-solving techniques based on Darwinian principles of evolution. The algorithms start with building blocks that use processes such as reproduction, mutation, and natural selection to "breed" solutions. As solutions alter and combine, the worst ones are discarded, and better ones survive to go on and electronically breed with others to produce even better solutions. The process may produce results superior to anything crafted by humans.

Genetic algorithms were invented by Professor John Holland at the University of Michigan. Holland found that one could string ones and zeroes along a piece of computer code similar to the way genes are strung along a chromosome. Computers could combine strings of ones and zeroes similar to the way chromosomes in living organisms combine and recombine, leading to successively better solutions. The genetic algorithm provides methods of searching all combinations of digits to identify the string representing the best solution for a problem.

Genetic algorithms are especially useful for complex problems with large numbers of variables and calculations, where large numbers of solution alternatives must be tested. Some of these problems and the solutions produced with genetic algorithms are described in the Focus on Problem Solving.

HYBRID AI SYSTEMS

Engeneous is an example of a **hybrid AI system,** one that combines different artificial intelligence technologies. It combines some of the functions of expert systems with those of genetic algorithms. Other hybrid systems might combine genetic algorithms with neural networks or neural networks with fuzzy logic. For example, Citibank developed a hybrid AI application for predicting movements in currency markets. The genetic algorithm component evolves models that can predict currency trends under various past market conditions. The neural network component identifies which past model is closest to current trends. By using this hybrid application, Citibank claims to have earned an annual profit of 25 percent on its currency trading, considerably more than most human traders could hope for. The Focus on Technology illustrates another hybrid application, where fuzzy logic and neural networks are being combined to make elevators more responsive and efficient.

Hybrid AI system
A system that combines multiple AI technologies into a single application to take advantage of the best features of each technology.

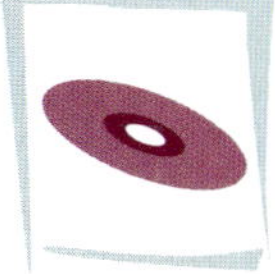

FOCUS ON TECHNOLOGY

DUMB ELEVATORS LEARN HOW TO THINK

If Otis Elevator has its way, people won't have to wait for elevators anymore. A team of Otis scientists is trying to make the elevator faster, smoother, and a great deal smarter.

The typical elevator is rather "dumb." It can't anticipate traffic patterns or know where to stop first when it is called to several floors at the same time. Elevator delays aren't caused by insufficient speed. They occur because elevators can't figure out the best way to respond to customer demands. That's where artificial intelligence technology comes in.

Consider a situation where Car A, on the fourth floor and climbing, is nearly empty and Car B, on the eighth floor, is crowded and also rising. A handful of waiting passengers press the elevator button on floors 9 and 10. Conventional logic would assign the nearest car, Car B, to pick up the additional riders, even though it is packed. However, the best decision would be to send Car A to pick up the riders because it is nearly empty. The Otis team is using fuzzy logic to assign values to such factors as how close a car is to the caller as well as how crowded it is.

Suppose it is lunch time and a large number of people on floors 9 and 10 want to reach the cafeteria on floor 12. Car A may not be able to hold all of them, but two elevators are standing idle on the lobby level. For that problem, Otis is trying out a neural network system. The neural network would teach the elevators to recognize busy times, such as lunch or rush hour, by the pattern of traffic flow. A free elevator could then move to the ninth floor. The elevators could also recognize the traffic patterns when it is a sunny, warm day and people go outside to eat and change their direction accordingly.

In December 1995, the Otis team started testing the software that controls which elevator stops at which floor in ten elevators in San Francisco's 48-story TransAmerica building. The elevators took an average of 21 seconds to reach a caller, compared with 41 seconds before Otis started using its artificial intelligence applications. Once in a while, glitches pop up. One errant elevator kept someone waiting 70 seconds.

FOCUS Questions:
Are fuzzy logic and neural networks appropriate technologies for these problems? Why or why not?

SOURCE: Amal Kumar Naj, "Dumb Elevators Learn to 'Think' More Efficiently," *The Wall Street Journal,* April 15, 1996.

15.4 LEADING-EDGE TECHNOLOGY: INTELLIGENT AGENTS

Intelligent agent
A software program with built-in knowledge that can carry out specific repetitive, predictable tasks for individuals; can work in computer networks.

Overworked? Short on time? Too busy to make vacation plans or keep up with the newspapers and magazines that have been piling up? Now you can relax and have an **intelligent agent** do many of these things for you. The agent is a set of software programs that works in the background on computer networks to schedule meetings and respond automatically to electronic mail by searching files and exchanging messages with other people's agents.

The concept of intelligent agents evolved in the 1950s as an offshoot of investigations into artificial intelligence. Since that time, the level of interest in intelligent software agents has grown. What exactly goes into these software programs that do their work behind the scenes? They are run by small but effective strings of programming code that demonstrate the task performance capabilities of scripting language and the communications abilities of object technology. These codes are then allowed to wander free in networks, searching for nuggets of information. The tasks that an intelligent agent performs for a user require the characteristics of specificity, repetitiveness, and predictability. Agents can also work for a business process or a software application and easily outperform humans when they function at a high level.

Intelligent agents have found their way into our daily lives already, perhaps without us having realized it. Operating systems, E-mail systems, mobile computing software, and network tools all serve as hosts for intelligent agents. While these agents show great potential for enhancing many business operations, like many advances in technology, they provoke some controversy as well. One possible use for agents is employee monitoring, which has both organizational and legal ramifications. Agents are also capable of

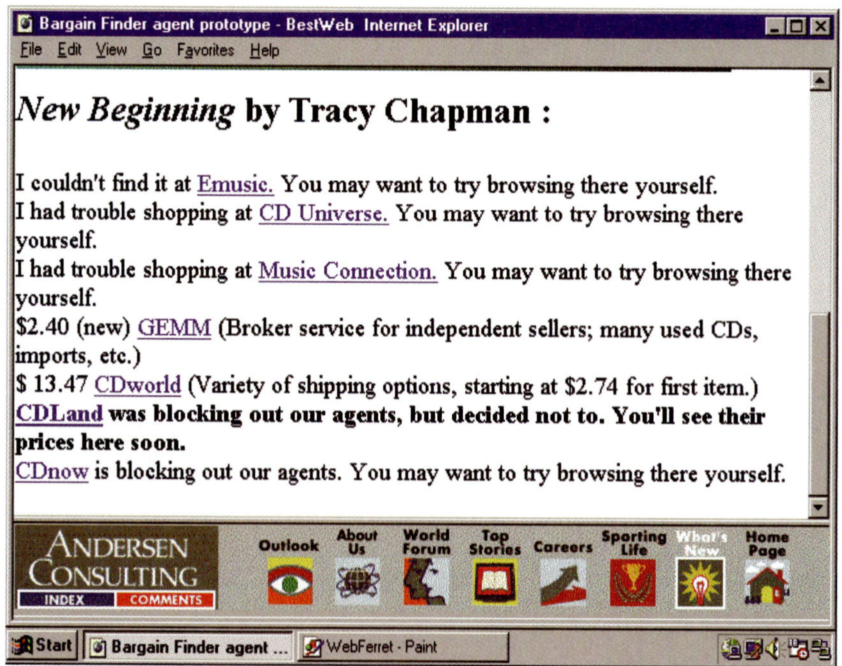

Bargain Finder agent, developed by Andersen Consulting, can search nine virtual retailers for price and availability of CD albums specified by the user. Displayed here are the results of a search for the Tracy Chapman CD entitled "New Beginning."

completing financial transactions on their own once a user sets them free to do so. This notion will probably be a cause of great concern for people who worry about the security of their personal information.

AT&T pioneered in moving intelligent agents beyond the common search engine with its PersonaLink service. The search engines that you may use to find items on the World Wide Web do not actually qualify as agents, even though some technologists have classified them as such. These engines do not search the Internet for your query. They simply sort through a massive database of Web pages that the engine's company has gathered. PersonaLink, using a communications language called Telescript from California's General Magic Inc., tried to establish an environment for E-mail, online news, and an electronic marketplace. AT&T hoped to attract all kinds of suppliers and consumers to its global electronic commerce service. Unfortunately, the communications giant found that it had a desired service but that it was not the most desirable provider. Affordable, easy access to the Internet invited people to take their business there, effectively dooming PersonaLink.

Since AT&T's misstep, intelligent agents have suffered few setbacks. The number of software companies developing agent technology has grown steadily. Table 15.2 present some of the leading developers and the functions of their products.

Not all agents are designed specifically for consumers. While Continuum can assist consumers, it really best serves companies with products to sell. The agent, known as a machine learning tool, provides sellers with a forum for displaying the latest data on their products for a monthly fee. At IBM's Almaden Research Center, Dr. Ted Selker created an agent that actually facilitates the learning process for computer programmers who are learning the programming language Lisp. COACH (COgnitive Adaptive Computer Help) contains three knowledge components that make it function. One

TABLE 15.2

Developers of Intelligent Agent Technology

General Magic Inc.	Operating system and scripting language that allow mobile agents to find very specific information, alert the user, and complete a transaction such as booking a hotel room.
Agents Inc.	Agents that automate "word of mouth" by matching users with similar preferences so that they can suggest new products or services.
Edify Corp.	Development tools for creating agents that can replace customer-service representatives.
Broadvision Inc.	Agents that track and remember users of Web sites and change their content accordingly, for example, targeting consumers with advertisements that would interest them.
Continuum Software Inc.	Agents that search for information and gather it from Web sites, clustering it for ranking and sorting by consumers.
Verity	Agent development tool for Notes, Windows, Mac, and UNIX.
Pointcast Inc.	Agents that choose subjects from different databases, such as sports scores, and display the information in real time on a screen.

compiles information about the user's Lisp abilities, including frequent mistakes and which coaching techniques proved effective. Another component maintains information about Lisp itself. The final component stores strategies for coaching. COACH ensures that students of Lisp receive a more thorough learning experience than they would otherwise.

Certainly one of the most popular ways intelligent agents work their magic is by cruising the Internet. Verity Inc. has developed server software that permits the release of an agent for the purpose of researching Web sites and databases. The product also provides means for the agent to then brief a user on its findings by way of a pager, E-mail, or Web page. This agent incorporates fuzzy logic in its attempts to imitate the human decision-making process. The Verity agent rates the importance of its findings according to the user's preferences and uses those ratings in its reports. It has already turned out customized editions of the San Jose *Mercury's* online newspaper in tests.

The Cambridge, Massachusetts, company Agents Inc. sells an agent that does count Internet consumers as its principal users. First, users send critiques of movies and music to the Agents Web site, Firefly. Then, when they want to select a new movie to see or a CD to buy, they can supply data on their personal favorites, and Firefly will produce a list of similar items based on the critiques.

One of the only obstacles remaining for intelligent agents is the fact that they lack standards. For an agent to be effective, a variety of Internet servers must buy its software. Sapient Health Network of Portland, Oregon, believes the answer to this problem is niche markets. For example, Sapient would target patients of prostate or breast cancer, supplying them with a "software angel" who would research their illness on the Web and then alert them to treatments and services. In this way, Sapient would only need to ensure that the best sources of medical information used the Telescript language instead of all servers.[3]

SUMMARY

- Artificial intelligence refers to a number of different techniques and practices that have as their common goal the emulation of human intelligence and perception.
- The artificial intelligence family has six members: natural language, robotics, perceptive systems, expert systems, neural networks, and intelligent software.
- There are two approaches to artificial intelligence: Top-down approaches seek to emulate the logic of human problem solving; bottom-up approaches seek to emulate the biological brain.
- Expert systems are composed of four major components: the knowledge base, the development team, the AI shell, and the user.
- Case-based reasoning is a type of expert system technology in which knowledge is collected in a database of cases rather than of rules.

- Neural networks exemplify the bottom-up approach to artificial intelligence because they are based on a biological metaphor of the brain.
- Neural networks can learn and excel at recognizing patterns that are not easily discerned by humans.
- Fuzzy logic technology expresses logic with carefully defined imprecision to solve problems that can't be handled with restrictive IF-THEN rules.
- Genetic algorithms develop solutions to problems using processes such as reproduction, mutation, and natural selection to "breed" solutions.
- Intelligent agents are software programs with embedded knowledge that can carry out specific, repetitive and procedural tasks, including conducting transactions on networks.

KEY TERMS

Artificial intelligence (AI)
Turing test
Natural language
Robotics
Perceptive systems
Expert systems
Neural network
Intelligent machines
Bottom-up approach
Top-down approach
Feedback
Perceptron
Logic Theorist
Combinatorial explosion
Knowledge base
Knowledge engineer
Artificial intelligence shell
Inference engine
Forward reasoning
Backward reasoning
Case-based reasoning
Fuzzy logic
Genetic algorithms
Hybrid AI system
Intelligent agent

REVIEW QUESTIONS

1. How would you define artificial intelligence?
2. What are the members of the AI family?
3. How would you characterize the history of AI? What were the major stages in its development, and when did they happen?
4. What is meant by a "combinatorial explosion"? How can intelligent systems solve this problem?
5. How would you define an expert system?
6. What are the major components of an expert system?
7. Define and describe forward and backward reasoning.
8. How does building an expert system differ from developing a traditional system?

9. What are some of the limitations of expert systems?
10. What is case-based reasoning?
11. What is a neural network? How does it differ from an expert system?
12. What kinds of problems are appropriate for neural networks?
13. Define and describe fuzzy logic and genetic algorithms.
14. What are intelligent agents? Describe some applications of intelligent agent technology.

DISCUSSION QUESTIONS

1. Many people say that someday intelligent expert systems will replace high-level business managers. Do you think this will be possible?

2. Examine an office in your college or in a local business, and describe how a small expert system might be used to make work more efficient and pleasant.

3. What is the proper role of expert systems or neural networks in a business or a government agency? Should key decisions be left to AI devices? Describe a range of possible roles.

PROBLEM-SOLVING EXERCISES

1. *Group exercise:* Divide into groups. Each group should locate a small business in your neighborhood, and within that business locate a single occupation, such as supervisor, clerk, or shelf stocker. Interview the person who occupies this position, and try to discover at least ten "rules of thumb" that this person follows to accomplish his or her job. Each group should write a short paper and make an oral presentation about what it discovered.

2. Look through several computer magazines, such as *Byte, PC Magazine, Information Week,* or *Computerworld,* for a case study of an expert or neural network system. Review this article and write a two-page critical report. Was the system as successful as originally planned? How did the system fall short?

3. *Hands-on exercise:* A popular expert system application is one that assists banks in deciding whether to grant credit for consumer loans, such as automobile loans. North Side Bank in Erie, Pennsylvania, uses the following rules for granting a car loan. Applicants must be over 21 years of age and make over $20,000 per year. The total value of the loan cannot exceed 25 percent of the applicant's annual salary. The bank would like you to use appropriate software to develop a simple expert system application to evaluate the following information. Which candidates qualify for loans?

Name	Age (yrs)	Salary	Loan Amount
Joan Elliott	19	$22,000	$4,000
Robert Morrissey	35	$34,000	$5,000
Sheila Burke	57	$17,500	$2,000
Carl Zeigler	22	$24,700	$4,000
Miranda Kase	44	$55,000	$15,000

4. *Internet problem-solving exercise:* You would like to use intelligent agent technology to search for the lowest prices for books available on the Internet. Bargain Bot is an agent that searches multiple virtual bookstores simultaneously to find the prices and availability of book titles specifed by the user. Use Bargain Bot to find the lowest price for a copy of *The Wealth of Nations* by Adam Smith.

NOTES

1. Actually, the story of AI is much more complex and controversial than can be presented here in such a brief introduction. Involved in this larger debate are questions about the nature of human beings and knowledge, the proper relationship between responsible human beings and machines, and the difference between promise and reality. The interested student is directed to two dramatically opposing books. For a positive view of AI, see Edward A. Feigenbaum and Pamela McCorduck, *The Fifth Generation: Artificial Intelligence and Japan's Computer Challenge to the World* (Reading, Mass.: Addison-Wesley, 1985), and Paul M. Churchland and Patricia Smith Churchland, "Could a Machine Think?" *Scientific American,* January 1990. For a counterview of AI, see Hubert L. and Stuart E. Dreyfus, *Mind over Machine: The Power of Human Intuition and Expertise in the Era of the Computer* (New York: The Free Press, 1986), and John R. Searle, "Is the Brain's Mind a Computer Program?" *Scientific American,* January 1990.
2. See Bruce Arnold, "Expert System Tools Optimizing Help Desks," *Software Magazine,* January 1993, and Sabra Chartrand, "Compaq Printer Can Tell You What's Ailing It," *The New York Times,* August 4, 1993.
3. Dean Tomasula, "Agents to Represent Traders," *Wall Street and Technology,* July 1996; Janet Endrijonan, "Agents on the Net," *Desktop Engineering,* January/February 1996; and Patti Maes, "Agents that Reduce Work and Information Overload," *Communications of the ACM,* July 1994.

PROBLEM-SOLVING CASE

CAN NEURAL NETWORKS PICK STOCKS?

For years, Brad Lewis seemed to have a magic stock-picking machine, a computerized artificial intelligence system that helped him pick stocks. Brad, a self-styled "computer nerd" and graduate of the U.S. Naval Academy, had been the portfolio manager of Fidelity Investments' Disciplined Equity Fund, a mutual fund that invests in stocks of companies similar to those on the Standard & Poor's Composite 500 Index. Lewis's "black box" helped the big fund outdistance the Standard & Poor's index for six years in a row, from 1989 to 1994—only one of three funds in the United States able to make that claim.

This stunning achievement was made possible through the use of a neural network system. Lewis built a database of more than 15,000 stock observations and used a complex series of equations to measure their cause-and-effect relationships. The computer looks at variables such as price-to-earnings ratios, price-to-cash flow ratios, and economic environment factors. After examing seven to ten years' worth of data on a particular stock, the computer reaches some conclusions about how the stock has behaved under a variety of circumstances and market conditions. The neural network learns very quickly how a large number of these variables combine to affect a stock price. For example, the neural network might find that over the past ten years General Electric is considered a "buy" when the yield curve is accelerating upward. A human analyst might not have thought of such relationships and would not be looking for them, but the neural network will find them if they exist.

Lewis and his team then reconcile this information with current data about the stock, and the computer generates a measure of expected return. Lewis can then use this information about which stocks to select for his fund based on the hypothetical expected returns on stocks generated by his network. Lewis assumes that the complex set of factors that have determined a stock's price over the past ten years that the system has identified will remain relevant for the next year or two.

Every Friday afternoon Lewis's desktop computer starts processing data on thousands of stocks in his database, working the whole weekend to produce the expected return on those stocks for the next nine months. When the weekend computer run has ended, it produces a list of recommendations of what stocks to buy and sell. Lewis does not know why the computer makes these specific recommendations, only that they work in most environments.

Lewis does not automatically buy the stocks recommended by the computer. He runs the data through an "optimizer" that creates what it believes to be an ideal model portfolio. For instance, if the neural network's recommendations show a substantial preference for technology stocks or small company stocks, the optimizer will limit those holdings in the portfolio to a manageable level. Lewis's Disciplined Equity Fund is based on the belief that combining the analysis of the neural network with the practicality of the optimizer should result in a fund that consistently outperforms the Standard & Poor's Composite Index of 500 stocks.

The Disciplined Equity Fund has generally traded in stocks that are smaller and faster-growing than those in the S&P 500 but with a similar industry diversification. Lewis notes that the computer can't identify some factors affecting stock performance, such as the quality of management, competitive threats, or investing themes or fads, such as the hype over the information superhighway that drove up prices of telecommunications stocks in the fall of 1993. At that time, Lewis's neural network shunned many fast-rising telecommunications stocks because their prices were high relative to other measures such as their earnings. The computer had "learned" to reject stocks that were too expensive. Disciplined Equity's performance suffered relative to many of its peers by not owning such stocks.

Disciplined Equity trailed the S&P benchmark in both 1995 and 1996. In 1996, Disciplined Equity returned 15.9 percent, compared with 22.9 percent for S&P 500 stocks. Lewis explained the fund's performance as being strong by historical standards but weak compared with the raging advances in 1996 of large company stocks that dominate the S&P. The historically smaller, faster-growing stocks that the Disciplined Equity Fund owns did not advance as rapidly as the traditionally low-growth, high-priced stocks of the largest U.S. companies that year.

SOURCES: Karen Damato, "A Can't Miss Mutual-Fund Machine Sputters," *The Wall Street Journal,* November 1996; "Fidelity Disciplined Equity Fund," *Fidelity Focus,* Winter 1995; and Fred W. Frailey, "Brad Lewis," *Kiplinger's Personal Finance Magazine,* October 1994.

CASE STUDY QUESTIONS

1. What are the strengths and weaknesses of using neural networks for stock picking?
2. What kinds of problems can be solved using neural networks? What kinds of problems can't be solved?
3. Would you use a neural network to help you pick stocks? Why or why not?

Chapter

→ SIXTEEN ←

MANAGEMENT SUPPORT SYSTEMS

CHAPTER OUTLINE

Opening Vignette: Wal-Mart Squeezes Decisions from Its Data

16.1 Introduction: Management Support Systems

16.2 What Managers Do

Traditional Views

The Behavioral View: Multiple Roles

The Realistic Setting: Culture, Politics, and Bureaucracy

Managers and Information Systems

16.3 Management Information Systems

Leading-Edge Application: California Pizza Kitchen

16.4 Individual and Group Decision Support Systems

Leading-Edge Application: Redstone Advisors

Group Decision Support Systems

16.5 Executive Support Systems

Leading-Edge Application: Pratt & Whitney's CEB Executive Support System

LEARNING OBJECTIVES

After reading and studying this chapter, you will

1. Be aware of what managers do in a business and how they use information.
2. Understand the characteristics of management support systems.
3. Be familiar with management information systems and how they work.
4. Be able to describe individual and group decision support systems and how they work.
5. Know what executive support systems are and how they work.

WAL-MART SQUEEZES DECISIONS FROM ITS DATA

Wal-Mart's success in retailing—getting the right product to the right shelf at the right price—owes much to its intensive use of information systems. While stocking shelves with its formidable inventory replenishment system, Wal-Mart carefully analyzes its data to improve its managers' decisions. Wal-Mart management can be more detailed than most of its competitors on what's going on by product, by store, by day—and act on it.

Wal-Mart assembled the 7 terabytes of data it collected on point-of-sale, inventory, products in transit, market statistics, customer demographics, finance, product returns, and supplier performance into a massive data warehouse—one of the largest in the world. There it can squeeze even more value out of these data by analyzing them in three broad areas of decision support: analyzing trends, managing inventory, and understanding customers. Wal-Mart can then establish "personality traits" for each of its 3,000 or so outlets, which can help managers make decisions about the product mix and presentation for each store.

Most of these decision support applications are handled through two NCR Teradata databases. Wal-Mart has another 6 terabytes of data on IBM and Hitachi mainframes and 500 gigabytes on hundreds of servers running Informix's OnLine Dynamic Server database. Wal-Mart is starting to roll out a demand-forecasting application using neural network software and a 4,000-processor parallel computer from NeoVista Solutions. By examining a year's worth of data on the sales of 100,000 products, the system can create a seasonal sales profile of each item. This information will help the company predict which items will be needed in each store.

Wal-Mart is expanding its use of market-basket analysis. Data are collected on items that make up a shopper's total purchase so that the company can analyze relationships and patterns in customer purchases. Wal-Mart made its data warehouse available to store managers and suppliers over the World Wide Web. The company expects the number of queries to its database to double by the end of 1997.

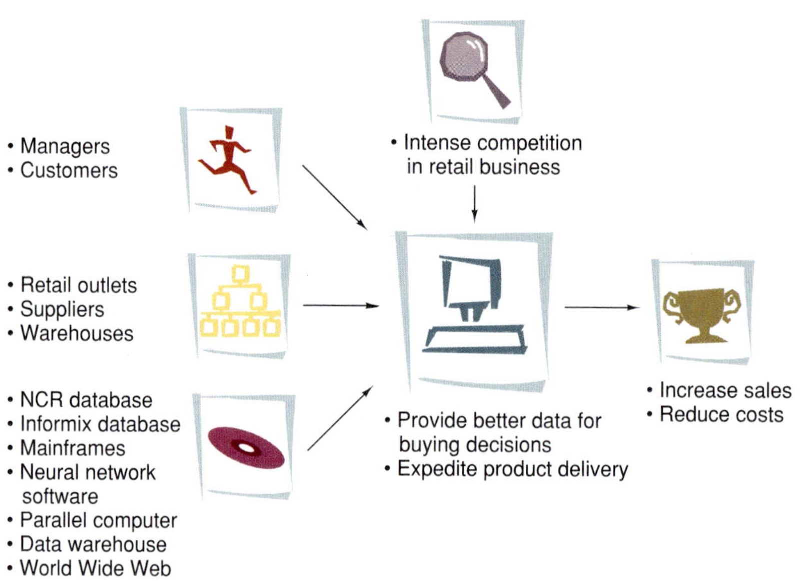

SOURCE: John Foley, "Squeezing More Value from Data," *Information Week*, December 9, 1996.

Keeping track of thousands of customers, controlling business finances, and planning for the future are just some of the tasks of modern managers. What should we do if profits fall below expectations? Why are so many employees leaving after four or five years? How can we increase the quality of our products without raising prices? How can we make our business more competitive? What changes should we make in our organization? These are typical of the questions that managers face every day.

Such questions rarely have simple answers, and they require managers to use a great deal of judgment. Managers require special kinds of information systems to help them find answers and develop solutions. Information systems can play a powerful role in helping managers meet the major challenges we present in this text. In this chapter we describe what managers do and explain how information systems can support them in their work.

16.1 INTRODUCTION: MANAGEMENT SUPPORT SYSTEMS

In Chapter 13, we described how information technology directly supports the transactions of a business—the functions in which the product is actually made and sold. In this chapter, we are concerned with how information technology supports the management of a business. We describe the three general kinds of management support systems: management information systems, decision support systems, and executive support systems. Each type of system will be illustrated by a real-world example.

Figure 16.1 shows the characteristics of the various management support systems and where they fit into the hierarchy of the firm. **Management information systems (MIS)** provide routine summary reports about the firm's performance; such systems are used to monitor and control the business and predict future performance. **Decision support systems (DSS)** are interactive systems under user control that provide data and models for

Management information systems (MIS)
Management support systems that provide routine summary reports on the firm's performance; used to monitor and control the business and predict future performance.

Decision support systems (DSS)
Interactive systems under user control that are used in solving semistructured problems.

FIGURE 16.1

The Three Types of Management Support Systems

An executive support system (ESS) serves the senior or executive management level in an organization. It supports the strategic, long-term planning required of this level. Management information systems (MIS) and decision support systems (DSS) serve mid- and low-level managers, who must deal with short-term, daily operational issues.

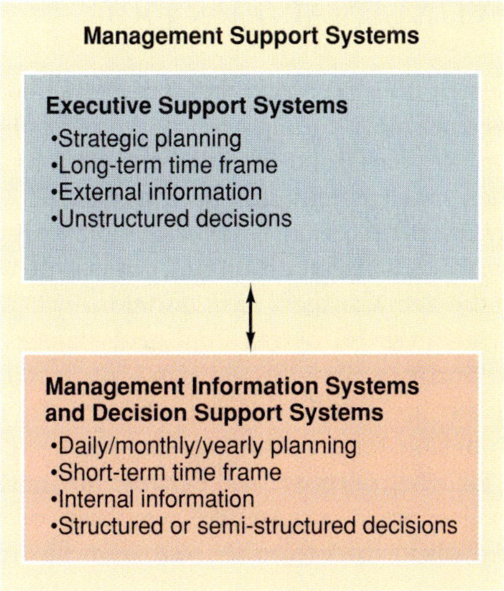

Management Support Systems
Executive Support Systems
•Strategic planning
•Long-term time frame
•External information
•Unstructured decisions
Management Information Systems and Decision Support Systems
•Daily/monthly/yearly planning
•Short-term time frame
•Internal information
•Structured or semi-structured decisions

Semistructured problem
A problem in which only parts have a clear-cut answer provided by a well-accepted methodology.

Structured problem
A routine, repetitive problem for which there is an accepted methodology for arriving at an answer.

Executive support systems (ESS)
Graphics-oriented systems designed for senior management that provide generalized computing and telecommunications facilities and combine internal and external information; used for long-term planning.

solving semistructured problems. A **semistructured problem** is one in which only parts of the problem have a clear-cut answer provided by a well-accepted methodology.

Both MIS and DSS are generally concerned with daily operations and with problems that are structured or semistructured. (**Structured problems,** such as those described in Chapter 13, are repetitive and routine and have a specified procedure for handling them; in contrast, unstructured problems are novel and nonroutine, with no agreed-upon procedure for solving them. Semistructured problems combine elements of both types.) Most of the information for these kinds of decisions comes from within the business, and the time frame is relatively short term (e.g., this week, this month, or this year).

Executive support systems (ESS) generally support the strategic planning function in a business, for which the time frame is relatively long term. Such activities involve largely unstructured, open-ended questions and decisions pertaining to unpredictable future events; they also tend to require a great deal of information from a business's external environment. Senior executives, for example, need information on government activities and regulations, new laws, the actions of competitors, market conditions, and so forth. ESS also tend to be more graphics oriented than other management support systems.

Although all these management systems are different, they often exchange information with one another and are related to one another through the information flow. These various systems can be seen as layers in a business organizational cake.

But before we examine each of these systems in detail, we must take a look at what managers do when they manage a business. That will give us a good idea of the kinds of problems managers face and why they build information systems to help solve those problems.

16.2 WHAT MANAGERS DO

There are many descriptions of what managers do, including "getting things done through other people," "leading an orchestra,"[1] and using business resources to accomplish goals. Each of these descriptions has some validity. Since ancient times, management has been associated with great accomplishments and achievements, such as the irrigation works of the Sumerians (6500 B.C.), the pyramids of Egypt (4000 B.C.), the Great Wall of China (third century B.C.), and the like. Managers have traditionally been concerned with criteria for measuring progress toward some goal. Management also involves the coordination of many (sometimes thousands of) workers.

Managers clearly are not the people who actually do "the work"; instead, they are responsible for determining what work will be done, where it will be done, and for what purpose. And because any business is composed of specialists, managers are in a sense like symphony orchestra conductors trying to get individuals to work together so that "music" results.

TRADITIONAL VIEWS

Classical writers on management, like the French industrialist Henri Fayol (1841–1925), who rose to become the director of a major French mining company, described management as involving five activities: planning, organizing, commanding, coordinating, and controlling. Contemporary writers on management have reduced these features to four management functions: planning, organizing, leading, and controlling (see Figure 16.2).[2] Thus, according to **traditional theories of management, managing** can be defined as the effort to accomplish business goals through planning, organizing, leading, and controlling.

Planning refers to defining the goals of the business and describing how it will fulfill these goals. Organizing involves assigning responsibility for accomplishing the necessary tasks and assigning appropriate resources. Leading means motivating employees to achieve organizational goals. Controlling involves monitoring the activities of the business and making corrections as necessary.

Traditional theories of management
Views of management that see its primary functions as planning, organizing, leading, and controlling.

Managing
The process of using business resources to accomplish goals, coordinate the work of many workers, and establish criteria for measuring progress toward the established goals.

FIGURE 16.2

The Four Major Functions of Management: Planning, Organizing, Leading, and Controlling

The classical view defines management as the effort to meet business goals through these four activities. By planning, the manager establishes the firm's goals and sets up tasks on which employees will work to achieve these goals. Organizing involves assigning staff and resources to accomplish these tasks. Effective managers lead their employees by motivating them to do their work well, and they control employees in the sense of monitoring business activities and making corrections as necessary.

SOURCE: Exhibit 1.1, "The Four Functions of Management," from *Management* by Richard L. Daft, p. 8, copyright © 1994 by The Dryden Press. Reprinted by permission of the author.

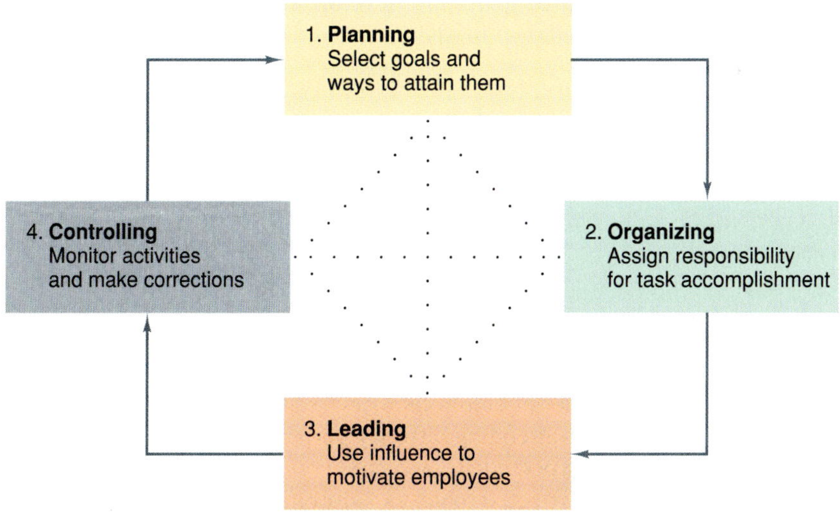

THE BEHAVIORAL VIEW: MULTIPLE ROLES

The traditional view is perfectly adequate for describing the basic functions of management, but it does not tell us how managers do what they do. How do managers actually go about planning, organizing, leading, and controlling? For this we must turn to contemporary behavioral scientists who have studied managers in daily action. The results are surprising. A typical manager's day consists of one brief meeting after another, interrupted by several telephone calls. The manager might spend an hour daily returning calls or making appointments.

This realistic world of the manager has six characteristics. (1) Managers perform high-volume, high-speed work, involving a large number of very different topics. (2) The pace is unrelenting, and the phone rarely stops ringing. (3) The work is characterized by variety, fragmentation, and brevity. There is very little time to "think about things." (4) Managers tend to be issue oriented because they spend attention on the things that need attention immediately. If something is not an issue, it often is not attended to. (5) Managers also have a complex web of personal contacts and interactions, which range from working with clerical workers to sympathizing and working with other managers. (6) Managers have a strong preference for verbal communications.

Behavioral theories of management
Views of management based on behavioral scientists' observations of what managers actually do in their jobs.

According to **behavioral theories of management,** the traditional notion of management as planning, organizing, leading, and controlling is a little simplistic. All these functions are performed, but not in any rational, sequential manner. Moreover, behavioral theorists perceive the manager's roles a bit differently than traditional theorists do.

When John T. Kotter observed real-world managers, he found that they engage in three basic activities:[3]

- **Establishing agendas:** Managers set long-term (three to five years) goals.
- **Building a network:** Managers develop a network of business and community contacts at all levels.
- **Executive agendas:** Managers use their personal networks to accomplish their goals.

A contemporary researcher, Henry Mintzberg, studied the characteristics of management work and found that managers perform ten roles, which fall into three major categories (see Table 16.1). A role is a set of expectations for a person who occupies a specific status. In other words, occupants of the manager position are expected to perform three types of roles:

Interpersonal roles
The activities of managers that involve performing symbolic duties; motivating, counseling, and supporting workers; and acting as liaisons to the larger firm and the outside world on behalf of employees.

- **Interpersonal roles:** Here managers are expected to act like human beings with a full set of emotions. They are expected to perform symbolic duties such as attending birthday parties and giving out employee awards; they are expected to motivate, counsel, and support employees, and they are expected to act as liaisons to the larger firm and outside world on behalf of employees. In the traditional view, these roles were all considered "leadership."

TABLE 16.1

Management Roles

Category	Role	Activity
Interpersonal	Figurehead	Perform ceremonial and symbolic duties such as greeting visitors or signing legal documents.
	Leader	Direct and motivate subordinates; train, counsel, and communicate with subordinates.
	Liaison	Maintain information links both inside and outside the organization; use mail, phone calls, and meetings.
Informational	Monitor	Seek and receive information, scan periodicals and reports, and maintain personal contacts
	Disseminator	Forward information to other organization members; send memos and reports, and make phone calls.
	Spokesperson	Transmit information to outsiders through speeches, reports, and memos.
Decisional	Entrepreneur	Initiate improvement projects; identify new ideas, and delegate idea responsibility to others.
	Disturbance handler	Take corrective action during disputes or crises; resolve conflicts among subordinates; adapt to environmental crises.
	Resource allocator	Decide who gets resources; perform scheduling, budgeting, and priority setting.
	Negotiator	Represent department during negotiation of union contracts, sales, purchases, and budgets; represent departmental interests.

SOURCE: Adapted from Henry Mintzberg, "Managerial Work: Analysis from Observation," *Management Science* 18 (1971), pp. B97—B110.

- **Informational roles:** Managers are expected to monitor the activities of the business, distribute information through reports and memos, and act as a spokesperson for the business. In the traditional theories, these informational roles were poorly understood and subsumed under all categories.
- **Decisional roles:** Managers are, of course, supposed to make decisions. They are expected to make decisions about new products, which involves acting like entrepreneurs; to handle disturbances in the business; and to allocate resources by budgeting, scheduling, and setting priorities. Additionally, managers are expected to be able to negotiate among individuals with different points of view.[4]

The behavioral perspective gives us a much more realistic and complex view of what managers do. The managerial role clearly involves much more than simply planning, organizing, leading, and controlling. Managers are also expected to nurture, care, inform, motivate, and decide.

Informational roles
The activities of managers that involve monitoring the activities of the business, distributing information through reports and memos, and acting as spokespersons for the business.

Decisional roles
The activities of managers that involve making decisions about new products, handling disturbances in the business, allocating resources, and negotiating among persons with different points of view.

THE REALISTIC SETTING: CULTURE, POLITICS, AND BUREAUCRACY

Complicating the behavioral picture described above, but making it even more realistic, are the features of business discussed in Chapter 2. To a large extent, managers are not free agents (see Figure 16.3). They must work within a given culture (certain basic business assumptions) and within a political environment in which other managers compete for limited resources. Furthermore, they must thoroughly understand the rules, regulations, and day-to-day procedures of how the business works (the bureaucracy) before they can accomplish their agendas. The behavioral view reminds us that managers ultimately are people.

MANAGERS AND INFORMATION SYSTEMS

Actual studies of managers have found that they spend most of their time talking with other people—not analyzing statements, calculating results, or reading formal reports (see Figure 16.4). More than half of a manager's time is spent in meetings—in some businesses, this occupies 75 percent of a manager's time.[5]

This means that the vast majority of information that an executive takes in comes through the grapevine in the form of comments, opinions, gossip, and short stories. Only a very small part of a manager's total information comes through formal information systems or message systems.

Table 16.2 relates the ten managerial roles to the actual use of information systems. As you can see, information technology is not helpful for all managerial roles. For instance, there really are no information systems that directly assist a manager's figurehead or leader roles. Systems do not directly assist the manager as entrepreneur or negotiator.

FIGURE 16.3

A Realistic View of a Manager's Environment

Managers do not operate in a vacuum. They must deal with, and sometimes surmount, three factors within a firm. One is the company's culture, the framework of assumptions and acceptable behaviors that are expected of employees in general and managers in particular. Another is the company's politics, often arising from competition with other managers for valuable resources. A third factor is bureaucracy: the day-to-day rules and procedures governing the firm's operations. Any of these factors can affect a manager's ability to do the job.

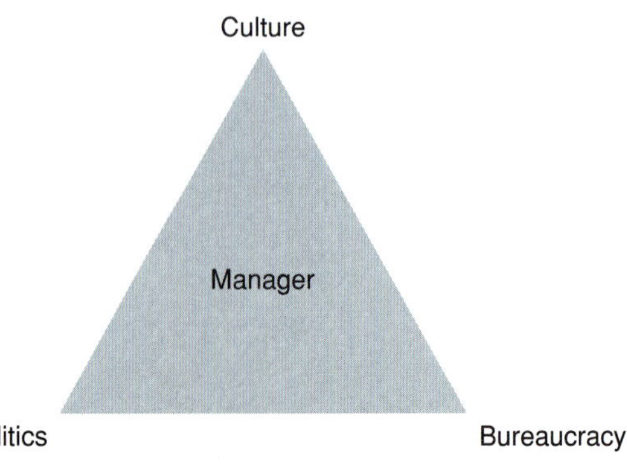

FIGURE 16.4

Managers and Information

Research on how managers obtain information shows that for the most part they get it from other people. A hefty 75 percent of a manager's time is spent in meetings—50 percent planned but 25 percent unplanned. Another 10 percent of the day is spent either making or receiving telephone calls, and 5 percent passes in clerical work. This leaves a scant 10 percent of a manager's time devoted to analysis: reading reports and research, making calculations, analyzing statements.

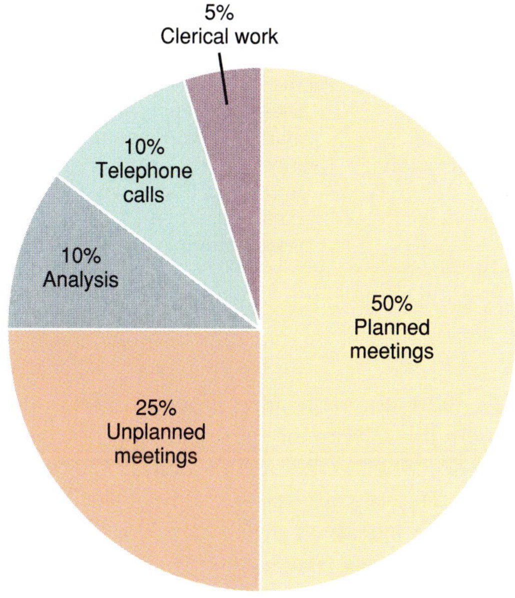

TABLE 16.2

How Information Systems Help Managers

Information technology can assist business managers in many of the roles that Mintzberg defined. Management information systems (MIS) are helpful in the informational role, as managers assess a firm's performance and attempt to predict its future. An MIS can also help a manager handle conflicts or problems. A decision support system (DSS) can help clarify decisions regarding resource allocations. However, we do not yet have information technologies that directly assist other key managerial roles such as "figurehead," "leader," "entrepreneur," and "negotiator."

Role	Management Support Systems
Interpersonal roles	
Figurehead →	None exist
Leader →	None exist
Liaison →	Electronic communication systems
Informational roles	
Nerve center →	MIS
Disseminator →	Mail office systems
Spokesperson →	Office and professional systems Workstations
Decisional roles	
Entrepreneur →	None exist
Disturbance handler →	MIS helpful
Resource allocator →	DSS
Negotiator →	None exist

SOURCE: Adapted from Henry Mintzberg, "Managerial Work: Analysis from Observation," *Management Science* 18 (1971).

TABLE 16.3

How the Internet Helps Managers

Management Activity	Example
Monitoring	Black & Veatch uses the Internet and intranets to track constructions costs across the United States.
Communicating	KeyCorp's intranet distributes job postings, information on best practices and training, marketing materials, and newsletters.
Controlling	Weyerhauser Co.'s intranet provides easy access to accounting data.
Planning, deciding	Pacific Enterprises/Southern California Gas. Co. uses an intranet for planning as well as for marketing and operations.
Coordination, communication	Cygnus Support uses Internet E-mail to link its offices in California and Massachusetts and to communicate with employees who telecommute.

Nevertheless, there are many areas where information systems can be of direct assistance in the solution of management problems. Management information systems (described in the next section) help managers monitor and control the business. This is a very powerful role. Decision support systems are very valuable in the manager's decision-making roles and are especially helpful in allocating resources (see Section 16.4). In addition, DSS are being developed to handle crisis situations and to assist negotiators in selected situations. Executive support systems are beginning to affect how managers perform their leadership and spokesperson roles (see Section 16.5).

Powerful network-based systems, including groupware, electronic meeting systems, and Internet applications, are widening the role of information technology in the management process. The Focus on Problem Solving and Table 16.3 illustrate some of the ways that managers can benefit from the Internet.

16.3 MANAGEMENT INFORMATION SYSTEMS

Management information systems (MIS) provide managers with reports on the firm's performance, both past and present. They serve managers' informational role by helping to monitor actual business performance and predict future performance, thus permitting managers to intervene when things are not going well; hence, they assist in controlling the business.

MIS are generally dependent on underlying transaction processing systems for their data. In other words, MIS summarize and report on the basic operations of the company. The system compresses the basic transaction data by summarization and presents the information in long reports, which

THE INTERNET: A NEW TOOL FOR MANAGERS

Before Charles Schwab & Co. started using the Internet, financial reporting for managers could be painfully slow. The giant discount brokerage firm's general ledger system ran only at corporate headquarters in San Francisco. Managers at regional centers could obtain financial reports on paper only by requesting them through interoffice mail. And the general ledger system was difficult to learn to use. So Schwab decided to develop an intranet-based general ledger reporting application called FinWeb to provide this information more rapidly.

FinWeb was written in SQL with a user interface developed with Java. It sends queries for financial data to an Oracle 7 database residing on an HP 9000 server. Users at any of Schwab's offices can access and print reports at any time. FinWeb presents the financial data in an easy-to-digest form.

FinWeb has cut down Schwab's training and printing expenses, but its real benefits come from providing better information to its managers. By the end of 1996, Schwab expects that the system will be used by 400 to 1,000 managers and other employees.

Realizing the benefits of intranets for managers, other companies are following suit. Ford Motor Company is developing a Java-based financial reporting system that helps managers gauge sales of product lines more quickly by combining data from its general ledger accounting system and inventory system. Managers could use this intranet to determine online, for example, the profitability of blue Taurus cars with leather seats.

The Compumotor Division of Parker Hannifin Corporation, an industrial automation manufacturer in Rohnert Park, California, put its basic human resources functions on an intranet. Employees can use the intranet to review the company's policies and procedures handbook, benefits reference manuals, and the employee telephone directory. Another intranet application provides managers with a single user interface for querying a number of different databases, enhancing their ability to drill down into important information and slice and dice the data any way they wish.

An intranet application called PE Xchng expedites the exchange of dispatches of "competitive intelligence" among employees at Southern California Gas Co. As they perform their regular jobs, employees volunteer to gather any information of competitive interest to managers at the company's Los Angeles headquarters. This application has proved so successful that other departments are requesting versions of PE Xchng for their own use.

FOCUS Questions: How can the Internet help managers? What problems can it solve?

SOURCES: Alice LaPlante, "Start Small, Think Infinite," *Computerworld Premier 100,* February 24, 1997, and Clinton Wilder and Stephanie Stahl, "Going to the Core," *Information Week,* October 7, 1996.

are usually produced on a regularly scheduled basis and answer structured, routine questions. Figure 16.5 shows how a typical MIS transforms raw data from transaction processing systems in order inventory, production, and accounting into MIS files. Managers can access the MIS files by using the MIS software.

Perhaps the best way to see how an MIS works is to look at a real-world, or in this case, a pizza-world, MIS. As you read the following case study, ask yourself these questions: Where does an MIS obtain its data? What does it actually do with the data? What management and business problems does this system solve? What difference does the MIS make for the firm?

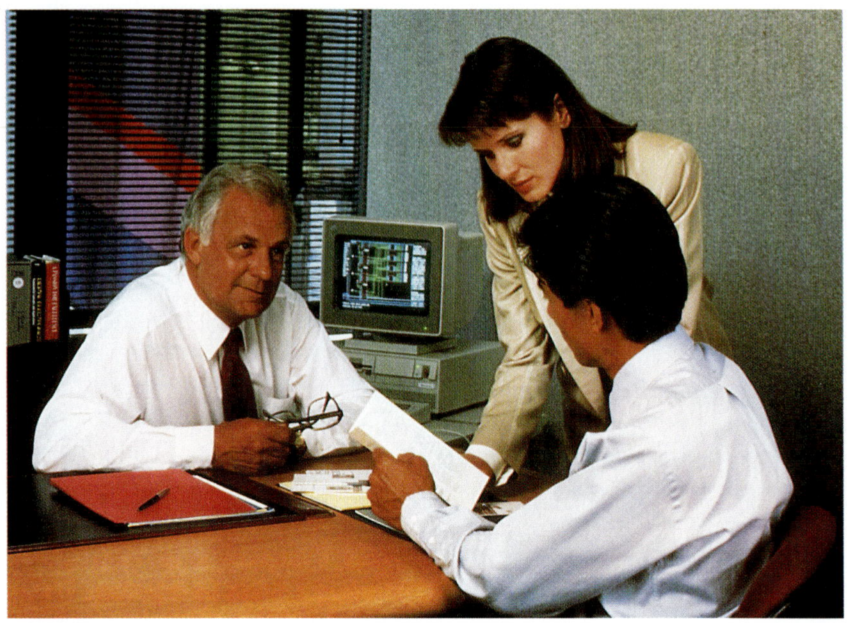

Managers must work closely with employees, juggling planning, organizing, leading, and controlling functions to accomplish business goals.

LEADING-EDGE APPLICATION: CALIFORNIA PIZZA KITCHEN

California Pizza Kitchen was created in 1985 by two former federal prosecutors looking for "something different" to do. This restaurant chain specializes in "designer pizza," in which the pizza crust is a "canvas" for exotic food toppings such as Thai chicken or southwestern burritos. The formula of offering stylish main courses costing less than $10 in a sit-down setting brought success. In only nine years, CPK mushroomed into a national chain of 77 restaurants with plans to expand tenfold in the years to come.

Part of its recipe for success was its intensive use of information systems. The fast-food restaurant business is extremely competitive. To remain profitable, restaurants need to tightly control food and labor costs while maintaining the quality of food and service. Since diners are put off by high prices, the only way to contain costs is through inventory and portion control. CPK keeps precise track of the amount of ingredients used in each menu item and stocks only as much of these ingredients as each restaurant needs.

Waiters and waitresses enter data about each menu item ordered into handheld point-of-sale (POS) devices in all CPK restaurants. These devices transmit the ordering information via radio frequencies to a server in the back of the restaurant. Each restaurant transmits its sales data and inventory reports to PCs at the company's home office, where the information is consolidated and analyzed. One application called Inventory Express "remembers" ordering patterns, such as the amount of tomatoes a restaurant needs each week, and compares the amount of each item used to what each restaurant actually sold. If, for example, a restaurant sold 100 Peking duck pizzas in one week, it should have used a predetermined amount of duck meat, such as 40 pounds, based on portion measurements established by CPK manage-

FIGURE 16.5

An MIS Helps Managers Access Transaction-Level Data

Generally, an MIS obtains its data from the company's transaction processing systems, the systems that perform the firm's basic business procedures. As this diagram shows, raw transaction-level data from three functional areas—order inventory, production, and accounting—are funneled through each department's transaction processing system to be collected as data in MIS files. Managers can use the MIS software to access these data.

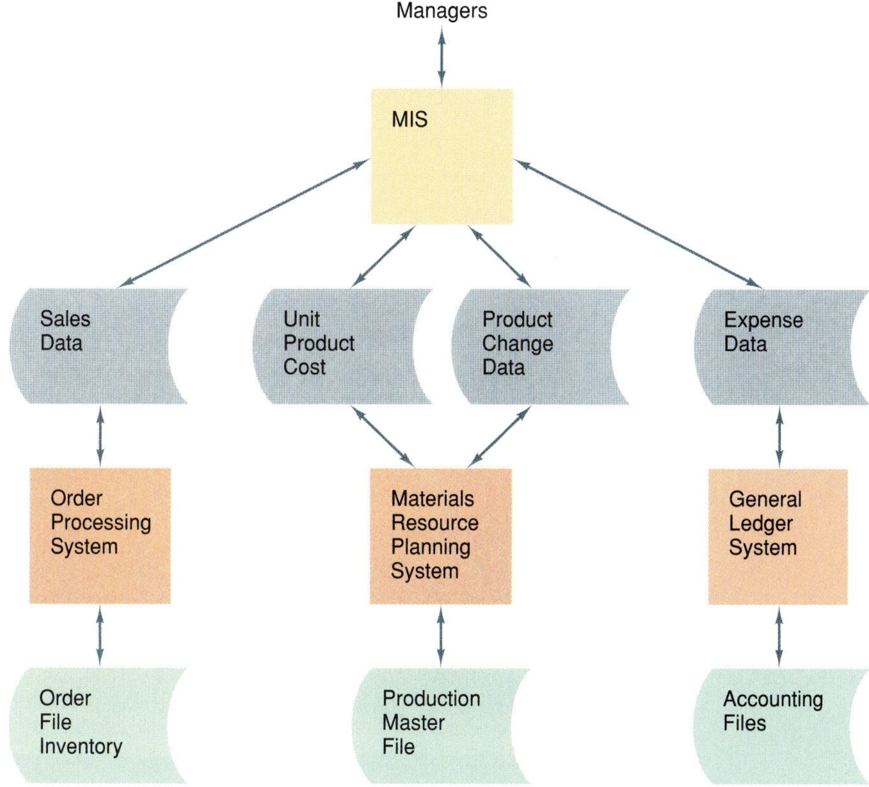

ment. Using more duck meat would indicate a problem with overportioning or waste. Restaurants with out-of-line portions would be told to take corrective action.

CPK's restaurant operations group uses the point-of-sale data to determine peak sales periods at each location so that they can schedule employee work shifts. The data also tell how well each item sells. For example, CPK found that it should eliminate its egg salad pizza because the item had poor sales. CPK can also use its information systems to calculate the relative costs of different markets so that it can determine whether it has a lower profit margin on Hawaiian pizza in Bethesda, Maryland, than in Waikiki. (Pineapple costs less in Hawaii than in the northeastern United States.) CPK's corporate accounting department uses the aggregate data to calculate revenue. It can combine these data with financial data residing on CPK's central computer.

These applications run on a client/server network using Microsoft's Windows NT Server installed at CPK's central computer at corporate head-

California Pizza Kitchen's MIS helps the company boost efficiency and cut costs, allowing managers to spend more time with customers.

quarters in Los Angeles and in all of its restaurants. A software connectivity package called RemoteWare allows company managers and district managers to access information about inventory levels, recipes, sales, and personnel schedules from their laptops as they travel from restaurant to restaurant. With this network and remote connectivity software, CPK management can easily track and monitor every aspect of the firm's operations while spending less time on administrative tasks. CPK profit margins have risen 5 percent, and managers can spend 15 percent more time assisting customers.[6]

This case study is a leading-edge example of how networked computers can be used to create very powerful management information systems. Let's go back and examine our list of questions, which should reveal more clearly just what an MIS actually does:

- **Where does the MIS obtain its data?** Like California Pizza Kitchen's MIS, most MIS obtain the raw data from transaction processing systems (TPS) such as those described in Chapter 13. In the case of California Pizza Kitchen's MIS, POS devices capture sales data on the amount and type of food items sold. Restaurant managers enter data about supplies in inventory. Each restaurant transmits these data to PCs at CPK's central headquarters.

- **What does the MIS actually do with the data?** Most MIS perform simple, repetitive summaries of transaction data and report exceptions or deviations from a plan. For instance, CPK's MIS summarizes daily sales, labor input, and inventory use. In addition, the system describes expected inventory levels and ordering amounts for each store. When a local store deviates from this corporate plan, managers are alerted that something may be wrong. Thus, this exception or deviation report signals management that efforts may be needed to change local store procedures concerning portion control.

  But CPK's MIS is a leading-edge system, and it provides a good deal more than simple summary and exception reports. In many respects, it functions like a decision support system (described in Section 16.4) because it provides recommendations for labor schedules, optimal portion sizes, and the like.

- **What management and business problems does this system solve?** In general, MIS are good at handling routine, repetitive kinds of problems that are well structured—that is, for which there is an accepted method of arriving at an answer. For instance, in answer to the question "How many people should I employ?" CPK's MIS can make a good estimate based on the number of predicted sales and the long historical experience that is captured in the system.

  The system would not handle less-structured problems, such as "If there is a snowstorm and there has been a large sales campaign for CPK, what is an optimal hourly labor force for a specific store?" Answering these less-structured questions usually requires sophisticated decision support systems, which are described in the next section.

  From a management perspective, MIS are critical to the operational control of the business. Because such systems report and summarize basic transactions and compare them with a plan, they are vital in providing managers with the right information in a timely fashion. In the case of CPK, the MIS provides central management with a bird's-eye view of how the company performs each day.

  From a business perspective, MIS help solve the problem of size by reducing coordination costs—the cost of managing many people in many different locations. As businesses grow and increase the scale of their operations, they should be able to deliver products and services more cheaply because they buy and sell in volume. On the other hand, coordination costs often grow as a business expands, preventing the business from reaping the benefits of large scale. MIS help reduce the costs of growth and make it possible for businesses to operate on a large scale with only minimal increases in coordination and management costs. CPK's MIS reduced the time and cost of administering the business, freeing up managers to spend more time on customer service and increasing sales.

- **What difference does the MIS make for the firm?** CPK's MIS has strategic consequences for the firm because it permits the company to provide low-cost food and restaurant service with a high level of quality by allowing managers to carefully control food and labor costs. It could remain competitive even though there were many other fast-food restaurants vying for its customers.

16.4 INDIVIDUAL AND GROUP DECISION SUPPORT SYSTEMS

Although nearly any computer that delivers information might be called a "decision support system," DSS are conceptually very different from MIS or TPS. Decision support systems (DSS) generally take less time and money to develop than MIS, are interactive in the sense that the user interacts with the data directly, and are useful for solving semistructured problems. As we noted earlier, a semistructured problem is one in which only parts of the problem have a clear-cut answer provided by a well-accepted methodology. Figure 16.6 summarizes major differences between an MIS and a DSS. Based on these characteristics, we can arrive at a working definition of a DSS: It is an interactive system under user control that provides data and models to support the discussion and solution of semistructured problems.

The generic DSS has three components. Figure 16.7 illustrates a DSS serving the same three business functions shown in Figure 16.5. The database of a DSS is a collection of information often taken from the firm's own internal transaction systems. Generally, this transaction information is summarized and transmitted to the DSS so that its database, unlike an MIS, contains data from inventory, production, and accounting.

Model base
The analytical tools used by an information system; in a decision support system, it includes very sophisticated tools such as built-in spreadsheets, statistical analysis, and simulation.

A second element of a DSS is a **model base,** or the analytical tools used by the system. Perhaps this is the critical difference between an MIS and a DSS. As we noted in the preceding section, MIS generally have very simple analytical tools—averages, summations, deviations from plan, and the like. DSS, however, usually have very sophisticated analytical and modeling tools, such as built-in spreadsheets, statistical analysis, and simulation.

One of the most widely used capabilities of DSS analytical and modeling tools is *"what-if" analysis*—examining the impact of changes in one or more factors or values on outcomes: What if we raised prices by 10 percent—how much would profits increase? How much more would it cost to

FIGURE 16.6

Differences between an MIS and a DSS

An MIS usually reports summaries of basic business transactions and notes exceptions from expected performance; its output is usually routine reports. It uses relatively simple analytical tools such as averages and summations to solve structured problems. A DSS, on the other hand, uses more sophisticated analytical and data modeling tools to solve semistructured problems. It provides data to support management decision making on issues that are less routine than those handled by an MIS.

MIS	DSS
•Reports summaries of basic transactions and exceptions from plan •Uses simple analytical tools •Solves structured, repetitive problems •Produces routine reports	•Provides data and models for decision making •Uses sophisticated analysis and modeling tools •Solves semi-structured problems •Provides interactive answers to nonroutine questions

FIGURE 16.7

Three Components of a DSS: Database, Model Base, and Easy-to-Use Software System

Like an MIS, a DSS draws its data from the firm's transaction processing systems. However, the DSS model base contains much more sophisticated analytical and modeling tools than would be found in an MIS. The DSS software system allows users with little computer experience to access these data, often online.

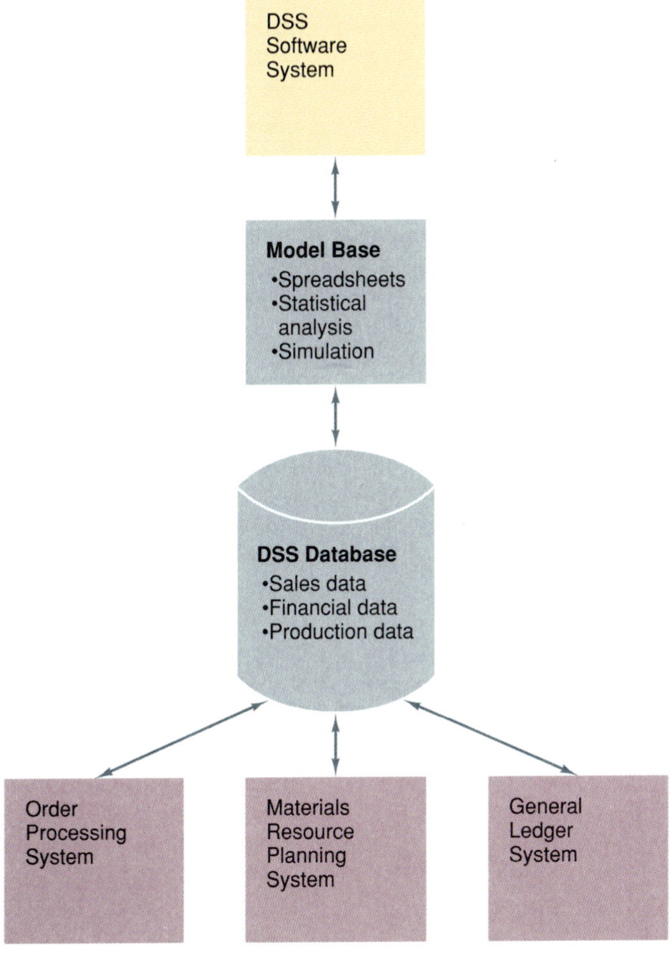

produce our product if the cost of employee wages rose by 15 percent? The Focus on Organizations describes how one small company made use of these DSS capabilities in its struggle to remain competitive as a government contractor.

The third element of a DSS is a software system that permits easy interaction between users of the system (who often have no computer expertise) and the database and model base. The Focus on Technology illustrates how these features of DSS support decision making.

Distinguishing between an MIS and a DSS is not always easy. Generally, MIS produce routine reports on a batch basis with a regular schedule—every day, week, or month. DSS produce such reports, but they also permit

FOCUS ON **ORGANIZATIONS**

TURNING GOVERNMENT INEFFICIENCY INTO COMPETITIVE ADVANTAGE

We've all heard stories about runaway government spending habits—$250 for a hammer, $600 for a toilet seat. For contractors, the U.S. government might seem like a dream client. But as Rick Lewandowski, secretary-treasurer of MDP Construction, tells it, the government can also create plenty of nightmares. MDP is totally dependent on the government for its revenues. The company stands to get a slice of the $87 million earmarked by the Pentagon for construction projects at Colorado military installations in 1997. Nevertheless, the stifling bureaucratic inefficiency of the system puts most small contractors at a decided disadvantage because they must wade through a thicket of regulations and paperwork. Delays in construction schedules keep workers idle and tie up company assets that could be used elsewhere.

Unlike large contractors, small companies do not have the resources and staff to deal with these problems, but they can deploy information technology. Virtually all aspects of MDP's business operations are computerized. Every piece of government-required paperwork has been scanned into MDP's network, allowing project supervisors to download any form from the company's server using laptops and modems. Supervisors can also instantly access subcontractor insurance and payroll information, "serial letters" to request modifications, and submittal registers, all of which are maintained on MDP's databases.

Lewandowski uses a program called SureTrak Project Manager to establish and track time lines for the myriad tasks of the company's construction projects. If he needs to make changes in one task, the program automatically rearranges the schedules for all related tasks. The program can also revise cost projections and deadlines when modifications are requested, generate precise time lines for any job or subcontractor, and produce daily progress reports. Lewandowski and his project supervisors used to do all of this work manually, a complex and arduous task for a large construction project. SureTrak now gives MDP's managers a snapshot of the big picture at any point during the project, enabling them to anticipate obstacles and to compare actual progress with original goals. When MDP was building a fire station at Peterson Air Force Base in the fall of 1996, the government wanted to change wall color midway through the project. Using SureTrak, Lewandowski showed how this one "simple" change would add 12 weeks to the schedule.

A typical construction company the size of MDP would have supervisors running each job site and a project manager overseeing three to five jobs doing all the scheduling, modifications, billing, and negotiations. With SureTrak, MDP's managers can oversee a greater number of projects than if the scheduling were done by hand. Supervisors tracking their own budgets can manage project dollars more effectively.

MDP is constructing a company Web site that will store the key project information, with all files formatted to run on the Microsoft Office 97 application software suite. Everyone will have access to general correspondence, serial letters, and submittal registers so that they can see the status of a particular submittal.

FOCUS Questions: What features of DSS are found in MDP's information systems? What management roles are supported?

SOURCE: Christopher Gaggiano, "Thriving on Bureaucracy," *Inc. Technology,* March 18, 1997.

the user to ask new and unanticipated questions and to intervene directly online to change the manner in which the data are presented. Sometimes, as illustrated in the following case, DSS have some MIS features. DSS are also starting to be developed for the Web. Once again, as you read the description of Redstone Advisors, keep the following questions in mind: Where does the DSS obtain its data? What does the DSS actually do with the data? What management and business problems does this system solve? What difference does the DSS make for the firm?

FOCUS ON TECHNOLOGY

BANK OF MONTREAL SPEEDS UP DECISION MAKING

How long does it take your bank to approve a mortgage application? The $41 billion (U.S.) Bank of Montreal had reduced its wait time to 24 hours, but management was still dissatisfied. The problem the staff at the bank faced was how to reduce the time to an almost instantaneous decision. Their solution? Combining decision support software with data warehousing. Using the new system, Lending On Pathway, the bank's approval time has dropped to about 12 minutes, even if the application is made by telephone.

The bank's new system automates many decisions that were made by human beings in the past. Previously, a human underwriter had to review a combination of paper-based applications and online credit bureau files in order to establish an applicant's credit worthiness. Now the system can do much of this work.

The mortgage decision process is the same whether a customer calls or goes into a bank branch. A staff member asks applicants questions about their assets and liabilities. The answers are then entered into a computer system where the data are stored in a customer data warehouse. Then the decision support system takes over. It first collects data online about the applicant from credit bureaus in order to determine the applicant's credit worthiness. The system then combines that information with any data on the applicant previously stored in the data warehouse and the information newly gathered from the applicant. Next, Lending On Pathway submits this data to a series of predefined lending criteria already stored in the decision support system. The system produces an answer in less than one minute, according to the bank's vice-president of personal lending services, Jane Weatherbie.

The system uses object-oriented software running a Sybase relational database management system on an IBM RS/6000 workstation. It lets users perform "what-if" analyses with various terms and loan amounts to see what best suits a customer's needs. When customers call the bank for these streamlined mortgage loans, bank staff at OS/2-based workstations input the applicant's data in English on a series of graphically oriented screens developed in Smalltalk. Unlike the Bank of Montreal's earlier rigid forms-based interface, the Smalltalk screens can be navigated in any order. During the application interview, staff can shift easily from screen to screen to jump between assets and liabilities for a husband and wife, conversing with the clients while inputting the information.

The system was piloted for four months, and the bank personnel found that in many cases the loan would even be approved while the customer was still on the telephone. Such quick service not only helps customers but also burnishes the image of the bank itself. In addition, the bank has found that its booking ratio has increased by about 20 percent. The bank is now distributing the software to all of its 1,200 branches.

FOCUS Questions:

What features of DSS are illustrated by this system? What people, organizational, and technology problems do you think the bank faced in the development and installation of Lending on Pathway? Suggest other uses the bank might have for this type of software.

SOURCES: Julia King, "Decision-Support Software Cuts Loan Processing Time," *Computerworld*, February 19, 1996.

LEADING-EDGE APPLICATION: REDSTONE ADVISORS

Money management is a giant industry, with many firms each managing hundreds of millions or billions of dollars. Redstone Advisors manages $500 million in taxable and tax-exempt fixed income securities such as bonds. By the very nature of its work, money management requires the continuous collection and analysis of an enormous amount of data. Redstone must track a range of complex financial instruments and continually analyze both individual investments and overall market trends in swiftly changing markets.

Decision support systems with capabilities for "what-if" analysis can help managers make important financial decisions.

Redstone managers hold monthly policy meetings to evaluate their company's investment strategy and determine its investment portfolio plan for the coming month. At these meetings, they set general guidelines for the managers, including establishing targets for the percentage of cash for portfolios and the weight of each business sector in the portfolio (for example, determining that 20 percent of their bonds should be in government treasury bills, 10 percent in tax-free municipals, 10 percent in banking bonds, 5 percent in mining company bonds, and so on). They also establish guidelines for the duration of the portfolios (that is, how many years out, on average, the bonds ought to go).

Once the policy meeting is completed, Redstone money managers make trades to bring their portfolios into line with the new guidelines for the coming month. The main task of the managers is first to identify appropriate financial instruments and then to determine whether purchasing those instruments will bring their portfolios into accord with the new guidelines. To support them in this task, they use a software package called PORTIA.

PORTIA, a product of Thomson Financial Services of Boston and London, is a LAN-based portfolio management system. Traders use the system first as a decision support system and then as a system through which they can execute their trades. PORTIA is a DSS because it includes a simulation capability. Using this capability, traders first enter their proposed trades as if they were real. The system simulator treats them as real trades and evaluates the overall portfolio with these changes, thus giving the portfolio manager a preview of the proposed new portfolio. The manager then enters additional changes to attempt to bring the portfolio closer to the guidelines and receives new feedback from PORTIA. This process is repeated iteratively until the manager is satisfied, at which point the remaining simulated trades are entered for real and actually executed. The portfolio's cash balances and holdings are also updated.

PORTIA is currently being used by over 350 investment firms around the world. It can handle all types of securities traded around the world, track and report in any currency, and automatically convert from one currency to another. This is one reason why National Mutual Funds Management (Global)

Limited (NMFM) of Australia selected PORTIA. NMFM is a subsidiary of National Mutual Holdings, one of Australia's largest insurance and funds management groups. NMFM will link PORTIA with existing systems in its other Asian Pacific sites.

PORTIA is popular partially because of its simulation models. However, like many quality DSS, it also performs many functions found in an MIS. It performs ongoing, routine analysis, including, in this case, determining for Redstone traders the actual cash percentage, the weight by sector, and the portfolio duration. The system includes routine status and performance reporting. It also acts as a TPS, performing key order processing, including submission of buy and sell orders, electronic linkages to the brokers who will execute the orders, and automatic updating of the Redstone database once the orders have been completed. It even contains all the generic accounting tools that are standard to money management firms. Finally, PORTIA's value to money management firms is enhanced because it offers the broad functionality Redstone and many other portfolio managers require. For example, fixed-income security firms are interested in multicurrency capabilities because they often trade in foreign bonds, and this facility is a strength of PORTIA. Moreover, PORTIA is available in a Microsoft Windows version, making it easy for traders to use[7] (see Figure 16.8).

FIGURE 16.8

A DSS for the Financial Industry

PORTIA is a portfolio management system that can be used to develop DSS for the financial services industry. Using PORTIA, money managers can simulate model portfolios under a variety of assumptions and currencies to guide their buying and selling decisions. This sample screen is used for creating reports.

SOURCE: Courtesy of Thomas Financial Services.

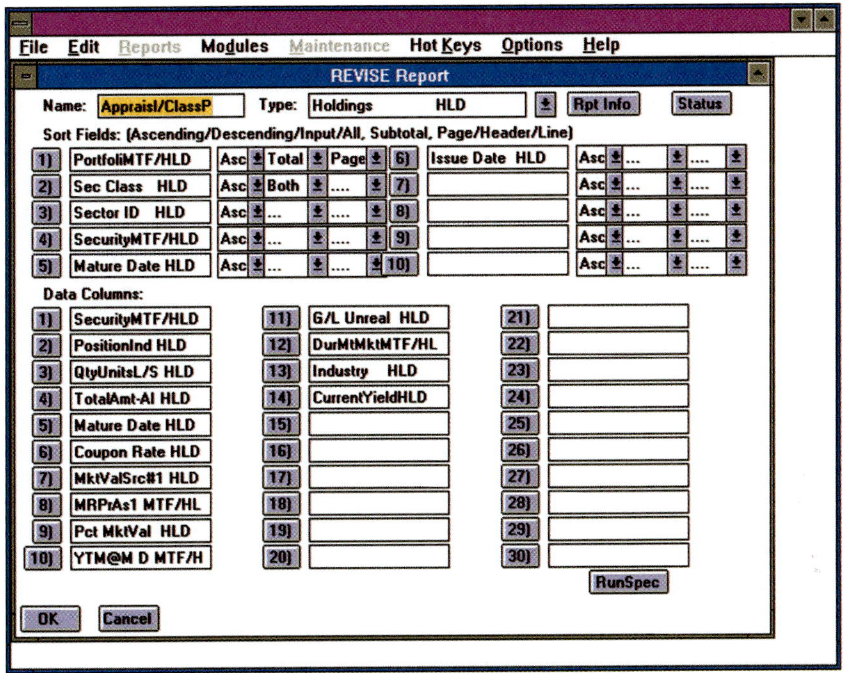

Now let's return to the questions we raised at the beginning of this case study by looking at the DSS capabilities of PORTIA:

- **Where does the DSS obtain its data?** In this case, the data come from a number of sources. Redstone must purchase daily market data from a data service such as Reuters or Dow Jones in order to be up to date in today's financial markets. Redstone is also the source of some of the data itself, such as the guidelines for evaluating the portfolios and the orders to buy and sell. Data also come from the systems of the brokerage firms that execute Redstone's orders.

- **What does the DSS actually do with the data?** Routine reporting tools inform managers of the current value and composition of each portfolio as well as other analytical data Redstone requires. The DSS takes the current data and the simulation input from the trader and performs "what if" analysis and feedback. Managers can determine the effects of their proposed trades on the portfolio before actually entering the trades, and they can see the effects of various decisions on different currencies.

- **What management and business problems does this system solve?** The central management problem involves establishing monthly strategy guidelines to maximize returns on complex investments when market conditions are rapidly changing. The DSS gives Redstone's traders the ability to plan their trades in advance and to make trades that meet those guidelines. Through its online reporting capabilities, it also gives management the ability to monitor and control the activities of its portfolio managers and to measure performance.

- **What difference does the DSS make for the firm?** More than anything else, it allows management to manage the business the way it wants despite the fast pace of the money management industry and the overwhelming amount of data the firm needs to handle. Senior management strategies can be executed and monitored. The system has other value as well. Errors are reduced and productivity increased because of the automated links with the brokers and the accounting systems. In an industry in which changes are as rapid as they are in the financial markets, this system also offers traders speedy analysis as well as fast execution and reporting. A less tangible, although critical, benefit provided by the system is its flexibility in international markets. Using PORTIA, Redstone and other firms can take advantage of the opportunities that are becoming available as the globalization of the world's economy continues.

Not all DSS for portfolio management are as powerful as PORTIA, nor can all investment decisions be handled by the computer. The Focus on People examines these issues as it describes other portfolio management DSS designed for individual investors.

GROUP DECISION SUPPORT SYSTEMS

DSS are primarily oriented toward the work of individuals. But many decisions are made by managers working together in groups. Special systems called **group decision support systems (GDSS)** have been developed to support managers. A GDSS is an interactive computer-based system to facilitate the solution of unstructured problems by a set of decision makers working together as a group.[8]

Group decision support system (GDSS)
Interactive computer-based system to help a set of decision makers working together as a group to solve unstructured problems.

In recent years organizations have placed increased emphasis on group decision making. More and more meetings are held in order to broaden the expertise available for decision making and thereby improve the quality of the decisions reached. But as meetings have multiplied, it has become clear that they can be both expensive and unproductive. New ways must be found to improve the group decision-making process in meetings.

Problems Posed by Group Meetings Before considering how to assist and improve the group decision-making process, we need to be aware of problems that arise when people work together in meetings. Some of the main problems include:

- **Too many attendees.** Studies indicate that the optimal size of traditional meetings is between four and five individuals. As meetings grow larger, some attendees are unable to contribute. Others choose not to participate, preferring to be lost in the crowd (known as "free riding"). In larger meetings, one or two individuals can more easily dominate the discussion. The result is an expensive loss of time combined with a failure to elicit potentially valuable input.

- **Meeting atmospheres may not encourage individual participation.** Two related problems have emerged. First, many employees are hesitant to participate openly when their managers or others higher up the corporate ladder are present because they fear being judged. Second, many do not contribute their ideas for fear both their ideas and they personally will be criticized. The result, again, is an undesirable conformity and a fruitless attempt to engender new ideas.

- **Ideas may not be evaluated objectively.** Such fears are not unfounded. Too frequently ideas are evaluated on the basis of the source of the idea rather than on the merit of the idea itself. Moreover, in traditional meetings, it is standard practice to find reasons why a suggested line of action will not work rather than looking for ways to make it work. As a result, too many good ideas are rejected and too many poor ones are adopted. When setting priorities and making decisions, ways should be found to encompass the thinking of all the attendees and to evaluate input more objectively.

- **Meetings may be poorly documented.** Attendees often do not have the documentation they need in order to follow up on decisions made. Moreover, without adequate documentation, organizational memory is lost—those who do not attend a specific meeting, such as staff at other

FOCUS ON **PEOPLE**

CAN COMPUTERS REPLACE FINANCIAL PLANNERS?

Today there are almost as many mutual funds as there are stocks—more than 6,000 at the end of 1996. Which are the best? How should investors allocate among stocks, bonds, or money market funds to meet their personal goals? There are so many choices that individual investors can easily become confused. Inexperienced investors need help.

To cash in on investors' confusion, many financial service firms such as Charles Schwab & Co. and Vanguard are offering free asset allocation and fund selection services to their customers. New services are springing up, such as Net Results, an online mutual fund advisory service based in California. Unlike traditional forms of financial advice, these low-cost services come from companies that have heretofore left investors to make their own decisions. The services are heavily dependent on computer number crunching. An investor is asked to provide data on his or her risk tolerance and financial goals, such as saving for a house, college education, or retirement. A computer program then uses these numbers to turn out a financial plan with an overall asset allocation recommendation (what percentage of the portfolio should be in stock, bond, or money-market funds) and specific fund selections.

Technology allows such services to be provided at much less cost than by a traditional full-service brokerage firm or financial planner. It reduces the costs of developing hundreds of thousands of investment portfolios and the time human financial planners must spend to identify the issues while maximizing the time they spend communicating results to the client. The number of mutual fund investors has soared. (There were 86 million stock mutual fund shareholder accounts at the end of 1996.) Technology-based financial planning fits well into the cultures of companies that previously did not provide investment advice because such financial planning can deliver answers that don't rely on subjective advice.

However, the relative simplicity of these services leaves them open to attack. For example, Robert Levitt, a partner at Evensky Brown Katz & Levitt, a Boca Raton, Florida, financial planning firm, feels that the financial planning service offered by Charles Schwab & Company is "very generic." The program asks only a few questions and picks funds from a list. Many investors may believe these services are very scientific because they are number oriented when, in fact, they are based on human judgment.

Thomas Taggart, a spokesman for Schwab, acknowledged that the firm's program is simplistic but noted that its purpose is to provide general investment guidelines for self-directed investors. Built into the program is a referral to a human adviser for more complex decisions. Other observers note that these automated financial planning services are improving their risk measurement techniques and fund evaluation capabilities.

The competition among financial services firms is so intense that these companies are likely to further reduce the cost of these asset allocation and portfolio evaluation services to attract and retain their clients. Technology-based services will drive down investment advisory fees and probably push traditional advice givers into more complex high-end functions such as estate planning, complex tax strategies, and investment advice for people with $1 million or more. Wealthy clients expect more service than filling out a computer questionnaire.

FOCUS Questions: What kinds of decisions can be supported by computerized asset allocation and mutual fund selection systems? What kinds of decisions can't be supported? Would you rely on such services for financial planning? Why or why not?

SOURCE: Virginia Munger Kahn, "A Move to Advice at a Lower Price," *The New York Times,* December 8, 1996.

Staff of the Ventana Corporation discusses the features of its GroupSystems for Windows meeting support software, which is designed to help teams work together for better and faster decisions. Participants interact through a network of PCs whenever and wherever they need to work together in meetings, between offices, across the country, or around the world. The software features special tools to help them create, share, record, organize, and evaluate ideas.

SOURCE: Courtesy of Ventana Corporation.

sites, may not have the information they need in order to work on a project.

- **Too much time can be wasted arguing over facts or searching for information needed for making a decision.** The lack of availability of corporate and external information prevents factual disagreements from being settled quickly and thus makes meetings longer and less productive.

Characteristics of Group Decision Support Systems Some of these problems can be solved by using group decision support systems. GDSS-guided meetings take place in conference rooms that contain special hardware and software tools to facilitate group decision making. The hardware includes computer and networking equipment, overhead projectors, and display screens. Special electronic meeting software can collect, rank, document, and store the ideas offered in a decision-making meeting. The more elaborate GDSS require a professional facilitator and support staff. The facilitator selects the software tools and helps to organize and run the meeting.

How GDSS Enhance Decision Making A sophisticated GDSS will provide each attendee with a dedicated desktop computer under his or her individual control. No one will be able to see what individuals do on their computers until and unless those participants are ready to share information, at which time they transmit it via a network to a central network server that makes the information available to all on the meeting network. Data can also be projected on a large screen or screens in the meeting room.

Let us look once again at the meeting problems listed above and see how GDSS contribute solutions.

- **Too many attendees.** Using GDSS hardware and software, meeting size can be increased significantly while at the same time increasing productivity because individuals can contribute simultaneously rather than one at a time. For example, during a brainstorming session, rather than going around the room and taking input one at a time from attendees, all prepare their input simultaneously and transmit the results to the group. The meeting can thus be both shorter and more productive. Studies indicate that GDSS meeting attendees believe the quality of participation in these meetings is much higher than in traditional meetings.
- **Meeting atmospheres may not encourage individual participation.** Using a GDSS, individuals contribute their ideas anonymously—when input is transmitted by an individual to the server, the source of the input is neither displayed nor even recorded, so no one can determine who offered which ideas. In this way attendees do not need to fear criticism from their managers or be concerned that other attendees will criticize them rather than evaluate their ideas. Anonymity establishes an atmosphere in which even unconventional and novel ideas can and will be submitted, often to the benefit of the organization. Studies show that in this environment, not only are more ideas generated, but attendees are more satisfied with the ideas.
- **Ideas may not be evaluated objectively.** Again, anonymity prevents evaluation of ideas based on their source and instead focuses attention on the ideas themselves. With a trained facilitator, attendees will also be asked to generate (again, anonymously) ideas on how to make the idea work rather than on why it won't work.
- **Meetings may be poorly documented.** All contributions, at each stage of the meeting, are transmitted to a network server that stores the data for future use by both attendees and others in the organization.
- **Too much time can be wasted arguing over facts or searching for information needed to make a decision.** In many GDSS meetings, the network is connected to needed organizational databases in the same way as are individual DSS. In some cases, the network can be connected to external sources as well to aid in decision making.

The effectiveness of GDSS depends heavily on how well the meeting is planned and conducted. Nonetheless, studies and the experiences of organizations indicate that GDSS allow managers to be more productive and to use their time more efficiently by producing the desired results in fewer meetings.

16.5 EXECUTIVE SUPPORT SYSTEMS

Special systems called executive support systems (ESS) have been developed to serve the information needs of managers at the highest organizational levels. They combine data from both internal and external sources to help senior management solve unstructured problems. ESS differ from MIS and DSS in several ways. Characteristically, ESS

- Are designed explicitly for the purposes of senior management.
- Are used by senior management without technical intermediaries.
- Require a greater proportion of information from outside the business.
- Contain both structured and unstructured data.
- Use state-of-the-art integrated graphics, text, and communications technology.

One can think of ESS as generalized computing, telecommunications, and graphics systems that, like a zoom lens, can be focused quickly on detailed problems or retracted for a broad view of the company.

Contemporary ESS usually fall into one of three types. Some ESS focus on executive communications and office work. These systems begin by building powerful electronic mail networks and then expand outward to include new officelike functions, such as document processing, scheduling of executives' time, and so forth. A second type of ESS simply provides a more convenient interface to corporate data. Such systems deliver more business performance data faster than a typical MIS can and usually present the data in a graphic mode. A third type of ESS focuses on developing elaborate scenarios, applying sophisticated statistical models to company forecasts, and using other tools that are designed to expand a senior manager's ability to plan for the future. Figure 16.9 shows a general model for an ESS that obtains data from the order processing, materials resource planning, and general ledger systems (transaction processing systems). In addition to these internal sources, data enter from external databases, are manipulated in the ESS database and model base, and are accessed through ESS software.

You might ask, "Haven't senior managers been using computers all along? Who uses all the MIS and DSS, not to mention the personal computers?" The answer to the first question is "no." Until very recently, senior managers generally did not believe it was appropriate for them to operate a keyboard, a skill they identified with clerical work. Senior managers generally left it to assistants and clerical workers to find and present data. Virtually all MIS and DSS are designed for corporate professional staff, both professional knowledge workers and middle managers. ESS are the only systems explicitly designed for senior executives.

In the next section, we present an example of a real-world ESS being used at Pratt & Whitney, a multibillion-dollar subsidiary of United Technologies and a leading manufacturer of jet aircraft engines. The company is headquartered in East Hartford, Connecticut. In response to growing market competition, executives at Pratt & Whitney's Commercial Engine Business (CEB) division developed a strategic plan to increase their market share by

FIGURE 16.9

An ESS Accesses Data from Both Internal and External Sources

Here we illustrate a generic ESS that includes a database and a model base. Its data come both from internal transaction processing systems and from outside databases. The ESS software uses integrated graphics, communications, and text to provide an easy-to-use interface for senior managers, who often have little experience with computers.

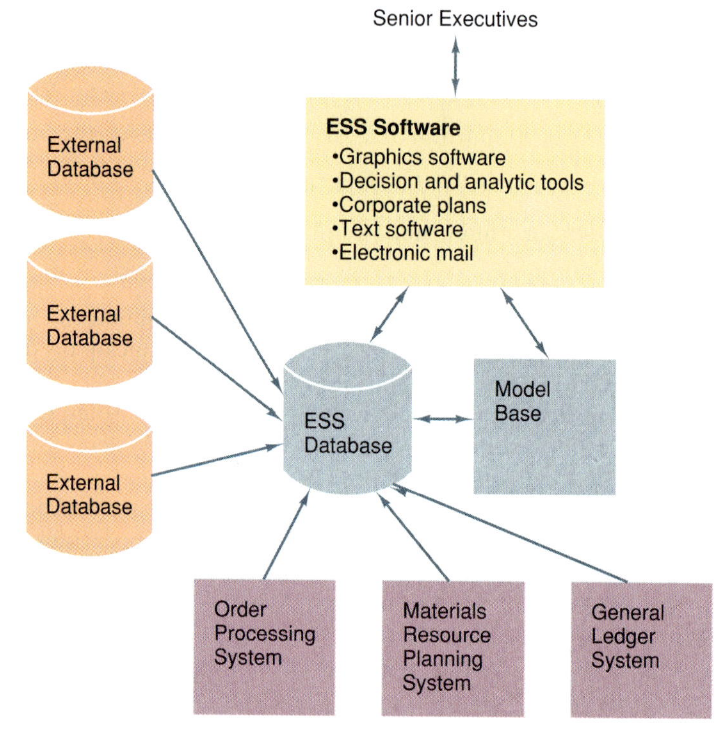

improving the quality of both their products and their customer service. As part of the implementation of that plan, they developed an ESS.

As you read about Pratt & Whitney, keep in mind our now-familiar questions: Where does the ESS obtain its data? What does the ESS actually do with the data? What management and business problems does this system solve? What difference does the system make for the firm?

LEADING-EDGE APPLICATION: PRATT & WHITNEY'S CEB EXECUTIVE SUPPORT SYSTEM

Pratt & Whitney's CEB management considers the quality of its customer service and the performance of its products as the heart of its business. CEB wanted software that would allow senior managers to monitor and analyze these critical success factors more closely. The software needed certain characteristics. First, it had to be interactive. Second, it needed to be heavily graphic so that senior managers could quickly and easily grasp the information presented. In addition, because senior managers had not been significant users of computers, any system would have to be not only easy to learn, but one that could be learned intuitively rather than by instruction (corporate executives are not known for being willing to sit still for computer education). Finally, because Pratt & Whitney was changing from centralized mainframe computing to a networked desktop environment, the system needed to be flexible. Its new ESS had to handle cooperative processing so that tasks could be run on either a PC or the larger host computer, depending on which was more suited to a particular task. The division settled on Commander EIS software from Comshare.

The first system Pratt & Whitney decided to develop with Commander EIS was a system to track key quality and reliability measures of each jet engine model. The ESS drew data from three production systems and included such data as the reliability of each engine model, the availability of spare engines, and the availability of spare parts for each engine. This data could be examined either by engine model or by customer. The system also included data from customers, including such critical (to the customer) data as flight delays and cancellations due to engine problems. The system made available to senior management three types of information: product quality indicators, marketing information, and customer-specific information, including critical issues for each customer.

One of the users of the new system is Selwyn Berson, president of CEB. Berson and other executives can confirm the reliability of the engine models in operation and the status of engine orders for each of their customers. Senior executives can also respond to customer questions about new product and service delivery dates. They can discuss with customers not only current policy on engine quality but also the results of that policy by using information available on steps taken to improve engine reliability.

Executives are also able to track data by engine model number, determining how often the engines are brought into the shop and the sources of the problems. Thus, through the ESS, they are able to monitor engine performance and reliability over time. With this information quite literally at their fingertips, senior management can modify corporate plans and procedures to keep the new, two-track strategy on target.

In 1992 about 25 senior executives from various areas (including human resources and finance) used the ESS. CEB executives predict that in time, more than 200 executives and managers will use the system and that its use will help highlight what is important to the whole organization so that all managers and executives will work toward a common goal.[9]

Now let's return to the questions we posed at the beginning of this case study:

- **Where does the ESS obtain its data?** The data are collected both internally and externally. Much of the data come from three existing production systems that carry data on product and part availability, repair records, and even customer service. The external data—maintenance issues and needs, flight delays and cancellations—come from customers.

- **What does the ESS actually do with the data?** The CEB ESS compresses and summarizes detailed data and presents them in a graphic format. This particular application provides little complex statistical analysis. Executives can examine the data to get more detailed information about specific customers or problems.

- **What management and business problems does this system solve?** By providing data on product quality and performance to senior managers, the new system helps the organization identify problems at the highest level. Senior managers can easily see which areas of the business need immediate and long-term improvement and use this information to make organization-wide changes that are essential to the continuing success of the company. They have access to timely data on new engine and replacement part availability, reported engine problems and repairs, and customer service. Because data on company performance are directly available to them without the technical assistance of others, senior managers have better control over the company.

  The system addresses several key issues for management. Customer service should improve because of management's new ability to be involved in and knowledgeable about this function. Moreover, by combining information specific to an individual customer with company-wide information about an engine model, customer relations is able to better understand and handle engine problems for individual customers. Senior management, in turn, can take a more strategic look at how customer support representatives can improve product availability. Management also believes that easy access to knowledge about how engine failure affects a customer's ability to fly should result in a heightened Pratt & Whitney sensitivity to the need to improve customer service.

  The new system also gives management the ability to track, analyze, and ultimately deal with internal problems. Managers use the system to ensure that spare parts are always available and to monitor management of engines in the field. Through the information they access, they are able to assess engineering and research investments. They can determine engine problem trends, product or part shortages, even engine repair times. By accessing and analyzing such data, management will be able to identify problems earlier and deal with them more quickly and effectively than in the past. In addition, they expect to be able to plan better for the future.

- **What difference does the ESS make for the firm?** Walt Dempsey, from CEB's business management and planning department and a strong supporter of the new ESS, believes it has created an organizational focus and alignment within the company that encourages executives to work toward common goals. He thinks that all functions within CEB will demonstrate an increased ability to contribute to the company's profitability by giving everyone better insight into what the company does and why it does things the way it does. He expects the various departments to identify business processes that need changing so that the company can better serve its customers.

RUNNING CASE PART 4

MACY'S STAGES A COMEBACK

Macy's new chief executive officer, Myron E. Ullman III, came up with a new five-year plan designed to put Macy's back on track. The plan aimed at cutting operating expenses from 37 percent of sales to 32 percent. Macy's would slash its advertising budget and stage fewer one-day sales to focus on frequent promotions and more attention to its frequent credit-card users. It would scale back on private-label goods and stock more name brands. It would increase customer service in departments such as designer apparel and luggage while cutting back in areas such as junior sportswear. With sharper merchandising, more focused customer service, and closer attention to costs, Macy's plan was designed to restore profits as the store gradually increased sales.

To stock and distribute merchandise more efficiently, Macy's installed a new computerized inventory management system called BPS, for buying, planning, and selling, that was developed by Federated Department Stores, Inc. (Federated's chains include Bloomingdale's, Stern's, and Burdines.) The system uses a point-of-sale system to capture data about what is actually sold at the checkout counter. The data captured at the point of sale are then transmitted to a central computer. At the end of each day the central computer sends the data to 100 national planners assigned to various product groups, such as men's apparel. The planners examine the sales data on their computer screens to determine what is selling and where. Armed with this information, they call store managers to investigate what's behind the numbers, and they instruct Macy's national buyers to ship specific items to specific stores. The planners also advise each store how much of each item to stock.

For example, when national planner Patti McCluskey found sales data showing a strong demand for knit shirts at the Macy's in Bridgewater, New Jersey, she notified Mark Owens, the men's apparel buyer, to allocate more knits and twills to that store. She also called Neal Goldberg, the Bridgewater store manager, and found out that the store's clientele favored golf. She then called Owens again to suggest other ways to increase sales, such as sending the store more V-necked tennis sweaters (customers who play golf at country clubs are likely to play tennis as well).

The new system increases Macy's chances of selling more and making those sales more profitable. In 1992, 46 percent of Macy's customers who shopped at the store left without buying anything, and 56 percent of them left empty-handed because the store did not have what they came in to purchase. After the new plan and system were implemented, a similar survey showed that only 23 percent of shoppers left Macy's without making a purchase and that only 29 percent of them could not find what they wanted.

Under this new system, Macy's has increased its business 15 percent on 25 percent less inventory. Although the system added 100 national planners, it cut the number of buyers from 425 to 180. With a direct computer link between Macy's and key suppliers, orders that used to take up to seven weeks to fill can now be completed within nine days.

Macy's is also developing information systems to support a more democratic company culture, in which employees are encouraged to learn as much as they can and to share their ideas with management. A new satellite network connects suppliers with salespeople in stores. Fashion designer Donna Karan can stage a teleconference with Macy's sales staff on how to best coordinate her clothing and accessories for the customer and answer sales staff questions. The network also lets Macy's executives brief employees on store performance, sales promotions, or other issues. Macy's is also planning to launch a national Macy's catalogue in 1998 to establish a presence in catalogue retailing.

Some critics wonder whether the new plan is enough to solidly turn the tide for Macy's. Getting employees to accept new computers and new ways of doing business takes years. Some store managers and buyers resent giving up some of their decision making to the national planners.

As Macy's emerged from bankruptcy protection, its top executives agreed to merge with Federated Department Stores Inc., Macy's longtime rival. The merger was finalized in late 1994, creating the largest department store chain in the United States. Allen Questrom, Federated's chairman and chief executive officer, wants to make Macy's one of Federated's two main chains. (Bloomingdale's would appeal to upscale customers, Macy's to middle-brow buyers.) The combined company could trim costs because of its enormous clout dealing with suppliers and economies achieved by having many stores share nationwide advertising and promotion campaigns.

The question is whether this strategy will work when the retail industry is shrinking. Many people have forsaken traditional department stores for discount stores. Questrom believes that people will still flock to department stores because they are sources of new ideas in design and fashion and centers of entertainment. Can Macy's—and Federated—bring back the old retailing magic?

SOURCES: Laura Bird, "Federated Plans National Launch of Macy's Catalog," *The Wall Street Journal,* September 12, 1997; Linda Grant, "Miracle or Mirage on 34th Street," *Fortune,* February 5, 1996; Susan Caminiti, "A High-Priced Game of Catch-Up," *Fortune,* September 6, 1993; and Stephanie Strom, "A Key for a Macy Comeback," *The New York Times,* November 1, 1992.

RUNNING CASE Questions

1. How did Macy's try to solve its problems? What were the people, organizational, and technological dimensions of its solution?
2. How successful was Macy's solution? What recommendations would you make?
3. How important were Macy's new information systems for solving its problems? What kinds of problems could these systems solve for Macy's? What problems couldn't be solved by these systems?

SUMMARY

- The three major types of management support systems (MSS) found in business firms are MIS, DSS, and ESS. These systems serve different groups and interests in the firm. In order to understand how these systems work, you need to know something about what managers do.
- In the traditional view, managers plan, organize, lead, and control.
- In the contemporary behavioral view, managers perform three major types of roles: interpersonal, informational, and decisional.
- Managers receive most of their information from group and interpersonal, informal communications. But the information they receive from formal systems can be decisive.
- Information systems can be of most help in decisional and informational roles.
- MIS (management information systems) are routine reporting systems used to monitor and control businesses.
- DSS (decision support systems) are interactive systems under user control that are used in solving semistructured problems. A DSS has three components: a database, a model base, and an easy-to-use software system.
- GDSS (group decision support systems) facilitate the solution of unstructured problems for decision makers working together as a group.
- ESS (executive support systems) are graphics-oriented systems designed for senior management that provide generalized computing and telecommunications facilities for monitoring and controlling a business.

KEY TERMS

Management information systems (MIS)
Decision support systems (DSS)
Semistructured problem
Structured problem
Executive support systems (ESS)
Traditional theories of management
Managing
Behavioral theories of management
Interpersonal roles
Informational roles
Decisional roles
Model base
Group decision support systems (GDSS)

REVIEW QUESTIONS

1. What is the traditional view of management? What are the major functions of management?
2. How do behavioral descriptions of management differ from traditional views?
3. What are the behavioral characteristics of modern management?
4. What are the three categories of management roles discovered by behavioral scientists?

5. In which of these roles can information technology make an important contribution? In which role is the contribution of information technology not large?
6. What can managers do to change corporate culture, politics, and bureaucracy?
7. What is a management information system? Where does it get its information, what does it do to that information, and what difference does it make for the firm?
8. What is a decision support system (DSS)? How does it differ from an MIS?
9. What is a group decision support system (GDSS)? How does it differ from a DSS?
10. Describe several problems that GDSS can help solve.
11. What is an executive support system (ESS)? How does it differ from an MIS and a DSS?

DISCUSSION QUESTIONS

1. Your boss has asked you to come up with some alternative ideas about how computers can be used to support the decision-making needs of top management. What kinds of systems would you recommend? Which would you recommend first?

2. How will hiring a large number of computer-literate, recent college graduates affect the use of systems in a business firm?

3. In what ways could a management support system of any kind help a manager perform his or her leadership roles?

PROBLEM-SOLVING EXERCISES

1. *Group exercise:* Divide into groups. Each group should find a description of a senior manager of a corporation in *Business Week, Forbes, Fortune,* or other business magazines. Each group should write a description of the kinds of decisions the manager has to make and suggest an executive support system or a decision support system that might be useful for this executive. Groups are encouraged to draw a diagram of their proposed systems and present their finding to the class.

2. Interview a manager at a local business or corporation. Write an analysis of his or her daily activities and the information required for these activities. What information systems does the manager currently use? What additional information systems would you suggest to help the manager with his or her work?

3. *Hands-on exercise:* Prime Plastics is a small manufacturer of plastic parts used to package medical supplies. The following income statement shows its income, expenses, and net profit for 1997. (The net profit can be calculated by subtracting the firm's total expenses from total income.) Prime's management would like to find the impact on profits if the company could increase sales by 10 percent a year while limiting increases in expenditures to only 5 percent a year. (Income from interest would remain the same each

year.) Use appropriate software to develop an application that would project Prime's income, expenditures, and profits for the next three years.

Prime Plastics Income Statement: Year Ending 12/31/97

Income:	
Sales	$1,300,000
Interest	110,000
Total income	$1,410,000
Expenses:	
Operating expenses	$490,000
Wages	450,000
Taxes	210,000
Total expenses	$1,150,000
Net Profit	$260,000

4. *Internet problem-solving exercise:* You are 35 years of age and have recently been promoted. You decide it is time for you to consider financial planning for your retirement. You understand that T. Rowe Price, the mutual fund company, has Internet software that will help you determine how much you will need to save. You can use the interactive financial planning software at the T. Rowe Price Web site to assist you with your financial planning decisions. First, take T. Rowe Price's "retirement quiz" to help you understand more about retirement finances. Then use the "Retirement Planning Worksheet" found by clicking on the "interactive worksheet" to help you determine how much you need to save for your retirement goals. Assume the following:

Your current annual salary is $45,000.

You are taxed at a rate of 28 percent.

You assume a long-range inflation rate of 4 percent.

You plan to retire in 25 years.

You want to retire with much more than you earn, 500 percent of your current salary.

You expect a rate of return after retirement of 10 percent.

Your current taxable investments amount to $10,000.

Your expected rate of return on these investments is 8 percent.

Your current tax deferred investments equal $15,000.

Your expected rate of return on these investments is 9.5 percent.

Once you have obtained your answer, try it again with numbers you choose for yourself.

NOTES

1. Peter F. Drucker, *Management Tasks, Responsibilities, Practices* (New York: Harper & Row, 1974).
2. For a contemporary introduction to management, see Richard I. Daft, *Management,* 4th ed. (Fort Worth, Texas: Dryden Press, 1997).
3. John T. Kotter, "What Effective General Managers Really Do," *Harvard Business Review,* November—December 1982.

4. Henry Mintzberg, "Managerial Work: Analysis from Observations," *Management Science* 18 (October 1971). See also Kotter, "What Effective General Managers Really Do."

5. Margrethe Olson, "Manager or Technician? The Nature of Information Systems Manager's Job," *MIS Quarterly,* December 1981.

6. Laura DiDio, "Pizzeria Eats Up Client/Server Pie," *Computerworld,* March 4, 1996, and Mary Hayes, "Getting a Slice of the Action," *Information Week,* December 12, 1994.

7. "National Mutual Funds Selects PORTIA and TradeView," *Thomson Investment Software,* March 4, 1997; Karen Corcell, "PORTIA Keeps the Faith," *Wall Street and Technology* 11, 11 (March 1994); and "Fixed Income Money Manager Boosts Efficiency with Flexible, Comprehensive System," *Wall Street and Technology* 10, 9 (April 1993).

8. Geraldine DeSantis and R. Brent Gallupe, "A Foundation for the Study of Group Decision Support Systems," *Management Science* 33, 5 (May 1987).

9. "Pratt & Whitney Unveils Computerized Illustrated Jet Engine Tool Catalog," *Pratt & Whitney Government Engines & Space Propulsion,* May 16, 1996, and "The New Role for Executive Information Systems," *I/S Analyzer,* January 1992.

PROBLEM-SOLVING CASE

MANAGING THE VIRTUAL TACO STAND

When John Martin took over as president and CEO of Taco Bell in 1983, he found himself at the helm of a fast-food chain with the logo of a man sleeping under a sombrero. That man had to wake up. Competition was accelerating as the fast-food industry matured. The only way companies could compete was by increasing their share of a market that was no longer growing. Costs were rising at the same time, primarily due to increased real estate and construction expenses. Taco Bell's management believed that the only way the firm could compete was to find a way to provide more value to customers—by offering better service while keeping prices low.

Traditional approaches to cutting costs—by lowering ingredient costs and reducing labor—wouldn't increase quality. Martin and his management team came up with a new formula for simplifying the fast-food preparation process. Instead of preparing items when customers placed their orders, Taco Bell started to prepare most of its food in consolidated facilities with lower production and labor costs. The prepared menu items such as chicken, beans, or shredded lettuce are delivered precooked in plastic bags to individual Taco Bell restaurants and assembled into the platters ordered by customers. The job of the kitchen shifted from preparing food to assembling meals, freeing resources for more customer service.

The company installed an information system called TACO (Total Automation of Company Operations) to increase the accuracy of ordering items for restaurants. The system provides restaurant managers with reports on food cost, labor cost, inventory, perishable items, and period-to-date costs, as well as 46 pieces of data on daily store operations. Restaurant managers can use the system for inventory control, labor scheduling, sales forecasting, product ordering, and sales tracking. Every night an IBM RS/6000 workstation polls a PC in each Taco Bell restaurant. The data are then analyzed so that managers can analyze sales trends, staffing levels, portion control, or the success of promotional campaigns. Taco Bell management knows what goes on in 15-minute increments—how many customers came in, what they ordered, and how quickly they were served.

This detailed information lets each Taco Bell district manager (to whom the restaurant managers report) oversee nearly 60 restaurants, a marked contrast to the fast-food industry average of eight units per manager.

Since restaurant managers don't have to spend so much time overseeing food preparation, they can spend more time dealing with customers. The cost of managing each Taco Bell restaurant is lower. By reducing management costs, Taco Bell can keep prices low to remain competitive.

Taco Bell was the first fast-food chain to institute "value pricing," offering main meal items for less than a dollar. Value pricing can lead to profits because customers who pour in for 39-cent tacos will buy nachos and sodas at the regular price. Most costs, such as a restaurant's physical plant, are fixed, so more customers equals more profits, even if the prices of a few food items are reduced.

Now Taco Bell is moving toward team-managed units, where teams of employees are trained to run the restaurant without a full-time manager. In addition to restaurants, it is establishing outlets in airports and convenience stores where people can purchase its food. TACO was modified to support these goals, delivering information in a form that team members can use to make decisions. Its reports were easy for management to understand, but not always understandable by rank-and-file employees. TACO II put information in the form of graphics and pictures that restaurant team members could easily relate to. For example, instead of reporting a meat variance of .05 percent, the system could show that .05 percent was equivalent to 300 tacos. The company's SMART labor-scheduling program uses a video game format. A little curve shows the sales of the day. If people schedule too much or too little labor, the color turns. The objective is to have labor meet the sales curve without going over the line.

CAT touch-screen ordering terminals were installed near the entrance of Taco Bell stores. Their graphic interface allows customers to order meals without a cashier. The orders are transmitted from the terminals directly to the assembly crew. Customers can enter their orders in the CAT, get a paper receipt, bring their receipt to the cashier, and pay for and pick up their food.

Martin has broadened his vision for Taco Bell even further. There are 1 billion feeding occasions in the United States every day that could be opportunities for the company.

SOURCES: Elizabeth U. Harding, "Taco Bell Serves Up Support," *Software Magazine*, January 1996, and Roger Hallowell, "Taco Bell Corp.," Harvard Business School 9-692-058, April 20 1994.

CASE STUDY QUESTIONS

1. Compare TACO to the MIS used by California Pizza Kitchen. In what ways is it similar? In what ways is it different?

2. Taco Bell considers itself more of a service company that sells meals than a preparer of fast food. Do you agree? Why or why not?

3. What people, organization, and technology issues had to be addressed when Taco Bell implemented its TACO system and when it made the modifications for TACO II?

4. Taco Bell changed the title of its restaurant manager to restaurant general manager, signaling a desire to find broader, more general managers. How could information systems help promote this new style of management?

Part 4

ILLUSTRATED CASE

CAN COMPUTERS TAME THE HEALTH-CARE MONSTER?

Health care is a giant business in the United States, with annual expenditures now approaching $1 trillion. That figure equals nearly 15 percent of the country's gross domestic product, a figure far higher than in other modern, industrialized countries. Yet many people have inadequate health-care insurance, and between 30 million and 40 million people have no medical coverage at all. Estimates are that between 10 percent and 20 percent of all health-care costs are waste. For example, health care is the only major industry in the United States that still primarily depends upon paper records, and paper handling not only is costly but also is very slow and generates many errors. Fraud is rampant in medical insurance claims. Quality problems are seen everywhere, from the performance of incorrect or unnecessary operations, to incorrect prescriptions, to the lack of good medical care in rural areas.

Some solutions are being provided through information technology, including computerizing patient records and using information systems to improve the quality of health care and control health-care costs.

THE COMPUTERIZED PATIENT RECORD

A computerized patient record (CPR) is a computer record that contains all of a person's necessary medical data stored in one place. Given the use of client-server computing and such networks as the Internet, the record can be accessible on a timely basis wherever needed. The CPR record for an individual patient will contain vital personal information, a full medical history, and test results for recent months, including the actual graphic results from such tests as x-rays, EKGs, echograms, CAT and MRI scans, and angiograms. It will contain diagnoses, treatments, the medicines prescribed and taken, and the effect of those treatments. It will even contain any voice recordings of clinicians' notes (see Figure 1). It can be linked to decision support systems so that the appropriateness and efficacy of the treatment and medicine being prescribed can be reviewed in an instant.

Using a CPR, a doctor would directly and immediately access needed information without having to leaf through paper files. If you went to the hospital, your record and the results of any tests or laboratory work would be immediately available online as opposed to on paper, which is slow, costly and prone to error. The computerized patient record improves both the delivery and the quality of health care in many ways in such a scenario:

Speeds health-care delivery. The CPR speeds the delivery of health care by making information immediately available to the doctors. Doctors can respond to emergencies much faster. The CPR is vital to rapid health care in rural areas, where the person in need of care might live a long way from the nearest medical facility.

Reduces the barrier of distance. The CPR provides complete and comprehensive patient information even when the patient is far from home. Today, this type of benefit is vital, as more and more health care is taking place outside the hospital. Patients go to satellite centers for such services as blood tests, CAT scans, physical therapy, and even outpatient surgery.

Ensures integrity of data. The CPR is a single set of records. Using a CPR, each department no longer needs to collect its own data. Thus, for example, the patient personal data would be carried in only one place. With the old (still dominant) paper system, each department carries its own data, and data integrity is often lost. For example, if one department uses a middle initial and the other does not, the hospital staff may think the records be-

FIGURE 1

Computerized Patient Record Software

ChartWizard is commercially available computerized patient record software that can be used in conjunction with voice recognition software.

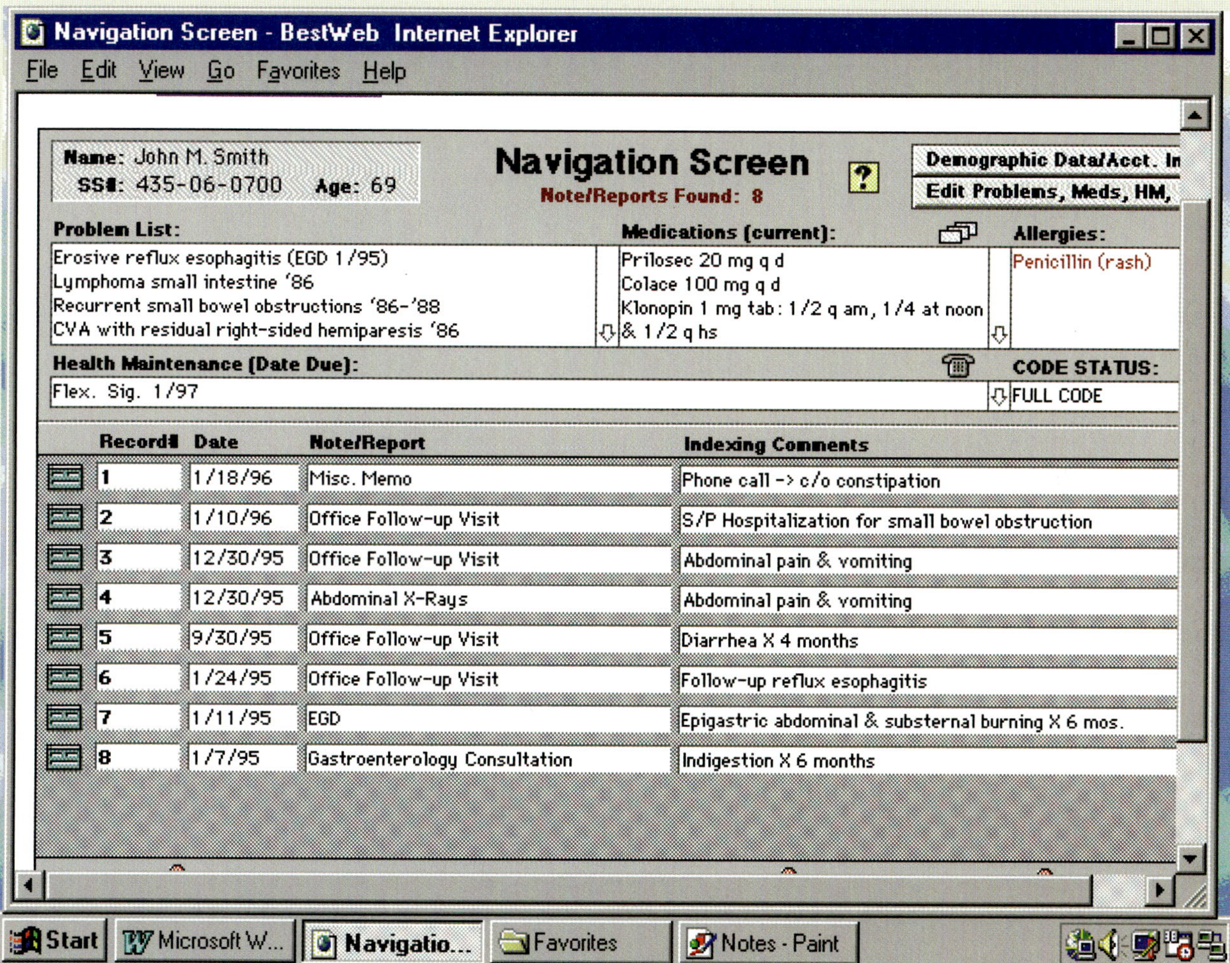

long to two separate people. These data integrity problems disappear for the most part with a CPR.

Reduces patient burden. The CPR reduces the burden on the emergency patient, who, in time of stress, may not be able to give complete personal or medical history information.

Facilitates medical research. With patient medical data on computer databases, it becomes relatively easy to use the computer for medical research. Records of many thousands of patients can quickly be searched to study such key issues as the efficacy of a particular treatment, the side-effects of a given drug, and the differing occurrence rates of a particular cancer in different geographical areas. This improved information can help the medical community to identify community health problems and better determine methods to fight them, to discover new uses for drugs, and to evaluate the value of given treatments and rate them against one another.

Improves design of health-care programs. Knowledge of one's patient population is very helpful in designing appropriate health-care programs to serve them. Hospitals and HMOs that have computerized patient records are using data mining techniques to learn more about their patients. For example, Kaiser Permanente, the largest HMO in the United States, recently used data mining to examine member billings, lab tests, and hospital admissions, thereby identifying 84,000 diabetics among its patients. Kaiser put this information to work in a number of ways to improve the care of these patients. For example, knowing that diabetes is the leading cause of blindness, Kaiser is now scheduling regular eye examinations for all its diabetic patients.

IMPROVING THE QUALITY OF HEALTH CARE

Information technology is already improving the quality of health care. For example, we have already seen how information systems are being used to reduce errors in prescribing medicines. Here we will discuss four ways in which IT is making a significant contribution to health-care quality.

Reducing errors in diagnosis and prescription. Artificial intelligence systems are now being used to identify incorrectly prescribed medicines. That prescription errors are a serious problem was demonstrated in a recent Harvard study that found that more than 200,000 hospital patients are injured each year due to errors in drug therapies. Moreover, studies show that many doctors make such errors, which would indicate the need for software that verifies the safety of each prescription every doctor writes. One study at the Latter-Day Saints Hospital in Salt Lake City shows that the computer catches errors at a rate 60 times higher than that of doctors using paper records. Bar coding of pharmaceuticals plays a key role. It enables a computer system to verify that the medical professional who is retrieving the drug has, in fact, obtained the drug prescribed for the particular patient. Where helpful, these same AI systems also suggest more appropriate medicines.

The use of this technology is now spreading as AI is being used to judge both the appropriateness and the effectiveness of courses of treatment prescribed by a doctor and to make recommendations to the doctor. These AI systems rely upon the combined intelligence of the medical community to suggest efficacious treatments. For example, New England Medical Center has installed a system that helps emergency room doctors determine in minutes whether or not a patient is having a heart attack, a diagnosis that otherwise requires several hours. A study showed that use of the system reduced hospital admissions by 30 percent, a benefit not only to the hospital but also to the patient who was not having a heart attack.

Health-care quality is also being improved because medical personnel are more easily able to obtain information prior to prescribing a treatment. For example, a physician associated with the Medical Center of Delaware is able to log onto the medical center's online drug interaction and poison control reference library and within minutes obtain information on possible side-effects of a particular drug before deciding whether or not to prescribe it. Doctors are also using the Internet to perform research on specific medical issues or to discuss a problem with doctors anywhere in the world (see Chapter 8). The same research done manually might take the doctor several hours or might not even be possible.

Delivering medical care to remote locations. Delivering health care in remote areas—large territories with low population—is always difficult. Patients traveling long distances for medical treatment is time consuming, expensive, and sometimes even dangerous. Today, however, the barrier of distance is coming down as medicine is relying more and more upon computer networks. Telemedicine uses IT networks to enable medical personnel in remote areas to consult with specialists located virtually anywhere in the world.

Telemedicine puts CPRs onto a network where doctors at different sites can view them. All can simultaneously examine test results, charts, x-rays, videos, or whatever is relevant. A video camera can also be used so that all can view the patient, including examining a specific wound in great detail or even following the course of an operation. The doctors can discuss the case as if they were in the same room. Specialists from other areas anywhere in the world are able to advise the local doctor on proper treatment, thus overcoming any lack of specialists in a given area. Telemedicine is also now being used to enable doctors to monitor and treat their patients without either the patient or doctor having to travel. For example, someone at the home of the patient can be taught to administer blood tests, which are analyzed by a local computer. If the test shows something out of a "normal" range, the computer can immediately notify the doctor as to the problem. Through the use of video in the home, the doctor can also observe the patient, enabling some kinds of examinations without the doctor traveling to the patient's home or the patient being transported to a medical facility.

Improving medical training and education. Information technology has become indispensable to the training and education of health-care professionals. Multimedia is now a major tool for training in all kinds of fields, and health care is no exception. One type of widely used system offers medical diagnoses based upon the symptoms of the patient and often offers treatment suggestions as well. Multimedia has even found a use in training nonprofessionals. For example, one multimedia program trains parents of children who have cancer but are in remission and able to live at home. The parents learn how to administer regular blood tests to their children. The blood is then analyzed by a device connected to the multimedia system, and if a problem is detected, the system automatically notifies the doctor. Virtual reality is also used to train medical professionals. For example, one software system used in medical schools enables students to perform virtual gall bladder removal surgeries. Surgeons also use this software prior to performing an actual operation. The World Wide Web is being extensively used for medical information and training (see Figure 2).

Making health care information more accessible to consumers. Nonprofessional medical consumers—all of the rest of us—are also able to obtain immense amounts of helpful information about symptoms or about a particular disease or problem. With the help of the Web, patients are becoming more knowledgeable about their own health-care needs (see the Chapter 6 Focus on People). One significant effect of the easy availability of all this medical information is that people are able to take a more active role in their own care and in the care of their loved ones.

Organizations are also finding ways to get more information to their members. Blue Cross/ Blue Shield of Massachusetts has placed kiosks in public places to give members access 24 hours a day. Members can use a kiosk to enroll in plans, review and change their health-care options, select primary care physicians, or check on the status of medical claims. They can also access this system, called Health Navigator, over the Web (see Figure 3). Many organizations have even given members access to online information through their own home computers. All these systems usually also offer information on medical problems and general advice on health care.

CONTROLLING HEALTH-CARE COSTS

The need to control the high cost of health care in the United States is a major thrust driving the industry to turn more to information technology.

Savings through computerized patient records. An Arthur D. Little study indicated that national health-care costs would be cut by more than $36 billion by deploying standardized CPR systems nationwide. A study at Staten Island University Hospital concluded that use of a CPR would result in an annual savings of $200,000 solely by eliminating the staff needed to transport documents to different areas in the hospital. Faster treatment that becomes possible due to remote access of medical records also results in lower costs by preventing complications and prolonged, more

FIGURE 2

Medical Training on the Web

The Department of Radiology at Brigham and Women's Hospital uses the Web to distribute multimedia teaching documents with medical images and lists of symptoms.

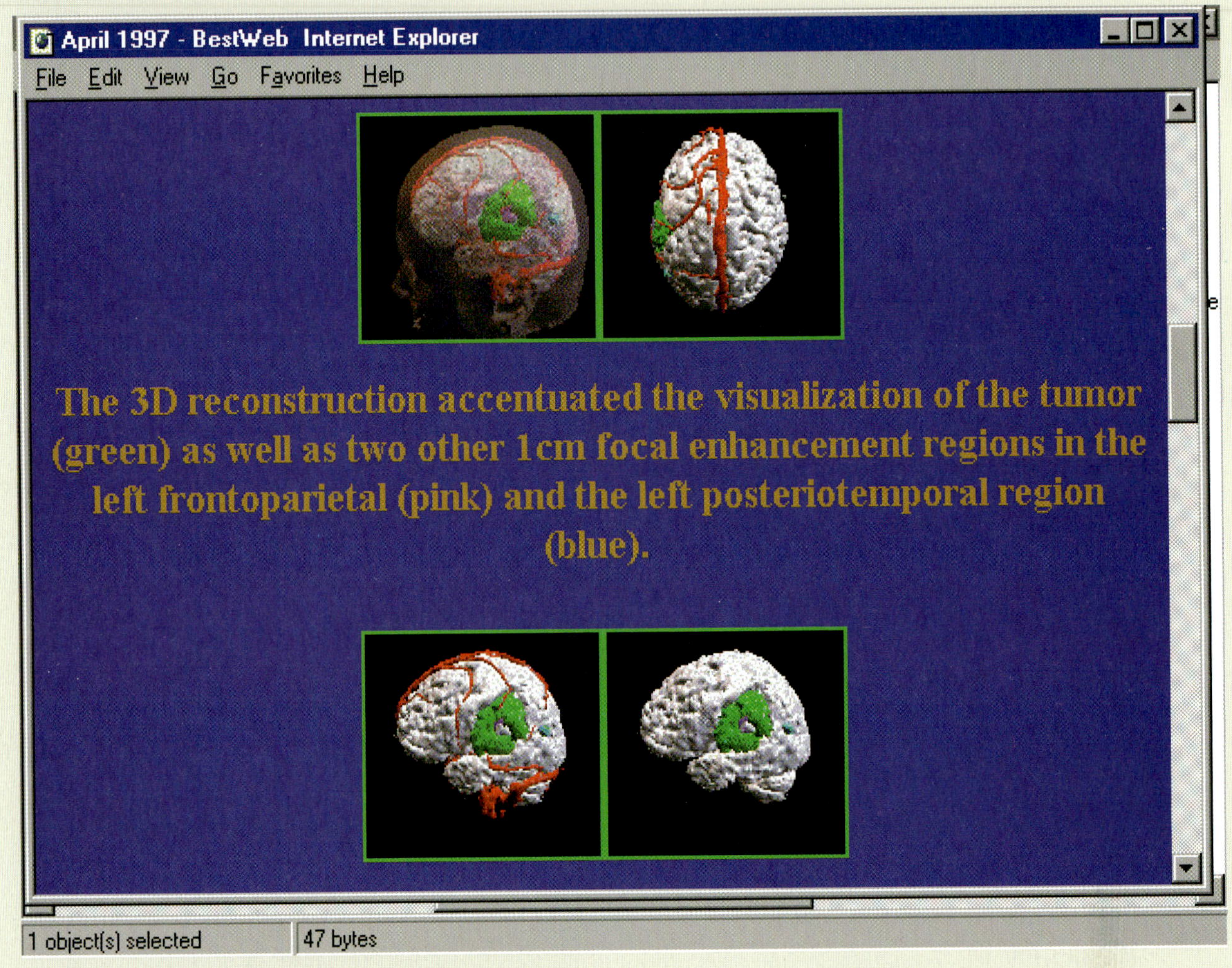
April 1997 - BestWeb Internet Explorer
File Edit View Go Favorites Help
The 3D reconstruction accentuated the visualization of the tumor (green) as well as two other 1cm focal enhancement regions in the left frontoparietal (pink) and the left posteriotemporal region (blue).
1 object(s) selected
47 bytes

expensive treatment. A study in a medical center in Delaware showed that faster access to data reduced hospital stays by up to 18 hours.

Electronic claims submission. Insurance claims submission adds immense costs to health care as doctors and hospitals must maintain large staffs devoted solely to this task. The federal government now requires electronic submission for Medicare and Medicaid claims. The government requirement is forcing insurance companies to turn to electronic filing as well, a move that ultimately will reduce medical costs by billions of dollars.

Reducing health-care fraud. Studies show that health-care fraud is rampant in the United States, costing over $80 billion annually. Patients and insurance companies are overcharged for some services, charged for others that are not even delivered, and charged for individual tasks of a complex procedure instead of using an overall charge

FIGURE 3

The Health Navigator System
This system for Blue Cross/Blue Shield of Massachusetts members can be accessed via the World Wide Web as well as through multimedia kiosks. Subscribers can use the system to select primary care physicians.

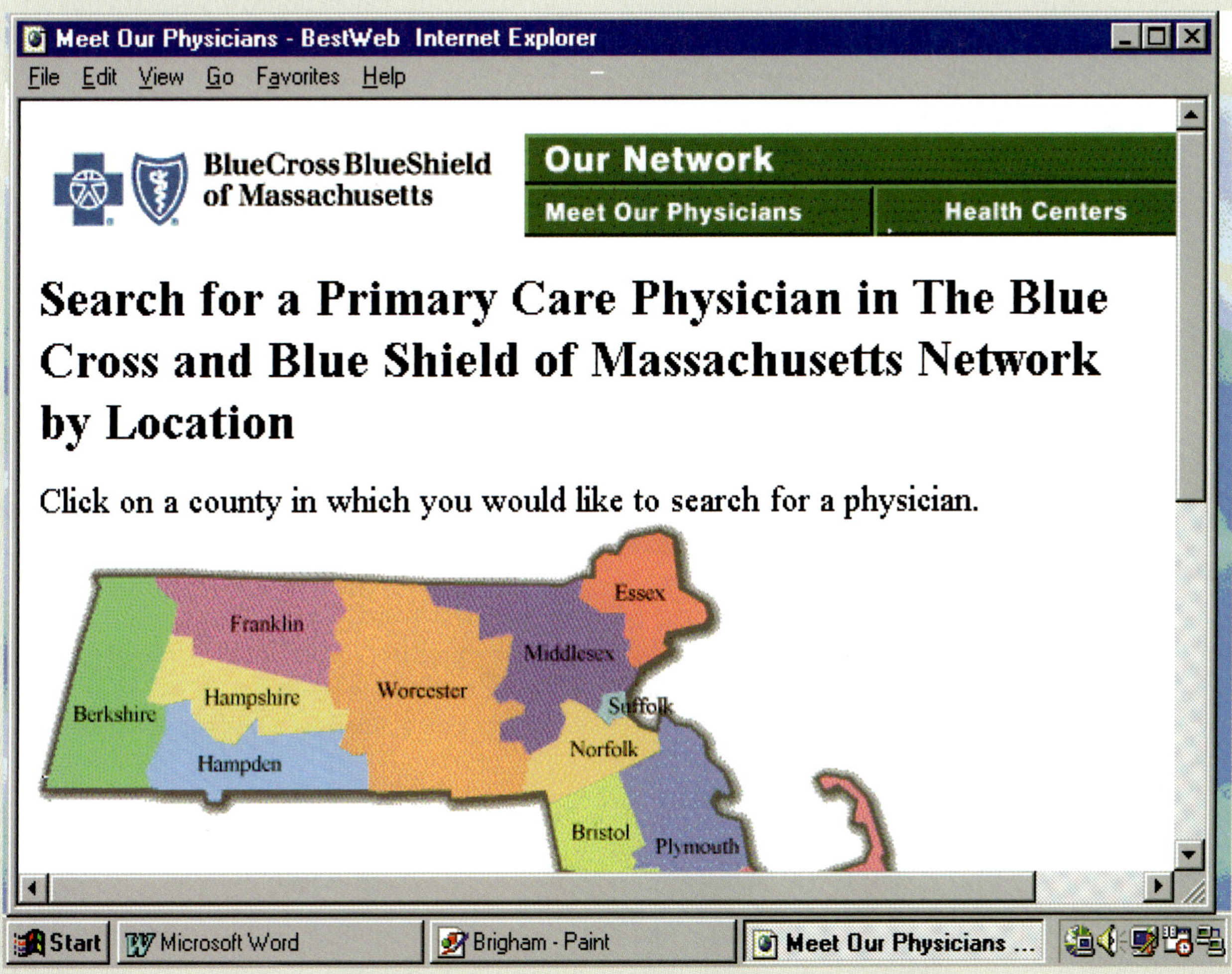

code for the total procedure, a less-expensive method. This problem is beginning to be attacked as insurance companies begin to use new auditing software. The software examines all submitted claims, rejecting any that fit these known patterns of fraud.

Other efficiencies. Automation will reduce hospital and pharmacy costs, just as it reduces costs in other industries. Controlling ordering and inventory can reduce inventory expenses and reduce staff costs. A study in one hospital showed that it would save $165,000 simply by standardizing the catheters used by its staff to two from the current 18. Some systems tell doctors the cost of tests and medication prior to their being used and indicate the effectiveness of the course of treatment. They will also suggest lower-cost alternatives where appropriate. A study concluded that patients of doctors who use this system are discharged from the hospital nearly a day earlier than

TABLE 1

Health Care on the World Wide Web

Web Site	Description
Australia Private Hospital Association	Directory of private hospitals and member services
Center for Disease Control	Provides reports, statistics, and disease prevention guidelines
Pharmaceutical Information Network	Provides access to database of drug information
Medaccess	Fee-based service providing medical information to subscribers
New England Journal of Medicine On-line	Weekly journal reporting results of worldwide medical research
Brigham & Women's Hospital	Educational and research material for radiologists, medical students, and patients

patients of other doctors. Their stays cost an average of nearly $900 less. Yet readmission studies indicate that there was no decline in quality of care for these patients.

SOURCES: Lawrence M. Fisher, "Health on Line: Doctor Is In, and His Disk Is Full," The New York Times, June 24, 1996; Jill Gambon, "A Transfusion of Technology," *Information Week,* July 1, 1996; Steve Alexander, "A Healthier Existence," *Computerworld Client/Server Journal,* April 1995; Emily Andren, "The Medical Center's Cure," *Information Week,* November 13, 1995; Catherine Arnst and Wendy Zellner, "Hospitals Attack a Crippler: Paper," *Business Week,* February 21, 1994; Scott Wallace, "The Computerized Patient Record," *Byte,* May 1994; and "Medicine's New Weapon," *Business Week,* March 27, 1995.

CASE QUESTIONS

1. What people, organization, and technology issues are involved in the high cost and uneven quality and availability of health care in the United States?
2. How much of a solution to these problems is provided by automated patient records?
3. How can the Internet contribute to solutions?

APPENDIX *Building Your Digital Portfolio*

Keep your answers to the problem-solving exercises, solution design exercises, and case studies that you completed from *Information Systems and the Internet:* A *Problem-Solving Approach* (Fourth Edition). They can be used to create a structured portfolio demonstrating your mastery of problem-solving and information systems skills that you can present with your resume when you are job hunting. Your portfolio also shows that you are meeting current information system curriculum guidelines.

If you answered the case studies, worked through the problem-solving exercises, and completed the solution design projects in Chapter 10, here are some of the skills and competencies you would be able to demonstrate:

Application development skills: The solution design exercises concluding Chapter 10 show that you can analyze a problem, design an application solution, and implement the solution using spreadsheet or database software. They also show that you know how to incorporate the Internet, where appropriate, into a solution design.

Software skills: The hands-on exercises concluding each chapter demonstrate that you can select appropriate software to solve a problem and use spreadsheet and database software skills to develop small, real-world applications.

Internet skills: The Internet problem-solving exercises concluding each chapter demonstrate that you know how to use the Internet tools to access information, conduct research, or perform online calculations and analysis.

Analytical, writing and presentation skills: The group and individual problem-solving exercises and chapter case studies demonstrate that you can research a specific topic, analyze a problem, think creatively, suggest a solution, and prepare a clear written or oral presentation of your solution, working either individually or with others in a group.

Following are some of the projects in the text that might be of special interest to future employers:

Application Development Skills

Skill	*Chapter*
Developing a hotel reservation database and Web strategy	10
Developing a marketing database for a video rental company	10
Developing a student housing referral database	10
Developing a DSS for estimating construction project costs	10

Software Skills

Application	*Software Skill*	*Chapter*
Sales commission projections	Spreadsheet	3
Financial portfolio planning	Spreadsheet	9
Income statement projections	Spreadsheet	16
Graphing incidence of production defects	Spreadsheet	13
Developing a personnel database	Database	2, 6
Employee skills inventory	Database	14
Waste management analysis	Database or spreadsheet	5
Bank loan credit authorization	Database or spreadsheet	15

Internet Skills

Application	*Chapter*
Online research	1, 14
Locating foreign suppliers and distributors	2,9
Market research using Usenet groups	3
Logistics planning	5
Job hunting with an online database	6
Sales support analysis	7
Using Internet E-mail	7
Downloading files	8
Using Internet search tools	8
Real estate relocation	10
Travel planning and budgeting	13
Shopping with intelligent agents	15
Investment portfolio analysis	16

Analytical, Writing, and Presentation Skills

Application	*Chapter*
Developing Equal Opportunity Affairs compliance reports	13
Office automation and workflow redesign	14
Evaluating PC operating system software	5
Evaluating computer hardware	4
Designing a university database	6
Designing a network for a retail chain	7
Analyzing business failures	9
Evaluating executive support systems	16

You may find additional exercises and projects to include in your portfolio. It's up to you! You've learned a great deal and now have a portfolio to demonstrate what you have accomplished.

Glossary

Accountability The ability to trace actions to identify individuals responsible for making the decisions to take those actions.

Accounts payable systems Accounting systems that keep track of amounts owed by a firm to its creditors.

Accounts receivable systems Accounting systems that keep track of amounts owed to the firm.

Ada Programming language developed for the Department of Defense to be portable across diverse brands of hardware; also has nonmilitary applications.

Analog signal A continuous sine waveform over a certain frequency range, with a positive voltage representing a 1 and a negative charge representing a 0; used for voice transmissions.

Applicant tracking systems Human resources systems that maintain data about applicants for jobs at a firm and provide reports to satisfy federal, state, and local employment regulations.

Application controls Manual and automated procedures to ensure that the data processed by a particular application remain accurate, complete, and valid throughout the processing cycle.

Application generator Software that can generate entire information system applications without customized programming.

Applications software Programs designed to handle the processing for a particular computer application.

Applications software package A prewritten, precoded, commercially available program that handles the processing for a particular computer application (e.g., spreadsheet or data management software for a personal computer).

Archie A tool for locating FTP files on the Internet that performs keyword searches on an actual database of documents, software, and data files available for downloading from servers around the world.

Arithmetic-logic unit (ALU) The component of the CPU that performs arithmetic and logical operations on data.

Artificial intelligence The study and creation of machines that exhibit humanlike qualities, including the ability to reason.

Artificial intelligence shell The programming environment of an artificial intelligence system.

ASCII A seven- or eight-bit coding scheme used in data transmission, PCs, and some larger computers. Stands for American Standard Code for Information Interchange.

Assembler A program that translates assembly language into machine code so that it can be used by the computer.

Assembly language A programming language used for second-generation software; consists of natural language-like acronyms and words such as add, sub(tract), and load and is considered a symbolic language.

Asynchronous transfer mode (ATM) Protocol for transmitting voice, data, and images over LANs and wide area networks using computers from different vendors by parceling information into uniform cells of 53 groups of 8 bytes.

Asynchronous transmission A method of transmitting one character or byte at a time when data are communicated between computers, with each string of bits comprising a character framed by control bits.

Attribute A characteristic or quality of a particular entity.

Audio output Output that emerges as sound rather than as a visual display.

Backward reasoning A strategy for searching the rules in a knowledge base in which the inference engine begins with a hypothesis and proceeds by asking the user questions about selected facts until the hypothesis is either confirmed or disproved.

Bandwidth The range of frequencies that can be accommodated on a particular telecommunications medium.

Bar code Specially designed bar characters that can be read by OCR scanning devices; used primarily on price tags and supermarket items.

BASIC A programming language frequently used for teaching programming and for PCs; although it is easy to learn, it does not easily support sound programming practices.

Basic business system A system that serves the most elementary day-to-day activities of an organization; it supports the operational level of the business and also supplies data for higher-level management decisions.

Batch input and processing An approach to input and processing in which data are grouped together as source documents before being input; once input, they are stored as a transaction file before processing, which occurs later.

Baud A change in voltage from positive to negative and vice versa. The baud rate at lower speeds corresponds to a telecommunications transmission rate of bits per second. At higher speeds, the baud rate is less than the bit rate because more than one bit at a time can be transmitted by a single signal change.

Behavioral theories of management Views of management based on behavioral scientists' observations of what managers actually do in their jobs.

Benefits systems Human resources systems that maintain data about employees' life insurance, health insurance, pensions, and other benefits, including changes in beneficiaries and benefits coverage.

Bit A binary digit that can have only one of two states, representing 0 or 1.

Bit mapping A technology often used for displaying graphics on a video display terminal; it allows each pixel on the screen to be addressed and manipulated by the computer.

Bookmark A Web browser tool for keeping personal lists of favorite Web sites and their addresses.

Bottom-up approach An approach to intelligent machines that concentrates on trying to build a physical analog to the human brain.

Bus network A network in which a number of computers are linked by a single loop circuit made of twisted wire, coaxial cable, or optical fiber; all messages are transmitted to the entire network and can flow in either direction, with special software identifying which component receives each message.

Bus width The number of bits that can be moved at one time among the CPU and the other devices of a computer.

Business environment The external conditions in which a business organization operates; the general environment includes government regulations, economic and political conditions, and technological developments, while the task environment includes customers, suppliers, and competitors.

Business functions The specialized tasks performed in a business organization—for example, manufacturing and production, sales and marketing, finance and accounting, and human resources activities.

Business organization A complex, formal organization whose goal is to produce a product or service for a profit.

Business process A series of interrelated activities through which work is organized and focused to produce a product or service.

Byte A single character of data made up of a combination of bits that the computer processes or stores as a unit; the unit in which computer storage capacity is measured.

C A programming language with tight control and efficiency of execution like assembly language; portable across different microprocessors and easier to learn than assembly language.

Case-based reasoning Artificial intelligence technology that represents knowledge as a series of cases stored in a database.

Cash management systems Financial systems that keep track of the receipt and disbursement of cash by a firm; they may also forecast the firm's cash flow.

CD-ROM An optical disk system used with microcomputers; it is a form of read-only storage in that data can only be read from it, not written to it; stands for compact disk/read-only memory.

Cellular telephones Telephones working in a system that uses radio waves to transmit voice and data to radio antennas placed in adjacent geographic areas.

Central processing unit (CPU) A hardware component of a computer system that processes raw data and controls other parts of the computer system.

Change management The process of planning changes within an organization to ensure that the changes are implemented in an orderly and controlled manner.

Channel A link by which voices or data are transmitted in a communications network.

Chatting Live, interactive conversations conducted over the Internet by typing messages on a keyboard while reading responses on a screen.

Client/server computing Model of computing that divides processing tasks between "clients" and "servers" on a network, with each machine assigned the functions it performs best.

Coaxial cable A transmission medium consisting of thickly insulated copper wire; it can transmit a larger volume of data than twisted wire and is faster and more interference-free.

COBOL A programming language with English-like statements designed for processing large data files with alphanumeric characters; the predominant programming language for business applications; stands for COmmon Business-Oriented Language.

Combinatorial explosion The difficulty that arises when a problem requires a computer to test a very large number of rules to reach a solution; even a very fast computer cannot search through all the possibilities in a reasonable amount of time.

Communications satellite A satellite orbiting the earth that acts as a relay station for transmitting microwave signals.

Communications technology Physical media and software that support communication by electronic means, usually over some distance.

Compiler A language translator program that translates an entire high-level language program into machine language.

Computer A physical device that takes data as an input, transforms them by executing a stored program, and outputs information to a number of devices.

Computer-aided design (CAD) Automation of the creation and revision of designs using sophisticated graphics software.

Computer crime The deliberate theft or criminal destruction of computerized data or services; the use of computer hardware, software, or data for illegal activities; or the illegal use of computers.

Computer hardware The physical equipment used for the input, processing, and output work in an information system.

Computer literacy Knowledge about the use of information technology; including hardware, software, telecommunications, and information storage techniques.

Computer mouse A hand-held device that can be moved on a desktop to control the position of the cursor on a video display screen.

Computer software Preprogrammed instructions that coordinate the work of computer hardware components to perform the processes required by each information system.

Computer virus A rogue software program that spreads rampantly through computer systems, destroying data or causing the systems to become congested and malfunction.

Concentrator A device that collects and temporarily stores messages from terminals in a buffer or temporary storage area and sends bursts of signals to the host computer.

Control totals A manual or automated count of the number of transactions processed during input, processing, or output, or of critical quantities, such as order amounts; this count is then compared manually or by computer with a second count; discrepancies in the counts signal errors.

Control unit The component of the CPU that controls and coordinates the other components of the computer.

Controller A device that supervises communications traffic between the CPU and peripheral devices such as terminals and printers.

Controls The specific technology, policies, and manual procedures used to protect assets, accuracy, and reliability of information systems.

Conversion strategies Plans and methods for changing from an old system to a new system; they include parallel conversion, direct cutover, pilot study, and the phased approach.

Cooperative processing The division of processing work for applications among mainframes and PCs.

Cost effectiveness The degree to which benefits exceed costs; measured by cost-benefit analysis.

Critical thinking The sustained suspension of judgment with an awareness of multiple perspectives and alternatives.

CRT An electronic tube that shoots a beam of electrons that illuminates pixels, or tiny dots, on a video display screen; stands for cathode ray tube.

Customization The modification of a software package to meet a firm's unique requirements.

Data Raw facts that can be shaped and formed to create information.

Data definition language The part of a data management system that defines each data element as it appears in the database before it is translated into the form required by various application programs.

Data dictionary The component of a database management system that stores definitions and other characteristics of data elements; it identifies which data reside in the database, their structure and format, and their business usage.

Data flow The movement of data within an information system; it can consist of a single data element or multiple data elements grouped together and can be manual or automated.

Data flow diagram A graphic design that shows both how data flow to, from, and within an information system and the various processes that transform the data; used for documenting the logical design of an information system.

Data management software Software that is used for such applications as creating and manipulating lists, creating files and databases to store data, and combining information for reports.

Data manipulation language A special tool in a database management system that manipulates the data in the database.

Data quality audits Surveys of data in information systems to ascertain their level of accuracy and completeness.

Data redundancy The presence of duplicate data in multiple data files.

Data security A control aimed at preventing the unauthorized use of data and ensuring that data are not accidentally altered or destroyed.

Data warehouse A database that consolidates data from various operational systems for use in reporting and analysis.

Data work Work that primarily involves the process, use, or distribution of information.

Database A group of related files; more specifically, a collection of data organized to appear to be in one location so that they can be accessed and used in many different applications.

Database management system (DBMS) Software that serves as an interface between a common database and various application programs; it permits data to be stored in one place yet be made available to different applications.

Decision making The process of debating objectives and feasible solutions and choosing the best option; the third step of problem solving.

Decision support systems (DSS) Interactive systems under user control that are used in solving semistructured problems.

Decisional roles The activities of managers that involve making decisions about new products, handling disturbances in the business, allocating resources, and negotiating among persons with different points of view.

Demodulation The process of converting analog signals into digital form.

Desktop publishing Applications for producing documents that combine high-quality type and graphics with a variety of layout options, allowing users to produce professional-quality reports and documents.

Development methodology A proven method of accomplishing the tasks of systems development to provide standards for guiding the activities of a systems development project.

Digital scanner An input device for translating images and printed information into digital form.

Digital signal A discrete flow in which data are coded as 0-bits and 1-bits and transmitted as a series of on-and-off electrical pulses.

Digital video disk (DVD) A very-high-capacity optical storage device that can store full-length videos and massive amounts of data.

Direct-access storage device (DASD) Magnetic disks, including hard and floppy disks; called *direct access* because in this technology the computer proceeds immediately to a specific record without having to read all the preceding records.

Direct cutover A conversion strategy in which the old system is replaced entirely with the new system on an appointed day; no backup system is available if the new system fails.

Disaster recovery plan A plan detailing how an organization can resume operations after disasters have disrupted its computer processing.

Distributed database A complete database or portions of a database that are maintained in more than one location.

Distributed processing The distribution of processing among multiple computers linked by a communications network.

Document management technology Information technology that is used for producing and managing the flow of documents in an organization; includes word processing, desktop publishing, and optical disk storage.

Documentation A control that involves establishing and maintaining a clear-cut explanation of how an information system works from both an end-user and a technical standpoint; includes system, user, and operational documentation.

Domain name The unique name of a collection of computers connected to the Internet.

DOS An operating system for 16-bit microcomputers based on the IBM microcomputer standard.

Downsizing The process of moving software applications from large computers, such as mainframes or minicomputers, to smaller computers, such as PCs.

Due process The right to be treated fairly in accordance with established legal procedures, including such things as the right to appeal and the right to an attorney.

EBCDIC An eight-bit binary coding scheme used in IBM and other mainframe computers; stands for Extended Binary Coded Decimal Interchange Code.

Electronic commerce The process of buying and selling goods electronically through computerized business transactions.

Electronic data interchange (EDI) The direct computer-to-computer exchange of standard business documents between two separate organizations.

Electronic mail The computer-to-computer exchange of messages.

Encryption The process of encoding data into unreadable form to prevent unauthorized access.

End-user interface The parts of an information system with which end users must interact—for example, online data entry screens or reports.

Entity A person, place, or thing on which information is maintained.

EPROM A memory device in which the memory chips can be erased and reprogrammed with new instructions; stands for erasable programmable read-only memory.

Ethics Principles of right and wrong that can be used to guide the behavior of free moral agents who make choices.

Execution cycle (E-cycle) The portion of a machine cycle in which the required data are located, the instruction is executed, and the results are stored.

Executive support systems (ESS) Graphics-oriented systems designed for senior management that provide generalized computing and telecommunications facilities and combine internal and external information; used for long-term planning.

Expert system A software application that seeks to capture expertise in limited domains of knowledge and experience and to apply this expertise to solving problems.

External knowledge base A knowledge base that is outside the organization, such as libraries of articles, collections of scientific or legal findings, and links to other professionals in universities or other organizations.

Extranet An organization's private intranet that is accessible to select outsiders.

Facsimile (fax) A machine that can transmit documents containing both text and graphics over telephone lines; the sending machine digitizes and transmits the image, which is reproduced as a facsimile (fax) by the receiving machine.

Fault-tolerant computer systems Systems with extra hardware, software, and power as backups against system failure.

Feedback (1) Output that is returned to appropriate members of the organization to help them refine or correct the input phase; (2) the return to a machine of part of the machine's output—the machine then uses the input information to improve its performance.

Fiber optics A transmission medium consisting of strands of clear glass fiber bound into cable through which data are transformed into pulses of light and transmitted by a laser device.

Field A grouping of characters into a word, a group of words, or a complete number.

File A group of related records.

File transfer protocol (FTP) An Internet tool for transferring and retrieving files to and from a remote computer.

Finance and accounting function The division of a business organization that manages the firm's financial assets (finance) and maintains the firm's financial records (accounting).

Firewall Specialized hardware and software used to prevent outsiders from invading private networks.

Floppy disk A flexible, inexpensive magnetic disk used as a secondary storage medium; primarily used with PCs.

Formal systems Information systems that rely on mutually accepted and relatively fixed definitions of data and procedures for collecting, storing, processing, and distributing information.

FORTRAN A programming language developed in 1954 for scientific, mathematical, and engineering applications; stands for FORmula TRANslator.

Forward reasoning A strategy for searching the rules in a knowledge base in which the inference engine begins with information entered by the user and searches the rule base to arrive at a conclusion.

Fourth-generation development The construction of information systems with little or no formal assistance from technical specialists; useful for smaller information systems and personal computer applications.

Fourth-generation languages Programming languages that are less procedural than conventional languages and contain more English language-like commands; they are easier for nonspecialists to learn and use than conventional languages.

Frame relay Network technology that organizes data into packets without error correction routines to transmit data over networks faster and cheaper than packet switching.

Front-end processor A computer that manages communications for a host computer to which it is attached.

Full-duplex transmission A form of transmission over communications lines in which data can be sent in both directions simultaneously.

Fuzzy logic A variety of concepts and techniques in AI for using rules to represent knowledge that is imprecise, uncertain, or unreliable.

General controls Organization-wide controls, both manual and automated, that affect overall activities of computerized information systems.

Genetic algorithms AI technology that "breeds" solutions to problems using the model of genetic processes such as reproduction, mutation, and natural selection.

Gigabyte A measure of computer storage capacity; approximately 1 billion bytes.

Gopher A tool that enables the user to locate information stored on Internet servers through a series of easy-to-use, hierarchical menus.

Graphical user interface (GUI) The feature of an operating system that uses graphical symbols, or icons; rather than typing in commands, the user moves the cursor to the appropriate icon by rolling a mouse on a desktop.

Graphics language A fourth-generation language for displaying computerized data in graphical form.

Group decision support system (GDSS) Interactive computer-based system to help a set of decision makers working together as a group to solve unstructured problems.

Groupware Software that attempts to expedite all the functions of a typical work group–for example, tracking the calendars of all or related individuals in an office, scheduling meetings, and sharing ideas and documents.

Hacker A person who gains unauthorized access to a computer network for profit, criminal mischief, or personal reasons.

Half-duplex transmission A form of transmission over communications lines in which data can move in both directions, but not simultaneously.

Hard disk A type of magnetic disk resembling a thin platter, where relatively large quantities of data can be stored and data can be rapidly accessed.

Hierarchical database model The organization of data in a database in a top-down, treelike manner; each record is broken down into multilevel segments, with one root segment linked to several subordinate segments in a one-to-many, parent-child relationship.

Hierarchy The arrangement of people in an organization according to rank and authority; people at one level of the hierarchy report to those on the next level who have more authority.

High-level language A programming language that consists of statements that, to some degree, resemble a natural language such as English.

Home page The text and graphical screen display that welcomes a visitor to a Web site.

Host computer The main computer in a network.

Human resources function The division of a business organization that concentrates on attracting and maintaining a stable work force for the firm; it identifies potential employees, maintains records on existing employees, and creates training programs.

Hybrid AI system A system that combines multiple AI technologies into a single application to take advantage of the best features of each technology.

Hyperlink A built-in link to other related documents or Web pages that enable the user to jump directly from one document or Web page to another.

Hypermedia database A database organized to store text, graphics, audio, or video data as nodes that can be linked in any pattern established by the user.

Hypertext markup language (HTML) A programming tool for creating Web pages that uses hypertext to establish dynamic links to other documents stored in the same or in remote computers.

Imaging Systems and software that convert documents into digital form so that they can be stored, accessed, and manipulated by the computer.

Implementation The process of putting the solution of a problem into effect and evaluating the results in order to make improvements; the fifth step of problem solving.

Index A list, for a file or database, of the key field of each record and its associated storage location.

Indexed sequential-access method (ISAM) A way of storing records sequentially on a direct-access storage device that allows individual records to be accessed in any desired order using an index of key fields.

Inference engine The strategy for searching through the rule base in an expert system; either a forward reasoning strategy or a backward reasoning strategy is used.

Informal structure A network of personal relationships within an organization.

Information Data that have been shaped by humans into a meaningful and useful form.

Information and knowledge economy An economy in which the majority of new wealth (gross domestic product) is produced by creating or processing information.

Information center A facility that provides training, tools, standards, and expert support for solution design by end users.

Information superhighway High-speed telecommunications networks that are national or international in scope and that offer open access to the general public.

Information system A set of interrelated components that collect, retrieve, process, store, and distribute information for the purpose of facilitating planning, control, coordination, analysis, and decision making in organizations.

Information systems literacy Knowledge and hands-on facility with information technologies, a broadly based understanding of organizations and individuals from a behavioral perspective, and a similar understanding of how to analyze and solve problems.

Information work Work that primarily involves the creation or processing of information.

Informational roles The activities of managers that involve monitoring the activities of the business, distributing information through reports and memos, and acting as spokespersons for the business.

Input The capture or collection of raw data resources from within an organization or from its external environment.

Input controls Application controls that ensure the accuracy and completeness of data entering the information system.

Instruction cycle (I-cycle) The portion of a machine cycle in which an instruction is retrieved from primary storage and decoded.

Integrated Services Digital Network (ISDN) Standard for transmitting voice, data, and video over public switched telephone lines.

Integrated software package A software package that provides two or more applications, such as spreadsheets and word processing, allowing for easy transfer of data between them.

Intelligent agent A software program with built-in knowledge that can carry out specific repetitive, predictable tasks for individuals; can work in computer networks.

Intelligent machine A physical device or computer that mimics the way people think.

Internet A vast interconnected network of networks linking business, governmental, scientific, and educational organizations as well as individuals around the world.

Internet service provider (ISP) A company with a permanent connection to the Internet that offers Internet access to subscribers.

Interpersonal roles The activities of managers that involve performing symbolic duties; motivating, counseling, and supporting workers; and acting as liaisons to the larger firm and the outside world on behalf of employees.

Interpreter A language translator program that translates a high-level language program into machine code by translating one statement at a time and executing it.

Intranet An internal private network based on Internet and Web technology.

Iteration construct A series of statements that repeats an instruction as long as the results of a conditional test are true; one of three basic control constructs in structured programming.

Java Platform-independent, object-oriented programming language that can deliver miniature applications as software "applets" downloaded from networks.

Just-in-time production systems (JIT) Systems that minimize inventory by ensuring that materials required for production are made available exactly at the time they are needed.

Key field A field in a record that uniquely identifies that record so that it can be retrieved, updated, or sorted.

Kilobyte The usual measure of PC storage capacity; approximately 1,000 bytes.

Knowledge The stock of conceptual tools and categories used by humans to create, collect, store, and share information.

Knowledge and data workers The employees in an organization who create and/or use knowledge (e.g., engineers) or data (e.g., clerical workers) to solve problems.

Knowledge- and information-intense products Products that require a great deal of learning and knowledge to create and often require information technologies for delivery in a timely fashion.

Knowledge base A model of human knowledge used by artificial intelligence systems; consists of rules, semantic nets, or frames.

Knowledge engineer Specialist trained in eliciting information and expertise from other professionals in order to translate the knowledge into a set of production rules, frames, or semantic nets.

Knowledge systems Information systems used by knowledge workers in business organizations to solve questions requiring knowledge and technical expertise.

Knowledge work Work whose primary emphasis is on the creation of new information or knowledge.

Liability The idea that people may be obligated by law to compensate those they have injured in some way; liability is established by laws that set out legal remedies for proscribed behavior.

LISTSERVs Online discussion groups that use E-mail instead of bulletin boards for communications.

Local area network (LAN) A transmission network encompassing a limited area, such as a single building or several buildings in close proximity; widely used to link PCs so that they can share information and peripheral devices.

Logic Theorist Software developed by Herbert Simon and Alan Newell that mimicked deductive logic; that is, it selected correct rules and postulates to create a coherent logical chain from premises to conclusion.

Logical design The part of a solutions design that provides a description of the general level of resources, the operational process, and the nature of outputs that the solution should require; it describes what the solution will do, not how it will physically work.

Logical view The presentation of data as they would be perceived by end users or business specialists.

Mac OS Operating system for the Macintosh microcomputer, with multitasking, graphics, Internet, and multimedia capabilities.

Machine cycle The series of operations involved in executing a single instruction.

Machine language The programming language used in the first generation of computer software; consists of strings of binary digits (0 and 1).

Magnetic disk The most popular secondary storage medium; data are stored by means of magnetized spots on hard or floppy disks.

Magnetic ink character recognition (MICR) A form of source data automation in which an MICR reader identifies characters written in magnetic ink; used primarily for check processing.

Magnetic tape A secondary storage medium in which data are stored by means of magnetized and unmagnetized spots on tape; can store information only sequentially.

Mainframe A large computer, generally used for business or military problems.

Management control A type of general control that provides appropriate management supervision and accountability for information systems (e.g., establishing formal written policies and procedures and segregating job functions in order to minimize error and fraud).

Management information systems (MIS) Management support systems that provide routine summary reports on the firm's performance; used to monitor and control the business and predict future performance.

Managing The process of using business resources to accomplish goals, coordinate the work of many workers, and establish criteria for measuring progress toward the established goals.

Manual system An information system that uses only paper and pencil technology and does not rely on computers.

Manufacturing and production function The division of a business organization that produces the firm's goods or services.

Massively parallel processing Computer processing in which a very large number of inexpensive processor chips are chained together to work on a single computing problem simultaneously.

Megabyte A measure of computer storage capacity; approximately 1 million bytes.

Megahertz (MHz) A measure of clock speed, or the pacing of events in a computer; represents 1 million cycles per second.

Microprocessor A silicon chip containing an entire CPU; used in PCs.

Microsecond A measure of machine cycle time; equals one one-millionth of a second.

Microwave A transmission medium in which high-frequency radio signals are sent through the atmosphere; used for high-volume, long-distance, point-to-point communication.

Middle management The people in the middle of the hierarchy in an organization; they carry out the programs and plans of senior management by supervising employees.

Millisecond A measure of machine cycle time; equals one one-thousandth of a second.

Minicomputer A medium-sized computer, generally used in universities or research labs.

Mobile data networks Radio-based wireless networks for two-way transmission of digital data.

Model base The analytical tools used by an information system; in a decision support system, it includes very sophisticated tools such as built-in spreadsheets, statistical analysis, and simulation.

Modem A device used to translate digital signals into analog signals and vice versa, a necessity when computers communicate through analog lines; stands for MOdulation and DEModulation.

Modulation The process of converting digital signals into analog form.

Module A logical way of partitioning or subdividing a program so that each component (i.e., module) performs a limited number of related tasks.

Multimedia The integration of two or more types of media such as text, graphics, sound, full-motion video, or animation into a computer-based application.

Multinational Approach to organizing a business in which financial management and control are maintained out of a central home office while production, sales, and marketing operations are located in other countries.

Multiplexer A device that enables a single communications channel to carry data transmission from multiple sources simultaneously.

Multiprocessing The simultaneous use of two or more CPUs under common control to execute different instructions for the same program or multiple programs.

Multiprogramming The concurrent use of a computer by several programs; one program uses the CPU while the others use other components such as input and output devices.

Multitasking The multiprogramming capability of single-user operating systems such as those for PCs; it enables the user to run two or more programs at once on a single computer.

Nanosecond A measure of machine cycle time; equals one one-billionth of a second.

Natural language Languages, including idioms, that are used by humans (e.g., English, Swahili, French).

Network Physical media and software that link two or more computers together to transmit voice, data, images, sound, and/or video or to share resources such as a printer.

Network computer A pared-down desktop computer that does not store software programs or data permanently, obtaining them when they are needed over a network.

Network database model The organization of data in a database to depict a many-to-many relationship.

Network gateway The communications processor that links a local area network to another dissimilar network, such as the public telephone system or another corporate network.

Network topology The shape or configuration of a network; the most common topologies are the star, bus, and ring.

Neural network Hardware or software that emulates the physiology of animal or human brains.

Node A device connected to a network.

Object code The machine-language version of source code after it has been translated into a form usable by the computer.

Object-oriented database A database that stores data and processing instructions as objects that can be automatically retrieved and stored.

Object-oriented programming Approach to software development that combines data and the instructions acting on that data into one "object."

Office activities The activities performed by an office in an organization, consisting of (1) managing documents, (2) scheduling individuals and groups, (3) communicating with individuals and groups, (4) managing data on individuals and groups, and (5) managing projects.

Office automation The application of information technology to increase the productivity of office information workers.

Office data management technology Information technology that centers on desktop databases for client or customer tracking, project tracking, calendar information, and other information required for office jobs.

Office roles The functions played by an office in an organization, consisting of (1) coordinating and managing people and work, (2) linking diverse organizational units and projects, and (3) coupling the organization to the external environment.

Office scheduling technology Information technology used to coordinate individual and group calendars, such as electronic calendars.

Online analytical processing (OLAP) Viewing data in different ways using multiple dimensions.

Online database and information service A service that supplies information external to the firm, such as stock market quotations, general news and information, or specific legal and business information.

Online realtime processing An input approach in which data are input into the computer and processed as they become available.

Online transaction processing (OLTP) A transaction processing mode in which transactions entered online are immediately processed by the CPU.

Operating system The systems software that manages and controls the activities of the computer.

Operational systems Information systems used in monitoring the day-to-day activities of a business organization.

Optical character recognition (OCR) A form of source data automation in which optical scanning devices read specially designed data off source documents and translate the data into digital form for the computer.

Optical disk A disk on which data are recorded and read by laser beams rather than by magnetic means; such disks can store data at densities much greater than magnetic disks.

Order processing systems Sales and marketing systems that record and process sales orders, track the status of orders, produce invoices, and often produce data for sales analysis and inventory control.

Organization perspective A way of viewing a problem that emphasizes the firm's formal rules and procedures, production process, management, politics, bureaucracy, and culture as sources of its problems and the ways in which they can contribute to a solution.

Organizational structure The number of different levels, the type of work, and the distribution of power in an organization.

OS/2 A powerful operating system used with 32-bit IBM PCs that supports multitasking and multiple users in networks.

Output The transfer of processed information to the people or activities that will use it.

Output controls Application controls that ensure that the results of computer processing are accurate, complete, and properly distributed.

Outsourcing Using an external vendor of computer services to develop or operate an organization's information systems.

Packet switching The breaking up of a block of text into packets of data approximately 128 bytes long; a value-added network gathers data from its subscribers, divides the data into packets, and sends the packets on any available communications channel.

Paging systems Wireless systems for notifying users of telephone calls that can also be used to transmit short alphanumeric messages.

Parallel conversion A conversion strategy in which the old system and the new system run in tandem until it is clear that the new system is working correctly.

Parallel processing A type of processing in which more than one instruction is processed at a time using multiple processors; used in supercomputers.

Partitioned database A database that is subdivided so that each location has only the portion of the database that serves its local needs.

Pascal A programming language that consists of smaller subprograms, each of which is a structured program in itself; used on PCs and for teaching programming.

Pen-based input Input devices that accept handwritten input by allowing users to print directly on a sensitized screen using a pen-like stylus.

People perspective A way of viewing a problem that emphasizes the firm's employees as individuals and their interrelationships as sources of its problems and the ways in which they can contribute to a solution.

Perceptive systems Sensing devices used in robots that can recognize patterns in streams of data.

Perceptron A machine devised by Frank Rosenblatt that could perceive letters or shapes and could be taught, or corrected, when it made mistakes; an example of the bottom-up approach to artificial intelligence.

Personal communications services (PCSs) Systems for wireless transmission of voice and data sending low-power, high-frequency radio waves to closely spaced microcells.

Personal computer (PC) A small desktop or portable computer.

Personal digital assistant (PDA) Pen-based, hand-held computer with built-in communication and organizational capabilities.

Phased approach A conversion strategy in which a new system is introduced in steps.

Physical design The part of a solutions design that translates the abstract logical system model into specifications for equipment, hardware, software, and other physical resources.

Physical view The presentation of data as they are actually organized and structured on physical storage media.

Picosecond A measure of machine cycle time; equals one one-trillionth of a second.

Pilot study A conversion strategy in which a new system is introduced to only a limited part of an organization; if the system is effective there, it is installed throughout the rest of the organization.

PL/1 A programming language developed in 1964 by IBM for business and scientific applications; not as widely used as COBOL or FORTRAN.

Plotter A device used for outputting high-quality graphics; pen plotters move in various directions to produce straight lines.

Point-of-sale systems Sales and marketing systems that capture sales data at the actual point of sale through the cash register or hand-held scanners.

Positions systems Human resources systems that maintain information about positions (slots in a firm's organizational chart); they maintain data about filled and unfilled positions and track changes in positions and job assignments.

Postimplementation The use and evaluation of a new system after it is installed; the last stage of the traditional systems life cycle.

Primary storage The component of a computer system that temporarily stores program instructions and the data being used by these instructions.

Printer An output device for producing permanent hard-copy output.

Privacy The right of individuals and organizations to be left alone and to be secure in their personal papers.

Privacy Act of 1974 A federal statute that defines citizens' rights in regard to federal government records and management's responsibilities for them; sets out some of the principles for regulating computer technology in order to protect people's privacy.

Private branch exchange (PBX) A central private switchboard that handles a firm's voice and digital communications needs.

Problem analysis The consideration of the dimensions of a problem to determine what kind of problem it is and what general kinds of solutions may be appropriate; the first step in problem solving.

Problem understanding The investigation—fact gathering and analysis—of a problem to gain better understanding; the second step of problem solving.

Process control systems Manufacturing and production systems that use computers to monitor the ongoing physical production processes.

Process specifications The logical steps for performing a process; they appear in documents accompanying lower-level data flow diagrams to show the various steps by which data are transformed.

Processing The conversion of raw input into a more appropriate and useful form.

Processing controls Application controls that ensure that the accuracy and completeness of data during updating.

Production workers The employees in a business organization who actually produce the firm's products or services.

Program A series of statements or instructions to the computer.

Program/data dependence The close relationship between data stored in files and the specific software programs required to update and maintain those files, whereby any change in data format or structure requires a change in all the programs that access the data.

Programmed edit check An application control technique for checking input data for errors before the data are processed; it uses a computerized checking procedure.

Project definition The process of investigating a perceived problem to determine whether a problem actually exists and, if so, whether it requires further analysis and research; the first stage of the traditional systems life cycle.

Project management technology Software that helps managers track and plan projects.

PROM A memory device in which the memory chips can be programmed only once and are used to store instructions entered by the purchaser; stands for programmable read-only memory.

Protocol The set of rules governing transmission between two components in a telecommunications network.

Prototyping Building an experimental, or preliminary, system or part of a system for business specialists to try out and evaluate.

Pseudocode A method of documenting the logic followed by program instructions in which English-like statements are used to describe processing steps and logic.

Push technology A method of obtaining relevant information on the Internet by having a computer broadcast information directly to the user based on prespecified interests.

Quality control systems Manufacturing and production systems that monitor the production process to identify variances from established standards so that defects can be corrected.

Quality of work life The degree to which jobs are interesting, satisfying, and physically safe and comfortable.

Query language A high-level, easy-to-use, fourth-generation language for accessing stored data.

RAID (redundant array of inexpensive disks) High-performance disk storage technology that can deliver data over multiple paths simultaneously by packaging more than 100 smaller disk drives with a controller chip and specialized software in a single large box.

RAM A memory device used for short-term storage of data or program instructions; stands for random-access memory.

Random file organization A way of storing data records so that they can be accessed in any sequence, regardless of their physical order; used with magnetic disk technology.

Record A grouping of related data fields, such as a person's name, age, and address.

Reduced instruction set computing (RISC) Technology for increasing microprocessor speed by embedding only the most frequently used instructions on a chip.

Reengineering The rethinking and radical redesign of business processes to significantly improve cost, quality, service, and speed and to maximize the benefits of information technology.

Register A storage location in the ALU or control unit; it may be an instruction register, address register, or storage register, depending on what is stored in it.

Relational database model The organization of data in a database in two-dimensional tables called relations; a data element in any one table can be related to any piece of data in another table as long as both tables share a common data element.

Replicated database A central database that is duplicated at all other locations.

Report generator A software tool that extracts stored data to create customized reports that are not routinely produced by existing applications.

Request for proposal (RFP) A detailed list of questions for software vendors to answer as part of the process of evaluating a software package; the questions are designed to determine the extent to which the software package meets the requirements specified during the solution design process.

Responsibility The idea that individuals, organizations, and societies are free moral agents who act willfully and with intentions, goals, and ideas; consequently, they can be held accountable for their actions.

Ring network A network in which a number of computers are linked by a closed loop of wire, coaxial cable, or optical fiber in a manner that allows data to be passed along the loop in a single direction from computer to computer.

Robotics The study or use of physical systems and devices with built-in intelligence and computer-controlled, humanlike capabilities that can perform work normally done by humans, especially in hazardous or lethal environments.

ROM A memory device used for permanent storage of program instructions; stands for read-only memory.

Sales and marketing function The division of a business organization that sells the firm's product or service.

Search engine A tool for locating specific sites or information on the Internet. Primarily used to search the World Wide Web.

Secondary storage The relatively long-term storage of data outside the CPU.

Sector A method of storing data that divides a disk into pie-shaped pieces, each with a unique number that becomes part of the address.

Security All the policies, procedures, and technical tools used to safeguard information systems from unauthorized access, alteration, theft, and physical damage.

Selection construct A series of statements that tests a condition; depending on whether the results of the test are true or false, one of two alternative instructions will be executed; one of three basic control constructs in structured programming.

Semistructured problem A problem in which only parts have a clear-cut answer provided by a well-accepted methodology.

Senior management The people at the top of the hierarchy in an organization; they have the most authority and make long-range decisions for the organization.

Sensors Devices that collect data directly from the environment for input into the computer.

Sequence construct A series of statements that are executed in the order in which they appear, with control passing unconditionally from one statement to the next; one of three basic control constructs in structured programming.

Sequential file organization A way of storing data records so that they must be retrieved in the physical order in which they are stored; the only file organization method that can be used with magnetic tape.

Server A computer with a large hard disk whose function is to allow other devices to share files and programs.

Server computer A computer designed or optimized to support a computer network.

Simplex transmission A form of transmission over communications lines in which data can travel in only one direction at all times.

Sociotechnical perspective An approach to information systems that involves the coordination of technology, organizations, and people.

Software bug An error or defect in the code of a software program.

Solutions design The development of a solution to a problem, including both logical and physical design; the fourth step of problem solving.

Source code Program statements in a high-level language that are translated by systems software into machine language so that the high-level programs can be executed by the computer.

Source data automation Advanced forms of data input technology that generate machine-readable data at their point of origin; includes optical character recognition, magnetic ink character recognition, digitizers, and voice input.

Specialization The division of work in an organization so that each employee focuses on a specific task.

Spreadsheet software Software that provides the user with financial modeling tools; data are displayed on a grid and numerical data can easily be recalculated to permit the evaluation of several alternatives.

SQL (Structured Query Language) A data manipulation language for relational database management systems that is an emerging business standard.

Star network A network in which a central host computer is connected to several smaller computers and/or terminals; all communications between the smaller computers or terminals must pass through the host computer.

Storage technology Physical media for storing data and the software governing the organization of data on these media.

Stored-program concept The concept that a program cannot be executed unless it is stored in the computer's primary storage along with the required data.

Strategic information systems Information systems used in solving a business organization's long-range, or strategic, problems.

Strategic-level systems Information systems used in solving a business organization's long-range, or strategic, problems.

Structured design A software design principle according to which a program is supposed to be designed from the top down as a hierarchical series of modules with each module performing a limited number of functions.

Structured problem A routine, repetitive problem for which there is an accepted methodology for arriving at an answer.

Structured program flowchart A method of documenting the logic followed by program instructions; uses graphic symbols to depict the steps that processing must take in a specific program, using the three control constructs of structured programming.

Structured programming A way of writing program code that simplifies control paths so that programs can be easily understood and modified by others; it relies on three basic control constructs—the sequence construct, the selection construct, and the iteration construct.

Supercomputer A very sophisticated and powerful computer that can perform complex computations very rapidly.

Synchronous transmission The transmission of characters in a block framed by header and trailer bytes called flags; allows large volumes of data to be transmitted at high speeds between computers.

System flowchart A diagram that documents the sequence of processing steps that take place in an entire system; most useful for physical design, in which such diagrams show the sequence of processing events and the files used by each processing step.

Systems analysis The study and analysis of problems of existing information systems; it includes identifying both the organization's objectives and its requirements for the solution of the problems.

Systems design A model or blueprint for an information system solution to a problem; it shows in detail how the technical, organizational, and people components of the system will fit together.

Systems software Generalized software that manages computer resources such as the CPU, printers, terminals, communications links, and peripheral equipment.

Systems study The process of describing and analyzing problems of existing systems, specifying solution objectives, describing potential solutions, and evaluating various solution alternatives; the second stage of the traditional systems life cycle.

Tactical systems Information systems used in solving a business organization's short-term, or tactical, problems, such as how to achieve goals and how to evaluate the process of achieving goals.

Technology perspective A way of viewing a problem the emphasizes information technology hardware, software, telecommunications, and database as sources of business problems and the ways in which they can contribute to a solution.

Telecommuting Working at home on a computer tied into corporate networks.

Teleconferencing The use of telecommunications technology to enable people to meet electronically; can be accomplished via telephone or electronic mail.

Telemarketing systems Sales and marketing systems that track the use of the telephone for contacting customers, offering products, and following up sales.

Telnet A network tool that allows a person to log on to one computer system and access its files from a remote computer.

Terabyte A measure of computer storage capacity; approximately 1 trillion bytes.

Time sharing A technique in which many users share computer resources simultaneously (e.g., one CPU with many terminals); the computer spends a fixed amount of time on each user's program before proceeding to the next.

Top-down approach An approach to intelligent machines that concentrates on trying to develop a logical analog to the human brain.

Top-down design A principle of software design according to which the design should first consider the program's main functions, subdivide these functions into component modules, and then subdivide each component module until the lowest level of detail has been reached.

Total quality management (TQM) Concept that makes quality improvement the responsibility of all members of an organization.

Touch screen A sensitized video display screen that allows data to be input by touching the screen surface with a finger or pointer.

Traditional file environment The storage of data so that each application has its own separate data file or files and software programs.

Traditional systems life cycle The oldest methodology for building an information system; consists of six stages (project definition, systems study, design, programming, installation, and postimplementation) that must be completed sequentially.

Traditional theories of management Views of management that see its primary functions as planning, organizing, leading, and controlling.

Training and skills systems Human resources systems that maintain records of employees' training and work experience so that employees with appropriate skills for special assignments or job requirements can be identified.

Transaction A record of an event to which a business must respond.

Transaction processing system (TPS) A basic business system that keeps track of the transactions necessary to conduct a business and uses these transactions to update the firm's records. Another name for a basic business system.

Transborder data flow The movement of information in any form from one country to another.

Transmission Control Protocol/Internet Protocol (TCP/IP) Networking standard for linking different types of computers; used in the Internet.

Transnational Approach to organizing a business in which sales and production activities are managed from a global perspective without reference to national borders.

Turing test A test devised by Alan Turing to determine whether a machine is intelligent. A computer and a human are placed in separate rooms connected by a communications link; if the human is not aware that he or she is communicating with a machine, then the machine is intelligent.

Twisted wire The oldest transmission medium, consisting of strands of wire twisted in pairs; it forms the basis for the analog phone system.

UNIX A machine-independent operating system for microcomputers, minicomputers, and mainframes; it is interactive and supports multiuser processing, multitasking, and networking.

URL The address of a specific resource on the Internet; short for uniform resource locator.

Usenet Internet news and discussion groups in which people share information and ideas on a defined topic through large electronic bulletin boards.

Value-added network (VAN) A multipath data-only network managed by a private firm that sets up the network and charges other firms a fee to use it.

Value chain The viewing of a business

firm as a series of basic activities that add value to the firm's products or services.

Veronica An Internet capability for searching gopher directories for files about a specific subject by using keywords.

Very-high-level programming language A programming language that produces program code with far fewer instructions than conventional languages; used primarily by professional programmers.

Videoconferencing Teleconferencing in which participants can see each other on video screens.

Video display terminal (VDT) A screen on which output can be displayed; varieties include monochrome, color, text, and text/graphics.

Virtual organization An organizational arrangement whereby companies create partnerships with other companies to deliver goods and services outside the traditional organizational framework and without having physical ties among the companies.

Virtual reality Technology that creates computerized simulations that enable users to feel they are participating in "real-world" activities.

Virtual storage A way of dividing programs into small fixed- or variable-length portions with only a small portion stored in primary memory at one time so that programs can be used more efficiently by the computer.

Visual programming A programming method in which programs are created by working with objects onscreen.

Voice input devices Input devices that convert the spoken word into digital form.

Voice mail A telecommunications system in which the spoken message of the sender is digitized, transmitted over a telecommunications network, and stored on disk until the recipient is ready to listen, when the message is reconverted to audio form.

Web browsers Software with a graphical user interface that can access and display Web pages.

Web site All the Web pages created by an organization or individual.

Webmaster The person in charge of an organization's Web site.

Wide area network (WAN) A telecommunications network covering a large geographical distance; provided by common carriers but managed by the customer.

Windows A GUI shell that runs in conjunction with the DOS operating system.

Windows 95 (Windows 98) A powerful 32-bit operating system with a streamlined graphical user interface and built-in multitasking, networking, and Internet capabilities.

Windows NT A powerful operating system for use with 32-bit microprocessors in networked environments; supports multitasking and multiprocessing and can be used with Intel and some other types of microprocessors.

Word length The number of bits that a computer can process or store together as a unit.

Word processing Software and hardware that are used to create, edit, format, store, and print documents.

Word-processing software Software that handles such applications as electronic editing, formatting, and printing of documents.

Workstation A desktop computer with powerful graphics and mathematical processing capabilities and the ability to perform several tasks at once.

World Wide Web A set of standards for storing, retrieving, organizing, formatting, and displaying information in a networked environment using graphical user interfaces and dynamic links to other documents

WORM An optical disk system in which data can be recorded only once on the disk by users and cannot be erased; stands for write once, read many.

Name Index

Organization Index

Subject Index